*Classical Studies
on
Physical
Activity*

Classical Studies
on
Physical
Activity

Edited by

ROSCOE C. BROWN, JR.
New York University

GERALD S. KENYON
University of Wisconsin

PRENTICE-HALL, INC., Englewood Cliffs, New Jersey

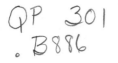

PRENTICE-HALL INTERNATIONAL, INC., London
PRENTICE-HALL OF AUSTRALIA, PTY. LTD., Sydney
PRENTICE-HALL OF CANADA, LTD., Toronto
PRENTICE-HALL OF INDIA PRIVATE LTD., New Delhi
PRENTICE-HALL OF JAPAN, INC., Tokyo

Preface

The study of physical activity has a long and interesting history. Man's interpretation and understanding of physical activity has been influenced by philosophical as well as scientific judgments. Since time immemorial physical activity, whether in a ritualistic dance, an act of war, or a sport skill, has been a significant force in the culture of every society. When laws and principles of science were developed, man did not immediately apply them to physical activity. However, during the twentieth century, medical researchers, physiologists, and physical educators have started scientific inquiry into such phenomena as muscular strength, metabolism, physical training, the effects of physical activity on health, motor learning, and factors influencing work output.

The authors became interested in the idea of "Classical Studies in Physical Activity" when it was necessary for us to review the literature for various studies in which we were involved. It became apparent that in each area of study the references usually led to certain studies that were of major significance in the identifying basic principles or essential facts. Invariably these studies were the landmarks for further research and study. We noted that these studies when taken collectively, described a considerable portion of man's quest for knowledge about physical activity. In our opinion a collection of the verbatim reports of the classical studies would be of great help and immeasurable interest to physical educators and students of physical activity.

The selection of the studies themselves, of course, posed a dilemma. Which studies should we include? What areas should we cover? How could we be sure that the classical studies are presented? To resolve the problem, we each surveyed the reference citations in prominent textbooks of physiology of exercise, measurement and evaluation, foundations and principles of physical education, and various reviews of research, such as those found in the *Research Quarterly* and the *Professional Contributions of the American Academy of Physical Education*. This initial survey provided us with a long list of references which we classified into several

v

categories: strength, energy and metabolism, etc. We then selected those studies which in our judgment had made significant contributions to the development of knowledge about physical activity. Finally, the list of studies was edited to achieve balance in the number of studies in the various areas and in the number of researchers who were represented.

We found the writing of the book, the chapter summaries, and the commentaries on each study an exciting reintroduction to the spirit of scientific inquiry. Time and time again, an idea or a relationship would be synthesized in a new context, or with new meaning. We have tried to comment on each study in enough detail to highlight its significance, but not to such a degree that the reader would be unable to make his own interpretations and see the study in his own personal context.

We have not included a summary chapter because we feel that the reader should draw his own conclusions about the most important findings in each area and the scientific challenges that remain. It will be obvious to the reader that many gaps remain in our knowledge about the scientific basis of physical activity. Possibly new avenues of thought and investigation might be stimulated by a review of some of the classical contributions in this field. We hope that the readers of the book will be able to capture some of the excitement of the process of scientific inquiry that we experienced as we collected and summarized the studies in the book.

Of course, an effort like this would not have been possible without the help of many people. First, we would like to mention George Flynn of Prentice-Hall, who seized upon the idea when it was first presented to him and urged us to continue to its completion. Second, we would like to acknowledge the kind consideration of all of the authors, editors, and publishers of the many papers presented in the book for their permission to reprint the studies. Third, we would like to recognize the influence and contributions of the authors of the studies themselves, for both of us have worked with and studied under several of these men and can speak first-hand of their dedication and their work. Finally, we would like to thank all of those persons involved in the physical reproduction of the book itself. Thanks for a job well done.

R.C.B.
G.S.K.

Contents

Classical Studies
on
Physical
Activity

Energy and Metabolism

The search for the secrets of the body's methods of supplying energy to the muscles has fascinated scientists for many decades. Ostensibly, the system is simple: carbohydrate sources in the muscles break down to liberate energy for muscular contraction. However, the energy sources must be replenished, and this requires the presence of oxygen which must be delivered to the tissues by the cardiorespiratory system. The classical problems faced by scientists are concerned with the amount of energy that can be provided without the presence of oxygen in the tissues, the relationship of oxygen availability and utilization to the accumulation of lactic acid, and the extent to which oxygen utilization can serve as an index of the magnitude of the demands of exercise on the body.

The creative and insightful work of A.V. Hill and his associates in England in the early 1920's provides an excellent basis for the examination of the relationship between aerobic and anaerobic metabolism in the muscles. Following the introduction of the concept of oxygen debt by Hill and his associates, D. B. Dill and his colleagues at the Fatigue Laboratory at Harvard University in the 1930's extended the knowledge on the relationship of oxygen utilization and oxygen debt to include the relationship between these variables and the capacity for vigorous physical work. Henry, at the University of California in the late 1940's and early 1950's clarified the relationship between the lactic acid and the alactic acid component of oxygen debt. Passmore and his fellow workers in England during the 1950's conducted extensive studies on the metabolic cost of a wide variety of activities, thus adding to the knowledge on the relationship of oxygen utilization and the intensity of physical work. More recently, in 1960, Hill has proposed some interesting hypotheses about the reversal of usual chemical processes in the muscle by stretching of the muscle during work.

The studies in this chapter were chosen to help provide a good
survey of the efforts made by scientists to understand the dynamic
relationship between energy, metabolism, and work.

A. V. HILL / HARTLEY LUPTON

Muscular Exercise, Lactic Acid, and the Supply Utilization of Oxygen

Reprinted from the *Quarterly Journal of Medicine*,
16 (1923), 135–71.

*Probably the physiological concept that is best known to students of exercise
physiology is the concept of* oxygen debt. *This article, which was published in
1923, presents some of the basic concepts of oxygen utilization, lactic acid
accumulation, the relationship between oxygen consumption and work, and oxygen
debt. This extensive, definitive treatise on muscular exercise explores every topic
and gives data to support the conclusions that are presented.*

The following statements from this study will point out its significance.

> *Oxygen is not used in the primary breakdown processes of rest or activity,
> . . . it is used only in what, strictly speaking, may be called a recovery
> process.*
>
> *. . . we must regard the muscle as capable of "going into debt" for
> oxygen, of committing itself to future oxidations on the security of lactic
> acid liberated in activity. [Hill and Lupton are referring to the fact that
> the body will not exceed its maximum lactic acid limit and thus the organism
> is protected against exceeding its basic limits.]*
>
> *. . . the maximum duration of an effort of given intensity is related to
> the intensity in a manner depending simply upon the supply of oxygen, actual
> or potential.*
>
> *. . . lactic acid will never occur as such: it will always obtain base from
> some weaker acid to form sodium, potassium, or ammonium lactate, in
> which forms alone it will exist in muscle, lymph, and blood.*
>
> *Little, however, is gained by regarding the phenomena of exercise,
> respiration, and dyspnoea as simpler than they really are: further knowledge
> will certainly introduce these other factors.*

*As the other articles in this chapter are reviewed, the magnitude of the contri-
bution of Hill and his colleagues will become more pointed. Only by reading the
treatise in its entirety can the process that Hill used in arriving at this conclusion
be fully comprehended. Of course, spontaneous discovery seldom happens in*

science, and Hill was influenced by the work of Fletcher, Meyerhof, Krogh, and Lindhard. The concept of oxygen debt has been further refined by Hill, Lupton, and Long; and later by Margaria, Edwards, and Dill, and by Henry. These studies are also included in this chapter.

Hill's most recent concern with the physiology of work has been his postulation[1] of negative work. He shows that by stretching a muscle during work (while it is contracting) the amount of heat energy produced during work can be lessened. Thus, he suggests it is possible for individuals to exert the same amount of force in a work task but to have different rates of oxygen consumption. He reports an experiment where one subject, in performing the same amount of work, was pedaling a bicycle forward and the other was pedaling backward. The one pedaling backward showed the lesser fatigue and had the lower oxygen consumption. This idea was developed by Hill as a result of some experimental laboratory work with frogs. He also relied on the studies of W. O. Fenn, in 1923 and 1924, in which Fenn reported that forcible lengthening during the contraction period decreases the energy liberated. Fenn reasoned that the shortening of a muscle in the usual contraction caused an extra amount of energy to be liberated, and stretching the muscle prevented the liberation of the extra energy. Hill closes the article with one of his well-known witticisms "The moral is, if you have a bright idea, try it and see; the result may be much more amusing than you expected."

Introduction

Modern progress in knowledge of the behavior of muscle started from the researches of Fletcher[11, 12, 13] on the respiration of muscular tissue, and has been guided since by that landmark in exact physiology, the investigation by Fletcher and Hopkins[14] of lactic acid in surviving muscle. Hence arose a long series of investigations by many workers on the heat production, the gaseous exchange, and the lactic acid and glycogen content of muscle; these have been summarized elsewhere.[21, 23, 24] The insight thus acquired of the intimate physical and chemical mechanisms of the living muscle exceeds that of any other cell or process. In muscle we have several independent but convergent lines of progress, chemical, physical, and mechanical, and it is possible already to see, often not too dimly,

from one to the other. Our knowledge is not, of course, in any single direction complete: it seemed sufficient, however, to warrant an attempt to press to their logical conclusion, in the case of man, the principles established in working on isolated muscles, while it was to be hoped that such an attempt would throw further light, and suggest further lines of attack, on the more academic problems of the pure physiology of muscle. Hitherto, apart from an occasional reference to lactic acid in connection with respiration, dyspnoea, or fatigue, there has been little realization of the extraordinary vigor of the chemical processes which occur in muscle, or of the clearness of the principles which govern them. With the generous help of the Medical Research Council the attempt has been made, and the following is a summarized account of some aspects of it, which we

---

[1] A. V. Hill, "Production and Absorption of Work by Muscle," *Science,* **131** (1960), 897–903.

believe perhaps may be pertinent to medicine. During the course of our work it has been a continual surprise and incentive to find how precisely the principles established in the case of isolated frog's muscle are verified in the case of muscular exercise in normal man: and we have been encouraged thereby to hope that perhaps these same principles may be found already to bear some tentative application to the case of muscular exercise in the abnormal, and (among other things) to the phenomena of breathlessness.

We have adopted throughout the standpoint reached in modern investigation of the isolated muscle, and have attempted to show, by experiment and deduction, how application may be made to normal man. We have avoided more than an occasional reference to the possible clinical aspects of the facts and principles discussed.

A. The Function of Oxidation in the Body

Oxygen is used in the combustion of foodstuffs to supply the energy required for bodily processes. Even in a state of complete rest the living cell requires oxygen in order to maintain its dynamic state of molecular organization, of readiness and power to respond to a stimulus. It is well known that a nerve deprived of oxygen gradually fails to conduct an impulse, though the amount of oxygen used is exceedingly small.[1] In muscle the resting rate of oxygen consumption is much larger, but it has long been known that, especially at relatively low temperatures, a muscle will maintain its excitability for considerable periods in the complete absence of oxygen. This was believed to be due to the supposed fact that oxygen is taken in and stored in the

living protoplasm for use in later need ("intramolecular oxygen"). There is no truth in this belief. The most rigorous exclusion of oxygen, even the entire prohibition of oxidation by poisoning with cyanide,[46] still leaves the muscle active for a considerable period. Moreover, the magnitude of the "initial" heat production[1] in a muscle twitch[45], and its time relations[15], are totally unaffected by the presence or absence of oxygen. *Oxygen is not used in the primary breakdown processes of rest or activity*, which proceed uninfluenced for a time by its complete absence: *it is used only in what, strictly speaking, may be called recovery processes.*

If a living, resting, isolated muscle be deprived of oxygen it survives for a while; if the process be not pushed too far, and oxygen be restored to the muscle before it is too late, it then proceeds to make good its previous deficit in oxygen intake by a rise above its earlier resting value. If an isolated muscle be stimulated in oxygen there is a prolonged rise in its oxygen consumption, lasting for some time after the stimulus: if the muscle be stimulated in a chamber free from oxygen, and then, later on, oxygen be admitted, the rate of oxygen consumption rises above normal, and the total oxygen used in a long survival period is the same as if oxygen had been present throughout. The same phenomena, within limits, can be demonstrated in man. It is not practicable to deprive a man, as a whole, of oxygen: the brain is too sensitive to oxygen want. It is practicable, however, to deprive the human muscle of oxygen, in the sense that it is possible for a healthy man to take

---

[1] i.e., the heat liberated in the phases of contraction and relaxation, as distinguished from recovery.

muscular exercise requiring far more oxygen than can conceivably be supplied through the circulation during the exercise itself, and to establish a heavy "oxygen debt": indeed, as the result of 24 sec only of severe exercise in a powerful man, we have found a total oxygen intake during the following 30 min of about $8\frac{3}{4}$ l in excess of the resting value: 24 sec of exercise led to a delayed consumption of oxygen sufficient to keep the subject comfortable in bed for more than half an hour. In another experiment more prolonged violent effort led to an oxygen deficit of $13\frac{1}{4}$ l. Were it not for the fact that the body is able thus to meet its liabilities for oxygen considerably *in arrears*, it would not be possible for man to make anything but the most moderate muscular effort. We will consider this more fully later. It is obvious, however, that we must regard the muscle as capable of "going into debt" for oxygen, of *committing itself to future oxidations on the security of lactic acid liberated in activity.*

We must distinguish therefore between three different quantities—oxygen "intake," oxygen "consumption," and oxygen "requirement." The first two may differ slightly, in so far as oxygen may (*a*) be taken in, in excess of consumption, to saturate blood previously reduced; and (*b*) be used in excess of intake at the expense of blood previously saturated: the difference is small. The third, however, may differ widely from the others, to the extent that "expenditure" may largely exceed "income," so long as the "security" remains adequate. In the body the "security" reaches its limit at the lactic acid maximum, and any further expenditure must be made out of "income" of oxygen through the lungs and circulation. The "security" given,

lactic acid then forces the body later to pay off its debt out of income, in oxidative recovery.

B. The Role of Lactic Acid in the Muscle

Lactic acid holds a very special position in the economy of the muscle. Like gas in the internal combustion engine its oxidation provides the power required to do external work: like the gas, also, it is intimately concerned in the mechanism by which the work is done. It appears to be derived from the glycogen stored within the muscle, either directly or through the intermediation of a hexose diphosphate. In activity, or in prolonged rest without oxygen, lactic acid appears in the muscle:[14] in recovery it reverts to glycogen, a small portion only being oxidized.[35,36] If an isolated muscle be kept at rest in oxygen, no lactic acid appears; it finally becomes inexcitable, but does not show the phenomena of *rigor mortis*. If the muscle be deprived of oxygen at rest, or if it be stimulated, lactic acid accumulates within it and corresponding glycogen disappears.[36] Deprival of oxygen pushed to its limit means *rigor mortis* and a lactic acid maximum of about 0.5 per cent to 0.65 per cent : stimulation, pushed to its limit, means inexcitability and a "stimulation maximum" of lactic acid of about 0.24 per cent to 0.4 per cent. Continued lack of oxygen, in a muscle stimulated to a standstill, leads to further lactic acid production and death. The introduction of oxygen to a muscle fatigued by stimulation, or by prolonged lack of oxygen, leads to an oxygen consumption and a heat production far above the normal resting values, to a disappearance of lactic acid, and to a restoration of the glycogen: the muscle regains its previous excitability, recovery has occurred, and a subsequent stimulus will release lactic acid again. Moreover, Meyerhof has shown: (*a*) that the excess oxygen[2] and the excess CO_2 are equal, that the recovery process therefore has a respiratory quotient of unity, and involves the oxidation only of carbohydrate (or lactic acid); (*b*) that the oxygen and the CO_2 correspond to the total carbohydrate lost by oxidation in the complete cycle; (*c*) that when lactic acid appears glycogen always disappears in exactly corresponding amount; (*d*) that when lactic acid disappears in recovery, glycogen always reappears in corresponding amount, *less a quantity which, calculated from the oxygen consumption, has been lost by oxidation*; (*e*) that only about one-fourth of the lactic acid removed in recovery is oxidized: three-fourths has reappeared as glycogen.

Moreover, Meyerhof has shown[37] that the same phenomena occur, in an exaggerated degree, in muscle which has been finely chopped. Here, in the absence of oxygen, there is a rapid production of lactic acid: in the presence of oxygen the production of lactic acid is less, there is still a recovery process: the lactic acid, however, which has failed to appear has *not* been oxidized, since the total oxygen absorbed is only about one-fifth of the quantity which would have been required to complete the oxidation of that amount.

It is probable, from the work of the Embden School,[9] that a hexose diphosphate $[C_6H_{10}O_4(H_2PO_4)_2]$ is an intermediary between glycogen and lactic acid, that it may indeed be the

immediate precursor of lactic acid, the "lactacidogen" whose explosive transformation into lactic acid, on stimulation of the muscle, initiates the contractile process. Embden showed that, in muscle extract, glucose cannot be broken down into lactic acid, while hexose diphosphate can. Moreover, Meyerhof[37] has shown that only in the presence of phosphate can minced muscle transform all its preformed glycogen into lactic acid. Apart from these observations, the chemistry of the breakdown and restoration of glycogen in the muscle remains at present a mystery. That phosphoric acid, however, has some special role in the process is shown by Embden's work, and it is of unusual interest that Embden, Gräfe, and Schmitz[10] found the maximum muscular output of trained men to be considerably increased by the ingestion of phosphates.

C. Heat Production

The contraction of a muscle has long been known to be accompanied by a production of heat: this heat appears more or less simultaneously with the mechanical response. Recent experiments, however, by A. V. Hill[20] and by Hartree and Hill[17] have shown that there is a further extensive production of heat, long delayed after the stimulus which caused it. In an isolated muscle stimulated in oxygen there is a prolonged evolution of heat, lasting for several minutes, which all evidence tends to connect with the oxidative removal of lactic acid in recovery (see Section N below). This recovery heat production has told us much about the time relations and other characteristics of the restoration process, following muscular activity. Other experiments by A. V. Hill,[19] by Peters,[40] and by Meyerhof[38] have

---

[2] "Excess oxygen" and "excess CO_2" are used throughout this paper to express the amount of gas used, or produced, in excess of the resting value, in any given time.

shown that the total heat liberated in the anaerobic production of 1 g of lactic acid in muscle is about 370 cal. In its later oxidative removal[17] there is a further liberation of about 340 cal. In the complete cycle, therefore, in which 1 g of lactic acid is liberated and removed, and the muscle finally restored to its original state, there is a total evolution of 710 cal. But the heat of oxidation of 1 g of lactic acid is about 3,788 cal. Hence only a small fraction of the lactic acid can have been oxidized in recovery: in a muscle lightly stimulated, and with an adequate supply of oxygen, only about one molecule in five or six of the lactic acid is oxidized, the remainder being restored as glycogen during the recovery process.

Further experiments by Hartree and Hill[15] have shown that, in addition to this recovery process, there is an evolution of heat—(a) during the onset, (b) during the maintenance, of a contraction, and (c) during relaxation, and the analysis of these has led to the following picture of the mechanism involved. The muscle is to be regarded as an accumulator of energy, energy available for rapid nonoxidative discharge, stored during previous oxidations. In this respect it is similar to an electrical accumulator. The transformation of glycogen into lactic acid, the action of the lactic acid on the muscle proteins, and the neutralization of the lactic acid by the alkaline buffers of the muscle, are the vehicle by which this stored energy is made manifest: during recovery the process is reversed at the expense of a portion of lactic acid oxidized. The accumulator has been recharged, at the expense of oxidations required to run the dynamo. We must regard the muscle therefore as possessing two mechanisms: (a) the anaerobic one of discharge, and (b) the

oxidative one of recovery. These two mechanisms are probably distinct from one another; the first may certainly act without the second, the second without the first, and their efficiencies may vary independently. The speed, vigor, and efficiency of contraction and the speed of relaxation depend upon the first one: the speed and efficiency of recovery depend upon the second.

The production of lactic acid during contraction, which is probably the ultimate cause of the mechanical response, must be regarded as being very sharply localized within the muscle fiber. Its sudden appearance probably changes the electrical and colloidal state of certain sensitive protein interfaces in the muscle, producing a rise of tension and the phenomena of contraction. During relaxation, a process just as important as contraction though largely neglected by physiologists, the acid is removed from its place of action through neutralization by the alkaline buffers of the muscle. The physical problem of how the acid produces the contraction has not yet been solved, but whatever be the mechanism, its reversal in relaxation would appear to be due simply to the withdrawal and neutralization of the acid whose presence locally in high concentration evoked the response. This affords a simple explanation of the delayed relaxation associated with fatigue: the neutralization of lactic acid has rendered the muscle less alkaline, and further neutralization is slower and less effective.

D. The Efficiency and Speed of the Recovery Process

The condition of the muscle apparently determines the efficiency and speed of the recovery process (which will be discussed further in

Section N). The "efficiency" may be measured by the ratio (total lactic acid removed): (portion of lactic acid oxidized), as found in oxidative recovery. In the experiments of Hartree and A. V. Hill[17] this ratio appeared to vary from 4.9:1 to 6:1, with a mean of about 5.5:1; in Meyerhof's experiments[35, 36] it was about 4:1; in the former experiments the supply of oxygen was adequate, the muscles were never fatigued, and recovery was rapid; in the latter the contrary was the case and recovery was correspondingly less efficient. It would seem probable that the efficiency of recovery in a healthy trained man is at least as high as in an isolated frog's muscle; we shall assume therefore in what follows a figure of 6:1 for the ratio

(total lactic acid removed):

(lactic acid oxidized)

in the recovery process of a healthy normal man.

In the isolated muscle the "speed" of recovery is best measured by experiments on the recovery heat production.[17] Like that of all chemical reactions it depends on the temperature, increasing two to three times for a rise of 10°C. It increases rapidly with the oxygen pressure. It increases with the magnitude of the effort from which recovery is necessary. It depends presumably upon the catalytic oxidative activity of surfaces inside the living cell. The oxygen pressure in the muscle increases in man with the vigor of the circulation and the efficiency of the lungs. Moreover, the oxidative activity of a cell may be changed in various artificial ways, e.g., it may be diminished by narcotics or cyanides (Warburg[44]). It is natural therefore to assume that the velocity of oxidative recovery in human subjects may vary similarly—not only in accordance with the oxygen supply, but with the more intimate

physicochemical characteristics of their muscle cells.

E. The Production of Lactic Acid in Man

After severe exercise lactic acid appears in the urine (Ryffel[42]). The amount however is small, and is no measure whatever of the quantity which has appeared in the body. The most obvious tokens of the latter are (a) the magnitude of the oxygen debt, and (b) the increased respiratory quotient, following severe exercise. It would seem probable that carbohydrate alone provides the energy for the excess metabolism of exercise: this certainly appears to be the case in isolated muscle[33]. In moderate, prolonged, steady exercise therefore, in which the concentration of lactic acid attains a steady value in the muscle, the respiratory quotient approximates to unity. As soon, however, as the exercise reaches a severity greater than can be maintained on a contemporary supply of oxygen—as soon as the level of exercise is reached at which lactic acid must continue to accumulate throughout it—the respiratory quotient rises above unity, CO_2 is turned out by lactic acid, sodium (or potassium) lactate being formed from the bicarbonate of blood and tissue fluids. In our observations the extreme upper value of the apparent respiratory quotient (R.Q.) of the excess metabolism, after exercise, has been 2.6: assuming a real respiratory quotient of 1, this means that for every gram-molecule of O_2 being used, and for every gram-molecule of CO_2 being produced, 1.6 g-mol of CO_2 were being turned out by lactic acid from bicarbonate.

Now in moderate exercise the main part of the lactic acid liberated in the muscle does not combine with bicarbonate. This is clearly shown in Section M below, and can be substantiated on the isolated muscle. The heat produced in the process of relaxation (as found by Hartree and Hill[15]) is far larger than that corresponding to the neutralization of lactic acid by bicarbonate, and Meyerhof[38] has suggested that the neutralization associated with relaxation is effected by the buffered alkaline proteins of the muscle tissue itself, according to the scheme, (lactic acid) + (sodium protein salt) →(sodium lactate) + (acid protein). This corresponds exactly to what we believe to be the mechanism by which acid is neutralized (and CO_2 carried) in blood,[39] *and is capable moreover of providing adequate heat.* Thus, in moderate exercise, the protein buffers of the muscle should be capable of neutralizing all the acid formed, little CO_2 should be driven out, no dyspnoea should occur, and the R.Q. of the excess metabolism should remain at unity. In severe exercise, on the other hand, an excess of lactic acid is produced for which the supply of protein buffers is inadequate, the hydrogen-ion concentration rises, the respiratory effort increases, and CO_2 is turned out of bicarbonate in muscle and blood. Hence the R.Q. rises above unity, its rise being an index of the amount of acid combining with bicarbonate. On the qualitative side therefore—by the examination of the urine after severe exercise—we know that lactic acid is produced in man and escapes in small quantities into the blood: on the quantitative side, the very great rise of the R.Q. during and after violent effort, is a sign that the acid production is considerable. In the next section we shall show how the "oxygen debt" may be used as an indicator of the absolute amount of lactic acid present in the body at the end of exercise.

F. Lactic Acid and Oxygen Debt

The "oxygen debt" is defined as the total amount of oxygen used, after cessation of exercise, in recovery therefrom. It may be measured in man in the following simple manner. Firstly, the resting rate of oxygen intake of the subject is determined by the Douglas bag method in some standard position (standing, sitting, or lying). The exercise is then taken. Immediately on its cessation the subject begins to breathe from the air into a large Douglas bag, remaining at rest in the standard position throughout recovery. We have used bags of capacities 400, 300, and 200 l. If one bag be not sufficient, a second one may be used and two analyses made. In experiments described in Section H, on the time course of recovery, a series of bags was employed, in fairly rapid succession throughout the recovery period, and such experiments have told us how long it is necessary in general to collect the expired gases. After moderate exercise the oxygen intake will return to its resting level in about 6 to 8 min: after very severe or exhausting exercise it may remain high for a much longer time. The total oxygen used in the selected recovery period is then determined by analysis and measurement in the usual manner. From this is subtracted the oxygen which the body would have used in the same time at rest. The difference represents the oxygen debt at the end of the exercise.

There are four possible objections to this method: (*a*) At the end of exercise a certain amount of oxygen is lacking, which at rest is dissolved or combined in blood or tissues, and this quantity is included in the figure determined as above. It can be calculated, however, that this error is almost negligibly small, at any rate in the case of oxygen debts of several liters. (b) One cannot be sure that the oxygen intake has returned to normal, after a selected period of recovery, unless special observations be made to prove that it has. This objection is admitted. The error, however, is always in the same direction, viz., in that of making our observed oxygen debt too small: we have endeavored always to allow an adequate recovery period, and in some observations (see Section H below) we have followed the rate of oxygen intake throughout. We can claim anyhow that our observations are certainly not too large. (c) The oxidations of recovery may replace in part the normal resting oxidative processes: e.g., if part of the resting metabolism be due to the necessity of producing heat to keep the body warm, this part could safely be omitted by the body during recovery from exercise, when loss of heat, rather than its production, may be important. This objection also is valid. The error however cannot be very large, and in any case it will cause our observations again to be too low, so that again we may claim them as minimum values. (d) Part of the oxygen debt observed may be due to the excessive movements of heart and respiratory muscles occurring during recovery: these movements, however, rapidly slacken, and cannot in any case account for more than a small fraction of the considerable oxygen debts found, expecially after they have slackened. On the whole, therefore, we may regard our results as reasonably accurate statements of the oxygen required in the metabolic processes of oxidative recovery.

No process is known to occur in muscular exercise in man which is not apparent in isolated muscle, and we shall now assume that the recovery oxygen, measured as above, is used entirely in the oxidative removal of lactic acid. The oxidation is as follows: $C_3H_6O_3 + 3O_2 \rightarrow 3CO_2 + 3H_2O$. Now, if the "efficiency" of recovery be assumed to be six in the sense defined above, i.e., if a total of 6 mol of lactic acid disappear in recovery for every one oxidized, then 6 mol of lactic acid will be removed for every 3 mol of oxygen used, or 2 g-mol of lactic acid (i.e., 180 g) for every gram-molecule of oxygen (i.e., 22.2 litres). This means that *an oxygen debt of 1 l betokens the presence in the body, at the end of exercise, of about 8.1 g of lactic acid.* The following table gives the magnitude of the oxygen debt, at the end of various types of exercise, in several different individuals, together with the total lactic acid content of the body calculated therefrom.

We see therefore that large quantities of lactic acid may be produced in the body, certainly up to 1.5 g per k of body weight. The extreme rapidity with which it can be produced is notable, as is shown by the last entry in the table, where over 3 g per sec were being liberated by a powerful individual running 225 yd at top speed. Even moderate exercise, such as running at about 7 mi per hr, leads to the production of about 13 g of acid in the body. It must not be supposed that this lactic acid occurs only in the absence of oxygen. There is a balance, even at rest, between lactic acid being produced and lactic acid being removed, as will be shown in Section I, dealing with the "steady state." The more vigorous the exercise the higher the level of the lactic acid at which the balance occurs, and the greater the oxygen debt at the end of exercise. If, however, the severity of the exercise be too great the supply of oxygen cannot cope with the production of lactic

TABLE 1

Subject	Weight k	Exercise	Oxygen Debt cc	Total Lactic Acid g
H.	73	Flat running at speed of 191 m per min, for 5 min 8 sec	1668	13.5
H.	—	Flat running at speed of 201 m per min, for 4 min 18 sec	2485	20.1
H.	—	10 sec violent jumping with skipping movement	2510	20.3
H.	—	20 sec violent jumping with skipping movement	5504	44.6
H.	—	Flat running for 3 min 23 sec at a speed of 239 m per min, i.e., at a speed causing an increasing debt of oxygen	2870	23.3
H.	—	Flat running for 33 min at a speed of 239 m per min. Practical exhaustion	7890	64.0
L.	65	36 sec violent jumping with skipping movement	5700	46.2
L.	—	Flat running at speed of 261 m per min for $4\frac{1}{4}$ min	7160	58.0
L.	—	Jumping over stool 14 in. high for 2 min 7 sec	10499	85.0
W.M.H.	72.5	Violent gymnastic exercises for 30 sec involving rapid contractions of all the muscles, leading to exhaustion	7670	62.1
		Ditto preceded by a rapid $\frac{1}{4}$-mi run	13250	107.2
S.	68.55	Ditto for 30 sec	6455	52.3
M. W.	79.9	Ditto for 32 sec	7810	63.3
W.	—	Flat running, 225 yd in 23.4 sec	8745	71.0

acid, no balance is attained, and exhaustion rapidly sets in.

G. The Lactic Acid Maximum and the Limit of Muscular Exertion

Stimulation of the isolated muscle leads to a so-called stimulation or fatigue maximum of the lactic acid content, which was supposed at one time[14, 21] to depend upon a limit in the amount of the lactic acid precursor. This, however, is not the case. Meyerhof has shown[37] that the immersion of the muscle in a solution of alkaline phosphate buffers may considerably increase the stimulation maximum of lactic acid. Apparently the limit is set by the rise in the hydrogen-ion concentration (cH) effected by the presence of the lactic acid itself, and may be increased if the rise of cH be hindered by the presence of extra alkali. This is a very important observation, as we shall see below, in explaining the differences in maximum effort between different human subjects. It was found also by Meyerhof that the stimulation maximum is practically the same for indirect as for direct excitation: his values range from 0.24 per cent to 0.43 per cent. Let us assume that a human subject, as the result of a supreme effort, can produce some 0.3 per cent of lactic acid in all the active muscles involved in violent running, jumping, or skipping. These muscles, in an active 70-k man, might weigh about 25 k: this figure of course is necessarily a matter of estimation. The total acid present therefore would amount to 75 g. Hence, if the recovery

removal of 8.1 g of lactic acid be secured by the intake of 1 l of oxygen,
the oxygen debt in this case of extreme
effort should amount to $75/8.1 = 9.3$ l.
Table 1 above contains several observations on the oxygen debt found in cases
of severe and exhausting exercise. Thus
H. running for 33 min at a rate at
which the oxygen requirement exceeded
the maximum oxygen intake produced
a debt of 7,890 cc; M. W. performing
violent rapid gymnastic exercises
produced in 32 sec a debt of 7,810 cc;
W. as the result of a rapid sprint of
225 yd in. 23.4 sec produced a debt
of 8,745 cc; L. by violent jumping for
2 min 7 sec caused a debt of 10,499 cc;
W. M. H. by an extreme effort a debt
of about $13\frac{1}{4}$ l. The prediction therefore
is verified; the oxygen debt in these
cases attains a value corresponding
reasonably well to that calculated from
the fatigue maximum of lactic acid in
the muscles. It is clear that in such
efforts the limit is not placed at an
early stage by fatigue occurring in the
nervous system, but rather by the
presence of acid in the muscles themselves.

Different individuals, even those
apparently of similar muscular development, differ enormously from one
another in the vigor and duration of
their maximum efforts. There are two
types of effort: (a) the violent and
short-lived type not depending on
concurrent oxidation, and (b) the more
moderate, longer lasting type, depending on the supply and utilization of
oxygen, i.e., made possible by contemporary and adequate recovery. All
possible stages intermediate between
these may occur. These individual
differences, important in everyday
life, in athletics, and probably in medicine, are of a complex nature. The
withdrawal of protective nervous
inhibitions, the mental and moral
factors ("guts") which make one in-

dividual inevitably a better man than
another, are clearly of importance;
the excitability of the respiratory center, and of the nervous system as a
whole, the size and capacity of lungs
and heart, the fitness of various organs
to stand the strain of violent effort,
have all clearly to be taken into
account. There remains, however,
one simple chemical factor, the efficiency of buffering of the muscles, which
determines the fatigue maximum of
lactic acid, the maximum oxygen
debt, and therewith the extent and
duration of a shortlived violent effort.
This factor is fully considered in Section
M below.

H. The Rate of Oxidative Recovery from Exercise in Man

There are only a few investigations
recorded in physiological literature of
the rate of return of the oxygen intake
to its resting value on the cessation
of exercise. Campbell, Douglas, and
Hobson[5] followed the return to the
normal resting value for periods of 80
and 90 min following different rates
of exercise on a bicycle ergometer.
Krogh and Lindhard[26] performed
similar experiments using similar apparatus.

Our experiments, which have been
concerned with the influence of varying
the type and severity of the exercise on
the time relations of recovery, have
confirmed the earlier observations,
and have brought out certain other
points of interest. Many types of exercise have been employed, of which the
following may be regarded as typical:
(a) flat running at a speed of 211 m
per min (8 mi per hr), the time relations
of recovery being determined (i) after
a short period of exercise (4 min), and
(ii) after a long period (22 min); (b)
flat running at a speed of 250 m per
min (9.3 mi per hr), continued for

TABLE 2

Exp. 1. *Subject*, L. *Exercise*, flat running at 211 m per min for 4 min. Resting (sitting): O_2 intake, 251 cc per min; CO_2 output, 227 cc per min; R.Q., 0.91. Total oxygen used in recovery in 24 min = 2,837 cc. Oxygen requirement at this speed 2,790 cc per min.

Interval of Collection	Mid-point of Interval from End of Exercise	Recovery, excess Oxygen:	
		Total in Interval	per min
33.3 sec	16.7 sec	1096	1975
35.2 ″	51 ″	416	709
35.6 ″	1 min 26.3 ″	229	386
1 min 3.2 ″	2 ″ 15.7 ″	238	226
2 ″ 3.3 ″	3 ″ 49 ″	333	162
2 ″ 6.1 ″	5 ″ 53.6 ″	86	41
3 ″ 7.4 ″	8 ″ 30.4 ″	259	83
3 ″ 4.1 ″	11 ″ 36.1 ″	64	21
5 ″ 6.1 ″	15 ″ 41.2 ″	82	16
5 ″ 35.8 ″	21 ″ 2.2 ″	34	6

Exp. 2. *Subject*, L. *Exercise*, violent jumping for 36 sec. Resting (sitting): O_2, 243 cc per min; CO_2, 197 cc per min; R.Q., 0.81.

Interval of Collection	Mid-point of Interval from End of Exercise	Recovery, excess Oxygen:	
		Total in Interval	per min
33.7 sec	17 sec	1105	1969
33.1 ″	50 ″	761	1382
32.3 ″	1 min 23 ″	463	860
1 min 5.2 ″	2 ″ 11.7 ″	554	514
1 ″ 3.6 ″	3 ″ 16.1 ″	368	347
2 ″ 3.3 ″	4 ″ 49.6 ″	536	261
4 ″ 2 ″	7 ″ 52.2 ″	633	157
6 ″ 31.2 ″	13 ″ 8.8 ″	743	114
6 ″ 33 ″	19 ″ 41 ″	537	82

Exp. 3. *Subject*, L. *Exercise*, flat running for 6 min at 250 m per min. Resting (sitting): O_2, 262 cc per min; CO_2, 211 cc per min; R.Q., 0.81. Oxygen requirement for this speed, 5,360 cc per min. Actual maximum excess intake, 3,483 cc per min. Hence a rapidly increasing oxygen debt, amounting to 7,160 cc at the end of 6 min running.

Interval of Collection	Mid-point of Interval from End of Exercise	Recovery, excess Oxygen:	
		Total in Interval	per min
33.5 sec	17 sec	1542	2763
36 ″	52 ″	927	1548
35.1 ″	1 min 28 ″	502	858
1 min 1 ″	2 ″ 15 ″	568	559
2 ″ 3.5 ″	3 ″ 48 ″	642	312
2 ″ 4.2 ″	5 ″ 51 ″	418	202
3 ″ 6.3 ″	8 ″ 27 ″	533	172
4 ″ 12 ″	12 ″ 26 ″	436	104
4 ″ 2.7 ″	16 ″ 13 ″	344	85
5 ″ 2.3 ″	20 ″ 46 ″	479	95
5 ″ 4.8 ″	25 ″ 49 ″	254	50
5 ″ 4 ″	30 ″ 53 ″	182	36
5 ″ 2.7 ″	35 ″ 56 ″	283	56
5 ″ 4.7 ″	40 ″ 59 ″	51	10

Results in Fig. 1

6 min; (c) rapid violent jumping with a skipping movement, continued for 36 sec.

Previous to the exercise the resting respiratory exchange was determined in some standard position (usually sitting). The subject finished the exercise in front of a stand carrying a wide pipe with nine projecting tubes. To one of these tubes the valves and mouthpiece were fixed: to the others were attached rubber bags through single-way stopcocks. All the tubes were of $\frac{3}{4}$ in. bore, the apparatus being similar in principle to that used by Campbell, Douglas, and Hobson.[5] The subject, on cessation of exercise, adopted the standard resting position, adjusted the valves and noseclip, and commenced to expire into the first bag. At the end of about one-half minute (end of nearest expiration) the first bag was turned off, and the second one turned on for a like interval. This process was continued, the intervals of collection being gradually increased. After the eighth bag the valves were attached successively to separate bags, if the

recovery was being followed for longer periods.

Table 2 gives the results obtained in three typical experiments.

The results indicate that on cessation of the exercise there is an immediate rapid fall in the oxygen intake, which occurs both after severe and after moderate exercise. This rapid fall is complete within 6 to 8 min. If, however, the exercise was severe, the oxygen intake falls to a level somewhat above the original resting level, the excess being maintained for prolonged periods, depending on the severity and extent of the exercise. There is thus a difference between the curves obtained—(a) after moderate exercise carried out for a short time, and (b) after severe or extended exercise. Even in moderate exercise, where the oxygen supply is adequate, if the exercise be maintained for a long period there is a prolonged recovery, and the total oxygen in the recovery period is larger in amount than in the case where the same exercise is maintained only for a short period. Now since, in such exer-

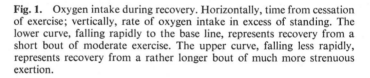

Fig. 1. Oxygen intake during recovery. Horizontally, time from cessation of exercise; vertically, rate of oxygen intake in excess of standing. The lower curve, falling rapidly to the base line, represents recovery from a short bout of moderate exercise. The upper curve, falling less rapidly, represents recovery from a rather longer bout of much more strenuous exertion.

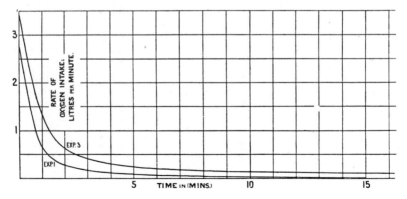

cise, the heart, lungs, and circulation are all able to cope with the demands of the muscles for oxygen, the only debt for oxygen should be that produced at the beginning of the exercise, i.e., before the respiratory, circulatory, and oxidative mechanisms have attained the rate of working equivalent to the exercise. The only explanation of the increased debt, after a prolonged period of such moderate exercise, appears to be that when the exercise is prolonged the steady maintained concentration of lactic acid, corresponding to the rate of oxidation as in Section I below, causes gradual diffusion of the acid to points distant from the oxidative recovery mechanism of the muscle (e.g., into lymph and other tissues), from which it returns by diffusion only very slowly to be oxidized in recovery. The exhaustion resulting from long-continued, comparatively moderate exercise is to be attributed therefore to the presence, outside the muscles, of noticeable quantities of lactic acid, the oxidative removal of which occurs only very slowly, as the acid diffuses gradually back—under a low concentration gradient—to the oxidative mechanism inside the fiber.

I. The "Steady State" in Exercise

In this section we shall deal with recovery occurring during the exercise itself. In prolonged steady exercise a balance must be struck between breakdown and restoration, the rate of breakdown being determined by the vigor of the exercise, that of restoration (*a*) by the concentration of lactic acid in the active muscles, and (*b*) by their oxygen supply. We shall consider here the characteristics of the dynamic equilibrium attained during steady exercise.

It was shown recently by Hartree and Hill[17] that the total magnitude of the recovery process is proportional, as was to be expected, to the extent of the "initial" breakdown preceding and initiating it. They showed also, in a muscle in oxygen, that the velocity of this recovery process is increased—not only absolutely but relatively—by an increase in the effort from which recovery is necessary. Thus, given a constant oxygen pressure in the muscle, the rate at which recovery occurs increases very rapidly as the breakdown from which recovery is necessary is increased. In other words, oxidation is more rapid the greater be the concentration in the muscle of the bodies—e.g., lactic acid—whose removal constitutes recovery. This is the chemical law of "Mass Action." In human muscular exercise the process is more complex: here we have an oxygen pressure in the muscle which decreases to some degree as the amount of exercise increases, so tending to diminish the rate of oxidation: for severe continued exercise this limit to the oxygen supply is the predominant factor and will be further considered below; for moderate exercise, however, where the oxygen supply is adequate, we may expect the rate of oxidation in the muscle to increase continuously as the concentration of lactic acid in it is increased. When muscular exercise is taken in man at a constant speed the lactic acid content of his active muscles increases gradually from its resting minimum at the start. This rise in lactic acid content increases the rate of oxidation, so that finally, if the oxygen supply be adequate, a "steady state" is reached in which the rate of lactic acid production is balanced by the rate of its oxidative removal, and its concentration remains constant in the muscle as long as exercise at that speed is maintained. Hence, the rate of oxygen consumption should rise continuously during the exercise, from its resting minimum at the start to a steady value depending on the severity of the effort; here it should be maintained throughout the exercise. Conversely, when the effort terminates, the lactic acid should continue to be oxidized, but at a decreasing rate as its concentration falls, so that the rate of oxygen consumption should fall continuously from its steady exercise value to its original resting minimum. The latter phenomenon we have discussed in Section H above. These expectations are well verified in certain experiments we have made on the rise in the rate of oxygen intake after the beginning of exercise. In these experiments the subject started to run, at a given constant speed, around a circular grass track $92\frac{1}{2}$ yd ($84\frac{1}{2}$ m) in circumference. The subject (H.) is a practiced runner and was able to maintain constancy of speed for long periods, especially

with the aid of a timekeeper calling out (and recording) the times of successive laps. He carried a small Douglas bag with a side pipe (much more convenient for running than a top pipe), a three-way tap, and a mouthpiece fitted with rubber valves. During each run the expired air was collected in the bag for a period of about 30 sec, the tap being turned on and off at the end of suitable expirations, the exact interval being recorded by the timekeeper on signals from the runner. During running, respiration is so rapid and free that a 30-sec sample is quite adequate, as is seen from the consistency of the points in Fig. 2. After a sufficient interval of rest (about 10 or 12 min) for the oxygen consumption to return to its resting level, the run was repeated, and the expired air collected in a different 30-sec interval. In this way a

Fig. 2. The attainment of a "steady state," in running at various constant speeds. Horizontally, time from commencing to run; vertically, rate of oxygen intake in excess of standing. Speeds of 181, 203, 203, and 267 m per min. The lower three curves represent a genuine steady state, the uppermost curve only an apparent steady state in which the oxygen intake is at its maximum and the oxygen debt is rapidly increasing.

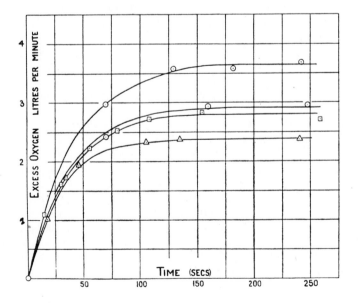

series of observations can be made on the rate of oxygen intake at various moments during the process of "warming up" to the steady state represented by the final constant level of exercise. In Fig. 2 each result, expressed as the rate of oxygen consumption per minute due to the exercise (i.e., after subtraction of the resting rate), is plotted as the ordinate against an abscissa representing the time, measured from the commencement of running, of the *middle* moment of the interval during which the expired gases were collected. The curves show that the rate of oxygen intake due to the exercise in this subject rises rapidly from the start, reaching

its final exercise value in 100 to 150 sec, and half its final value in about 25 sec. Further details of the experiments are given in the following table. The ventilation of the lungs at the highest speed is notable, especially when account is taken of the hindrance offered by valves and mouthpiece.

So far we have discussed a genuine steady state of exercise in which the lactic acid concentration of the muscle attains a constant value, and the subject would be able (apart from extraneous disturbances, such as blisters on the feet) to continue the exercise almost indefinitely. This was almost certainly the case in the experi-

TABLE 3

Subject H. O_2 and CO_2 in cc dry and at N.T.P. Ventilation in l per min moist and at 37°C, and at the actual atmospheric pressure. S = standing.

Speed: m per min	Mid-point of Sample: sec	O_2 per min	Excess Oxygen due to Exercise, per min	CO_2 per min	$\dfrac{CO_2}{O_2}$	Total Ventilation
181	S	269	—	248	0.92	9.16
	47	2220	1943	1780	0.80	48.7
	106	2618	2341	2242	0.86	56.1
	135	2652	2375	2405	0.91	59.3
	240	2655	2378	2622	0.99	67.8
	S	285	—	261	0.92	9.3
203	S	372	—	304	0.82	11.26
	70	2792	2420	2250	0.81	62.1
	159	3300	2928	3010	0.91	76.75
	247	3320	2948	2990	0.90	82.1
	362	3205	2833	2905	0.91	84.7
203	S	306	—	259	0.88	10.18
	15	1406	1096	1300	0.92	37.46
	31	1933	1623	1616	0.84	45.3
	56	2548	2238	2095	0.82	52.7
	80	2846	2536	2370	0.83	57.2
	108	3030	2720	2618	0.86	62.7
	154	3140	2830	2890	0.92	67.7
	258	3012	2702	2870	0.95	69.4
	S	315	—	275	0.87	10.3
267	S	373	—	328	0.88	11.84
	69	3340	2967	3310	0.99	87.6
	129	3950	3577	4040	1.02	114.0
	182	3950	3577	4360	1.10	132.6
	242	4055	3782	4335	1.07	138.4

ments recorded in the three lower curves of Fig. 2. In the highest curve, at a speed of about 10 mi per hr, it was quite certainly not the case for the subject of our experiments, carrying the bag, pipes, and tap, and breathing through valves: he would manifestly have been unable to continue at this speed for more than 10 min if so long. In such severe exercise the lactic acid is continuously accumulating in the muscles, the maximum oxygen intake (depending upon the capacity of heart and lungs) being inadequate to maintain the recovery at a level high enough to cope with the production of lactic acid. Hence, in such cases, the fact that the intake of oxygen has reached a constant value within $2\frac{1}{2}$ min represents nothing more than the fact that its *maximum* level has been attained: *it does not imply that the body has reached a state of dynamic equilibrium in which breakdown is balanced by recovery*. Considering the case of running, there is clearly some critical speed for each individual, below which there is a genuine dynamic equilibrium, breakdown being balanced by restoration, above which, however, the maximum oxygen intake is inadequate, lactic acid accumulating, a continuously increasing oxygen debt being incurred, fatigue and exhaustion setting in. The absolute magnitude of the maximum oxygen intake will be considered below.

The failure to realize the true nature of the steady state of exercise and its dependence on the maximum oxygen intake has led to some curious and paradoxical results. It is obvious that if the oxygen and energy consumption associated with a given type of exercise be required, it is necessary to continue it until a genuine steady state is attained. In running, the true oxygen consumption corresponding to a given speed can be measured only after the subject has been running at that

speed for about $2\frac{1}{2}$ min. If, moreover, the exercise be so vigorous that a steady state is impossible, the rate of oxygen consumption corresponding to the exercise can be measured only by adopting a technique which we will describe later (Section K). The value actually attained is only the *maximum oxygen intake* for that type of exercise, and may not correspond in the least to the oxygen *requirement* of the body: in such a case what we require is (oxygen income) + (rate of increase of oxygen debt), and in severe exercise this cannot be measured directly by such means as we have described hitherto. An amusing paradox in this connection has been recorded by Liljestrand and Stenström.[28] These observers recorded the oxygen intake during horizontal running, and found that the oxygen consumption (per meter traveled) *decreased* as the speed increased over the range 140 to 300 m per min. It was apparently more economical to run fast than slow! Now the opposite is notoriously the case, and these observations of Liljestrand and Stenström (of which, on technical grounds, we have no criticism) obviously need an explanation. The explanation is simple: the subjects of their experiments were not in a genuine steady state at the higher speeds. In the case, e.g., of their subject N. S.[28, p. 183] it is clear that the maximum oxygen intake of about 3.3 l per min was attained at a speed of about 186 m per min. Hence, however fast N. S. ran above this speed he did not use more oxygen, not because he did not require it, but because he could not get it. Consequently, since he ran more meters per minute at the higher speed, the apparent oxygen consumption, i.e., the oxygen intake *per meter*, diminished as the speed increased. The real fact is that the true oxygen requirement per meter (as distinguished from the oxygen intake) increases continuously as the speed of running increases.

The finite time occupied in the attainment of the maximum oxygen intake allows an interesting comment on a well-known practice in athletics, viz. that of running the first part of a middle or long distance race very rapidly. For example, the times of the winner for successive laps ($\frac{1}{3}$ mi) in the mile race of the 1890 Oxford and Cambridge Sports were 80 sec, 93 sec, 88 sec, and this represents only partially the speed at which the first few hundred yards are run in a half-mile or mile race. The advantage of a high initial speed is that it rapidly raises the oxygen intake and the recovery oxidation to their maximum values. The speed at which a race is run depends upon—(*a*) the maximum oxygen debt, and (*b*) the amount of oxidation possible during the race. Clearly the more rapidly the oxygen intake can be pushed up to its limiting value, the greater will be the maximum effort that can be made.

J. The Maximum Oxygen Intake

In this section we will consider shortly—(*a*) the factors in exercise which cause a high oxygen requirement, and (*b*) those which facilitate a high oxygen intake. We shall then give experimental values of the oxygen intake, considerably higher than have been recorded before, and shall discuss shortly the bearing of these values on the problem of the vigor and efficiency of the circulation in man.

Running on the flat is a form of exercise peculiarly well adapted to a high oxygen intake, and specially subject to a high oxygen requirement. As regards the *oxygen intake*, the body is free, respiration is unimpeded, movements are considerable and very rapid, and the muscles are rigid during only a small fraction of the cycle of each step; consequently there is very littel hindrance to a free and rapid circulation of the blood, while the extensive and frequent movements of the limbs, together with an unimpeded and rapid respiratory cycle, assist largely in the venous flow of blood back to the heart. These factors are not so potent in the case of exercise of the types of swimming, rowing, and gymnastics. For example, Lindhard[31] has shown that in the severe effort of holding the weight of the body with arms bent, there is little excess oxygen intake during the exercise, fatigue comes on rapidly, and the excess oxygen consumption occurs mainly after the exercise is over. The circulation through the active muscles is impeded by their continued rigidity.

In oxygen *requirement*, as distinguished from *intake*, running also takes first place among types of muscular exercise. Running consists of rapid, vigorous alternating movements, each maintained only for the minimum of time. Experiments on the heat production of isolated muscles have shown that, to set up a contraction in a muscle and to maintain it, both require a certain liberation of energy,[16] while other experiments[22] have shown that in man the maintenance of the contraction is far less expensive than its setting up, that indeed to maintain a contraction for 5 sec requires only as much energy as to set it up initially. Hence it may be calculated that to make four steps in a second, as in running 100 yd at top speed, should require more than three times as much energy as to set up a maximal contraction in the same muscles and to maintain it for a second. This calculation of course is very rough, but it illustrates the reason why rapid vigorous alternating efforts require far more energy than equally vigorous maintained ones. The setting up of a contractile effort in a muscle is much more expensive than its maintenance. In running, the efforts are almost entirely dynamic, and therefore expensive; in rowing; the cycles are much less rapid, and the effort of maintaining the contraction provides a much larger part of the whole expense, which is correspondingly smaller. The fatigue associated with maintained contraction is due, not to its expensiveness, but to the difficulty placed in the way of an adequate oxygen supply by the rigidity of the muscle.

Very many observations have been made by physiologists of the maximum oxygen intake in man, and in the following table we give a selection of the highest values.

Thus running, skiing, and skating take the highest places in the series, all of these, in the accomplished performer, being types of exercise in which rapid and violent alternating movements occur. Even the notoriously exhausting effort of pushing a motor bicycle up a hill does not approach them in its actual oxygen consumption! We have made a number of observations on various individuals running,

TABLE 4

Oxygen Intake during Exercise (Maximum Values).

Subject	Reference	Exercise	Oxygen, cc per min
L. Zuntz	(1)	Bicycling	2310
Kolmer	(1)	Swimming	2320
Durig	(1)	Climbing	2245
Kolmer	(1)	"	2660
Ranier	(1)	—	2580
Reichel	(1)	—	2670
M. A. M.	(1)	Bicycling (15 min)	3000
M. A. M.	(1)	" (70 min)	2850
Douglas	(2)	"	2795
Hobson	(2)	"	2680
Douglas	(2)	Pushing motor bicycle uphill	2940
Haldane	(2)	" " "	2790
Boothby	(2)	" " "	2750
J. J.	(3)	Bicycling (4 min)	3200
J. L.	(3)	" (3 min)	2550
V. M.	(3)	" (4 min)	2520
N. S.	(4)	Running	3500
G. L.	(4)	"	2570
E. S.	(4)	"	2904
N. S.	(4)	Skiing	3750
G. L.	(4)	"	2800
E. S.	(4)	"	3480
N.S.	(4)	Skating	3060
E. S.	(4)	"	2530
N.S.	(5)	Swimming	2800
G. L.	(5)	"	2080

(1) Benedict and Cathcart, *Publ. No.* **187**, *Carnegie Inst. Wash.* (1913).
(2) Campbell, Douglas, and Hobson *Phil. Trans. Roy. Soc.* (*London*), **B210** (1920), 1.
(3) Lindhard, *Pflügers Arch. ges. Physiol.*, **161** (1915), 318.
(4) Liljestrand and Stenström, *Skand. Arch. Physiol.*, **39** (1920), 167.
(5) *Ibid.*, p. 1.

some of which considerably exceed the values given in the Table 4; the following are well-substantiated maximum values:

Subject	Age: yr	Weight: k	Oxygen: cc per min
S.	—	—	3985
W.	19	72	3995
J.	21	77	4040
L.	21	65	3535
H.	35	73	4175

All the subjects of the above experiments are of athletic disposition; none, however, are first-class athletes. S. is a University Rugby footballer, W. is a good short-distance runner, J. could probably be a first-class mile runner if he tried, H. is a practiced runner (see section L), and L. is a well-built athletic person. In comparing these results with those in the previous table we must remember, also, that N. S. weighed 81 k, so that, reckoned per k, our numbers are still higher than those previously recorded. It is obvious, therefore, that up to about 4,175 cc of oxygen per minute can be taken in during running by a man of 73-k body weight.

Let us consider what this means in circulation of the blood. Assuming a normal oxygen capacity of his blood, viz 0.185 cc of O_2 per cc of arterial blood, and a utilization coefficient of 60 per cent an oxygen intake of 4,175 cc per min implies a blood flow of $4.175/0.185 \times 0.6 = 37.6$ l per min. Lindhard[30] in severe exercise found a utilization coefficient of $57\frac{1}{2}$ per cent when his subject J. J. was taking in 2,410 cc of O_2 per min, and of 79 per cent when he himself was using 2,550 cc per min, while he states that the mean of all his higher experiments was 67 per cent. His subject V. M. gave a value of 58 per cent, and a mean for higher

experiments of 51 per cent. Even if a utilization coefficient of 80 per cent be assumed in our experiments, the blood flow corresponding to an oxygen intake of 4,175 cc must have been 28 l a min. During such exercise the brain and other relatively inactive parts of the body are being liberally supplied with blood, and the mixed venous blood can scarcely have been 80 per cent unsaturated: neither is it likely that the arterial blood was completely saturated. It would seem fairly certain, therefore, that, in running, the blood flow may attain a value between 30 and 40 l per min, an enormous amount which it is difficult to realize more effectively than by turning it into gallons (8 to 10) and inquiring how long an ordinary water tap would require to pass the same amount. It is obviously impossible to be a runner without possessing a powerful heart.

Other investigators have measured the circulation rate by more exact methods. Meakins[32] found values at rest round about 8 l per min, and during bicycle ergometer exercise about 17. Similar values were found by Douglas and Haldane.[8] Liljestrand and Lindhard[29] found considerably smaller values at rest. Lindhard[30] found up to 20 l per min during work. It would be difficult or impossible to measure the circulation rate during vigorous running by such methods as these authors employed, and one is constrained to fall back on the rougher method of calculation given here, a method previously suggested by Y. Henderson and Prince;[18] this method, however, shows values, during running, which are unquestionably higher than have ever been recorded in another type of exercise. We have made no exact observations of the pulse rate during such running: it is not, however, extremely rapid, so that the output per beat in running must be excep-

Interval of collection	Mid-point of interval from start	Oxygen intake, cc per min	CO_2 output, cc per min	$\dfrac{CO_2}{O_2}$	Total ventilation, liters, moist and at 37°C.
75 sec	3 min 3 sec	3590	3420	0.95	90
63 sec	10 min 48 sec	3785	3800	1.0	100
77.5 sec	17 min 54 sec	3910	3910	1.0	108
63 sec	26 min 32 sec	3910	3930	1.0	118

tionally great. This is probably due to a good venous return.

That these large outputs can be maintained for a considerable time was shown by the experiment of Benedict and Cathcart[3b] on their subject M. A. M., who for 15 min maintained, while bicycling, an oxygen intake of 3,000 cc per min, and for 70 min one of 2,850 cc. Their subject was very exhausted by the longer effort. To maintain such an oxygen consumption for a long time while running is, however, quite easy, and the following experiment shows a much higher one. The subject (H.) ran at a steady speed of 240 m per min (9 mi per hr), carrying a large Douglas bag and breathing through valves and mouthpiece. At intervals the equipment was discarded and the expired gas sampled and measured, while the subject continued running at the same speed. The gradual rise in oxygen consumption is probably to be attributed to a painful blister on the foot causing inefficient movement.

This oxygen intake must have required a total blood flow of not much (if any) less than about 30 l per min, and it was maintained for half an hour. In a highly trained athlete it is obvious that still higher values must be possible.

It is open to question whether the oxygen intake is limited by the heart or by the lungs. It is possible that, at the higher speeds of blood flow, the blood is only imperfectly oxygenated in its rapid passage through the lung; on the other hand, the limit may be placed simply by the sheer capacity of the heart. It would seem probable that, in the healthy normal man, both factors work together. A diminished oxygen tension in the coronary blood supply, owing to the shortness of its stay in the capillaries of the lung, would lower the output of the heart itself, so tending to diminish the flow and to drive the oxygen tension up again. In abnormal persons one factor or the other may preponderate.

K. The Relation between Speed and Oxygen Consumption in Running

The effect of speed on the oxygen intake during horizontal walking has been investigated by a variety of authors, and their results have been fully summarized by Benedict and Murschhauser[3a]. Similar determinations during "level and grade walking" have been recorded recently by Monmouth Smith.[43] The effects of speed upon the oxygen intake during walking, running, swimming, skating, and skiing have been investigated by Liljestrand and Stenström.[27,28] We have made a number of observations on the actual oxygen *intake* during running, over as wide a range of speeds as possible; since, however, at the higher speeds, a genuine steady state is never attained (as pointed out in Section I above), we have amplified these observations by others in which the oxygen *requirement* of the exercise is determined by a different method.

In determining the rate of oxygen intake during running at various speeds, the subject ran (as in Section I) with a constant measured velocity around a grass track, carrying a Douglas bag, and breathing through mouthpiece and valves, the tap being turned to allow the expired air to escape into the atmosphere. After continuing this for a time known, from the experiments of Section I, to be sufficient for the oxygen intake to attain a steady value, the tap was turned for a measured interval (usually about 1 min) to allow a sample of expired air to be collected in the bag, the running being continued at the same speed. After the end of the interval the running ceased, and the measurement and analysis of the expired air were carried out in the usual manner. Experiments were made at a variety of speeds, and on several subjects (which amply confirm one another), and in Fig. 3 the curve *A* summarizes the observations of the excess oxygen intake made on our most usual subject (H., aged 35, weight 73 k, vital capacity 5 l, normal resting pulse rate about 60, in fair general training owing to a daily slow run of about one mile before breakfast). It must not be supposed that this line represents accurately the same subject's excess oxygen intake when running without the respiration apparatus, which provided a small but appreciable hindrance, especially at the higher speeds: probably when unhampered he is noticeably more efficient, and might, with freer respiration, attain a rather higher oxygen intake. It is seen that the rate of oxygen intake per minute due to the exercise, i.e., in excess of standing, increases as the speed increases, reaching a maximum, however, for speeds beyond about 260 m per min (9.7 mi per hr). However much the speed be increased beyond this limit, no further increase in oxygen intake can occur: the heart, lungs, circulation, and the diffusion of oxygen to the active muscle fibers have attained their maximum activity. At the higher speeds the requirement of the body for oxygen is far higher, but cannot be satisfied, and the oxygen debt continuously increases.

Curve *A* of Fig. 3 expresses the relation between speed and oxygen *requirement* (as distinguished from *intake*) only at speeds of less than about 210 m

Fig. 3. Relation between oxygen intake (curve A), or oxygen requirement (curve B), and speed, in running at various speeds. The circles on curve B, and the dotted curve through them, were obtained indirectly by a calculation described in Section L.

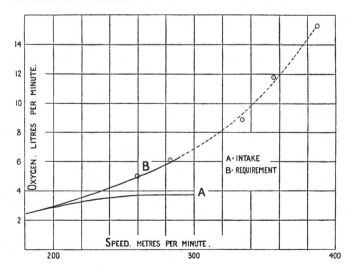

per min (7.8 mi per hr), where the body can attain a genuine steady state. At higher speeds the same relation can be investigated by another method, not involving the attainment of such a steady state. The procedure measures the total *excess oxygen intake during, and in recovery from*, a given muscular effort of short duration. The subject stands for some minutes, ready to run and breathing through the apparatus, his expired air escaping to the atmosphere, until his standing-resting minimum oxygen intake is likely to be reached. He turns the tap, causing the expired air to flow into the bag, and immediately proceeds to run a given distance (say 100 yd) at a measured speed. At the end of the run, and for the succeeding 10 or more minutes (the interval required depending on the magnitude of the recovery), he stands breathing into the bag until recovery is expected to be complete, the total interval of collection being measured. The total oxygen intake during this interval is then determined in the usual manner, and from this is subtracted the amount of oxygen which would have been used in the same time, *had no exercise been taken*. The difference gives the total oxygen consumption caused by the exercise, during the run and in recovery therefrom. Suitable observations of the standing-resting oxygen intake are made before, and sometimes after the run. The following example illustrates the procedure:

> *Subject*, H. Resting (standing): O_2 346 cc per min; CO_2, 277 cc per min; R.Q., 0.80. *Exercise:* ran $1\frac{3}{4}$ laps (148 m) in 30.5 sec, breathing into bag from start. Speed, 291 m per min. Interval of collection, 8 min 5 sec. Total oxygen used, 5,950 cc; resting (standing) value, same interval, 2,795 cc; diference due to exercise, 3,155 cc. Hence oxygen requirement at this speed = 6,200 cc per min.

Here no assumption is made that a steady state of any kind has been attained: the only assumption indeed is that the excess oxygen intake is to be credited to the exercise. This method has been used to measure the real oxygen requirement of running at various speeds, and the result of our experiments are shown in curve *B* (unbroken portion), Fig. 3. It is seen that the oxygen requirement rises continuously, at an increasing rate, as the velocity increases, attaining enormous values—far beyond the possibility of satisfying them contemporaneously—at the higher speeds. The curve *B* diverges from the curve *A* beyond about 220 m per min: at lower speeds they are the same. In H., carrying the respiration apparatus, all speeds greater than 220 m per min imply an increasing oxygen debt, with gradually oncoming exhaustion caused by the accumulation of lactic acid. At high speeds the accumulation of acid is rapid, the oxygen requirement exceeding considerably the maximum oxygen intake.

These methods and results might bear some application to the case of persons whom metabolic, cardiac, or other disturbances have rendered incapable of prolonged exercise, of any but the mildest type. By walking or running a short given distance, or indeed by any standard given effort, the oxygen requirement of that effort could be determined, without any assumption of the attainment of a steady state, and compared either with the value found in normal man or with the maximum oxygen intake attainable or allowable for the abnormal individual in question.

The curve of Fig. 3 really represents what we may call the "efficiency" factor in running. A man may fail to be a good runner by reason of a low oxygen intake, a low maximum oxygen debt, *or a high oxygen requirement;* clumsy and uneconomical movements may lead to exhaustion, just as well as may an imperfect supply of oxygen.

L. Distance and Speed in Athletics.

The results of the preceding section have an interesting application to athletics. The subject H. was able ten years ago, with a maximum effort, to run the following distances in the following times, i.e., at the following speeds*
This considerable variation of speed with the duration of the effort can be explained quantitatively by considerations of oxygen supply alone. Let us assume that his maximum oxygen intake per minute, in excess of standing, was 4.0 l (i.e., 0.2 l greater than it is now), and that his maximum oxygen debt was 10 l (i.e., about the maximum recorded in this paper). Let us further assume that at the end of the race his oxygen supply, actual and potential, was completely exhausted. Then in a race lasting for 1 min the total oxygen available would be $(10 + 4) = 14$ l, i.e., for 1 min he could run at a speed requiring 14 l of oxygen per min. In a race lasting 5 min, however, the total oxygen would be $(10 + 5 \times 4) = 30$ l, i.e., for 5 min he could run at a speed requiring $30/5 = 6$ l per min. Thus in the longer race the speed must be considerably reduced. On these lines the following table may be calculated†

This table gives us immediately a relation between speed and oxygen requirement, which we may compare with that given, for the same subject, in Fig. 3. Before doing so, however, we must note that the respiration apparatus used in the experiments recorded in Fig. 3 offered a definite, if small, hindrance to movement, and we may allow for this provisionally by assuming that, for a given oxygen requirement, the speed is reduced 15 per cent by the apparatus carried. Hence, if we reduce all the speeds in the above table by 15 per cent we obtain the following set of numbers, which are shown as circles in Fig. 3.

‡We see that the last two of these calculated quantities lie close to the curve actually observed for H., while the first three appear to make a good continuation of it. We have been unable hitherto to continue the observations on H. at the higher speeds, owing to the smallness of our track making faster running on it impossible. There can be little doubt, however, that if the observations were made they would lie close to the values calculated as above: a few isolated observations on other subjects at higher speeds confirm the general rise of the curve. Hence, we may conclude that *the maximum duration of an effort of given intensity is related to the intensity in a manner depending simply upon the supply of oxygen, actual or potential*, i.e., upon the

* Distance	$\frac{1}{4}$ mi	$\frac{1}{3}$ mi	$\frac{1}{2}$ mi	1 mi	2 mi
Time	53 sec	1 min 17 sec	2 min 3 sec	4 min 45 sec	10 min 30 sec
Average speed, m per min	455	419	392	333	306

† Distance	$\frac{1}{4}$ mi	$\frac{1}{3}$ mi	$\frac{1}{2}$ mi	1 mi	2 mi
Average speed, metres per min	455	419	392	333	306
Total oxygen potentially available	13.5	15.1	18.2	29.0	52
Oxygen requirement per min	15.3	11.8	8.9	6.1	4.95

‡ Distance	$\frac{1}{4}$ mi	$\frac{1}{3}$ mi	$\frac{1}{2}$ mi	1 mi	2 mi
Speed (reduced for respiration apparatus)	387	356	334	283	260
Oxygen requirement per min	15.3	11.8	8.9	6.1	4.95

maximum rate of oxygen intake and the maximum oxygen debt of the subject in question. This is a striking confirmation, from another aspect, of the truth of the principle discussed in this paper. It would appear to be of importance in the scientific study of athletics and physical training, both in health and in disease.

M. The Importance of Tissue Buffers in Muscular Effort

In recent years the fundamental part played by the buffers of the bloods, in respiration and muscular exercise, has been very fully discussed. The importance, however, of the buffers present in the muscles themselves has been largely neglected, partly owing to their relative inaccessibility to investigation, partly because of a failure to realize the magnitude of the neutralization process occurring in the muscles during exercise. Moreover, the study of buffers, and of the principles governing their behavior, has been somewhat obscured by a logarithmic notation of hydrogen-ion concentration, which has made even the comparatively expert feel that there is something unduly subtle in their action. As a matter of fact, given an elementary knowledge of the principles governing the behavior of electrolytes in solution, the action of buffers is extremely simple and intelligible, and since it is of the utmost importance to an understanding of muscular activity, of respiration, of dyspnoea, and the like, we have given below a rather full discussion of the subject. We have avoided throughout the use of the logarithmic notation (pH), as leading only to obscurity, and have dealt with the simple and intelligible conception of the hydrogen-ion concentration itself, for which we have adopted the usual symbol cH. As a prelude, we may state that the

action of a buffer in solution consists merely in the substitution of a weak acid for a strong one, the strong acid in the case of muscle being lactic acid, the weak ones being carbonic acid, phosphoric acid, and protein.

If a very small quantity of strong acid be added to pure water, or to a neutral salt solution, e.g., of NaCl, a very large change in the hydrogen-ion concentration (cH) results. For example, at 22°C the cH of pure water is 10^{-7} g-ions per 1 (i.e., one ten-millionth part of a milligram of ionic hydrogen per cc): if now 1 cc of normal hydrochloric acid, containing 36.5 mg of HCl, be added to a liter of such water, the cH rises ten thousand times, to a value of 10^{-3}. According to out observations, some 90 g of lactic acid may be liberated in the body as the result of severe exercise. Dissolved in 60 l of water this amount of lactic acid would produce a cH of about 1.5×10^{-3}; the cH of blood is about 4×10^{-8}; thus the result of exercise, in the absence of some mechanism able to eliminate this effect of added acid, would be to raise the cH of the body fluids some 40,000 times. Actually the change of cH is very small: the maintenance of bodily processes, in particular of respiration, and of the physical state of the colloidal proteins of the tissues, demands an extremely high constancy of cH: this constancy is maintained by the "buffers," both of blood and tissues. As Ritchie[41] has shown, the change of cH of an isolated muscle on moderate stimulation is almost inappreciable.

Weak acids, e.g., carbonic acid H_2CO_3, boric acid H_3BO_3, phosphoric acid H_3PO_4 (in its second and third dissociations), amino acids, and in particular proteins such as hemoglobin or those of muscle (which act as acids at the cH of the body), are only very slightly dissociated into hydrogen ions and anions. Calling such a weak acid HA, the reaction $H^+ + A^- \rightarrow HA$ goes almost entirely to the right. Now, in the body many such weak acids exist, but normally they are largely in the form of their sodium or potassium salts, NaA or KA, which are fairly highly ionized into Na^+ (or K^+) and A^- ions. Now imagine that we add a strong acid, e.g., HX, ionized largely as H^+ and X^-, to a solution of such a salt of a weak acid, the following mixture is obtained: $Na^+ + A^- + H^+ + X^-$. But the acid Hx is an extremely weak one, i.e., the ions H^+ and A^- cannot exist side by side in appreciable concentrations, they must form the undissociated acid HA. Hence, provided the buffer salt NaA be present in sufficient excess, practically all the H^+ is removed by the reaction $H^+ + A^- \rightarrow$ HA, leaving only the neutral or approximately neutral salt Na^+X^- and the excess of buffer salt Na^+A^-. Thus the buffer salt has, so to speak (and this is the origin of the term "tampon," mistakenly translated "buffer"), "absorbed," or "mopped up," the hydrogen ions of the added acid, and turned them into undissociated weak acid and approximately neutral salt. Such buffers are extremely effective, reducing the change of cH caused by added acid many thousands or even tens of thousands of times. In the body the most

effective buffer salts are bicarbonates, phosphates, proteins, and particularly hemoglobin.

The matter can be expressed in another way. Buffer salts may be regarded as stores of sodium (or potassium). An added acid requires sodium to neutralize it: the stronger acid seizes sodium from the weaker; if the anion of the buffer salt were that of a strong acid the effect would be nil, one strong acid would be exchanged for another; actually, however, the buffer is a salt of a very weak acid, and the strong added acid is replaced, therefore, by a neutral salt and a very weak acid, which raises only slightly the cH of the solution.

The quantity of acid which must be added to a solution to change the cH by a given amount may be used to measure the efficiency of buffering of that solution, *to that acid, at that cH.* For example, the efficiency of buffering of blood, to carbonic acid, can be deduced from the left-hand diagram of Fig. 4. The relation between vCO_2 (the total volume of CO_2 held by 1 cc of blood in solution and combination) and cH is there given as a straight line, and the slope of this line represents the efficiency of buffering: the greater the slope the more efficiently the blood is buffered; if it were not a straight line the efficiency of buffering at any cH

Fig. 4. Curves showing the "efficiency of buffering." Horizontally, Hydrogen-ion concentration (cH); vertically, acid (or CO_2) added to attain that cH. Left, actual curve for blood. Right, hypothetical curve for muscle.

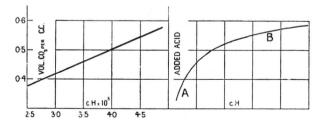

would be given by the slope of the tangent to the curve at the corresponding point. The study is still in its infancy, but there can be no doubt of the existence of similar buffer curves for lymph, tissue fluids, and living muscle substance; the efficiency of buffering of these determines the amount of lactic acid which can be taken up without fatigue or exhaustion, without escape of unneutralized acid into the blood, and corresponding excessive respiration. This buffer curve is probably represented by a line such as that in the right-hand diagram of Fig. 4. To produce a given change in cH the quantity of added acid is largest at the start, and becomes less and less as the cH of the solution increases, so that the efficiency of buffering (as measured by the slope of the curve) is greatest at first, and becomes less and less as more and more acid is added. If now the resting condition of a muscle be represented on the curve by a point such as A, then considerable violent exercise can be taken and noticeable quantities of acid produced, without much disturbance of the cH, and therefore without much fatigue in muscles or distress in respiration. If, however, the resting condition of the muscle be represented on the curve by a point such as B, the efficiency of buffering will be less, the effects of exercise and acid production will be relatively greater, and distress will rapidly ensue. Moreover, if the muscle were to start at a resting state such as A, it might, as the result of exercise and lactic acid production, pass along the curve to B; here the effects of further exercise and of further acid production would be relatively more severe, owing to the less efficient buffering at B than at A. This additional effort might lead to far more than the corresponding additional distress.

Lactic acid compared with an acid such as HCl is fairly weak: its dissociation constant is given as 1.38×10^{-4} at 25°C. It is, however, a very much stronger acid than carbonic acid, for which the dissociation constant (at 37°C.) is about 6×10^{-7}: than leucin (3.1×10^{-10}) and other amino acids: than hemoglobin (oxy-, 6×10^{-10}, and reduced, 7.5×10^{-9};[4]) and other proteins: than phosphoric acid in its second and third dissociations (2.1×10^{-7} and 5.6×10^{-13}). Indeed a 0.1 per cent solution of lactic acid in water is about 10 per cent ionized. In the body, therefore, *lactic acid will never occur as such: it will always obtain base from some weaker acid to form sodium, potassium, or ammonium lactate, in which forms alone it will exist in muscle, lymph, and blood.* This is borne out by the fact that the reaction of isolated muscle never becomes appreciably acid, even in severe fatigue. The consequence, however, is that exercise, liberating lactic acid, increases the concentration of these other weaker acids in the muscles and body fluids; hence, owing to the presence of these other weaker acids, the cH does actually rise, though much less than it would in the absence of buffer salts. One only of these other weaker acids, viz. carbonic, is volatile; hence an immediate aftereffect of a short burst of severe exercise is to drive off excessive quantities of CO_2. This fact has appeared in the work of other authors, e.g., Krogy and Lindhard,[26] and Campbell, Douglas, and Hobson.[5] It is shown more vividly by the first experiment given in Table 5, where the apparent respiratory quotient of the excess metabolism produced by exercise is as high as 2.6 2 min after a very violent effort: in other words, for every CO_2 mol produced by oxidation, another 1.6 mol were being displaced by lactic acid. It is obvious that CO_2 driven out by lactic acid will have to be restored later if the lactate

TABLE 5

Exp. 1. *Subject*, L., 3 hr after meal. *Exercise*, jumping with rapid skipping movement for 36 sec. Room temp., 14°C. Resting resp. exchange (sitting, before exercise, for 10 min): oxygen, 243 cc per min; CO_2, 197 cc per min; R.Q., 0.81. The expired gases were collected during successive intervals, one bag being turned on at the instant the previous bag was turned off. All gases in cc at N.T.P.

Interval of collection		Mid-point of interval from end of exercise		Recovery excess oxygen:		Recovery excess CO_2:		Apparent R. Q. of excess metabolism
min	sec	min	sec	per min	Total in interval	per min	Total in interval	
	33.7		17.0	1969	1105	2763	1551	1.40
	33.1		50.2	1382	761	2448	1350	1.77
	32.3	1	23	860	463	1863	1001	2.17
1	5.2	2	12	514	554	1343	1460	2.62
1	3.6	3	16	347	368	828	879	2.39
2	3.3	4	50	261	536	598	1229	2.29
4	2.0	7	52	157	633	292	1178	1.86
6	31.2	13	9	114	743	135	880	1.19
6	33.0	19	41	92	537	79	567	0.86

By "excess oxygen" and "excess CO_2" are meant the amounts taken in or given out over and above the resting-sitting values.

Exp. 2. *Subject*, L., 3 hr after meal. *Exercise*, horizontal running around grass track at $9\frac{3}{4}$ mi per hr, maintained for $4\frac{1}{4}$ min. Temp. 16°C. Resting resp. exch. sitting: oxygen, 262 cc per min; CO_2, 211 cc per min; R.Q., 0.81. Rate of oxygen *intake during* exercise, measured after 2 min 48 sec of exercise, 3,745 cc per min: rate of CO_2 output, ditto, 3,755 cc per min. Oxygen *requirement* of exercise, measured as on p. 24 above, 5,360 cc per min. The vigor of the exercise, therefore, was considerably in excess of that corresponding to the maximum oxygen intake, and a heavy oxygen debt was incurred.

Interval of collection		Mid-point of interval from end of exercise		Recovery excess O_2:		Recovery excess CO_2:		Apparent R. Q. of excess metabolism
min	sec	min	sec	per min	Total in interval	per min	Total in interval	
	33.5		17	2763	1542	2984	1666	1.08
	36		52	1548	928	2189	1313	1.42
	35.1	1	28	858	502	1507	881	1.76
1	1	2	15	559	568	1079	1097	1.93
2	3.5	3	48	312	642	568	1170	1.82
2	4.2	5	51	202	418	292	604	1.45
3	6.3	8	27	172	534	230	714	1.34
4	12	12	26	104	437	79	332	0.76
4	2.7	16	13	85	344	44	178	0.52
5	2.3	20	46	95	479	33	166	0.35
5	4.8	25	49	50	254	−1	−5	−0.02?
5	4.0	30	53	36	182	−11	−56	−0.31?
5	2.7	35	56	56	282	25	126	+0.45?
5	4.7	40	59	10	51	−12	−61	−1.20?

The values denoted with queries (?) are doubtful because of the smallness of the quantities involved.

Exp. 3. *Subject*, H., 10 hr after meal. *Exercise*, easy horizontal running around

TABLE 5 (Con't)

grass track at 7.6 mi per hr. Temp., 13°C. During recovery (standing) for 7 min 2 sec following 4 min 10 sec exercise, the total excess oxygen used (over and above standing) was 2,485 cc and of CO_2 excreted was 2,508 cc: R.Q. of recovery metabolism = 1.01. The oxygen debt, therefore, was relatively small, and the recovery R.Q. can be sufficiently explained by the oxidation of carbohydrate.

Conditions.	Oxygen intake:		CO_2 output:		R. Q.		Ventilation:
	cc per min	Excess over standing	cc per min	Excess over standing	of total	of excess	l* per min
Basal (bed)	217	—	195	—	0.90	—	6.1
Standing before exercise	306	—	269	—	0.88	—	10.2
Standing after exercise	315	—	275	—	0.88	—	10.3
During exercise (after 4 min)	3012	2702	2870	2598	0.95	0.96	69.0

* Moist, at 37°C., and at 754 mm Hg pressure.

formed at its expense be oxidized or removed. (If, however, the lactate were excreted by the kidneys, it might appear in the urine as sodium lactate, so depriving the body of sodium and preventing a corresponding amount of CO_2 from being restored later.) Hence, at some later stage in recovery, we find that the apparent respiratory quotient of the excess metabolism falls far below unity—indeed it may become negative—as also has been found by previous authors[3b, 26, 5], but is shown more clearly in the second experiment quoted. It is obvious that, in the later stages of recovery, such a very low value of the apparent R.Q. cannot represent a genuine metabolic change: it is due simply to the restoration of CO_2 driven away earlier by lactic acid.

Moderate continued exercise in man does not lead to this driving off of CO_2, as is shown by Exp. 3 above. Apparently when lactic acid is formed in moderate amount during exercise its neutralization is effected by the protein buffers of the muscle, and possibly in part by phosphates, but not by the bicarbonates present in blood and tissue fluids; hence there is no dyspnoea, and the R.Q. of the excess metabolism remains at or near that of carbohydrate. This is confirmed by recent work on isolated muscle, in which[17] the total heat production in the initial anaerobic phase of contraction can be attributed to simple causes, (a) the breakdown of glycogen into lactic acid, and (b) the neutralization of that acid, provided only that we may assume the neutralization to take place by protein buffers and not by phosphates or bicarbonates. The heat of neutralization of acid, as shown by Meyerhof,[38] is large if it be effected by protein buffers, but small if it be effected by others. Hence in an unfatigued muscle we must assume a protein salt to be the neutralizing agent; only when the supply of suitable protein buffer has run out, and when the cH inside the muscle has risen far enough, may we suppose the lactic acid to attack the bicarbonate, and so to drive off CO_2: it is probably at this stage that labored respiration begins.

Little is known about the buffers of the muscle, more is known about the buffers of the blood. In blood the buffers are bicarbonates and phosphates, serum proteins and hemoglobin. All the serum proteins are capable, to a small degree, of acting as buffers; there is strong evidence, however, that one protein only, hemoglobin, is a really effective agent in neutralizing added CO_2, and its effectiveness appears to be enhanced by its confinement within the semipermeable walls of the blood corpuscle.[7] The efficiency of hemoglobin as a buffer is really due to the fact that as an acid it is extremely weak. Moreover reduced hemoglobin is a weaker acid than oxyhemoglobin[4] and should correspondingly be a better buffer: Christiansen, Douglas, and Haldane[6] found that reduced blood takes up appreciably more CO_2 than oxygenated blood at the same CO_2 pressure. Now it is obvious that human individuals may differ enormously from one another in the degree to which their muscles can tolerate sudden and violent exercise, and the same individual will vary enormously from time to time. A sudden effort which will make one man exhausted and stiff and lead to extreme dyspnoea will not affect another, or the same man when he is in better training. This is doubtless partly a matter of the buffers in the blood: lack of hemoglobin, as in anemia, may cause a much greater rise in cH for a given addition of acid or CO_2;[7] this, however, is not the sole cause, and the blood is only a small part of the total tissue fluids. Muscular stiffness may result, in a powerful individual "out of training," from a few seconds only of severe exercise, at a time when his blood is quite reasonably normal in its buffering power. Indeed, it is continually observed that, even when in good training for running, moderate unaccustomed exercise, of the type, say, of climbing a rope in a gymnasium, may lead to severe stiffness in the muscles concerned in that process. It would appear that training is

able somehow to increase the *local* buffering power of the muscle proteins, possibly by a relative increase in the amount of the salt of the *weaker* protein acids. The salt of the weaker acid is the more effective buffer; it will surrender more rapidly and readily its available alkali, and it will cause a smaller rise of cH when it has done so. If it be present only in small amount it will be used up first of all in neutralizing added acid: its role must then be taken on by some less effective agent, the efficiency of buffering will fall, and the cH will rise more rapidly as acid continues to be liberated. The excessive rise of cH so produced may cause a semipermanent physicochemical effect in the colloidal structure of the tissue, something analogous to precipitation or coagulation of some constituent, so leading to stiffness, pain, and loss of power in the muscle, and, by diffusion into the blood and lymph, to excessive respiratory movements and dyspnoea.

We shall consider later the question of oxidation in its bearing on this subject. By very violent exercise for a short time, even—or possibly particularly—in the best trained man, it is possible to exceed many times over any possible oxidative recovery during the exercise, and to produce enormous quantities of lactic acid in the muscles, so that fitness for short-lived effort denotes almost entirely the ease with which the acid products of activity can be dealt with *without oxidation*, i.e., through neutralization by the tissue buffers. It may denote, also, doubtless the relative immunity of the body at large to the harmful or painful effects of a sudden change of cH; in the main, however, fitness for violent short-lived effort would seem to depend upon the quality of the tissue buffers. If this be the case, we may perhaps inquire why the body does not maintain the presence of the more effective buffers, i.e., of the salts of the weaker protein acids, *all the time and independently of "training."* This inquiry lies within the province rather of the biologist than of the physical chemist, but there is no reason why the biologist should not inquire in physicochemical terms. An answer may be suggested as follows: The more effective buffer is the less stable one, insofar as it is the salt of the weaker acid. The salt of a very weak acid readily surrenders its sodium, even to a weak acid, and as soon as it has done so it ceases to be a buffer. Hence in the less vigorous metabolic processes of the untrained or abnormal man, in the distorted processes of disease, or after excesses of meat or drink, the highly unstable and most efficient buffers may be partly saturated with other rather stronger acids, may surrender their sodium, and so become inoperative. A relatively unstable system has been displaced by a stabler, if less effective one, and can only be restored as a gradual adaptation to an external need. In the muscle there are buffers of all kinds, salts of stronger and of weaker protein acids, phosphates, and bicarbonates. The salts of the weaker acids may be transformed into their undissociated acids by chance acidic metabolic products, and even by an undue excretion of sodium or potassium by the kidney. Exercise, especially regular exercise, stimulating and regulating the oxidative and excretory functions of the cells, may protect the more unstable protein buffers from such acid contamination, and so lead to those three essentials of bodily fitness, (a) quickness of muscular response and relaxation, (b) immunity from fatigue, dyspnoea, and their unpleasant consequences, and (c) a high upper limit of the effort which can be made, beyond the range of a contemporary oxygen supply.

The subject of tissue buffers is at present of necessity speculative. A further study of the physicochemical properties of muscle proteins, unchanged as far as possible by chemical or manipulative treatment, may throw much further light upon the problem of muscular effort, muscular stiffness, and dyspnoea. In applying such results to muscular exercise in man it is well to make a clear mental separation of the two great types of effort—(a) the sudden, violent, and anaerobic type, and (b) the long-continued type, involving contemporary oxidation. Short-lived, vigorous efforts are made almost entirely by the expenditure of "capital," in the form of lactic acid production: long-continued, milder efforts by the expenditure of "income," in the form of rapidly ensuing, almost contemporary oxidation. Thus short and violent exercise depends largely, if not mainly, on the ease with which lactic acid is dealt with by the tissue buffers; long-maintained exercise on the efficiency of oxidation, and the ease and liberality of oxygen supply.

N. The Oxidative Factor in Muscular Fitness

An efficient oxidative metabolism will tend to maintain a low resting lactic acid minimum in the muscle, and probably to restrain the appearance of acid metabolites likely to neutralize the more efficient but less stable buffers of the muscle substance. When the organism is subjected to a low oxygen pressure, the initial discomfort and muscular disability are doubtless to be associated partly with the lower oxygen pressure in the brain and heart, partly with the fact that the rate of oxidative recovery from exercise is diminished. In addition, however, it would seem probable that a reduced oxygen pressure, by slowing the last stages of recovery and by diminishing the resting oxidative breakdown of waste products of metabolism, would decrease the efficiency of the most potent protein buffers of the muscle, and so lead to greater discomfort following a sudden effort. It would be of great interest, therefore, to ascertain the extent of the maximum oxygen debt —(*a*) at sea level, and (*b*) at high altitudes, before and after acclimatization.

The chief oxidative factor in muscular effort is concerned, however, with its prolongation by means of a rapid and efficient recovery. The "efficiency" of recovery we have discussed already above: it appears to change with the condition of the muscle, and may well vary from one individual to another. The rapidity of recovery depends upon a variety of factors, upon the oxygen supply and pressure, upon the temperature, *and upon the intrinsic oxidative power of the living cells.* It is usual to treat capacity for exercise, and freedom from the unpleasant symptoms of dyspnoea, as though they resided merely, or at any rate mainly, in the supply of oxygen through the lungs and circulation, and in the degree of buffering of the blood. Indeed, books and articles are written on respiration which take little or no account of the oxidative function of the cell, the mechanism thereof, and the factors which influence it. This is natural, in a sense, since so little is known about the oxidative mechanism. Something, however, is known, and a short discussion of the oxidative mechanism may be of interest here. It will emphasize how many possibilities there are in explaining the various abnormalities of response to exercise.

The oxygen supply to the active muscles in man, depending as it does on the efficiency of heart, lungs, and circulation, on the corpuscles, hemoglobin, and alkalies in the blood, on diffusion of oxygen in the tissues, and on the pressure of oxygen in the air, has been already the subject of innumerable investigations. We have been able to add little to these, beyond the experimental proof that the rate of oxygen supply can attain considerably higher values than had previously been supposed. Experiments with isolated muscles have made it clear, even apart from experiments on man, that the oxidative process of recovery is intimately dependent on the pressure of oxygen, increasing rapidly in speed as the latter is raised. Hence, even in moderate prolonged exercise, a vigorous circulation is advantageous in maintaining a higher average oxygen pressure in the active muscles, and so ensuring a lower level of the lactic acid in the final "steady state" attained, with less resultant fatigue and smaller aftereffects. A higher oxygen pressure would appear to be always an advantage. *It must be regarded, however, as merely antecedent, and contributory to the speed of the oxidative cell process itself.* Of this latter little can be said, because so little yet is known; with further research, however, it will almost certainly prove to be the most important factor of all in facilitating and completing the cycle of muscular activity.

It might have been supposed that in man the speed of the recovery process depends simply upon the supply and the pressure of oxygen, that the muscle restores itself, with the oxidative removal of lactic acid, exactly as fast as the supply of oxygen enables it; if this were so the curves of Fig. 1 would represent merely the oxygen supply to the active muscles, falling gradually to its resting value on the cessation of exercise. The form of the curves makes this, a priori, very improbable; there is conclusive evidence, however, from another direction that it is definitely not the case; the oxidative recovery process has an intrinsic speed of its own, like other catalysed chemical reactions, even in the presence of a completely adequate supply of dissolved oxygen. Hartree and Hill,[17] in recent experiments, have analyzed the course of the recovery heat production of a frog's sartorius muscle suspended in pure oxygen; here the amount of oxygen dissolved in the muscle itself must be far more than adequate to complete the oxidations of recovery from a short tetanic stimulus, so that no delay is interposed by the diffusion of oxygen to the places where it is required. In spite of this the recovery process is very protracted, as is shown in Fig. 5. In 5 min at 20°C recovery is by no means complete: at 0°C it has barely attained its maximum speed. The rate of recovery increases rapidly as the temperature rises, but decreases rapidly as the pressure of oxygen falls. Hence, at 37°C in man, with a comparatively low oxygen pressure in the active muscle, the rate of recovery is not far different from that in the frog's sartorius at 20°C and in pure oxygen. The rate at which the chemical processes of recovery occur starts at a low level, rises to a maximum, and then slowly falls again to zero. Moreover,

the greater the initial effort from which recovery is necessary, the greater is the relative (not merely the absolute) rate of that recovery. Here, in Fig. 5, we are dealing with the intrinsic oxidative capacity of the cell itself, uninfluenced by any considerations of oxygen supply. The characteristics of these curves may guide us in the further analysis of the chemistry of the recovery metabolism of muscle.

Many factors are known to influence the speed of oxidative recovery; of these we have mentioned temperature and oxygen pressure, but there are other important chemical agencies which do the same. Cyanides prohibit oxidation (and therefore recovery) completely, even in minute doses. According to Warburg[44] this is due to the removal of traces of catalytic iron, by chemical combination with the cyanide, from its place of action in some formed constituent of the cell. Many narcotic substances hinder or prevent oxidation, probably (according to Warburg[44]) owing to their preferential adsorption to the same formed constituents of the cells. There is strong evidence, derived from a study of the red corpuscles of birds, that the solid parts of the cells are the seat of

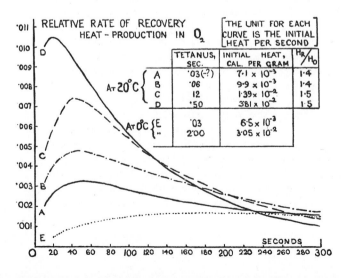

Fig. 5. Recovery heat production of frog's sartorius muscles in oxygen.

oxidation. Laking the red corpuscles barely diminishes their oxygen consumption: removal of the "ghosts" of the laked corpuscles abolishes it entirely. Apparently oxidation takes place at the surfaces of such formed constituents of living cells, by adsorption of the oxidizable body, and through a reaction catalysed by traces of adsorbed iron. Narcotics displace the oxidizable body, cyanides remove the iron; both, therefore, hinder or prevent oxidation.

In another direction, recent work by Hopkins[25] has shown the existence in active cells of a chemical body ("glutathione") capable of catalysing oxidations by acting as a "hydrogen acceptor," so enabling oxidation to occur without the direct and immediate utilization of molecular oxygen. The total quantity of this "hydrogen acceptor" in muscle is probably very small, so that no appreciable amount of oxidation can occur without the aid of molecular oxygen: there is no possibility, for example, of the "oxygen debt" in man being noticeably increased by such means. On the other hand, however, the speed and vigor of muscular oxidation may depend largely on the presence of an adequate quantity of such bodies, though the relative importance of this and other factors cannot, as yet, be assessed.

It is obvious, therefore, that—apart from temperature, and pressure of oxygen—there are many possible ways in which the rate of oxidation in a living muscle cell could be altered. The surfaces, which are the seat of oxidation, might vary in their chemical or colloidal nature: preferential adsorption of bodies analogous to Warburg's narcotics might displace the proper foodstuffs, for example, in disturbances of metabolism; physical or chemical interference with the catalytic iron might diminish the rate of oxidation of the appropriate bodies, even when properly adsorbed; a decrease in the amount or activity of suitable hydrogen acceptors might weaken an essential link in the oxidative chain. These matters still are of necessity largely speculative, and we must wait for further improvements in knowledge of the physical chemistry of living cells. Little, however, is gained by regarding the phenomena of exercise, respiration, and dyspnoea as simpler than they really are: further knowledge will certainly introduce these other factors.

We wish to express our sincere thanks to the various persons who have submitted themselves to our—often severe—experiments: their hearty goodwill and interest have made the investigation possible. We desire particularly to thank our colleague, Mr. C. N. H. Long, B.Sc., both for his skilled and strenuous activity as a subject, and for his help in the analysis of the results. We are much indebted also to Mr. Corker, of Messrs. C. Macintosh & Co. of Manchester, for his help in the design of suitable experimental bags for the collection of expired gases.

We are indebted to the Medical Research Council for grants to cover the expenses of the investigation.

References

1. Adam, *Biochem. J.*, **15** (1921), 358.
2. Barcroft, Bock, Hill, Parsons, and Shoji, *J. Physiol.* (*London*), **56** (1922), 157.
3. (a) Benedict and Murschhauser, *Publ. No. 231, Carnegie Inst. Wash.* (1915), pp. 22–27. (b) Benedict and Cathcart, *Publ. No. 187, ibid.* (1913).
4. Brown and Hill, *Proc. Roy. Sec.* (*London*) (1923).
5. Campbell, Douglas, and Hobson, *Phil.*

Trans. Roy. Soc. (London), **B210** (1920), 1.

6. Christiansen, Douglas, and Haldane, *J. Physiol. (London)*, **48** (1914), 245.

7. Conway, *ibid.*, **56** (1922), Proc. 25.

8. Douglas and Haldane, *ibid.*, **56** (1922), 69.

9. Embden *et al.*, *Ber. ü. d. ges. Physiol.*, **8** (1921), 136–50.

10. Embden, Gräfe, and Schmitz, *Hoppe-Seylers Z. Physiol, Chem.*, **113** (1921), 67.

11. Fletcher, *J. Physiol. (London)*, **23** (1898), 10.

12. Fletcher, *ibid.*, **28** (1902), 354.

13. Fletcher, *ibid.*, **28** (1902), 474.

14. Fletcher and Hopkins, *ibid.*, **35** (1907), 247.

15. Hartree and Hill, *ibid.*, **54** (1920), 84.

16. Hartree and Hill *ibid.*, **55** (1921), 133.

17. Hartree and Hill, *ibid.*, **56** (1922), 367.

18. Henderson and Prince, *Am. J. Physiol.*, **35** (1914), 106.

19. Hill, A. V., *J. Physiol. (London)*, **44** (1912), 466.

20. Hill, A. V., *ibid.*, **46** (1913), 28.

21. Hill, A. V., *Ergeb. Physiol.*, **15** (1916), 340.

22. Hill, A. V., *J. Physiol. (London)*, **56** (1922), 19.

23. Hill A. V., *Physiol. Rev.*, **2** (1922), 310.

24. Hill and Meyerhor, *Ergeb. Physiol.* (1923).

25. Hopkins, *Biochem. J.*, **15** (1921), 286.

26. Krogh and Lindhard, *J. Physiol. (London)*, **53** (1920), 431.

27. Liljestrand and Stenström, *Skand. Arch. Physiol.* **39** (1920), 1.

28. Liljestrand and Stenström, *ibid.*, **39** (1920), 167.

29. Liljestrand and Lindhard, *J. Physiol. (London)*, **53** (1920), 420.

30. Lindhard, *Pflügers Arch. ges. Physiol.*, **161** (1915), 318.

31. Lindhard, *Skand, Arch. Physiol.*, **40** (1920), 145.

32. Meakins, *Heart Bull.* **9** (1922), 191.

33. Meyerhof, *Pflügers Arch. ges. Physiol.*, **175** (1919), 88.

34. Meyerhof, *ibid.*, **182** (1920), 232.

35. Meyerhof, *ibid.*, **182** (1920), 284.

36. Meyerhof, *ibid.*, **185** (1920), 11.

37. Meyerhof, *ibid.*, **188** (1921), 114.

38. Meyerhof, *ibid.*, **195** (1922), 22.

39. Parsons, *J. Physiol. (London)*, **53** (1919–20), 42, 340.

40. Peters, *ibid.*, **47** (1913), 243.

41. Ritchie, *ibid.*, **56** (1922), 53.

42. Ryffel, *ibid.*, **39** (1909), Proc. 29.

43. Smith, H. Monmouth, *Publ. No. 309, Carnegie Inst. Wash.* (1922).

44. Warburg, *Biochem. Z.*, **119** (1921), 134.

45. Weizsäcker, *J. Physiol. (London)*, **48** (1914), 396.

46. Weizsäcker, *Pflügers Arch. ges. Physiol.*, **147** (1912), 135.

A. V. HILL

Production and Absorption of Work by Muscle

Work absorbed in stretching a contracting muscle can reverse the chemical processes of activity.

The author is affiliated with University College, London, England. This article is the John R. Murlin lecture, presented 3 June 1959 at the University of Rochester School of Medicine and Dentistry, Rochester, N.Y.

A contracting muscle performs mechanical work by shortening against a load. Its energy is derived from chemical reactions. What the reactions are, and what their sequence is, is not precisely known, though it is certain that they occur in two main phases, initial and recovery. The initial phase is rapid and is independent of the presence of oxygen; it is known to include the splitting of creatine phosphate and it is commonly believed, though on indirect grounds, that the earliest occurrence in it is the hydrolysis of adenosine triphosphate. Other processes, not yet known, may be involved. Moreover, the formation of lactic acid from glycogen certainly occurs in normal muscles when more than a very small muscular effort is made; but since a muscle poisoned with iodoacetate may continue to contract for a time in a perfectly normal way without producing any lactic acid at all, the formation of lactic acid is now regarded as an early event in recovery. The large amount of free energy thus made available is believed to effect a resynthesis of the creatine phosphate.

The main recovery process is very slow and involves the utilization of oxygen; the free energy supplied by oxidation provides a means of reversing the previous reactions, and finally the muscle returns to the same chemical state as when it started, except that a certain amount of fuel has been burned and oxygen used. If adenosine triphosphate is in fact split in the earliest stage of contraction, the fact that its products cannot be detected chemically has to be explained by supposing that it is very rapidly re-formed with the aid of the free energy supplied by the slightly later breakdown of creatine phosphate. Unfortunately the energy changes in these three nonoxidative processes are not yet accurately known, but approximate values for the changes in enthalpy $-\Delta H$ and free energy $-\Delta F$ are given in Table 1. It would be a great service to physiology if these quantities could be more certainly determined, under the conditions existing inside a muscle fiber, but that will not be easy, for it requires a knowledge of the initial and final states, whether combined or uncombined, and the concentrations of the substances involved.

Work and Heat in Contraction

In the living muscle the energy liberated can be measured as

$$\text{work} + \text{heat};$$

in the complete cycle, including recovery, it is about twice as great as in the initial process alone. In this article, only the initial process is considered, and no further reference is made to specific chemical reactions. The relations discussed are those between work and heat, under various conditions of shortening, lengthening, and tension, so chemical details are really irrelevant.

The processes of muscular contraction occur at constant temperature and pressure; any idea that muscle is a heat engine is nonsense—work is certainly derived at constant temperature from the free energy of chemical reactions. If no external work were done, the heat production would be $-\Delta H$, while the maximum amount of work conceivably possible is $-\Delta F$. In any actual contraction the ratio of work done to total energy used, often—though perhaps improperly—called the "efficiency," depends on several variables, particularly on the speed of shortening. The maximum value is about 0.4, so $\Delta F/\Delta H$ is certainly greater than 0.4—possibly considerably greater, for the production of work may be far from reversible in the thermodynamic sense. The values of $-\Delta H$ and $-\Delta F$ in Table 1 show that the ratio $\Delta F/\Delta H$ is rather large; it may indeed be substantially greater than 1. Then, under "reversible" conditions, if those could be realized, a

TABLE 1

Heat production $(-\Delta H)$ and maximum amount of work possible $(-\Delta F)$ (in kilocalories per mole) for splitting and neutralization at pH 7.0. ADP, adenosine diphosphate; ATP, adenosine triphosphate; Cr, creatine; CrP, creatine phosphate; P, phosphate.

Reaction	$-\Delta H$	$-\Delta F$
ATP → ADP + P	5 to 10	8 to 10
CrP → Cr + P	11 to 17	10 to 15
Lactic acid from glycogen	24	39

muscle would cool when it did maximum work. In fact, nothing like that ever happens.

It has often been supposed that when a given stimulus has been applied to a muscle the total amount of energy liberated is then settled for good, the only point not settled being how much of this energy is turned into work, how much into heat. The question was really decided experimentally 95 years ago by Heidenhain, whose results showed (to put the conclusion in modern jargon) that a muscle contains a "governor" and that the energy used depends not only on the stimulus but on the length throughout contraction and on the load. Heidenhain's technique would be regarded today as primitive; it was subject to various errors, and the readings obtained were very small. Nevertheless he arrived by it at the right answer, one of the most important in physiology. But rather little attention was paid to it, perhaps because his differences looked so small, and people went on thinking in the older terms; I did myself when I came to the subject 45 years later. The problem was not properly tackled again until nearly 60 years after Heidenhain, when W. O. Fenn joined me at Manchester in 1922. Fenn's two papers on the subject, published in 1923 and 1924,[6] opened an entirely new chapter in the physiology of muscle. There is no point now in recalling the details of his experiments, but their conclusion can be put into two simple statements, in Fenn's words: (a) "When a muscle shortens upon stimulation and does work in lifting a weight, an extra amount of energy is mobilized"; and (b) Forcible "lengthening during the contraction period decreases the energy liberated. . . . When the work done by the muscle is negative the excess energy is also negative."

These conclusions still stand; they

were the starting point of most of what follows.

Contractile and Elastic Elements

The "business" part of a muscle is the contractile component, which in skeletal muscle is joined to the bones by tendons forming the series elastic component. Under so-called "isometric" conditions the distance between the outer ends of the tendons is constant, and when the muscle is stimulated it shortens and stretches the tendons, doing quite a lot of work on them (which can, for example, be useful in jumping). It may be that part of the series elastic component really resides in the contractile component itself—for example, in one of the bands of the sacromere—and it is certain that, when one makes experiments, part of the series elastic component resides in the connection to one's recording instruments. There are other elastic elements in muscle, making up the parallel elastic component, but if one works at a short enough length, these provide no complication and need not be referred to again.

The series elastic component, however, provides a major complication in any investigation of the mechanical work performed by a muscle and the heat it produces. By special methods,[9] which need not be described here, its properties can be measured and displayed in a generalized diagram from which the amount of stretch under any tension, and the amount of elastic energy it contains, can be read off. A similar diagram can be constructed for the elastic properties of the recording arrangements. This stored elastic energy is important: when a muscle relaxes under tension, the elastic energy is turned into heat in the contractile component and is added to the heat previously recorded.

Activation, Shortening, and Work

When a muscle is stimulated it passes from a state of rest to one of activity. These two states differ fundamentally from one another, just as a piece of hard rubber (ebonite) after vulcanization differs from the original soft rubber. In fact, by current theories, contraction could be pictured as reversible vulcanization. The transformation from the first state to the second requires chemical change, and that results in a production of heat which we call the heat of activation, A. A is independent of whether the muscle shortens and does mechanical work, or does not. But the transformation from rest to activity quickly reverses itself, and if the stimulus is not repeated, the active state decays and the initial condition returns. In order to maintain the state of activity a succession of stimuli must be applied, and A becomes the heat of maintenance, the cost of keeping the engine going.

The next stage is this. If a muscle is allowed to shorten it gives out extra heat. For a given amount of shortening the heat is independent of whether mechanical work is done or not; it is simply proportional to the amount of shortening.[1,8] The phenomenon is most elegantly displayed by releasing a muscle against a load during a previously isometric contraction. The quantity of heat is ax, where x is the amount of shortening and a is a constant of the dimensions of force (heat is always calculated in mechanical units). The constant a is directly related to the strength of the muscle—that is, to the maximum force it can exert.

The third stage is this. When a muscle shortens it does more or less work according to the load which, to quote Fenn's anthropomorphic idiom, it "discovers it must lift." The performance of this work does not affect the amount of heat liberated in the other two stages; the mechanical work (W) just appears as an extra term in the equation, which finally runs: total energy by muscle $= A + ax + W$.

The appearance of W as an extra energy term without any extra heat is striking, but it seems to be authentic. The quantity $(A + ax)$, in a sense, is "waste heat," though a better term is "overhead"; it depends, as regards A, on the duration of the stimulus and as regards ax, on the amount of shortening allowed. To get the greatest mechanical output from a given expenditure of chemical energy, the conditions must be adjusted to make $(A + ax)/W$ as small as possible. But the "overhead" cost of contraction cannot be avoided, and this suggests that it may not really be "irreversibility" (in the thermodynamic sense) that limits the ratio of work done to energy used, but the nature of the machine itself. If a muscle is to do mechanical work it has to be put in a state of readiness and then to shorten, and the energy needed for this can be regarded as "overhead" cost. The muscle can then perform mechanical work with an extra expenditure of energy no greater than the work itself. If in the underlying chemical reaction $-\Delta F$ and $-\Delta H$ were equal, this could happen if the muscular process were "reversible" in the thermodynamic sense. If $-\Delta F$ were greater than $-\Delta H$, as may well be the case, thermodynamic "irreversibility" can still occur to a certain extent; then only a part of $-\Delta F$, equal to $-\Delta H$, would be utilized in producing external work.

Stretching During Contraction

The exciting possibilities of an approach in muscle to thermodynamic "reversibility" in the production of work, together with the rather precise way in which all these relations seem to hold together, suggested a reexamination of Fenn's original result on the stretching of muscle. Could the chemical processes which are provoked by applying a stimulus really be reversed by the application of external mechanical work? Consider a storage battery and a motor which can also function in the reverse direction as a dynamo. When they are connected the storage battery provides energy which is used by the motor in doing mechanical work. When external mechanical power is applied to the motor in the opposite direction it becomes a dynamo and charges the battery. Can this sort of thing happen in a muscle when mechanical power is applied to it during contraction? One must say specifically "during contraction" because a muscle at rest does not resist stretch except by purely elastic and viscous forces. The only way in which mechanical work can be applied to the contractile portion of a muscle is by stretching the muscle while it is actively resisting.

In 1938, 15 years after Fenn, I took the question up again and came to the preliminary conclusion that during very gradual lengthening, under a load somewhat greater than a muscle could bear, the net rate of its energy liberation was rather less than during an isometric contraction.[7] After another interval of 12 years, due to World War II and to the need for rehabilitating ideas and apparatus, the problem was tackled again, by Abbott and Aubert, who clearly confirmed the earlier result.[2,3] But something far more important came out of their experiments when much more rapid stretches were applied and when heat and work were measured. It then became clear that a substantial part of the work disappeared and did not reappear as heat; we could only suppose that it was used in driving the resynthesis of chemical breakdown products of the reaction set up by the stimulus. But the results were not as decisive as they might have been, and there was no evidence of when and how the work disappeared. We were, in fact, not thinking very clearly about the subject; it is funny how long clear thinking sometimes takes! But after another 7 years the subject was taken up again.[11] In the meantime, apparatus and methods had been somewhat improved, but, more important, we had much clearer ideas of the mechanics of muscle and of the nature of the problem.

Chemical Reversal by Stretch

Consider a muscle stretched by 11 per cent or more during a single twitch or a short tetanus. The stretch occurs at any desired speed, starting not too long after the stimulus. The ergometer is provided with a tension recorder,

TABLE 2

Contractions with stretch. H_s, total heat appearing in muscle ; W_o, total work done on muscle.

Stretch %	H_s g-cm	W_o g-cm	$H_s - W_o$ g-cm
	Twitches		
11	26.4	25.8	0.6*
11	31.5	26.7	4.8
11	27.9	25.2	2.7†
12	26.5	24.2	2.3†
14.5	39.5	38.8	0.7*
18	46.3	46.7	−0.4*
	Tetani (short)		
15.5	42.8	42.4	0.4*
16	72.1	66.5	5.6
16	57.3	55.1	2.2*
16.5	76.6	68.5	8.1
18	58.8	59.2	−0.4*
18	64.2	65.4	−1.2*
22	75.1	75.0	0.1*

* H_s and W_o were equal within the limits of experimental error. † The equality of H_s and W_o was doubtful.

joined to the muscle by a strong chain, and also with a device to record the distance moved. Tension and distance are displayed on the two beams of a cathode-ray tube and photographed. The work is obtained from the curve relating the two. The heat is measured by thermopile and galvanometer and recorded from a second tube.

Let us first consider total quantities—the total work done by the ergometer and the total heat produced in the muscle up to the time when it has fully relaxed (Table 2). To avoid trouble with elastic energy remaining after the end of relaxation, the length to which the muscle is stretched must not be so great that any tension is then left. With that provision, the whole of the work done on the muscle disappears; it must have gone into the muscle, for there is nowhere else it could go. Either it has been dissipated as heat and is added to the heat produced by the muscle itself, or it has been absorbed in some other form. Now here is the striking fact that emerges. In a good proportion of all the experiments made, the heat found in the muscle in the end was no greater than the work put into it. The muscle itself apparently had produced no heat at all of its own, although it had resisted the stretch very strongly. One might think that the very act of stretching the muscle somehow prevented the normal chemical processes of activity from occurring. That is certainly not so, for the muscle may produce a large part of its normal heat before the stretch begins. The only possibility is that the chemical reactions (which certainly started, as is shown by the normal early heat production) were totally reversed. In the whole process, from start to finish, the muscle liberated no energy at all; the heat observed was merely degraded work.

This is what happened in a good proportion of the experiments; in the rest the heat was slightly greater than the work, but much less than it would have been had the work been added to the normal heat production of the muscle. The reversal of chemical processes, though substantial, was not quite complete. With smaller stretches, of less than 10 per cent, the heat is always greater than the work; the degree of reversal depends on the amount of stretch—that is, really on the amount of work applied. One striking result was that, within the limits of experimental error, the heat was never less than the work; this means that the chemical reversal never overshot its original mark. Such an overshoot might possibly have occurred, for the muscles were not fully recovered from previous contractions and there must always have been chemical substances at large which could conceivably have been resynthesized. A stretch, therefore, cannot reverse any chemical reaction except that of the actual contraction during which the stretch was applied.

Time Course of Heat Minus Work

This was all very odd and required closer analysis of when and how it happened. Fortunately the means for that analysis were at hand, for the instruments are capable of yielding a true picture of the course of the heat production throughout a contraction, and that, when it is compared with the mechanical events, throws much light on the matter.

Figure 1 (upper half) gives three curves obtained from a muscle stretched 3 mm during a single twitch; the stretch started early and continued till 360 ms after the shock. These experiments were all made with toad sartorius muscles at 0°C, and in an isometric twitch the maximum tension is reached in 0.4 or 0.5 sec. Curve A is the tension (P), which drops rapidly at first when the stretch ends. Curve B is the heat (H) liberated in the muscle, as obtained by analysis from the records. Curve C

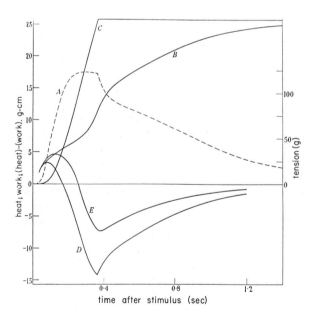

Fig. 1. Curves for tension, heat, work, and the difference between heat and work during a 3-mm stretch of a muscle stimulated at time zero (single shock, toad sartorious, 0°C). Curve A: tension (P); curve B: heat (H); curve C: work (W) done by the ergometer; curve D, difference between heat and work ($H - W$); curve E, difference between heat and net work ($H - W_n$), where W_n is the difference between work W and elastic energy E in the muscle and connections.

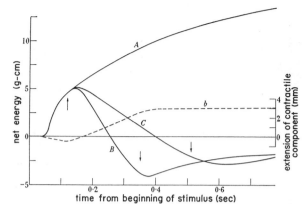

Fig. 2. Net energy liberated by muscle in isometric contraction (curve *A*) and in contractions with stretch (curves *B* and *C*). For curve *A* the ordinate is $(H + E)$; for curves *B* and *C*, it is $(H + E - W)$. The stretches began at the arrow that points up and ended at the arrows that point down. Curve *b* (broken line) shows the calculated extension of the contractile component of the stretch shown in curve *B*. Toad sartorium, 0.3-sec tetanus, 0°C.

is the work (W) done by the ergometer. This is a good example of a contraction with stretch in which the heat converges to the same value as the applied work, so that in the complete process the muscle really liberated no energy at all. Now look at the lower half of the figure. Curve *D* is the difference between heat and work $(H - W)$. As a first approximation this could be taken as the net energy liberated by the muscle. The astonishing result appears that the net energy rapidly becomes negative after the stretch begins, changes direction when the stretch ends, and then slowly returns to zero at the end of relaxation.

Such a strange result had to be regarded very critically. One obvious correction had to be made, due to the fact that, except at the very end, not all the work had gone into the contractile component of the muscle—some of it remained, until relaxation was complete, as elastic energy in the series elastic component and in the connecting chain. The elastic energy (E) could be calculated from the tension, and so the net work (W_n) could be obtained by subtracting the elastic energy from the work $(W_n = W - E)$. Curve *E* is the result of subtracting the net work from the heat $(H - W_n)$; this gives the net energy liberated by the muscle. The

negative phase is reduced but by no means abolished; clearly it has to be taken seriously.

Figure 2 gives the results of three contractions in another experiment with a short tetanus. Here the stretch did not start very early, and a good deal of the normal heat production had occurred before it began. The ordinate in this case is the net energy liberated by the muscle. For the isometric contraction, this is the sum of heat and elastic energy $(H + E)$; for the stretches it is the sum of heat and elastic energy, less work $(H + E - W)$. Two stretches were applied, one quicker than the other, ending at the downward-pointing arrows. Exactly the same phenomenon is observed: soon after the stretch begins the curve of net energy turns around and passes through a long negative phase, finally becoming zero at the end of relaxation.

Figure 2 contains one effect (curve *b*) not hitherto referred to, the stretch of the contractile component. This can be derived from the tension by means of the data from which the elastic energy is derived. From the actual stretch indicated by the ergometer the calculated extension of the elastic elements is subtracted, and the difference is the stretch of the contractile component.

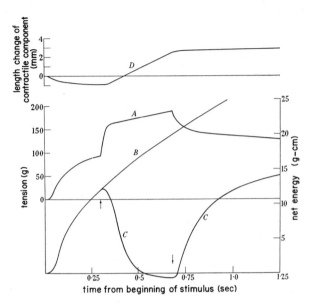

Fig. 3. Net energy liberated by muscle in isometric contraction (curve *B*) and in contraction with 4-mm stretch (curve *C*). For curve *B*, the ordinate is $(H + E)$; for curve *C*, it is $(H + E - W)$. Curve *A* shows tension (P) before, during, and after the stretch. Curve *D* shows the calculated change of length of the contractile component before, during, and after the stretch. The duration of the stretch is indicated by arrows. Toad sartorius, 1-sec stimulus, 0°C.

When the stretch begins, as soon as the tension exceeds the maximum force that the muscle can bear, the contractile component begins to be extended. It is during the forcible lengthening of the contractile component that all these interesting things happen. Curve *b* corresponds to stretch *B*; one can see that the rate of extension of the contractile component rapidly falls when the stretch ends. But the tension is still high, and the extension continues to the end of relaxation.

Figure 3 shows another experiment, a 15 per cent stretch during a longer tetanus. Here the stimulus long outlasted the stretch, so the total heat greatly exceeded the work: the curve of net energy rose rapidly as soon as the stretch ended and went on rising as long as the stimulus continued. Curve *A* shows the tension before, during, and after the stretch; curve *B* shows the energy liberated by the muscle, as the sum of heat and elastic energy $(H + E)$, in an isometric contraction; curve *C* shows the net energy liberated by the

muscle during a stretch—that is, the sum of heat and energy, less work $(H + E - W)$. A large amount of energy had been liberated normally by the time the stretch began. Then the net energy rapidly fell, became negative for a short time, then rose quickly as the stimulus continued after the stretch ended. At the top the change in length of the contractile component is shown, before, during, and after the stretch.

Such experiments left no doubt that an absorption of energy occurs during the extension of the contractile component. This extension lasts longer than the applied stretch, for the stretch produces a high tension in the elastic elements which go on extending the contractile component right to the end of relaxation. But a puzzling dilemma remained. When total quantities in the whole cycle of contraction and relaxation are considered, the net energy produced by a muscle was never negative. How could it be so obviously negative throughout a large part of the process? No simple explanation seemed possible, but the dilemma was resolved in an unexpected way.

Thermoelastic Effect

It has been known for more than a century that when a tension is applied to a rod or wire, the temperature of the rod or wire falls; when the tension is removed the temperature rises again. The heat absorbed, or produced, can be calculated, in mechanical units, from the coefficient α of thermal expansion of the material, by the expression

$$\alpha T l \Delta P.$$

Here T is absolute temperature, l is length, and ΔP is change of tension. In materials like thermosetting plastics, which are more like an active muscle than metal wires are, the value of α is large. The phenomenon occurs universally and in an analogous form is found in liquids. It is absent only if the coefficient of thermal expansion is zero, a rare and special case.

If this so-called "thermoelastic" effect occurred also in the filaments of active muscle, and if they had a value of α similar to that of thermosetting plastics, then the whole difficulty would be cleared up. During the phase of rising tension there would be a "thermoelastic" absorption of heat, of purely physical origin, which would neutralize some of the heat derived from physiological and chemical processes, so the real physiological heat would be greater by that amount. Conversely, during the phase of falling tension there would be a purely physical production of heat, which would add to the heat produced by chemical processes, so during this phase the real physiological heat production would be less. Now it happens that in 1953 I came upon a phenomenon of just this kind,[10] which is illustrated in Fig. 4. The lower curve shows the mechanical effect of a sudden short release applied near the maximum tension of a twitch; the upper curve shows the immediate rise of temperature. This sort of experiment was made in a variety of ways, and the final conclusion was embodied in the formula

$$\Delta Q = 0.018 \, l_0 \, (-\Delta P),$$

where ΔQ is the heat produced, $-\Delta P$ is the fall of tension, and l_0 is the stand-

Fig. 4. Heat and tension in isometric twitch of frog sartorius muscle at 0°C, released 0.6 mm in 8 msec, 0.23 sec after the shock.

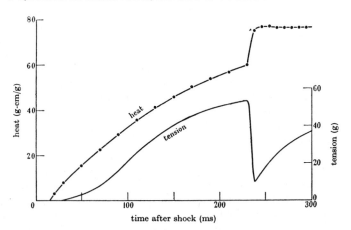

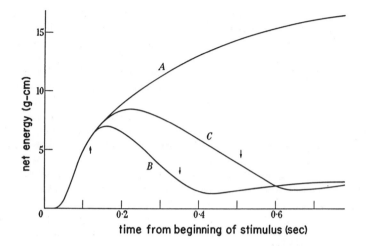

Fig. 5. Effect of a 4-mm stretch on the net energy liberated by a muscle during and after a short tetanus (0.3 sec). The experiment is the same as that illustrated in Fig. 2, but account is taken of the "thermoelastic" heat absorption associated with a rise of tension. Curve *A*, isometric contraction; ordinate: $H + E + 0.018l_0P$. Curves *B* and *C*, contraction with stretches starting and ending at the arrows; ordinate: $H + E + 0.018l_0P - W$. l_0, standard length of the muscle.

ard length of the muscle. This formula is the same as that referred to above for the thermoelastic effect in solids, if αT is 0.018; it gives a value of α about the same as that for ebonite.

The application of this result to the present experiments was made by adding Q in the formula to H, the observed heat; Q was calculated from the observed tension. Fig. 5. shows the same experiment as Fig. 2, but Q, the thermoelastic heat, has been added to the observed heat throughout. The same downward movement of the curves of net energy is found as before—that is, energy is still absorbed by the muscle during a stretch, but the net energy never becomes negative, and the difficulty has disappeared.

This is not the place to go further into the thermoelastic effect, or to justify its use on other gounds, other than to add that its application gives a greatly simplified picture of the energy liberated during the course of an iso-

metric contraction. The introduction of the thermoelastic heat has no effect on total quantities, since P (and therefore Q) is zero at the beginning and end of contraction.

Mechanism of Reversal

One naturally asks, what is the actual mechanism by which the reversal of a chemical process is effected by stretching a contracting muscle? Beyond demonstrating the fact itself, these experiments throw no light on the mechanism: for that purpose, experiments of quite a different kind are required. The great strength of thermodynamics is that the results are independent of the molecular mechanism, but one cannot have it both ways or use thermodynamic results to throw light on the mechanism. It is tempting to speculate, in terms of current theories of contraction,[12] on how mechanical work is derived from chemical free energy when filaments creep along one another, and on how chemical free energy is restored when the filaments are forcibly drawn apart. But if I were to mention the words *actin, myosin,* and *adenosine triphosphate,* attention might be drawn away from the facts under discussion, which would be rather a pity, for they *are* facts and have to be explained by any theory of muscle contraction.

The chief scientific interest of these results lies in the fact that a biochemical process, in a living muscle cell, can be reversed by the application of external mechanical work. But they do not allow any expectation that energy can be stored in this way, for there is no evidence that the reversal can ever be more than 100 per cent complete—that is, that chemical substances other than those produced in the contraction itself can be reinstated.

Application to Man

There is, however, another aspect of these results to be considered—the bearing they have on the physiology of muscular work in human beings. It is always interesting to try to find out how far the results obtained on isolated living material can be reproduced in the intact animal, particularly on the best of all experimental animals, man. It is scarcely conceivable that so large and obvious an effect, once recognized, should not appear again in human muscles, when those are doing "negative" muscular work, as in lowering a weight or going downhill. This is not an unimportant matter, for lowering weights, or the body, is a common affair, and indeed the whole muscular system is guided and balanced all the time by an arrangement of antagonist muscles, one of which lengthens under tension whenever the other shortens.

Soon after the work of 1951 was finished, an attempt was made by three of my colleagues[5] to see how the physiological expense of "negative" work in man compares with that of ordinary positive work. At that time research workers were not so certain as they are now that stretching a muscle during contraction can cause a reversal of chemical processes, and they were more cautious in interpreting what they found than they would need to be today. Their results, indeed, were quite unexpectedly large and were certainly due in part to the fact that the force exerted by a muscle while it is being stretched is much greater than the force exerted while it is shortening at the same speed, so a smaller number of muscle units could be employed for a given force. But that is probably not the whole story, and the partial reversal of chemical reactions probably plays a substantial part. That possibility should be examined critically in further experiments on man.

The original experiments were entertaining ones to make, or to watch. Two bicycles were arranged in opposition; one subject pedaled forward, the other resisted by back-pedaling. The speed had to be the same for both, and (apart from minor loss through friction) the forces exerted were the same. All the work done by one subject was absorbed by the other; there was no other significant resistance. The main result was evident at once, without analysis: the subject pedaling forward became fatigued, while the other remained fresh. The rate of working was varied, and the physiological effort was measured by determining the rate of oxygen consumption. It was found that the slopes of the lines relating oxygen usage to rate of working differed greatly between positive and negative work. The experiment was shown in 1952 at a *conversazione* of the Royal Society in London and was enthusiastically received, particularly because a young lady doing the negative work was able quickly, without much effort, to reduce a young man doing the positive work to exhaustion. It is evident now that further investigation is necessary. But however much, or little, the results of stretching isolated muscles may explain the findings in studies of negative work in man, it is interesting to see how the experiments on man arose directly from those on toads. The moral is, if you have a bright idea, try it and see; the result may be much more amusing than you expected.

References

1. Abbott, B. C., *J. Physiol. (London)*, **112** (1951), 438.
2. Abbott, B. C., and X. M. Aubert, *Proc. Roy. Soc. (London)*, **B139** (1938), 104.
3. Abbott, B. C., X. M. Aubert, and A. V. Hill, *ibid.*, **B139** (1938), 86.
4. Abbott, B. C., and B. Bigland, *J. Physiol. (London)*, **120** (1953), 319.
5. Abbott, B. C., B. Bigland, and J. M. Ritchie, *ibid.*, **117** (1952), 380.
6. Fenn, W. O., *ibid.*, **58** (1923), 175; *ibid.*, **58** (1924), 373.
7. Hill, A. V., *Proc. Roy. Soc. (London)*, **B126** (1938), 136.
8. Hill, A. V., *ibid.*, **B136** (1949), 195.
9. Hill, A. V., *ibid.*, **B137** (1950), 273; *ibid.*, **B141** (1953), 104.
10. Hill, A. V., *ibid.*, **B141** (1953), 161.
11. Hill A. V., and J. V. Hobarth, *ibid.*, **B151** (1959), 169.
12. Huxley, A. F., *Progr. Biophys. Biophys. Chem.*, **7** (1957), 255.

R. MARGARIA*   /   H. T. EDWARDS   /   D. B. DILL

The Possible Mechanisms of Contracting and Paying the Oxygen Debt and the Role of Lactic Acid in Muscular Contraction†

Reprinted from the *American Journal of Physiology*, **106** (1933), 689–715.

This paper is another of the important contributions of the Harvard Fatigue Laboratory and provides the first exact quantitative validation of the theoretical formulations of Hill and his associates. Margaria, Edwards, and Dill describe the characteristics of the curve of the removal of lactic acid. The curve they found is an exponential function of time, its speed of disappearance is proportionate to the amount of lactic acid at a particular time. They define the phenomenon of

† A preliminary report of this work has been given at the annual meeting of the Federation of American Societies for Experimental Biology in Cincinnati, April, 1933, and the abstract appeared in the *Journal of Biological Chemistry*, **100** (1933), 65.
* Fellow of the Rockefeller Foundation.

alactacid debt, a form of oxygen debt not accompanied by the accumulation of lactic acid. This debt is paid off very rapidly and is a linear function of oxygen intake in exercise. The lactacid oxygen debt is a function of work carried on in anaerobic conditions and increases rapidly at maximum rates of work.

Dill[1] in writing about oxygen debt in 1962 raises the following questions that he felt deserve "qualitative and quantitative" investigation:

a. What factors limit the ability to accumulate lactic acid and how can these be altered, especially by training?

b. What factors limit the ability to build up an alactic acid debt and how can these be altered?

c. What are the enzyme systems involved in the phenomena of oxygen debt?

The recent work of Huckabee[2] has raised questions about the linear relationship of lactic acid and oxygen debt. It is generally felt that the phenomenon of oxygen debt is much more complex than was suggested by the earlier studies and, as Dill mentioned above, deserves more extensive research. A review of these articles should help in suggesting possible leads to be followed.

Although direct evidence of a quantitative relationship between oxygen debt and lactic acid production in man has never been given, there is general agreement with A. V. Hill's hypothesis that the oxygen debt is due to the delayed oxidation of a fraction of the lactic acid produced during the anaerobic processes of muscular activity. After the "revolution" produced in muscle physiology by the discoveries of the last few years, mainly after Lundsgaard's work, and the further observations on men, it seemed to us that the lactic acid mechanism alone is inadequate to explain all the processes which occur in the payment of the oxygen debt, particularly for the following reasons:

a. It has been observed in isolated muscle that most of the lactic acid is produced after the contraction is over, during the first minute of recovery; this does not seem to agree with the fact that the payment of the oxygen debt at the beginning shows no lag even if the exercise is of very short duration.

b. In moderate exercise of long duration in man, involving an oxygen debt of 3 to 4 l, the changes in lactic acid concentration or in pH of blood are negligible in comparison with the values implied by the assumption of an increment of lactic acid in the body corresponding to the amount of oxygen debt. (See, for the lactic acid concentration in blood following muscular exercise;[20, 4] for data on pH.[10])

c. There exist oxidative recovery processes following muscular contraction other than the glycogen resynthesis from lactic acid; Lundsgaard[14] has demonstrated in muscles poisoned with iodoacetic acid the partial resynthesis of the phosphocreatine in the presence of oxygen and in the absence of any lactic acid formation or removal; Clark, Eggleton, and Eggleton[3] found that heart muscle poisoned with iodoacetate and supplied with oxygen can go on almost indefinitely. Moreover, in the normal muscle only a part of the phosphagen can be restored anaerobically at the expense of the formation of the lactic acid, while a considerable fraction is restored only in the presence of oxygen.

It was our purpose to investigate

---

[1] D. B. Dill, and B. Sactor, "Exercise and Oxygen Debt," *Journal of Sports Medicine and Physical Fitness,* **2** (1962), 66–72.

[2] W. E. Huckabee, *Journal of Clinical Investigation,* **37** (1958), 244.

this problem, particularly in regard to any relation between production and removal of lactic acid and amount and payment of oxygen debt in man.

The Behavior of Lactic Acid

There is no means of measuring directly in man the total lactic acid production or the total amount of lactic acid present in the body at a certain time. The only datum available is the concentration of lactic acid in the blood and we must first make certain whether or not this really represents the total amount of lactic acid present in the body.

The promptness of appearance of lactic acid in muscular exercise as well as the rapid decrease in its concentration as blood passes through an inactive region of the body,[1] proves that lactate ions diffuse freely between tissues and blood. A free diffusion through the isolated frog's muscles has been observed by Hill[11] and Evans and Eggleton[6,7] have found in mammals that within half a minute after a short tetanic contraction, the venous blood coming away from the muscle contains lactic acid at a concentration almost equal to that in the muscle. Thus, except when changes in lactic acid production are so rapid that an equilibrium between the concentrations of lactic acid in tissues and in blood has not been reached, we are justified in assuming the concentration of lactic acid in the blood to be proportional to the total amount of lactic acid in the body.

In preliminary experiments a young athlete, Clapham, ran to exhaustion on a treadmill at 18.7 km per hr on a 5 per cent grade for $4\frac{1}{2}$ to 6 min. The excess lactic acid concentration in the blood, disregarding the values of the first 6 to 8 min of recovery, was found

to decrease logarithmically according to the formula:

$$L = L_r + 10^{a-bt}, \qquad (1)$$

where L is the lactic acid concentration at time t, L_r the concentration of lactic acid in the blood at rest, 10^a the extrapolated value of excess lactic acid concentration in the blood at the beginning of recovery and b the velocity constant. The values of the constants a and b were calculated from the experimental values obtained after the first 5 min of recovery with the method of least squares, assuming the resting value for lactic acid concentration to be 10 mg per 100 cc of blood. As can be seen in Table 1, which gives the values of blood lactic acid concentration in two experiments in which the subject ran to exhaustion, the calculated values fit very well with the experimental ones, the differences being of the same order as the methodical error.[3]

A formula of the type given cannot be applied satisfactorily to the early phase of recovery. This may be due:

a. To delayed lactic acid production, though this in isolated frog's muscle has been shown to last less than a minute[9].

b. To the slowness of diffusion of lactic acid from the tissues to blood, and

c. To the lower O_2 tension in the tissues in the first part of recovery, due to failure of the O_2 supply to keep pace with the greater oxygen consumption.

This lag in the disappearance of lactic acid is greater the shorter the exercise and the higher the degree of exhaustion. In fact, if the exercise is hard and short enough a rise in blood

---

[3] The method used for determining lactic acid was that of Friedemann, Cotonio, and Schaffer;[8] the blood was collected from an antecubital vein unless otherwise noted.

TABLE 1

Observed and calculated values for lactic acid concentration in the blood of Clapham
after running to exhaustion at 18.7 km per hr on a 5 per cent grade

RECOVERY TIME	LACTIC ACID CONCENTRATION IN ARM BLOOD		
	Observed	Calculated by the formula $L = 10 + 10^{2.113\ -0.0185t}$	Δ
October 14. Duration of performance, 4 minutes			
min.	*mgm. per 100 cc.*	*mgm. per 100 cc.*	*mgm. per 100 cc.*
$\frac{1}{2}$	120		
$3\frac{3}{4}$	107		
$5\frac{1}{2}$	108		
$7\frac{1}{2}$	104	104.2	+0.2
$15\frac{1}{2}$	77.4	77	−0.4
$27\frac{1}{2}$	50.3	50.2	−0.1
$56\frac{1}{2}$	24.7	21.7	−3.0
October 28. Duration of performance, $5\frac{3}{4}$ minutes			
		$L = 10 + 10^{2.175\ -0.0205t}$	
$\frac{1}{3}$	108		
5	111		
7	109		
9	108	107.8	−0.2
15	85.4	83.7	−1.7
25	55.1	56	+0.9
61	18.4	18.4	0
100	12	11.5	−0.5
130	10.4	10.3	0.1

lactic acid concentration may be observed in the first part of recovery[13] (see Protocol 9). Margaria and Talenti[16] have found under such conditions an associated increase in hydrogen-ion concentration. The lag is nearly eliminated if the period of exercise is made to last longer, say, 10 min, which shows that factors *a* or *b* or both are the most important in determining such a lag.

The fact that the removal of lactic acid from the body is a logarithmic function of time shows that the rate of removal of the excess lactic acid is proportional to the concentration of the excess lactic acid itself. This fits the conception that the removal of lactic acid is due to the combustion of a fraction of it. We must assume, however, that after the first few minutes of recovery the tissue O_2 tension remains practically constant and the physicochemical changes in the body do not interfere with the process of lactic acid oxidation.

The payment of the oxygen debt, on the other hand, has never been shown to be a logarithmic or any other simple function of the time in spite of efforts made in this direction. Hill, Long, and Lupton[13] affirm that "there are clearly two factors at work, one of which accounts for the initial rapid fall in the oxygen intake on the cessation of exercise, the other for the prolonged remainder of recovery occurring after extended or severe exertion. . . . Each process is exponential in character— one is rapid; one, however, is slow. Moderate exercise is followed to a preponderant degree by recovery of the rapid type." These authors attribute the first and rapid phase of recovery to the oxidative removal of lactic acid in the muscles where it was formed, while the second and prolonged phase represents the oxidative removal of lactic acid which has had time to escape by diffusion from the muscles.

If this hypothesis were true we ought to find a close proportionality between oxygen debt and lactic acid concentration in the blood, provided that the exercise had been long enough for complete diffusion of lactic acid to have taken place between muscles and blood at the end of the exercise.

Method

We have performed a series of experiments on the same subject in which the exercise lasted 10 min. We assume that in this time and for exercise not involving the maximum metabolic rate, equilibrium is reached as regards diffusion of lactic acid from the muscles at work into the blood stream and from this into the tissues which were not producing lactic acid. This assumption has been proved very nearly correct. After such a period of work, provided a steady state has been reached, the concentration of lactic

acid in the blood decreases without showing an appreciable lag from the end of the exercise.

Evidence for this statement is given also by Protocol 7 in which the subject ran for 10 min at 14 km per hr on a 2.5 per cent grade. Samples of blood from the femoral vein, and an arm vein and from the femoral artery were taken at various periods after exercise. In spite of the fact that the exercise was very strenuous involving a metabolic rate very near the maximum, there was but little difference in lactic acid concentration or pH of blood samples taken simultaneously from the various sources. Fig. 1 shows the phenomenon; the values for lactic acid concentration are the same for arterial and arm vein blood, and only slightly higher in blood from the femoral vein during the first minutes of recovery.

Various amounts of oxygen debt were produced by varying the intensity of the exercise, which consisted of walking or running on a motor-driven treadmill at various speeds and at various grades.

There is some trouble in measuring

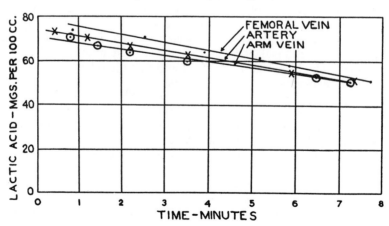

Fig. 1. Lactic acid concentrations of arterial, (X), femoral vein (·), and arm vein blood (⊙) in recovery, as a function of time, in Clapham after a 10 min run at 14 km per hr on a 3.8 per cent grade.

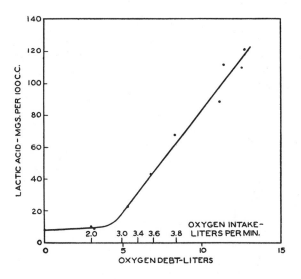

Fig. 2. Relation between lactic acid concentration in the blood, oxygen debt as calculated after A. V. Hill, and metabolic rate, at steady state of exercise. Duration of exercise was 10 min in each case.

the extra oxygen consumption as an effect of previous muscular exercise (we shall not use temporarily the term "oxygen debt" which specifies a mechanism as to the use of the oxygen) as the oxygen consumption after a considerable amount of work does not come back, even in 2 hr, to the pre-work values. For example, the basal O_2 consumption for the subject Clapham was 240 cc per min; this value was reached one-half hour after a 10-min run at 7.4 km per hr, while after harder exercise his oxygen consumption per minute was still as high as 270 cc 2 hr after the end of work. The resting oxygen consumption then is merely a matter of subjective appreciation. So, following A. V. Hill's procedure, in our first calculations we assumed as resting the O_2 consumption one and one-half hour after the end of the work.

Relation between Lactic Acid Production and Oxygen Debt, as Calculated after A. V. Hill

Plotting in a coordinate system the concentration of lactic acid in the blood at the beginning of recovery against the after-work extra oxygen consumption so calculated, we obtain the curve represented in Fig. 2.

For the contraction of an excess oxygen consumption during recovery up to 3 or 4 l we see no appreciable increase of blood lactic acid. For extra oxygen consumption of 6 l or more, the concentration of lactic acid in the blood is a linear function of the extra oxygen consumption. It seems that the most obvious way of explaining this behavior is to admit that when the excess oxygen is less than 3 l the lactic acid mechanism is not involved but some other process, at present unknown. The lactic acid mechanism starts coming into play when the extra oxygen consumption is 3 to 4 l, while for increasing the extra oxygen consumption over 4 l it seems that only the lactic acid mechanism is involved. That there is no extra accumulation of lactic acid, even localized in the muscles, corresponding to small amounts of extra oxygen consumption after work is also proved by the behavior of the R. Q. which does not increase in the first stages of recovery more than can be accounted for by the retention of CO_2 at the beginning of exercise (see Protocols 1 to 4).

53

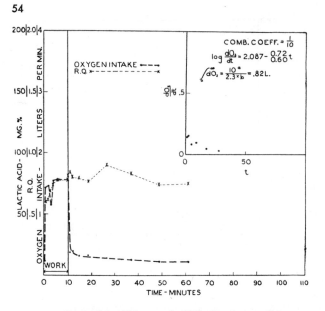

Protocol 1. February 1, 1933. Clapham walking at a speed of 7.5 km per hr for 10 min. Corner figure: Oxygen consumption per min less the minimum basal oxygen consumption. The values for the speed constants of the alactacid process in this and the following protocols are given for the single experimental data in order of time, as well as the value of the alactacid oxygen debt $\left(\int_0^\infty dO_2\right)$.

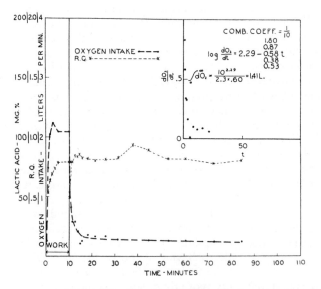

Protocol 2. January 25, 1933. Clapham running at a speed of 9.3 km per hr for 10 min. Corner figure: Oxygen consumption per min less the minimum basal oxygen consumption.

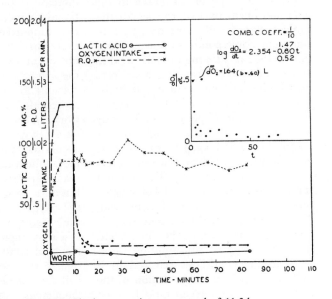

Protocol 3. January 27, 1933. Clapham running at a speed of 11.3 km per hr for 10 min. In the inserted figure in Protocols 3 to 8: oxygen consumption per min less the minimum basal oxygen consumption and less the amount attributable to the combustion of the excess lactic acid on the assumption of a combustion coefficient of 1/10.

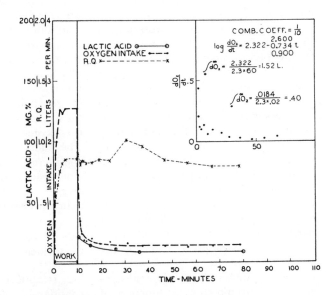

Protocol 4. February 15, 1933. Clapham running at a speed of 11.3 km per hr on a 1 per cent grade for 10 min.

From the slope of the curve in the later and linear part we can see for this subject that 1 l of extra oxygen consumption corresponds to a concentration change of 12.8 mg of lactic acid in 100 cc of blood. Assuming a uniform distribution of lactic acid in the body, with water contents of 80 per cent in the blood and of 72 per cent in the body as a whole, the body weight of the subject being 61.2 kg, 12.8 mg of lactic acid in 100 cc of blood would correspond to 7.0 g in the body. This amount is removed in the body by 1 l of oxygen. Since in the combustion of lactic acid, 3 mol of O_2 are used for 1 mol of lactic acid, assuming that the increment in extra oxygen consumption after work in the conditions referred to is only used up in the combustion of the lactic acid, 1 l of oxygen must be used for the combustion of 1.34 g of lactic acid, the remaining being resynthesized as glycogen. The ratio between lactic acid burned and total lactic acid removed is $1.34/7.0 = 1/5.2$. This value corresponds to the lowest given by A. V. Hill and by Meyerhof for the recovery in isolated frog's muscle.

As we shall see later, the assumption that the extra oxygen consumption is only used in the combustion of lactic acid is probably incorrect, as other oxidative processes are going on. The value 1/5.2 given above is lower than the average obtained by Hill and Meyerhof. This is due to the fact that in our calculation we avoided the error of using the whole of the extra oxygen consumption for comparison with the whole lactic acid removed, but employed instead the increment of the extra oxygen consumption for comparison with the increment of lactic acid on the straight portion of the curve.

Figure 2 shows also lactic acid concentration in blood as a function of metabolic rate. The assumption that increase in blood lactic acid is proportional to increase in metabolic rate is not supported by the facts. We see that extra lactic acid formation does not occur except in severe work. Also the lactic acid produced does not account for all the extra oxygen consumed after work, particularly for easy work. In easy work there must certainly be an oxygen debt too, which may be accounted for by the fact that the metabolic rate during work does not reach its steady state immediately, but after an initial period during which the oxygen consumption is lower than the corresponding amount of work. We may then distinguish two mechanisms of contracting O_2 debt, the one due to the lactic acid, which we shall call the "lactacid" mechanism, and an "alactacid" one where there is no apparent lactic acid formation. The lactic acid mechanism in this subject, running on a treadmill, comes into play at an O_2 consumption of about 2.4 l per min which is 60 per cent of his maximum metabolic rate.

The alactacid mechanism occurs then far more frequently in the ordinary conditions of life than the lactacid mechanism. This fact, together with the fact that, as we shall see later, the alactacid oxygen debt is paid at a much faster rate than the lactacid oxygen debt, raises the importance of the alactacid mechanism of contracting the oxygen debt to a primary degree. The lactacid mechanism has to be considered more like a mechanism of emergency, though its capacity is greater than that of the alactacid O_2 debt mechanism.

Role of Lactic Acid in Muscular Contraction

It appears from Fig. 2 that up to a considerable rate of work, not exceeding two thirds of the maximum

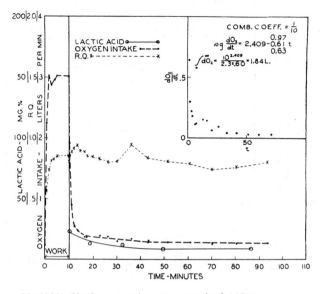

Protocol 5. January 25, 1933. Clapham running at a speed of 14 km per hr for 10 min.

aerobic rate of work, no lactic acid excess appears in the blood, and presumably in the muscles, for the case of the athletic subject investigated. Does that mean that no excess lactic acid is formed in the muscles as a consequence of that amount of work?

The concentration of lactic acid in the muscles depends upon an equilibrium between lactic acid formation and lactic acid removal: there is no doubt that, if the rate of lactic acid formation increases without a corresponding increase in the rate of its removal, a new equilibrium will be set up at a higher lactic acid concentration. The removal of lactic acid, being due to the oxidation of a fraction of the lactic acid itself, depends upon the oxygen tension in the muscles: it is highly improbable and contrary to the usual findings that the oxygen tension is higher in the working muscles than in the ones at rest; therefore, unless the lactic acid removal in these conditions is due to

another mechanism which goes at a faster rate than the mechanism of removal of the lactic acid during recovery for a lactacid oxygen debt, for which we have no evidence, it follows that muscular work at such a rate is accomplished without any lactic acid formation.

The slowness of the removal of lactic acid during recovery may be due either (a), to the fact that the speed of the oxidation of the lactic acid is low, or (b), to the speed of the reaction lactic acid→glycogen being low. In case of (a) we have to exclude the possibility of any important part played by the lactic acid in normal aerobic muscular contractions, because, on this assumption, we would reach in moderate exercise excessively high levels of lactic acid in the body.

For example, assuming that the work is all performed at the expense of the combustion of lactic acid and that no lactic acid is resynthesized to

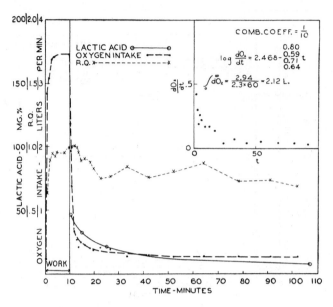

Protocol 6. February 1, 1933. Clapham running at a speed of 14 km per hr on a 2.5 per cent grade for 10 min.

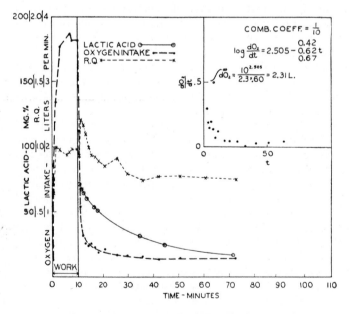

Protocol 7. February 23, 1933. Clapham running at a speed of 14 km per hr on a 3.8 per cent grade for 10 min.

glycogen during work, for the subject Clapham working in a steady state at a metabolic rate of 2 l of oxygen per min, a calculation, on the basis that the speed constant for the removal of lactic acid is 0.02, leads to a value of increased lactic acid concentration in the blood of 5 g per l. Actually, for such a metabolic rate, we do not observe any increase in lactic acid. On the other hand evidence that oxidation of lactic acid is a slow process is found in the facts (a), that at the beginning of recovery when the oxygen consumption is still very high, the decrease in concentration of lactic acid is no greater than in the later period of recovery, and (b), that for all the period of recovery the combustion of lactic acid accounts only for a small fraction of the total oxygen consumption. We would have expected that, given a great excess of lactic acid in the body, there ought to be at least a proportionality between oxygen consumption and lactic acid disappearance. Moreover, as we shall see later, the speed of removal of lactic acid is affected by the oxygen tension in the inspired air and therefore in the tissues, which shows that the slowness of the reaction is due to the oxidation of the lactic acid and not to the reaction lactic acid→glycogen which must be independent of the oxygen tension.

It is justifiable, therefore, until direct data on the speed of oxidation of lactic acid in the body are available, to assume as more probable the hypothesis that the slowness of removing lactic acid is due to the slowness of the process of its oxidation.

This interpretation does not, of course, exclude the possibility of the interpretation given by A. V. Hill in 1924, i.e., that the lactic acid, though being formed at all rates of muscular work, does not escape out of the muscles below a certain metabolic rate because "it is hemmed in by a zone in which oxygen supply is adequate, and through which it cannot pass: only when some regions of the muscles become oxygen-free can lactic acid pass through them and escape into the capillaries." We think, however, that this hypothesis can hardly be reconciled with the following facts: (a), no sign of the presence or removal of any acid in the body can be detected from the behavior of the R. Q. up to an afterwork oxygen consumption of 4 l. The period required for consuming this amount of oxygen is long enough for such phenomena to be observed, if present; (b), the time required for the removal of lactic acid from the blood is certainly much greater than that which could be accounted for by simple diffusion from blood to the muscles. This requires the assumption that lactic acid diffused into the blood cannot be utilized by the muscles again, an assumption for which we have no evidence.

Oxygen Consumption Due to the Lactic Acid Removal

If the lactic acid concentration of the blood decreases logarithmically, its speed of removal decreases also logarithmically. Thus we have, from (1),

$$-\frac{dL}{dt} = 2.3 \times b \times 10^{a-bt}. \qquad (2)$$

Assuming the total amount of lactic acid in the body uniformly distributed per amount of water, then for our subject, 1 mg of lactic acid concentration in 100 cc of blood corresponds to 0.55 g of lactic acid: and assuming a combustion coefficient of lactic acid of 1/5, i.e., $-dL/dO_2 = 6.7$, where L is expressed in grams in the whole body and O_2 in liters, and substituting in (2) we have

$$\frac{dO_2}{dt} = \frac{2.3 \times 0.55}{6.7} \times b \times 10^{a-bt}, \quad (3)$$

which expresses the oxygen consumption due to the removal of the lactic acid on the assumption above. The amount of oxygen debt due to this mechanism will be given by

$$\int_0^\infty dO_2 = \frac{0.55}{6.7} \times 10^a. \quad (4)$$

Subtracting from the values of the oxygen consumption after work the amount due to the basal metabolic rate (0.24 l per min) and also the amount due to the lactacid oxygen debt (if any) we obtain curves all more similar to each other. The value of the velocity constant b has been assumed in these calculations to be 0.02.

The fact that the curves of the remaining oxygen consumption become all more similar to each other is particularly interesting as it was known, after A. V. Hill's work, that the payment of small oxygen debts goes on at a relatively much faster rate than the

payment of large oxygen debts. This fits in with the hypothesis that the lactacid payment of the oxygen debt is a slow process and that such a mechanism only enters into play when large amounts of oxygen debt are required. We must remember that the speed of the payment of the lactacid oxygen debt is the same as the speed of disappearance of the lactic acid from the blood; the velocity constant is for both processes about 0.02, which means that 50 per cent of the reaction is not reached until after 15 min and that it takes 1 hr to reach 94 per cent of completion.

The Oxygen Consumption Curve from Which the Minimum Resting O_2 Consumption and the Amount Attributable to the Lactic Acid Removal Have Been Subtracted

The curve of the oxygen consumption in recovery less the minimum resting oxygen consumption and the oxygen used in paying the lactacid debt seems to be the sum of two curves, corresponding to two processes occur-

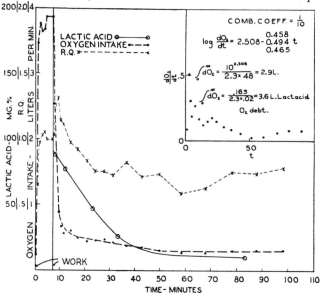

Protocol 8. January 27, 1933. Clapham running at a speed of 18.6 km per hr for 7 min.

ring at very different rates. The composite curve falls rapidly at the beginning of recovery, a process lasting only 3 to 4 min, and then falls slowly and rather irregularly, a process lasting perhaps one-half hour in mild work and 2 hr or more after strenuous exercise.

The possibility arises that the first rapid fall of the oxygen consumption is due to the presence in the body of an oxygen reserve mechanism. Such an oxygen reserve could be the expression of the difference of saturation of the hemoglobin between rest and work, particularly for the hemoglobin contained in the working muscles. In Henderson's charts[10] we see that the difference in oxygen saturation of venous blood between rest and work at an oxygen consumption of 1,750 cc per min in a nonathletic man corresponds to 40 cc per l of blood. Assuming the volume of venous blood is 1.5 l, only 60 cc of oxygen could be attributed to this mechanism. Taking into account also the difference in saturation of the arterial blood and of the muscle hemoglobin, we believe that we can safely state that the total amount of oxygen debt attributable to this mechanism cannot exceed 100 cc, which is negligible for the present purposes.

The Alactacid Mechanism of O_2 Debt

In mild exercise we may consider the curve of the oxygen consumption in recovery less the minimum resting O_2 consumption without lactic acid formation as resulting from the summation of two processes. Extrapolating to zero recovery time the slow process, the difference between the summated curve and that corresponding to this slow process will permit an analysis of the fast process. The curve that we obtain in this way is within the limits of experimental error, of the same logarithmic type as the curve of the

oxygen consumption due to lactic acid removal, only the speed of this process is much greater. As for the lactic acid mechanism, this function is defined by

$$\log \frac{dO_2}{dt} = a_1 - bt_1; \qquad (5)$$

b_1, the velocity constant, is easily calculated knowing the value of a_1, which is defined by $dO_2/dt = 10^a$ for $t = O$.

The fact that this process has the characteristic of logarithmic decrement is good evidence for attributing to it the significance of an oxygen debt payment. This portion of the debt may be called "alactacid" because it takes place without apparent extra lactic acid formation. The more reliable value of b_1 is obtained at t = about 2 min, because for very small values of t the experimental error may be very considerable, and for higher values of t errors due to incorrect extrapolation of the slow function may become considerable. The values for b_1, so calculated for the different times, are given in the protocols: the more reliable value is about 0.60.

This alactacid mechanism of paying an oxygen debt is much more convenient than the lactacid mechanism as far as the speed of payment is concerned. This speed is 30 times greater, taking only half a minute to pay 50 per cent of the alactacid debt, while the payment is practically complete (98.5 per cent) in 3 min.

The total amount of oxygen debt contracted by this mechanism is defined by

$$\int_0^\infty dO_2 = \frac{10^{a_1}}{2.3 + b_1}. \qquad (6)$$

The Coefficient of Combustion of Lactic Acid

In experiments where a considerable amount of lactic acid was formed curves may be derived showing the residual oxygen consumption after subtraction of the minimum resting oxygen consumption and of the oxygen consumption due to the payment of the lactacid oxygen debt on the assumption of a combustion coefficient for lactic acid of 1/5. These curves are dissimilar in two respects from corresponding curves obtained in mild exercise without lactic acid formation. One dissimilarity is found in the shape of the curve corresponding to the slow process. Values for O_2 consumption in this process are smaller in mild exercise. The curve may be flat for the first 1 or 2 hr of recovery and in some cases negative values for O_2 consumption are indicated. Another dissimilarity is observed in the speed constants. Those calculated in experiments where excess lactic acid formation occurs are about one-half the magnitude of corresponding values derived in the absence of apparent lactic acid formation.

If we calculate such curves on the assumption of a combustion coefficient for lactic acid of 1/10 the resulting curves appear to be more nearly the same type as the corresponding curves for mild exercise. Values for oxygen consumption are always positive and the oxygen consumption for the slow process tends to decrease with time as in milder exercise. Also uniform values for the speed constants of alactacid recovery are derived by this calculation whether or not excess lactic formation occurs. Finally, in a given experiment, the values for speed constants calculated at different times agree better with each other (see Protocol 9). Therefore, it seems to us justifiable to assume as more nearly correct a value of 1/10 for the combustion coefficient of lactic acid.

The fact that a combustion coefficient of 1/5.2 was found from the data

from Fig. 1 and 1/5 from the data of Hill and Meyerhof may be explained by the fact that in these cases the computation of the oxygen involved not only the oxygen removal of lactic acid but also the oxygen used in the slow process, which may amount to nearly the same value.

Also from a theoretical point of view the value of 1/10 as the combustion coefficient of lactic acid seems more probable than the value 1/5. If the latter value is correct, the heat of combustion of lactic acid as lactate being 3,501 cal per g of lactic acid and the heat of transformation of 1g glycogen to 1g lactic acid, as lactate in the muscles, 340 cal, the efficiency of resynthesis of glycogen from lactic acid comes out to be less than 40 per cent. Now the mechanical efficiency of muscular work performed anaerobically at the expense of glycogen breakdown to lactic acid may be not less than 30 per cent. It follows that the efficiency of glycogen breakdown into lactic acid and the transformation of this chemical energy into mechanical has an efficiency of over 75 per cent. It is hardly believable that this process takes place at a higher efficiency than the process of resynthesis of glycogen from lactic acid. This, being a pure chemical process not involving transformation into other kinds of energy, occurs presumably at a very high efficiency.

On the assumption of a combustion coefficient of lactic acid of 1/10 the efficiency of resynthesis of glycogen from lactic acid would be about 87 per cent.

The Increase in Basal Metabolism after Work

The remaining oxygen consumption does not seem to have anything to do with a real oxygen debt as ordinarily

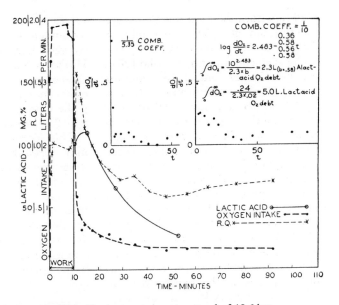

Protocol 9. February 15, 1933. Clapham running at a speed of 18.6 km per hr for 10 min. Corner figures: Oxygen consumption per min less the minimum basal oxygen consumption and less the amount attributable to the combustion of the excess lactic acid on the assumption of a combustion coefficient of 1/10 and of 1/5.35.

defined. In other words, the oxidative processes which account for such an amount of oxygen do not appear to provide the energy for the reconstitution of substances which broke down in consequence of the muscular contraction and whose anaerobic breakdown furnished directly or indirectly the energy developed in the muscular contraction. This conception is supported by the fact that this oxygen consumption takes such a long time to reach the zero value; it may still be 10 to 20 per cent of the minimum basal oxygen consumption, 1 or 2 hr after the end of the work, when quantitatively important properties of the blood have returned to normal. The hypothesis of an increase in the basal metabolism after work was advanced by Hill, Long, and Lupton[13] on the basis of their findings and those of Benedict and Cathcart[2] of an increased resting

oxygen consumption several hours after the end of severe muscular exercise. The former authors assumed a constant value for the increase in metabolism for all the period of recovery, a value that they deduced from measurements of the oxygen consumption 2 or 3 hr after the end of work.

It seems to us that our calculation indicating that the oxygen used in this slow process decreases uniformly explains the phenomenon in a more satisfactory way than does the assumption of a constant increase of oxygen intake for this process. Since the phenomenon is due to muscular work and continues in evidence for several hours of recovery, it appears likely that it will be more pronounced in the early phase of recovery.

Data on the amount of oxygen consumption due to this mechanism are given in the protocols. After exercise of 10 min duration requiring an oxygen consumption of 1550 cc per min, in the first 5 min of recovery such extra rest oxygen consumption may be 120 cc per min (50 per cent of the minimum resting oxygen consumption). It may be 250 cc per min (over 100 per cent of the basal oxygen consumption) for harder work. The time required for attaining the minimum resting oxygen consumption is greater the more severe and prolonged the work.

The oxygen debt as computed by our method may differ greatly from the value obtained by A. V. Hill's method, which does not take into account all the increase in oxygen consumption after work. Thus, in the 10-min run at 18.7 km per hr the oxygen debt as calculated after A.V. Hill for 1 1/2 hr after the end of work was 12.5 l. According to our calculations the lactacid oxygen debt was 5 l, the alactacid one 2.3 l and the oxygen used in that period of time attributable to an increased rest oxygen consumption amounted to 10.6 l. The amount of oxygen debt as calculated following Hill's procedure is 70 per cent higher than our value. In the 7.4 km per hr run our value for oxygen debt is 0.82 l while following A. V. Hill's procedure it is 2.55, three times as great.

This increased oxygen consumption may account for the oscillations and irregularities of the values for oxygen consumption after work. They were not seen in this subject in determinations of the basal metabolism carried on for several hours,[4] nor are they detectable in the curves of lactic acid removal from the blood and therefore in the corresponding oxygen consumption.

_____

[4] In Protocol 9 determinations of the basal metabolism performed on the subject Clapham from 8: 30 a.m. until 12: 30 p.m. the average oxygen consumption came out to be 0.240 l per min with a probable deviation from this value of ±0.004.

Protocol 10. February 2, 1933. Shaeron running at a speed of 14 km per hr for 3 min.

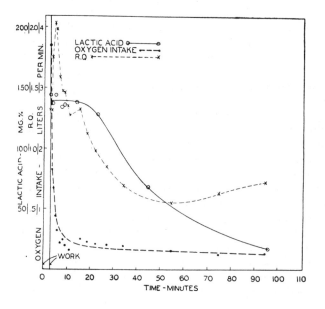

The Delayed Lactic Acid Appearance in Arm Venous Blood

We mentioned before that the curve showing lactic acid concentration in blood during recovery in the first few minutes deviates from the curve calculated on the data of a later period. This phenomenon, however, only follows high degrees of exhaustion, and it is greater the shorter the exercise. The duration of this delay in various experiments on Clapham was about 6 to 8 min, while in another subject, only capable of a poor performance the curve of the lactic acid removal took 25 to 30 min to reach the normal logarithmic shape (see Protocol 10).

Of the possible explanations, pointed out on p. 51, the low oxygen tension in the tissues at the beginning of recovery does not seem to affect the speed of removal of lactic acid to such an extent as to explain this phenomenon. On the other hand the delayed lactic acid production in isolated frog muscle at 20° lasts a very short time after contraction, and is complete in a minute or so. The delayed lactic acid equilibrium in blood then must be attributed to the slowness of diffusion of the lactic acid from the muscles to the blood stream and into idle tissues.

Amounts of the Lactacid and Alactacid Oxygen Debts and Their Significance

If we plot the amount of lactacid and alactacid oxygen debts as calculated on the assumption of a combustion coefficient for lactic acid of 1/10 against the metabolic rate, for the experiments lasting 10 min, we obtain the curves represented in Fig. 3.

The alactacid oxygen debt increases linearly with increase in metabolic rate to reach a maximum of about 2.5 l at the maximum metabolic rate, 3.6 l of oxygen per min in excess of the resting value. So the alactacid oxygen debt amounts in this subject to 700 cc for an increase in metabolism of 1 l of oxygen. It does not seem to be related directly to the intensity of work performed since it does not increase as an increasing proportion of the work is carried on by anaerobic processes.

In moderate work the alactacid oxygen debt accounts for nearly all the lag in oxygen consumption at the beginning of work before a steady state is established.

The lactacid oxygen debt in Clapham is not appreciable until the oxygen intake is about 2.5 l of oxygen per min. It increases slowly at first, more rapidly later and the curve becomes vertical at the point corresponding to the maximum metabolic rate. In this region it increases with increasing amount of work performed, which shows that at the highest metabolic rates an increase in oxygen debt is made only at the expense of the lactacid mechanism.

The alactacid oxygen debt is very probably the expression of an oxidative process in which the energy liberated is spent in repaying the amount of energy set free anaerobically during the muscular contraction, i.e., it is a true oxygen debt in the meaning given by A. V. Hill to this term.

We do not know the identity of the substances oxidized nor the nature of the anaerobic process that requires this latter oxidative process. However, the more important anaerobic change in muscle during contraction, excluding the lactic acid formation, is the splitting of phosphagen into creatine and H_3PO_4 and we know that the reverse process requires, at least in part, the presence of an oxidative process. It seems, therefore, justifiable to advance the hypothesis that the resynthesis of the phos-

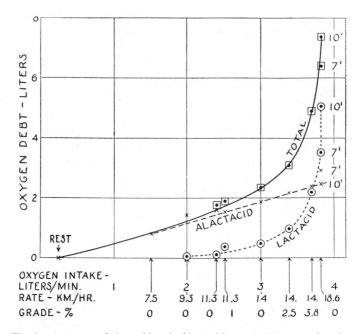

Fig. 3. Amounts of alactacid and of lactacid oxygen debts as a function of the metabolic rate: subject Clapham: from Protocols 1 to 9.

phagen is the process which absorbs the energy developed in the oxidative processes attributable to the alactacid oxygen debt payment. This hypothesis could be checked knowing the amount of oxygen which is required in the resynthesis of the phosphagen, and the amount of phosphagen in the muscles at work.

During rest a certain equilibrium must exist in the muscles between phosphagen and its products of scission. Since phosphagen breakdown accompanies muscular contraction, the steady state of exercise is associated with a new equilibrium in which the amount of phosphagen will be less and the amount of the products of its scission will be greater than at rest. At the end of the work there will be a tendency toward reaching the rest equilibrium state again, and this will go at the expense of the oxidative

processes responsible for the alactacid oxygen debt.

This all fits with the findings that an oxygen debt is found also at the lowest rates of work and also with the approximate linear relation between the rate of oxygen consumption and alactacid oxygen debt.

Eggleton[6] has found that the creatine equilibrium concentrations for resting and for fatigued muscle are respectively 0.005 and 0.023 M. Since 11,000 cal are evolved per g-mol of phosphagen hydrolyzed[18] the difference in phosphagen content between fatigued and resting muscle would account for 200 cal per kg of muscle, which corresponds to about 0.043 l of oxygen. On the hypothesis that the alactacid oxygen debt accounts for the resynthesis of phosphagen from its components, 2.5 l correspond to the exhaustion of about 60 kg of muscle.

Taking into account that the efficiency of this process may lie, presumably, between 40 and 80 per cent, we reach a figure of about the expected order of magnitude.

On the basis that during muscular contraction phosphagen splits down into H_3PO_4 and creatine and that this may account for the alactacid oxygen debt, we have measured inorganic phosphorus and creatine contents of blood after strenuous work. There is quantitatively little change in the content of creatine, and an increase in the concentration of inorganic phosphorus from about 0.0018 mol in rest to about 0.0025 after work: this change is much too small to account for the amount of phosphagen split down, as calculated from the oxygen debt. However, this may be due either to the esterification of the H_3PO_4, originating from the phosphagen, with the glucose, a process which is known to happen, or to the fact that phosphate is practically indiffusible through the muscle membrane;[6] the smallness of the creatine increase in the blood may be explained by its failure also to diffuse out of the muscle cells.

We venture no hypothesis as to the nature of the substances oxidized in payment of the oxygen debt; we have no reason to suppose that they are substances other than those usually burned during other activities of the tissues.

As far as the lactacid oxygen debt is concerned, there is no doubt, after the work of Hill and Meyerhof, that this accounts for the energy of resynthesis of the glycogen from the lactic acid. However, we have no direct evidence for supposing that the destiny of such oxygen is to burn part of the lactic acid itself. The slowness of the removal of the lactic acid may be due to the fact that the resynthesis of the lactic acid into glycogen is a slow pro-

cess, or to the fact that the oxidative processes furnishing the energy for such a resynthesis are slow. In the latter case we have to assume that the resynthesis of the glycogen cannot take place by oxidation of the usual fuel, because these oxidative processes may go at a much faster rate. This is evident from the behavior of the payment of the alactacid oxygen debt and from the oxidative processes taking place when muscular work is performed aerobically at the highest metabolic rate.

That this really is so is very probable, in view of the influence of the oxygen content in the inspired air on the speed constant of the removal of lactic acid. Then we must conclude that the speed of disappearance of lactic acid is slow because the combustion of the lactic acid is a slow process, and that the resynthesis of glycogen from lactic acid can only occur at the expense of the oxidation of the lactic acid itself.

A fraction of the oxygen debt being due to lactic acid formation, we can increase the capacity of oxygen debt by increasing the capacity of the body for lactic acid. Meyerhof showed that the lactic acid concentration in the exhausted isolated muscle is much greater if the muscle is kept in an alkaline medium.

Also in man the values of blood lactic acid following exhaustion are much higher if the man started the work with higher alkali reserve.[5] This may mean that we may be able to increase the capacity for work by increasing the alkali reserve.

We performed two experiments on Clapham in which 3 hr before the performance of work he took 20 g of sodium bicarbonate: the exercise consisted in running on the treadmill at 18.7 km per hr on a 5 per cent grade. In Table 2 the two experiments are compared with two other experiments

TABLE 2

DATE	PREVIOUS TREATMENT	MAXIMUM L. A. CONCEN- TRATION	O_2 DEBT CALCU- LATED AFTER A. V. HILL	TIME OF PERFORM- ANCE	SPEED CONSTANT OF DISAP- PEARANCE OF L. A.
		mg per 100 cc	l	min	
Oct. 14	—	121	12.70	4	0.0185
Oct. 21	20 g. NaHCO$_3$	136	11.26	$5\frac{1}{3}$	0.0186
Oct. 28	—	110	11.46	$5\frac{2}{3}$	0.020
Nov. 23	20 g. NaHCO$_3$	120	11.44	$6\frac{1}{2}$	0.023

TABLE 3

DATE	MIXTURE BREATHED	TIME OF PERFORMANCE	MAXIMUM LACTIC ACID CONCENTRATION	INITIAL EXCESS LACTIC ACID CONCENTRATION AS CALCULATED (10^a)	OXYGEN INTAKE AT END OF EXERCISE	CALCULATED ALACTACID O_2 DEBT	CALCULATED LACTACID O_2 DEBT	SPEED CONSTANT OF DISAPPEARANCE OF LACTIC ACID	SPEED CONSTANT OF ALACTACID PROCESS
		min	mg per 100 cc	mg per 100 cc	l per min	l	l		
Oct. 14	Air	4	115	150	3.85	2.5	6.16	0.0195	0.60
Oct. 28	Air	$5\frac{2}{3}$							
Nov. 11	O_2 40.5%	$7\frac{1}{6}$	84	108	4.5	2.5	4.43	0.027	0.60–0.65
Dec. 2	O_2 43.3%	$7\frac{2}{3}$							
Jan. 23	O_2 13.64%	$2\frac{2}{3}$	116	172	3.1	2.5	6.56	0.017	0.42

performed in the same conditions but without previous ingestion of alkali.

It seems from these data that, really, together with a higher lactic acid concentration in the blood, the performance was better. No appreciable change can be seen in the total O_2 consumption after exercise; however, this measurement is subject to large sources of error, certainly greater than the variation expected, which is 1 l of oxygen for every 24 mg of increase in lactic acid concentration in the blood.

Calculations of the lactacid oxygen debt, as described in this paper, on the experiments with ingestion of NHCO$_3$ cannot bring evidence for an increase of the lactacid oxygen debt, as they are made on the assumption that the lactacid oxygen debt is proportional to the lactic acid accumulation.

These two experiments with bicarbonate are perhaps complicated by the fact that the subject was somewhat nauseated when he began running. The subject was left to decide when he had reached exhaustion and this decision may have been influenced by extraneous circumstances.

Effect of the Oxygen Tension on the Amount of Oxygen Debt and on the Duration of the Performance

Averages of two experiments performed breathing a 40 per cent oxygen mixture and of two experiments breathing in air are compared in Table 3 with one experiment performed breathing a 14 per cent O_2 mixture.

An increase in the percentage of oxygen in the inspired air seems to go parallel with a decrease in the capacity to accumulate lactic acid. It may be that a limit to the production of lactic acid is given by the acidity of the tissues. Working at a maximum metabolic rate, the CO_2 tension in the tissues is greater when a high oxygen percentage mixture is breathed, because the CO_2 production is greater, while the pulmonary ventilation, being at its maximum value, cannot vary whatever the oxygen content in the inspired air. Then if the tissue acidity limits lactic acid production, the capacity for accumulating lactic acid decreases with increasing amount of oxygen in inspired air. This hypothesis is in agreement with the findings obtained in the bicarbonate experiments, which may be explained on the same lines.

On the assumption that the lactacid oxygen debt is proportional to the lactic acid content of the body at the end of work plus that produced during recovery, we conclude that also the lactacid oxygen debt is less when breathing high oxygen mixtures.

The speed constant of the lactacid process increases in the same direction as the amount of oxygen in the inspired air, which is in agreement with

the hypothesis that the lactic acid removal is due to an oxidative process. Moreover, if the resynthesis of lactic acid to glycogen were due to the combustion of ordinary fuel, whose speed of oxidation is certainly very high, and if the slowness of removing lactic acid were due to the slowness of the reaction lactic acid→glycogen, the speed of removing lactic acid would be unrelated to variation in oxygen tension. This finding supports the hypothesis that the slowness of the removal of lactic acid is due to the slowness of the oxidative process of combustion of the lactic acid itself.

We saw that for a constant content of oxygen in the inspired air the amount of alactacid oxygen debt is nearly proportional to the increase in rate of oxygen intake during exercise. It was interesting to see whether the amount of alactacid oxygen debt depended on one or the other of these two processes which run parallel. This problem can be solved by performing work at the same rate but at different rates of oxygen intake. This can be attained by breathing mixtures of various oxygen contents. From the formula of Protocol 6 the amount of alactacid oxygen debt is proportional to the extra oxygen consumption per minute in exercise over the resting and the lactacid oxygen consumption, and inversely proportional to the speed constant of the alactacid mechanism. If this speed constant increases with an increase in work, the amount of alactacid oxygen debt remains constant. This is what really seems to happen: breathing a 13.6 per cent oxygen mixture the value of the speed constant for this process decreases to about 0.42 with a total alactacid oxygen debt of 2.5 l. Breathing a 40 per cent oxygen mixture, though there seems to be an increase in the speed constant of the alactacid process, the increase in work metabolism is rather too small to affect this constant significantly.

It seems, therefore, that the amount of alactacid oxygen debt depends on the rate at which the work is carried on; this hypothesis, on the assumption that this oxygen debt is due to the resynthesis of the phosphagen, is in agreement with the current views on the part played by phosphagen in muscular contraction.

The values of the speed constants both for the alactacid and for the lactacid process decrease in the same direction as the oxygen content in the inspired air. Then we must expect that also the speed of payment of the total oxygen debt decreases with decreasing partial pressure of oxygen in the inspired air. This is in agreement with Margaria's[15] findings on the speed of payment of the oxygen debt at low barometric pressure.

Summary

1. The removal of lactic acid from the blood during recovery is, disregarding the first period, an exponential function of time: i.e., its speed of disappearance is proportional to the concentration of the lactic acid at that moment.

2. Evidence is given for the validity of the assumption that lactic acid is rapidly diffusible and uniformly distributed through the body, so that the concentration of lactic acid in the blood is proportional to the amount of lactic acid in the body at that time.

3. No extra lactic acid appears in the blood up to a rate of work corresponding to about 2/3 of the maximum metabolic rate, after which the lactic acid increases very rapidly, with an increment of 7.0 g per increment of 1 l of O_2 debt as calculated after A.V. Hill.

4. The removal of lactic acid in the body is a very slow process, its velocity constant being 0.02; i.e., one half is removed in 15 min. Arguments are presented for the validity of the hypothesis that such a speed is limited by the slowness of the process of the oxidation of a fraction of the lactic acid itself.

5. After (3) and (4) it follows that the lactic acid mechanism would not play any important part in muscular contraction except in very strenuous exercise, probably in connection with the anaerobic conditions in which the exercise is performed.

6. The oxygen consumption curve during recovery may be considered in the simplest way as resulting from the sum of four functions:

a. The basal oxygen consumption as measured before the performance of work, a function independent of time.

b. An oxygen consumption attributable to oxidation of the lactic acid: this, as a function of time, is of an exponential character. This process is a very slow one, the value of the velocity constant being 0.02.

c. Another exponential function of time, occurring at a much faster rate, the velocity constant being 0.6 (50 per cent of the reaction takes place in 1/2 min).

d. An oxygen consumption decreasing during recovery very slowly so that this process may be present several hr after the end of the work; this function is not defined mathematically.

Of these four functions only b and c have the meaning of an oxygen debt payment. The function d has been interpreted as an increase of the resting metabolism caused by the exercise.

7. The mechanism of b is the lactic acid mechanism, as described by A. V. Hill. The mechanism c is independent of any lactic acid formation or removal, and therefore it is indicated in this paper as "alactacid."

8. The facts fit better in the four

functions in (6) if we assume as coefficient of combustion of lactic acid 1 : 10 instead of 1 : 5. The value 1 : 10 seems therefore more probable, and this is supported also by a more reasonable value obtainable for the efficiency of the resynthesis of glycogen from lactic acid on such an assumption.

9. The alactacid oxygen debt is approximately a linear function of the oxygen intake in exercise. It is supposed to be related to the oxidation of substances (ordinary fuel) furnishing the energy for the resynthesis of phosphagen split down during muscular contraction. A rough calculation made on this assumption shows that that may be a possible interpretation. The maximum amount of oxygen debt by this mechanism was in our subject about 2.5 l.

10. The lactacid oxygen debt starts coming into play only when there may be reasons to believe that the work is carried on in anaerobic condition. Its amount, relatively to the total amount of oxygen debt, increases particularly rapidly at the maximum rates of work. The maximum absolute amount is about 5 l. It may be increased by increasing the capacity of the body to accumulate lactic acid, as for example, after ingestion of alkali.

11. The speed of payment of the alactacid oxygen debt and the speed of disappearance of lactic acid from the blood vary with the oxygen tension in the inspired air. Therefore, the payment of the entire oxygen debt is slower at low oxygen tensions.

12. The disappearance of lactic acid from the blood at the beginning of recovery after strenuous exercise shows a lag which does not seem to be fully explained either by a lag in the diffusion of lactic acid from muscles to the blood or by a slower oxidation of lactic acid, or by a delayed lactic acid production.

In a trained subject this lag has a duration of 6 or 8 min. In nonathletic and untrained subjects, incapable of good performances, the lag may last two or three times as long.

We are very much indebted to Prof. A. V. Hill of University College, London, for his friendly and helpful criticism of our paper before publication.

References

1. Barr, D. P., H. E. Himwich, and R. P. Green, *J. Biol. Chem.*, **55** (1923), 525.

2. Benedict, F. G., and E. P. Cathcart, *Publ. No. 187, Carnegie Inst. Wash.* (1913), p. 163.

3. Clark, A. J., M. G. Eggleton, and P. Eggleton, *J. Physiol. (London)*, **75** (1932), 332.

4. Dill, D. B., H. T. Edwards, A. Fölling, S. A. Oberg, A. M. Pappenheimer, and J. H. Talbott, *J. Physiol (London)*, **71** (1931), 47.

5. Dill, D. B., H. T. Edwards, and J. H. Talbott, *J. Biol. Chem.*, **97** (1932), 58.

6. Eggleton, P., *J. Physiol.*, **70** (1930), 294.

7. Evans, C. Lovatt, *Recent Advances in Physiology.* London: J. and A. Churchill, 1930.

8. Friedemann, T. E., M. Cotonio, and P. A. Schaffer, *J. Biol. Chem.*, **73** (1927), 335.

9. Hartree, W., *J. Physiol. (London)*, **75** (1932), 273.

10. Henderson, L. J., *Blood—A Study in General Physiology.* New Haven: Yale University Press, 1928.

11. Hill, A. V., *Proc. Roy. Soc. (London)*, **B104** (1928), 39.

12. Hill, A. V., *Adventures in Biophysics.* Philadelphia: University of Philadel-

phia Press, 1931; *Physiol. Rev.*, **12** (1932), 56.

13. Hill, A. V., C. N. H. Long, and H. Lupton, *Proc. Roy. Soc. (London)*, **B97** (1924), 84.

14. Lundsgaard, E., *Biochem. Z.*, **217** (1931), 162.

15. Margaria, R., *Arch. di Fisiol.*, **26** (1928), 525.

16. Margaria, R., and C. Talenti, *Arch. di Fisiol.* (1933).

17. Meyerhof, O., *Die chemischen Vorgänge im Muskel.* Berlin: Springer Verlag, 1930.

18. Meyerhof, O., and K. Lohmann, *Biochem. Z.*, **196** (1928), 41.

19. Milroy, T. H., *Physiol Rev.*, **11** (1931), 515.

20. Owles, W. H., *J. Physiol. (London)*, **69** (1930), 214.

F. CRESCITELLI / C. TAYLOR

The Lactate Response to Exercise and its Relationship to Physical Fitness

Reprinted from the *American Journal of Physiology*, **141** (1944), 630–40.

A logical extension of the relationship of lactic acid accumulation to oxygen debt is the use of lactate response as an indication of physical fitness. The authors studied lactate response in both blood and urine among a group of 47 subjects who possessed varying degrees of fitness. Treadmill-running and arm-and-leg stool-stepping tests were used as the exercise stressors. Although the daily variation in lactate response is considerable, the investigators were able to establish a significantly greater blood lactate concentration among the less fit subjects. Urine lactate tended to follow the same pattern.

Crescitelli and Taylor comment on other studies which investigated lactate response on the basis of a five-minute run. The authors[1] point out that some of these studies fail to control the intensity of the exercise adequately. A subject who is able to complete a 5-min run without reaching complete exhaustion has not received the same physiological stress as one who becomes exhausted after 2-min of exercise. Although blood lactate is variable, the authors report test-retest correlations of 0.71–0.81 for the reliability of blood lactate. However, caution is still needed about the reliability of lactate response. Crescitelli and Taylor are careful in their statistical analysis; they suggest that the conclusions of some of the earlier studies might have been more limited if more sophisticated techniques of analysis had been used. In general, the findings tend to support previous investigators who suggested that the more fit individual can sustain a larger accumulation of blood lactate.

Since the demonstration by Ryffel[25] of an increased lactic acid concentration in the blood and urine of man after muscular activity, a number of reports have appeared on the general subject of lactic acid in relation to exercise. From the communications of Hill, Long, and Lupton;[12] Liljestrand, and Wilson;[19] Jervell;[13] Margaria, Edwards, and Dill;[20] Dill, Edwards, Newman, and Margaria;[7] Bang;[1] Newman, Dill, Edwards, and Webster;[22] and Johnson and Edwards,[15] it is now possible to present a picture of the changes in blood and urine lactate during and following muscular activity. With the onset of exercise there is a rapid increase in the blood lactate concentration to a maximum; the magnitude of its maximum is greater, other factors remaining constant, the greater the intensity of exercise.[1] The view has been expressed that this maximum concentration, once attained, remains constant during a continued steady state exercise.[11] A review of the literature reveals little evidence to support this, and Bang[1] has actually demonstrated that the blood lactate in man decreases even though the activity is continued in a steady state. Confirmation of this has come with the report of Flock, Ingle, and Bollman[9] that in the stimulated muscles of the rat the lactate content rises rapidly during the first minute and then declines, this decline being similar whether the

muscle continues to be active or not following the initial stimulation.

With cessation of exercise the blood lactate decreases, the recovery rate being such that the logarithm of the excess lactate is a linear function of time.[20,7] Under some circumstances, especially with exercise of short duration, the blood lactate concentration continues to rise for some minutes after cessation of the activity.[17,7,1] Investigators differ as to whether this rise is due to a lag in the diffusion of lactate from the muscles into the blood[1] or to an actual post-exercise production of lactic acid.[20,21]

Following exercise of sufficient intensity, lactate appears in the urine. Liljestrand and Wilson[19] noted quantities of this substance ranging from 140 to 1,370 mg over the resting level after a period of activity. The peak of lactate excretion occurs 10 to 20 min after the cessation of exercise[13,15] and excretion is complete in 40 to 50 min after the cessation.

One of the many factors which may determine the lactate response of an individual to a given exercise is the individual's exercise tolerance (physical fitness). Severl reports allude to the higher blood lactate following a submaximal exercise in persons considered unfit or untrained[3,23] or to a lower critical intensity of exercise for unfit subjects beyond which increases in blood lactate appear.[4,22] Bang[1] cites the lower blood lactate response to exercise of two subjects after a 2-month training period, an observation which is confirmed by Edwards, Brouha, and Johnson.[8] The lower blood lactate response to a submaximal exercise after a training program was also observed by Robinson and Harmon,[24] who also reported a higher blood lactate response to exhausting exercise after a training period; this latter finding

------

[1] The work described in this paper was done under a contract, recommended by the Committee on Medical Research, between the Office of Scientific Research and Development and Stanford University.

The authors wish to express their indebtedness to Dr. John Field II for the use of equipment and to Dr. F. W. Weymouth for advice on the statistical treatment of data. Acknowledgment is made of technical assistance by Ellen Burton, Royce Skow, Bernard Hansen, and Robert Morris.

has been confirmed by Knehr, Dill, and Neufeld.[16] The urinary output of lactate in exercise also appears to be decreased after a training period, according to the results of Lewis, Hewlett, and Barnett.[18] The modification of the lactate response by a training program is considered reliable enough by Johnson and Brouha[14] to include it in an index of physical fitness.

On theoretical grounds there seems to be a real basis for a relationship between fitness and the lactate response. On the assumption that the lactic acid of exercise arises mainly as the result of anaerobic glycolysis[1,13] in the muscles during the initial period before the circulatory and respiratory adjustments are completed, it is understandable how physical training, by making these adjustments more efficient either in speed or degree (or both) and thereby decreasing either the degree or duration of anaerobiosis in the muscles, can lower the lactate production in relation to a specific exercise. Since the results thus far are suggestive rather than statistically conclusive, it remains to be seen whether such a theoretical expectation is capable of experimental verification.

It is the aim of this report to present data on the blood and urine lactate response to exercise of a group of young men in several states of fitness; to illustrate the time course of the response in these individuals; and to examine the data for a possible quantitative relationship between fitness and some function of the lactate response.

Procedure

The 47 subjects in these experiments were college students and laboratory workers, varying in age from 19 to 33 yr. All were in good health and in respect to physical training ranged from men who take vigorous exercise

regularly to laboratory workers who lead sedentary lives except for the activity involved in routine laboratory work. The lactate response of these individuals was studied in three types of muscular exercise:

I. Submaximal treadmill walk for 15 min. Speed was 100 m per min and the grade was 15 per cent.

II. Submaximal arm-and-leg stool stepping for 2 min with a step height of 18.5 in. and an ascent-descent rate of 40 per min. In this exercise one hand grasped a horizontal bar 70 in. above the floor while the ipsilateral foot rested on the stool. The body was raised through a distance equal to the height of the stool by the simultaneous pull of the arm (flexion) and extension of the leg. At each cycle pull-up arm and step-up leg were changed thus giving to all the appendages an equal opportunity to share in the work. A knapsack for weights was carried on the back of the subject.

III. Treadmill exercise in three sections: (a) preliminary treadmill walk at 106 m per min and a 5 per cent grade which lasted for 4 min, (b) a sitting rest period of 4 min, (c) a treadmill run to exhaustion at 162 m per min starting at a 5 per cent grade and increasing the grade 1 per cent each min until the subject quit.

Between 0.1 to 0.5 ml of blood was collected in tubes coated with oxalate and fluoride, the blood being obtained from two closely spaced stab wounds in the finger tip. In the case of the treadmill walk (I) blood was collected before, during and for 60 to 90 min after cessation of the exercise. For the stool stepping exercise (II) blood was collected before and for 60 to 90 min after the end of the work. With the treadmill exercise (III) blood was obtained 2 min after the end of the preliminary walk (IIIa); 5 min after the end of the exhaustive run (IIIc) and 20 min after the end of the exhaustive run. In

12 subjects blood was also collected before the beginning of the walk (IIIa) and in two subjects blood was also obtained during the exhaustive run (IIIc).

In the case of types I and II tests, urine samples were collected before the beginning of the exercise and at intervals following the end of the exercise. Urines from subjects in the basal condition were collected after a 30-to 40-min rest which was preceded by

TABLE 1

Duplicate Analysis of Blood for Concentration of Lactate During Treadmill Experiments (type III)

	MEAN mg %	S.E. mg %	C.V., S.D./MN.
Rest (not basal)	28.5	4.4	15.4
2 min after walk..........	32.5	2.8	8.6
5 min after run	215.9	10.3	4.8
20 min after run..........	143.1	10.9	7.6

TABLE 2

Postabsorptive, Resting Blood and Urine Lactates

SUBJECT	BLOOD mg %	URINE LACTATE Conc. mg %	Total mg	Rate mg per min
P. L.	7.3	2.12	0.70	0.016
	10.3	1.25	1.06	0.023
	14.5	1.11	1.33	0.024
R. S.	7.0	3.29	2.20	0.059
	11.3			
	13.4	0.76	1.19	0.028
	9.8			
	13.4			
	11.2	1.61	1.21	0.023
	14.8	1.47	1.31	0.034
	11.9	1.36	0.90	0.023
	8.4	2.93	2.43	0.053
	16.0	1.13	2.03	0.040
A. O.	9.4	0.49	0.96	0.022
	13.4	0.78	0.83	0.036
E. S.	14.3	1.60	1.20	0.028
B. H.	13.2	0.37	1.56	0.020
	11.3	1.82	0.88	0.021
	11.2	1.72	3.44	0.063
D. K.	15.1	0.60	2.54	0.073
T. B.	14.4			
R. U.	9.9			
C. T.	22.7	1.43	3.93	0.063
C. K.	13.2	2.05	1.46	0.042
Means	12.4	1.47	1.64	0.036

voiding all previously formed urine and imbibing 500 ml of water.

The heart beat was recorded by means of the cardiotachometer of Henry.[10] The respiratory metabolism was also determined; for this purpose the air expired through either a face mask or mouthpiece was collected in a 400 l double-chamber gasometer. Collections of expired air were made during the 9 to 14 min of the 15-min treadmill walk (type I); during the 1.5 to 4 min of the preliminary treadmill walk (IIIa); and during the last min of the maximal treadmill run (IIIc). Duplicate samples of this expired air were analyzed for oxygen and carbon dioxide by means of the Haldane apparatus. The blood and urine lactate concentrations were determined by the procedure of Barker and Summerson.[2] To indicate the standard error of these determinations, the results of duplicate analyses of blood collected from 31 subjects during the type III test have been treated statistically. This analysis covers a range of blood lactate from 20 to 300 mg per cent. In Table 1 are shown the mean blood lactate concentrations, the standard error (S.E.) and the coefficient of variability. The standard error is given by $\bar{D}/1.1284$, where $\bar{D}$ is the average difference between duplicate samples without regard to sign.

Results

I. *Resting blood and urine lactate.* The individual and mean values of the blood and urine lactate concentration of 11 subjects in the postabsorptive, resting state are indicated in Table 2. All the earlier literature[13] gives somewhat higher values for resting blood lactate than are given in this table but a number of the more recent communications present values in about the same range. The results of Decker and Rosenbaum,[6] obtained also with the Barker-Summerson method, are somewhat lower than the figures for blood lactate given here. The figures for resting urine lactate shown in Table 2 agree well with the few data available in the literature. Liljestrand and Wilson[19] report an excretion of 0.1 to 0.25 mg lactate per min while values of 0.013 and 0.015 mg per min for two experiments are given by Johnson and Edwards.[15]

II. *Lactate response to submaximal exercise.* Nineteen subjects performed the 15-min walk (type I). In all experiments each subject rested for at least 30 min on a bed before exercising, during which time samples of finger blood and all the accumulated urine were collected. Representative curves to indicate the time course of the blood and urine lactate changes in four subjects are presented in Fig. 1 and 2. Subjects B. H., F. C., and C. K. were in poor physical condition in contrast to J.D. who was a cross-country runner and was in excellent condition at the time of the test. These curves, along with the mean curves for all the subjects of Fig. 3, show that the blood lactate concentration rises rapidly after the beginning of exercise, reaches a peak, and then declines along a curve in which the rate of decrease is a function of the time after cessation of the exercise. Only 2 of the 20 subjects showed a higher blood lactate concentration within 2 min after the cessation of activity than the peak value during the walk. There is no suggestion in such a steady state exercise of a post-exercise rise in blood lactate concentration; neither is there any indication, within the limits of the time intervals involved, of the attainment of a steady state blood lactate concentration.

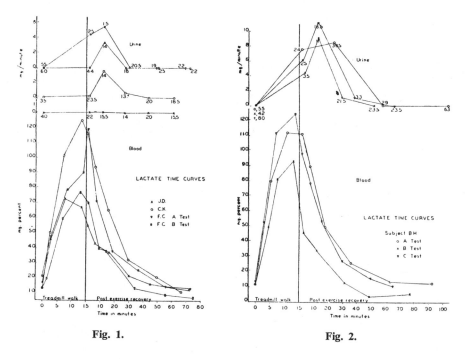

Fig. 1.   **Fig. 2.**

Identical experiments performed on the same individual on different days yield lactate response curves that indicate considerable day-to-day variability. This is seen in the duplicate test of F. C. (Fig. 1) and the triplicate test of B. H. (Fig. 2). A similar variability was obtained in the stool-stepping exercise (type II) where a much larger proportion of the body musculature is active than in the treadmill walk. These wide differences obtained on separate occasions, associated with no known change in the fitness of the subject, indicate the difficulty involved in obtaining a reliable figure based on only one or a few tests which is significant in characterizing the individual.

The time course of lactate elimination through the urine is also indicated in Figs. 1 and 2 where the rate in milligrams per minute is plotted in each case versus the midpoint of the collection period, the duration of the collec-

tion interval, in minutes, being indicated by a printed figure adjacent to each point on the graphs. The amount of excess lactate that appears in the urine as a result of the exercise varies from individuals who show no increase (J. D.) to those whose urines excrete several hundred milligrams (B. H.). The major portion of the excess lactate is contained in the urine collected over the 10- to 20-min interval after the end of the exercise. By the 40- to 50-min period the urinary output of lactate has returned to the resting level. This time course of lactate excretion is similar to that already reported by Liljestrand and Wilson[19] and Johnson and Edwards.[15]

III. *Lactate response to maximal exercise.* The blood lactate responses during and after the maximal treadmill run (type IIIc) are given for two subjects in Fig. 4. Subject V. L. was an athlete

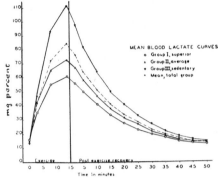

Fig. 3.

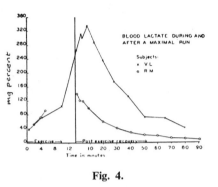

Fig. 4.

who ran for the superior time of 13 min on the test while R. M. was a laboratory worker who continued for the slightly below average time of 7 min. In the case of V. L. there is evidence of a post-exercise increase in blood lactate concentration for some minutes following the termination of the run. For the 31 subjects who performed the type IIIc exercise the mean value of blood lactate 5 min after the end of the run was 217.6 mg per cent with a range of 117 to 328 mg per cent; 10 min after the run, the mean value was 144.1 mg per cent with a range of 54 to 243 mg per cent. This wide scatter gives no evidence of a "ceiling" lactate level toward which the subjects approach when reaching the point of exhaustion.

IV. *Lactate response and physical fitness.* In order to elucidate the relationship between the lactate response and fitness an analysis has been made of the data obtained on the 19 subjects who performed the 15-min treadmill walk (type I). These subjects have been segregated into the following three groups on the basis of personal knowledge of the subject's exercise background and on the basis of results obtained from performance tests used

in this laboratory which are to be reported elsewhere.

Group I. Athletes or men who have performed in a superior manner in the laboratory.

Group II. Men who have taken regular but not competitive exercise.

Group III. Laboratory workers who exercise little or not at all.

The time course of blood lactate concentration for these three groups along with the mean curve for all 19 subjects is reproduced in Fig. 3. It is obvious that for both the exercise and post-exercise periods group I exhibits the lowest lactate level; group III, the highest lactate level; while group II occupies an intermediate position. To characterize these three groups more completely the results of other physiological measures have been combined with the blood lactate concentration at two points in the post-exercise period to yield Table 3A. From these data it appears that in contrast to an unfit subject, a fit man has, on the average, a lower post-exercise blood lactate concentration, a lower total excess urine lactate, a lower heart rate during the exercise, a higher oxygen consumption, a lower R.Q., and a lower ventilation. Using Fisher's t[5, p. 330] the data have been

TABLE 3

Comparison of Three Fitness Groups in 15-min Treadmill Walk

A. GROUP MEANS

	I	II	III
Blood lactate			
5 min post-exercise	50.1	64.6	93.5
20 min post-exercise....................	41.0	52.1	75.4
Excess urine lactate	4.33	18.8	165.5
Maximal exercise heart rate	166.2	172.4	180.5
Oxygen consumption	37.1	36.1	35.0
Carbon dioxide production	34.9	34.1	34.3
Respiratory quotient	0.94	0.94	0.98
Total ventilation	738	728	849

B. SIGNIFICANCE OF DIFFERENCE BETWEEN GROUPS

	I-II		II-III		I-III	
	t	P_t	t	P_t	t	P_t
Blood lactate						
5 min post-exercise	1.27	0.50	2.16	0.06	3.78	0.003
20 min post-exercise	1.20	0.26	1.91	0.09	3.23	0.009
Excess urine lactate	1.69	0.12	2.29	0.05	2.81	0.02
Maximal exercise heart rate	1.76	0.10	1.31	0.23	2.58	0.03
Oxygen consumption	0.31	0.50	0.41	0.50	0.79	0.44
Carbon dioxide production	0.25	0.50	0.07	0.50	0.23	0.50
Respiratory quotient	0.00	0.50	2.34	0.05	2.98	0.01
Total ventilation	0.18	0.50	1.78	0.10	2.04	0.07

analyzed for significance of differences. The resulting t and P_t values for the comparison among the three groups, which are reproduced in Table 3 B, are of interest in that they indicate that the differences between the means of the three groups do not attain statistical significance except for the extreme groups I and III. The oxygen consumption has no significance even for these extreme groups. It is notable that blood lactate and urine lactate may serve to differentiate fitness groups better than do heart rate and respiratory measures.

Reference has already been made to the variation in blood lactate response of the same individual when tested on several different occasions. This, of course, brings into question the reliability of any one lactate determination. This reliability has been assessed by computing the reliability coefficient (r; between test and retest blood lactate determinations) for the 31 subjects in the case of both the preliminary treadmill walk (types IIIa) and the maximal treadmill run (type IIIc). A value of unity for this coefficient would, of course, indicate complete agreement between the test and retest determinations. For the preliminary walk the reliability coefficient was found to be 0.77; for the maximal run they were 0.71 and 0.81, respectively, for the 5- and 20-min post-exercise values. These coefficients, though not high, compare favorably with the coefficients of other physiological measures which have been determined in this laboratory and are to be reported later. The

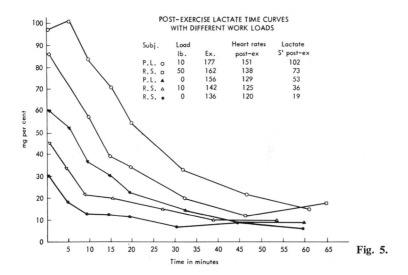

POST-EXERCISE LACTATE TIME CURVES
WITH DIFFERENT WORK LOADS

Subj.	Load lb.	Heart rates		Lactate
		Ex.	post-ex	S' post-ex
P.L. o	10	177	151	102
R.S. □	50	162	138	73
P.L. ▲	0	156	129	53
R.S. △	10	142	125	36
R.S. ●	0	136	120	19

mg per cent

Time in minutes

Fig. 5.

conclusion seems warranted that for testing purposes, blood lactate determinations have at least as high, if not a higher, reliability than such measures as heart rate, ventilation, etc.

The greater blood lactate response to submaximal exercise of the unfit subject as compared with the fit person is also seen in the case of the stool-stepping exercise (type II) with varying loads. In this case an extremely unfit subject (P. L.) was compared with a man who was clearly above average in the matter of exercise tolerance. From the results (Fig. 5) it will be seen that P. L. carrying no load gave a much greater lactate response than R. S. with either no load or with a 10-lb load. It will also be seen that P. L. with only a 10-lb load gave a greater response than did R. S. with 50 lb. The heart rate for these two subjects (maximal exercise rate and rate 1 min after exercise) also indicates clearly the difference in fitness between these two individuals (Fig. 5).

Discussion and Interpretation

The time course of blood lactate to submaximal exercise confirms the interpretation of Bang[1] that lactate production, beginning immediately aft-

er the onset of exercise, rises to a maximum, and then declines without attaining a steady level for any significant period of time. No equilibrium conditions are apparently set up between the processes of production and dissipation of lactic acid; rather this compound appears to be related to a period of adjustment associated with the beginning of activity.

Heretofore inadequate data or failure to apply rigorous statistical methods have left the problem of lactate and physical fitness in an inconclusive state. The findings of Robinson and Harmon[24] and of Knehr, Dill, and Neufeld,[16] on the effects of training, are extremely suggestive, but the variations between individuals appear to have been so great that it is unfortunate a statistical treatment of the data was not published. The results of blood lactate determinations on 40 men after a treadmill run[14] are also available in this connection. These authors segregated their subjects into four groups on the basis of an estimate of relative fitness and from the results concluded that the blood lactate is higher in the groups lower in the scale of fitness. Actually this is what the present report indicates in so far as submaximal work is concerned, but it is difficult to see how the data of Johnson and Brouha prove this point. Not only is group D (men in poor condition) misplaced (since the data show the mean blood lactate to be 113 mg per cent, rather than 131 and 130 as given by Johnson and Brouha), but no statistically valid difference can be shown to exist between the two extreme groups (A and D). In reality Johnson and Brouha's experimental arrangement was a poor one to decide the relationship between lactate and fitness, since men able to run for 5 min were stopped at that time, while others continued to the exhaustion point because this was still within the 5-min limit. This arrangement tends to make the work submaximal for groups A and B whereas it is exhaustive for groups C and D. As Robinson and Harmon[24] have pointed out, the lactate response is quite different in the two types of activity.

One suggestion that emerges from the results of Table 3 is the finding that the total excess urine lactate is, like the blood lactate, related to fitness in the case of submaximal work. The training studies of Lewis, Hewlett, and Barnett[18] also point to the same conclusion. Practically, the use of urine in a test for physical fitness would not only obviate the problem of blood collection but would also yield a large quantity of material for analysis, making unnecessary micromethods with their attendant difficulties and errors. The use of urine in connection with a macro-method might greatly improve the figures for the reliability coefficient of a lactic acid determination.

Summary

Experiments are reported in which the blood and urine lactate concentrations were determined in rest, during work of various types, and in the recovery period following this work. The response of 19 subjects in varying degrees of fitness to a 15-min treadmill walk (submaximal work) indicates that the blood lactate rises rapidly with the onset of work, reaches a maximum concentration at or before the completion of the work and then declines along a die-away curve, reaching the resting level in from 30 to 90 min after the end of the walk. As a group, less fit individuals appear to give a significantly greater blood lactate concentration throughout the entire period of the lactate response to the exercise than do fit individuals. Lactate excretion via the urine is maximal in the 10- to 20-min period after the work and is complete within the 40- to 50-min period. The total excess urine lactate in response to the activity also is significantly related to the fitness of the group, as less fit individuals, again as a group, show larger quantities of this compound. In a test-retest series on 31 subjects involving both submaximal and maximal work it was found that the reliability of blood lactate determinations is at least as high as the reliability of other commonly used physiological measures.

References

1. Bang, O., *Skand. Arch. Physiol.* **10** (1936), 51.
2. Barker, S. B., and W. H. Summerson, *J. Biol. Chem.*, **138** (1941), 535.
3. Bock, A. V., C. Vancaulaert, D. B. Dill, A. Fölling, and L. M. Hurxthal, *J. Physiol.* (*London*), **66** (1928), 136.
4. Cook, L. C., and R. H. Hurst, *J. Physiol.* (*London*), **79** (1933), 443.
5. Croxton, F. E., and D. J. Cowden,

Applied General Statistics (2nd ed.). Englewood Cliffs, N. J.: Prentice-Hall, Inc., 1955.

6. Decker, D. G., and J. D. Rosenbaum, *Am. J. Physiol.*, **138** (1942), 7.

7. Dill, D. B., H. T. Edwards, E. V. Newman, and R. Margaria, *Arbeitsphysiol.*, **9** (1936), 299.

8. Edwards, H. T., L. Brouha, and R. T. Johnson, *Le Travail humain*, **8** (1940), 1.

9. Flock, E. V., D. J. Ingle, and J. L. Bollman, *J. Biol. Chem.*, **129** (1939), 99.

10. Henry, F., *Science*, **86** (1937), 299.

11. Hill, A. V., *Muscular Activity*. Baltimore: The Williams & Wilkins Co., 1926.

12. Hill, A. V., C. N. H. Long, and H. Lupton, *Proc. Roy. Soc. (London)*, **B96** (1924), 455.

13. Jervell, O., *Acta Med. Scand. Suppl.*, **24** (1928), 3.

14. Johnson, R. E., and L. Brouha, *Rev. Can. Biol.*, **1** (1942), 171.

15. Johnson, R. E., and H. T. Edwards, *J. Biol. Chem.*, **118** (1937), 427.

16. Knehr, C. A., D. B. Dill, and W. Neufeld, *Am. J. Physiol.*, **136** (1942), 148.

17. Laug, E. P., *Am. J. Physiol.*, **107** (1934), 687.

18. Lewis, J. K., A. W. Hewlett, and G. D. Barnett, *Proc. Soc. Exptl. Biol. Med.*, **22** (1925), 537.

19. Liljestrand, S. H., and D. W. Wilson, *J. Biol. Chem.*, **65** (1924), 773.

20. Margaria, R., H. T. Edwards, and D. B. Dill, *Am. J. Physiol.*, **106** (1933), 689.

21. Newman, E. V., *Am. J. Physiol.*, **122** (1938), 359.

22. Newman, E. V., D. B. Dill, H. T. Edwards, and F. A. Webster, *Am. J. Physiol.*, **118** (1937), 457.

23. Owles, W. H., *J. Physiol. (London)*, **69** (1930), 214.

24. Robinson, S., and P. M. Harmon, *Am. J. Physiol.*, **132** (1941), 757.

25. Ryffel, J. H., *J. Physiol (London)*, **39** (1909), 29.

F. M. HENRY

Aerobic Oxygen Consumption and Alactic Debt in Muscular Work

Reprinted from the *Journal of Applied Physiology*, **3** (1951), 427–38.

Henry's* work is widely admired for its precision and quality. He is best known, however, for his studies in the area of motor learning (see Chapter V). In addition, he has made substantial contributions in the understanding of the lactic acid-alactic acid debt phenomena. In this study Henry provides data to support

* From the Department of Physical Education and the Division of Medical Physics (Department of Physics), University of California, Berkeley, California.

the hypothesis that alactic oxygen debt is a function of oxygen consumption during steady state of work and that certain aspects of alactic debt are highly related to workload and others are not. Using a series of exponential formulas and correlations based on oxygen consumption at various time periods of exercise and recovery, he produces clear evidence to support the hypotheses. He also shows that athletic training reduces alactic debt resulting from a standard exercise and thus increases the speed of recovery from work.

The introduction to the article presents the theoretical basis for alactic oxygen debt, quite clearly. The specifics of aerobic metabolism are still not completely known and Henry alludes several times in the paper to the need to understand more about enzyme systems if we are to understand exercise metabolism and oxygen debt more fully. His paper is an excellent example of the type of study that must be done to explore the mysteries of exercise.

When a muscle contracts, some of the stored glycogen disappears and oxygen is consumed. It has been shown by D. K. Hill that the oxygen is consumed subsequent to the contraction[11] although with continued work (consisting of repeated contractions of the muscle fibers) oxygen is used during the work as well as during the debt payoff period that follows. Margaria et al.[12] have reported fractionation of the post-work oxygen consumption into an *alactic* debt having rapid payoff characteristics that occurs as a result of either light or heavy work, and a slow payoff *lactic* component, previously discovered by A. V. Hill, that is not ordinarily observed unless heavy muscular work has occurred. Hill and colleagues were aware of the fast component,[10] but at that time thought it to be a rapid phase of the lactic debt.

Theoretical Considerations

Aerobic oxidation in exercise metabolism involves the transfer of hydrogen atoms from metabolites, such as the pyruvic acid breakdown products of the Krebs cycle, to coenzyme and then to the flavoproteins, where they are ionized by electron transfer—the electrons passing via the cytochrome oxidase system to the oxygen molecules. Thus the oxygen supplied to the tissues by the blood serves as a hydrogen scavenger to create the end product H_2O. This is the *main line* oxidation,[3, p. 661] assumed in the present paper to represent the fast payoff or *alactic* oxygen debt. This fast component was at one time thought to represent the aerobic reconstitution of phosphogen[12] but it now appears probable that it is a matter of Krebs cycle oxidation producing phosphate bond energy, energy also used to reconstitute the high-energy adenosine phosphates.[3] The fast-component debt is the only debt present in mild exercise; in heavier exercise it is superimposed on the lactic acid debt.[12]

If the oxygen income is inadequate to keep the substrate metabolites oxidized, hydrogen is scavenged by reducing the pyruvic acid to lactic acid through the action of lactic dehydrogenase. This is the *branch line* oxidation, anaerobic in nature, related to the *lactic* oxygen debt by Margaria et al.[12] as well as others. Temporarily, the lactic acid is buffered and stored as lactate. During recovery, it is probably returned to pyruvic acid, a part of which is converted to carbon dioxide and water by the main line aerobic oxidation mechanism, furnishing the energy to resynthesize the remainder to glycogen. It is this oxidative phase of the process that is responsible for the slow payoff component of the post exercise oxygen consumption.[3] The rate of debt payoff coincides with the rate of blood lactate removal,[5, 4] having a half-time recovery constant of the order of 10 to 20 *min* even with a lactic acid excess as low as 15 or 20 mg per cent. This is a different order of magnitude from the 20 to 30 *sec* half-time of the so-called alactic debt.

Accepting the general principles of the above schema (the exact biochemical details of which are not crucial to the present consideration) it would seem reasonable to hypothesize that under conditions where the molecular oxygen income is adequate and not limited by factors such as blood supply, (as occurs in certain types of static work, heavy work, or pathological cases) the amount of oxygen intake will be determined by the amount of oxidizable substrate present because oxygen cannot be consumed unless there is something for it to oxidize. Thus the amount of substrate will be determined by the rate of muscular work, since the oxidizable metabolites that form the substrate are a product of work.

A quantitative formulation of this idea may be made as follows: *Assuming the rate of work to be uniform*, there will be produced by the work a units of substrate x during the first time-unit. Some proportion c of this substrate will be oxidized during this time. The unoxidized remainder will add to the a units produced by the next time-unit of work, the proportion c of the total substrate on hand during this second time-unit will be oxidized, and so on. It follows, under the assumption that the constant of proportionality c does not chage, that the rate of accumulation of sub-

strate will be of the exponential form[1]

$$\frac{dx}{dt} = a_0 e^{-kt}, \qquad (1)$$

the amount of substrate (in oxygen units) at any time t will be

$$x = \frac{a_0}{k}(1 - e^{-kt}), \qquad (2)$$

the rate of oxygen consumption will be

$$\frac{dy}{dt} = a_0(1 - e^{-kt}), \qquad (3)$$

and the total oxygen (in excess of the resting level) consumed by time t after the start of the work will be

$$y = a_0 \left(t + \frac{1}{k} e^{-kt} - \frac{1}{k} \right). \qquad (4)$$

This hypothesis leads to certain predictions. It will be noted that the constants a_0 and k are entirely independent mathematically, hence should be uncorrelated. It would be expected that k should be independent of the rate of working, but a_0 (i.e., the steady-state rate of oxygen income) should show a linear relation with rate of work up to the region where limitations of oxygen supply come into action. Above this region, these mathematical expressions will not hold true. Hence, for heavy work, the income rate should tend to level off, although the amount of oxidizable substrate should continue to increase as the work load increases, since it results *from* the muscular work.

___

[1] It is of interest that a similar formula for oxygen intake during exercise and recovery, based of course on the pre-Lundsgaard theoretical concepts, was presented by Simonson[13] as early as 1927. Several of the conclusions of that study, although made without statistically acceptable proof, are the same as conclusions of the present report. Since the writer was not aware of the Simonson paper until after the current research was completed, it would seem that this independent confirmation is of value in validating the conclusions.

However, it will be oxidized anaerobically to an increasing extent. It is conceivable that factors other than oxygen supply may impose important limitations.

A second prediction is that certain aspects of the alactic oxygen debt should be highly related to work load, whereas certain other aspects should be unrelated. Berg[2] and others referred to by him have shown that the rate of oxygen intake (above resting) at any time t' during the debt payoff period is given by the exponential expression

$$\frac{dy'}{dt'} = a'_o e^{-k't'}, \qquad (5)$$

and Margaria *et al.*[12] as well as others[e. g., 8] have found that the lactic component of the total oxygen debt of heavy exercise can be described by this formula. Inasmuch as the intercept a'_o is the rate of oxygen intake at the very beginning of recovery, it is substantially the equivalent of the asymptotic rate of intake during the steady state of exercise, hence it should show a high relation with the rate of work. On the other hand, because of the mathematical independence of a'_o and k', there is no theoretical reason for the velocity constant k' to be related to the rate of work, at least within fairly wide limits, and Berg[2] as well as others have indeed found it to be independent. If k' remains constant at varying work loads for a particular individual, the size of the debt will be determined by a'_o; hence the debt should also approximate a simple linear function of the rate of *mild* or *moderate* work. Among individuals doing the same external work of a mild or moderate degree, it is known that there are individual differences in the oxygen requirement[6, 9] which probably implies that due to differences in skill,

exercise technique, body build, and other factors, some individuals require more energy expenditure than others. In this situation, there should be a relatively high correlation between a'_o (but not k') and the total metabolic cost of the work.

Berg[2] has proved that there are individual differences in the velocity constant k', and has presented suggestive evidence that these differences are related to the efficiency of the circulation in delivering oxygen to the tissues, even in moderate exercise. This leads to a third prediction, namely that changes produced in the individual in the direction of improved oxygen supply to the tissues should leave a'_o or steady-state intake rate unchanged if the work is unchanged, but k' should increase and the size of debt should decrease.

Results

In order to test certain aspects of the hypothesis, the oxygen intake of five young men and five young women was determined continuously during exercise and recovery for several work loads, ranging from 15 to 910 kg-m per min, on a bicycle ergometer using the closed-circuit mehod described in other papers.[8, 9] At the lightest work load each subject was tested twice, and data were secured on an additional subject of each sex. In all cases the work period lasted 6 min, the pedal speed being approximately constant at 62 rpm.[2] As may be seen in Fig. 1, the results are in accord with formula (3) for the rate of oxygen intake during exercise. The integral form (formula

---

[2] The writer is indebted to Miss Janice DeMoor for technical assistance in securing these data and making the statistical analyses, and to Mr. Irving Trafton for testing the 17 additional male subjects.

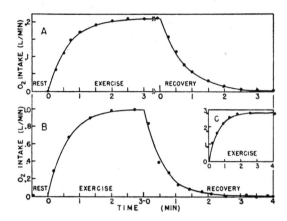

Fig. 1. Exercise and recovery curves calculated from *formulae* (3) and (5). For *curve A*, experimental points represent average of 12 individuals measured at lightest bicycle work load by the closed-circuit method. Experimental points for *curve B* were obtained by Berg with the thermal conductivity method, testing one individual doing a step-up exercise. Points for *curve C* were obtained on a runner by A. V. Hill, using the open-circuit method.

[4]) is necessarily in accord also. The amount of substrate or its rate for formation (formulae [2 and 1]) cannot of course be measured directly in exercising human subjects; however, this part of the hypothesis receives some degree of implicit confirmation since it originally led to the formulation of the mathematical experssion for oxygen intake. As shown in Fig. 2, the rate of oxygen intake and the magnitude of oxygen debt show the predicted relation to severity of work.

To study the intercorrelations between the metabolic cost of work at constant external work load and the two oxygen debt parameters a'_o and k', the control data obtained in a previous study of bicycle ergometer work at 614 kg-m per min [9] were supplemented by testing 17 additional subjects, bringing the total number of men up to 35. Correlational analysis shows that indi-

vidual differences in the velocity constant of recovery k' and the intercept oxygen intake a'_o are independent, since their intercorrelation, $r = 0.08$, is not significantly different from zero. At this work load the individual magnitude of debt is determined mostly by the velocity constant. Size of debt correlates $r = -0.74$ with k' (*i.e.*, a large debt tends to have a slow recovery rate), whereas the debt correlates only $r = 0.47$ with a'_o and 0.45 with steady-state income rate. The net metabolic cost of the work, i.e., the total oxygen used over and above the resting requirement, is unrelated to the velocity constant k', as the correlation is only $r = 0.06$.

This pattern of intercorrelations is in accord with prediction—the velocity constant of alactic recovery tends to be independent of rate of work insofar as it is measured by the individual metabolic cost, and also independent of the rate of oxygen income during exercise. A large oxygen income tends to be associated with a large debt, but the correlation is not high. While the amount of oxidizable substrate that is left at the instant the work ceases is the determiner of the size of the debt, a_o is only one of the determiners of its magnitude, the other and at least equally important factor being the velocity constant k.

With respect to the third prediction, it may be mentioned that in a recent paper by the writer and Berg [7] it was shown that a typical athletic conditioning program resulted in decreasing the alactic oxygen debt resulting from a standard stool-stepping exercise, and also significantly speeded up the recovery rate. At the time the data were worked up, the a'_o figures were disregarded as of no immediate interest, because the income rate was somewhat decreased as a result of the training. They have since been examined statistically in connection with the present paper. The mean a'_o in these 23 athletes before conditioning was 16.1 cc per kg body weight, and after conditioning, 14.9 cc. The difference is not significant, since the t ratio is only 1.5. The mean k' before conditioning was 1.40, and after conditioning 1.52, a difference that is statistically significant above the 1 per cent probability level. Thus this finding, also, is in accord with the hypothesis.

Discussion

The close agreement of the theoretical curve with the experimental results shown in Fig. 1, curve A, is fairly convincing, since the formula for oxygen consumption has only two parameters and there are six experimental points in the curved portion of the line. Curve B of the same figure, drawn from the Berg data obtained by an entirely different method, lends considerable supporting evidence. Curve C, also showing excellent agreement, makes use of the Hill data obtained with a third method. Thus it would seem that the formula describes the experimental results quite satisfactorily within the limits tested. It is planned to examine the upper limit of its application in a subsequent study.

There is a definite indication that the the velocity constant k is somewhat greater during work than during recovery. The t ratio for the difference between k and k' (i.e., exercise and recovery velocity constants) in Fig. 1 A is 2.6, which is significant at the 2 per cent level of probability. It seems not unreasonable to expect this difference to occur as a result of improved local tissue circulation or perfusion due to the massaging action of the working muscles. Individual differences in k during exercise tend to be maintained during recovery, as a correlation $r = 0.79$ is found between the two conditions. Obviously the standard error of a correlation based on only 12 cases is rather large, so that even though this correlation is statistically significant, further work will be necessary to establish the precise degree of relationship.

The factor or factors that determine the magnitude of k and k' of the so-called alactic component are not really known at the present time. As mentioned elsewhere in this paper, Berg[2] and others referred to by him have shown that restriction of the circulation decreases these velocity constants, so it is fairly certain that under some circumstances the circulation constitutes a limiting factor for k. D. K. Hill[11], however, has shown that the rate of oxidative recovery in isolated muscle depends on the cytochrome oxidase system, and his sodium azide experiments suggest the possibility that this system may need to be considered in relation to determiners of the normal magnitude of k in the human subject. As for factors determining the magnitude of k_2 (the velocity constant of the slow-component lactate debt), nothing need be said here, since the theory in its present form applies only to exercise that is sufficiently moderate that the slow-component debt is not quantitatively important.

An interesting aspect of the data on oxygen intake presented in Fig. 2, A and B, is that for work loads up to 5 cal per min, a linear regression line originating at zero and intersecting 5 cal at 0.9 l per min intake, fits the individual determinations for all subjects within the accuracy of the method. Within these limits, the standard deviation of the displacement of the points from the line is only 0.016 l. At high work loads the oxygen intake of the women subjects tends to diminish, with a slight suggestion of individual differences in the degree of departure from linearity. The data on the men show

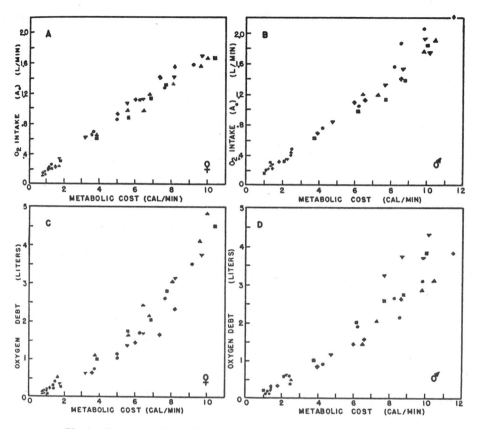

Fig. 2. Oxygen intake and debt related to changes in total net metabolic cost of work.

very little departure from linearity, probably because the work load did not go high enough. The highest work load used resulted in a net O₂ intake of only about 2 l per min whereas maximum intakes of 3 to 4 l per min are common in men. It may be mentioned that the absence of individual differences is just what would be expected according to the hypothesis—the derivation of the formula postulated substrate production in proportion to rate of work, predicting a steady-state oxygen intake a_o determined only by the rate of work, even though the amount of substrate a_o/k can vary as a result of individual differences in k.

It may be mentioned that this finding might have been obscured if the rate of work had been measured as *external* work performed, since energy would be expended and substrate formed whether the muscle contractions turned the bicycle wheel, opposed its turning due to imperfect coordination, or were used to maintain posture. For these reasons, metabolic cost of the work is the proper measure. The absence of any important indication of individual differences in oxygen intake as a function of rate of metabolic work implies that there are no individual differences in the efficiency of oxygen metabolism, although differences in efficiency of performing external work may well be present because of variation in such factors as coordination. At higher work loads, individual differences in metabolic efficiency may occur because the region of limited oxygen intake is probably not the same for everyone. If it varies, the proportion of anaerobic to aerobic oxidation will vary, resulting in differences in efficiency.[8]

Unfortunately, the necessity for reliance on metabolic work as the abscissa in Fig. 2 results in the ordinate variance forming a part of the abscissa variance, since the metabolic cost of work as estimated from oxygen consumption is made up of exercise oxygen income plus oxygen debt. However, in examining these data, it should be kept in mind that only *part* of the variance is common to the two axes, and that the length of the exercise bout does not mathematically effect the linearity of vertical scatter of the points if a true steady state can be assumed. The writer certainly makes no claim for priority in establishing the relationship shown in Fig. 2, *A* and *B*, but cannot refrain from pointing out that published data of this specific type, obtained under constant conditions, are not as extensive as is desirable from a statistical point of view. Due to the complication mentioned above, it would not be possible to arrive at any far-reaching conclusions from this finding alone, although an analysis by the partial correlation technique might be revealing if the number of subjects was large enough to warrant it. Nevertheless, the present data do fall into the pattern that is predicted by theory, thus forming a part of the total chain of evidence.

In contrast to the results with oxygen intake, the magnitude of oxygen debt as plotted against work load in Fig. 2, *C* and *D*, appears to depend to a considerable extent upon individual charac-

teristics. This can be explained by the established individual differences in velocity constant k, even though a_o shows no individual variance when metabolic work load is equated. The steady-state level of unoxidized substrate is a_o/k. Inasmuch as the total oxygen debt is a_o'/k' (these parameters being derived from the recovery curve), there are theoretical complications if k' is really smaller than k. While a_o can be measured with reasonable accuracy, it is not possible to observe a_o' directly; it must be estimated from the recovery curve. The semilog plot of debt payoff used to determine the parameters for Fig. 1 *A* gives a good fit for a linear curve taking a_o as the intercept, but not as good if slightly different parameters are chosen so that $a_o/k = a_o'/k'$ (see Fig. 3). The work of Asmussen[1] suggests, however, that aerobic metabolic efficiency is less during recovery

Fig. 3. Semilog plots used to determine curve constants of the theoretical curve of Fig. 1. *A*. For exercise *ordinate* represents oxygen deficience, i.e., the difference between steady-state income and actual income for each minute plotted. In this case, $a_0 = .21$ and $k = 1.63$. For recovery, *ordinate* represents net oxygen income above the resting level. The curve constants are $a_0' = .21$ and $k' = 1.37$. To equate a_0/k and a_0'/k, the best-fitting recovery curve would be as shown by the dashed line.

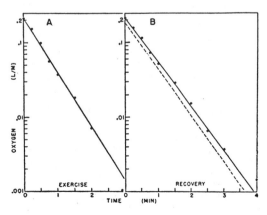

than during exercise even with moderate work loads, which would imply $a_o'/k' > a_o/k$ as shown in Fig. 1 A, and justify the expectation of a smaller k' in recovery. In either case, the individual differences in k imply individual differences in unoxidized substrate and in amount of debt.

For metabolic work loads up to 5 or 6 cal per min, the relation between oxygen debt and work load is essentially linear, the average regression line for the men and women being almost identical (Fig. 2, C and D). The origin of the line is close to zero both for the average and for individuals. Others have reported a larger debt for very light work loads,[6] which is probably a reflection of using the pre-exercise resting level as a base line instead of the post-exercise asymptote.[10] At work loads higher than 5 or 6 cal per min there begins to be noticed a definite upward trend in the curve, particularly in the women subjects. Presumably this is due to an increasing proportion of lactate debt in the total oxygen debt,[12, 8] although the possibility of a decreasing k' at the higher work loads cannot be ignored. The two subjects studied by Erickson et al.[6] do not show this upward trend with work loads going to nearly 12 cal per min; this is also true of some of the men in the present experiment, but it would probably have been revealed with heavier work.

While the alactic oxygen debt is a true debt in that it represents the oxidative restoration of energy in payment for energy that was released during the preceding work, it is a normal rather than emergency mechanism, and is a necessary accompaniment of work. This type of debt does not result from a lag in the circulatory or other adjustments to the early phase of exercise—rather it is simply a reflection of the fact that oxygen consumption

during exercise does not increase until there is substrate to be oxidized, and that substrate is formed as a *result* of work, hence requires time for accumulation. There is eventually an equilibration between accumulation and oxidation of substrate, the dynamics of which result in a steady-state oxygen intake that is determined only by the rate of work. The accumulation of substrate, however, is an individual matter, being determined by rate of work and individual differences in k, the latter controlling the rate of substrate oxidation. For constant metabolic work and oxygen intake, individuals having a small k' carry a relatively large amount of unoxidized substrate while those with a high velocity constant have a proportionally smaller amount.

Thus it would seem that the individual with a slow velocity constant k is at a disadvantage for two reasons. First, for a given rate of work, he will use a larger proportion of his alactic oxygen requirement during the recovery period; hence the total requirement for the work will be greater because debt oxidation seems to be of relatively low efficiency as shown by Asmussen. Naturally, these phenomena will be most important for short periods of work, when debt oxidation is a relatively large proportion of the total oxidation. Secondly, if it may be assumed that the branch line (lactate) oxidative mechanism comes into action because of a limitation as to the possible amount of alactic substrate or of factors that control it, he will be forced to depend on the lactate mechanism at a lesser work load than would be the case for an individual with a larger k.

It should be emphasized that the theory presented above applies only to what may be termed *typical* and *moderate* work conditions. In these circumstances the rates of arterial blood flow and circulation time do not seem to be limiting factors except as they influence k. Otherwise the theoretical and experimental rates of oxygen intake would hardly be expected to agree as closely as is found to be the case. If the the exercise is predominantly static or isometric in nature, it is very likely that there will temporarily be considerable restriction of the local circulation, hence the formula cannot be expected to apply—there will be local debts of the slow-component type. Similarly, it is not expected to hold for individuals with pathological circulatory impairment, or for heavy work loads. The present experiments have tested the fit of the theoretical curves only for net oxygen incomes of the order of 1 or 2 1 per min.

One of the fundamental assumptions has been that the rate of work is uniform. The data that have been presented seem to show that it has been in the series of experiments herein described, but in some types of work the technique of the subject may vary during the exercise, resulting in considerable fluctuation above and below the average work load. Furthermore, if the work load is heavy, tending to approach the crest load rate, there are apt to be considerable fluctuations in the amount of debt due to variations in oxygen transport. However, in evaluating any apparent exceptions, there must be due consideration to the question as to whether the departures represent merely statistical fluctuations or real differences.

Summary

The oxygen intake during exercise and recovery was determined for six men and six women working at 15 kg-m per min on a bicycle ergometer, using the closed-circuit method. The experimental results agreed very closely with the theoretical assumption that the amount of oxidizable substrate present at any time t is equal to $(a_0/k)(1 - e^{-kt})$, the rate of oxygen consumption during exercise is $a_0(1 - e^{-kt})$, where k is a velocity constant and a_0 is the steady-state rate of oxygen intake, and the rate of oxygen intake during the recovery period is equal to $a_0 e^{-k't'}$. Ten of the subjects also exercised at four heavier work loads ranging up to 910 kg-m per min. Their steady-state oxygen intake a_0 was found to be linearly proportional to the metabolic cost of the work, except at the highest work loads where there was an indication of restricted oxygen intake in the women subjects. In general, there appeared to be no individual differences in the rate of intake. At light work loads the relation between debt magnitude and metabolic cost was essentially linear up to about 6 cal per min, with an indication of individual differences explained by the fact that the theoretical debt magnitude (a'/k') is a function of the velocity constant k'. At heavier work loads the size of the debt showed a relative increase, presumably due to lactate debt formation. The magnitude of oxygen debt estimated from the recovery curves was significantly greater than the oxygen deficiency contracted during the work, suggesting that alactic debt oxidation is less efficient than oxidation during exercise. In terms of the curve constants, the larger post-exercise debt was due to a slower velocity constant k'. Individual differences in the k of oxygen deficiency appeared consistently in the smaller k' of recovery, the intercorrelation r being 0.79.

In another experiment, 35 men worked at a constant rate of 614 kg-m per min. Correlational analysis showed that steady-state oxygen intake a_0' and velocity constant k' were unrelated, r being only 0.08, as predicted by the mathematical independence of these parameters in the theoretical formula for oxygen intake. Variance in size of debt was largely determined by the velocity constant, as debt magnitude correlated $r = 0.74$ with k' but only 0.47 with a'_o. A third experiment concerned the changes in a'_o and k' as a result of the physical conditioning of 23 athletes. The steady-stage oxygen intake a'_o did not change significantly, but the velocity constant k' was definitely increased.

All of these experimental results are in accord with the theoretical position that the so-called alactic oxygen debt is probably not usually due to the lag of the circulation or other adjustment processes in the initial phase of moderate exercise, but is instead a necessary consequence of exercise oxygen consumption being controlled by the production of oxidizable substrate. This production is in direct linear proportion to the work done by the muscles and is not characteristic of the individual, although there are individual differences in debt accumulation and pay-off because of characteristic differences in the velocity constant of fast-component (alactic) oxidation.

References

1. Asmussen, E., *Acta Physiol. Scand.* **11** (1946), 196.

2. Berg, W. E., *Am. J. Physiol.*, **149** (1947), 597.

3. Best, C. H., and N. B. Taylor, *Physiological Basis of Medical Practice.* Baltimore: The Williams & Wilkins Co., 1950.

4. Crecitelli, F., and C. Taylor, *Am. J. Physiol.*, **141** (1944), 141.

5. Dill, D. B., H. T. Edwards, E. V. Newman, and R. Margaria, *Arbeitsphysiol.*, **9** (1936), 299.

6. Erickson, L. E. Simonson, H. Taylor, H. Alexander, and A. Keys, *Am. J. Physiol.*, **145** (1946), 391.

7. Henry, F. M., and W. E. Berg, *J. Appl. Physiol.* **3** (1950), 103.

8. Henry, F. M., and Janice DeMoor, *ibid.*, **2** (1950), 481.

9. Henry, F. M., and J. R. Fitzhenry, *ibid.*, **2** (1950), 461.

10. Hill, A. V., C. N. H. Long, and H. Lupton, *Proc. Roy. Soc. (London)*, **B97** (1924), 84.

11. Hill, D. K., *J. Physiol. (London)*, **98** (1940), 207, 467.

12. Margaria, R., H. T. Edwards, and D. B. Dill, *Am. J. Physiol.* **106** (1933), 689.

13. Simonson, E., *Arch. ges. Physiol.*, **215** (1927), 716.

K. MAHADEVA / R. PASSMORE / B. WOOLF

Individual Variations in the Metabolic Cost of Standardized Exercises; The Effects of Food, Age, Sex, and Race

Reprinted from the *Journal of Physiology*,
121 (1953), 225–31.

Mahadeva, Passmore, Woolf, and their colleagues in England have furnished the much needed precision to the assessment of the metabolic cost of energy (total oxygen used during and in recovery from exercise). Their work has been facilitated by the Kofranyi-Michaelis calorimeter, a small portable device that, when affixed to the subject, collects small samples of expired air periodically. This study is presented because it affirms the value of detailed studies of the metabolic cost of physical activity.*

The authors conclude that the metabolic cost of standardized stepping and walking is related to body weight in a linear proportion. Using the statistical techniques of multiple regression and analysis of covariance, they find that height, age, sex, race, or resting metabolism do not increase the precision of prediction of metabolic cost. Consequently, they conclude that body weight is the main variable to be considered in obtaining an assessment of the metabolic cost of standardized stepping and walking exercise. This finding makes it possible to study metabolic cost of these activities without complex sampling problems. It is also of interest to note the statistical sophistication of this study. This quality is particularly noticeable when comparing this treatise to the earlier studies, which—it should be noted in all fairness—did not employ the more complex methods of variance and regression analysis. These methods were not widely used in any of the sciences until after World War II, and much of the basic work on exercise took place before that time.

A provisional yardstick of human calorie requirements has been provided by a report from the Nutrition Division of the Food and Agricultural Organization (F.A.O.) of the United Nations.[2] In a world beset with food shortages and an increasing population this is of great practical importance.

The report draws attention to several gaps in fundamental physiological knowledge. Thus the variation in the Basal Metabolic Rates (B.M.R.), the foundation upon which standards for human energy requirements have been built, is not well defined in different population groups. Recently Quenouille, Boyne, Fisher, and Leitch[6] have made a new assessment of normal B.M.R. standards in relation to sex, stature, age, climate, and race. Robert-

* From the Departments of Public Health and Social Medicine and of Animal Genetics, University of Edinburgh. We have to thank the Medical Research Council for an expense grant.

son and Reid[7] have made measurements of the B.M.R.'s of a large series of the British people. These authors have discussed body size, age, sex, and race in relation to B.M.R.'s. We now have a good body of data on this subject, but there is little or no data of the effect of these factors on the metabolism during muscular activities. If metabolic variations of the same order occurred during exercise, they would profoundly affect the food requirements of a population.

In the present investigation we have studied the energy expenditure of 50 persons of varying size and age, male and female, European and Asiatic, during the carrying out of two different standard muscular activities. The first one was a stepping test in which there was measurable external work performed in raising the body weight and the second was walking, an ordinary everyday activity. In these two activities the movements involved are those to which the subjects are of necessity accustomed in everyday life, and so should be little affected by training or practice.

A statistical analysis of our data shows that energy expenditure during stepping or walking can be very closely predicted from a knowledge of body weight, and that no significant increase in precision is gained by also taking into account height, age, sex, race, or resting metabolism. In the case of stepping, energy expenditure may be taken as directly proportional to body weight. In walking, the regression line is also linear but does not pass through the origin.

Methods

Energy utilization was determined by indirect calorimetry. Basal and resting metabolic rates were measured either with a Benedict-Roth spirometer, assuming an R.Q. of 0.8 or a Douglas bag. Rates for stepping and walking were obtained with the Kofranyi-Michaelis calorimeter.[4] This was regularly checked against the Douglas bag method. Gas analyses were carried out in duplicate, using the Haldane gas analysis apparatus.

The subjects were chosen from a variety of walks of life: most were either laboratory technicians or postgraduate students, but a few were still at school and some were inmates of a home for old people. After an explanation of the nature of the tests, they rested for 30 min and then a recording of respiration was made on a Benedict-Roth drum, whilst the subject was recumbent. If a regular respiratory rhythm was shown in the tracing, and the subject was breathing smoothly, the test was made immediately. Some ten volunteers were clearly restless and unable to breathe easily through the mouthpiece. These were rejected: a further four showed irregularities in the tracing and in these the tests were repeated on a second day. The remaining 46 appeared quite at ease with the apparatus and these carried out the exercise tests only once. Five subjects were accustomed to metabolic work, but showed no marked difference from the remainder. Although it is well known that training plays a marked effect on the cost of such complicated activities as stationary bicycling, Erickson, Simonson, Taylor, Alexander, and Keys[1] have shown that in walking on a treadmill under standardized conditions repetition produces no reduction in metabolic cost. In these simple tests, with ourselves as subjects, we have found no improvement following training.

Stepping was carried out to a metronome at a rate of 15 steps up and down per minute for 10 min on to a 10 in. (25.4 cm) stool. This is well within the range of optimum efficiency for stepping.[5] Walking took place on an indoor track; the subjects walked for 10 min at a uniform speed of 3 mi per hr (4.8 km per hr). The room temperatures during the experiments ranged from 61 to 70°F.

Effects of Food

Orr and Kinloch[3] have carried out a series of experiments on one subject on the effects of food on the metabolic cost of walking. The expenditure of energy per unit of work performed was influenced by the nature of the preceding meal. Following a high protein diet the increase due to work wa greater than in the preceding postabsorptive state; after a high carbohydrate diet the increase due to work was less than in the preceding postabsorptive state; and after a high fat meal there appears to be a summation of extra energy expenditure due to food and that due to work. We have repeated their experiment on similar lines and also included experiments where a mixed diet was used.

A summary of our findings and those of Orr and Kinloch are given in Tables 1 and 2. Though in general our findings confirm theirs, it will be seen that the specific dynamic action only amounts to at most an extra 2 kcal per 10 min. As the standard deviation of the metabolic cost of these standard exercises is of this order, a long series of experiments would be needed to measure the statistical significances of these increases. It will be noted that Table 2 shows that the coefficient of variation during exercise is less than the coefficient of variation under basal conditions. As the effects of food are so slight, relative to the cost of walking and stepping, it was thought unnecessary to carry out our experiments in the postabsorptive state. Instead our subjects reported either in the forenoon or

afternoon, half an hour after a light meal. They then rested recumbent for 30 min before the commencement of observations.

Experimental Results

The calorie expenditure resting, stepping, and walking for periods of 10 min, together with particulars regarding age, sex, race, height, and weight for the 50 subjects are given in Table 3. The weight includes the actual weight of the subject, together with that of his clothes and the weight of the Kofranyi-Michaelis instrument. The apparatus and clothing amounted on an average to 7–8 kg.

The findings of an exhaustive statistical analysis are summarized in Table 4. Multiple regression equations were calculated in which weight, height, age, sex, race, and resting metabolism were simultaneously taken into account. In the case of sex, the "dummy variate" method was used, males being scored one and females zero. For race, a joint regression and analysis of covariance technique was employed. The significance of the constant term in the regression was also assessed by testing whether there was any significant increase in

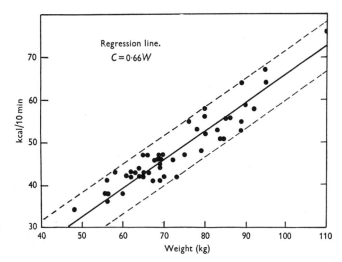

Fig. 1. Energy expenditure during standardized stepping. The dotted lines show twice the standard error of estimate.

the residual mean square when the line was constrained to pass through the origin.

For stepping, the relation found was very simple. Energy expenditure can be taken as directly proportional to body weight. The mean for all the subjects was 48.2 kcal, S. D. ± 8.52. After taking weight into account, the residual standard error measured around the regression line is reduced to ± 3.02 kcal. This is illustrated in Fig. 1, which shows the individual values of energy expenditure in relation to body weight, with the regression line drawn in. For walking also, the only variable that need be taken into account is weight. The original standard devia-

TABLE 1

Effect of a Previous Meal on the Calorie Expenditure During Lying, Stepping, and Walking. Energy Expenditure in kcal per 10 min

SUBJECT: K.M., AGE 41 YR, WEIGHT 66 KG, HEIGHT 165 CM				
Nature of meal	No. of observations	Lying	Standard stepping	Walking (3.0 mi per hr)
Postabsorptive	9	9.4	40	41
High carbohydrate	3	9.6	41	41
High fat	3	9.8	40	41
High protein	3	12.2	42	42
Mixed breakfast	2	10.8	42	41
SUBJECT: T.B., AGE 26 YR, WEIGHT 57 KG, HEIGHT 165 CM (ORR AND KINLOCH[3])				
Nature of meal	No. of observations	Lying		Walking (3.4 mi per hr)
Postabsorptive	9	11.1		48.8
High carbohydrate	8	12.9		49.4
High fat	9	11.9		49.6
High protein	7	13.2		52.7

TABLE 2

Daily Variations in Individuals Doing Standard Tasks

Subject	Activity	No. of observations	Energy expenditure kcal per 10 min		S.D.	S.E. of mean	Coeff. of variation (%)
			Mean	Range			
K.M.	Basal	10	9.3	7.7–10.7	0.8	0.2	7.8
	Standard stepping without food	9	39.8	34–43	2.0	0.6	4.6
	Standard stepping after food	11	41.2	39–44	2.8	0.8	5.0
	Walking 3.0 mi per hr without food	8	41.0	37–43	2.2	0.7	5.1
	Walking 3.0 mi per hr after food	11	41.1	37–44	3.4	1.0	8.2
T.B.	Basal	9	11.0	10.2–12.1	0.7	0.2	6.5
	Walking 3.4 mi per hr without food	18	48.8	45.8–51.6	2.8	0.6	5.8
	Walking 3.4 mi per hr after food	24	50.5	45.8–54.6	2.2	0.4	4.4

TABLE 3

Calorie Expenditure Resting, Stepping, and Walking

Age	Sex	Race	Total weight (kg)	Height (cm)	Resting	Standard stepping	Walking (3.0 mi per hr)
					Energy expenditure kcal per 10 min		
41	M.	Eur.	89	181	11	55	51
41	M.	Eur.	84	181	11	51	49
29	M.	Eur.	73	171	10	42	41
41	M.	As.	67	165	10	41	41
41	M.	Eur.	69	181	13	47	42
20	M.	Eur.	69	170	11	41	45
20	M.	Eur.	90	180	11	59	55
34	M.	Eur.	83	182	16	53	52
41	F.	Eur.	69	170	11	47	46
22	M.	Eur.	84	182	16	51	44
28	M.	As.	62	162	12	43	36
39	M.	Eur.	95	178	16	64	54
38	M.	Eur.	75	172	13	47	41
37	M.	As.	70	164	11	42	40
48	M.	Eur.	92	181	14	58	53
36	M.	As.	85	172	12	56	48
26	M.	As.	89	173	12	53	50
45	F.	Eur.	79	166	11	48	48
22	F.	Eur.	72	165	12	46	39
31	F.	Eur.	64	152	12	44	40
28	F.	Eur.	65	168	10	42	39
26	M.	Eur.	86	187	12	56	46
14	M.	Eur.	48	150	11	34	37
13	M.	Eur.	56	162	13	41	40
13	M.	Eur.	56	157	12	36	40
18	F.	Eur.	56	157	12	38	38
21	F.	Eur.	56	158	11	38	34
20	F.	Eur.	62	155	11	42	36
24	M.	Eur.	69	177	14	46	48
20	F.	Eur.	66	171	11	47	37
18	M.	Eur.	110	188	18	76	65
20	F.	Eur.	61	157	11	42	33
15	M.	Eur.	68	166	13	46	46
17	F.	Eur.	64	159	10	42	46
14	F.	Eur.	66	162	12	43	43
57	M.	Eur.	65	168	11	43	40
32	M.	As.	78	172	12	53	50
64	M.	Eur.	95	177	12	67	55
79	M.	Eur.	68	170	13	46	46
53	F.	Eur.	80	158	9	52	48
62	M.	Eur.	76	170	11	55	52
34	F.	Eur.	65	161	12	47	44
47	M.	Eur.	80	176	10	58	41
26	M.	As.	69	156	10	44	48
40	M.	Eur.	89	188	12	64	60
73	M.	Eur.	58	162	7	43	36
38	M.	As.	63	162	14	44	39
22	M.	As.	69	171	12	45	39
15	F.	Eur.	60	151	10	38	34
26	M.	Eur.	80	168	12	56	50

TABLE 4

Regression analysis of energy expenditure of 50 subjects during standardized activities

	Stepping	*Walking*
Mean kcal per 10 min	48.24	44.50
S.D.	8.52	6.98
Coefficient of variation (%)	17.7	15.7

REGRESSION EQUATIONS

$$\text{Stepping } C = 0.66\ W \pm 3.02,$$
$$\text{Walking }\ C = 10.24 + 0.47\ W \pm 3.67,$$

where C = gross kcal expenditure in 10 min, W = gross body weight in kg. Last term is standard error of estimate.

TEST OF SIGNIFICANCE FOR ADDITIONAL TERMS IN REGRESSION OF CALORIE
EXPENDITURE ON BODY WEIGHT
5% point for $t^2 = 4.04$.

Proposed new independent variate *k*	*Stepping* t^2	*Walking* t^2
Diversion of regression line from origin	0.98	11.29
Height	0.09	0.00
Sex	0.00	1.14
Age	2.14	0.05
Race	1.76	0.60
Resting metabolism	1.31	0.77

TABLE 5

Energy Expenditure During Standard Stepping and Walking. Effects of Age, Sex, and Race

| | | | | | ENERGY EXPENDITURE (KCAL PER 10 MIN) | | | |
| | | | | | STEPPING | | WALKING | |
Age	*Sex*	*Race*	*No. of observations*	*Mean weight*	*Uncorrected mean*	*Mean per 70 kg*	*Uncorrected mean*	*Mean per 70 kg*
13–20	M. and F.	Eur.	14	66.6	44.6	46.8	42.5	44.6
21–45	M.	Eur.	12	81.3	52.7	45.4	48.2	41.5
21–45	M.	As.	9	72.3	46.8	45.4	43.4	42.0
21–45	F.	Eur.	7	68.3	44.4	45.6	41.4	42.5
46–79	M. and F.	Eur.	8	76.7	52.8	48.1	46.4	42.3

tion is ± 6.98 and the standard error of estimate is ± 3.67. The scatter diagram and regression line for walking are shown in Fig. 2.

Table 5 shows the mean total energy expenditure for the 10 min periods for the stepping and walking tests for different age groups of males and females, Europeans and Asiatics, both uncorrected for weight and corrected to a standard gross weight (70 kg).

Our results indicate that in any physical activity in which a large proportion of energy expenditure is used to move the body weight, the metabolic cost is directly proportional to the body weight. Factors such as age, sex, surface area, race, and previous dietary, which

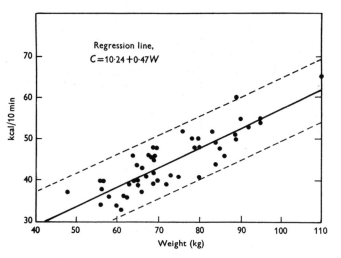

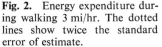

Fig. 2. Energy expenditure during walking 3 mi/hr. The dotted lines show twice the standard error of estimate.

are known to play an important part in determining individual basal metabolic rates, do not assume sufficient importance to add to the precision in assessing the cost of such activities. In a large number of activities, industrial, domestic, and recreational, a major part of the metabolic cost is spent in moving the body. Therefore the fact that weight is the only important individual variable in determining this cost can greatly simplify their assessments.

It may also be concluded that the stepping test seems to have valuable features as a measure of energy expenditure, giving on the average a result exactly proportional to weight and having quite a small residual variance after weight is taken into account.

Summary

1. The metabolic cost of standardized stepping and walking has been determined in 50 subjects and shown to be linearly proportional to body weight.

2. Statistical analysis showed that no significant increase in the precision of individual assessments is gained by taking into account height, age, sex, race, or resting metabolism.

References

1. Erickson, L., E. Simonson, H. L. Taylor, H. Alexander, and A. Keys, "The Energy Cost of Horizontal and Grade Walking on the Motor-Driven Treadmill," *Am. J. Physiol.*, **145** (1946), 391–401.

2. Food and Agricultural Organization of the United Nations, *Report of the Committee on Calorie Requirements.* Washington, 1950.

3. Orr, J. B., and J. P. Kinloch, "Note on the Influence of Diet on the Energy Expenditure in Work," *J. Roy. Army Med. Corps*, **36** (1921), 81–86.

4. Orsini, D., and R. Passmore, "The Energy Expended Carrying Loads Up and Down Stairs: Experiments Using the Kofranyi-Michaelis Calorimeter," *J. Physiol. (London)*, **115** (1951), 95–100.

5. Passmore, R., and J. G. Thomson, "Energy Expenditure During Stepping," *Brit. J. Prevent. Social Med.* (formerly *British Journal of Social Medicine*), **4** (1950), 234–37.

6. Quenouille, M. H., A. W. Boyne, W. B. Fisher, and I. Leitch, Commonwealth Bureau of Animal Nutrition. *Technical Communication. No. 17* (1951).

7. Robertson, J. M., and D. D. Reid, "Standards for the Basal Metabolism of Normal People in Britain," *Lancet*, **1** (1952), 940–43.

The Effect of Physical Activity on the Cardiovascular System

Most of the experimental studies on the effect of exercise on the cardiovascular system are concerned with pulse rate and blood pressure response. Some of these studies have resulted in tests which are widely reported in the literature, e.g., the Schneider test. Historically, research on the effect of exercise on pulse rate and blood pressure goes back to the early 1900's. Among the pioneer researchers in this field were medical doctors; this reflects the emphasis placed on physical fitness of industrial personnel at that time. The work of C. Ward Crampton,[1] G. L. Meylan,[2] W. Stone,[3] and T. B. Barringer[4] are examples of these early studies. During the 1930's and 1940's physiologists and physical educators studied cardiovascular exercise response using more refined statistical techniques. The results of their labors are found in the well-known pulse ratio and cardiovascular efficiency tests found in the literature. The papers of Tuttle,[5] McCurdy and Larson,[6] and Brouha

---

[1] C. W. Crampton, "Blood Ptosis," *N. Y. Med. J.*, November 8, 1913.

[2] G. L. Meylan, "Twenty Years Progress in Tests of Efficiency," *Am. Phys. Ed. Rev.*, **18** (1913), 441.

[3] W. Stone, "The Clinical Significance of High and Low Pulse Pressure With Special Reference to Cardiac Load and Overload," *J. Am. Med. Assoc.*, **74** (1920), 1507.

[4] T. B. Barringer, "Studies of the Heart's Functional Capacity," *Arch. Internal Med.*, **20** (1917), 829.

[5] W. W. Tuttle, "The Use of the Pulse-Ratio Test for Rating Physical Efficiency," *Res. Quart.*, **2** (1931), 5–7.

[6] J. H. McCurdy, and L. A. Larson, "Measurement of Organic Efficiency for the Prediction of Physical Condition, *Res. Quart. Suppl.*, **6** (1935), 11–41.

and his colleagues[7] represent some of the work done during these two decades.

Recently, cardiologists have become interested in studying the effect of exercise on the heart as one method of understanding the basic physiology of the heart muscle and the vascular system. These studies have not been adequately interpreted in terms of their practical use in the prediction of physical performance at the present time. One possible reason for this is that highly specialized equipment, such as ballistocardiographs and intravenuous cannulas, is needed to obtain the measurements. Of more practical value are the many surveys[8, 9] reported on the relationship between regular exercise and coronary heart disease, an example of which is included in Chapter 7 on "The Effect of Exercise on Health." These studies are ex post facto surveys and present no experimental evidence to support or refute the conjectures of the authors.

The studies presented here were selected not only because they provide historical perspective, but also because they are rather clear in presentation of purpose, methodology, and conclusions. Aside from studies on pulse rate and blood pressure response, the editors have included an original study on cardiac output. As with so many of the components of physical activity, cardiovascular response to exercise is related to energy and metabolism cycles, the amount of previous physical training, and the type and duration of the exercise, so that these papers should furnish the basis for assessing such interrelationships when examining other related studies.

T. B. BARRINGER

Studies of the Heart's Functional Capacity

Reprinted from the *Archives of Internal Medicine*,
20 (1917), 830–39.

Barringer's work* is one of the pioneer studies concerning pulse rate and blood pressure response. He focuses on the reserve power of the heart as reflected in circulatory reactions to graduated work, employing dumbbells to represent the work load in this particular study. The essence of Barringer's findings is that

[7] R. E. Johnson, L. Brouha, and R. C. Darling, "A Test of Physical Fitness for Strenuous Exercise," *Rev. Can. Biol.*, **1** (1942), 491.

[8] J. N. Morris, and M. D. Crawford, "Coronary Heart Disease and Physical Activity of Work," *Brit. Med. J.*, **2** (1958), 1485.

[9] H. L. Taylor, *et al.*, "Death Rates Among Physically Active and Sedentary Employees of the Railway Industry," *Circulation*, Part 2, **22** (1960), 822.

* Paper submitted for publication June 12, 1917. From the Second Medical *blood pressure response to a short period of vigorous exercise is delayed until after the exercise is completed. He calls this "delayed rise" in systolic pressure a simple test of cardiac reserve power. In studies done after Barringer completed his work, Bock[1] placed more emphasis on the maximum rise in systolic blood pressure rather than on the delay in the rise. Other investigators, McCurdy and Larson[2] and Schneider,[3] have shown that the change in systolic blood pressure and pulse rate when the subject changes from a reclining or sitting posture, is a more reliable measure of cardiovascular response to exercise. Nevertheless, Barringer's work is important as part of the preliminary investigation that led to a more refined assessment of blood pressure and pulse rate response to exercise.*

The term functional capacity is used to indicate the total amount of power possessed by the heart muscle. When the body is at rest a small portion of this power is utilized to furnish the circulatory requirements of the metabolism. As soon as any muscular activity occurs the so-called reserve power of the heart is drawn on to furnish blood to the working muscles.

Of these two component parts of the power inherent in the heart muscle the reserve power forms normally by far the larger portion, and it is with this factor that our studies are concerned. We propose to gain an idea of the heart's functional capacity by a measurement of its reserve power.

The method used to determine this is based on the circulatory reactions to graduated work, and a rather detailed description of these reactions is necessary to a clear understanding of our test, and, what is more important, to a belief in its validity.

Work was furnished by means of a Krogh-Lindhard ergometer in a few experiments, but in the greater number by movements with dumbbells. The blood pressures were taken by the auscultatory method with a Riva Rocci manometer. A rubber hand bulb was used to inflate the cuff. The systolic pressure and pulse were taken and then work was performed. The pressure was read again between 20 and 30 sec after completion of work. This was the time required with our technique to make the first reading, and 90 per cent of the readings on the first trial fell between 20 and 30 sec. If the first reading was made before 20 sec or after 30 sec had elapsed the experiment was discarded. A second reading was made between 50 and 60 sec after work, the aim being to make it as close to 60 as possible, and the third reading 90 sec after. Then readings were made every 60 sec. (In our earlier experiments we made readings every 60 sec after the first reading; later we made readings every 30 sec after.)

In a person with normal heart, shortly after work the systolic blood pressure and pulse rate are increased. If they are then taken according to the

Division of the New York Hospital. Read before the Section on Practice of Medicine at the Sixty-Eighth Annual Session of the American Medical Association, New York, June, 1917.

[1] A. V. Bock, *et al.*, "Dynamic Changes Occurring in Man at Work," *J. Physiol. (London)*, **66** (1928), 136.

[2] J. H. McCurdy, and L. A. Larson, "Measurements of Organic Efficiency for the Prediction of Physical Condition," *Res. Quart. Suppl.*, **6** (1935), 11–14.

[3] E. C. Schneider "A Cardiovascular Rating as a Measure of Physical Fatigue and Efficiency," *J. Am. Med. Assoc.*, **74** (1920), 1507.

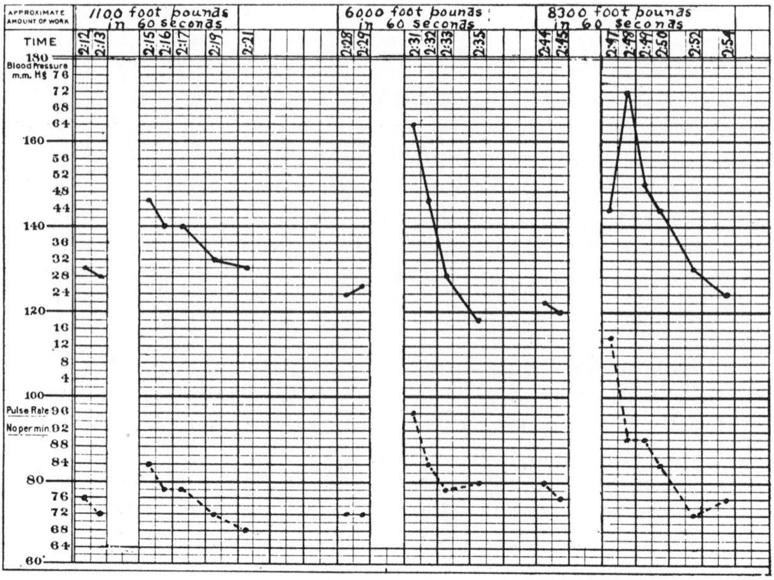

Chart 1. Circulatory reactions in a normal man to increasing amounts of work performed by means of dumbbells. The white perpendicular spaces represent the work periods in each experiment during which blood pressure and pulse rate could not be measured.

above plan they will be found to return rapidly to the figures noted before work. If successively increasing amounts of work are performed the same reactions will be observed. The greater the work, the higher are the subsequent systolic pressure and pulse rate. Finally, an amount of work is reached which is followed by a different type of blood pressure curve. It does not reach its greatest height within 30 sec after the completion of work, but at a later period (50 to 90 sec) when the pulse rate has dropped back toward normal.

Chart 1 represents the course of the blood pressure curve in a normal individual after increasing amounts of work, which were furnished by dumbbell exercises.

This delayed rise in systolic pressure (for so we shall term it) is a most interesting and extraordinary phenom-

enon. It has been the subject of many hundred experiments on both normal persons and patients with cardiac insufficiency, and we shall summarize the facts we have discovered about this peculiar reaction.

1. It is always obtained in normal people whenever the work exceeds a certain amount (the work may be of any kind).

2. Children are able to do much larger amounts of work, in comparison to their weights than are adults before a delayed rise ensues.[1]

3. It makes no difference what group of muscles is employed to do the work. If, for example, a delayed systolic rise follows 5,000 ft-lb of work, per-

---

[1] The data on which this statement is based were furnished through the courtesy of Drs. W. P. St. Lawrence and H. L. Bibby.

formed in 60 sec with the arm and back muscles, it will invariably follow 5,000 ft-lb of work done in 60 sec with the thigh and leg muscles. It is the amount of work and the time in which it is performed, or, technically, the power expended, which determine the delayed rise, not the group of muscles used.

4. The amount of work which is followed by a delayed rise varies but slightly from day to day in the same individual.

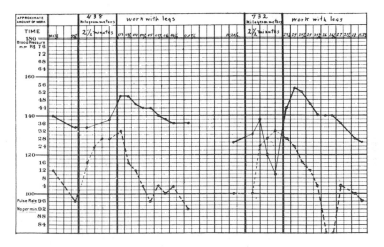

Chart 2. Circulatory reactions in patient C. G. suffering from cardiac insufficiency to increasing amounts of work performed with the legs on the bicycle ergometer.

Chart 3. A continuation of the experiments shown in Chart 2 on the same patient a few minutes later, the work being performed on the bicycle ergometer with the arms instead of the legs. The white perpendicular spaces represent the work periods in each experiment during which blood pressure and pulse rate could not be measured.

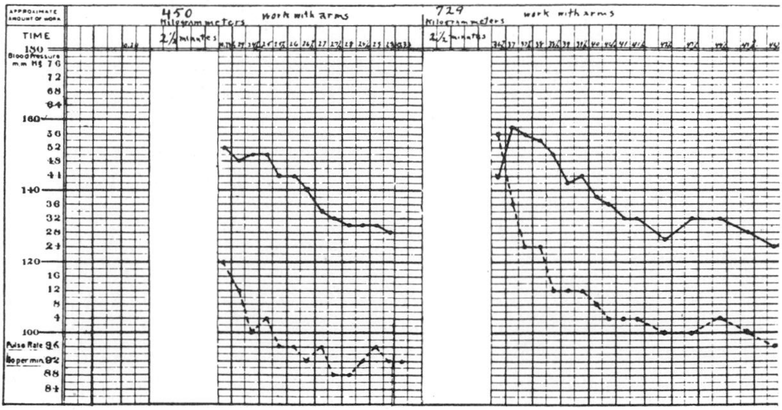

5. Patients with varying grades of cardiac insufficiency are able to perform much smaller quantities of work than normal individuals before a delayed rise ensues. These quantities are measured in hundreds, as compared with thousands in normal individuals. Occasionally in these cardiac patients the pressure after work is lower than before. It then rises to or even above the original figures.

6. Patients with marked cardiac insufficiency, edema, dyspnoea when resting, etc., are able to do no work at all which is not followed by a delayed rise or fall.

7. As the general health of normal persons improves, or as the condition of cardiacs improves, we find that the amount of work which can be performed before a delayed rise ensues becomes greater and greater.

8. In a few experiments on patients with cardiac insufficiency we have found that digitalis causes a marked but temporary increase in the amount of work the patient can do before a delayed rise ensues.

9. In the treatment of normal people, and of cardiacs by graduated exercises, the prescribing of quantities of work which are not followed by delayed rises has caused a marked improvement in the majority of suitable cases.

Of all these facts the most significant is, perhaps, the one which shows that the delayed rise occurs quite independently of the group of muscles used in the work.

Charts 2 and 3 illustrate this most important point.

Gräupner described the delayed rise many years ago, but he did not discover its most significant feature, which has just been described.

The present incomplete state of our knowledge of circulatory physiology does not permit of a complete explanation of the phenomenon. If its significance is to become apparent it can only do so at present through clinical experiments.

We believe that the facts here enumerated, many of which have been confirmed by other observers, demonstrate, as far as it is possible to demonstrate clinically, that the delayed rise in systolic pressure indicates that the preceding work has exceeded the limit of the heart's reserve power.

We conclude, therefore, that if the systolic blood pressure does not reach its greatest height during the first 30 sec after the completion of work, but at the second or third reading (that is, 50 to 90 sec after work), or if this first reading is lower than the original level, that work, whatever its amount, has overtaxed the heart's reserve power and may be taken as an approximate measure of the heart's reserve power.

In the following studies we have considered work which was not followed by a delayed systolic rise as being within the heart's reserve power, and work which was followed by a delayed rise as exceeding the heart's reserve power.

We have used various movements with iron dumbbells, which were first described by Dr. Jacob Teschner of New York, to furnish work, on account of their convenience and the ease of making comparative estimations of the amount of work performed.

Studies of the Heart's Reserve Power in Normal Individuals

Chart 4 summarizes our results by decades in 45 normal persons.

Effect of digitalis on the cardiac reserve power in normal people and in patients with cardiac insufficiency. Three people were selected with normal hearts but low reserve powers: One, aged 52 yr, had pulmonary tuberculosis and had a

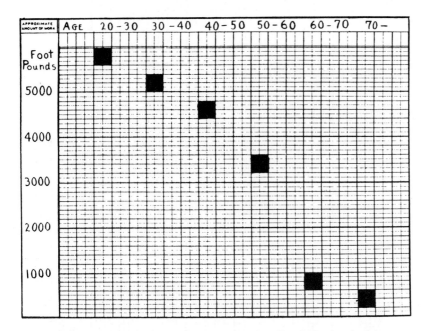

Chart 4. Average cardiac reserve power by decades of 45 normal adults. Each space between two heavy perpendicular lines represents 60 sec. The black squares represent the heart's capacity. For example, between the ages of 20 and 30 yr the average heart was able to supply sufficient blood to the muscles to enable them to do 5,600 ft-lb in 60 sec. The performance of 6,000 ft-lb was followed by a delayed rise. It will be noted that the highest figures were obtained between the ages of 20 and 30 yr. After that the heart's reserve power steadily decreases.

reserve power averaging from day to day between 500 and 600 ft-lb performed in 30 sec. One, aged 43 yr, had a chronic pyloric ulcer with partial gastric retention and averaged between 250 and 300 ft-lb in 15 sec. The third, aged 51 yr, had a cancer of the esophagus and averaged between 150 and 200 ft-lb in 15 sec. Their hearts were normal on physical examination and showed normal electrocardiograms. They all received large doses of digitalis, enough to produce mild toxic symptoms, but showed no increase whatever in their cardiac reserve powers.

A fourth patient, aged 23 yr, suffering from rheumatic endocarditis and slight cardiac insufficiency, which was evinced by some dyspnoea on climbing stairs, showed a marked, but temporary, increase in his heart's reserve power following digitalis.

Chart 5 represents this experiment.

Effect of graduated exercises on normal hearts and on cardiac insufficiency. Chart 6 illustrates the effect of daily graduated exercises with dumbbells on a patient with low reserve power, due probably to a combination of hard intellectual work, no exercise, insomnia, several attacks of bronchitis, and much tobacco and considerable alcohol. Physical examination of the heart and the electrocardiogram were normal.

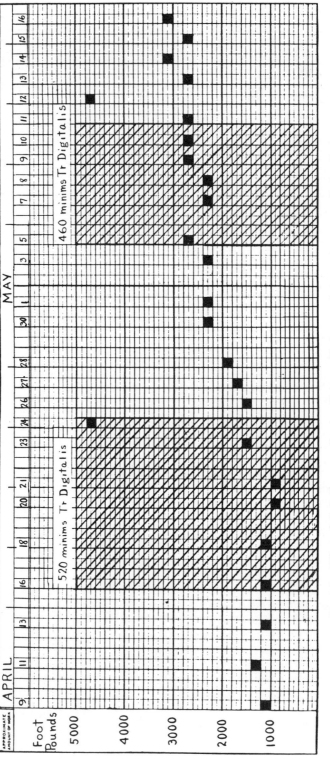

Chart 5. Effect of digitalis on cardiac insufficiency. Each space between two perpendicular lines represents 30 sec. The black squares represent the heart's reserve power. The shaded portions represent the periods during which digitalis was given. It will be noted that the heart increased its efficiency rather suddenly on both occasions at a time when the digitalis had produced a toxic effect.

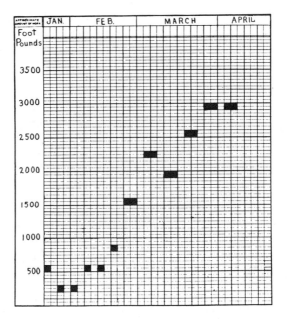

Chart 6. Course of the heart's reserve power in normal individual A. O. In this chart each space between two consecutive perpendicular lines represents fifteen seconds. The black squares represent the heart's capacity.

Chart 7 represents the effect of daily graduated exercise on a patient, J. C., suffering from cardiac insufficiency. He was 54 yr old and had had his first attack of cardiac insufficiency in 1913, having at that time swelling of the feet and legs and dyspnoea. Sept. 8, 1915, he was admitted to the House of Relief with the same symptoms. He was a thin man with gray hair, dyspnoea and with markedly swollen legs and scrotum. The heart was enlarged and showed an aortic and mitral regurgitation.

There were signs of small quantities of fluid in both pleural cavities. The liver was enlarged and the blood showed a four plus Wassermann reaction. He received altogether 16 dr of tincture of digitalis and 20 intramuscular injections of mercury salicylate. September 22, the cardiac capacity was tested and the patient was given a course of graduated exercise. A few days after the exercise began the digitalis was stopped.

September 22, when he was able to

Chart 7. Course of the heart's reserve power in J. C., suffering from aortic regurgitation and cardiac insufficiency. In this chart each space between two consecutive perpendicular lines represents 15 sec.

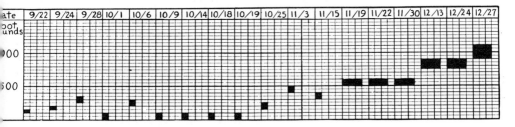

walk slowly around the ward for a short distance, his cardiac capacity was very low. December 27, when his capacity had increased to between 900 and 1,100 ft-lb performed in 60 sec, he was much stronger and able to do light work.

It can be gathered from the studies described here that the cardiac reserve power may be very low in a man with perfectly normal heart as well as in a man with diseased heart. Mackenzie has made the same observations in his last work on the heart, although his conclusions were reached without the aid of any test of the heart's reserve power.

The simplicity of the test of the heart's reserve power on which the foregoing studies are based, puts it within the reach of every practitioner. A few experiments will enable any one to confirm the most important of the circulatory reactions we have described. It makes no difference what kind of work is used, stair-climbing, walking, dipping exercises, or dumbbell work, for any one of these permits of a comparative measure of the cardiac reserve power. It is hardly necessary to point out the value of the information derived through this test, but we will mention one subject which has been much illuminated thereby, namely the kind and amount of exercise which a cardiac patient may take. Also the bearing it has on the suitability of any particular occupation is obvious. We have advised many cardiacs during the past two years on these two matters and the results have proved to be almost without exception so excellent that we feel this experience affords additional evidence of no slight value in support of the validity of our test.

I wish to express may indebtedness to Dr. William R. Williams, whose cooperation has made much of the preceding work possible, and to Dr.

H. E. B. Pardee for his help in the experiments with digitalis, and for doing the electrocardiographic work.

ADDENDUM

I take this opportunity to reply to an article by D. L. Rapport,[1] entitled "The Systolic Blood Pressure Following Exercise, with Remarks on Cardiac Capacity."

Dr. Rapport conducted experiments on normal people to determine the blood pressure reactions following graduated work. His blood pressure readings were made sooner and more frequently after work than ours were and he was able to show that the systolic rise never reaches its greatest height immediately after work, but at varying subsequent times, depending on the amount of work, thereby differing from our conclusions.

Dr. Rapport was unfamiliar with the technique we have used since early in 1916, which is described above. Our first readings were made between 20 and 30 sec after the completion of work, the second reading 50 to 60 sec after work, and the third reading 90 sec after work. By our method we secured curves of the systolic pressure which were so nearly isochronous that their comparison must have been valid in the great majority of instances. Whenever we detected a delayed rise (and no difference less than 4 mm of mercury was considered as such) the experiment was not considered valid unless we could obtain the same or a more marked delay in the rise by a repetition with increased work. It seems apparent that when we did get this reaction it must have been a marked example of the phenomenon because our first reading was not made earlier than 20 sec after work. Otherwise, we would have noted this reaction constantly. Also, if our tech-

I reproduce one of **Dr. Rapport's** charts (Chart 8) depicting four reactions which he considers "in most respects characteristic."

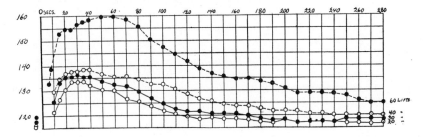

Chart 8. Weight of subject, 140 lb; lift, two 10-lb dumbbells through 6 ft; time, one lift in 2 sec. With 30 lifts, slight breathlessness; with 40 lifts, moderate breathlessness; with 60 lifts, considerable breathlessness and slight distress. As in all curves, the zero mark represents the cessation of exercise, the readings charted to the left of this line being controls taken before exercise.

nique had not been unvarying we could not have obtained the constant results we have described.

Compare with this our interpretation of his chart which notes the read-ings which would have been made by our method:

What we term "delayed rise" is apparently identical with what Dr. Rapport terms a "delay in the full

TABLE 1

Interpretation of Dr. Rapport's Chart by Our Method of Noting Blood Pressure

WORK = 20 LIFTS		WORK = 40 LIFTS	
Time	*(Before work)* *Systolic Blood Pressure*, 115	*Time*	*(Before work)* *Systolic Blood Pressure*, 115
20 sec.............	130	20 sec.............	136
30 sec.............	134	30 sec.............	137
50 sec.............	130	50 sec.............	136
60 sec.............	130	60 sec.............	135
90 sec.............	124	90 sec.............	133

WORK = 30 LIFTS		WORK = 60 LIFTS	
Time	*(Before work)* *Systolic Blood Pressure*, 118	*Time*	*(Before work)* *Systolic Blood Pressure*, 120
20 sec.............	135	20 sec.............	155
30 sec.............	136	30 sec.............	156
50 sec.............	134	50 sec.............	160 } Delayed rise
60 sec.............	132	60 sec.............	160
90 sec.............	127	90 sec.............	150

development of the rise." Our contention is that this most marked form of
reaction, whatever we term it, indicates
an overtaxing of the heart's reserve
power, and the clinical experiments we
have described above are offered as
substantiation of this thesis.

References

1. Rapport, D. L., *Arch. Internal Med.*,
   19 (1917), 981.

EDWARD C. SCHNEIDER

A Cardiovascular Rating As A Measure of Physical Fatigue and Efficiency

Reprinted from the *Journal of the American Medical Association*,
74 (1920), 1507–10.

The well-known Schneider test—first described in the literature in 1920—
was developed as a result of experience with aviators in World War I. Schneider
used the findings of previous studies to establish his criteria and, as did Barringer,
he placed great emphasis on pulse rate and blood pressure changes associated with
postural changes and with exercise. Schneider makes a telling point when he says
". . . that while the several pulse rate criteria of fitness may all be found in a
single person, not one or even any two of them is found to be an absolute test."
Accordingly, Schneider developed a scoring scheme for each of the six items on the
test ranging from +3 to −3. The system was based in part on the scheme of
Dr. J. H. McCurdy, then at Springfield College. Eighteen was considered a
perfect score on the test, and as the score decreased, the cardiovascular fitness of
the subject was found to be proportionately lower.

This study is of particular importance because it represents one of the first
research efforts in which there was cooperation between physical educators, physiologists and the military services. In fact, the Schneider test is of such value to
the Air Force that it was also used in World War II in screening Air Force pilots.*
Since the test determines the presence of general physical fatigue, rather than
functional abnormalities of the heart, it has been a very useful screening tool,
not only in selection of aviation personnel, but also in identification of those

---

* From the Medical Research Laboratory, Air Service, Mitchell Field, Long Island,
N.Y.

individuals whose cardiovascular systems reflected general fatigue. The major virtue of the Schneider test is that it was the first cardiovascular test to consider many variables and score them in a way that makes it possible to obtain an over-all rating. Although, the test procedure is not very complex from a statistical point of view, it has nevertheless been effective in achieving its purpose.

The need of a measure for physical efficiency whereby degrees of fatigue, physical fitness, and health may be determined has been felt alike by the medical profession and instructors in physical education and school hygiene. Of late, the newly awakened interest in industrial efficiency has shown that we lack satisfactory and reliable tests of fatigue. Experience with the aviator during the war also emphasized the need of some easily applied reliable physical efficiency test. Some aviators gradually underwent physical and nervous deterioration, the result of the wear and tear of the air work, or sometimes of dissipation, which made them less reliable in handling the airplane and frequently ultimately led to a crash. These aviators at times developed a disinclination to fly, but would not confess it because of the fear of being considered "yellow." To single out such men, the flight surgeon required the aid of a dependable test.

Unquestionably, the most satisfactory test for fatigue and loss in physical fitness would be one that eliminates the "personal equation" of the examiner and the anxiety and dishonesty of the patient. Replies to questions concerning symptoms and habits are often misleading because of a preformed opinion by the examiner or because the patient is incapable of self-analysis and accurate description of his experiences. Furthermore, for personal reasons some men would prefer to mislead the examiner, and the test should not, therefore, demand much cooperation and attention from the patient.

The functional changes of the body brought about by regular physical training give the basis for a number of physical efficiency tests. The attention of trainers and athletes, as well as of physiologists, has naturally been directed to these. A brief review of the conclusions regarding the physiologic changes which occur as a result of improved physical condition will suggest possible tests for degrees of health and fitness.

Certain differences between active and inactive animals throw light on these functional variations. The wild hare, which lives an active life in the open, and the wild rabbit, which lives an inactive life in seclusion and does not venture far from its burrow, have been compared by Dreyer[10] of Oxford University. He found that a wild hare has double the blood volume, 30 per cent more hemoglobin and three times more heart muscle than a wild rabbit of the same weight. The rate of heartbeat of the wild hare is about 68, and of the wild rabbit about 200 per min. The respiration rate of the hare is between 18 and 20, and of the rabbit about 50 per min. Furthermore, the meat of the hare is dark, and that of the rabbit light in color. No doubt, similar differences exist between an athlete and a sedentary worker, and there is reason to believe that these functional differences vary to some extent as the health and fitness of the individual person vary.

The cardiovascular changes during altered physical fitness have been studied most, and it is these that are considered in this paper. The tests here discussed should not be confused with functional heart tests. We are concerned with the cardiovascular changes only so far as they give evidence of fatigue and health changes in the body.

The Pulse Rate as a Criterion of Health

(a) *The Postural Rates.* Cook and Pembrey,[5] while finding considerable variation in the pulse rate of different healthy individuals, showed, however, more frequently a slow rate in men trained for muscular work. From his extensive experience, Meylan[20] concluded that a horizontal posture pulse rate between 40 and 80 and a vertical posture rate between 50 and 90 were favorable health signs. McCurdy,[18] from a study of boys passing through the adolescent changes, decided that the heart rate serves as a fair indication of condition; a high heart rate indicates poor condition, and a heart rate with wide variations between the horizontal and standing positions suggests a poor vascular adjustment.

During repeated periods of training of a single subject, Dawson[8] found that training slowed the resting pulse rate as much as 9 beats per min and that this especially influenced the noon and afternoon pulse. Thus the form of the diurnal curve was slightly altered. He also found that acute infection caused an increase in the pulse rate, but this was much less pronounced in the trained than in the untrained man. In young men, the normal average pulse rate has been reported to be 78.9 standing, 70.1 sitting, and 66.6 lying. The continued practice of some form of exercise, such as rowing, extending over a period of years may progressively

lower the rate of heart beat. Thus Michell[21] found the average rate of the athlete's pulse during the first year of training was 69, in the second year, 64.5 and in the third year, 56.8. According to Lindhard,[17] not only is the pulse less frequent, but the output of the heart per minute is slightly larger in the trained than in the untrained man.

All available evidence indicates that with improvement in physical fitness the heart beats less frequently and more efficiently. It follows, therefore, that the pulse rates in the reclining and standing postures may at times give useful hints as to the degree of fitness and health. That the altered physical condition may not be evidenced by pulse rate changes in both of these postural positions was demonstrated by Boney,[2] who found in some tired, listless, depressed, and fatigued patients that the pulse rate was normal while lying down but was abnormally rapid on standing; in several the standing rate was as high as 130 or 140 beats per min.

(b) *Pulse Rate Increase on Standing.* The difference between the pulse rates in the standing and reclining postures has been found to be a useful index of physical fitness. According to Vierordt,[24] the average postural increase is from 12 to 14 beats. Crampton[7] reported that in vigorous subjects the heart rate may not increase on standing, while in wearied subjects it may increase as much as 44 beats per min. Meylan[20] believes a standing increase of not more than 16 beats is a favorable sign of physical efficiency. Parkinson[22] recently reported that in 20 healthy soldiers an average increase of 10 beats was noted when the recumbent and standing rates were compared. Geigel[14] considers that a variation of more than

30 between lying and standing pulse rates indicates weakened heart function. It is now recognized that in states of debility the postural difference may be as much as from 30 to 50 per min. A slow horizontal and a slow vertical postural pulse rate with a small difference between the two are usually signs of excellent health.

(c) *Exercise Pulse Rate.* According to Bowen,[3] the rapidity of the pulse during exercise is chiefly determined by (a) the speed of movement; (b) the resistance encountered; (c) the condition of the individual, and (d) age. He[4] also pointed out that pulse rate counts made after exercise are worthless for comparison, unless the count is made at exactly the same period in each case, and the subject is placed in exactly the same position and assumes the same degree of relaxation and repose.

The increase in the pulse rate after a certain amount of work is greater in an untrained than in a trained person. Hartwell and Tweedy,[15] comparing athletic and nonathletic women, found that running up and down stairs accelerated the heart rate an average of 10 beats more in the nonathletic women. Cotton, Rapport, and Lewis[6] believe that the average height to which the pulse rate is raised at the cessation of effort may be taken as a gauge of the degree of distress produced, and that the amount of distress is determined by the degree of health. Similar conclusions have been reached by many students of the effects of exercise on acceleration of the pulse rate.

(d) *The Decline in Pulse Rate After Exertion.* A widely recognized sign of physical condition is the time required by the pulse rate to return to normal

after effort. Flack and Bowdler,[12] from a study of the reactions following stepping on a chair five times in 15 sec, conclude that the heart rate in the healthy subject should not increase more than 25 beats and should return to normal within 30 sec. Meakins and Gunson[19] report that after a climb of 27 steps at a brisk walk, the pulse rate returned to normal within 1 min in healthy subjects, while in patients it required as much as 5 min.

It should be emphasized that while the several pulse rate criteria of fitness may all be found in a single person, not one or even any two of them is found to be an absolute test. In forming a judgment as to the physical condition of a man it is best to consider together the postural rates, the increase on standing and after exercise, and the time required for the rate to return to normal after exercise.

The Arterial Blood Pressure as a Criterion of Condition

(a) *The Normal Arterial Pressures.* Although the arterial pressures have received much attention, the determination of the pressures of a person at rest offers little of value in estimating the physical condition of the young man. Meylan[20] considers systolic pressures for the horizontal posture between 110 and 140, and for the vertical position between 110 and 150 mm of mercury as favorable signs. Dearborn[9] believes that adequate physical training raises the blood pressure. He obtained an average of 114 in trained and 108 in untrained women. Dawson[8] has recently shown that the effect of training on the resting blood pressure is neither striking nor constant. Bainbridge[1] has written that "the systolic arterial pressure, according to most observers, is not higher during rest in trained than in untrained men."

Opinion as to the value of the diastolic and pulse pressures is not as clearly crystallized as it is regarding the systolic pressure. Hypotension in systolic or diastolic pressure occurs in weak patients.

(b) *The Postural Changes in Arterial Pressures.* The hydrostatic effects of posture and the manner in which the splanchnic vasomotor mechanism compensates for these are well known. Normally, when man changes from the reclining to the standing position, the splanchnic vasomotor tone overcompensates the hydrostatic effects of gravity. In normal subjects the systolic blood pressure is about 10 mm higher in the standing than in the recumbent posture. Erlanger and Hooker[11] found that on standing there might be either a slight rise or fall in the brachial systolic pressure. According to Hill,[16] any influence which weakens the splanchnic vasomotor mechanism interferes with the compensation. Sewall[23] has shown that individuals in whom there is excessive gravitation of the blood to the limbs and splanchnic area on standing are victims of physical weakness and nervous instability and often suffer from headache, dizziness, or tinnitus in the erect posture. That the systolic pressure falls in persons weakened by dissipation, overwork, lack of sleep, or disease was recognized by Crampton in his "blood ptosis test" for physical fitness. Crampton[7] demonstrated that a subject might, when standing, show weakness by a decrease in the systolic pressure or by a large increase in the heart rate. Recently, Sewall[23] has pointed out that a weakened patient on standing may fail to show the systolic drop, but instead may have an inordinate rise in diastolic pressure. He employs this rise in diastolic pressure and low levels of pulse pressure as measures of fitness.

Means of Measuring Physical Efficiency

The foregoing observations on the cardiovascular changes that occur with training and with weakness suggest means of measuring fatigue, staleness, and weakness. A pulse rate more rapid than the average in the reclining and standing postures, a large acceleration on standing and after exertion, a slow return to normal after exercise, and a systolic pressure that fails to rise but falls when the subject stands, indicate fatigue or weakness.

In 1913 and 1914, three physical efficiency tests were reported that used some or all of these changes. Crampton's[7] "blood ptosis test" is a vasomotor efficiency test that is intended to show the beneficial or depressive effect of various conditions supposed to affect the health. It takes account of the differences between the pulse rates and the systolic pressures in the horizontal and vertical postures. The usual range of systolic pressure variation is from $+10$ to -10, and the heart rate increase from zero to 44. It was determined that a decrease of 1 mm in systolic pressure was equivalent to an increase in heart rate of approximately two beats. By statistically balancing the ranges of systolic pressure and pulse rate and assigning equal percentages to equal ranges, a percentage scale of fitness was established.

Meylan,[20] although not attempting to evaluate, finds that efficiency may be judged by (a) general condition as shown in weight, color of skin, and general appearances such as firm, vigorous muscles; (b) pulse rate in the horizontal and vertical positions; (c) systolic blood pressure in the horizontal and vertical positions, and (d) heart reaction after the exercise of hopping

100 ft. Favorable signs were considered to be a horizontal pulse rate between 40 and 80, a vertical rate between 50 and 90, and a standing increase of not more than 16; a horizontal blood pressure between 100 and 140, and a vertical pressure between 110 and 150, with a difference of 10 or more; an exercise increase in pulse rate of less than 100 per cent and a recovery of more than 80 per cent in a minute.

Foster's[13] efficiency test made use of the standing pulse rate, the rate immediately after running in a fixed place for exactly 15 sec at the rate of 180 steps per min, and the rate 45 sec after the work ceased.

Crampton's test was employed with the aviators at Hazelhurst Field, but was found to be unsatisfactory because of the fact that physical deterioration may be mainfest in various ways in the cardiovascular mechanism. The test neglects four of the available factors. A similar criticism may be made of Foster's method. A statistical study of several hundred cases led to the abandonment of both of these methods.

Point System For Grading Cardiovascular Reactions

When it becomes necessary to weigh data from six sets of observations, it is difficult to evaluate them properly and avoid giving undue weight to a single factor. If it is true, as it seems to be, that weakness may show itself differently in individual cases, then a centering of the attention only on the postural systolic blood pressure changes or on the amount of acceleration of the pulse rate in exercise would result in the overlooking of some cases of weakness. In order to avoid the disposition to stress, one or two of the factors that give evidence of physical deterioration, and to recognize equally all six factors, we have used a system of scoring the

tests wherein each of the cardiovascular changes is rated according to a scale that evaluates the condition or change. The grading of performance must of necessity be arbitrary and, therefore, is held by some to be objectionable. Nevertheless, as was stated earlier, the "personal equation" of the observer often weighs too heavily where comparisons are made. A mathematical system of grading can in large measure eliminate the personal factor.

The scoring scheme we have used recognizes that fatigue or derangement may be evidenced in the high heart rate during reclining, during standing; in the number of beats the heart rate increases when the standing and reclining postures are compared; in the acceleration in the pulse rate after exercise; in the time take by the pulse to return to normal, and lastly, in the rise or fall in the systolic blood pressure on standing. This scheme uses in part a plan proposed by Dr. J. H. McCurdy for rating infantry men in cardiovascular and neuromuscular efficiency. The scores for each of the six items range from $+3$ to -3. A perfect score, the sum of the value given to each of the six items, is 18. The values as assigned appear in Table 1, Parts A, B, C, D, E, and F. In using the table for scoring, Parts A and B, also C and D, must always be used together. Thus, if an individual has a pulse rate increase of 15 beats (see Part B) on standing and his reclining rate was 60 (see Part A), he is graded 3 on his standing increase. However, if his reclining rate had been 100, then a standing increase of 15 would have been scored zero.

Procedure in Making Observations

1. The patient reclines for 5 min. (*a*) The heart rate is then counted for 20 sec. When two consecutive 20-sec counts are the same, this is multiplied

TABLE 1

Points For Grading Cardiovascular Changes

A. RECLINING PULSE RATE		B. PULSE RATE INCREASE ON STANDING				
		0–10 Beats, Points	11–18 Beats, Points	19–26 Beats, Points	27–34 Beats, Points	35–42 Beats, Points
Rate	Points					
50– 60	3	3	3	2	1	0
61– 70	3	3	2	1	0	−1
71– 80	2	3	2	0	−1	−2
81– 90	1	2	1	−1	−2	−3
91–100	0	1	0	−2	−3	−3
101–110	−1	0	−1	−3	−3	−3

C. STANDING PULSE RATE		D. PULSE RATE INCREASE IMMEDIATELY AFTER EXERCISE				
		0–10 Beats, Points	11–20 Beats, Points	21–30 Beats, Points	31–40 Beats, Points	41–50 Beats, Points
Rate	Points					
60– 70	3	3	3	2	1	0
71– 80	3	3	2	1	0	0
81– 90	2	3	2	1	0	−1
91–100	1	2	1	0	−1	−2
101–110	1	1	0	−1	−2	−3
111–120	0	1	−1	−2	−3	−3
121–130	0	0	−2	−3	−3	−3
131–140	−1	0	−3	−3	−3	−3

E. RETURN OF PULSE RATE TO STANDING NORMAL AFTER EXERCISE		F. SYSTOLIC PRESSURE, STANDING, COMPARED WITH RECLINING	
Seconds	Points	Change in mm	Points
0– 60	3	Rise of 8 or more	3
61– 90	2	Rise of 2–7	2
91–120	1	No rise	1
After 120: 2– 10 beats above normal	0	Fall of 2–5	0
After 120: 11– 30 beats above normal	−1	Fall of 6 or more	−1

by 3 and recorded. The score is noted according to Part A, Table 1. (*b*) The systolic blood pressure is next taken by auscultation; two or three readings are made as a check.

2. (*a*) The patient stands at ease for 1 or 2 min to allow the pulse to assume a uniform rate. When two consecutive 20-sec counts are the same, this is multiplied by 3 and recorded. The score is obtained by use of Part C, Table 1. The difference between the standing and reclining pulse rates is scored then by use of Part B, Table 1. (*b*) The standing systolic pressure is next taken. The difference between this and the reclining systolic pressure is then scored by Part F, Table 1.

3. The patient next steps on a chair about 18 in. high, five times in 15 sec timed by a watch. To make this test uniform, he stands with one foot on the chair at the count one; this foot remains on the chair and is not brought

to the floor again until after the count five. At each count he brings the other foot on the chair and at the count "down" replaces it on the floor. This should be timed accurately, so that at the 15-sec mark both feet are on the floor. (*a*) Immediately, while he stands at ease, the pulse rate is counted for 15 sec; this is multiplied by 4 and recorded. (*b*) Counting is continued in 15-sec intervals for 2 min, record being made of the counts at 60, 90, and 120 sec.

The data from *a* will be scored by Part D, Table 1, taking the difference between this exercise pulse rate and the standing rate. The data in *b* are scored according to Part E, Table 1.

This system of scoring men as to physical fitness is now being used by flight surgeons in their work among aviators, and is applied at the Medical Research Laboratory at Mitchel Aviation Field on Long Island.

That there may be value in assembling the circulatory data under such a point system is indicated from an analysis of 54 cases of aviators who, when examined by the medical officers of the departments of the laboratory, were found to be ailing and physically below standard. The medical examinations included an overhaul by the internist, neurologist, ophthalmologist, and ear, nose, and throat expert. The medical findings include a large variety of conditions, the majority being common to any group of men and in no way characteristic of aviators.

That which was of greatest interest in this analysis was the final efficiency score of each patient. The distribution of the cases is shown in Table 2.

Only 6 of the 54 cases had a score of 10 or better, while 88.8 per cent had scores ranging between 9 and −1. These figures seem to indicate that a score of 9 or less is characteristic of physically unfit men.

TABLE 2
Efficiency Score in Fifty-Four Cases

	Points	No. of Cases	%
	0 or less............	2	3.7
From	1 to 3	9	16.6
	4 to 6	15	27.8
	7 to 9	22	40.7
	10 to 12	3	5.6
	13 to 15	3	5.6
	16 to 18	0	0.0
	Total.............	54	100.0

On the assumption that a score of 9 or less gives indication that the clinician may find something wrong with the patient, we have listed all men among a group of 150 men who had a low score. In this group there were 46 who scored 9 or less.

The medical examiners working independently, and without the cardiovascular data available to them, recorded abnormal conditions in 30 of the 46 men. Thus, when working independently, 65.2 per cent of the group of 46 with low scores by the cardiovascular efficiency test were found by others to be below standard. Two of the men were unfit because of excessive smoking, and one had recently been on a drunken spree. The neurologist reported five as stale and nervously unbalanced, the internist alone found five unfit, six were tonsil or local, infection cases, and the remainder were found wrong by at least two of the medical departments.

This point system of scoring men as to health and physical fitness by the cardiovascular reactions is easily applied. It has the advantage of stimulating men to attempt to improve the score by exercise and proper living. It is suggested that a score of 9 or less gives reason for an overhaul of the patient by a clinician. Aviators with a low score might well be called back for further examination and observation. A poor score suggests a search for a cause. The cause may be disease or unhygienic living.

References

1. Bainbridge, *The Physiology of Muscular Exercise.* London: Longmans, Green & Co., 1919, p. 142.

2. Boney, *Brit. Med. J.,* **2** (1916), 645.

3. Bowen, *Am. Phys. Educ. Rev.,* **8** (1903), 8.

4. Bowen, *ibid.,* **8** (1903), 232.

5. Cook and Pembray, *J. Physiol. (London),* **45** (1913), 438.

6. Cotton, Rapport, and Lewis, *Heart Bull.,* **6** (1917), 269.

7. Crampton, *Proc. Soc. Exptl. Biol. Med.,* **12** (1915), 119.

8. Dawson, *Am. J. Physiol.,* **50** (December, 1919), 443.

9. Dearborn, *Am. Phys. Educ. Rev.,* **20** (1915), 337, 414.

10. Dreyer, cited by M. Flack and L. Hill, *Text-Book of Physiology.* New York: David McKay Co., Inc., 1919, p. 79.

11. Erlanger and Hooker, *Johns Hopkins Hopsital Report,* **12** (1904), 145.

12. Flack and Bowdler, *Reports of the Air Medical Investigations Committee.* London, *No. 2* (1918), p. 12.

13. Foster, *Am. Phys. Educ. Rev.,* **19** (1914), 632.

14. Geigel, *Deut. Arch. klin. Med.,* **99** (1906), 1028.

15. Hartwell and Tweedy, *J. Physiol. (London),* **46** (1913), 9.

16. Hill, *ibid.,* **18** (1895), 15.

17. Lindhard, *Pflügers Arch. ges. Physiol.,* **161** (1915), 233.

18. McCurdy, *Am. Phys. Educ. Rev.,* **15** (1910), 421.

19. Meakins and Gunson, *Special Report of the Medical Reasearch Committee.* London, *No. 8* (1918), p. 27; *Heart Bull.,* **6** (1917), 284.

20. Meylan, *Am. Phys. Educ. Rev.,* **18** (1913), 441.

21. Michell, cited by M. Flack and L. Hill, *Text-Book of Physiology.* New York: David McKay Co., 1919, p. 216.

22. Parkinson, *Heart Bull.,* **6** (1917), 317.

23. Sewall, *Am. J. Med. Sci.,* **158** (1919), 786.

24. Vierordt, *Anatomische, physiologische und physikalische Daten und Tabellen.* Jena: G. Fischer, 1906, p. 235.

W. W. TUTTLE

The Use of the Pulse-Ratio Test for Rating Physical Efficiency

Reprinted from the *Research Quarterly,*
2 (1931), 5–18.

As a physiologist, Tuttle, as well as Schneider, was concerned with pulse rate response to exercise. He investigated the application of the pulse ratio technique to specific physical activities and sports. Tuttle acknowledges that the idea for the pulse-ratio test originated in the work of Hambly and Hunt in England during the 1920's. The pulse ratio as defined by Tuttle represents the ratio of resting pulse rate to the rate after exercise. The standard exercise he chose for his subjects consisted of stepping on a 13-in. stool, because this height was commonplace it would eliminate undue stress and possible variations that might invalidate the test. Tuttle developed the concept of a standard pulse ratio (2.5 was selected as an empirical value) in order to compare the amount of work required to produce the ratio by individuals of different levels of cardiovascular fitness.

The results of additional studies by Tuttle and his graduate students on the relationship of the pulse ratio to performance in such specialized activities as gymnastics and swimming showed that the pulse ratio indicates which of the participants are expert and which are less skilled. An interesting point, in the light of contemporary studies on smoking, is the report by Tuttle which shows the relative inefficiency on the pulse-ratio test of smokers as compared to nonsmokers. Although these findings have been refuted by more recent studies (cf. Karpovich and Hale in Chapter VI), the fact that the pulse-ratio tests did detect differences as subtle as the effect of smoking on physical condition is an indication of the importance of this technique. More recent research has raised some questions about the value of employing the pulse-ratio test to differentiate among athletes of similar levels of fitness. At present, it is felt that the pulse-ratio technique is more valuable in identifying groups of individuals at various levels of fitness than as a means for predicting athletic performance.

The increase in demand for graduate theses in the Physiology of Exercise, by students in physical education, has stimulated rather extensive research in a number of fields. Out of the various investigations carried on in this laboratory, a technique has been developed for rating physical efficiency by means of a pulse-ratio test. The technique is of such a type that the test not only applies to problems which are general in nature but also to the more specialized sports. Since numerous papers are appearing from time to time involving similar technique, it seems more economical to present a rather detailed discussion of the pulse-ratio technique in one paper, rather than to treat it more or less inadequately in several publications.

121

The original idea for the pulse-ratio test as it is now being used in this laboratory, came from the work of Hambly[2,3] and Hunt[4]. Dr. J. T. McClintock[5] has made use of Hambly's technique for rating physical efficiency in his laboratory for a number of years. When the problem of physical efficiency was suggested as a project in the Physiology of Exercise, Dr. McClintock suggested to the writer that he develop a pulse-ratio test which could be applied to such problems.

The commonly accepted idea concerning the response of the heart to exercise, reinforced by rather extensive research on various phases of the problem, is that cardiovascular response reflects the physiological condition of the individual. This idea suggests the possibility of adopting some measure of cardiovascular response as a means of rating physical efficiency. If a test of such a nature is to be employed, the validity of the test is the first consideration. No doubt one might approach this problem from many angles. We have been interested in adopting some method which eliminated complicated apparatus and procedures. The simplicity of the pulse-ratio technique, together with its flexibility, prompted a rather extensive investigation of its possibilities. The paramount idea in mind is the development of some test for rating physical efficiency which is practical for use by coaches, and one which they can handle with a high degree of accuracy.

In this laboratory our primary interest is the application of the pulse-ratio test to problems in physical education. It need not, however, be confined to this field. The test, as described, may be applied to any individual or group of individuals where a comparative rating of physical efficiency is desired.

The Pulse Ratio Defined

The pulse ratio, as we use it, represents the ratio of the resting pulse rate to the rate after exercise. This ratio is found by dividing the total pulse for 2 min after a known amount of exercise by the normal resting pulse for 1 min. Suppose the normal resting pulse for 1 min is 70 and the total pulse for 2 min after a prescribed exercise is 210. Then the pulse ratio is represented by 210/70 or 3.0.

The Technique Employed in Rating Physical Efficiency by Means of the Pulse-Ratio Test

The technique employed in rating physical efficiency by means of the pulse-ratio test is, on the face of it, quite simple. Our experience has taught us, however, that there are many pitfalls, and chances for variation, which are sufficient to destroy the usefulness of the test.

The standard work employed. If one is to use the heart response to exercise for comparing the reaction of different individuals, or the same individual under different conditions, a standard exercise, applicable to all, must be adopted. In selecting standard exercise some type must be chosen that requires practically no skill and that is available almost anywhere. Hambly and his co-workers investigated various types of exercise such as walking, stair climbing, and running. His investigations, together with our own, have led to the adoption of stool climbing. The stool commonly used is 13 in. high, and of such dimensions that it may be mounted and dismounted satisfactorily. This exercise can be performed by any normal individual without experience and without being conscious of any undue stress or strain. This type of standard work is not only convenient but it is extremely flexible. It is possible to vary the amount of work performed to suit the experiment under consideration. This is done either by varying the rate of stepping or by increasing the number of steps at a uniform rate. One may use 15, 20, 25, 30, 35, 40, 45 steps per min. Here we might add that the upper limit is about 60, due to the inability of the majority of people to mount and dismount at a faster rate. On the other hand, one may vary the amount of exercise by using, say, 20 steps per min for 1, 2, or 3 min as indicated by the experiment.

The act of mounting and dismounting is carried out in a regular cadence, determined by counting 1, 2, 3, and 4. The subject is seated in such proximity to the stool that when he rises he is in a position to begin the work. At the count of 1, the left foot is placed on the stool; at the count of 2, the right foot is placed on top of the stool. Now the subject is in an upright position on top of the stool. At the count of 3, the left foot is placed on the floor, and at the count of 4, the right foot is placed on the floor. Now the subject is standing in front of the stool as in the beginning. The act having been completed, the subject is ready for a second trial.

The cadence used is acquired by the experimenter either by a stop watch or a metronome. By practice an experimenter soon acquires the proper rate of counting for whatever rate he desires to use. By calibrating a metronome, the technique is enhanced and guides the experimenter in his counting rhythm.

In this laboratory a calibrated metronome has been adopted (Type F782, Central Scientific Co., Chicago, Ill.). This particular metronome was adopted because it is equipped with a signal bell which is set to ring every fourth beat. The apparatus has been calibrated so that various amounts of exercise are indicated on the scale. For the convenience of those who might wish to use this metronome the calibrations are given. In each case the top of the pendulum weight is set at the metronome scale as indicated.

Exercise per min	Metronome Scale
12 steps	40
18 steps	66
20 steps	76
25 steps	96
30 steps	120
35 steps	138
40 steps	160

Suppose the initial exercise adopted is 18 steps per min. The top of the pendulum weight is set at 66 on the metronome scle. The subject is instructed as follows: Listen to the metronome. Get the rhythm in mind. Listen for the signal bell. At the first beat after the signal, place the left foot on the stool. (The start may be made with either the right or left foot according to the handedness of the subject.) On the second beat, place the right foot on the stool. Now the subject is in an upright position on the stool. On the third beat the left foot is placed on the floor and on the fourth beat, as the bell rings, the right foot is placed on the floor. Now the subject is standing in front of the stool, ready to repeat the exercise. The experimenter need pay no attention to the cadence of the stepping but he must count the number of completed trials which are indicated by the ringing of the bell. If 18 steps is the exercise performed, at the count of 18, the subjects stops, seats himself in the chair. The pulse is immediately counted.

Since standard work is the object of the stool climbing, there are several points to be observed in order to preserve uniformity. In each trial the subject must assume a uniform position on top of the stool. In addition, uniformity in the position and action of the arms must be adopted. In this laboratory, the elbows are kept in contact with the body, the forearm held stationary at right angles to the body. This position is assumed because it seems more natural, and a stationary member is more easily controlled than one which is swinging.

It is advisable to give each subject a few practice trials before the test is given. This serves a dual purpose in that it acquaints him with the exercise he is to perform as well as making him more stable physiologically.

The standard of comparison. If we are to compare the efficiency ratings of different individuals or those of the same individual under different conditions, some standard of comparison must be set up. This is done by adopting a standard pulse ratio that remains constant, and allowing the amount of standard exercise required to produce it to be the variable factor. The standard pulse ratio adopted in this laboratory is 2.5. This is an empirical value. It has been adopted because experience has shown that this ratio may be obtained by the majority of individuals by moderate amounts of exercise. This value is found, as previously stated, by dividing the total pulse for 2 min after a known amount of exercise by the normal resting pulse for 1 min. Since the 2.5 pulse ratio is empirical, if occasion demanded, some other value, such as 2.3 or 2.4, might be substituted without detracting from the value of the test.

The method for determining the amount of work required to produce a pulse ratio of 2.5. The next question to be considered is, how is the amount of work required to produce a pulse ratio of 2.5 determined? In the first place, this value is determined as "number of steps per minute." The basis of rating one's efficiency is, then, the number of

steps required to produce this 2.5 pulse ratio. This value is determined by mathematical formula derived from a graphic calculation where we have given one value distinctly below and one distinctly above the 2.5 ratio. The lower value must be more than 2.0 since merely doubling the normal pulse rate gives this value. The details are as follows: An amount of work is selected, usually 18 steps for 1 min, which gives a pulse ratio below 2.5. Then a second rate is employed, usually 30 or 40 steps for 1 min, which gives a value above 2.5. These data permit the establishment of two points on the graph. The first one is found by plotting the known number of steps on the abscissa and the resulting pulse ratio on the ordinate. The second point is determined in the same manner. The next step in the procedure is to connect these two points by a straight line. Now, by dropping an ordinate from the place where the line connecting the two values just determined crosses the 2.5 abscissa, to the base line representing the number of steps, the mathematical value in number of steps is indicated.

It is seen that the pulse-ratios are plotted on the ordinate to the scale of 0.1 pulse ratio equals 1 cm. This makes possible the plotting of the pulse-ratio values in hundredth places which are represented by millimeters. The amount of exercise is plotted on the abscissa to the scale of 1 cm equals five steps. In the illustration presented, 15 steps produced a pulse ratio of 2.24. Thirty steps gave a pulse-ratio of 2.80. The line connecting these two points crosses the 2.5 abscissa at a point where, if an ordinate is dropped to the base line, 22 steps are mathematically required to produce a pulse ratio of 2.5. Twenty-two steps, then, is the figure adopted for comparing the subject with either himself under different conditions or with other individuals.

The first rate of exercise, 15 or 18 steps for 1 min, presents no difficulty, since almost any light exercise will produce in most subjects a pulse ratio of more than 2.0 and less than 2.5. In case of the higher ratio, one may experience some difficulty. If it should happen that 30 steps is not strenuous enough to give a value above 2.5, this obstacle is easily overcome by increasing the rate of stepping to, say, 40 steps per min. Our experience has shown that 40 steps is usually adequate.

The determination of the pulse rate. The determination of the pulse rate, although quite a simple technique, presents sufficient difficulties to destroy the validity of the pulse-ratio test if certain precautions are not observed. The main consideration is uniformity. It is more or less immaterial whether normal sitting or standing pulse is used. In this laboratory both positions have been employed. We believe, however, that sitting pulse is preferable to standing pulse. One finds that the normal standing pulse tends to increase somewhat due to the effort required in standing.

The ausculatory method is the most reliable for determining the pulse rate. Time is best checked by a stop watch. The pulse is considered as normal when in 3 full 1-min counts, with 1 min elapsing between each count, the same figures are obtained. A variation in a beat or two may be disregarded, and charged to experimental error. In all cases, the full time must be counted. For the normal rate this is 1 min and after exercise 2 min. Experience and good judgment are the important factors in determining pulse rate.

The reading of the pulse for 2 min after exercise should begin at the instant the subject places both feet on the floor following the last trial of his exercise. The beginning of the count is important since compensation begins very soon after exercise and a delay in starting the count leads to serious error.

Consideration must be given to the length of time elapsing between the first exercise and the second. Since the first exercise is very mild, not more than 5 min need elapse. In the absence of fatigue, the criterion to be followed in determining this interval is the pulse rate. When the heart has returned to normal, the second exercise may be done. If it is necessary to repeat the more strenuous exercise, 10–15 min rest may be necessary. The criterion is again the pulse rate.

If, in any case, repetition of the test is of sufficient severity to induce fatigue, there is another complication. Successive trials of so mild an exercise as 15 steps for 1 min cause a progressive increase in the resulting pulse ratios. For example, in an experiment where we gave five successive tests to the same individual with not more than 10 min rest between trials, although the heart rate appeared normal, there was a progressive increase in the resulting pulse ratios as follows:

For test 1, 15 steps
gave a pulse ratio of 2.20
2	2.30
3	2.40
4	2.45
5	2.50

Another condition which must be avoided is the application of the test too soon after the individuals have participated in strenuous exercise, such as 40 min of basketball. In these cases the slightest amount of exercise causes an abnormal cardiac response, the rate being far in excess of the results obtained before strenuous exercise. These findings are in accord with the generally accepted idea that fatigue increases the irritability of the cardiovascular system.

Method for determining efficiency ratings. For the purpose of comparing data, the number of steps required to produce a 2.5 pulse ratio is converted into per cent efficiency. Various methods have been employed for doing this. In some instances, the individual in a group under investigation who required the greatest number of steps to produce a 2.5 pulse ratio has been assumed to be 100 per cent efficient. In other cases some arbitrary number of steps, for example 80, has been assumed as representing 100 per cent efficiency. As a matter of convenience we let 50 steps for 1 min represent the amount of exercise required to produce a pulse ratio of 2.5 in a highly efficient individual. For sake of calculation the value 100 is assigned to this individual. Fifty steps for 1 min is adopted since this number falls above the requirements for a 2.5 pulse ratio of the fittest individual which we examined, while at the same time this figure is not far

above the requirements of our best athletes. Now, by substituting the amount of exercise, expressed in number of steps, required to produce a 2.5 pulse ratio in the formula

$$\text{Efficiency Rating} = \frac{100 \,(\text{No. steps required for 2.5 pulse ratio})}{50}$$

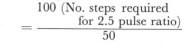

the data are reduced to an arbitrary per cent basis.

In order that the data may be conveniently classified and recorded, a record sheet is prepared.

The record sheet. A sample record sheet is presented here. It provided space for a subject's history as well as for recording the pulse rates, pulse ratios, determined exercise, and per cent efficiency ratings. The heart rate is recorded in one-half minute intervals. This is convenient for giving a clue to the time of the return to normal.

RECORD SHEET

Physical Efficiency as Rated by the Pulse-Ratio Test

Name, ... John Jones .... Date .... 1–5–31 ....

Age ....22........ Height .... 5'11″ .... Weight ....165........

Physical Condition .... In athletic training. ....

    I.   Normal Sitting Pulse Rate
        1.   35
        2.   35   Total 70

   II.   Heart Rate After 15 Steps of Exercise
        1.   45   2.   40   3.   36   4.   36
                                 Total 157
                                 Ratio 2.24

  III.   Heart Rate After 30 Steps of Exercise
        1.   70   2.   50   3.   40   4.   36
                                 Total 196
                                 Ratio 2.80

  IV.   Steps Required to Produce 2.5 Pulse Ratio, 22*

         Per Cent Efficiency Rating $\dfrac{22 \times 100}{50} = 44.0\%$

---

* The method for determining the number of steps required to produce a 2.5 pulse ratio in this case is shown in Fig. 2.

The validity of the theoretical values determined by the graphic method. A crucial point in this test is the validity of the mathematical number of steps, as determined by the graphic method, to produce a 2.5 pulse ratio. If these values thus determined are not valid, then the whole scheme is useless. This phase of the procedure has been thoroughly investigated, sufficient data having been collected to justify conclusions. A detailed discussion of the experimental check as it has been carried out will be omitted from this discussion, but will be presented in a separate paper.[10] An investigation of nearly a hundred cases shows that the values determined by the graphic method are valid. In fact, the predicted values have been found to be as accurate as those experimentally determined.

The Application of the Pulse-Ratio Test to the More Specialized Sports

The flexibility of the pulse-ratio test seemed to warrant an attempt to apply it to some of the more specialized sports. The experiments which have been carried out have proven quite successful in the opinion of the coaches in their special fields of endeavor.

Since the basis of this test is controlled exercise, then any sport which involves definite rhythmic movements may be investigated. Such a condition exists in the case of sports involving gymnasium apparatus and swimming.

The application of the pulse-ratio test to performance on the horizontal bar.[11] Performance on the horizontal bar involves exercises such as chinning, hanging, and flexing thighs to a right angle to body, etc. The only difference involved in making general and specific use of the pulse-ratio test is the type of standard exercise employed. For general application the standard exercise is mounting a stool, while for the horizontal bar the specific movement being investigated is substituted for the stool mounting. This is feasible because the definite movements involved make them as suitable for standard controlled exercise as mounting a stool. Instead of varying the rate of performance per minute, the rate is kept constant and the number of trials varied. The remaining procedure is exactly the same. For example, in case of chinning, two trials gave a pulse ratio of 2.4 while eight trials gave a ratio of 2.7. The graphic method of determination indicates that in order to produce a pulse ratio of 2.5 the subject must perform four trials. Now by comparing the number of trials of a given exercise necessary to produce a 2.5 ratio, athletes participating in the sport may be compared as to their efficiency in the sport.

That the pulse-ratio test points out differences in one's ability to perform on the horizontal bar is shown by a brief discussion of our findings. When the accomplishments of an athlete who was recognized as an expert on this piece of apparatus and who was in training was compared with the mean accomplishments of 30 men picked at random it was quite clear that the trained athlete was far superior to the untrained. There were some in the group who were specialists in some of the exercises. Where this was true the data show them as such. The only criterion available for checking the data is the fact that a number of the men were members of competitive teams, while others were beginners. The data paralleled these facts.

The application of the pulse-ratio test to exercise on the parallel bars.[7] An experiment similar to the one just described, involving the parallel bars, has been completed. Here again the only variation in the procedure is the substitution of exercises on the parallel bars for the stool climbing. The results show that, as in the case of the horizontal bar, the trained subject is far superior to the untrained. To be more specific, an expert on the parallel bars required eight trials of jumping to cross rest and dismounting, untrained subjects required as few as one trial, the mean of 30 subjects picked at random being four.

In sports where skill of a specialized kind is required, efficiency takes on a twofold aspect, viz. skill and physical fitness. A subject who is truly physically fit, yet untrained in a highly specialized sport, will naturally fall among the inefficient by the pulse-ratio criterion. On the other hand, one who is skillful, yet in poor physical condition, will likewise be classified as inefficient.

The application of the pulse-ratio test to efficiency in swimming. The flexibility of the pulse-ratio test makes it applicable for measuring efficiency in swimming. It is necessary, however, to confine the test to trained swimmers. Each recognized stroke in swimming involves very definite, smooth, and coordinated movements. It seems reasonable to suppose, then, that ability in swimming technique materially affects one's swimming efficiency. Here again both physical fitness and swimming technique are determining factors. Armbruster[1] is carrying on a study of the efficiency of his varsity swimming squad. He varied the pulse-ratio technique by substituting swimming strokes for stool climbing. Although the study is yet incomplete, the data show that practice and training materially affect the efficiency of the swimmers.

The use of the pulse ratio test for separating technique efficiency and physical

efficiency. The data obtained on this phase of the work are too meager for generalization. However, the possibility of separating physical and technical efficiency is not a remote one. The approach to this problem is a comparison of the efficiency, where exercise requiring no skill (stool climbing) is used as the basis, with efficiency where exercises requiring skill are employed. That there is a difference is easily demonstrated. It is also easy to show that by giving attention to either variable, that is physical condition or training technique, the difference between physical efficiency and technical efficiency may be decreased.[6]

Evidence that the Pulse-Ratio Test Points Out Differences in Physical Efficiency

The basis of the pulse-ratio test is the cardiac response to exercise. Past researches have shown conclusively that there is a wide individual variation in cardiac response to exercise as well as a wide variation in the same individual at different times and under different conditions. That physiological changes are reflected by a change in heart rate is easily demonstrated. Such factors as the emotions, fatigue, loss of sleep, and many other conditions change the heart rate. There is evidence that this change in heart rate as well as the rate of return to a normal level after exercise is an individual thing. Also it has been proven that the rate of return to normal may be altered. Such conditions as physical training, meals, fatigue, and loss of sleep have been shown to alter this process. It is, in fact, not a difficult task to understand why the heart responds to slight physiological changes when the controlling mechanism involved is considered. The vagal-sympathetic balance is easily disturbed as is the case with the calcium-potassium balance in the blood. In reality, there are at least eight possibilities for changing the rate of the heart beat. Familiarity of workers in this field with the compensatory mechanism of the heart justifies omission of a detailed discussion of it here.

The crucial test of the pulse-ratio technique is whether it shows the physiological changes which are reflected by the compensatory mechanism of the heart. Furthermore, if the pulse-ratio test does detect such differences we must determine whether there exists a definite relationship between the findings made by the test and the conditions which exist. In order to throw some light on this phase of the work, citation is made, briefly, to instances where this point has been investigated.

The investigations of Hambly and Hunt led them to believe that the pulse-ratio test was adequate in pointing out variations in physiological condition. In this laboratory, experiments have been carried out with high school boys,[9] college men,[12] and college women.[8] Such questions as the effect of fatigue, smoking, athletic training, physical condition, etc. have been investigated. This particular group of experiments was selected because the consensus of opinion is that such factors alter the cardiac response to exercise and are important as problems in physical education.

The evidence which we have gathered supports the thesis that the pulse-ratio test detects condition as reflected by the cardiovascular system. Attention is called at this time to some of our findings. In the experiment on the effect of smoking on the physical efficiency rating, the data show that for a group of 15 high school boys, their mean efficiency rating is 5 per cent less than the mean of those who abstain from this practice. Furthermore, the data

indicate that there are 95 chances in 100 that nonsmokers are at a distinct advantage from the standpoint of physical efficiency. True, the group studied is small, but certainly the results parallel the generally accepted view in regard to smoking. In order to substantiate these results, the physical efficiency of a group of ten university women, who are habitual smokers, was determined by the pulse-ratio test. They were found to be 13 per cent less efficient than the women who do not smoke. Abstinence from smoking is always stressed by athletic coaches. This "training rule" is no doubt one of tradition, based upon opinion of performance principally, but the pulse-ratio test substantiates this view. In fact, the test, if there is any virtue in it, shows conclusively that smoking is a detriment to athletes.

The extent to which women should indulge in athletics has always been a debatable question. The effect of athletic participation on women has been studied by use of the pulse-ratio test. It is interesting to note that when the physical efficiency of a group of 80 women participating in athletics is compared with 90 who indulge in no athletic training, the athletic group have a mean efficiency rating 6 per cent higher than the nonathletic group. Furthermore, the data indicate there are 95 chances in 100 that women participating in athletics will have a higher efficiency rating than those who ignore physical training. Here again, the tendencies indicated by the pulse-ratio test are in accord with the views generally expressed by authorities on this subject.

No one is willing to argue that fatigue is conducive to efficiency. The tendency pointed out by the pulse-ratio test is interesting. First, the problem of fatigue was considered from the standpoint of daily routine. Under these conditions a group of ten women were found to be 6 per cent less efficient at 10:00 P.M. than they were at 8:00 A.M. This seems logical. The question of fatigue was also investigated from the laboratory standpoint, where the conditions were under our control. The data show that fatigue induced by 250 deep knee bends decreases the efficiency rating 22 per cent. These results not only corroborate the diurnal findings, but are in accord with the general belief in regard to fatigue.

There is yet another finding that is of special interest. While following the efficiency of his football team by the pulse-ratio test, a coach recently directed our attention to an outstanding case. J. V., after one week of training, had an efficiency rating of 70 per cent. Very soon he received an injury which prevented him from training for a week or more. When he finally reported for practice his efficiency rating was 60 per cent. After two weeks of strenuous practice J. V.'s efficiency rating was 96 per cent. Ten days later the old injury was hurt, necessitating the abstinence from training for more than a week. Upon his return to the team, the efficiency rating was 44 per cent. The only available check on these data is the experience and observation of the coach. In his opinion, the results of the pulse-ratio test were authentic, in fact, so much so that he was willing to substitute it for his own judgment.

Many other experiments have been carried out with a similar trend, but a further discussion would add nothing to the evidence which we wish to present. The idea in mind in carrying out these investigations was to test the pulse-ratio test, and to establish its validity. The results of the investigations make it evident that the pulse-ratio test possesses much virtue. The data are somewhat meager for generalization, but the tendency is in favor

of the success of the pulse-ratio test for detecting the physiological changes reflected by the cardiovascular mechanism.

The use of the pulse-ratio test in this laboratory up to the present time has been limited to normal cases. However, a number of individuals with cardiovascular disturbances have been encountered. Although in our investigation they were eliminated, they deserve special comment.

Such cases were detected by the method employed for proving the validity of the graphic method as a means of determining the number of steps required for a 2.5 pulse ratio. A number of cases were encountered which could not be checked by our method, that is, when the calculated number of steps required for a 2.5 ratio was performed, the resulting pulse ratio was not 2.5.

Furthermore, it should be said that these cases were not detected by the routine physical examination to which they had been subject. Just how valuable the pulse-ratio test is in detecting cardiovascular disturbances has not yet been determined.

Summary

The technique employed in rating physical efficiency by means of the pulse-ratio test is described in detail. Evidence is submitted which supports the validity of the use of the test as a means of pointing out differences in physical efficiency.

Methods are described for applying the pulse-ratio test to highly specialized sports such as gymnastics and swimming. It is also suggested that where both physical efficiency and efficiency in technique are involved, these two phenomena may be tested separately by means of specialized use of the pulse-ratio test.

The writer wishes to acknowledge his indebtedness to Dr. J. T. McClintock for constant suggestions in carrying out the rather extensive program in the Physiology of Exercise. Credit is also due my graduate students who have enthusiastically carried out many of the experiments.

References

1. Armbruster, David, and W. W. Tuttle, "The Use of the Pulse-Ratio Test for Rating Efficiency in Swimming." Unpublished report, 1931.
2. Hambly, W. D., G. H. Hunt, L. E. L. Parker, M. S. Pembrey, and E. C. Warner, "Tests for Physical Efficiency," *Guys Hospital Report*, Part 2, **72** (1922), 367–85.
3. Hambly, W. D., M. S. Pembrey, and E. C. Warner, "The Physical Fitness of Men Assessed by Various Methods," *ibid.*, **75** (1925), 388–94.
4. Hunt, G. H., and M. S. Pembrey, "Tests of Physical Efficiency," *ibid.*, Part 1, **71** (1921), 415–28.
5. McClintock, J. T. Private communications, 1931.
6. Schroeder, E. G., "The Use of the Pulse-Ratio Test in Separating Physical Efficiency and Technique Efficiency." Unpublished report, 1931.
7. Schroeder, E. G., and W. W. Tuttle, "The Application of the Pulse-Ratio Test to Efficiency in Performing on Gymnasium Apparatus: The Parallel Bars." Unpublished report, 1931.
8. Tuttle, W. W., and Henryetta Frey, "A Study of the Physical Efficiency of College Women as Shown by the Pulse-Ratio Test," *Res. Quart.*, **1** (1930), 17–25.
9. Tuttle, W. W., and J. S. Skien, "The Efficiency Rating of High School Boys as Shown by the Pulse-Ratio Test," *Res. Quart.*, **1**, (1930), 19–33.
10. Tuttle, W. W., and Geo. Wells, "The Validity of the Graphic Method for Determining the Amount of Work Required to Produce a Given Pulse Ratio." Unpublished report, 1931.
11. Tuttle, W. W., and R. C. Wilkins, "The Application of the Pulse-Ratio Test to Efficiency in Performing on Gymnasium Apparatus: The Horizontal Bar," *Arbeitsphysiol.*, **3** (1930), 449–55.
12. Wells, Geo. A., "Study of the Physical Efficiency of High School and College Athletes by Means of the Pulse-Ratio Test." Unpublished report, 1929.

ARTHUR GROLLMAN

Physiological Variations in the Cardiac Output of Man

Reprinted from the *American Journal of Physiology*,
98 (1931), 8–15.

Although the indirect method of determining cardiac output used by Grollman has been largely displaced by the direct, or Fick method, this study is included here because this work was the first to establish the relationship of cardiac output and exercise. Some of the data might not be precise estimates of cardiac output, yet the essence of Grollman's conclusions are still largely valid. Cardiac output is the amount of blood pumped by the heart per unit time. It is expressed as minute volume, the amount pumped in a minute, or stroke volume which is the minute volume divided by the pulse rate. Resting cardiac output is about 4 l per min and in several exercises may rise as high as 35–40 l per min.

Grollman's study points out that cardiac output is not a simple function of oxygen consumption. While it is generally true that cardiac output and oxygen consumption are related, there is a fairly wide range in cardiac output for activities involving the same energy output (oxygen consumption) in mild exercise. Grollman suggests that the rate of muscular movement is the probable cause of this variation because cardiac output tends to increase as the rate of muscular activity increases. He refers to some earlier work by Lindhard, done in 1915 and 1920, to support his contention.

A key point with regard to physical education is that "better coordination of movements which results from training leads to an economy of movement and a lesser return of blood to the heart for a given amount of work." Taken in conjunction with the effect of training on the maximum stroke volume of the heart, this observation provides a cogent point in support of regular physical activity.

A knowledge of the changes in cardiac output which accompany muscular exercise is essential for an understanding of this important physiological state. Unfortunately, the methods available at present for determining the cardiac output render these determinations difficult under severe exercise and fraught with considerable error even in comparatively mild exercise. The previous extensive investigations on the subject by Krogh and Lindhard and subsequent workers using their method[15, 2, 24, 18, 19, 20, 21, 16, 17, 4, 13] were confined almost entirely to moderate and severe exercise. In many physiological problems, e.g., postural changes, exposure to cold, forced breathing, etc., it is necessary to know what effect the muscular activities, which accompany such changes, produce in the cardiac output. Results obtained during the investigations described in the previous papers of this series have led to the belief that many of the current views regarding the effect of light exercise on the cardiac output were incorrect. The present investigation was, therefore, undertaken to determine the effect of very mild exertion (such as involves an increase in oxygen consumption of only several hundred cubic centimeters per minute) on the cardiac output.

Methods

The same procedure was used for the determination of the cardiac output as in the preceding papers of this series.[22,7] Unfortunately this method does not permit the accurate determination of the cardiac output when the latter is greatly increased and it was therefore necessary to limit the determinations to very mild exercise. The failure to attain homogeneous mixture during the rebreathing procedure is most liable to lead to error in determining the cardiac output by the above method. One must however, also, avoid exceeding the time of a single circulation of the blood. In the procedure of Krogh and Lindhard[15] this last consideration was minimized by taking "half samples" of alveolar air, and hence their method is applicable to more violent exercise, where the circulation is greatly accelerated. This advantage is, however, counterbalanced by the difficulty and uncertainty of the "mixing" which introduces great errors.

The subject upon whom the data recorded in the present paper were obtained, could mix thoroughly, as determined by experiments with hydrogen,[12] in 10 to 12 sec. The analytical accuracy with which acetylene can be determined makes it possible to avoid any appreciable error in experiments during exercise when the period between the collection of the two samples is only about 3 sec. Hence it was possible in this subject to complete a determination in 13 to 15 sec. Assuming the decrease in circulation time of the blood to be proportional to the

increase in cardiac output, one may obtain values almost twice as great as the normal without sacrifice of accuracy. When the cardiac output is greater than 7 l, however, the errors involved in overpassing the time of a single circulation render the accuracy of the results questionable. During moderate or severe exercise (when the cardiac output is over 10 l) the results are quite undependable even on the above-mentioned subject whose ability to mix was unusually good. For this reason, the results quoted in the present paper are limited to values of the cardiac output which are not greater than 7.0 l and, in this range, are considered to be practically as accurate as those obtained in the resting condition.[1]

All the experiments quoted were

---

[1] Since completing the work described in the present paper, Baumann and the author[1] have demonstrated the dependability and accuracy of the cardiac output determinations when performed under the conditions defined above. We have, in the first place, compared the results obtained by the use of acetylene with those derived from a determination of the cardiac output by direct analysis of the blood obtained from the human right heart. The latter procedure has been limited heretofore to experiments on the lower animals but the technique of heart puncture makes the method also applicable to man. By comparing the oxygen content of the blood removed from the right human ventricle with that obtained from the brachial artery, one obtains an unequivocal and direct measure of the cardiac output. The average deviation of a series of determinations simultaneously carried out by this direct method from those obtained by the use of acetylene was only 2 per cent. We have also investigated two other fundamental principles upon which the indirect method using acetylene is based. Simultaneous determinations of the tension of acetylene in the alveolar air with that in the blood demonstrated that, in normal individuals at least, acetylene distributes itself in accord with the physicochemical laws of the solution of gases in liquids. The same distribution of the gas was found to occur in vivo (with the attainment of a true equilibrium) as had previously been demonstrated to occur in vitro. The

done in the basal condition and with the precautions noted in the preceding papers of this series.

Results

It is a widely current notion that the cardiac output is a simple function of the oxygen consumption during exercise,[2, 15] although exceptions to this view have been previously noted.[18] Thus Starling's textbook (1930) cites the curves of Means and Newburgh[24] in which the cardiac output is plotted against the oxygen consumption during work. Although this concept is, in a sense, true within certain limits of oxygen consumption, in which the same muscle groups are predominantly active, it leads to quite erroneous conceptions, particularly in considering very mild exercise. That the cardiac output is not determined solely by the oxygen consumption and may vary over wide limits for the same expenditure of energy (as measured by the oxygen consumption) is demonstrated in Table 1. This table gives the results of three sets of experiments involving various types of muscular activity. In comparing Exp. 5 with Exps. 2 and 3, one notes that the cardiac output in the former (when the forearms are alternately flexed once a second) is less than in the latter (when only one arm is flexed once per second as in Exp. 2, or even twice per second as in Exp. 3). The oxygen consumption in Exp. 5 is only slightly greater than that in Exp. 2 and less than that of Exp. 4. Nevertheless, the cardiac output is much less than it is in either Exps. 2 or 3. Although the work expended in flexing the arms alternately once a second is about the same as that in flexing one arm every second and less than that expended when both arms are flexed once per second, the heart output is less in the first case.

Experiments 7 and 8 of the second series of Table 1 also demonstrate the independence of the cardiac output to the oxygen consumption or work expended. Thus, alternately flexing both thighs results in a much smaller cardiac output than does the flexion of one thigh every second, although the work and oxygen consumption in the two cases are the same.

Experiments 10 and 11 of the third series of Table 1 show the comparatively high cardiac outputs which may be obtained with small oxygen expenditures. Thus the flexion and extension of the fingers of both hands, although requiring only 100 cc of oxygen over the basal value, results in a marked increase in the cardiac output as does also a corresponding muscular movement of the feet. The cardiac output is much greater in either case than for the same oxygen consumption as observed in the muscular movements of the first two series of Table 1. In Exps. 12 and 13, on the other hand, the increases in cardiac output are much less than those of Exps. 10 and 11 despite the greater oxygen consump-

---

question of the circulation time in man is also fundamental to an understanding of the validity of cardiac output determinations. All previous attempts to answer this question have been either indirect, or have given at best only qualitative results. We have been able to solve the problem quantitatively and directly by determining the acetylene content of blood removed from the right human heart at varying intervals after beginning to rebreathe acetylene as in the procedure for determining the cardiac output. In normal resting subjects the amount of acetylene returning to the lungs at the end of the experimental procedure (20 to 23 sec after beginning the rebreathing) is negligible. When the cardiac output is increased, however, the circulation time is proportionally diminished. The above described experiments offer direct and unequivocal evidence for the accuracy of the cardiac output determinations described in the papers of this series.

TABLE 1

The Relation of the Cardiac Output to the Oxygen Consumption in Mild Exercise

EXPERIMENT NUMBER	TYPE OF EXERCISE	OXYGEN CONSUMP-TION	ARTERIO-VENOUS OXYGEN DIFFERENCE	CARDIAC OUTPUT
		cc per min	*cc per l*	*l per min*
1	Resting	246	60	4.1
2	Flexing and extending right forearm, once per second	286	59	4.8
3	Flexing and extending right forearm, twice per second	340	65	5.2
4	Flexing and extending right forearm rapidly	453	76	6.0
5	Alternately flexing and extending both forearms, each every other second	315	73	4.3
6	Resting	256	61	4.2
7	Flexing right thigh once per second	430	56	7.7
8	Alternately flexing both thighs, each every other second	428	85	5.0
9	Resting	240	60	4.0
10	Flexing and extending hand muscles, twice per second	346	55	6.3
11	Flexing and extending feet and toes, once per second	310	62	5.0
12	Supporting body in horizontal position with feet flexed	424	72	5.9
13	Supporting body in horizontal position with feet flexed	352	66	5.3

tion in the former experiments. Experiments 12 and 13 represent a type of static exercise as compared to the dynamic exercise of Exps. 10 and 11. We must thus conclude that the cardiac output and the cardiovascular response to muscular activity, in general, are independent of the oxygen consumption when different groups of muscles are involved.

The question arises as to the effect of increasing the activity of a given muscular group on the cardiac output and its related functions. As may be noted in the experiments of Table 1, the arteriovenous oxygen difference for very slow muscular movements (e.g., Exp. 5) is high, and the cardiac output consequently is but slightly raised. With increasing activity the arteriovenous oxygen difference falls (as in Exp. 2) after which it again rises (Exps. 3 and 4). The cardiac output gradually increases with greater muscular activity at a progressively diminishing but not uniform rate. Very quick movements (as in Exps. 10 and 11) result in rapid increases in the cardiac output.

The effect on the cardiac output of gradual increases in the activity of the muscle groups involved in walking is demonstrated in Table 2. When the

TABLE 2

The Relation of the Cardiac Output to the Oxygen Consumption with Varying Degrees of Muscular Exertion of Essentially the Same Muscle Groups

CONDITION OF EXPERIMENT	OXYGEN CONSUMPTION	ARTERIO-VENOUS OXYGEN DIFFERENCE	CARDIAC OUTPUT
	cc per min	*cc per l*	*l per min*
Leaning against a wall (rested)...............	289	80	3.6
Standing quietly (rested)....................	339	85	4.0
Sliding feet once every 1½ sec................	347	83	4.2
Standing quietly after work..................	374	86	4.4
Walking 1 step every 5 sec..................	403	79	5.1
Walking 1 step per sec......................	500	87	5.8
Walking 1 step per sec......................	527	89	5.9
Walking 1 step per sec......................	538	92	5.9
Walking 1 step per sec......................	550	89	6.2
Walking 1 step per sec......................	605	95	6.4
Raising feet, once per sec..................	607	101	6.0
Raising feet, twice per sec..................	728	104	7.0

subject is standing still, he is using the muscles which maintain the upright posture, but these are comparatively static. The arteriovenous oxygen difference under these conditions is high and the cardiac output is the same as in the sitting position.[6] Any decrease in cardiac output due to the effect of gravity is counteracted by a compensatory cardiovascular reaction. With a further increase in the oxygen consumption (as in walking) the arteriovenous oxygen difference also increases but not proportionately to the former. Hence there is a gradual rise in the cardiac output with greater muscular activity.

Discussion

The cardiovascular reactions to muscular exercise consist of a complex series of changes occurring in various parts of the organism. Prior to and during work there may be widespread reaction due to stimuli from the higher centers. This includes an increase in blood pressure, pulse rate, and, very likely, in cardiac output. The mild forms of exercise cited in Tables 1 and 2 required little effort for their performance (with the exception of Exps. 12 and 13 of Table 1) and hence central stimulation of the cardiac output in these cases is improbable.

Other important changes during muscular activity are a dilatation and opening of capillaries and an increased venous return due to the pumping action of the muscles. The last two named factors may be considered as the prime agents in increasing the blood flow in mild exercise. The blood pressure rise which occurs under these conditions is so slight as to be a minor factor in producing the observed increases in cardiac output. The heart may thus be considered as merely reacting to the increased venous return, as discussed by Eyster.[5] According to this view, the difference in response of the cardiac output to the various forms of exercise of Table 1 would be explicable as due to a variation in the intensity with which the muscular activity aided in the return of blood to the heart. Exercises involving efficient venous emptying (as in Exp. 10 of Table 1) would result in a much greater cardiac output than a static exercise (as in Exp. 12). Such muscular activity as is involved in standing or shivering in response to cold would result, as has been previously demonstrated,[6, 11] in slight increases in cardiac output because they do not involve active aid in returning blood to the heart. Rapid movements, on the other hand, produce marked changes in cardiac output. The increases in cardiac output observed during forced breathing[10] may thus, in large part at least, be merely resultants of the increased blood flow through the active muscles of respiration.

The above view stresses the importance of the muscles as active aids in maintaining the circulation in exercise. The discrepancy in the results of Chauveau and Kaufmann[3] and of Tschuewsky[27] are explicable on this basis. The former noted a fourfold to eightfold increase in the blood flow through the *levator propius labii superioris* of the horse during activity while the latter noted much slighter increases when the *gracilis* of the dog was stimulated. In sustained tetanic contraction, as might be predicted, Tschuewsky found even a smaller response in cardiac output.

Lindhard[18, 19, 20] has also demonstrated the dependence of the rate at which work is performed on the cardiac output. Thus for a given expenditure of energy, the cardiac output during swimming was greater than it was while riding on a bicycle ergometer. This difference is explained by Kisch[14] as due to the effect of cold in the swimming experiments. This explanation seems improbable from the results previously described.[11] It is more probable that the muscular movements vary in their effectiveness in returning the venous blood to the heart and thus produce the observed changes. The effect of training on reducing the response of the cardiac output, as found by Lindhard[19, 20] and by Collett and Liljestrand,[4] may also, in part at least, be explicable on the same basis. The better coordination of movements which results from training leads to an economy of movement and a lesser return of blood to the heart for a given amount of work.

In static work, Lindhard[19, 20] has also observed a greater increase in cardiac output than would be expected from the oxygen utilized. This result is surprising in view of the fact that one would expect a slight response, as indeed Lindhard himself anticipated, due to the lack of muscular movements in such static work. However, in the experiment of Lindhard (hanging on a horizontal beam), there is considerable nervous stimulation due to the strain of the exercise. Under such conditions the nervous factors controlling the cardiovascular system probably help to produce the observed increases. That such purely nervous influences do occur is evidenced by the cardiovascular response preparatory to exertion or to psychic stimulation in general.[8] This psychic factor was recognized by early workers.[25, 23] Thus Masing showed that work performed with a single leg caused a greater blood pressure rise than when the same amount of work was done by the two legs alternately. Moritz, indeed, considered the pressure elevation during bodily work to be principally conditioned by psychical influences.

During an investigation of the effect of high altitudes on the cardiovascular system,[9] experiments were performed similar to those of Table 2 in order to compare the reaction of the cardiac output to exercise under low barometric pressure with that at sea level. The results obtained before acclimatization was established (about 10 days) were higher than those obtained for the same exercise at sea level. However, if correction was made for the observed increased basal values during this period, it was found that the increased cardiac output due to the exercise was equal to that observed in the same experiment at sea level. Experiments performed when the subject had become acclimatized (and when the basal resting cardiac output had resumed its sea level) showed the same increases in cardiac output as were observed at sea level.

Summary

A study was made of the cardiac output during very mild muscular activity. The cardiac output in such exercise bears no simple relation to the oxygen consumption. Active muscular movements result in a much greater increase of the cardiac output than static or slow movements. This is explained as due to the greater pumping action of the muscles in the former exercises which causes a greater return of venous blood to the heart.

References

1. Baumann, H., and A. Grollman, Z. ges. exptl. Med. (1930).

2. Boothby, W. M., Am. J. Physiol., 37 (1915), 383.

3. Chauveau, M. A., and M. Kaufmann, Compt. rend. Acad. Sci., 104 (1887), 1126.

4. Collett, M. E., and G. Liljestrand, Skand. Arch. Physiol., 45 (1924), 29.

5. Eyster, J. A. E., Physiol. Rev., 6 (1926), 281.

6. Grollman, A., Am. J. Physiol., 86 (1928), 285.

7. Grollman, A., ibid., 88 (1929), 432.

8. Grollman, A., ibid., 89 (1929), 584.

9. Grollman, A., ibid., 93 (1930), 19.

10. Grollman, A., ibid., 94 (1930), 287.

11. Grollman, A., ibid., 95 (1930), 263.

12. Grollman, A., and E. K. Marshall, ibid., 76 (1928). 110.

13. Jarisch, A., and G. Liljestrand, Skand. Arch. Physiol., 51 (1924), 235.

14. Kisch, B., in Handbuch der normalen und pathologischen Physiologie. (Berlin), 7 (1927), 1200.

15. Krogh, A., and J. Lindhard, Skand. Arch. Physiol., 27 (1912), 100; J. Physiol. (London), 51 (1917), 182.

16. Liljestrand, G., and J. Lindhard, Skand. Arch. Physiol., 39 (1920), 215.

17. Liljestrand, G., and N. Stenström, ibid., 42 (1922), 82.

18. Lindhard, J., Pflügers Arch. ges. Physiol., 161 (1915), 233.

19. Lindhard, J., Skand. Arch. Physiol., 39 (1920), 64.

20. Lindhard, J., ibid., 40 (1920), 145.

21. Lindhard, J., J. Physiol. (London), 57 (1923), 17.

22. Marshall, E. K., and A. Grollman, Am. J. Physiol., 86 (1928), 117.

23. Masing, E. Deut. Arch. klin. Med., 74 (1902), 253.

24. Means, J. H., and L. H. Newburgh, J. Pharm. Exptl. Therap., 7 (1915), 441, 449.

25. Moritz, O., Deut. Arch. klin. Med., 77 (1903), 339.

26. Starling, E. H., Principles of Human Physiology (5th. ed.). Edited by C.

Lovatt Evans. Philadelphia: N. B. Saunders Co., 1930, p. 610.

27. Tschuewsky, J. A., *Pflügers Arch. ges. Physiol.*, **97** (1903), 289.

F. S. COTTON / D. B. DILL

On the Relation Between the Heart Rate During Exercise and That of the Immediate Post-Exercise Period

Reprinted from the *American Journal of Physiology*,
111 (1935), 554–56.

This study, one of many classic studies which came from the Harvard Fatigue Laboratory, is particularly important because it represents one of the first applications of the cardiotachometer to the study of pulse rate during strength exercise. Boas and his colleagues[1] *studied pulse rate during mild exercise, although no reliable reports were available on pulse rate in strenuous exercise prior to the Cotton and Dill studies. The cardiotachometer, which uses electrical potentials generated by the heart muscle action, provides a record on a narrow strip of paper at intervals of 1 sec. Thus, it was possible to record pulse rate for 10-sec periods immediately before and after exercise.*

The investigators indicate that the decrease in rate in the first 10 sec after the cessation of exercise is about 1 beat per min. They further suggest that it should be possible to predict heart rate during exercise from the heartbeat in the 10-sec period immediately following exercise with reasonable accuracy (within $\pm$ 3 per cent). In the light of modern statistical procedures, the analysis of the data in this study appears somewhat crude. Nevertheless, the basic findings are still thought to be valid and provide a good basis for studying the dynamics of pulse rate during and after exercise. Further work in the Fatigue Laboratory showed that post-exercise pulse rate follows an exponential curve and that trained subjects return to a resting level sooner than those who are untrained.

The available data concerning the pulse rate during exercise are very scanty. Until the advent of the cardiotachometer it was practically impossible to obtain these data in the most strenuous exercise since the movements of the subject interfered so profoundly with the records obtainable by all previous methods of registration.

Although Boas and his associates have published a considerable amount of data concerning heart rate during exercise, no attempt has been made to study the change that occurs during the abrupt transition from active exercise to rest. Although further, many data exist concerning the heart rate after exercise, the importance attaching to that during the work is naturally greater.

A logical outcome of the foregoing is therefore to examine the possibility of predicting the heart rate during exercise from observations made immediately after exercise.

During the course of an investigation of the heart rate during and after exercise, a considerable number of records was taken by means of a modified Boas cardiotachometer. An examination of these records was made with the above purpose in view.

Method

The cardiotachometer record was written as an ink tracing on a fairly rapidly moving narrow strip of paper, the time being inscribed each second. The exercise in all cases was carried out on a flat treadmill surface traveling at various speeds from about four and a half miles to about eleven miles per hour, but with uniform speed in any given experiment. The duration of the exercise was very variable, being adjusted to the intensity of work, so that for the most part, except where the subject was running very fast, he continued long enough to attain a fairly steady state. In the case of the slower speeds the treadmill surface was inclined upward so as to increase the intensity of the exercise. The subjects were normal men in the third or fourth decade. Our conclusions reached from study of such subjects may not apply to boys and certainly do not apply to dogs.

On examining the records for the purpose in hand, the heart rate was determined for four periods of 10 sec

each, two immediately preceding the stop signal and two immediately following this signal. To secure an accurate result it was necessary to count the beat intervals and fractions thereof to the nearest 0.1 in each 10-sec period. The result multiplied by 6 (approximated to the nearest whole number) gave the heart rate per minute correct to one beat (excluding errors of timing). Errors of draughtsmanship (erecting vertical lines and judging tenths of a beat interval) may be reckoned as negligible. The results are set out in the two tables in the arbitrary order of date, with the object of testing whether stabilized averages were being obtained. The first group includes six subjects observed on dif-

TABLE 1

Heart Rate during Consecutive 10-Sec Periods

(1 and 2 immediately before, and 3 and 4 immediately after cessation of exercise)

NO. OF SUBJECT	1	2	3	4
1	136	136	132	123
1	141	142	140	135
2	160	160	166	154
2	180	181	186	174
3	164	176	172	168
4	186	183	178	168
4	194	192	188	181
4	182	184	186	175
5	104	105	98	89
5	146	141	141	122
5	166	166	162	154
6	142	142	142	133
6	156	157	154	142
6	164	174	172	160
1	160	161	159	153
1	163	164	161	157
Mean........	159.0	160.2	158.6	149.2
Approximate mean......	159	160	159	149

TABLE 2

Heart Rate during Consecutive 10-Sec Periods

(1 and 2 immediately before, and 3 and 4 immediately after cessation of work)

NO. OF SUBJECT	1 −20	2 −10	3 +10	4 +20
7	176	177	174	154
1	128	128	122	126
8	194	189	185	165
9	176	183	183	166
9	126	136	124	100
9	182	186	186	177
9	194	189	196	187
9	186	190	189	180
9	189	186	186	186
9	180	180	183	179
9	189	186	183	180
10	199	200	202	194
11	108	108	105	105
12	195	200	190	175
11	198	197	194	180
7	185	188	185	180
1	171	168	159	158
7	150	145	144	137
7	160	162	163	156
1	144	144	144	145
7	141	145	146	124
7	103	102	107	95
1	159	159	169	170
Mean........	166.6	166.9	166.0	157.3
Approximate mean......	167	167	166	157

ferent occasions up to June, 1930, while the second includes seven subjects from this date up to April, 1932. One subject only was common to the two groups.

The mean data show agreement to within less than one heart beat in the two consecutive periods of work. It is also noteworthy that the decrease in the heart rate in the first 10 sec after the cessation of the exercise was almost identical in each case. Moreover, the fact that in both cases the mean values

for the two periods during the exercise agree to the nearest whole beat is evidence of the stability of the mean results.

From this it is clear that the heart rate falls very little during the first 10 sec after the work, and for the next 10 sec only about 6 per cent.

The value of the result for prediction purposes in individual cases must, however, rest on the extent of individual variation in these data. To investigate this point these variations were collected from both tables, namely: the individual differences in heart rate in the two consecutive periods of exercise (from columns 1 and 2) and the individual differences in heart rate that takes place immediately on cessation of work (from columns 3 and 4).

An analysis shows that the S.D. of the variation in heart rate during the exercise periods is 4.03, i.e., about 2.6 per cent, while the S.D. of the change in heart rate in the first 10-sec period after the exercise is 4.58, i.e., about 2.9 per cent.

Merely for the sake of completeness a slight correction[1] should be applied to the latter figure bringing it to 2.8 per cent, since the difference of the two mean heart rates in question is about one beat.

It may therefore be deduced from the foregoing that the pulse rate during exercise may be predicted from that recorded immediately after exercise[2] with an error whose S.D. is rather less than 3 per cent.

[1] This correction is applied according to the formula (True S. D.)^2 = (Uncorrected S. D.)^2 + x^2, where x is the difference between the two means in question.

[2] It should be emphasized that "immediately" implies the 10-sec period following cessation of work. As may be seen in the tables, there is apt to be a rapid decrease in rate in the second 10-sec period. The decrease may be even more precipitous in later periods.

Summary

An examination of heart rate data recorded by means of a cardiotachometer in the case of strenuous exercise on a treadmill shows that in the 10 sec following cessation of the exercise, the heart rate of man decreases on an average of just about 1 beat per min. Analysis of the data indicates the possibility of predicting the heart rate during exercise from that obtained in the 10-sec period following its cessation with a reasonable degree of accuracy (mean error less than 3 per cent).

References

1. Boas, E. P., and E. F. Goldschmidt, *The Heart Rate*. Springfield, Ill.: C. C. Thomas, 1932.

J. H. McCURDY / L. A. LARSON

Measurement of Organic Efficiency for the Prediction of Physical Condition

Reprinted from the *Research Quarterly Supplement*, **6**, (1935), 11–41.

Springfield College has been a leader in exercise research for over three decades. The work of McCurdy, Cureton, Karpovich, Larson, and Clarke is renowned among scientists the world over. The original McCurdy-Larson study is presented here because it treats of one of the first attempts to use modern measurement theory in constructing an exercise tolerance test. It is a very complete research paper and provides a good introduction to the techniques of test construction for the interested student. The authors employed particularly the multiple correlation and regression technique in which several variables are combined statistically to determine which combination provides the highest correlation or prediction. McCurdy and Larson applied cardiovascular variables that were used in many of the older tests. These variables, sitting and standing blood pressure and pulse rate before and after exercise, were supplemented by a vital capacity and breath-holding test. A group of infirmary patients recuperating from a fever condition was chosen as the criterion against a group of varsity swimmers. This method may be considered unsound; however, the study of such dissimilar groups led to correlations that were high enough to make statistically reliable predictions.

Introduction

These experiments were begun at the request of Dr. Frederic Brush of the Burke Foundation Hospital. The completion of this study has been made possible through a grant from their funds. Dr. Brush asked us to devise a predictive index of organic efficiency which would aid in the determination of functional fitness to leave their convalescent hospital. The ability to return to ordinary vocations was stressed. Dr. Brush also asked that the predictive index help in measuring the dosage of physical activity needed during the period of recuperation, particularly in golf on the two courses on the hospital estate. Work by McCurdy in the physiology of exercise in the last 35 years and an examination by the authors of the literature on organic efficiency raised doubts regarding the statistical reliability of previous work.

Schwartz and his associates in the United States Public Health Bureau challenge the fundamental question of ability to find measures of functional efficiency that are accurate enough to be valid. He says, "Measures of physical fitness (apart from weight itself, 0.98) are on quite a doubtful basis. Pulse rate led with 0.71 which seems very low when compared with the results obtained by precise measurements on the body, the blood pressures are much lower." The systolic pressure is 0.65, the diastolic 0.46, pulse pressure, 0.46. The measurements were taken on 68 boys 4 months apart from ages 13 and less to 17 and more (13 and less—4, 14 yr—8, 15 yr—24, 16 yr—20, 17 yr and over—12). Schwartz fails to recognize the unreliable method of his test taken on 68 boys 4 months apart. These boys were distributed in age range through the entire adolescent period. His assumption that the comparison of differences in functional measurements taken 4 months apart on growing boys is evidence of reliability is not scientific evidence.

Schwartz's widely quoted apparent proof of inability to measure functional power required a reexamination of the subject with an avoidance of his errors. The first section of this study, "The Reliability and Objectivity of Blood Pressure Measurements," attempts to find out whether functional tests can be made with sufficient objectivity and reliability to serve as valid indexes of physical condition.

The second part of the study "Measurements of Organic Efficiency for the Prediction of Physical Condition" selects from a battery of 26 items, 5 test items which have the highest significance as measurements of physical condition. The preliminary examinations cover 2 yr. The examinations included four groups of students in the International Young Men's Christian Association College:

1. College freshmen for the fall seasons of 1933 and 1934—286 men.

2. Infirmary cases from October, 1933, to March, 1935—77 cases.

3. Varsity swimmers for the seasons of 1934 and 1935—49 cases. The time for the 440-yd swim was used as evidence of physical condition. Only experienced swimmers in condition were used in the test. The method aimed to eliminate learning to swim, and to test only physical condition.

4. The case-study group. This group includes men who were in two or all three groups. These case studies permit the comparison of the test on the same individual under different conditions; e.g., in the infirmary and on the varsity swimming team.

The authors are indebted to the 409 students who willingly cooperated as subjects in the long battery of 26 tests.

Specific help and cooperation were given by the following faculty members: Dr. Peter V. Karpovich in the blood pressure examination, Professor T. K. Cureton in the swimming tests, Mr. Bliss P. Sargeant in the heart rates, and Professors Hickox and Cureton on statistical procedures. Dr. Frederick S. Hopkins and Mrs. Pauline Whitney, nurse, gave help in the infirmary studies. The following students assisted as recorders: Messrs. Bicknell, Crowell, Harris, Pawling, and Russell.

The large volume of work entailed in these experiments would have been impossible without the splendid work of all of these groups. All of the statistical work has been done by Mr. L. A. Larson. He also wrote the preliminary draft of the study. The authors collaborated in the final study.

Method of Validation

It is important that norms be established on the basis of healthy groups. We have selected for the criterion of "good" condition 49 varsity swimmers who have been in training for varsity competition; therefore, have learned the fundamental skills. These men have been tested on the basis of their ability to swim 440 yd in varsity time. For the criterion of "poor" condition we have selected 77 infirmary subjects who have been in bed for 2 or more days with fever. For the "average" condition we have used freshmen who have been examined on entrance to the college. This group contains the freshman class for the past 2 yr, or 286 in number.

The determination of condition is an extremely complex matter. A person may be able to go about his daily work and yet may not be fit, or organically efficient for more strenuous work. Many tests have been devised to measure condition. Only a few of these tests have exercise as a measure of organic capacity. Endurance, however, is basic in measuring organic capacity. If one is able to run or swim more than the normal amount without a great amount of fatigue, this can be used as a real criterion of condition. Therefore, in this research we have studied the underlying organic measures of endurance swimming, and have used these items as the criteria. For the other extreme, we have studied infirmary subjects by the use of a number of organic measures.

The authors have used for the test battery 26 organic items which have been generally used for examination in the field. By the use of the two extreme groups and correlating these various measures we determined the items that were significant in predicting organic efficiency. We believe a real test or measure of condition can be obtained by using endurance as the criterion of condition, determining the significant organic measures through correlating typical groups, statistically weighting each of these test items, and finally developing a statistically sound scoring device.

Development of the Test

In beginning the study the author selected the following organic measurements to be used in a test battery: weight; horizontal, sitting, and standing systolic pressures; horizontal, sitting, and standing diastolic pressures; horizontal, sitting, and standing pulse pressures; vital capacity with temperature correction; breath-holding by use of the flarmeter; the standard Prudential stair-climbing exercise; pulse rate immediately after exercise; breath-holding 20 sec after the exercise; pulse rate sitting one and one-half minutes after exercise; pulse rate standing 2 min after exercise, and the difference between the following items: horizontal and standing pulse rates, horizontal and standing systolic pressures, horizontal and standing diastolic pressures, horizontal and standing pulse pressures, normal breath-holding and breath-holding 20 sec after the standard stair-climbing exercise, standing normal pulse rate and pulse rate immediately following exercise, sitting normal pulse rate and sitting pulse rate one and one-half minutes following exercise, and standing normal pulse rate and standing pulse rate 2 min following exercise.

These measurements were taken on the swimmers, average group or freshmen, and the infirmary subjects. The first step in determining the important test items for the prediction of condition was to correlate the test items from the infirmary group with the test items of the swimming group. The Bi-Serial "r"[7] for a two-point distribution was used as the method of correlation. The significant correlations obtained using three groups of data are shown below.*

Selection of Test Items

It was first thought that the test would contain the following items on the basis of the raw correlations:

These organic items were used in a multiple correlation development to determine their value as a test battery. The Fisher-Doolittle[2] method of solving a multiple correlation was used. The multiple correlation for the test battery was found to be as follows:

$$R_m = 0.898$$

It was next decided to eliminate variables 6 and 7 in the test battery to see what effect it would have on the value of the test, or to determine whether or not they were important items in a test. The Fisher-Doolittle method[2] was again used with the resulting multiple correlation:

$$R_m = 0.881$$

*		1933–34 Data	1934–35 Data	Combination or Total
1.	Sitting Diastolic Pressure............	−0.632	−0.574	−0.622
2.	Breath-Holding 20 sec After Standard Exercise	+0.496	+0.545	+0.531
3.	Difference Between Standing Normal Pulse Rate and Pulse Rate 2 min After Exercise.................	+0.523	+0.439	+0.446
4.	Sitting Pulse Pressure.............	+0.531	+0.400	+0.414
5.	Standing Pulse Pressure...........	+0.480	+0.280	+0.346
6.	Vital Capacity...................	+0.423	+0.277	+0.311
7.	Standing Diastolic Pressure (Data for 2 yr not separated)			−0.350

1.	Sitting Diastolic Pressure........................	−0.622	±0.037
2.	Breath-Holding 20 sec After Standard Exercise........	+0.531	±0.043
3.	Difference Between Standing Normal Pulse Rate and Pulse Rate 2 min After Exercise.................	+0.446	±0.048
4.	Sitting Pulse Pressure.........................	+0.414	±0.050
5.	Standing Pulse Pressure........................	+0.346	±0.053
6.	Vital Capacity................................	+0.311	±0.055
7.	Standing Diastolic Pressure.....................	−0.350	±0.053

It was next decided to eliminate variable 5 and retain variables 1, 2, 3, and 4 from the test battery. The multiple correlation was found to be as follows:

$$R_m = 0.826$$

The next step was to eliminate variable 4 and retain variables 1, 2, 3, and 5. The reason for this step was that in solving the multiple correlation with variable 1, 2, 3, 4, and 5 it was found to have the least amount of weight in the test battery. The weighting was so low that it appeared to be unimportant. The result from eliminating variable 4 was as follows:

$$R_m = 0.806$$

It was decided unnecessary to eliminate variable 1, 2, or 3 from the test battery to see the effect because of their high raw correlations, also because of the large weighting given each of these three variables.

It can be clearly seen on the basis of the multiple correlations that the final test would contain the items shown below.

stairs) is determined by a table prepared by the Prudential Life Insurance Company of America.[6] (See Table 1).

After the amount of exercise to be given in the test is known it is next necessary to secure the standing pulse rate (15 sec and multiply by 4), standing systolic and diastolic pressures, and sitting systolic and diastolic pressures. Following these measurements the stair-climbing exercise is given on the basis of the age and weight of the individual. To conduct this test it is necessary to obtain the regulation stairs used for this exercise. The stairs can be obtained at the Becton and Dickinson Company, Rutherford, N. J. Following the exercise, which continues for 90 sec, the subject is allowed to sit close to a table on which is the flarimeter with the small orifice open. The blow should begin 20 sec after the exercise with only one large inhalation made before blowing. The subject should be asked to make one large inhalation 15 sec following the exercise and blow when ready. This will take approximately 5

		Raw Correlations		Weighting
1.	Sitting Diastolic Pressure............	−0.622	±0.037	−6.4
2.	Breath-Holding 20 sec After Standard Exercise	+0.531	±0.043	+6.6
3.	Difference Between Standing Normal Pulse Rate and Pulse Rate 2 min After Exercise.................	+0.446	±0.048	+7.7
4.	Sitting Pulse Pressure.............	+0.414	±0.050	+1.0
5.	Standing Pulse Pressure...........	+0.346	±0.053	+3.0
	R_m (organic test) = 0.881			

Description of the Test

It is first necessary in a test to obtain the age and weight of the individual so as to determine the amount of exercise to be given. The exercise (number of ascents on the

sec, making the blow 20 sec following the exercise. The stopwatch used should have two large hands so that one hand will always be continuous. This is necessary in order to obtain the length of the breath-holding and also be able to secure the pulse rate accurately 2 min after exercise.

TABLE 1

Males
Standard Number of Ascents

(*Adapted from Two-step Exercise Test of Master and Oppenheimer*)

Weight (*lb*)	AGE IN YEARS											
	10–14	15–19	20–24	25–29	30–34	35–39	40–44	45–49	50–54	55–59	60–64	65–69
50— 59	28	..	..	..	..	..	..	..	..	..	..	..
60— 69	27	34	..	..	..	..	..	..	..	..	..	..
70— 79	26	32	..	..	..	..	..	..	..	..	..	..
80— 89	26	30	35	36	35	34	32	30	29	27	26	24
90— 99	25	28	33	34	32	31	30	28	27	26	24	23
100—109	24	26	30	31	30	29	28	27	25	24	23	22
110—119	23	25	28	29	28	27	26	25	24	23	22	21
120—129	23	24	27	28	27	26	25	24	23	22	21	20
130—139	22	23	25	27	26	25	24	23	22	21	20	19
140—149	21	23	25	26	25	24	23	22	21	20	19	18
150—159	21	22	24	25	24	23	22	21	20	20	19	18
160—169	20	22	23	24	23	22	21	21	20	19	18	17
170—179	..	22	22	23	22	21	21	20	19	18	18	17
180—189	..	21	21	22	21	21	20	19	19	18	17	17
190—199	..	..	20	21	21	20	20	19	18	17	17	16
200—209	..	..	19	20	20	19	19	18	17	16	16	15
210—219	..	..	18	19	19	18	18	17	16	15	15	14
220—229	..	..	17	18	18	17	17	16	15	14	14	13

An example will make this clear. Using the face of the watch the exercise will begin at 60 and continue for 90 sec which will take the hand to 30. The subject is asked to sit close to the flarimeter and breath normally for 15 sec which will take the hand to 45 on the face of the watch. The subject is asked to take one large inhalation and blow *as long as possible*. The subject should be encouraged to give everything he has in this measurement. When the subject begins the blow the hand on the face of the watch will be on about 50. The length of the blow will be determined by the organic fitness of the subject. Suppose the blow would stop at 20 and if started at exactly 49 sec, the length of this blow would be 31 sec. The hand on the stopwatch is allowed to continue until it comes to 15. The subject is asked to stand. At 30 (2 min following exercise) the pulse rate is taken for 15 sec and multiplied by 4. The form used for this test is shown at the top of p. 148.

In regard to the time required per individual for the organic efficiency test, the maximum is 10 min. After the examiner has become acquainted with the routine procedure of the test, the time per individual can be reduced 2 or 3 min.

The equipment necessary to conduct this test is as follows:

1. Stopwatch (Double Action).
2. Stairs (Prudential Life Insurance Co.).[1]
3. Blood Pressure Equipment (Sphygmomanometer and Stethoscope).
4. Flarimeter.[1]

[1] This equipment may be purchased from the Becton and Dickinson Company, Rutherford, N. J.

Name............................... Age........ Weight........ Sex........
        Date.. Hour............
1. Pulse Rate. Standing Normal. 1.................... 2....................
2. Blood Pressure
            (*a*) Systolic Pressure   (*b*) Diastolic—4th Phase   (*c*) Pulse Pressure
        Sitting.   1........ 2........ 1........ 2........ 1.......... 2..........
        Standing.   1........ 2........ 1........ 2........ 1.......... 2..........
3. Exercise and Measurements Following:
        (*a*) Exercise. Number of Ascents 1.............. 2..............
        (*b*) Breath-Holding 20 sec After Exercise 1.............. 2..............
        (*c*) Pulse Rate (Standing) 2 min After Exercise 1.............. 2..............

NOTE: Two or more spaces should be allowed in the form so that the examination could be repeated at some later date.

Organic Measurements in Typical Groups

It was decided to introduce into the study a group of individuals who could be considered "average" from the standpoint of condition; i.e., a group that could not be classified as infirmary subjects, or a group that would not be in excellent condition in terms of endurance swimming. The three groups, also the total number of subjects, will be represented as follows:

A. "Good" condition: Excellent condition for endurance swimming (440 yd). Number of subjects—49.

B. "Average" condition: Freshmen examined on entrance to college. Number of subjects—286.

C. "Poor" condition: Infirmary subjects who have had fever and in bed for 2 or more days. Number of subjects—77.

The significant organic items were obtained by correlating the organic test items of Group A ("good" condition) with the organic test items of Group C ("poor" condition). Beginning with 26 organic measurements the number dropped to 5 significant measures by this method. By using these 5 significant test items, and representing according

to the above classification, the following physiological facts are obtained:

1. SITTING DIASTOLIC PRESSURE
    A. "Good" condition—49 subjects—Varsity Swimmers.
    B. "Average" condition—286 subjects—Entering Freshmen.
    C. "Poor" condition—77 subjects—Infirmary Cases.

Correlation Coefficients:

$$^rAC = -0.622$$
$$^rBA = +0.208$$
$$^rBC = +0.541.$$

Physiological Facts:
(1) The "Good" condition group had a lower sitting diastolic pressure than the "Poor" condition group.

Mean for "Good" condition = 78.08.
Mean for "Poor" condition = 89.568.

(2) The "Good" condition group had a higher sitting diastolic pressure than the "Average" group.

Mean for "Good" condition = 78.08.
Mean for "Average" condition = 75.172.

(3) The "Poor" condition group had a higher sitting diastolic pressure than the "Average" group.

Mean for "Poor" condition = 89.568.
Mean for "Average" condition = 75.172.

2. BREATH-HOLDING TWENTY SECONDS AFTER THE STANDARD STAIR-CLIMBING EXERCISE

A. "Good" condition—49 subjects—Varsity Swimmers.

B. "Average" condition—164 subjects[2]—Entering Freshmen.

C. "Poor" condition—77 subjects—Infirmary Cases.

Correlation Coefficients:

$$^rAC = +0.531$$
$$^rBA = +0.368$$
$$^rBC = -0.161.$$

Physiological Facts:

(1) The "Good" condition group had the ability for longer breath-holding after the standard stair-climbing exercise than the "Poor" condition group.

Mean for "Good" condition = 32.832.
Mean for "Poor" condition = 22.864.

(2) The "Good" condition group had the ability for longer breath-holding after the standard stair-climbing exercise than the "Average" group.

Mean for "Good" condition = 32.832.
Mean for "Average" condition = 25.26.

(3) The "Average" condition group had the ability for longer breath-holding after the standard stair-climbing exercise than the "Poor" condition group.

Mean for "Average" condition = 25.26.
Mean for "Poor" condition = 22.864.

3. DIFFERENCE BETWEEN STANDING NORMAL PULSE RATE AND PULSE RATE TWO MINUTES AFTER STANDARD STAIR-CLIMBING EXERCISE

A. "Good" condition—49 subjects—Varsity Swimmers.

B. "Average" condition—286 subjects—Entering Freshmen.

C. "Poor" condition—77 subjects—Infirmary Cases.

Correlation Coefficients:

$$^rAC = +0.446$$
$$^rBA = +0.248$$
$$^rBC = -0.017.$$

Physiological Facts:[3]

---

[2] The 1933–34 data could not be used as the breath-holding test was taken 10 sec following exercise rather than 20 sec.

[3] Plus (+) means above normal; minus (−) means below normal.

(1) The "Good" condition group had a pulse-rate difference between normal standing and 2 min after exercise of above normal and ranging slightly below normal, while the "Poor" condition group had a pulse-rate difference below normal.

Mean for "Good" condition = +4.532.
Mean for "Poor" condition = −4.024.

(2) Comparing the "Average" group with the "Good" condition group the "Average" group had a pulse-rate difference between the normal standing and 2 min after exercise of greater variability; i.e., the range was from 32 below to 32 above normal.

Mean for "Good" condition = +4.532.
Mean for "Average" condition = −3.572.

(3) Comparing the "Poor" condition group with the "Average" group we found that the "Average" group had greater variability in the range.

Mean for "Poor" condition = −4.024.
Mean for "Average" condition = −3.572.

4. SITTING PULSE PRESSURE

A. "Good" condition—49 subjects—Varsity Swimmers.

B. "Average" condition—286 subjects—Entering Freshmen.

C. "Poor" condition—77 subjects—Infirmary Cases.

Correlation Coefficients:

$$^rAC = +0.414$$
$$^rBA = +0.063$$
$$^rBC = -0.256$$

Physiological Facts:

(1) The "Good" condition group had a higher sitting pulse pressure than the "Poor" condition group.

Mean for "Good" condition = 44.448.
Mean for "Poor" condition = 35.036.

(2) The "Good" condition group had a higher sitting pulse pressure than the "Average" group.

Mean for "Good" condition = 44.448.
Mean for "Average" condition = 42.396.

(3) The "Poor" condition group had a lower sitting pulse pressure than the "Average" group.

Mean for "Poor" condition = 35.036.
Mean for "Average" condition = 42.396.

5. STANDING PULSE PRESSURE

A. "Good" condition—49 subjects—Varsity Swimmers.

B. "Average" condition—285 subjects—Entering Freshmen.

C. "Poor" condition—77 subjects—Infirmary Cases.

Correlation Coefficients:

$$^rAC = +0.346$$
$$^rBA = +0.039$$
$$^rBC = -0.040.$$

Physiological Facts:

(1) The "Good" condition group had a higher standing pulse pressure than the "Poor" condition group.

Mean for "Good" condition = 37.252.
Mean for "Poor" condition = 29.556.

(2) The "Good" condition group had a slightly higher standing pulse pressure than the "Average" condition group.

Mean for "Good" condition = 37.252.
Mean for "Average" condition = 35.94.

(3) The "Poor" condition group had a lower standing pulse pressure than the "Average" condition group.

Mean for "Poor" condition = 29.556.
Mean for "Average" condition = 35.94.

Reliability of the Test

The reliability will be developed under two parts: first, the reliability and objectivity of the test items, and second, the reliability of the test battery in predicting condition.

There has been a great deal of comment made in the field in regard to the value of a test containing blood pressures because of the inaccuracy of their measurements. However, the authors were unable to find a careful study in regard to the reliability and objectivity of blood pressure measurements. It was, therefore, decided to conduct a study[4] to determine the consistency by which blood pressure measurements are made. The results of this study are indicated* below.[4]

The organic efficiency test contains the sitting diastolic pressure, the sitting pulse pressure, and the standing pulse pressure. It can be concluded on the basis of the above study that these organic measurements can be obtained accurately enough to render the test valid.

The reliability of the test battery is indicated by the two following values:

$$R_m = 0.881$$

$$^RCoefficient of reliability for the test = 0.845.$$

The coefficient of reliability for the test was obtained by the use of the actual test scores from the "Good" and "Poor" condition groups. The Bi-Serial "r"[7, p. 465] for a two-point distribution was used as the method of correlation. The table (on page 151*) will show the method used to obtain the reliability coefficient for the test, also the placement of the "Poor" and "Good" condition subjects in the scoring table.

---

[4] For complete results, see reference 4.

	Diastolic Pressure 4th Phase	Pulse Pressure 4th Phase—Diastolic
* 1. Reliability		
^{r}McCurdy	0.813	0.905
^{r}Larson	0.718	0.932
2. Objectivity		
^{r}McCurdy and Karpovich..............	0.773	0.860
^{r}McCurdy and Sargeant...............	0.776	0.871
^{r}Karpovich and Sargeant.............	0.788	0.864

Method of Scoring

In order that the organic test could be of real practical use it was necessary to arrange a short, simple, and yet accurate scoring device. It was finally decided to score each individual in the following manner:

1. Change the raw score of the organic test to the T-scale score. Table 2.

2. Multiply the T-scale score in each of the organic items by the proper weighting. Table 2.

3. Add the total score to obtain the final score for each individual. Table 3.

4. Determine the condition rating or classification given the individual by use of percentiles. Table 3 or 4.

An example will make the use of the scoring device clear. The following is an infirmary subject, age 21, in bed with a temperature for 6 days. He was tested when his temperature became normal, which was at the end of the sixth day.[†]

SCORING ORGANIC EFFICIENCY*

Percentile	Rating	Score	"Poor" Condition Infirmary Case	"Good" Condition Varsity Swimmers
90	Excellent	759—up	..	12
80	Very Good	758—696	..	10
70	Good	659—627	1	20
60	Above Average	626—596	2	3
50	Average	595—	2	..
40	Below Average	594—557	10	1
30	Fair	556—474	23	..
20	Poor	473—436	17	..
10	Very poor	435—down	22	..
			N = 77	N = 46

[R]Reliability coefficient $= 0.845$.

[†]

NAME M. H.   DATE FEBRUARY 21, 1935

Test Items	Raw Score	T- Score	T- Score × Weight	Classification		
1. Sitting Diastolic Pressure	90	64	−410	90 Excellent	759—up
2. Breath-Holding 20 sec After Standard Exercise........	12	31.5	+208	80 Very Good	758—696
				70 Good	695—627
3. Standing Pulse Rate Minus Pulse Rate 2 min After Exercise	0	54.5	+420	60 Above Av.	626—596
				50 Average	595
4. Sitting Pulse Pressure.......	30	42	+42	40 Below Av.	594—557
5. Stand. Pulse Pressure.......	28	46.5	+140	30 Fair	556—474
Classification *Very Poor*		Total	400	20 Poor	473—436
				10 Very Poor	435—down

This subject (M. H.) was examined again April 22, 1935. His score in this test was 599 which shows an increase of 49.7 per cent in organic efficiency.

TABLE 2

T-Score for Organic Efficiency Items

Sitting Diastolic Pressure			Breath-Holding 20 sec After Exercise			Difference between Stand. P.R. and P.R. 2 min After Exercise			Sitting Pulse Pressure			Standing Pulse Pressure		
Pressure	T-score	T-score × −6.4	B.-H.	T-score	T-score × +6.6	Pulse Rate Diff.	T-score	T-score × +7.7	Pulse Press.	T-score	T-score × +1.0	Pulse Press.	T-score	T-score × +3.0
100	77	−493	56	75.5	+498	32	77	+593	76	78	+78	72	80	+240
99	76	−486	55	75	+495	31	76	+585	75	77	+77	71	79	+237
98	74	−474	54	74.5	+492	30	75	+578	74	76	+76	70	78	+234
97	72	−461	53	74	+488	29	74	+570	73	75	+75	69	77	+231
96	70	−448	52	73	+482	28	73.5	+566	72	74	+74	68	76	+228
95	69	−442	51	72	+475	27	73	+562	71	73	+73	67	75	+225
94	67	−428	50	71.5	+472	26	72.5	+558	70	72.5	+73	66	74	+222
93	66.5	−426	49	71	+469	25	72	+554	69	72	+72	65	73	+219
92	65.5	−419	48	70.5	+465	24	71	+547	68	71	+71	64	72.5	+218
91	65	−416	47	70	+462	23	70.7	+544	67	70.5	+71	63	72	+216
90	64	−410	46	69.5	+459	22	70.5	+543	66	70	+70	62	71	+213
89	63	−403	45	69	+455	*21	70.3	+541	65	69	+69	61	70.5	+212
88	62	−397	44	68.5	+452	20	70	+539	64	68.5	+69	60	70	+210
87	61	−390	43	68	+449	19	69.7	+537	63	68	+68	59	69.5	+209
86	60	−384	42	67.8	+447	18	69.5	+535	62	67.7	+68	58	69	+207
85	59	−377	41	67.4	+445	17	69	+531	61	67.3	+67	57	68.5	+206

(Table continued on next page.)

* All varsity swimmers ("Good" group) range between +24 and −16 in the difference between standing normal pulse rate and pulse rate 2 min after exercise, while only one went above +20 and one below −8. Both of these individuals had a total good score; the one with +24 had a total score of 953 and the one with −16 had a score of 694.

TABLE 2 (continued)

84	58.5	−374	40	67	+442	16	68.5	+527	60	67	+67	56	68	+204
83	57	−365	39	66	+436	15	68	+524	59	66.5	+67	55	67	+201
82	56	−358	38	65.5	+432	14	67	+516	58	66	+66	54	66.5	+200
81	55	−352	37	65	+429	13	66.5	+512	57	65.5	+66	53	66	+198
80	54.5	−348	36	64	+422	12	66	+508	56	65	+65	52	65.5	+197
79	53	−339	35	63	+416	11	65	+501	55	64	+64	51	64	+192
78	52	−333	34	62	+409	10	64	+493	54	63	+63	50	63	+189
77	51	−326	33	61	+403	9	63	+485	53	62	+62	49	62.5	+188
76	50.5	−323	32	60.5	+399	8	62.5	+481	52	61	+61	48	62	+186
75	49	−314	31	59	+389	7	61	+470	51	60	+60	47	61	+183
74	48	−307	30	58	+383	6	60	+462	50	59	+59	46	60.5	+182
73	47	−301	29	57	+376	5	59	+454	49	58	+58	45	60	+180
72	46	−294	28	56.5	+373	4	58	+447	48	57.5	+58	44	59.5	+179
71	45	−288	27	55	+363	3	57	+439	47	57	+57	43	59	+177
70	43.5	−278	26	54	+356	2	56	+431	46	56	+56	42	58	+174
69	42	−269	25	53	+350	1	55	+424	45	55.5	+56	41	57.5	+173
68	41	−262	24	52.5	+347	0	54.5	+420	44	55	+55	40	57	+171
67	40	−256	23	51	+337	−1	54	+416	43	54	+54	39	56	+168
66	39	−250	22	49	+323	−2	53	+408	42	53	+53	38	55.5	+167
65	38	−243	21	47.5	+314	−3	52	+400	41	52	+52	37	55	+165
64	37	−237	20	46	+303	−4	51	+393	40	51.5	+52	36	54.4	+164
63	36	−230	19	44	+290	−5	50	+385	39	50	+50	35	54	+162
62	35	−224	18	42.5	+281	−6	49	+377	38	49	+49	34	53	+159
61	34	−218	17	41	+271	−7	48	+370	37	48	+48	33	52	+156
60	33	−211	16	39.5	+261	−8	47	+362	36	47.5	+48	32	51	+153
59	32	−205	15	37	+244	−9	46	+354	35	47	+47	31	50	+150

TABLE 2 (continued)

Sitting Diastolic Pressure			Breath-Holding 20 sec After Exercise			Difference between Stand. P. R. and P. R. 2 min After Exercise			Sitting Pulse Pressure			Standing Pulse Pressure		
Pressure	T-score	T-score × −6.4	B.-H.	T-score	T-score × +6.6	Pulse Rate Diff.	T-score	T-score × +7.7	Pulse Press.	T-score	T-score × +1.0	Pulse Press.	T-score	T-score × +3.0
58	31	−198	14	35	+231	−10	45	+347	34	46	+46	30	49	+147
57	30	−192	13	33	+218	−11	44	+339	33	45	+45	29	48	+144
56	29	−186	12	31.5	+208	−12	43.5	+335	32	44.5	+45	28	46.5	+140
55	28	−179	11	28	+185	−13	43	+331	31	43	+43	27	45	+135
54	26	−166	10	26	+172	−14	42	+323	30	42	+42	26	44.5	+134
53	24	−154	9	24	+158	−15	41	+316	29	41	+41	25	43	+129
52	23	−147	8	21	+139	−16	40	+308	28	40.5	+41	24	42.5	+128
						−17	39	+303	27	39	+39	23	41	+123
						−18	38	+293	26	38	+38	22	40	+120
						−19	37	+285	25	37	+37	21	39	+117
						−20	36	+277	24	35.5	+36	20	38	+114
						−21	35	+270	23	34	+34	19	36	+108
						−22	34	+262	22	33	+33	18	35.5	+107
						−23	33	+254	21	32	+32	17	34	+102
						−24	32.5	+250	20	31	+31	16	33	+99
						−25	31	+239	19	30	+30	15	32	+96
						−26	30	+231	18	29	+29	14	30.5	+91
						−27	29	+223	17	28	+28	13	29	+87
						−28	28	+216	16	27.5	+28	12	28	+84
						−29	27	+208	15	27	+27	11	27	+81
						−30	25	+193	14	26	+26	10	26	+78
						−31	23.5	+181	13	25	+25	9	25	+75
						−32	22	+170	12	24	+24	8	24	+72

TABLE 3

Classification Test and Record Card[1]

Name .... Date ....

Test Items	Raw Score	T-Score	T-Score × Weight	Classification	
1. Sitting Diastolic Pressure ..	..	..	....	90 Excellent	759—up
2. Breath-Holding 20 sec After Standard Exercise........	..	..	....	80 Very Good	758—696
				70 Good	695—627
3. Standing Pulse Rate Minus Pulse Rate 2 min After				60 Above Av.	626—596
				50 Average	595
Exercise	..	..	....	40 Below av.	594—557
4. Sitting Pulse Pressure......	..	..	....	30 Fair	556—474
5. Stand. Pulse Pressure......	..	..	....	20 Poor	473—436
Classification	Total	......		10 Very Poor	435—down

TABLE 4

Scoring Organic Efficiency of Subjects Examined*

Percentile	Rating or Classification	Score	"Poor" Condition Infirmary Cases	"Average" Condition Freshmen	"Good" Condition Varsity Swimmers
90	Excellent	759—up	..	16	12
80	Very Good	758—696	..	18	10
70	Good	695—627	1	39	20
60	Above Average	626—596	2	20	3
50	Average	595	2	..	..
40	Below Average	594—557	10	20	1
30	Fair	556—474	23	24	..
20	Poor	473—436	17	16	..
10	Very Poor	435—down	22	9	..
			N = 77	N = 162	N = 46

* The 1933–34 dots could not be used in the final scoring, due to the fact that the breath-holding test was taken 10 sec following exercise rather than 20 sec.

Case Studies

In this section of the study we have a number of subjects who have been tested in two or more of the typical groups. In one case we have a subject who was tested on entrance to college, later as an infirmary subject, and still later as a member of the swimming team. This subject represents all three groups in terms of condition; i.e., the "average," "poor," and "good" condition. It is interesting to note that his score was 522 on the entrance test, or as a subject in "average" condition, his score was 454 on the infirmary test, while as a member of the swimming team he had a score of 620. You will notice at the foot of the following table the average score for

TABLE 5

Case Studies—Physical Condition Table

Subject	*"Poor" condition or infirmary subjects with fever*	*"Average" condition. Examined on entrance to college*	*"Good" condition. In training for swimming*
1. H	454	522	620
2. P	541	...	674
3. C	529	...	780
4. M	454	515	...
5. B	383	750	...
6. C	...	456	693
7. C	378	520	...
8. H	472	361	...
9. A	448	439	...
10. A	437	607	...
11. C	590	470	...
12. B	581	645	...
13. N	374	457	...
14. M	542	616	...
15. B	422	525	...
16. B	492	722	...
17. H	410	700	...
18. R	503	725	...
19. H	560	643	...
20. W	522	412	...
21. H	589	707	...
22. S	597	466	...
23. L	506	627	...
24. K	459	489	...
25. M	...	833	664
26. B	...	689	694
27. H	...	629	657
28. R	...	462	634
29. C	...	456	693
30. C	...	650	633
31. E	...	592	633
32. O	...	715	678
Average score	488.8	580.0	671.0

Physiological Norms[5]

		"Poor" condition	*"Good" condition*
1.	Sitting diastolic pressure[6].................	90 and up	52 to 89
2.	Breath-holding twenty seconds after standard stair-climbing exercise..................	22 and down	23 and up
3.	Standing normal pulse rate minus pulse rate two min after exercise..................	−4 and down	−4 up to +20
4.	Pulse pressure	10 to 29	30 to 60

[5] These norms are set on the basis of people who do not have an organic defect. A careful examination of the raw data shows in a few cases an overlapping in the figures as given above. These exceptions are so few that they have not materially affected the norms.

[6] "Clearly it is impossible for an individual with a high diastolic pressure to obtain a considerable output per beat without developing a dangerously high pressure, and throwing an enormous strain on the heart. Conversely, it is obvious that an individual with a low diastolic pressure will be able to reach a high output without difficulty."[3] As quoted by L. F. MacKenzie, M. D., and P. V. Wells, D. Sc.[5]

"poor" condition was found to be 488.8; the average score for "average" condition was found to be 580.0; while the average score for "good" condition was 671.0. This shows a rise in the score with increased organic efficiency.

The case studies with the three groups of condition represented are as follows:

Conclusions

1. The study on reliability and objectivity shows that blood-pressure measurements can be accurately made. Tests which contain blood pressures are valid as far as the measurements are concerned.

2. The research on organic efficiency gives a predicted index which separates clearly the ill group in the infirmary from the varsity swimming group in good condition.

3. The correlations have separated from twenty-six items five items which are significant in the measurement of organic efficiency, comparing the infirmary group with the varsity swimmers.

4. Tests on the same individual show an improvement in "condition" as the athlete reaches varsity form. This is indicated by a rise in the total score for the individual.

5. This organic efficiency test requires experimentation on groups at different age levels, and in a wider variety of activities.

References

1. Bovard and Cozens, *Tests and Measurements in Physical Education.* Philadelphia: W. B. Saunders Co., 1930, p. 277.

2. Cureton, Edward E. By correspondence. New York, N. Y.

3. Hill, A. V., J. C. Gramwell, and A. C. Downing, *Heart Bull.,* **10** (1923), 289–300.

4. McCurdy, J. H., and L. A. Larson, "The Reliability and Objectivity of Blood Pressure Measurements," *Res. Quart. Suppl.,* **6** (1935), 3–10.

5. MacKenzie, L. F., and P. V. Wells, "On the Interpretation of Blood Pressure." Newark, N. J.: The Prudential Insurance Company of America, 1933.

6. Medical Department of the Prudential Insurance Company of America, "Determining Ciruclatory Fitness—Flarimeter Tests." Newark, N. J.: The Prudential Insurance Company of America, Table 3, p. 22.

7. Richardson and Stalnaker, "A Note on the Use of Bi-Serial *R* in Test Research," *J. Gen. Psych.,* **8**, No. 2 (1933), 463–65.

III

The Effect of Training and Strenuous Exercise

Studies on the effect of training on physical performance and physiological functions are widely reported in the literature. Many of these investigations, however, have been concerned with limited aspects of physical performance or with only one or two physiological variables. In selecting the material for this chapter, the editors have tried to obtain a representative sampling of the more comprehensive studies. Three of the articles describe work conducted at the Harvard Fatigue Laboratory. The research activities at this laboratory over a period of more than a decade in the 1920's and 1930's probably represent the foremost efforts of the kind regarding physical activity. Using the team approach that is common in research now—but was rather uncommon at that time—physiologists, biochemists, and physical educators studied the effects of exercise and training in various ways in order to understand more about the factors that influence physical performance and fatigue.

The remaining studies included here are pioneer studies on the effects of types of training that were not studied extensively until after World War II. Physical reconditioning and weight training were areas subject to many popular beliefs; few facts had been scientifically established until Karpovich-Weiss and Zorbas-Karpovich published their work. As a result many other scientists have chosen this field of inquiry as the subject for further research.

D. B. DILL / J. H. TALBOTT / H. T. EDWARDS

Studies in Muscular Activity.
VI. Response of Several Individuals
to a Fixed Task

Reprinted from the *Journal of Physiology* (*London*),
69 (1930), 267–305.

In this study ten subjects performed the same amount of work for 20 min, and expired air and blood samples were taken at periodic intervals in order to assess their response to the task. The article is especially valuable in that it presents the results for each subject in great detail. This practice is now discouraged in most scientific journals for the obvious reason of space and expense, but a report of this nature is very helpful to the researcher or student who is interested in specific reactions. The authors also present the classical data on Clarence De Mar, the famous marathon runner who competed in 26-mi marathons past the age of 70, in which he showed practically no increase in blood lactate or change in blood bicarbonate after running for 20 min. The DeMar observations have been widely quoted as evidence of the organism achieving a maximum degree of adaptation to exercise due to training.

The authors discuss the dynamics of the changes in equilibria in such blood variables as serum protein, red cell concentration, diffusible ions such as phosphate and bicarbonate, and blood lactate. In general, they conclude, that the adjustment of the body to strenuous exercise is accompanied by a series of homeostatic changes involving blood volume, diffusible ions, particularly bicarbonate ions and blood lactate. They liken the body to a machine in suggesting that the efficiency of a person's physiological response to exercise can best be judged by studying blood lactate and bicarbonate changes under the stress of exercise. The Harvard studies, of which this is one example, have contributed immeasurably to understanding the organism response to exercise and should be studied by every student of physical activity. It is an interesting aside that Dr. D. B. Dill and other members of the Harvard staff participated actively as subjects in their experiments.

Introduction

Experience teaches that individuals are not equal in physical ability. From prehistoric times contests in war and in sport have given convincing evidence of this fact. The question as to how one individual can surpass another in capacity and in skill is at least partially susceptible of analysis in the laboratory. This has been demonstrated by Hill and his associates,[37, 26] and by many others.

There remain, however, many unanswered questions raised by the rearguard runner. Does he fall behind because of inadequate physical endowment or because of insufficient training?

160

His coach may ascribe his failure to his musculature, to his heart, to his "wind," or to his "guts." Since the empirical observations of the runner and his coach certainly have an objective foundation, it has been our aim to seek a basis for these ideas in physiological and physicochemical facts.

Experimental

Ten men, normal but not in active training, have performed the same task under controlled conditions. Each came to the laboratory without breakfast and rested for 30 min on a bed. With the subject in this state, respiratory and pulse rates were observed, expired air was collected in a 100-l gasometer over a 10-min period and then samples of alveolar air and "virtual venous" air were collected. Gas samples were analysed on the Haldane apparatus.

The method used for estimating blood flow is in basic principle that of Christiansen, Douglas and Haldane.[17] Y. Henderson and Prince[36] modified it in important details and introduced the term "virtual venous" air. Field, Bock, Gildea, and Lathrop[25] added further modifications. It is now necessary to modify it still further, for recent determinations[10] indicate that Haldane-Priestley samples collected in rest at the end of expiration have, without correction, the same pressure of carbonic acid as that in arterial blood. Accordingly the carbonic acid pressures of alveolar air and of "virtual venous" air are applied directly to the carbonic acid dissociated curve of oxygenated whole blood. The difference between the indicated contents, diminished by 0.3 volume per cent on the assumption that arterial blood is 95 per cent saturated, represents carbon dioxide transport in volumes per cent. Rate of dioxide output divided by rate of transport gives rate of blood flow.

Of course this method for determining rate of blood flow, being indirect, is unsatisfactory. Yet many arguments of the kind commonly advanced for indirect methods may be presented in its defense. It yields results, particularly in exercise, of the same order of magnitude as those obtained by other methods: results in certain pathological conditions are qualitatively similar to blood velocity determinations;[1] repeated observations on a given individual in the same state give good checks; wholly improbable results are not obtained. So long as the evidence for the absolute accuracy of this and other indirect methods is of such a character, estimates of rate of blood flow must be accepted with reserve.

When all these observations were completed, about 65 cc of venous blood was drawn without stasis: 5 cc was set aside for serum calcium determination and the remainder was treated with heparin. Determinations made on blood will be described below.

Within an hour of the time resting blood was drawn, the subject, still fasting, began exercise. This consisted in running for 20 min on a treadmill, motor-driven in a horizontal plane at a rate of 9.3 km per hr. Outside air was inspired through a large-size Henderson-Haggard valve[35] and alveolar air samples were collected automatically, since it is not practicable in exercise of this character to use the heavy system

---

[1] Reference may be made to the series of papers by H. L. Blumgart and Soma Weiss,[8] in which velocity was measured by injecting radioactive material and detecting its arrival at a distant point. The recent velocity measurements by Soma Weiss, G. P. Robb, and H. L. Blumgart[55] involved use of the effect of histamine on the minute vessels and gave similar results. W. O. Thompson, J. M. Alper, and P. K. Thompson[50] have demonstrated posture effects on velocity from ankle to arm by the dye injection method; and A. V. Bock and associates, in an investigation in the course of publication, have obtained similar results with the histamine method. All the above experiments on blood velocity agree qualitatively with our determinations of rate of blood flow.

of valves suitable in rest or in exercise on the ergometer. The subject breathed continuously through the mouthpiece from the start until the 9th minute, and again from the 12th through the 17th minute. Other details, such as the method of collecting "virtual venous" air in exercise of this sort, are given by Hochrein, Talbott, Dill, and Henderson.[42]

Expired air was measured in a 600-l gasometer, and six samples were taken by the mixing chamber method as described by Bock, Dill, and Talbott.[11] Pulse rate was recorded by a cardiotachometer which will be described by Paul S. Bauer, its designer, in detail at another time. It resembles in many particulars the instrument of Boas.[9] The nature of other observations made during exercise will be disclosed in tables of data.

After running for 20 min the subject jumped on to the bed, and another 65 cc portion of venous blood was withdrawn. A sample of blood obtained within 1 min of cessation of work of this intensity represents blood circulating during work in nearly every respect, except for different contents of oxygen and of carbonic acid. This is borne out by unpublished observations made in this laboratory on oxygen capacity, carbonic acid capacity, and lactic acid content of blood taken during the course of, and within 1 min of, cessation of exercise on the bicycle ergometer.

Each of the 60-cc portions of blood treated with heparin was kept in ice water until equilibration. Two 5-cc portions were removed for determination of lactic acid and oxygen combining capacity. The remainder was divided into a 45-cc and a 5-cc portion and equilibrated at 37.5° with sufficient oxygen for saturation at carbon dioxide pressures of about 40 and 80 mm, respectively. After 15 min equilibra-

tion, blood was drawn into sampling tubes for carbon dioxide determination and about 40 cc of the larger portion, without exposure to air, were divided between two calibrated centrifuge tubes of 20-cc capacity. This technique and other determinations carried out on serum and cells have been described in detail by Dill, Talbott, Edwards, and Oberg. The only new method used was Van Slyke's micro total nitrogen method.[52] Single 10-cc portions of equilibrated serum and cells were dried to constant weight for total solid determination, and then ashed and used for sodium and potassium determination. Previous determinations of sodium and of potassium carried out in duplicate, using the same method,[22] usually agreed within 1 meq per 1. In these experiments determinations were not carried out in duplicate, but rest and work serum and cells were analyzed side by side, and it is likely that a difference between rest and work greater than 1 meq per 1 is significant.

Table 1 records ventilation, pulse rate, respiratory rate, composition of expired air, metabolic rate (M.R.) and respiratory quotient (R.Q.). Composition of alveolar air and carbon dioxide pressure in gas samples equilibrated in vivo with oxygenated venous blood are shown in Table 2. Four samples of each were taken in rest, and only the averages of these are shown. Alveolar samples were collected at about the 4th, 8th, 13th, and 17th minutes in work, and each determination is given in order to show change of state if such occurred. Two "virtual venous" samples were collected during the 9th to 12th minutes, and two more during the 18th to 20th. The average of each pair is given. Values for carbon dioxide transport and rate of blood flow, calculated from the data of Tables 1 and 2, are also given in Table 2. Experimental observations on blood equilibrated with

TABLE 1

Metabolic Rate, Respiration, and Pulse

Time (min)	Remarks	Total ventilation (l per min)	Composition of expired air CO_2 (%)	O_2 (%)	Oxygen used (cc per min)	Respiratory quotient	Pulse rate	Respiratory rate
	D. B. D. Basal	5.38	3.77	16.53	246	0.82	62	10
0	*Work begun*							
4–5		41	4.43	15.95	2100	0.86	—	—
6–7		41	4.44	15.99	2080	0.87	138	21
12–13		48	4.17	16.46	2180	0.91	140	24
14–15		50	4.10	16.50	2260	0.90	135	22
16–17		45	4.02	16.53	2020	0.89	138	22
	P. F. P. Basal	7.90	2.65	17.58	277	0.75*	68	15
0	*Work begun*							
2–3		45	4.12	16.64	2180	0.95	—	37
4–5		52	4.09	16.89	2100	1.01	172	38
6–7		53	4.06	16.91	2130	1.00	164	44
14–15		67	3.81	17.10	2570	0.98	166	46
16–17		62	3.78	17.15	2350	0.99	164	45
17–18		62	3.72	17.01	2470	0.93	—	47
	A. A. McC. Basal	5.23	3.23	16.77	276	0.72*	50	15
0	*Work begun*							
3–4		65	4.23	16.55	2880	0.95	—	36
4–5		64	4.35	16.43	2900	0.95	—	—
6–7		59	4.29	16.22	2830	0.88	—	—
13–14		59	4.27	16.09	2950	0.85	—	34
15–16		59	4.45	15.88	3080	0.85	132	—
17–18		58	4.42	16.05	2900	0.88	132	36
	J. H. T. Basal	5.89	3.33	16.94	242	0.80	64	9
0	*Work begun*							
3–4		50	3.84	16.60	2220	0.85	153	—
5–6		52	3.75	16.90	2130	0.90	153	25
7–8		53	3.72	17.03	2100	0.93	153	—
11–12		54	3.70	17.04	2150	0.93	153	—
13–14		52	3.76	16.91	2120	0.91	153	37
16–17		53	3.57	17.15	2020	0.92	153	36
	W. C. Basal	7.23	3.35	16.90	305	0.79	69	15
0	*Work begun*							
3–4		63	4.68	16.45	2790	1.04	174	41
5–6		71	4.06	17.06	2720	1.05	168	—
7–8		70	3.91	16.90	2850	0.95	174	—
13–14		74	3.93	17.06	2850	1.01	174	42
15–16		80	3.63	17.38	2830	1.02	180	—
16–17		82	3.45	17.60	2710	1.03	176	49

TABLE 1 (Continued)

Time (min)	Remarks	TOTAL VENTILATION (l per min)	CO₂ (%)	O₂ (%)	OXYGEN USED (cc per min)	RESPIRATORY QUOTIENT	PULSE RATE	RESPIRATORY RATE
	O. S. L. Basal	5.94	3.39	16.96	246	0.81	71	12
0	Work begun							
2–3		44	4.93	15.63	2380	0.91	144	14
4–5		45	5.19	15.28	2600	0.90	146	—
7–8		46	5.13	15.48	2560	0.92	160	12
14–15		49	4.86	15.71	2610	0.91	163	15
15–16		50	4.74	15.95	2530	0.93	156	18
16–17		51	4.69	16.04	2520	0.94	159	19
	J. L. S. Basal	6.12	3.22	17.40	222	0.88*	69	14
0	Work begun							
3–4		53	4.59	16.22	2520	0.96	—	25
5–6		55	4.30	16.51	2450	0.95	—	—
7–8		53	4.36	16.39	2460	0.94	—	29
11–12		54	4.34	16.40	2470	0.94	—	30
14–15		53	4.25	16.41	2420	0.92	—	—
17–18		53	4.12	16.47	2390	0.90	—	30
	H. T. E. Basal	4.15	4.32	15.66	232	0.78	66	10
0	Work begun							
3–4		35	5.24	14.91	2180	0.84	153	15
5–6		39	4.80	16.95	1950	0.95	154	—
7–8		42	4.77	15.75	2220	0.90	156	19
12–13		46	4.50	16.15	2210	0.92	154	21
14–15		44	4.62	15.90	2260	0.90	156	—
16–17		43	4.69	15.58	2380	0.84	—	20
	A. V. B. Basal	4.90	4.02	16.26	237	0.82	61	5
0	Work begun							
2–3		47	4.03	16.41	2190	0.86	—	21
5–6		52	4.02	16.80	2170	0.96	142	—
7–8		55	3.96	16.60	2440	0.88	144	32
11–12		60	3.87	16.92	2430	0.95	144	33
14–15		57	3.72	16.98	2290	0.92	—	—
17–18		56	3.75	16.78	2380	0.87	142	33
	W. J. G. Basal	5.02	3.60	16.83	212	0.83	62	14
0	Work begun							
2–3		55	4.16	16.78	2280	1.00	156	27
3–4		55	4.12	16.75	2290	0.97	170	—
7–8		55	3.92	16.90	2230	0.96	168	31
12–13		55	3.82	16.82	2300	0.91	168	30
16–17		56	3.99	16.80	2340	0.95	169	31

* Probably a fallacious value due to abnormal breathing.

TABLE 2

Determination of Blood Flow

Remarks		Respiratory quotient	(pCO₂ mm Hg)	(pO₂ mm Hg)	Virtual venous air (pCO₂ mm Hg)	CO₂ transport (meq per l blood)	O₂ transport (meq per l blood)	O₂ saturation of venous blood (%)	Blood flow (l per min)
D. B. D.	Basal	0.82	40.2	105	47.6	1.35	1.65	75	6.7
	Work	0.89	42.0	106	—	—	—	—	—
		0.94	40.2	110	65.4	4.44	4.99	38	18.9
		0.92	39.4	110	—	—	—	—	—
		0.92	40.5	109	62.7	3.95	4.44	44	21.3
Average Δ		+0.10	+ 0.3	+ 4	+16.5	+2.85	+3.07	−34	+13.4
P. F. P.	Basal	0.82	36.3	106	43.3	1.30	1.73	75	7.1
	Work	0.96	39.8	108	71.5	4.72	4.82	41	21.1
		0.97	37.4	111	—	—	—	—	—
		0.88	36.8	109	66.8	5.12	5.22	37	19.4
Average Δ		+0.12	+ 1.7	+ 3	+25.8	+3.62	+3.29	−36	+13.1
A. A. McC.	Basal	0.81	38.0	103	46.1	1.53	2.12	69	5.9
	Work	0.88	42.3	102	—	—	—	—	—
		0.81	42.1	99	67.0	4.23	4.75	43	27.3
		0.83	42.0	100	—	—	—	—	—
		0.87	40.3	103	69.7	5.00	5.61	34	23.1
Average Δ		+0.04	+ 3.7	− 2	+22.3	+3.09	+3.06	−31	+19.3
J. H. T.	Basal	0.80	39.5	103	45.8	1.12	1.40	80	8.8
	Work	0.86	37.2	112	—	—	—	—	—
		0.95	35.5	112	62.6	4.81	5.28	46	17.9
		0.92	34.3	112	—	—	—	—	—
		0.85	34.3	110	60.1	4.63	5.09	48	18.7
Average Δ		+0.09	− 4.2	+ 8	+15.6	+3.60	+3.79	−33	+ 9.5
W. C.	Basal	1.02	35.6	113	45.0	1.65	2.09	72	6.7
	Work	1.05	45.2	105	—	—	—	—	—
		0.99	37.3	110	75.1	5.48	5.32	35	24.4
		1.00	32.7	116	72.9	—	—	—	—
		1.01	33.5	115	—	5.66	5.50	33	21.8
Average Δ		−0.01	+ 1.6	− 2	+29.0	+3.92	+3.32	−38	+16.4
O. S. L.	Basal	1.11	38.2	114	45.0	1.12	1.38	79	8.0
	Work	0.84	42.9	101	—	—	—	—	—
		0.87	45.4	99	67.8	3.64	3.96	52	28.8
		0.86	43.4	102	—	—	—	—	—
		0.87	42.1	103	66.3	4.00	4.35	48	26.3
Average Δ		−0.25	+ 5.2	− 13	+22.1	+2.70	+2.78	−29	+19.6
J. L. S.	Basal	1.06	39.3	111	46.6	1.44	1.63	78	6.0
	Work	0.94	42.0	106	—	—	—	—	—
		1.07	40.6	104	70.9	5.00	5.38	41	20.7
		0.92	39.7	107	—	—	—	—	—
		0.92	39.7	107	67.7	4.76	5.12	44	20.8
Average Δ		−0.11	+ 1.2	− 5	+22.7	+3.44	+3.62	−36	+14.8

TABLE 2 (Continued)

Remarks		ALVEOLAR AIR — Respiratory quotient	$(pCO_2$ mm Hg$)$	$(pO_2$ mm Hg$)$	VIRTUAL VENOUS AIR $(pCO_2$ mm Hg$)$	CO_2 TRANSPORT (meq per 1 blood)	O_2 TRANSPORT (meq per 1 blood)	O_2 SATURATION OF VENOUS BLOOD (%)	BLOOD FLOW (l per min)
H. T. E.	Basal	0.72	40.3	98	46.8	1.15	1.47	78	7.4
	Work	0.78	47.0	94	—	—	—	—	—
		0.61	43.2	87	69.7	4.22	4.74	44	21.2
		0.85	41.0	103	—	—	—	—	—
		0.81	42.1	100	69.3	4.42	4.96	42	20.4
Average Δ		+0.04	+ 3.0	− 2	+22.7	+3.17	+3.38	−35	+13.4
A. V. B.	Basal	0.87	38.1	100	45.9	1.39	1.70	76	6.3
	Work	0.88	38.4	102	—	—	—	—	—
		0.87	38.0	102	63.0	4.59	4.99	45	20.7
		0.88	34.7	106	—	—	—	—	—
		0.86	34.7	105	60.3	4.86	5.28	42	19.5
Average Δ		0.00	− 1.7	+ 4	+15.8	+3.34	+3.44	−33	+13.8
W. J. G.	Basal	1.04	43.7	108	49.5	1.04	1.24	82	7.8
	Work	0.90	38.6	109	—	—	—	—	—
		0.94	37.8	111	66.2	5.16	5.43	43	19.1
		0.92	35.7	112	—	—	—	—	—
		0.88	36.9	110	59.7	4.55	4.79	49	21.6
Average Δ		−0.13	− 6.5	+ 1	+13.6	+3.82	+3.87	−36	+12.5

oxygen and carbon dioxide are given in Table 3.

Under the conditions of our experiments it was not practicable to secure arterial blood nor to equilibrate venous blood at precisely the carbonic acid pressure of arterial blood. From our knowledge of shift of anions and water between cells and plasma with change in acidity and from the present experimental observations, it is possible to recalculate the data to a basis more convenient for comparison.

Thus it is possible to recalculate to the basis of (a) a given pH_s value; (b) a given carbonic acid pressure, say 40 mm Hg; (c) the estimated carbonic pressure of arterial blood; or (d) the estimated carbonic acid pressure of mixed venous blood.

Consideration of these procedures brings to mind the discussion by L. J. Henderson[32] of corresponding states. Any attempt to bring two or more individuals, or even specimens of their blood, to the same state in all probability will fail because of the interdependence of the variables involved. When a given variable has been brought to a common value others will be disturbed. This is well illustrated in the present case. Thus we may bring all specimens of blood to the same pH_s value for rest and work. Calculated values for pH of arterial serum in rest and work are shown in Table 4. These calculations involve the assumptions that arterial blood is 95 per cent saturated in work of this character, and that alveolar carbon dioxide pressure measures accurately arterial carbon dioxide pressure. Arterial punctures in

TABLE 3

BLOOD EQUILIBRATED WITH CARBONIC ACID

Subject		Serum calcium (meq per l serum)	pCO_2 (mm Hg)	$(Total\ CO_2)_b$ (meq per l blood)	$(Total\ CO_2)_s$ (meq per l serum)	Cell vol. (%)	$(Cl)_s$ (meq per l serum)	$(Cl)_c$ (meq per l cells)	$(H_2O)_s$ (cc per l serum)	$(H_2O)_c$ (cc per l cells)	$(Na)_s$ (meq per l serum)	$(Na)_c$ (meq per l cells)	$(K)_s$ (meq per l serum)	$(K)_c$ (meq per l cells)	$(HPO_4)_s^{--} + (H_2PO_4)_s^{-}$ (meq per l serum)	$(Protein)_s$ (g per l serum)
D. B. D.	Rest	4.81	58.6, 82.0	25.91, 29.50	30.86	42.0	103.3	56.1	940	734	137.5	16.7	3.2	93.5	2.29	70.8
	Work	5.05	46.7, 90.4	22.28, 29.20	26.98	44.1	103.7	55.7	934	728	138.0	15.8	3.7	96.4	2.57	79.9
P. F. P.	Rest	—	39.1, 68.4	21.73, 27.00	26.40	45.7	104.4	54.7	940	730	137.0	14.5	3.6	95.7	2.18	70.0
	Work		30.5	15.34	18.56	47.6	106.2	56.2	933	726	141.6	13.2	3.0	96.3	2.57	77.1
A.A. McC.	Rest	4.58	42.4, 75.2	21.84, 27.70	26.67	44.5	107.0	54.0	939	727	—	—	—	—	2.48	—
	Work	4.82	39.0, 81.1	19.46, 26.60	23.98	47.9	107.6	54.7	931	725	—	—	—	—	2.92	—
J. H. T.	Rest	4.69	42.4, 58.6	21.42, 24.38	26.11	46.2	105.7	52.5	940	725	139.0	15.0	2.9	93.6	1.79	68.6
	Work	4.93	42.7, 99.9	21.01, 30.05	25.95	47.8	106.0	52.9	939	724	140.7	14.4	2.7	94.3	2.07	71.6
W. C.	Rest	4.75	44.3, 60.9	22.22, 24.93	26.70	44.4	105.2	53.3	937	724	134.5	15.4	2.9	88.7	2.46	72.0
	Work	5.05	42.7, 60.9	15.93, 18.77	18.63	45.8	106.1	58.0	933	725	140.5	16.0	2.8	90.4	3.30	77.7
O. S. L.	Rest	4.55	44.8, 56.7	22.40, 25.49	26.81	41.8	108.1	53.7	939	722	139.8	17.2	3.2	90.6	2.20	71.4
	Work	4.70	43.4, 68.3	18.97, 23.31	22.68	44.9	107.8	56.1	932	722	142.6	17.4	2.8	90.2	2.72	78.0
J. L. S.	Rest	4.70	43.1, 88.2	20.82, 28.30	26.05	48.3	106.3	52.6	938	726	141.5	13.1	3.6	96.8	2.14	69.4
	Work	4.70	37.5, 84.0	18.94, 26.57	23.38	49.4	107.5	53.6	935	724	138.5	13.3	3.7	96.8	2.80	73.9
H. T. E.	Rest	4.65	42.6, 67.8	21.67, 26.00	26.29	44.1	106.4	51.9	940	729	140.3	13.5	2.9	99.1	2.34	69.4
	Work	4.85	38.8, 69.2	17.43, 22.55	21.04	46.7	107.7	57.9	934	727	143.5	13.5	3.3	98.2	2.87	77.0
A. V. B.	Rest	4.45	33.8, 93.7	19.57, 29.22	23.79	43.9	107.0	52.2	939	726	138.5	14.7	4.3	92.6	2.30	65.0
	Work	4.75	40.3, 68.6	18.85, 24.02	23.39	48.8	104.8	53.8	929	718	139.0	12.5	4.2	92.6	2.57	78.8
W. J. G.	Rest	—	45.1, 68.8	21.92, 26.09	26.42	44.3	107.1	51.1	945	718	140.2	14.1	3.1	92.7	1.88	62.5
	Work	4.65	39.9, 69.6	18.66, 24.14	23.13	47.4	108.0	51.9	939	715	143.3	13.3	2.9	93.4	2.55	71.2

TABLE 4

pH of Arterial Serum in Rest and at the End of Work

Subject	pH_s		ΔpH_s	Ventilation per kg body weight (l)
	Rest	Work		
D. B. D.	7.42	7.39	−0.03	0.58
P. F. P.	7.44	7.32	−0.12	0.80
A. A. McC.	7.42	7.37	−0.05	0.72
J. H. T.	7.40	7.44	+0.04	0.67
W. C.	7.44	7.29	−0.15	1.19
O. S. L.	7.41	7.31	−0.10	0.67
J. L. S.	7.39	7.37	−0.02	0.72
H. T. E.	7.39	7.30	−0.09	0.59
A. V. B.	· 7.40	7.40	0.0	0.70
W. J. G.	7.36	7.38	+0.02	0.81
Average...	7.41	7.36	−0.05	0.75

TABLE 5

Carbon Dioxide Pressure in Alveolar Air in Rest and Work

Subject	Rest (mm Hg)	Work		ΔpCO_2 from rest to end of work (mm Hg)
		Average (mm Hg)	End of work (mm Hg)	
D. B. D.	40.2	40.5	40.5	+0.3
P. F. P.	36.3	38.0	36.8	+0.5
A. A. McC.	38.0	41.7	40.3	+2.3
J. H. T.	39.2	37.4	37.1	−2.1
W. C.	36.4	37.3	33.5	−2.9
O. S. L.	38.2	43.4	42.1	+3.9
J. L. S.	39.3	40.5	39.7	+0.4
H. T. E.	40.3	43.4	42.1	+1.8
A. V. B.	38.1	36.4	34.7	−3.4
W. J. G.	43.7	37.2	36.9	−6.8
Average...	39.0	39.6	38.4	−0.6
Median...	38.7	39.7	38.2	+0.3

exercise reported by Dill, Laurence, Hurxthal, and Bock[21] fully justify these assumptions when one is considering the average of a series of observations on the ergometer, but such general agreement does not ensure that every individual observation is correct. The values in Table 4 show clearly that, on the average, there is a decrease in pH of arterial serum of about 0.05. However, it is equally clear that some individuals show slight change and others large change in pH_s. This variation as well as related physiological changes would be masked by comparing properties of blood in rest and work at a common pH_s value.

Table 5 has been complied in order to test the second method of recalculation suggested above. Two columns are given for work. One contains an average of all four samples taken during work and the other gives values for the last work sample only. It appears that in exercise of this character (*a*) there is not usually much change in alveolar pCO_2 from rest to work nor during progress of work, and (*b*) the changes which do occur have no distinct relation to degree of lactic acid accumulation. The evidence for the latter statement will be given later.

Accordingly, this method of recalculation was finally decided upon, viz. on the basis of a carbonic acid pressure of 40 mm Hg. While open to some objection, it involves no doubtful assumptions, it is simple and it gives values at least approximately the same as if arterial blood had been used; in short, it gives values approximately of the order of corresponding states. The recalculations for serum are given in Table 6 and for whole blood in Table 7.

Interpretation of Results

Concentration changes in protein of serum and hemoglobin of blood. Zuntz with his associates[56] was perhaps the first to demonstrate clearly that increase in specific gravity and cell count of blood takes place in exercise. In 28 experiments, marching with a pack of 22–31 kg over a course of 18–24$\frac{3}{4}$ km caused an increase in specific gravity of 2 to 4 thousandths and in cell count of about 9 per cent. Later it was shown by Ferrari[24] that the average red cell count of students may increase 10 per cent during the course of an examination. Since then much more evidence has accumulated that change in degree of physical activity or in emotional state is reflected by hemoglobin concentration change in the blood.

In the cat suddenly confronted by the barking dog, there is an increase of 20 to 30 per cent (or, rarely, 40 to 50 per cent) in red cell count as shown by Lamson[45] and Izquierdo and Cannon.[43] The latter authors, having at hand knowledge of the spleen as a reservoir of red cells recently acquired by Barcroft and his associates[4, 5, 6, 7] and many others, demonstrated that when only the liver of the upper abdominal viscera is left innervated, there is no emotional polycythemia. Furthermore:

"After section of the nerves to the spleen, excitement for one minute does not produce polycythemia. . . . Inactivation of the adrenal medulla has no marked influence on emotional polycythemia."

Aside from contributions of polycythemic blood by the spleen, there may be a change due to salt solution transfer from blood to tissues or interstitial spaces. Imbibition by frog's muscle in strychnine tetanus and simultaneous loss of fluid by the blood was reported by Ranke[46] in 1865. Water content of blood of resting frogs was 88.3 per cent and of tetanized frogs 87.0 per cent. Corresponding values for muscle were 80.3 and 82.1, respectively. More recently Back, Cogan, and Towers,[1] also working on frog's muscle, found that faradic stimulation caused increases in water content ranging from 0.7 to 7.6 per cent, averaging about 4 per cent.

Increase in hemoglobin concentration in exercise varies with the species and with the conditions of exercise. For man Bock, van Caulært, Dill, Fölling, and Hurxthal[12] found increases of 5 to 10 per cent with some difference in individuals, the maximum increase of about 10 per cent occurring in A. V. B. at a metabolic rate of about 2 l of oxygen per min. Increases found by Harrison, Robinson, and Syllaba[28] and by Himwich and

TABLE 6

Electrolytes of True Plasma at a Carbonic Acid Pressure of 40 mm Hg. Concentrations Are Expressed in meq per 1 of Serum, Excepting Hydrogen Ion

Subject		(Total CO₂)	pH	Serum vol. (%)	(HCO₃)⁻	(Lactate)⁻	(Cl)⁻	(HPO₄)⁻⁻ +(H₂PO₄)⁻	(Proteinate)⁻	Σ anions	Σ cations*
D. B. D.	Rest	27.20	7.42	58.5	25.96	1.0	104.0	2.3	17.4	150.7	147.5
	Work	25.62	7.40	56.1	24.38	1.8	104.4	2.6	19.5	152.7	148.8
	Δ	−1.58	−0.02	−2.4	−1.58	+0.8	+0.4	+0.3	+2.1	+2.0	+1.3
P. F. P.	Rest	26.57	7.41	54.3	25.33	1.1	104.4	2.2	17.1	150.1	147.3
	Work	20.68	7.30	52.2	19.44	5.8	105.2	2.6	18.0	151.0	151.6
	Δ	−5.89	−0.11	−2.1	−5.89	+4.7	+0.8	+0.4	+0.9	+0.9	+4.3
J. H. T.	Rest	25.58	7.40	53.9	24.34	1.6	107.2	1.8	16.7	151.6	148.6
	Work	25.24	7.39	52.3	24.00	2.1	107.6	2.1	17.4	153.2	150.3
	Δ	−0.34	−0.01	−1.6	−0.34	+0.5	+0.4	+0.3	+0.7	+1.6	+1.7
W. C.	Rest	26.08	7.40	55.7	24.84	1.3	105.7	2.5	17.5	151.9	144.2†
	Work	18.12	7.24	54.3	16.88	7.2	106.2	3.3	17.5	151.1	150.4
	Δ	−7.96	−0.16	−1.4	−7.96	+5.9	+0.5	+0.8	0.0	−0.8	
O. S. L.	Rest	26.08	7.40	58.2	24.84	1.3	108.7	2.2	17.4	154.4	149.6
	Work	22.59	7.34	55.2	21.35	3.7	108.2	2.7	18.5	154.4	152.1
	Δ	−3.49	−0.06	−3.0	−3.49	+2.4	−0.5	+0.5	+1.1	−0.0	+2.5
J. L. S.	Rest	25.13	7.39	51.8	23.89	1.3	106.6	2.1	16.8	150.7	151.8
	Work	23.96	7.37	50.5	22.72	2.1	107.3	2.8	17.7	152.6	146.9†
	Δ	−1.17	−0.02	−1.3	−1.17	+0.8	+0.7	+0.7	+0.9	+1.9	
H. T. E.	Rest	25.67	7.40	56.0	24.43	1.2	106.6	2.4	16.9	151.5	149.9
	Work	21.15	7.31	53.3	19.91	3.8	107.6	2.8	18.0	152.1	153.7
	Δ	−4.52	−0.09	−2.7	−4.52	+2.6	+1.0	+0.4	+1.1	+0.6	+3.8
A. V. B.	Rest	25.19	7.39	56.3	23.95	1.1	106.4	2.3	15.8	149.6	149.3
	Work	23.81	7.36	51.2	22.57	3.4	104.8	2.6	18.8	152.2	150.0
	Δ	−1.38	−0.03	−5.1	−1.38	+2.3	−1.6	+0.3	+3.0	+2.6	+0.7
W. J. G.	Rest	25.31	7.39	55.9	24.07	1.1	107.6	1.9	15.2	149.9	150.3
	Work	23.11	7.35	52.6	21.87	3.4	108.0	2.6	16.9	152.8	153.5
	Δ	−2.20	−0.04	−3.3	−2.20	+2.3	+0.4	+0.7	+1.7	+2.9	+3.2
Average,	Rest	25.87	7.40	55.6	24.63	1.2	106.1	2.2	16.7	151.2	149.3
	Work	22.70	7.34	53.1	21.46	3.7	106.3	2.7	18.0	152.5	151.3
	Δ	−3.17	−0.06	−2.5	−3.17	+2.5	+0.2	+0.5	+1.3	+1.3	+2.0

* Concentration of magnesium is assumed to be 2 meq per l of serum.   † Doubtful result. Not included in the average.

TABLE 7

Electrolytes of Oxygenated Blood at a Carbonic Acid Pressure of 40 mm Hg. Concentrations Are Expressed in meq per l of Blood

Subject		Total Hb	Total CO_2	$(HCO_3)^-$	$(Lactate)^-$	$(Cl)^-$	$(HOP_4)^{--} + (H_2PO_4)^-$	$(Protein-ate)^-$	$(Na)^+$	$(K)^+$	Σ anions	Σ cations*
D. B. D.	Rest	8.27	22.44	21.30	0.80	83.5	1.7	30.1	86.8	41.1	137.4	132.9
	Work	8.76	21.00	19.86	1.47	82.5	1.9	31.6	84.1	44.6	137.3	133.7
	Δ	+0.49	−1.44	−1.44	+0.67	−1.0	+0.2	+1.5	−2.7	+3.5	−0.1	+0.8
P. F. P.	Rest	8.92	21.90	20.76	0.90	81.7	1.6	31.4	81.0	45.7	136.4	131.7
	Work	9.56	17.36	16.22	4.85	82.4	1.9	30.4	80.4	47.4	135.8	132.8
	Δ	+0.64	−4.54	−4.54	+3.95	+0.7	+0.3	−1.0	−0.6	+1.7	−0.6	+1.1
J. H. T.	Rest	9.34	20.82	19.68	1.30	81.1	1.4	31.2	81.7	45.8	134.7	132.5
	Work	9.86	20.33	19.19	1.74	80.6	1.6	32.2	80.3	46.5	135.3	131.8
	Δ	+0.52	−0.49	−0.49	+0.44	−0.5	+0.2	+1.0	−1.4	+0.7	+0.7	−0.7
W. C.	Rest	9.13	21.54	20.40	1.08	82.1	1.9	32.1	81.6?	41.0	137.6	127.6†
	Work	9.29	15.56	14.42	6.04	84.1	2.5	28.2	83.5	42.9	135.3	131.4
	Δ	+0.16	−5.98	−5.98	+4.96	+2.0	+0.6	−3.9	+1.9?	+1.9	−2.3	
O. S. L.	Rest	8.63	21.59	20.45	1.12	85.4	1.6	30.6	88.6	39.7	139.2	133.3
	Work	9.29	18.36	17.22	3.18	84.6	2.0	29.9	86.3	42.0	136.9	133.3
	Δ	+0.66	−3.23	−3.23	+2.06	−0.8	+0.4	−0.7	−2.3	+2.3	−2.3	0.0
J. L. S.	Rest	9.79	20.23	19.09	1.08	80.4	1.6	31.6	79.5	48.6	133.8	133.1
	Work	10.09	19.56	18.42	1.74	81.9	2.1	32.6	76.6?	49.7	136.8	131.3†
	Δ	+0.30	−0.67	−0.67	+0.66	+1.5	+0.5	+1.0	−2.9?	+1.1	+3.0	
H. T. E.	Rest	8.92	21.15	20.01	0.99	82.3	1.7	30.7	84.4	44.3	135.7	133.7
	Work	9.41	17.60	16.46	3.13	84.4	2.1	30.6	82.7	47.6	136.7	135.3
	Δ	+0.49	−3.55	−3.55	+2.14	+2.1	+0.4	−0.1	−1.7	+3.3	+0.1	+1.6
A. V. B.	Rest	8.91	20.94	19.77	0.90	82.9	1.7	30.0	84.1	43.1	135.3	132.2
	Work	9.92	18.80	17.66	2.87	79.9	1.9	31.1	77.3	47.3	133.4	129.6
	Δ	+1.01	−2.11	−2.11	+1.97	−3.0	+0.2	+1.1	−6.8	+4.2	−1.9	−2.6
W. J. G.	Rest	9.47	20.81	19.67	0.95	82.3	1.4	30.6	84.3	42.8	134.9	132.1
	Work	10.50	18.70	17.56	2.87	81.4	1.9	31.9	81.7	45.8	135.6	132.5
	Δ	+1.03	−2.11	−2.11	+1.92	−0.9	+0.5	+1.3	−2.6	+3.0	+0.7	+0.4
Average,	Rest	9.04	21.27	20.13	1.01	82.3	1.6	30.9	84.4	43.6	136.0	132.7
	Work	9.63	18.61	17.47	3.10	82.3	2.0	30.9	81.8	46.0	135.8	132.6
	Δ	+0.59	−2.66	−2.66	+2.09	0.0	+0.4	0.0	−2.6	+2.4	−0.2	−0.1

* Concentration of calcium plus magnesium in whole blood is assumed to be 5 meq per l in rest and in work.

† Doubtful result. This value is not used in calculating the average.

Loebel[39] were of the same order of magnitude. In contrast with these moderate changes in man are results on the horse reported by Scheunert and Krzywanek.[48] During 5 min trot, six experiments showed increase in cell volume (expressed in per cent of blood volume) from 30 to 40, 29 to 36, 28.7 to 38, 24 to 35.5, 25 to 37, and 29 to 39.5 per cent, respectively. The average increase was from 27.6 per cent to 37.6 per cent or about one-third.

In Scheunert and Krzywanek's experiments increase in plasma protein concentration was determined and associated decrease in plasma volume was estimated. Increase in per cent cell volume by this water transfer represented but a small part of the total observed increase and it was concluded that the spleen must make a large contribution of cells to the active circulation.

In exercise experiments on man which caused sweating and lasted for 15 to 30 min, Cohn[18] found a decrease in hemoglobin concentration. At the same time increase in plasma protein concentration took place. Cohnheim, Kreglinger, and Kreglinger[19] as well as Gross and Kestner[27] found a decrease in red count and per cent hemoglobin after prolonged and strenuous mountain climbing. These latter observations we have confirmed in recent experiments but Cohn's result remains unexplained.

It was found by Broun[15] that after 10 or 15 min exercise, dogs had an average increase of 3.6 per cent in total plasma volume and 12.3 per cent in total cell volume, the range of the latter increment being from 1.5 to 24 per cent. There was thus a distinct increase in circulating blood volume. After several hours' exercise both total cell volume and hemoglobin content were less than after 10 min exercise, a difference that was much greater in animals which had been confined for several months. The conclusion was reached that blood destruction is a significant phenomenon during prolonged exercise in untrained dogs. Results of a similar character have been obtained by Hastings.[29]

Barcroft and Florey[3] have succeeded in resecting a portion of colon of the dog and sewing it, with blood supply still maintained, into the belly wall. Exercise and emotional disturbance result in a simultaneous decrease in size of the spleen and in the pink color of the colon. A shutting down of vessels in the splanchnic area is clearly proved by these experiments.

Chiatellino and Margaria[16] have studied concentration changes in the blood of men during a march of 2 to 6 hr with no water intake. Loss of body weight ranged from 1.6 to 3.5 per cent. Increase was slight for osmotically active substances and marked for serum proteins and red cells. An actual diminution in blood volume was observed.

Finally we come to our own results. We have in Table 8 values for serum solids, serum protein, cell solids, and per cent cell volume in rest and work. In addition to the ten subjects already referred to, we were fortunate in securing observations on two young men without spleens. Splenectomy had been performed about two years before our observations on E. H. and five years before in the case of W. K. Recovery was complete in each case.

The last column in this table shows values for per cent cell volume calculated as follows:

$$V'_c = 100\left(\frac{V_c P_c}{P'_c}\right) \div \left[\left(\frac{V_c P_c}{P'_c}\right) + \left(\frac{[100 - V_c]P_s}{P'_s}\right)\right],$$

where V'_c = per cent cell volume in work;

TABLE 8

Effect on Cell Volume of Concentration Changes in
Serum and Cells from Rest to Work

A. NORMAL SUBJECTS

| | Serum solids | | Serum protein | | Cell solids | | Cell volume | | |
| | | | | | | | | Work | |
Subject	Rest (g per l)	Work (g per l)	Rest (g per l)	Work (g per l)	Rest (g per l)	Work (g per l)	Rest (%)	(observed %)	(calculated %)
D. B. D.	86.5	93.6	70.8	79.9	366	372	42.0	44.1	44.6
P. F. P.	86.9	94.2	—	—	370	374	45.7	47.6	47.4
A. A. McC.	86.4	97.1	—	—	375	378	44.5	47.9	47.2
J. H. T.	84.4	87.0	68.6	71.6	377	380	46.2	47.8	47.1
W. C.	88.4	94.2	72.0	77.7	380	377	44.4	45.8	46.5
O. S. L.	86.2	95.8	71.4	78.0	387	386	41.8	44.9	44.0
J. L. S.	88.1	92.4	69.4	73.9	376	378	48.3	49.4	49.7
H. T. E.	85.2	93.3	69.4	77.0	373	376	44.1	46.7	46.5
A. V. B.	90.8	99.8	65.0	78.8	377	389	43.9	48.8	47.9
W. J. G.	77.8	86.3	62.5	71.2	387	390	44.3	47.4	47.3
Average...	86.1	93.4	68.6	76.0	377	380	44.5	47.0	46.8

B. SUBJECTS AFTER SPLENECTOMY

W. K.	84.1	90.4	—	—	389	387	48.0	49.4	49.9
"	78.5	89.0	—	—	389	389	43.6	47.0	46.7
"	91.8	91.8	—	—	386	389	48.7	48.3	48.5
E. H.	91.0	100.5	—	—	372	373	48.2	51.4	50.7
Average...	86.4	92.9	—	—	384	385	47.1	49.0	49.0

V_c = per cent cell volume in rest;

P_c = g of solids per liter of cells in rest;

P'_c = g of solids per liter of cells in work;

P_s = g of protein per liter of serum in rest;

P'_s = g of protein per liter of serum in work.

This formula is a mathematical expression of the hypothesis that all the changes are due simply to loss of water from the blood, during work. The loss of water per unit weight of serum and of cells was determined by analysis but we have no information regarding total blood volume changes.

In most cases determinations of serum solids and of serum protein were made. The values for protein furnish the more suitable basis for recalculation and these values were used when available. Otherwise values for serum solids were employed. The result is essentially the same; the average calculated per cent cell volume for normal men comes out 46.8 on the basis of serum protein concentration change, and 46.6 on the basis of serum solids change. This fact is expressed in another form in Fig. 1 which shows that in most subjects the value for serum solids is merely a linear function of that for serum protein in rest and work. Also it is evident that increase in serum solids is nearly equal to increase in serum protein. Evidently in most subjects

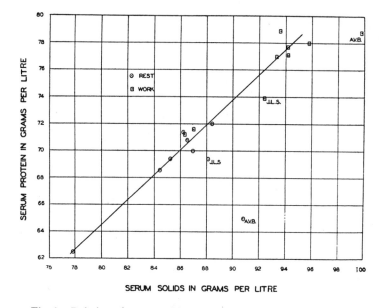

Fig. 1.   Relation of serum solids to serum protein in rest and work.

concentration of serum fat and other similar substances does not change much in exercise of this character.

The results speak for themselves. It is obvious that in normal man increase in per cent cell volume during exercise of the sort studied is accompanied by a corresponding increase in serum protein concentration, and the phenomenon is not different in men after splenectomy. Thus the average increase in normal men was 5.6 per cent and after splenectomy 4 per cent. Clearly the spleen is not essential to this aspect of the phenomenon and seems to play a subordinate role under the circumstances of our experiments.[2]

The question as to what changes may have taken place in total blood volume during the course of work cannot be answered. Broun's results[15] on the dog cannot be applied without reservation to our experiments, both because of the difference in species, and because in his experiments at least 4 min elapsed after cessation of exercise before blood samples were withdrawn. The marching experiments of Chiatellino and Margaria[16] were of long duration and direct comparison cannot be made, but their findings make it appear that decrease in blood volume is not incompatible with maintenance of a high metabolic rate in man. The best we can do is to make use of our data on per cent cell volume and plasma protein concentration, with certain assumptions with regard to total blood volume, in a calculation of probable range in amount and character of new blood.

Such calculations have been made and are shown in Table 9. On the assumption that total serum protein

---

[2] Posture effect upon composition of the blood has been studied by W. O. Thompson, P. K. Thompson, and M. E. Dailey.[51] They found changes in serum protein concentration and in per cent cell volume from a reclining to an erect posture, with a minimum of muscular movement, of the same order of magnitude as we have found in exercise. Total serum volume decreased in a reciprocal manner with serum protein concentration and total cell volume remained constant.

TABLE 9

Outcome of Certain Assumptions with Regard to Blood Volume Changes in Exercise*

		WORK					
	Rest	*Assuming total serum proteins constant*	*Assuming blood vol. decrease = 5%*	*Assuming blood vol. constant*	*Assuming blood vol. increase = 5%*	*Assuming blood vol. increase = 10%*	*Assuming blood vol. increase = 5% and cell vol. of new blood = 70%*
Blood vol. (liters)	5.0	4.7	4.75	5.0	5.25	5.50	5.25
Cell vol. (%)	44.5†	46.8	47.0†	47.0†	47.0†	47.0†	48.0
Total cell vol. (liters)	2.23	2.20	2.23	2.35	2.47	2.59	2.52
Total serum vol. (liters)	2.77	2.50	2.52	2.65	2.78	2.91	2.73
Serum protein (g per liter serum)	68.6†	76.0†	76.0†	76.0†	76.0†	76.0†	76.0†
Total serum protein (g)	190	190	192	201	211	221	208
New blood (liters)	—	None	0.05	0.30	0.55	0.80	0.55
New cells (liters)	—	None	0.03	0.15	0.28	0.40	0.34

* Serum protein concentration in new blood is assumed to be the same as the observed value in our blood specimens. Serum protein concentration change indicates a transfer to tissues of 0.3 l of salt solution and this transfer is implicit in all our assumptions. Cell volume of new blood is assumed to be 50 per cent in every case but the last.

† Observed value.

and total hemoglobin in the circulation remain constant, while in fact serum protein concentration increases from 68.6 to 76.0 g per l, it follows that blood volume decreases 6 per cent. Now in order to restore the original volume, 0.3 l of blood must be added, and in order to increase per cent cell volume from 46.6 to 47.0 the added blood must contain 52 per cent cells. When blood volume increases 5 per cent, 0.55 l of new blood is added. The fact that observed per cent cell volume exceeds calculated cell volume by only 0.2 per cent thus implies that added blood contains only about 5 per cent more cells than circulating blood. The experimental evidence on this point is, however, quite inconclusive in any case and wholly without meaning if the volume of added blood is small.

It was found by Bock, van Caulært, Dill, Fölling, and Hurxthal[12] that increase in oxygen capacity is a function of metabolic rate. The present experiments involve increases in metabolic rate of eight to twelve times the resting level. In other running experiments at faster rates, increases in per cent cell volume are sometimes, but not invariably, greater. Such experiments are for the most part unpublished, but one may be referred to. Hochrein, Dill, and Henderson[41] found in an experiment on M. H., running at a rate of 11.3 km per hr for 15 min, an increase in metabolic rate of fifteen times and an increase in per cent cell volume of one-ninth, a change greater than any and twice as large as the average observed in the present experiments.

The physical condition of the subject may be a factor in increase in per cent cell volume. In our experiments no well-defined relation was found between decrease in level of the carbon dioxide dissociation curves and serum

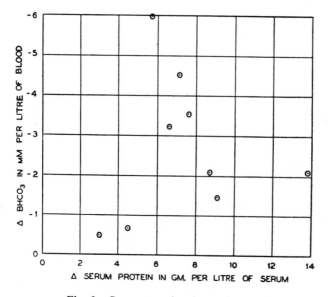

Fig. 2. Serum protein change in relation to change in bicarbonate capacity of whole blood.

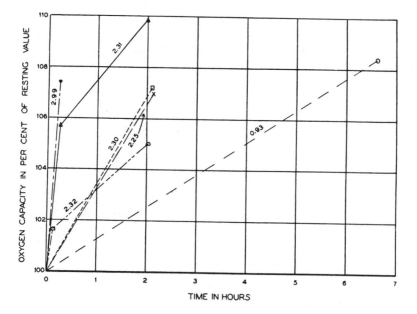

Fig. 3. Change in oxygen capacity during work of different intensities. Oxygen consumption in liters per minute is indicated.

protein increments (see Fig. 2). Since the first variable furnishes an index to physical condition and the second to increase in per cent cell volume, no relation between physical condition and increase in per cent cell volume is revealed by the present experiments. Furthermore Bock, van Caulært, Dill, Fölling, and Hurxthal[12] found about the same increase in oxygen capacity in De Mar, a successful Marathon runner for 20 years, as in untrained subjects.

The time factor must also be considered. The above-mentioned authors found in one experiment that while most of the increase in oxygen capacity had taken place at the end of 6 min, there was a further increase of about 0.5 volume per cent between 6 and 16 min after work began. In long-continued work concentration of cells in blood may be appreciably influenced by water loss from the body as a whole or by increased rate of destruction of cells or by both factors combined. In Fig. 3 are plotted results obtained by Talbott, Fölling, Henderson, Dill, Edwards, and Berggren[49] on the subject J. H. T. It is interesting to note that oxygen capacity increase was greater after a 6-hr walking experiment with an oxygen consumption of 0.93 l per min than after three out of four running experiments lasting about 2 hr with an oxygen consumption of about 2.3 l per min. J. H. T. drank no water during these experiments so that appreciable cell destruction may have taken place while its effect may have been masked by body water loss.

Concentration changes in hemoglobin of cells. In the above discussion the terms oxygen capacity and cell volume have been used interchangeably, thus implying a constant ratio between these variables in rest and work. The fact that the average increase in cell solids from rest to work is less than 1 per cent, as shown in Table 8, implies that ratio of oxygen capacity to cell volume does not change notably. Further evidence that such is the case is found in Table 10. Hemoglobin concentrations are calculated to the basis of (*a*) meq oxygen combining capacity per liter

TABLE 10

Hemoglobin Concentration at $pH_s = 7.4$

Subject	Rest (meq per l cells)	Work (meq per l cells)	Δ	Rest (meq per kg cell solids)	Work (meq per kg cell solids)	Δ
D. B. D.	19.84	19.95	+0.11	53.78	53.36	−0.42
P. F. P.	19.48	20.08	+0.60	52.70	53.65	+0.95
A. A. McC.	18.14	19.00	+0.86	48.38	50.26	+1.88
J. H. T.	20.26	20.67	+0.41	53.52	54.30	+0.78
W. C.	20.61	20.42	−0.19	54.20	53.76	−0.44
O. S. L.	20.70	20.69	−0.01	53.42	53.73	+0.31
J. L. S.	20.31	20.43	+0.12	53.94	53.98	+0.04
H. T. E.	20.27	20.28	+0.01	54.20	53.61	−0.59
A. V. B.	20.25	20.37	+0.12	53.95	52.28	−1.67
W. J. G.	21.47	22.25	+0.78	55.26	56.78	+1.52
Average ...	20.13	20.41	+0.28	53.34	53.57	+0.24
Minimum...	18.14	19.00	−0.19	48.38	50.26	−1.67
Maximum...	21.47	22.25	+0.86	55.26	56.78	+1.88

of cells at pH_s 7.4, and (b) meq per kg of cell solids. The first calculation is made as follows:

$$\text{meq Hb per liter of cells} = \frac{(\text{total Hb})_b}{V_c - \dfrac{7.40 - pH_s}{30}},$$

where $(\text{total Hb})_b$ = meq oxygen combining capacity per liter of blood,

V_c = cc of cells per cc of blood as equilibrated,

pH_s = pH of of serum as equilibrated,

and $\dfrac{7.40 - pH_s}{30}$ is an empirical factor dependent upon the rate of change of cell volume with pH_s. The correction in no case exceeds 0.003 in V_c and is thus nearly but not quite negligible. The second calculation is made by dividing the values for oxygen combining capacity per liter of cells, Table 10, by corresponding values for solids per liter of cells given in Table 8.

The first three columns in Table 10 suggest that the slight increase in cell solids from rest to work shown in Table 8 is a reality, for there is a similar increase in oxygen combining capacity. The increase in the first case is 0.8 per cent and in the other, 1.4 per cent.

The values for Δ in the last column of Table 10 probably can be taken as a measure of the accuracy of the six determinations involved in this calculation, viz. oxygen capacity, cell solids, and cell volume both in rest and work.

Aside from the evidence that rest to work change in hemoglobin concentration per liter of cells is small and that change in the ratio hemoglobin ÷ cell solids is probably negligible, Table 10 is interesting in showing the normal range of individual variation. Values for hemoglobin concentration per liter

of cells are already on record for four individuals of this group.[20] These observations were made a year earlier by the same method, and it is of interest to compare the results, shown in Table 11.

TABLE 11

Cellular Hemoglobin Concentration in Rest Concentrations in Meq per Liter of Cells

Subject	1928	1929
D. B. D.	19.7	19.8
J. H. T.	20.4	20.2
H. T. E.	21.0	20.2
A. V. B.	20.2	20.2

In three cases the results are practically identical. Only in one case is the difference nearly, if not quite, outside the probable limit of error, and in this case evidence exists that the condition of the subject changed during the period in question. Certainly concentration of hemoglobin in cells is a variable that fluctuates within narrow limits in normal man, whether at rest or at work.

Acid-base equilibrium in serum. Concentrations of individual anions and of Σ cations in true plasma at a carbonic acid pressure of 40 mm Hg are shown in Table 6. Values for total CO_2, serum volume, chloride, and phosphate were determined directly and, where the equilibration CO_2 pressure differed appreciably from 40 mm, correction was made to this value. Phosphate corrections are not required and all others can be made by reference to a nomogram of blood of normal man in rest and work, e.g., that of M. H.[41]

Values for pH are calculated from the equation

$$pH_s = pK_s + \log (BHCO_3)_s - \log (H_2CO_3)_s,$$

where $pK_s = 6.10,$

meq $(H_2CO_3)_s = 0.0329 (H_2O)_s(pCO_2)$,

and $(BHCO_3)_s = (\text{total } CO_2)_s$
$$- (H_2CO_3)_s,$$

accepting the recent determinations of Van Slyke, Sendroy, Hastings, and Neill[54] for the solubility of CO_2 in plasma at 38° and correcting it to 37.5°, the temperature we have employed for equilibration. The value used for pK_s is that recently established by Hastings, Sendroy, and Van Slyke.[30]

Lactate in serum is calculated from its determination in whole blood, observation of serum volume and the distribution ratio between serum and cells reported by Edwards, Hochrein, Dill, and Henderson.[23]

Proteinate is calculated according to Van Slyke, Hastings, Hiller, and Sendroy.[53]

meq $(BP)_s = 0.104 (P)_s(pH_s - 5.08)$,

where $(P)_s = $ g of protein per l of serum.

The expression Σ anions represents the sum of these determined and calculated anions, while Σ cations represents the sum of determined values for calcium, sodium, and potassium, as given in Table 3, and the value of 2.0 assumed as representing concentration of magnesium in normal serum.

The results are too involved to yield to simple treatment and hence have been presented graphically in two forms. Figure 4 shows changes per liter of serum from rest to work. Figure 5 shows concentration of base and each principal anion in rest and also the consequences of (*a*) work without exhaustion with lactic acid accumulation small or negligible but with salt solution transfer, and (*b*) work to exhaustion with slightly greater salt solution transfer to tissues and large lactic acid accumulation.

In some particulars, the results are easily understood. Thus there is the

Fig. 4. Increments in principal anions of serum from rest to work.

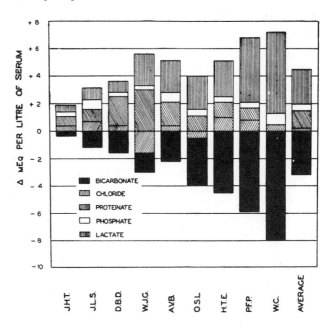

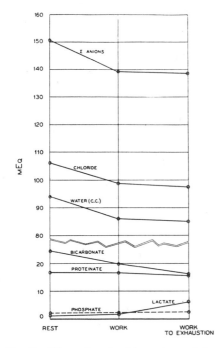

Fig. 5. Effect of work with moderate fatigue and of work to exhaustion on constituents of serum. Calculated on the assumption that total protein of serum remains constant, viz. observed concentrations in work are multiplied by

$$\frac{\text{Protein per liter rest serum}}{\text{Protein per liter work serum}}.$$

reciprocal relation of bicarbonate and lactate already known to occur in whole blood from the work of Bock, van Caulært, Dill, Fölling, and Hurxthal.[12] Also increase in phosphate has already been described by Havard and Reay.[31]

On the other hand, there are certain questions heretofore unanswered to which answers can now be given. Thus, on the average, increase in lactate is actually only three-fourths or four-fifths of the decrease in bicarbonate. Taking the subjects individually, Δ lactate as compared with $-\Delta$ bicarbonate is distinctly smaller in five cases, larger in one case and about the same in three cases. Chloride shows a slight increase in seven out of nine

subjects with an average increase of 0.2 meq or less than 0.2 per cent, thus indicating that the fluid leaving the blood during exercise carries a concentration of chloride equal to that of the blood.

Base bound by protein increases on the average just one-half as much as lactate but there are large individual differences. As shown in Fig. 4, there is a fairly uniform increase in serum protein concentration in most of the subjects, even including those most fatigued, P. F. P. and W. C. Consequently when there is little lactic acid accumulation ΔBP_s is large, since ΔP_s increases and $(pH_s - 5.08)$ remains constant or nearly so. But the latter factor decreases with increasing lactic acid accumulation and in the most fatigued subject, W. C., $\Delta BP_s = 0$.

It is interesting and probably significant that for the series $\Delta\Sigma$ anions $= \Delta(BP)_s$, i.e., net increase in anions equals increase in nondiffusible anions. Finally, $\Delta\Sigma$ anions $= \Delta\Sigma$ cations from rest to work, approximately.

In short, nothing takes place in the serum which does not have a fairly simple interpretation. In the well-trained subject there is transfer from blood to tissues of a fluid carrying practically unchanged concentrations of diffusible ions. Nondiffusible proteinate with an equivalent amount of base is left behind and there is a higher concentration of phosphate than corresponds to salt solution transfer. This latter change is probably a reflection of increased inorganic phosphate concentration in tissues. In the poorly trained subject, entrance of lactate decreases bicarbonate and increases acidity.

Values for calcium, sodium, and potassium as given in Table 3 show no other change worthy of note except that there is a greater relative increase of calcium than of other cations.

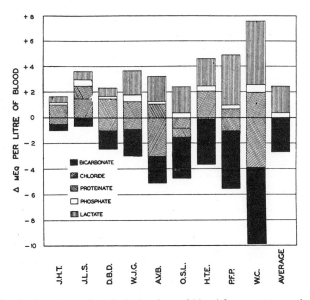

Fig. 6. Increments in principal anions of blood from rest to work.

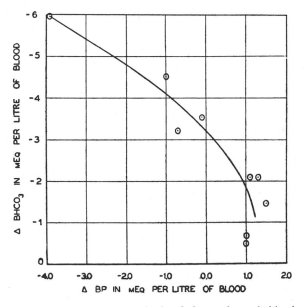

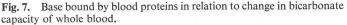

Fig. 7. Base bound by blood proteins in relation to change in bicarbonate capacity of whole blood.

Acid-base equilibrium in whole blood. Table 7 and Fig. 6 give data for whole blood corresponding to those for true plasma already described. Changes in blood are due not only to changes in plasma and cells but also to change in relative proportion of the two phases. It has already been shown that there is almost no change in concentration of nondiffusible constituents of cells and it is also true that there is but a slight change in chloride, sodium, and

TABLE 12

Average Values for r_{Cl} and r_{HCO_3} at $pH_s = 7.45$

Remarks	r_{Cl}			r_{HCO_3}		
	Rest	Work	Δ	Rest	Work	Δ
12 subjects, 1928	0.640	0.655	+0.015	0.743	0.784	+0.041
10 subjects, 1929	0.633	0.645	+0.012	0.757	0.768	+0.011
2 subjects with maximum fatigue, 1929	0.655	0.665	+0.010	0.775	0.815	+0.040

potassium, all of which were determined directly. The components which do change, therefore, are those subject to change with acidosis, viz. $(BP)_c$, lactate, and bicarbonate. The composite picture of blood happens to be simple when the average of the group is considered. Chloride and proteinate are unchanged, ratio of lactate change to bicarbonate change is essentially the same as in plasma, and $\Delta\Sigma$ cations $= \Delta\Sigma$ anions $= 0$, approximately.

It must be emphasized, however, that blood changes in nonfatigued subjects vary in many respects from those of nearly exhausted subjects.

The manner in which $\Delta(BP)_b$ changes with acidosis is shown in Fig. 7. When acidosis is no more than moderate there is an increase in $(BP)_b$ of about 1 meq. The reason for this is that there is, per liter of blood, not much change in serum protein but a large increase in cell protein. With increasing acidosis there is little if any further increase in blood protein but decreasing amount of base found by protein.

The data given in the above tables may be used for calculating concentration ratios of bicarbonate and chloride ions in cells and plasma. A series of preliminary experiments has already

Fig. 8. Increments in blood lactate and in bicarbonate capacity at 40 mm Hg from rest to work.

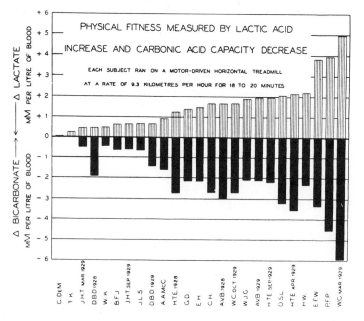

been reported by Edwards, Hochrein, Dill, and Henderson.[23] Their findings have been confirmed in the present experiments, as shown in Table 12. Further, it appears that r_{HCO_3} increases with acidosis, since the most fatigued subject in 1927 and the two most fatigued subjects in 1928 had the greatest average increase in this variable.

Lactic acid accumulation and physical performance. The relation of lactate to bicarbonate change in exercise of this character has been observed on a total of 19 individuals with two or more experiments on five individuals. All these observations are collected in Table 13 and shown graphically in Fig. 8. Subjects are arranged in order of increasing lactic acid concentration, and it will be noted that this is approximately the order of decreasing bicarbonate concentration. This type of experiment furnishes an excellent guide to capacity of individuals for great and sustained physical activity. De Mar, with no appreciable change in lactic acid, is a Marathon runner of 20 years experience. T. K. was a first-class half-miler 4 years ago and has

TABLE 13

Lactate and Bicarbonate Changes from Rest to Work. Concentrations are expressed in meq per liter of Blood at $pCO_2 = 40$ mm

Subject	Lactate increase	Bicarbonate decrease	Bicarbonate minus lactate
C. De M.	0.01	0.00	−0.01
T. K.	0.24	0.00	−0.24
J. H. T., Mar., 1929	0.43	0.49	+0.06
D. B. D., 1928	0.44	1.93	+1.49
W. K.*	0.50	0.45	−0.05
B. F. J.	0.63	0.63	0.00
J. H. T., Sept., 1929	0.66	0.60	−0.06
J. L. S.	0.67	0.67	0.00
D. B. D., 1929	0.67	1.44	+0.77
A. A. McC.	0.93	1.62	+0.69
H. T. E., 1928	1.25	2.74	+1.49
G. D.	1.40	2.16	+0.76
E. H.*	1.49	2.20	+0.71
C. H.	1.67	2.70	+1.03
A. V. B., 1928	1.68	2.97	+1.29
W. C., Oct., 1929	1.68	2.72	+1.04
W. J. G.	1.92	2.11	+0.19
A. V. B., 1929	1.97	2.11	+0.14
H. T. E., Sept., 1929	1.97	2.20	+0.23
O. S. L.	2.06	3.23	+1.17
H. T. E., Apr., 1929	2.14	3.55	+1.41
H. W.	2.20	2.34	+0.14
E. F. W.	3.84	3.33	−0.51
P. F. P.	3.94	4.54	+0.60
W. C., Mar., 1929	4.97	5.98	+1.01
Average...	1.57	2.11	+0.54

* After splenectomy.

kept in good condition since then. Probably neither of these men was more fatigued by exercise of this nature than an average person would be by a 20-min walk.

At the other end of the series stands W. C., a young man of 18. A twentieth subject had to quit from exhaustion in 6 min. His record is not shown in the figure, for his lactic acid determination was lost, but bicarbonate decrease was 5.2 meq per l. The fact that there is such a wide range in performance is all the more interesting when one bears in mind that these individuals would be rated as normal by an examining physician. It is another illustration of the old principle that the performance of a machine can be judged best, not when idling, but when running under a heavy load.

One variable in performance can be easily evaluated. It is well known that skill in performance of any physical task varies widely. Running calls for skill of a high order, and it has already been shown by Furusawa, Hill, Long, and Lupton[26] that oxygen consumption of different individuals varies considerably while running at a given rate. In Fig. 9 comparison has been made of skill in running of 17 individuals. Variation of net oxygen consumption per kg of body weight ranges from 26 to 40 cc, the least skillful subject using one-half more fuel than the most skillful. The data upon which this figure is based, together with physical measurements of some of the subjects, are given in Table 14. While there is a fair correlation between skill and lactic acid accumulation, A. A. McC. is a striking exception. He is one of the most inexpert of runners and at the same time one of the least fatigued subjects. It is not improbable that of

Fig. 9. Skill index expressed as net oxygen consumption per kg of body weight.

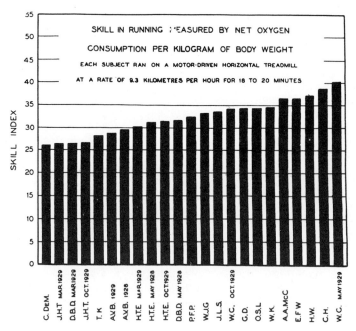

TABLE 14

Physical Characteristics and Skill Index

Subject	Age (yr)	Height (cm)	Weight (kg)	Vital capacity standing (cc)	Net oxygen used in work (l per min)	Skill index
D. B. D.	37	180	72.5	4400	1.91	26.3
P. F. P.	33	173.5	67.6	4550	2.19	32.3
A. A. McC.	23	177.0	74.0	5900	2.70	36.5
J. H. T.	26	171.0	70.4	4000	1.85	26.3
W. C.	18	171.0	62.0	4500	2.49	40.2
O. S. L.	27	188.0	67.2	5950	2.31	34.3
J. L. S.	41	183.2	65.3	5400	2.20	33.7
H. T. E.	32	166.0	67.7	3940	2.04	30.1
A. V. B.	40	173.4	74.2	4000	2.13	28.7
W. J. G.	26	171.0	63.3	4550	2.11	33.2

the entire group he would show greatest improvement in training, for he is already well equipped for oxygen transport.

Two or more sets of observations on lactic acid and carbonic acid capacity have been made in the case of five individuals performing the same task at different times. J.H.T., D.B.D., and A.V.B. had about the same lactic acid concentration in 1929 as in 1928. H. T.E. showed only small variation while W.C. in his second experiment showed great improvement. W.C. was the only one of these subjects to show much change in oxygen consumption, using in the second experiment about 2.4 l of oxygen per min as compared with 2.8 in the first experiment.

Total ventilation. It is possible from these experiments to study ventilation in relation to time, fatigue, and reaction of arterial blood. The ten subjects may be divided into three groups on the basis of degrees of fatigue. Group I, with less than 1 meq lactic acid increase, contains J.H.T, J.L.S., D.B.D., and A.A.McC. The second, with increases of about 1 to 2 meq, includes W.J.G., A.V.B., O.S.L., and H.T.E. The last group consists of P.F.P. and W.C. with increases of 3.95 and 4.96 meq, respectively. Average values for surface area, body weight, and for the six observations on ventilation throughout the 20-min experiment are given in Table 15. Groups I and II show no significant difference except that average weight of the second group is about 3 per cent less, and average ventilation is about 5 per cent less. Group III, however, as compared with Group I has an average weight 8 per cent less and an average ventilation 34 per cent greater. It is also clear that a steady state was not reached by these two most fatigued subjects until after the seventh minute of the experiment. These observations are fully borne out by unpublished running experiments made in this laboratory on the subjects J.H.T., M.H., and D.B.D. As long as little lactic acid accumulates ventilation reaches a steady state within 3 or 4 min. When work is increased enough to cause large lactic acid accumulation, there is a disproportionate increase in ventilation, and instead of early attainment of a constant value the rate continues to accelerate, either until

TABLE 15

Ventilation During Work in Relation to Time and Lactic Acid Accumulation

AVERAGE VALUES BY GROUPS.

	Minimum lactic acid; 4 subjects	Medium lactic acid; 4 subjects	Maximum lactic acid; 2 subjects
Surface area (sq m)	1.87	1.87	1.77
Weight (kg)	70.5	68.1	64.8
Ventilation, 3rd min (1 per min)	52.3	45.3	54.0
Ventilation, 5th min (1 per min)	53.0	50.3	61.5
Ventilation, 7th min (1 per min)	53.3	49.5	61.5
Ventilation, 13th min (1 per min)	54.3	52.5	70.5
Ventilation, 15th min (1 per min)	52.3	51.8	71.0
Ventilation, 17th min (1 per min)	53.0	51.3	72.0
Ventilation, average (1 per min)...	53.0	50.1	65.1

a steady state at a high level of lactic acid is reached, or until the subject stops from exhaustion.

The relation between reaction of the blood and increase in ventilation in exercise is a familiar subject of discussion. Values for pH_s in rest and work[3] have already been given in Table 4. In Fig. 10 we have shown pH of arterial serum in rest and at the end of work as a function of total ventilation. Figure 11 shows pH_s as a function of change in ventilation from rest to work. It is clear that individual variation, both in rest and work, is considerable and that many subjects have a reaction in work well within normal limits for rest. Values in Fig. 10 indicate blood lactate concentration and illustrate again the relation between ventilation increase and lactate concentration.

_____

[3] A systematic error is involved in these calculations of pH_s in rest and work for the assumption of a temperature of 37.5° is made. Temperature in rest is somewhat below this and in work of this intensity possibly somewhat higher. Since we did not observe body temperature in these experiments no attempt has been made to correct for the small error involved in the assumption of a constant body temperature.

The two subjects with greatest lactate concentration had also greatest ventilation increase.

Increase in ventilation is of course a function of body weight. This latter variable has been eliminated in Table 4 which gives values for pH_s and ventilation per kg body weight. Here again there are large individual variations. Nevertheless it is quite clear that the relation between decrease in pH_s and increase in ventilation is not linear. As has been pointed out by L.J. Henderson,[32] it is clearly impossible to select one variable, such as the hydrogen-ion concentration of arterial blood, and assign to it a unique influence upon the respiratory center.

Respiratory quotient. This is not a suitable occasion for reviewing the extensive literature upon the R.Q. in exercise, particularly in view of the recent review by Richardson.[47] Values have been reported ranging from well below the usual resting value to unity and above. For example, there are the experiments on college oarsmen of Henderson and Haggard[34] which led them to the conclusion that fat and sugar are burned in the same

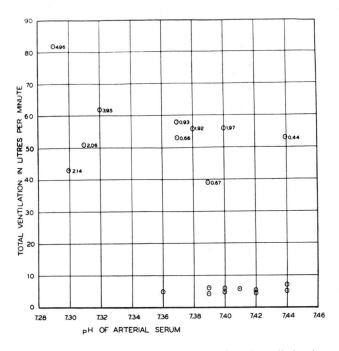

Fig. 10. pH of arterial serum as a function of total ventilation in rest and work. Increase in lactic acid concentration in meq per liter of blood is indicated.

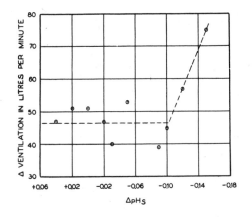

Fig. 11. Change in pH_s as a function of change in ventilation from rest to work.

ratio in rest and work, provided one takes into account the recovery process. The results of Hill and his associates[1, 26] point to an R.Q. of unity for severe exercise of short duration plus recovery. In more moderate exercise involving small oxygen debt their R.Q.'s are well below unity. Experiments of particular interest from our point of view are those of Benedict and Cathcart,[14] who carried out a long series of bicycle ergometer experiments on M.A.M., a professional cyclist. We have collected their values for M.R. and R.Q. in

187

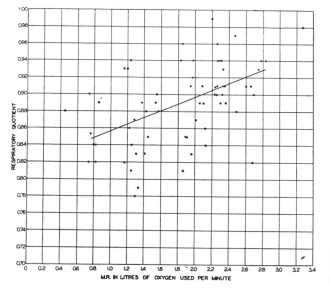

Fig. 12. Change in R. Q. with M. R. Calculated from Benedict and Cathcart.[14]

exercise from their Tables Nos. 36–52, 59–62, 68, and 70–90, not including experiments with special diets. Results for each table were averaged except where it was possible to group observations into two or more distinct metabolic levels. Sixty-eight pairs of such observations are shown in Fig. 12. The best fitting straight line for these points[4] corresponds to the equation R.Q. = 0.04 (M.R.) + 0.817, where M.R. is expressed in liters of oxygen used per minute. The results leave no doubt that in these experiments there was a well-defined increase in R.Q. with M.R. This was noted by Benedict and Cathcart,[14] who remarked:

"Apparently in the later experiments there was an increase in the respiratory

---

[4] The straight line shown on Fig. 12 was derived according to the formula

$$y = Rx - Rx_m + y_m,$$

where x_m = mean value of x,

y_m = mean value of y,

n = number of observations,

and $R = \dfrac{n\Sigma xy - \Sigma x \Sigma y}{n\Sigma x^2 - (\Sigma x)^2}$.

quotients during the working period which was not observed in the earlier experiments, this probably being due to the fact that the excessive muscular work was performed in the last part of the research."

Bock, van Caulært, Dill, Fölling, and Hurxthal[12] also found values increasing with metabolic rate. De Mar, a trained athlete, had the lowest values of the group of four men studied. Talbott, Fölling, Henderson, Dill, Edwards, and Berggren[49] in 2-hr experiments on J.H.T. found R.Q.'s of about 0.88 at a metabolic rate of about 2.3 l of oxygen per min. Unpublished observations on J.H.T. using about 2.3 l of oxygen per min on the bicycle ergometer give values for R.Q. above 0.9 and similar observations have been made on other individuals.

The values given for respiratory quotient in rest in Table 2 range from 0.72 to 0.88 and average 0.80. Recent observations of Benedict[13] on variation in the R.Q. in rest when a mouthpiece is employed, and its constancy when a suitable mask is used, leave little doubt that our three quotients in rest which depart widely from the average value give a misleading impression of the resting metabolic processes going on in those subjects.

Our evidence, however, that the R.Q.'s reported for work indicate approximately what ratio of fat and carbohydrate is being used is as follows: Carbon dioxide is being produced at about ten times the resting rate. Since the total carbonic acid content of the body is of the same order of magnitude in rest and work, ten times as much would have to be blown off or held back in a given time in order to produce a given change in R.Q. Our observations on alveolar air and on the level of the carbonic acid dissociation curve in rest and work tell us to what extent such a blowing off or retention of carbonic acid has taken place. On the average the change in alveolar carbonic acid pressure is small, as has been pointed out already. Accordingly we have again segregated the ten subjects into groups according to lactic acid accumulation. The R.Q.'s thus summarized are presented in Table 16.

TABLE 16

Respiratory Quotients During Work in Relation to Time and Lactic Acid Accumulation

	Minimum lactic acid; 4 subjects	*Medium lactic acid; 4 subjects*	*Maximum lactic acid; 2 subjects*
3rd min	0.90	0.90	1.00
5th min	0.92	0.94	1.03
7th min	0.91	0.92	0.98
13th min	0.90	0.92	1.00
15th min	0.89	0.92	1.00
17th min	0.90	0.89	0.98
Average...	0.903	0.915	1.00

Groups I and II, with little or moderate lactic acid concentration, and hence small blowing off of CO_2, again

show only slight difference in values for R.Q., the averages being 0.903 and 0.915, respectively. There does appear to be a slight falling off in R.Q. as work continues. Group III, with maximum fatigue, has quotients of unity. P.F.P. showed a distinct falling off toward the close of the experiment, while W.C. evidently continued to blow off carbon dioxide to the end. We are inclined to accept the quotient 0.91 as a true indication of what materials were being oxidized in Groups I and II. The average M.R. for these groups was 2.41 l of oxygen per min, and it is interesting that the line indicating the trend of the experiments of Benedict and Cathcart passes through the point (M.R. = 2.41, R.Q. = 0.91). Not much can be said as to fuels used by the third group. A more satisfactory procedure when exhaustion and blowing off of CO_2 occur is that of Hill, Long, and Lupton[38] who followed oxygen consumption and carbon dioxide production through work and complete recovery. Such experiments gave quotients of about unity. Even in such experiments there is the possibility that the recovery process may involve a different proportion of fuels than that of work.

Certain facts seem to be well established and are worthy of emphasis:

(*a*) Exercise requiring no more than 1.5 l of oxygen per min is often carried on with little or no change in R.Q. The extensive experiments of Benedict and Cathcart[14] prove this.

(*b*) Respiratory quotient increases with metabolic rate. This is proved by the work of Benedict and Cathcart,[14] and again by Bock and his associates.

(*c*) It is possible to carry on long-continued experiments on the ergometer at a metabolic rate of about 2 l of oxygen per min, with high but constant lactic acid and no blowing off of CO_2. Under such conditions the

R.Q. may average 0.94 with a net R.Q. for work of 0.96. This was shown by Henderson, Dill, van Caulært, Fölling, and Coolidge.[33]

(d) In view of the increase in R.Q. with M.R. clearly established by the work of Benedict and Cathcart, our results do not conflict with those of Krogh and Lindhard,[44] for their oxygen consumptions were below 1.5 l per min.

Pulse and respiratory rates. These observations are particularly interesting in showing to what extent these rates vary among individuals. Respiratory rate in work ranged from 16 in the case of O.S.L. to 44 in the case of W.C. There is a closer relation between pulse rate and performance. Athletes have notoriously slow pulse rates as compared with nonathletes at the same metabolic level. To what extent their increased stroke volume is due to training is quite unknown.

Oxygen and carbon dioxide transport. The composition of alveolar air and of "virtual venous" air as defined by Henderson and Prince,[36] with derived calculations, are shown in Table 2. Individual determinations are given for alveolar air. Four samples were collected throughout the experiment, and in general the range from rest to work and during the course of work is not very great. This has already been referred to in Table 5, and the relative constancy of alveolar carbon pressure has been used as a basis for recalculation to a common basis for all.

Alveolar oxygen pressure in work fluctuated from 87 to 116 mm although most values were between 100 and 112 mm. Oxygen saturation of arterial blood was probably about 95 per cent except in the cases of P.F.P. and W.C. where, on account of lactic acid accumulation and shift of the oxygen dissociation curve, it may have been as low as 92 per cent. Our basis for this conclusion consists of the arterial

punctures in exercise reported by Dill, Laurence, Hurxthal, and Bock,[21] supplemented by two unpublished experiments on the ergometer with lactic acid accumulation somewhat greater than that observed in the cases of P.F.P. and W.C. and with arterial saturations of 91.2 and 91.4 per cent and with oxygen pressure heads of 35 and 15 mm respectively.

With these assumptions as to saturation of arterial blood, with the established rate of carbon dioxide production and the calculated values for carbon dioxide and oxygen transport, we have calculated values shown in Table 2 for venous saturation and rate of blood flow. The eight subjects with least fatigue had venous saturations ranging from 41 to 50, average 44 per cent, while P.F.P. had a value of 39, and W.C. 34. In general those who had higher saturations of venous blood in rest had high values in work also. Differences between venous saturation in rest and work ranged from 31 to 38, and averaged 35 per cent for all subjects.

Values for venous saturation are more interesting than rate of blood flow for many purposes since the variable of body weight is eliminated, and with a knowledge of the position of the oxygen dissociation curve one can derive the oxygen pressure in blood leaving tissue capillaries. By the methods described by Dill, Talbott, Edwards, and Oberg,[22] we have estimated pH_c values for mixed venous blood in rest and work. The effect on position of oxygen dissociation curves of changes in pH_c, due to lactic and carbonic acids, has been found to be linear near the physiological range,[40] and hence it is simple to interpolate on a family of oxygen dissociation curves and to estimate value for oxygen pressure in each case. The resulting estimates are shown in Table 17.

TABLE 17

Pressure of Oxygen in Mixed Venous Blood

Subject	Rest (mm Hg)	Work (mm Hg)	Δ (mm Hg)
D. B. D.	41	25	−16
P. F. P.	40	26	−14
A. A. McC.	38	25	−13
J. H. T.	46	27	−19
W. C.	39	26	−13
O. S. L.	45	30	−15
J. L. S.	45	27	−18
H. T. E.	44	27	−17
A. V. B.	42	27	−15
W. J. G.	49	27	−22
Average...	43	27	−16

The results in work may be considered a striking confirmation of the estimates of L. J. Henderson[32] for four subjects near maximum work on the ergometer. He has fully discussed the significance of this observation, and has estimated that blood leaving the capillary of an active muscle contains oxygen at a nearly constant partial pressure in the neighborhood of 20 mm.

Summary

A study has been made of simultaneous changes in several important physiological variables during performance of a fixed task by ten individuals. Supplementary observations have been made on nine other subjects, including two young men after splenectomy. The task consisted in running at 9.3 km. per hr for 20 min with an increase in metabolism of eight to twelve times the resting rate.

Concentration of the blood in exercise by transfer of salt solution to the tissues does not commonly exceed 10 per cent in man and in these experiments averaged about 6 per cent in normal man and 4 per cent in two splenectomized subjects. Changes in serum protein concentration corresponded to changes in red cell concentration. The possibility that the spleen may function in such exercise by increasing blood volume is not involved in these observations and deductions. There is no well-defined connection between physical condition and blood concentration change in exercise.

Concentration of hemoglobin in cells is remarkably constant in normal man and increases only about 1 per cent in work of this character.

The effect of exercise on concentration of the principal ions in serum and in cells is as follows:

(a) In nonfatigued subjects changes consist chiefly of those related to transfer of fluid carrying diffusible ions from blood to tissues, the exception being a disproportionate increase in inorganic phosphate and calcium of serum.

(b) In exhaustion there is but little greater transfer of fluid from blood to tissues, and consequently only slightly greater increase in serum protein and in blood hemoglobin concentrations. Lactate increase in blood is approximately balanced by decrease in other ions, notably bicarbonate and proteinate.

(c) In general, there is an increase of about 2 meq of anions and cations per liter of serum but, on account of the decreased proportion of serum in blood during work, there is on the average practically no change in anions and cations per liter of blood.

The principle that a machine can be judged best when running under a heavy load has been exemplified by comparing blood lactate and bicarbonate changes from rest to work. Subjects who, at rest, would be placed in the same category were differentiated precisely by our observations.

Total ventilation in work of this character reaches a steady state in 3 or 4 minutes if lactic acid is not accumulating rapidly. Even when the lactic acid increase is 4 or 5 meq per l, ventilation rate may become nearly constant in from 7 to 15 min. The level reached in such a case may be one-third higher than in nonfatigued subjects. In these experiments there was no evidence of a linear relation between decrease in pH_s and increase in ventilation. When lactic acid does not accumulate, the subject may maintain the resting reaction in arterial plasma despite an eightfold or tenfold increase in metabolic rate.

Work of this level, when there is not excessive exhaustion, is associated with a change in fuel from the resting ratio of one-third carbohydrate and one-half fat to a ratio of two-thirds carbohydrate and one-third fat.

References

1. Back, M., K. M. Cogan, and A. E. Towers, *Proc. Roy. Soc. (London)*, **B88** (1914–15), 544.

2. Barcroft, J., and H. Barcroft, *J. Physiol. (London)*, **58** (1923), 138.

3. Barcroft, J., and H. Florey, *ibid.*, **68** (1929), 181.

4. Barcroft, J., H. Harris, D. Orahovats, and R. Weiss, *ibid.*, **60** (1925), 443.

5. Barcroft, J., C. D. Murray, D. Orahovats, J. Sands, and R. Weiss, *ibid.*, **60** (1925), 79.

6. Barcroft, J., and L. T. Poole, *ibid.*, **64** (1927), 23.

7. Barcroft, J. and J. C. Stephens, *ibid.*, **64** (1927), 1.

8. Blumgart, H. L., and Soma Weiss, *J, Clin. Inv.*, **4** (1927 *et seq.*), 15.

9. Boas, E. P., *Arch. Internal Med.*, **41** (1928), 403.

10. Bock, A. V., D. B. Dill, H. T. Edwards, L. J. Henderson, and J. H. Talbott, *J. Physiol. (London)*, **68** (1929), 277.

11. Bock, A. V., D. B. Dill, and J. H. Talbott, *ibid.*, **66** (1928), 121.

12. Bock, A. V., C. van Caulært, D. B. Dill, A. Fölling, and L. M. Hurxthal, *ibid.*, **66** (1928), 136.

13. Benedict, F. G. Personal Communication.

14. Benedict, F. G., and E. P. Cathcart, "Muscular Work," *Publ. No. 187, Carnegie Inst. Wash.* (1913).

15. Broun, G. O., *J. Exptl. Med.*, **36** (1922), 481; **37** (1923), 113.

16. Chiatellino, A., and R. Margaria, *Boll. Soc. Ital. Biol. sper.*, **3** (1928), 12.

17. Christiansen, J., C. G. Douglas, and J. S. Haldane, *J. Physiol. (London)*, **48** (1914), 244.

18. Cohn, E., *Z. Biol.*, **70** (1919), 366.

19. Cohnheim, O., Kreglinger, and Kreglinger, Jr., *Hoppe-Seylers Z. physiol. Chem.*, **63** (1909), 413.

20. Dill, D. B., A. V. Bock, C. van Caulært, A. Fölling, L. M. Hurxthal, and L. J. Henderson, *J. Biol. Chem.*, **78** (1928), 191.

21. Dill, D. B., J. S. Laurence, L. M. Hurxthal, and A. V. Bock, *ibid.*, **74** (1927), 313.

22. Dill, D. B., J. H. Talbott, H. T. Edwards, and S. A. Oberg.

23. Edwards, H. T., M. Hochrein, D. B. Dill, and L. J. Henderson, *Arch. exptl. Pathol. Pharmakol.*, **143** (1929), 161.

24. Ferrari, G. C., *Riv. Patol. nerv. ment.*, **2** (1897), 306; cited by Izquierdo and Cannon (42).

25. Field, H., Jr., A. V. Bock, E. F. Gildea, and F. L. Lathrop, *J. Clin. Inv.* **1** (1924), 65.

26. Furusawa, K., A. V. Hill, C. N. H. Long, and H. Lupton, *Proc. Roy. Soc. (London)*, B97 (1924), 167.

27. Gross, W., and D. Kestner, *Z. Biol.*, **70** (1919), 187.

28. Harrison, T. R., C. S. Robinson, and G. Syllaba, *J. Physiol. (London)*, **67** (1929), 62.

29. Hastings, A. B., *U. S. Pub. Health Bull.*, *No. 117* (1921).

30. Hastings, A. B., J. Sendroy, Jr., and D. D. Van Slyke, *J. Biol. Chem.*, **79** (1928), 183.

31. Havard, R. E., and G. A. Reay, *J. Physiol. (London)*, **61** (1926), 35.

32. Henderson, L. J., *Blood. A Study in General Physiology.* New Haven, Conn.: Yale University Press, 1928.

33. Henderson, L. J., D. B. Dill, C. van Caulært, A. Fölling, and T. C. Coolidge, *J. Biol. Chem.*, **74** (1927), 36.

34. Henderson, L. J., and H. W. Haggard, *Am. J. Physiol.*, **72** (1925), 264.

35. Henderson, L. J., and H. W. Haggard, *ibid.*, **73** (1925), 193.

36. Henderson, Y., and A. L. Prince, *J. Biol. Chem.*, **32** (1917), 325.

37. Hill, A. V., C. H. N. Long, and H. Lupton, *Proc. Roy. Soc. (London)*, **B97** (1924), 155.

38. Hill, A. V., C. N. H. Long, and H. Lupton, *ibid.*, **B97** (1924), 84, 96, 127.

39. Himwich, H. E., and R. O. Loebel, *J. Clin. Inv.*, **5** (1927), 113.

40. Hochrein, M., *Proc. Am. J. Physiol.*

41. Hochrein, M., D. B. Dill, and L. J. Henderson, *Arch. exptl. Pathol. Pharmakol.* **143** (1929), 129.

42. Hochrein, M., J. H. Talbott, D. B. Dill, and L. J. Henderson, *ibid.*, **143** (1929), 147.

43. Izquierdo, J. J., and W. B. Cannon, *Am. J. Physiol.*, **84** (1928), 545.

44. Krogh, A., and J. Lindhard, *Biochem. J.*, **14** (1920), 290.

45. Lamson, P. D., *J. Pharmacol.*, **7** (1915), 169; **9** (1916), 129; **16** (1920), 125.

46. Ranke, J. *Tetanus. Eine physiologische Studie.* Leipzig. 1865.

47. Richardson, H. B., *Physiol. Rev.*, **9** (1929), 61.

48. Scheunert, A., and F. W. Krzywanek, *Pflügers Arch. ges. Physiol.* **213** (1926), 198.

49. Talbott, J. H., A. Fölling, L. J. Henderson, D. B. Dill, H. T. Edwards, and R. E. L. Berggren, *J. Biol. Chem.*, **78** (1928), 445.

50. Thompson, W. O., J. M. Alper, and P. K. Thompson, *J. Clin. Ivn.*, **5** (1928), 605.

51. Thompson, W. O., P. K. Thompson, and M. E. Daily, *J. Clin. Inv.*, **5** (1928), 573.

52. Van Slyke, D. D., *J. Biol. Chem.*, **71** (1927), 235.

53. Van Slyke, D. D., A. B. Hastings, A. Hiller, and J. Sendroy, Jr., *ibid.*, **79** (1928), 769.

54. Van Slyke, D. D., J. Sendroy, Jr., A. B. Hastings, and J. M. Neill, *ibid.*, **78** (1928), 765.

55. Weiss, Soma, G. P. Robb, and H. L. Blumgart, *Am. Heart J.*, **4** (1929), 1.

56. Zuntz, N., and Schumberg. *Studien zu einer Physiologie des Marsches.* Berlin, 1901; Tornow, *"Blutveränderungen durch Märsche."* Inaug.–Diss. (Master's thesis). Berlin, 1901; cited by Von Willebrand, *Skand. Arch. Physiol.*, **14** (1903), 176.

C. A. KNEHR / D. B. DILL / WILLIAM NEUFELD

Training and Its Effects on Man at Rest and at Work

Reprinted from the *American Journal of Physiology*,
136 (1942), 148–56.

One of the major problems in studying the effect of training on the organism is the difficulty of making periodic observations over a time span sufficiently long to obtain meaningful data. In this study 14 male college students followed a training regimen of middle-distance running for 6 months. Periodic tests were made at intervals of two months and various physiological parameters were assessed at rest and during exercise on a treadmill at two different speeds.

It is interesting to note that the investigators found no significant differences in metabolic rate, blood hemoglobin, and alkaline reserve at rest after training. They did find a slight increase in weight and a decrease of 5 pulse beats per min at rest. Probably the most important finding was the fact that the subjects could accumulate more lactic acid after training and thus perform more anaerobic work. Of note in relation to the studies on cardiovascular response to exercise, the authors found that training did not alter the rate of pulse-rate recovery following maximum capacity exercise. They suggest that since it took longer to reach the point of exhaustion after training, the pulse rate response to an exercise of fixed intensity probably should have shown more rapid recovery in trained subjects. However, their findings point out that the rate of pulse-rate recovery after complete exhaustion does not seem to be affected by training.

In exhausting activity, such as in competitive sports and in war, the vigor and extent of exercise are circumscribed by the limits of the physiological functions involved. We know that at a given age and under fixed conditions, the heart rate cannot be pushed beyond a certain value. At any given time the capacity for supplying oxygen to the tissues is strictly limited. The individual will work anaerobically until a tolerable limit of oxygen debt and concentration of lactic acid is reached. Severe prolonged work may be limited by the stores of carbohydrate.

Yet it is a common observation that exercise repeatedly carried out leads to an improved performance. In the runner this amounts to running a greater distance at the same pace, or covering the same distance more quickly, or covering the same distance at the same rate with less fatigue. As soon as improvement in performance can be demonstrated, the process of training may be said to have begun. The rate of improvement depends on the individual's initial state and on how rigorous a regime he follows. Any regime systematically followed will have its most striking results following a few weeks of training; after the first rapid gains, hard diligent work is required if a continued improvement is to be secured. Such training is essential for success in amateur or professional sport. The less seriously one takes his sport, the less impressive is the second phase of improvement: the average young man can soon acquire the ability to run a mile in 6 min but he must work hard and long to run it in 5 min.

The means by which training results in an increased capacity for work is not completely understood. Experimental work done on animals and their musculature, and on intact humans, has yielded some significant advances, but some of the evidence is conflicting. An excellent review of work on training was made by Steinhaus,[10] and later Dill[2] reviewed various aspects of muscular exercise. More recent summaries of the literature related to the problem are those of Hellebrandt,[4] Steinhaus,[11] and the closely related studies of muscular contraction as reviewed by Sacks.[8] Extensive discussions are found in Bainbridge[1] and Schneider.[9] Many of the studies on training have compared two selected populations, one, a group of trained men and the other, a control group. This type of study yields less useful data than one in which individuals are studied before and during training.

Two years ago simultaneous studies of training were begun in the Fatigue Laboratory and in the Department of Physiology of the University of Indiana. The subjects consisted chiefly of non-athletic students. The plans for laboratory performance tests and observations were similar but separate paths were followed in order to obtain independent judgments as to the outcome of the experiments. Some of the Indiana results have been published by Robinson and Harmon,[7] and the

review in their paper of recent literature is so adequate that it need not be repeated here. It is now clear that the Indiana students showed greater improvement and reached higher levels of performance than did the Harvard students. These differences probably depend on a number of factors, some of them psychological. The students at Indiana were working their way through college and were paid for their time in these tests. Those at Harvard were fulfilling the requirement that all freshmen take part in some physical activity. They too were paid but not all of them were dependent on this source of income. While both groups had track work three times weekly there is no comparative record of the amount of training received nor of the degree to which individuals pushed themselves during training. The Indiana students, in the words of Doctor Robinson, "were given about as much running as they could take but this was considerably short of what is expected of a veteran runner. The amount of running done by a beginner is limited by shin splints and arch trouble. These may occur even in some veterans if too much work is attempted."[1]

The observations made in our laboratory consisted of bimonthly studies of the men at rest and biweekly studies of work performance. We measured basal metabolic rate, analyzed alveolar air, recorded breathing curves and vital capacity, obtained resting pulse and blood pressure values. Venous blood drawn during each bimonthly test was analyzed for O_2 capacity, alkaline reserve, plasma protein, and chloride. A study was made of the formed elements of the blood and hemoglobin concentration. At the same intervals,

---

[1] Personal communication.

the men collected three 24-hr urines for study of possible effects of training on excretion of chloride, creatine, and creatinine.[2]

The progress of the subjects was followed biweekly by means of work experiments on our motor-driven treadmill. The subject walked 8 min at 3.5 mi per hr on an 8.6 per cent grade, and then immediately ran on the same or a higher grade at 7.0 mi per hr for 5 min if possible. Otherwise he stopped when exhausted. At the end of the run the subject jumped to the side ·or straddled the belt, keeping the mouthpiece in place. As soon as the belt stopped a stool was placed on it. The subject sat on the stool during a 15-min recovery period. Oxygen consumption was measured for the last part of the walk, for each minute of the run and for the recovery period. A continuous heart-rate record was made of the entire experiment. Capillary blood was taken after the run for the determination of sugar and lactate. Since the treadmill grade was adjusted up and down during the series of experiments, the subjects were not exhausted at the end of five minutes in some instances. The experiments reported here, however are those in which the subjects became exhausted within 5 min. These series at approximately the same intervals as the basal tests.

RESULTS. *Basal state.* The mean results of the experiments on fasting and resting subjects are shown in Table 1. The first figures represent the initial

---

[2] Nearly all of our subjects ate at the dining hall provided for freshmen and hence had the same choice of food. There was no control exercised over their diet except that over a 6-week period some time during the 6 months each man took 60 g of gelatin daily. There was no evidence that the gelatin influenced performance nor the training curve, that is, the rate at which performance improved.

values before training began. The next three were obtained after approximately 2, 4, and 6 months of training.

Most of the measures in rest, which have been previously thought to be related to the degree of training, appear to remain relatively constant. For example, the alkaline reserve and the alveolar CO_2 tension remain practically level, and if a tendency must be noted, it is for a decrease, rather than an increase, as found in numerous previous studies. On the other hand, there is a decrease in the resting pulse rate of 5 beats per min, which fits nicely into the generally accepted picture of training. The gain in weight, amounting to slightly more than 2 kg, may be related in whole or in part to the training regime.

Blood pressure, respiratory rate, vital capacity of the basal metabolism were not significantly altered by training. Oxygen capacity of venous blood rose by about 2 per cent, an insignificant change. The increase in concentration of the plasma chloride was at the outside less than 3 per cent, but the change was so consistent that the increases by the fourth and sixth months of training were statistically reliable.

The remaining data on hemoglobin, the formed elements of the blood and the excretion of chloride, creatine, and creatinine were more variable in the subjects from test to test, and showed no significant relation to the regime of training.

Grade walking. In the walk, which was always at the same grade and rate, experienced subjects reach a steady state within 3 or 4 min of starting, carrying on aerobically without a mounting oxygen debt. The oxygen requirement for this grade of work showed the greatest decline within 2 months, with a further slight decrease at the end of 6 months of training

TABLE 1

Summary of the Means of Data on the Basal state of 14 subjects in training for Middle-Distance Running Over a Period of 6 Months

	CONTROL	TRAINING PERIOD After two months	After four months	After six months
Height, cm	176.1	176.1	176.1	176.1
Weight, kg	69.6	70.8	72.0	71.8
Heart rate	66.8	62.8	63.2	61.8
Blood pressure, mm Hg	114/65	113/65	111/63	113/67
Respiratory rate	15.1	14.6	14.1	14.3
Respiratory vol., 1 per min N. T. P.	6.23	5.73	5.60	5.69
Vital capacity, 1	3.79	3.67	3.70	3.63
Basal metabolism, cal per m^2 per hr	41.5	40.6	40.8	40.9
Alveolar pCO$_2$, mm Hg	41.5	40.8	40.6	41.3
Alveolar pO$_2$, mm Hg	100.3	104.4	100.8	98.1
O$_2$ Capacity, vols. %	19.83	20.24	20.14	20.18
Alkali reserve*	47.8	46.9	47.6	46.6
Plasma chloride, meq per 1	103.6	104.8	106.0	105.8
Plasma nitrogen, g per l	10.3	10.7	10.7	10.8
Hemoglobin, g per 100 ml	14.8	15.1	15.0	15.2
Red cells, millions per mm^3	4.62	4.82	4.72	4.73
White cells, per mm^3	5960	6120	5780	6090
Hematocrit, %	44.1	44.7	45.2	46.0
Urine chloride, meq per day	186	210	181	201
Urine total creatinine, g per day	1.85	1.92	1.84	1.81

* Defined as the CO_2 combining capacity of oxygenated blood, measured at 37°C and a pCO$_2$ of 40 mm Hg.

TABLE 2

The Mean Changes in the Efficiency of Grade Walking

	O$_2$ PER MIN 1 per min	Δ%	NET EFFICIENCY Per cent	Δ%	HEART RATE Beats per min	Δ%
Control	1.91		15.3		151	
After 2 months	1.81	−5.2	16.6	+8.5	145	−4.0
After 4 months	1.81	−5.2	16.8	+9.8	145	−4.0
After 6 months	1.78	−6.8	16.9	+10.4	146	−3.3

(Table 2). This is reflected in an increased net efficiency at this rate of work of about one-tenth. These two functions are not exactly mirrored because the measurement of oxygen requirement has not been adjusted by subtracting the basal O$_2$ requirement nor has it been related to body weight. These points are taken into account in measuring efficiency. The increased efficiency of grade walking was accompanied by a decreased heart rate of about 4 per cent. The mean values of R.Q. for the four series were 0.94,

0.93, 0.92, 0.93, respectively, reflecting an extraordinary constancy in the proportion of carbohydrate utilized.

The improved performance in the walk probably depends on better skill and coordination. It is not likely that the training program had much to do with this improvement, for even skilled runners may be clumsy and inefficient in their first walk on the treadmill.

Maximal work. The experiments calling for the exhaustion of the subject within 5 min necessitated an increase in grade as the training progressed. The mean grade was increased from 9.1 per cent in the control series to 10.9 in the second, to 13.3 in the third, and to 13.4 per cent in the last series. Observations made on one of the men after he had attained a high capacity are shown in Table 3. The mean duration of run for these same series was 3.22, 3.87, 3.17, and 3.44 min, respectively. Thus, in the last test the run was 7 per cent longer, while the grade was almost one-half greater than in the first test. When the body weight is taken into account, the duration and rate of work yield the total physical work done.

It is of great importance to recognize that the principal increase in work output was accomplished by the increase in rate of work, the duration of work not varying greatly. Under these conditions gains in rate of work performance must decline approaching an asymptote, however rigorous the training. On the other hand, if the rate of work output is kept constant, there may be an enormous increase in the quantity of work that can be done. Thus, with the rate constant, Karpovich and Pestrecov[5] had a subject who was exhausted after 12-min work at the beginning of their tests, but who was able to work for 5 hr, 16 min several weeks later. This represents a gain of over 2,500 per cent in total work output.

To translate the accomplishment of our subjects into more familiar units, we may say that our average man, while running up hill at 7 mi per hr could raise his body 180 ft in 3.22 min at the beginning, and 284 ft in 3.44 min 6 months later.

Exhausting experiments are characterized by a mounting oxygen debt, indicating that the body processes are working beyond a point where equilibrium can be attained, and much of the work is carried on anaerobically. The mean increase of about 60 per

TABLE 3

Typical Data on the Performance of One Man (J. Y.) in Exhausting Work

		HEART RATE IN RECOVERY
Work		
Treadmill speed	(11.3 km per hr)..........	At 20 sec, 187 beats per min
Treadmill grade	(15.8%)	At 40 sec, 178 beats per min
Duration of run	(3.63 min)	At 60 sec, 171 beats per min
Physical work	(7000 kg-m)	At 90 sec, 158 beats per min
Maximal oxygen transport	(3.53 1 per min)..........	At 2 min, 147 beats per min
Maximal heart rate	(197 beats per min)........	At 3 min, 132 beats per min
		At 4 min, 124 beats per min
Recovery		At 5 min, 123 beats per min
Net O_2 debt (15 min)	(8.63 l)	At 10 min, 112 beats per min
Maximal lactate	(144 mg %)	At 15 min, 113 beats per min
Maximal blood sugar	(163 mg %)	

TABLE 4

The Mean Changes in the Capacity for Exhausting Work During Training

	WORK DONE TO EXHAUSTION		MAXIMAL LACTATE		MAXIMAL BLOOD SUGAR	
	kg-m	Δ%	mg %	Δ%	mg %	Δ%
Control..............	3786		114		127	
After 2 months........	5593	+47.7	131	+14.9	142	+11.8
After 4 months........	5573	+47.2	135	+18.4	134	+5.5
After 6 months........	6046	+59.6	134	+17.5	134	+5.5

	WORK PER L O_2 DEBT		MAXIMAL O_2 PER MIN		O_2 DEBT FOR 15 MIN	
	kg-m	Δ%	l	Δ%	l	Δ%
Control..............	484		3.45		7.82	
After 2 months........	691	+42.7	3.64	+5.5	8.09	+3.4
After 4 months........	671	+38.7	3.69	+7.0	8.30	+6.2
After 6 months........	737	+52.2	3.69	+7.0	8.20	+4.9

cent in work done through the training period was in part due to a greater use of the anaerobic mechanisms for energy transformation (Table 4). This is indicated both by the increased tolerance for lactate of as much as 18 per cent, which is paralleled by a smaller increase of 5 or 6 per cent in the oxygen debt as judged by the amount repaid in the first 15 min of recovery. There was also an increase of about 6 or 7 per cent in the transport of oxygen to the tissues during work, which represents a clear-cut gain in the amount of work which could be carried on aerobically. The amount of oxygen debt measured during the first 15 min of recovery from work of this nature represents a proportion of the total debt that may vary from one-half to two-thirds. The index to anaerobic work so obtained is not precise but even making the most unfavorable assumptions it is clear that only a small fraction of the increased work output can have been accomplished by increased anaerobic energy transformation: it must be attributed to improved efficiency in running.

It is interesting to note that the concentration of lactate reached increased about 10 per cent in the second series relative to unit oxygen debt as measured for 15 min. The ratio stayed virtually constant for the remainder of the experiment. The figures were 20.4, 22.5 22.4, and 22.6 mg per cent lactate per liter of oxygen debt. The constancy of the figure leads one to believe that this change was real, whatever its basis.

An analysis of the heart rate data in recovery after maximal work showed that not only was the mean maximal heart rate at the end of the run approximately constant but neither did the regime of training materially alter the course of the recovery heart rate. The data are charted in Fig. 1. The curves appear to be exponential, and can be fitted reasonably well from the 1st to the 15th minute of recovery. The general form of the curve can be expressed, using the exponential function, as $y = ae^{-bx} + c$, where y = heart rate and x = the time elapsed. The curves have been calculated but do not yield any more information than can be obtained from the chart shown. The important thing we wanted to know was whether the heart rate declined more rapidly or reached a

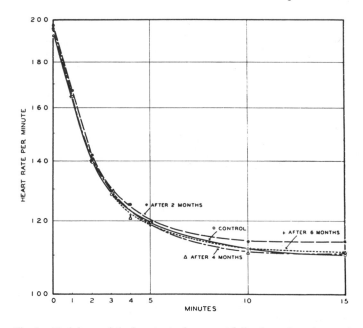

Fig. 1. Training and the heart-rate decrement following exhausting work on the treadmill.

lower level as a result of training. Obviously, the curves under the stated conditions are virtually unaffected by training.

DISCUSSION. In the exhausting grade of work we found that the capacity for aerobic energy transformation had been increased, as evidenced by the increase in maximal oxygen intake. This probably depends on an increased cardiac output, on improved circulation to the working muscles, and on more favorable conditions for exchange of gases between the capillaries and muscle cells.

The increased level of lactate noted in our subjects may be looked upon as one of the most significant effects of training. We have been accustomed to say that the level of lactate at the end of work is a measure of the extent to which a man has pushed himself. It has been recognized that at best this is a rough approximation. In high altitudes Edwards[3] has shown that

the capacity of an individual to accumulate lactate in exhausting work falls off as the degree of anoxia, or the altitude, increases. Robinson[6] has shown that old men, even though healthy, cannot accumulate much lactate: the capacity for anaerobic work falls off with increasing age. On the other hand, the highest lactates we have seen occur in athletic young men. The ordinary young man will stop work with a lactate of 100 mg per cent while first-class athletes will continue until their lactate level has reached 150, 175, or even 200 mg per cent as has been shown by Robinson and Harmon.[7]

We know that in high altitudes despite the inability to reach sustained high levels of performance in climbing, the individual may have unimpaired muscle strength. Furthermore, we have seen excellent performances in strength tests in men past middle age who were incapable of reaching a high level of lactate in work that taxed the capacity for supplying oxygen. These observations suggest that the capacity to accumulate lactate runs parallel and may in fact furnish an excellent index to cardiovascular fitness.

Increases in oxygen intake and in oxygen debt account only in part for the increase during training in the rate at which external work can be done. The useful work output increases in relation to the oxygen requirement.

One of our negative findings is interesting in the light of current indices of physical fitness. Many of these use the decline of pulse rate after performance of a fixed task as one of a battery of tests of physical condition of a subject. We find that a regime of training, which certainly increases physical fitness, does not alter the decline of heart rate following exercise to complete exhaustion within an approximately constant time limit of 3 to 4 min. A study of the decrement in heart rate after exercise of fixed intensity and duration would certainly show a more rapid pulse recovery during any effective period of training. Our data do not negate such findings nor do they run counter to the assumption that individual differences in performance can be related to decline of pulse rate after moderate exercise. They do seem to show that when complete exhaustion is reached in a given time, the rate of work varying, the pulse recovery curve remains unaffected by training. This is in harmony with the findings of Robinson and Harmon (unpublished data—personal communication).

Summary

A group of 14 subjects followed a training regime for middle-distance running over a period of 6 months. The men were studied before and during this period at rest and while doing two grades of work on a motor-driven treadmill.

The training regime was accompanied by a slight increase in weight, a decrease in resting pulse rate of 5 beats per min, a slight decline in the respiratory rate and volume, and a slight increase in plasma chloride.

No significant differences were found in alveolar CO_2, alkaline reserve, metabolic rate, hemoglobin, or the formed elements of the blood, all being measured in the resting state.

An increase in efficiency of grade walking was observed.

In exhausting work there was an increased capacity for supplying oxygen to tissues and greater utilization of anaerobic energy reserves. The work increment unaccounted for by these alterations presumably results from a more economical organization of bodily functions.

The increased capacity for accumulating lactic acid that is developed during training, and the notably high lactate levels attained by first-class athletes points to this determination as a useful index to cardiovascular fitness.

We are indebted to Dr. Clark W. Heath for hematological studies reported here and to Mr. Frank Consolazio for invaluable technical assistance.

References

1. Bainbridge, F. A., *The Physiology of Muscular Exercise* (3rd ed., rewritten by A. V. Bock and D. B. Dill). London: Longmans, Green & Co., 1931.

2. Dill, D. B., *Physiol. Rev.*, **16** (1936), 263.

3. Edwards, H. T., *Am. J. Physiol.*, **116** (1936), 367.

4. Hellebrandt, F. A., *Ann. Rev. Physiol.*, **2** (1940), 411.

5. Karpovich, P. V., and K. Pestrecov, *Am. J. Physiol.*, **134** (1941), 300.

6. Robinson, S., *Arbeitsphysiol.*, **10** (1938), 251.

7. Robinson, S., and P. M. Harmon, *Am. J. Physiol.*, **132** (1941), 757.

8. Sacks, J., *Physiol. Rev.*, **21** (1941), 217.

9. Schneider, E. C., *Physiology of Muscular Activity*. Philadelphia: W. B. Saunders Co., 1939.

10. Steinhaus, A. H., *Physiol. Rev.*, **13** (1933), 103.

11. Steinhaus, A. H., *Ann. Rev. Physiol.*, **3** (1941), 695.

E. METHENY / L. BROUHA / R. E. JOHNSON / W. H. FORBES

Some Physiologic Responses of Women and Men to Moderate and Strenuous Exercise: A Comparative Study

Reprinted from the *American Journal of Physiology*, **136** (1942), 318–26.

This study shows that collaborative research efforts are beneficial not only when conducted among specialists in related fields, but achieve excellent results when made in cooperation with another laboratory. Here the studies were carried out in the Harvard Fatigue Laboratory in conjunction with Wellesley College. Men and women from both colleges were chosen as subjects, and performed moderate and strenuous exercise on the treadmill; their physiological responses were then measured. An interesting pattern of analysis was used where the eight "best" women were compared to the ten "poorest" men. The women rated best compared favorably with the poorest men in strenuous exercise of short duration but showed a poorer physiological adaptation to moderate exercise of longer duration.

The authors concluded that the differences between the physiological responses of men and women are similar to those differences between trained and untrained men. Judging by the group studied, it was suggested that the physiological adaptation of women to moderate and strenuous exercise is not as efficient as men. The study does not analyze the relative efficiency of male and female adaptation in terms of the size of the heart and lungs. Unfortunately there have been few follow-up studies of the relationship between male and female adaptation. An unpublished study conducted at New York University in which the senior editor participated under the direction of Dr. Isidore Schlamowitz and Dr. L. A.

Larson for the U.S. Air Force also compared the physiological responses of men and women to exercise. The findings of this study were essentially the same as those described here. Certainly, these relationships should be considered anew using more modern techniques of measurement now available.

Numerous investigators have reported on changes in heart rate, blood pressures, blood sugar, blood lactate, ventilation, and oxygen consumption during and following exercise of various kinds, intensity, and duration. The typical physiologic responses of normal males to mild, moderate and strenous exercise have been fairly well established.[1, 5, 7, 9, 10, 15, 16, 17, 19, 21, 22, 23, 24, 25, 26, 27] Similar observations on young women may be found scattered through the literature.[2, 4, 11, 12, 13, 14, 18, 20, 27, 28, 29, 30] The physiologic responses of women to exercise are, as might be expected, similar in nature to those reported for young men. At present, however, the literature does not yield sufficient comparable data on the two sexes to permit generalizations as to how such responses differ in degree for work of a given intensity.

It is the purpose of this paper to present and compare data relative to ventilation, oxygen consumption, R.Q., blood lactate, blood sugar, pulse rates, and blood pressures for healthy young women and men during and following nonexhausting and exhausting work performed under identical conditions. Since certain of these variables are related to physical fitness for exertion[15, 16] such data should be useful in attempting to evaluate the relative fitness of men and women for this type of work.

Subjects. The 17 women used in these experiments were graduate students in hygience and physical education between the ages of 20 and 27. They do not represent a random sample of young women, since they are selected as to health and probably engage in more physical activity than the average young women in this age range. They should not, however, be considered athletes in a trained state.

The 30 men subjects were between the ages of 19 and 23. They were drawn from the 250 cases which comprised at the time the Grant Study at Harvard University. None were athletes in training. Ten cases were chosen at random from those designated as "good," ten from "average," and ten from the "poor" classification. The basis of classification has been described and certain data for these same individuals presented elsewhere.[15, 16]

Procedure

The moderate exercise, referred to as "the walk," was walking at 3.5 mi per hr on an 8.6 per cent grade for 15 min on a motor-driven treadmill. The strenuous exercise, referred to as "the run," was running at 7 mi per hr on the same grade for 5 min or until unable to continue. Only nine subjects, all men, were able to continue this work for 5 min. Heart rates were measured continuously from the beginning to the end of the experiment with a recording Guillemin cardiotachometer, as described by Cotton and Dill.[3] Blood pressures were obtained with sphygmomanometer and stethoscope. Blood sugar was measured on a sample of capillary blood by the method described by Edwards.[6] Ventilation and oxygen consumption were determined by the open-circuit gasometer method.

No data on women were collected during the subject's menstrual period, the week preceding or the three days following the period.

The women subjects arrived at the laboratory 6 hr after breakfast, with no lunch. The typical experiment proceeded as follows:

1:30–2:00 Bed rest

2:00–2:15 Resting ventilation and oxygen consumption measured

2:15–2:25 Sitting and standing heart rate and blood pressures measured

2:25–2:40 Subject walked on treadmill

    2:34–2:39 expired air collected in Tissot spirometer

    2:35 blood samples from finger for sugar and lactate analyses

2:40–2:50 Subject seated beside treadmill

    2:41, 2:43, 2:45, 2:47, 2:49 blood pressure taken

2:50–2:55 Subject ran on treadmill for 5 min or until unable to continue. Expired air collected for each half minute

2:55–3:10 Recovery from run, subject seated beside treadmill

    2:56, 2:58, 3:00, 3:03, 3:05, 3:13 blood pressure taken

3:00, 3:05 blood sample taken for sugar and lactate analyses

The experiments on men differed only in that they were performed at various times during the day, and the bed rest and measures of ventilation, oxygen consumption, heart rate, and blood pressures at rest were omitted.

The "Recovery Index"[15] and the "Work Index,"[16] designed to measure physical fitness for exertion, were computed for each subject. (*See below.)

For each index the higher scores represent greater fitness for exertion. The derivation of these indices is described in the references cited.

The data. The means and extremes for the data obtained for the 17 women and 30 men are shown in Table 1.

A. *During and following the walk.* Nonexhausting exercise in which all subjects performed the same amount of work per kilogram body weight for the same length of time, and in which all subjects reached an approximately steady state within the first 5 or 6 min.

1. There is no marked difference between the men and women in ventilation, oxygen consumption, R.Q., or blood sugar.

2. The women show a more rapid increase in heart rate and reach a

---

*Recovery Index—Walk

$$\frac{300}{\text{recovery pulse rates } (30'' \text{ to } 90'') + (2' \text{ to } 3') + (5' \text{ to } 6')} \times 100,$$

Recovery Index—Run

$$\frac{\text{Duration of run in seconds}}{\text{recovery pulse rates } (30'' \text{ to } 90'') + (2' \text{ to } 3') + (5' \text{ to } 6')} \times 100,$$

Work Index—Walk

   150 (maximum pulse rate + maximum lactate concentration),

Work Index—Run

Duration of run in seconds (maximum pulse rate + maximum lactate concentration).

TABLE 1

Means and Extremes of Values for Selected Physiologic Variables for
17 Women and 30 Men Performing Moderate and Strenuous Exercise

	MEANS		EXTREMES			
	Women	*Men*	*Women*		*Men*	
Walk (3.5 mi per hr on 8.6 % grade for 15 min)						
Ventilation, cc/min/kg......	610	552	467	831	421	748
O₂ consumed, cc/min/kg (9–14 min)	27.8	29.6	25.3	30.2	24.5	38.3
R.Q.—maximum	0.91	0.89	0.84	0.99	0.56	0.97
Blood lactate, mg %........	40	21	26	58	9	38
Blood sugar, mg %..........	115	112	88	141	89	131
Pulse rate—1 min..........	152	140	134	177	112	162
Pulse rate—3 min..........	168	143	150	190	115	168
Pulse rate—maximum......	179	151	156	200	120	172
Recovery pulse—1 min......	139	116	111	172	85	162
Recovery pulse—2½ min....	123	107	93	141	82	135
Recovery pulse—5 min......	112	91	82	143	75	124
Systolic pressure—1 min....	148	148	130	160	122	176
Diastolic pressure—1 min....	84	74	76	98	60	90
Recovery Index............	81	96	67	101	75	120
Work Index	−69	−22	−106	−36	−59	14
Run (7 mi per hr on 8.6 % grade until exhausted)						
Duration (sec)............	108	216	70	186	105	300
Ventilation, cc/min/kg (max.)	975	1112	716	1220	690	1400
O₂ consumed, cc/min/kg (max.)	40.9	51.3	29.6	47.5	30.5	60.5
R.Q.—maximum	1.06	1.14	0.72	1.30	0.81	1.45
Blood lactate, mg per cent (max.)	112	119	69	144	68	178
Blood sugar, mg per cent (max.)	156	144	113	235	114	194
Pulse rate—1 min..........	188	177	170	202	157	192
Pulse rate—maximum......	197	194	181	206	178	210
Recovery pulse—1 min......	163	158	145	180	128	180
Recovery pulse—2½ min....	132	124	111	151	102	148
Recovery pulse—5 min......	116	114	105	137	95	136
Systolic pressure—1 min....	163	181	140	190	140	212
Diastolic pressure—1 min....	88	77	78	108	48	96
Recovery Index............	26	55	16	40	28	92
Work Index	−201	−95	−266	−132	−208	50

higher maximum, although oxygen consumption in cc/min/kg is roughly equivalent for the two groups.

3. The rates of recovery for heart rate are approximately the same, although the women must recover from a higher maximum level.

4. The lactate concentration is higher for the women, suggesting a greater degree of fatigue resulting from

the same amount of nonexhausting work.

5. Systolic pressures are the same, but diastolic pressure following the walk is greater for the women. (In interpreting the results of these experiments no great significance may be attached to differences in observed blood pressures. It is difficult to obtain accurate readings of blood pressure immediately following exertion; the conditions in the laboratory increased this difficulty; and different observers took the measurements on the two groups. The pressures change very rapidly during the recovery period and a difference of a few seconds in time elapsing before obtaining the measurement may have a marked effect on the reading.)

6. Both indices of fitness are lower for the women.

B. *During and following the run.* Exhausting exercise in which the amount of work per kilogram body weight per second was the same for all subjects, but the duration of the work was determined by the ability of the subject to continue. No subject achieved a steady state at this level of activity.

1. The average duration of the run for the women is only half that for the men, so that the women performed only half as much work before becoming exhausted.

2. The maximum pulse rate is approximately equal for the two groups, but the women reach this maximum more quickly. The rates of recovery are about the same.

3. The maximum lactate concentration is approximately the same for both groups, indicating that both were equally fatigued, although the women ran only half as long.

4. The men have a higher R.Q., and greater maximum ventilation and oxygen consumption in cc/kg/min, although

maximum heart rates are about the same.

5. The women show a higher blood sugar level after the run.

6. Systolic pressure is lower and diastolic pressure higher for the women immediately after the run. (See note under A–5 above.)

7. Both indices of physical condition are lower for the women than for the men. This difference is greater for the run than for the walk.

8. In all variables there is considerable overlap in the ranges for the two groups.

The extensive overlap between the men's and women's data and the difficulty of comparing data from the run, in which the women performed only half as much work as the men, suggested a second type of comparison. Using a composite of the four indices of fitness for exertion, the eight "best" women were selected, for the purpose of comparing them with the ten men classified as "poor." The means and extremes for these two groups are shown in Table 2.

It may be observed that for these two groups doing the same amount of work per kilogram of body weight the physiologic responses are very similar. During and following the walk, in which neither group is pushed to maximal exertion and both attain a steady state, it is noteworthy that:

1. The blood lactate is slightly higher for the women.

2. The maximum pulse rate is higher for the women, but their recovery is prompt, so that recovery pulse rates at 1 min, $2\frac{1}{2}$ min, and 5 min are equivalent for the two groups.

3. The "Work Index" is slightly lower for the women because of the higher lactate concentration and pulse rate. This suggests that these women are less fit than the men for long-

TABLE 2

Means and Extremes of Values for Selected Physiologic Variables for 8 "Best" Women and 10 "Poor" Men Performing Moderate and Strenuous Exercise

	MEANS		EXTREMES			
	Women	*Men*	*Women*		*Men*	
Walk						
Ventilation, cc/kg/min......	544	574	467	623	462	748
O₂ consumed, cc/kg/min....	27.3	29.9	25.3	30.0	24.6	38.3
R.Q. (max.)..............	0.90	0.85	0.87	0.91	0.56	0.97
Blood lactate, mg per cent....	34	25	26	53	19	37
Blood sugar, mg per cent....	114	110	102	135	89	126
Pulse rate—1 min.........	148	149	136	164	116	162
Pulse rate—3 min.........	165	151	150	183	122	168
Pulse rate—maximum......	172	159	161	183	130	172
Recovery pulse—1 min......	130	128	111	154	105	162
Recovery pulse—2½ min....	116	117	93	141	96	135
Recovery pulse—5 min......	104	107	82	132	95	124
Systolic pressure—1 min....	149	149	130	160	138	168
Diastolic pressure—1 min....	83	72	76	99	60	88
Recovery Index............	86	87	71	101	75	102
Work Index	−56	−34	−83	−45	−59	6
Run						
Duration (sec)............	133	138	87	186	105	175
Ventilation, cc/kg/min (max.)	1000	1055	716	1220	756	1400
Max. O₂ consumed, cc/kg/min (max.)	41.6	48.7	36.5	47.5	36.2	57.9
R.Q.—(max.)	1.13	1.10	0.91	1.30	0.81	1.45
Blood lactate, mg per cent....	112	113	69	144	83	153
Blood sugar, mg per cent....	155	138	131	200	114	194
Pulse rate—1 min.........	184	180	170	194	165	192
Maximum pulse rate........	194	194	181	202	187	205
Recovery pulse—1 min......	164	159	150	180	140	170
Recovery pulse—2½ min....	131	123	117	151	102	136
Recovery pulse—5 min......	115	113	105	137	96	130
Systolic pressure—1 min....	166	183	140	190	168	210
Diastolic pressure—1 min....	88	83	78	98	66	96
Recovery Index............	32	35	22	40	28	42
Work Index	−174	−169	−132	−197	−143	−208

continued submaximal work. In other words, this work is more strenuous for the women than it is for the men.

In the run, which is sufficiently strenuous to exhaust both groups in about 2 min, and in which both are pushed to their maximum level, these differences disappear. The only differences are:

1. Oxygen consumption in cc/min/kg is lower for the women, indicating a slightly higher mechanical efficiency in the performance of the work.

2. Blood sugar is slightly higher for the women.

DISCUSSION. Among the physiologic responses to exercise which differentiate the trained from the untrained (1–10) may be listed:

1. More economical ventilation during exertion
2. Ability to attain a greater maximum ventilation
3. Greater mechanical efficiency as measured in terms of lower oxygen consumption for a given amount of external work
4. Ability to attain a greater maximum oxygen consumption
5. Lower gross R.Q. during exercise
6. Lower blood lactate for a given amount of exercise
7. Ability to push self to a higher lactate before exhaustion
8. Less increase in pulse rate for submaximal exertion
9. Quicker recovery in pulse rate following activity

An examination of the data for the 30 men and 17 women presented in Table 1 shows these same differences existing between the men and the women. For the walk, in which all subjects did the same amount of external work per kilogram body weight, the men exhibit lower ventilation in cc/min/kg; their blood lactate is lower; and their pulse rate is lower, the maximum rate reached being equal to that attained by the women after only 1 min of walking. The data indicate throughout that this exertion is more strenuous for the women than it is for the men, even though both are able to achieve a steady state. Stated differently, the men are in better physical condition for this submaximal type of exertion and the level at which they reach a steady state is somewhat lower. This is shown also by the differences in the Recovery Index and the Work Index.

Comparisons of data for the run are made difficult because the men performed on the average twice as much work as the women. The data should yield some explanation of why the men

were able to continue twice as long before exhaustion. It may be seen that they were able to reach a greater ventilation, higher R.Q., and markedly greater maximum oxygen consumption and were therefore able to carry on for a longer time. Insofar as blood lactate serves as a measure of fatigue, there is little evidence that the men pushed themselves nearer to exhaustion, since the blood lactates are roughly equivalent, but the men ran twice as long before reaching their maximal lactate. The means and extremes for maximum heart rate are almost identical, but the women reached this maximum in half as much time. This more rapid increase is shown in the difference in rate at 1 min. Again it is evident that this exertion is more strenuous for the women than for the men, taxing all the body systems to their limits in a much shorter time. That the women are less fit for this exhausting exercise is also shown by the great differences in the Recovery Index and the Work Index.

The analysis of the means of the data for the 17 women and 30 men prompts the generalization that women, as a group, are the "weaker sex," being less fit than men for both moderate and strenuous exertion and exhibiting less endurance for this type of activity.

From the comparisons in Table 2 which shows data for the eight "best" women and the ten "poorest" men, it may be seen, however, that such a generalization may be made only about the *average* performances of the two groups, for the responses of the eight "best" women closely approximate those of the ten "poor" men.

In running uphill at a rate which does not permit the attainment of a steady state by any of these subjects, the eight "best" women and the ten "poorest" men are exhausted in the same amount of time. The women equal the men in maximum ventilation, oxygen consumption, R.Q., blood lactate, increase in pulse rate, maximum pulse rate, rate of recovery, and systolic and diastolic blood pressures. The women have a higher blood sugar after the run. This may be due to excitement, or it may be a chance difference. In short, there is nothing to indicate that these eight women are in any way less fit than these ten men for short bouts of exhausting exertion. This is shown also by the similarity of the Recovery Index and the Work Index for the two groups.

In the longer continued but less exhausting activity of walking uphill, the differences are somewhat greater for the eight "best" women and the ten "poorest" men. For the women, pulse rate accelerates more rapidly, and reaches a higher maximum, but recovery during the first minute is also more rapid. This suggests that even these "best" women found this long-continued moderate exertion more strenuous than did the ten "poor" men. This is further shown by the higher blood lactate, which indicates that they were more fatigued. There is no difference in the Recovery Index for the two groups, but the Work Index shows that even the best women are slightly less fit for long-continued submaximal exertion than are the poorest group of men.

Since the walk and the run represent two quite different levels of activity, the statements: *a*, the groups of eight women and ten men are equally fit for short bouts of exhausting activity; and *b*, the women as a group are slightly less fit for long-continued activity, are not necessarily contradictory. They do, however, raise the question as to why this difference exists. In the run, the limiting factors are primarily circulatory and respiratory. In the walk, the subjects reached a

steady state in which the circulatory and respiratory systems adjusted to the demands made upon them, but the duration of the activity is such that muscular fatigue becomes a factor. It is possible that differences in muscle strength relative to body weight may provide a partial explanation of why the women were more fatigued than the men by this continued exertion. Data on this point are not available for the present group of subjects.

On the basis of the data presented, it is interesting to speculate on the distribution of physical fitness for exertion in the total population. It is obvious from the data on the Recovery Index and Work Index presented in Tables 1 and 2 that there is no clear-cut division between men and women in physical fitness for these two types of exertion. Some of the best women exceed in fitness the poorest men, and for the best half of the women studied and the poorest third of the men the overlap is complete. Thus, it is obvious that in the total population, including both sexes, physical fitness for exertion must be considered a continuous variable, although the distribution is not necessarily normal in form. In this distribution it is evident that the women are more numerous in the "poor" end of the distribution, while the men preponderate at the "good" end, but in the middle of the range the sexes overlap.

It may be pointed out that the subjects of the present experiment do not represent extremes of fitness. The classifications "good," "average," and "poor" are only relative. As has been shown by Johnson and Brouha,[15, 16] athletes in training exceed in fitness the "good" men in the present group. The same is probably true for women. As has been stated, the women subjects were selected as to health and amount of daily activity. There are, no doubt, many healthy young women of this age who would make poorer records than the poorest reported here. Similarly, healthy young men have been found who are less fit than the "poor" members of this selected college group. Lacking data on these extremes of performance it is not possible to set the limits of overlap in performance for the two sexes, but it seems probable that it is very great.

Summary

1. Seventeen women and 30 men walked 15 min at 3.5 mi per hr and ran for 5 min or until exhausted at 7 mi per hr on a motor-driven treadmill with a grade of 8.6 per cent.

2. Records of heart rate, blood pressure, ventilation, oxygen consumption, R.Q., blood sugar, and blood lactate were obtained.

3. Means and extremes for the data are compared for the two groups.

4. The differences between the averages for the men and women are similar in nature to those between the trained and the untrained.

5. As a group, the women were less fit than the men for both moderate and strenuous exertion.

6. Means and extremes for the data on the eight "best women and the ten "poorest" men are also compared.

7. The eight "best" women equaled in every respect the performance of the ten "poor" men in the strenuous exhausting exercise. They showed slightly greater fatigue as a result of 15 min of nonexhausting exercise in which a steady state was reached and maintained.

References

1. Bainbridge, F. A., *The Physiology of Muscular Exercise* (3rd ed., rewritten by A. V. Bock and D. B. Dill). London: Longmans, Green & Co., 1931.

2. Benedict, F. G., and H. S. Parmenter, *Am. J. Physiol.*, **84** (1928), 675.

3. Cotton, F. S., and D. B. Dill, *ibid.*, **111** (1935), 554.

4. Damez, M. K. *et al.*, *J. Am. Med. Assoc.*, **86** (1926), 1420.

5. Dill, D. B. *et al.*, *Le Travail humain*, **5** (1937), 1.

6. Edwards, H. T., *J. Biol. Chem.*, **125** (1938), 571.

7. Edwards, H. T. *et al.*, *Le Travail humain*, **8** (1940), 1.

8. Folin, O., and H. Malmros, *J. Biol. Chem.*, **83** (1929), 115.

9. Gemmill, C. *et al.*, *Am. J. Physiol.*, **92** (1930), 253.

10. Gemmill, C. *et al.*, *ibid.*, **96** (1931), 265.

11. Hartwell, G., and N. Tweedy, *J. Physiol. (London)*, **46** (1913), 9.

12. Hellebrandt, F., *Am. J. Physiol.*, **101** (1932), 357.

13. Hellebrandt, F. *et al.*, *Proc. Soc. Exptl. Biol. Med.*, **43** (1940), 629.

14. Hodgson, P., *Res. Quart. Am. Assoc. Health, Phys. Educ.*, **7** (1936), 3.

15. Johnson, R. E., and L. Brouha, *Rev. Can. Biol.*, **1** (1942), 171.

16. Johnson, R. E. *et al.*, *ibid.*

17. Knehr, C. A. *et al.*, *Am. J. Physiol.*, **136** (1942), 148.

18. Murphy, N. A., *Res. Quart. Am. Assoc. Health, Phys. Educ.*, **9** (1940), 57.

19. Owles, W. H., *J. Physiol. (London)*, **69** (1930), 214.

20. Prosch, F. *Res. Quart. Am. Phys. Educ. Assoc.*, **4** (1932), 75.

21. Robinson, S., *Science*, **85** (1937), 401.

22. Robinson. S., *Arbeitsphysiol.*, **10** (1938), 251.

23. Robinson, S., and P. M. Harmon, *Am. J. Physiol.*, **132** (1941), 757.

24. Robinson, S. *et al.*, *Human Biol.*, **13** (1941), 139.

25. Schneider, E. C., and C. B. Crampton, *Am. J. Physiol.*, **129** (1940), 165.

26. Steinhaus, A. H., *Physiol. Rev.*, **13** (1933), 103.

27. Taylor, C., *Am. J. Physiol.*, **135** (1941), 27.

28. Thomas, J., and A. Keyes, *ibid.*, **129** (1940), 480.

29. Thomas, J., and G. B. Nichelsen. Unpublished data.

30. Wellesley College Studies in Hygiene and Physical Education, *Suppl. Res. Quart. Am. Assoc. Health, Phys. Ed.*, **9** (1938), 10.

P. V. KARPOVICH / M. P. STARR / R. W. KIMBRA /
C. G. STOLL / R. A. WEISS

Physical Reconditioning After Rheumatic Fever

Reprinted from the *Journal of the American Medical Association*,
130 (1946), 1198–1203.

Prior to World War II it was generally thought that persons recuperating from rheumatic fever should avoid physical activity until they were released from the hospital. The Army Air Forces developed a policy through the guidance of Dr. Howard Rusk and his associates which stressed reconditioning of patients before discharge from the hospital to prepare them for duty immediately after release. The AAF School of Aviation Medicine was entrusted with the responsibility of devising a method of assessing the patient's capacity for a specific exertion.

The patient's pulse-rate response after exercising in a simple stair-stepping test was used to assess his capacity for exercise throughout the period of his reconditioning. The results of the study provide dramatic evidence of the value of physical activity during recuperation. A classification system based on the step test was effective in reducing the number of days preceding initiation of reconditioning exercises from 77 to 16. The implications of these findings were of such significant impact that it is now standard procedure in the treatment of most cardiac patients to obtain some measure of exercise tolerance in order to have a basis for prescribing the exercise regimen most beneficial for the patient.

There is a great deal of diversity in AAF hospitals regarding the management of the period of convalescence after rheumatic fever. It varies from a prolonged restriction of physical activities to an early participation in special exercise which often may require a great deal of exertion. This difference in attitude regarding physical activity can be explained easily. On the one hand, it has been a medical tradition, based mainly on observation among children, that rest is an essential part of the rheumatic fever regimen not only during the active stage of the disease but also during a long period of time afterward. On the other hand, accumulated experience with rheumatic fever has indicated that this disease affects adults in a lesser degree than children, and therefore the management of the patients in the two instances may not be the same. Moreover, the present attacks on the "abuse of bed rest" in the treatment of various diseases, including those of the heart, have led to the question whether a prolonged period of physical inactivity during convalescence after rheumatic fever is beneficial or not.

The AAF convalescent policy is to recondition patients before their discharge from the hopsital and to prepare them, when possible, for full or limited military duty. Therefore it is of practical importance to assess and develop to the required level the capacity of the patients for physical exertion while they are in the hospital.

The need for some practical tests for determination of the physical fitness of patients convalescing from rheumatic fever has been recognized before. Swift and McEwen[5] started physical reconditioning of patients convalescing from rheumatic fever by allowing them to sit in a stationary chair for a progressively increasing length of time. After the patients had become accustomed to sitting most of the day, they were permitted to make short walks in the ward. "The first walk consisted of about 50 ft, the second either the same amount or double that, the third about 100 ft, and then the amount is increased slowly according to the patient's response."[4] Wilson[7] described a set of arbitrary tests consisting of dumbbell swinging and stair climbing. As criteria

for appraising the degree of fitness she used the color of the face, the degree of dyspnoea and the type of systolic blood pressure curve plotted from determinations made at frequent intervals after exercise.

Our purpose in the present study was to apply certain physical fitness tests to the patients convalescing from rheumatic fever in order to determine (a) how soon after clinical subsidence of the disease a patient can safely participate in physical training, and (b) how much time is required in order to regain the degree of physical fitness necessary for limited and full military duty.

Methods

In designing the present study it was decided to start testing the physical fitness of the patients after a 2-week period of quiescence of the disease, with the exceptions to be noted. Criteria for the beginning of the quiescent period were normal temperature, an erythrocyte sedimentation rate of 15 mm or less (Westergren method), a normal electrocardiogram, and the absence of arthralgia. During this period no salicylates were given. Eighty-eight patients convalescing from rheumatic fever at the AAF Regional Hospital, San Antonio Aviation Cadet Center, San Antonio, Texas, were used as subjects. These patients were at various stages of convalescence (Table 1).

Because of the great variation in the length of time from the beginning of the quiescent period to the beginning of testing, all patients studied in the present investigation were divided into three groups, A, B, and C.

Group A, consisting of 22 men, was living in the barracks at the beginning of this study. For these men an average of 3 months had elapsed since the first day of quiescence. The exact time when these patients were made ambulatory could not be ascertained from their hospital records. They had had no special physical training program. Some of them had had furloughs; some had been sent for 2 weeks to a convalescents camp located in a hilly section of Texas.

Group B, consisting of 30 men, had an average of 77.3 days of quiescence before the testing and physical activation began.

Group C, consisting of 36 men, was activated after an average of 16.2 days of quiescence.

Physical fitness tests. In selecting tests of physical fitness suitable for the present investigation, it was decided to use the same stepping-up tests which were used in a study conducted on patients with upper respiratory diseases.[3] However, because rheumatic fever is a more debilitating disease it seemed advisable to introduce one additional mild test which could be used as the first test.

Thus, there were three stepping-up tests used in this study:[1]

1. Preliminary test, consisting of 12 complete steps in 30 sec, using a 12-in. bench, referred to in this study as the "12-in. test."

2. Preliminary test, consisting of 12 complete steps in 30 sec, using a 20-in. bench, referred to in this study as the "20-in. test."

3. Progressive test, consisting in stepping on a 20-in. bench at a rate of 24 complete steps per min for as long as the patient could continue but no longer than 5 min.

---

[1] Stepping technique is the same for all three tests. The subject stands in front of the bench and steps up on it with one foot and then with the other. He steps down in the same order. Four counts are used for each complete step. The stepping rate is 24 complete steps per min. The cadence, therefore is 96 counts per min.

Scoring in preliminary tests. Possible scores in preliminary tests were either "passed" or "failed." The criteria were the same for both the 12- and the 20-in. tests. The pulse rate with the subject sitting was taken 1 min after exercise for 30 sec and multiplied by 2. If the post-exercise pulse rate was 100 or less, the cardiac reaction was considered normal on the basis of a previous investigation. If, however, muscular coordination was not good and the patient had difficulty in executing the step-ups and in maintaining the cadence, he was considered as failing, regardless of his pulse reaction.

If the patient failed the 12-in. test, he was considered a bed patient and

TABLE 1

Frequency Distribution of the Number of Patients Respective to the Length of Time Elapsed from the Beginning of the Quiescent Period to the Beginning of Testing

	Number of Men
1 week	11
2 weeks	7
3 weeks	10
4 weeks	11
5 weeks	3
6 weeks	5
7 weeks	4
8 weeks	3
9 weeks	3
10 weeks	4
11 weeks	5
12 weeks	1
13 weeks	3
14 weeks	0
15 weeks and over	18

was given an additional medical examination and then retested in a day or two. If the patient passed the 12-in. test, he was given the 20-in. test on the same day. If he passed the 12- but failed the 20-in. test he was allowed to be ambulatory but not allowed to take part in ward exercises and was retested one or two days later. The patient who had passed both preliminary tests was placed on the ward exercise program.

Scoring in the progressive test. Two days after passing the 20-in. preliminary test and after having had ward calisthenics, the patients were given the progressive test. The degree of fitness was estimated by the duration of well-tolerated exercise, as judged by the absence of signs of distress, and by the pulse rate taken in a sitting position for half a minute, starting 1 min after exercise. The possible scores in this test (Table 2) are low, fair, and good. For those who scored "low," the test was repeated after 3 or 4 days depending on the soreness of the leg muscles. After the patients had scored "fair," they were tested only once a week.

Erythrocyte Sedimentation Rate. As a matter of precaution regarding the possible untoward effect of exercises, it was decided to test the patient's erythrocyte sedimentation rate 24 hr after each physical fitness test. This was done because a previous investigation[2] showed that after strenuous muscular work the erythrocyte sedimentation rate should return to normal within 24 hr.

Physical training program. A detailed description is given elsewhere;[6] only essentials will be outlined here. The graded physical training program was divided into three phases officially designated as III, II, and I. The relationship between the present numerical classification and the former color designation is shown in Table 3 in order to avoid confusion in reading some of the references mentioned in this article.

Phase III consisted of two 10-min periods of calisthenics usually given in the ward, for which reason this phase was known also as "ward exercises." The intensity of activity during the beginning of this phase was mild, raising metabolism about 100 per cent over that at rest. By the end of 2 weeks' exercise metabolism was increased to 600 per cent over resting metabolism.

At that time patients were reexamined, and if there was no medical contraindication they were allowed to participate in mild games either outdoors or in a gymnasium. These games

TABLE 2

Scoring Table for Progressive Test

Duration of Exercise	Pulse Rate One Minute After Exercise	Score
Below 2′	Any rate	Low
2′ to 2′29″	Above 100	Low
	Below 100	Fair
2′30″ to 2′59″	Above 130	Low
	Below 130	Fair
3′ to 3′29″	Above 140	Low
	100 to 140	Fair
	Below 100	Good
3′30″ to 3′59″	Above 170	Low
	110 to 170	Fair
	Below 110	Good
4′ to 4′29″	Above 130	Fair
	Below 130	Good
4′30″ to 4′59″	Above 140	Fair
	Below 140	Good
5′	Above 150	Fair
	Below 150	Good

were given in addition to the calisthenics; therefore the time for each period was extended to 30 min, which included the time of walking to the place designated for the games. This part of the third phase continued for one week.

After a patient had been in phase III for 3 weeks and had scored "fair" on the progressive test, with the approval of the ward medical officer he was transferred to the barracks and placed in phase II of the training program. This phase continued for 4 weeks and was conducted outdoors. In addition to calisthenics and games, some running was included. The time allotted was 40 min once a day during the first 2 weeks and 50 min during the last 2 weeks.

Patients who were on program II for 4 weeks and scored "good" in the progressive test were reexamined by the medical officer and with his approval were moved to the more strenuous program, I, which lasted 70 to 80 min once a day during the first 2 weeks and 80 min during the last 2 weeks.

Results

The pertinent data regarding the improvement in physical fitness of each group and the disposition of the patients at the time of their discharge from the hospital are given in Table 5. It is evident that Group A was in a fair state of physical fitness when the testing was started, since within an average of 2.3 days after the testing began 21 men out of 22 scored "fair" on the progressive test and 10.6 days later 20 men scored "good."

B required 21.5 days and Group C 19.1 days. To score "good" Group B needed altogether 31.2 days and Group C 39.9 days. This means that prolonged bed rest during the period of quiescence did not result in a noticeable physical deterioration. Such an observation is not surprising, because in an AAF hospital bed rest during convalescence is often fictional, as the patients while unobserved may indulge in physical activity to a great extent.

Not all patients reached phase I of the training program. Some of them obviously reached the limit of physical fitness at phase II. Since this level appeared to be sufficiently high for men who were not going to engage in strenuous physical work, it was decided not to hold such patients in the hospital until they scored "good" on the progressive test but discharge them from the hospital 6 months after the onset of rheumatic disease. These patients were able to perform efficiently limited military duty.

At the time of discharge from the hospital, only 1 patient from Group A received a certificate of disability

TABLE 3

Comparison of Functional, Numerical and Color Classification of the Patients

Functional	Official Numerical	Color
Bed*	IV*	White*
Ward-ambulatory	III	Red / Orange
Barracks	II / I	Blue / Green

* No exercise was given during this phase.

The average rate of improvement in physical fitness of the patients in Group B was approximately the same as in Group C. To score "fair" Group

TABLE 4

Causes for Issuing Certificates of Disability for Discharge

	Number of Men	
Group A	1	Cardiac lesion developed during present hospitalization
Group B	2	Cardiac lesion developed during present hospitalization
	1	Old cardiac lesion
	1	Rheumatoid arthritis
Group C	1	Cardiac lesion developed during present hospitalization
	1	Old cardiac lesion
	2	Rheumatoid arthritis
	2	Duration of active phase of disease beyond 3 months

TABLE 5

Summary of the Improvement in Physical Fitness of Patients in Groups A, B, and C and the Decision of the Disposition Board

Group	Number of Men in Each Group	Number of Recurrent Cases	Number of Definite or Possible Cardiac Cases	Days of — Duration of Disease	Days of — Duration of Quiescence	Fair — Number of Men	Fair — Number of Days from Preliminary Test to Scoring "Fair"	Good — Number of Men	Good — Number of Days from Preliminary Test to Scoring "Good"	Number of Men Discharged from Hospital	Full Military Duty	Limited Duty	Certificate of Disability for Discharge
A	22	1	5	41.3	91.1	21	2.3	20	10.6	22	16	5	1
B	30	11	4	33.2	77.3	30	21.5	21	31.2	29	22	3	4
C	36	13	1	66.8	16.2	35	19.1	29	39.9	35	23	2	6
Totals....	88	..	..	....	....	86	....	80	....	86	61	10	11

TABLE 6

Brief Diagnostic and Physical Fitness Data on Patients Developed Definite (D) or Possible (P) Heart Disease During Present Hospitalization, or Who, on Admission to the Hospital, Had Valvular Lesions Which Had Not Changed by the Time of Discharge (S)

Group	Subject	Diagnosis at Admission	Diagnosis at Discharge	Classification	Days from Preliminary Test to Scoring "Fair"	Days from "Fair" to Scoring "Good"	Disposition
A	1	Normal	Mitral stenosis; mitral systolic murmur, grade II	D	1	1	Certificate of disability for discharge
	2	Mitral systolic murmur, grade I	Mitral systolic murmur, grade II	D	1	0	Limited military duty
	3	Mitral systolic murmur, grade I	Aortic insufficiency; mitral systolic murmur, grade II	D	..	..	Limited military duty
	4	Mitral systolic murmur, grade I	Mitral systolic murmur, grade II	P	1	1	Full military duty
	5	Mitral systolic murmur, grade I	Mitral systolic murmur, grade II	P	1	31	Limited military duty
	6	Mitral systolic murmur, grade II	Same as at admission	S	1	0	Full military duty
	7	Aortic and mitral insufficiency	Same as at admission	S	12	56	Limited military duty
B	8	Normal	Mitral stenosis; mitral systolic murmur, grade III	D	8	18	Certificate of disability for discharge
	9	Aortic insufficiency; mitral systolic murmur, grade I	Aortic insufficiency; mitral stenosis; mitral systolic murmur, grade II	D	57	*	Certificate of disability for discharge
C	10	Mitral systolic murmur, grade I	Mitral systolic murmur, grade II	P	44	12	Limited military duty
	11	Normal	Mitral systolic murmur, grade III	P	122	*	Certificate of disability for discharge
	12	Mitral systolic murmur, grade II	Same as at admission	S	3	3	Certificate of disability for discharge
	13	Mitral systolic murmur, grade I	Mitral stenosis; mitral systolic murmur, grade II	D	9	20	Certificate of disability for discharge
	14	Mitral systolic murmur, grade II	Same as at admission	S	18	4	Certificate of disability for discharge

* Did not make the score.

for discharge, as compared with 4 men from Group B and 6 from Group C.

The causes for issuance of certificates of disability for discharge are given in Table 4.

Cardiac patients. Altogether in the three groups there were only six patients who developed definite valvular changes in the heart during the active phase of the disease, and four patients who developed either grade II or grade III systolic murmurs, thereby being designated as possible cardiac patients.[1] Moreover, there were four patients who, on the day of admission to the hospital, had definite cardiac lesions which did not change during 6 to 9 months of disease and convalescence. A brief description of diagnostic data for these patients is given in Table 6. The diagnoses were made independently by three medical officers.

All patients who exhibited abnormalities of the heart as evidenced by electrocardiogram, X-ray, or auscultation were frequently reexamined by the medical officer in charge, and testing was started only when there was no evidence of an active pathologic process in the heart.

Of 14 patients with cardiac lesions (Table 4) only 1 did not score "fair," and of 13 who scored "fair" only 2 did not reach the "good" level of physical fitness. It may be noted here that the individual variations in regaining and developing physical fitness could not be predicted on the basis of the diagnostic findings in the heart indicated in Table 6.

There is general agreement that in the presence of carditis it is wiser to reduce the amount of heart activity, and therefore bed rest is indicated. However, since there is no method for diagnosing latent pathologic processes in the rheumatic heart a conservative physician frequently tends to suspect the existence of such a process in the heart of every patient. For this reason it was of interest to establish a relationship between early activation and the incidence of pathologic cardiac changes. From Tables 5 and 6 it may be seen that the incidence of definite and possible heart disease acquired during the present illness was distributed among the groups as follows: Group A, 5; Group B, 4; Group C, 1. The numbers are too small for justifying conclusive statements. The fact, however, that the average length of rheumatic activity was longest and the duration of the quiescent period shortest in Group C, in which the number of cardiac patients was the smallest, indicates that the organized graded physical training program was safe for these patients.

Clinically evident cardiac lesions in all cases with the exception of one (subject 8 in Group B) developed before physical activation started. It is of interest that the two cardiac patients in Group C, 1 with an old cardiac lesion and the other with a lesion acquired during the present illness, had periods of quiescence of 15 and 12 days, respectively, whereas for cardiac patients in Group B the period of quiescence ranged from 67 to 144 days.

Erythrocyte sedimentation rate. Altogether 671 erythrocyte sedimentation-rate determinations were made on 88 subjects after they took the progressive test. In only 22 determinations did the rate go above 15 mm. These 22 elevations were all on 16 patients, 6 of whom were responsible for 11 of the 22 readings. It was noted, however, that these six men had occasional slight elevations of the erythrocyte sedimentation rate which had no relation to physical training or testing.

An attempt was made also to determine the relationship between the behavior of the erythrocyte sedimenta-

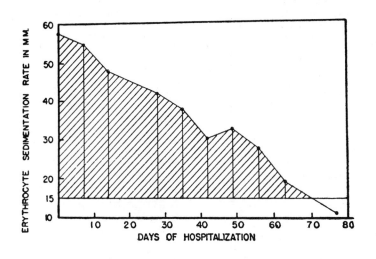

Fig. 1.

tion rate during the course of the disease and the length of time it took to regain a certain level of physical fitness during the period of convalescence. In order to combine the height and the duration of the erythrocyte sedimentation-rate elevation, the erythrocyte sedimentation-rate area was calculated. This was done in the following manner: The erythrocyte sedimentation rate was plotted on graph paper against the time in days (Fig. 1) and a horizontal line was drawn at the level of 15 mm (normal erythrocyte sedimentation rate). The abnormal erythrocyte sedimentation-rate area is then the area which is bound by the vertical axis on the left, the erythrocyte sedimentation-rate curve above and the 15 mm line below.

The limitation of this method is evident, because the erythrocyte sedimentation rate was determined only once a week or even less frequently. The criterion of progress in physical fitness was accepted as the time in weeks from the beginning of the period

of quiescence to the scoring of "fair" on the progressive test.

For this comparison only 15 patients who received the preliminary test not later than 3 weeks after the beginning of the period of quiescence were used. Analysis of the data showed no significant statistical relationship between the erythrocyte sedimentation-rate area and the time required to score "fair" on the progressive test because the coefficient of correlation was only 0.49, whereas in order to be significant it should be at least equal to 0.64.

Comment

Since in rheumatic fever greatest concern is given to a probability of cardiac damage, the tests of physical fitness employed in this study were those which emphasized cardiac function. It is realized that pulse response to an exercise is not always dependable; but, when it is combined with the observations of the actual performance in stepping up, results are gratifying. The

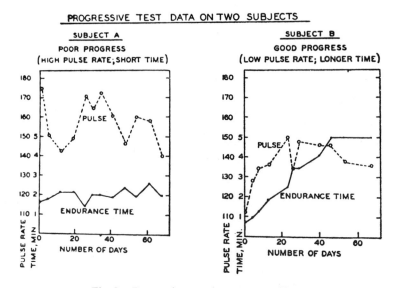

Fig. 2. Progressive test data on two subjects.

periodic testing supplied objective evidence concerning the physical fitness of convalescents. In Fig. 2 are represented the records of a good and a poor recovery. The endurance time of subject A increased but little in 10 weeks, and his pulse rate was high, fluctuating between 160 and 170 beats per min. It was obvious that the degree of physical fitness of this patient was poor. At the time of discharge from the hospital he was judged to be unfit for full military duty. The duration of the stepping up (endurance time) of subject B increased in about 7 weeks from 45 sec to 5 min, whereas the pulse rate, which had been increasing with the lengthening of endurance time for 3 weeks, started to slow down and continued to do so after the endurance time reached the 5-min limit. This patient, at the time of discharge from the hospital, was pronounced physically fit for full military duty.

This investigation showed definitely that the testing records in most instances substantiated the judgment of ward officers and, when different, tended to cluster on the conservative side. The testing can easily be performed by a nurse, but it is worthwhile for the ward officer to observe the patients' progress in regaining physical prowess, which, after all, is the ultimate goal of therapeutic efforts. A prolonged bed rest ordinarily results in comparatively little rest, either physically or mentally. In the present investigation the duration of bed rest after cessation of all pathologic symptoms in Group C was reduced to 16.2 days as compared with 77.3 days for Group B, which was managed more conservatively. This meant that the patients had objective evidence that they were getting definitely well 61 days earlier. Watching their own progress in testing, they had definite proof of improvement and absence of cardiac damage. Those who developed some cardiac lesion were able to see how much work they could do and still be comfortable. The beneficial effect of the testing program on the patients' mental state cannot be minimized.

The patients in Groups B and C

(Table 5) made the "fair" score on the progressive test in about the same length of time after testing started; yet the patients in Group C had, on the average, 66.8 days of illness whereas those in Group B had 33.2 days. This means that the debilitating effect of rheumatic disease is not in proportion to the length of the active pathologic process as determined by present-day methods.

Only one man showed additional pathologic valvular changes during the physical training program. He, however, was detected as a "possible" cardiac patient rather early and was excused from all activities. Moreover, there is no proof that he would not have developed the same lesion if he had not participated in physical training.

Observations of the erythrocyte sedimentation rate indicate that the testing, which, on most occasions, was done to the limit of the patient's stepping-up endurance, and the physical training program caused no changes which could be detected by the erythrocyte sedimentation rate. As the result of this observation, the number of erythrocyte sedimentation-rate determinations in the later stages of convalescence was reduced to one every 2 weeks.

As a rule, patients with an erythrocyte sedimentation rate above 15 mm were excused from the physical training program. Inadvertently, four patients with erythrocyte sedimentation rates ranging from 20 to 35 mm were placed on the ward exercise program. No ill effects were observed,

and the erythrocyte sedimentation rates tested 2 days after the progressive test were normal.

Summary and Conclusions

1. Study was conducted on 88 men convalescing from rheumatic fever in an Army Air Forces hospital.

2. Patients participated in a graded program of physical training.

3. The time of beginning and intensification of training were controlled by a series of physical fitness tests.

4. It was found that these tests constituted a simple and safe method of control over physical reconditioning of the patients and furnished objective data when a patient was brought before the Disposition Board for discharge from the hospital.

5. It was found that patients convalescing from rheumatic fever could safely participate in a graded system of physical exercises within 2 weeks after clinical cessation of the pathologic rheumatic activity.

6. The conventional delay in the beginning of physical reconditioning was reduced from 77.3 days to 16.2 days without causing an increase in the incidence of cardiac damage during 6 to 12 months of observation.

7. There was no relationship between the abnormal erythrocyte sedimentation-rate area during the disease and the time necessary to obtain a "fair" score on the progressive test.

References

1. American Heart Association. *Nomenclature and Criteria for Diagnosis of Diseases of the Heart.* St. Louis, Mo: The C. V. Mosby Company, 1943.

2. Black, William A., and Peter V. Kar-

povich, "Effect of Exercise on the Erythrocyte Sedimentation Rate," *Am. J. Physiol.*, **144** (1945), 224.

3. Karpovich, Peter V., Merritt P. Starr, and Raymond A. Weiss, "Physical

Fitness Tests for Convalescents,"
J. Am. Med. Assoc., **126** (December 2,
1944), 873.

4. Swift, Homer F. Personal communication to the authors.

5. Swift, Homer F., and Currier McEwen, "Rheumatic Fever," in *Oxford Loose-Leaf Medicine*, **5** (1938), 38 (47). New York: Oxford University Press, Inc.

6. Weiss, Raymond A., "Physical Training Program for Patients Recovering from

Rheumatic Fever," *Project Report No.
246, Report No. 3,* AAF School of
Aviation Medicine, March 10, 1945;
"Oxygen Consumption During Various Calisthenic Exercises," *Project
Report No. 246, Report No. 2,* AAF
School of Aviation Medicine, November 4, 1944.

7. Wilson, May G., *Rheumatic Fever.* New York: Commonwealth Fund, 1940, p. 412.

W. S. ZORBAS / P. V. KARPOVICH

The Effect of Weight Lifting Upon the Speed of Muscular Contractions

Research Quarterly, **22** (1951), 145–48.

For many years physical educators maintained that an individual who regularly participated in weight lifting would become "muscle-bound," and, therefore, slower in his movements. Zorbas and Karpovich studied the speed of a rotary arm motion of 300 weight lifters and 300 control subjects who did not lift weights. The results refute the belief that weight lifters are slower in arm movements. In fact, the lifters were significantly faster ($P \leq 0.05$) than Springfield College students, most of whom were physical education majors. Both the weight lifters and the Springfield College students were significantly faster ($P \leq 0.01$) than students of a liberal arts college.

The results suggest that weight training involving the arms leads to faster arm movements. It might be hypothesized that the weight lifters not only develop strength of the arm and shoulder girdle muscles, but also develop speed of movement because certain lifts require fast arm movements. Weight training is now a well-respected form of physical training and one seldom hears the allegation that weight training, when properly conducted, has deleterious effects on the efficiency of body movements.

Many coaches, trainers, and others associated with physical education are of the opinion that training with heavy weights will lead to slower muscle contractions and hence will slow down the athlete: consequently, they prohibit weight lifting by men under their supervision whose success depends upon speed.

On the other hand, some coaches and

trainers claim that weight lifting is very helpful in training their athletes. Unfortunately neither group has produced any documented evidence for their contentions.

As far as we know, there has been no research conducted specifically related to this controversial problem. The need, however, is felt and expressed by those associated with physical education. For this reason the present investigation has been undertaken.

Since weight lifting affects especially the muscles of the arms and of the upper girdle, it was decided to study the effect of weight lifting on these particular muscle groups.

Subjects

Six hundred men, whose ages ranged from 18 to 30 yr, were used. They were divided into two groups of 300 men each.

One group consisted of men who never indulged in weight lifting and was used as a control group. In this group were 150 men from Springfield College and 150 from a liberal arts college.

The other group was composed of weight lifters who had participated in weight lifting for a minimum of 6 months and were still engaged in this activity. Some men were tested at the 1950 Senior National AAU Weight Lifting Championships and Mr. America contest held in Philadelphia. These

men were from various parts of the world, Australia, Hawaii, Puerto Rico, Canada, and many states of this country. The many weight lifting and body building clubs located in New York City and Western Massachusetts also contributed subjects used in this study. They varied from little-known weight lifters to world champions and from unknown body builders to winners of the Mr. America physique contest.

Preliminary Testing

Several types of arm motion have been tried during exploratory experimentation and several special devices were constructed for this purpose before the apparatus finally used in this study was developed. One trial machine required an up and down arm motion in a vertical plane. Contact switches for recording complete movements were placed at the top and bottom of the machine. It was found however, that when the subject moved his arm rapidly there was a tendency not to complete the full movement, and contact with the switches was not made each time. Another trial machine involved a rotary arm motion in a sagittal plane and was found to be impractical because at certain times the extended arm would lock at the elbow, thus interfering with completion of the movement.

After all these preliminary tests, it was found that a clockwise rotation of

TABLE 1

Statistical Data Obtained on the Lifters and Nonlifters

Group	Mean time in Seconds	Excess time Over Group I	σ	σ_m
1. Weight Lifters............	5.491	—	0.344	0.0198
2. Non-Weight Lifters.........	5.665	0.174	0.392	0.0226
3. Springfield College.........	5.55	0.06	0.373	0.03
4. Liberal Arts College.......	5.78	0.29	0.377	0.03

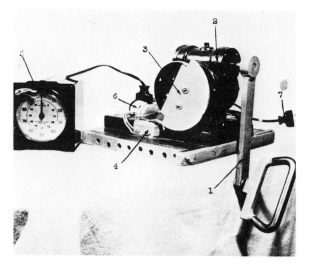

Fig. 1. Apparatus for Automatic Recording of Rotary Movements of the Arm.

   The turning of the arm and handle (1) which is attached to the gear reduction box (2) causes the cam (3) to rotate at a 1-24 ratio. This cam depresses the microswitch (4) thus completing the circuit which starts the electric clock (5). When the arm and handle has been turned 24 complete times, the cam will have completed its required distance and will release the microswitch, thus breaking the electric circuit and stopping the clock. An electric plug connection (6) and an electric plug (7) were used to connect with the conventional electric outlet for 110 v AC.

the arm in which the hand described a circle in a frontal plane was the most satisfactory. The clockwise rotation was chosen because this movement is more natural than in the counter-clockwise one and the pronator muscles are stronger than the supinator muscles.

   It was important to minimize the fatigue and learning factors. A test consisting of two trials of 24 complete revolutions each was found to be most satisfactory.

Method

   A specially constructed apparatus recording speed of rotary movements of the arm was used. It automatically registered to a hundredth of a second the time of 24 complete rotary move-

ments of the arm (see Fig. 1). Each subject had two trials with a 3-min rest between tests. The lower time of the two recordings was used as representative of the subject's speed.

   The cabinet of the apparatus was clamped upon a table and the subject stood with the feet in a stride position, facing the apparatus. The elbow was placed touching the side of the body, arm flexed at right angle, palm downward. The apparatus was then adjusted by having the handle of the apparatus level with the height of the elbow.

   From this position the subject grasped the handle and moved away from the apparatus, still holding the handle, until a comfortable position was attained. The arm had full freedom and range of movement.

   When the subject attained the pre-

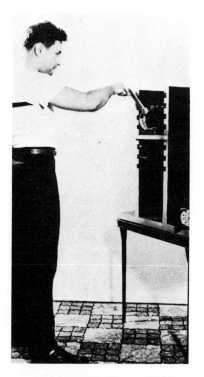

Fig. 2. Apparatus for Testing Speed of Arm Movement in Action.

scribed position, he proceeded at his own discretion to move his arm in a clockwise direction turning the handle as fast as possible until given a verbal signal by the tester that the 24 movements were completed (see Fig. 2).

Analysis of Data

From Table 1 it may be seen that weight lifters were faster in the speed of rotary arm motion than nonlifters. The difference was 0.174 sec, which is statistically significant at the 0.01 level of confidence.

All subjects ranked according to their speed as follows: weight lifters, Springfield College nonlifters, and liberal arts nonlifters.

The weight lifters were 0.29 sec faster than the students of the liberal arts college. This difference is also significant at the 0.01 level of confidence.

The lifter group was only 0.06 sec faster than the Springfield College nonlifters. This difference, however, is statistically significant at the 0.05 level of confidence

In the nonlifter group the Springfield College students were 0.23 sec faster than students from the liberal arts college. This difference is statistically significant at the 0.01 level of confidence.

Summary and Conclusions

The findings of this study appear to be contrary to the common opinion of coaches, trainers, and others associated with physical education who believe that weight lifting will slow down the athlete.

On the basis of the obtained data it is evident that:

1. The weight-lifting group was faster in their rotary motions of the arm than the nonlifters.

2. The nonlifters from Springfield College were faster than the nonlifters from the liberal arts college. This is probably because they engage in physical activities more than the students of the liberal arts college.

CHAPTER IV

Muscular Strength

Despite its common use, the word "strength" is a nebulous one. It is variously thought of as a reward for faithful practice of home calisthenics; a prerequisite to ringing the midway bell; a quality permitting the long distance swimmer or runner to maintain a rapid pace; or even the consequence of regular consumption of certain breakfast foods. Although such confusion is sometimes seen in the research literature, most investigators carefully define that aspect of strength with which they are concerned.

In an effort to identify the various "strengths," factor analysis has been employed with some success.[1] For example, there tends to be considerable independence among such concepts as isometric or "static" strength, and isotonic or "dynamic" strength. The former is usually determined by measuring the force (frequently with a dynamometer) of a single maximum contraction of a group of muscles, with little or no muscle shortening; the latter by maximum number of contractions of a given set of muscles against a given movable resist-

---

[1] For example see Edwin A. Fleishman, E. J. Kremer, and G. W. Sharp, "The Dimensions of Physical Fitness—A Factor Analysis of Strength Tests," ONR Contract Nonr-609 (32), Technical Report No. 2 (mimeographed, 1961), Department of Industrial Administration and Department of Psychology, Yale University. See also Delmar C. Nicks and E. A. Fleischman, "What Do Physical Fitness Tests Measure?— A Review of Factor Analytic Studies," ONR Contract Nonr-609 (32), Technical Report No. 1 (mimeographed, 1960), Yale University; E. A. Fleishman, Paul Thomas, and Philip Monroe, "The Dimensions of Physical Fitness—A Factor Analysis of Speed, Flexibility, Balance and Coordination Tests," ONR Contract Nonr-609 (32), Technical Report No. 3 (mimeographed, 1961), Yale University; and E. A. Fleishman, *The Structure and Measurement of Physical Fitness* (Englewood Cliffs, N. J.: Prentice-Hall, Inc., 1964).

ance (e.g., push-ups or DeLorme's ten repetitions—maximum). Such findings have led to the suggestion that quite different mechanisms may be involved in the expression of each.

Some writers use the term "power" or "explosive strength" when referring to a single maximum contraction resulting in muscle shortening (e.g., vertical jump, standing broad jump). Also, it has been shown that a distinction should be made between isometric strength and "breaking strength," or the force required to overcome a subject's willful resistance to force applied to a muscle group.[2] Despite the diverse use of the term, those who use "strength" to describe the quality necessary to run a 4-min mile are beyond their license. Such an event more properly demands cardiorespiratory endurance.[3]

Most recent investigators have defined strength operationally as either (a) the maximum amount of force (lb, kg) one can exert against a fixed resistance (isometric strength), or (b) the maximum amount of work (ft-lb, kg-M) performed in a single exercise bout (usually measured as the maximum number of contractions against a given movable resistance.) Occasionally work per unit of time, or *power*, is improperly referred to as strength. Thus, to fully appreciate the literature reporting research on strength the reader should be aware of type of "strength" to which the writer refers.

For such a common phenomenon, the objective study of strength does not have a long history. In 1897 Morpurgo reported that observed increases in muscle girth following training were not the result of an increase in the number of fibers but rather the development of latent fibers that existed in the beginning.[4] Although many subsequent studies have looked at the muscle tissue itself (its chemistry and structure) for an explanation of this phenomenon, the use of indirect methods (performance characteristics) continues to be popular.

Confronted with the great number of research reports treating of strength, it was difficult to choose a small number that would represent its several facets. Although historically the work of both Morpurgo and Siebert is important, only an example by the latter is represented here, translated from the German. DeLorme's work has led to such widespread adoption of heavy-resistance exercise, both in rehabilitation and in athletics, that a sample of his work could not be overlooked. The attention given to the theory of strength development by Hellebrandt and co-workers prompted the editors to include a paper illustrating the significance of the overload principle. In this chapter the student will also find the now classic report of Hettinger and Muller which was the forerunner of considerable research into, and application of, their method of increasing strength through isometric contraction.

---

[2] See L. Rarick, K. Gross, and M. J. Mohns, "Comparisons of Two Methods of Measuring Strength of Selected Muscle Groups in Children," *Res. Quart.*, **26**, No. 1 (1955), 74–79.

[3] See Chapter II.

[4] B. Morpurgo, "Über Aktivität—Hypertrophie der willkürlichen Muskeln, *Virchows Arch. Pathol. Anat.*, **150** (1897), 522–44; cited by A. H. Steinhaus, "Strength From Morpurgo to Muller—A Half Century of Research," *J. Assoc. Phys. Mental Rehabil.*, **9**, No. 2 (1955), 145–50.

W. W. SIEBERT

Investigations on Hypertrophy of the Skeletal Muscle

Reprinted from *Zeitschrift für klinische Medizin*,
109 (1928), 350–59. Translated from German.

The work of Lange[1] and of Petow and Siebert[2] demonstrates that muscle hypertrophy is dependent upon the intensity of training, not its duration. Thus the cross section of the skeletal muscles can be increased with relatively short periods of intensive exercise. Casual observations of the musculature of sprinters and weight lifters, in contrast with marathon runners and distance swimmers, provide empirical support for this. This phenomenon is frequently referred to as the "overload principle."[3] Siebert's 1928 article illustrates the principle using frogs.

It has long been known that increased activity can enlarge a skeletal muscle. Lamarck had already described this phenomenon. Darwin and Haeckel have called particular attention to this process, and we owe special thanks to A. Fick for several far-sighted observations concerning the conformity of the laws accompanying this process.

The present-day method of observation goes back to that of Roux. On the basis of inclusive research, he summarized the muscle enlargement caused by increased activity with all closely related phenomena under the heading "functional adaptation" by which he meant "the adaptation to the function through the function itself."

Writers who concerned themselves with this area in the following years stayed for the most part within the limits of Roux's method of observation. They did not introduce any major change into his teachings or theories.

The muscle increase that occurs as a result of increased activity is a true hypertrophy in the sense that Virchow used it, that is, increase of identical parenchymal components in the cells. Rössle defined this even more closely, as follows: "True hypertrophy is an enlargement of the nucleus and the protoplasm accompanied by the creation and enlargement of the specific endocelluar structures and is not to be confused with the simple swellings that occur as a result of saturation . . . with increased nourishment or even with other fluids of the medium, and in fact in the first stages of hypertrophy." The question of whether or not hyperplasy—that is, the formation of new cells—occurs as a result of increased activity of the muscle will be discussed in detail later.

---

[1] Lange, *Über funktionelle Anpassung* (Berlin: Springer Verlag, 1919).

[2] H. Petow and W. Siebert, "Studien über Arbeitshypertrophie des Muskels," *Z. klin. Med.*, **102** (1925), 427–33.

[3] Cf. DeLorme and Hellebrandt articles.

The expression "hypertrophy of activity," which implies that the occurring hypertrophy results from the activity of the organism, was originated by Recklinghausen. Roux distinguishes between a physiological functional adaptation, in which there is no change in form and mass, and a morphological change, in which such a change does occur. The first consists only of a qualitative improvement of the organism, which enables it to perform more work than formerly. The second consists of an increase of the substance, in which the newly added material must be qualitatively at least equal to the old material. A quantitative adaptation probably accompanies every qualitative adaptation.

We concern outselves here solely with the increase in volume of the muscle, thus with the morphological adaptation. Possible the qualitative changes interest us only insofar as they are necessary to the study of the quantitative relationships.

Roux considered the question of "dimensional adaptation" of utmost importance in the field of morphological adaptation. According to his investigations, the hypertrophy of skeletal muscle can occur as an increase in length or an increase in circumference. The latter is more common under normal circumstances, that is, in increased activity in business life, in gymnastics, and on the athletic field, etc. No lengthening of the fiber occurs here (Roux, Lange, Murpurgo, Schiefferdecker, et al.). Such lengthening occurs only under one condition, namely when the points of attachment of the tendons are moved apart by pathological processes or are separated experimentally (Roux, Strasser, Joachimsthal, et al.).

Roux formulated the law of "dimensional adaptation" which was derived from this behavior of the muscle: "Increased activity enlarges an organism only in that dimension or in those dimensions which take part in the increased activity." In our discussion, we are concerned only with the increase in circumference. The expression "hypertrophy" will be limited to this meaning in the following discussion, although, strictly speaking, the expression does include increase in length. Does every increase in work activity lead to a correlative hypertrophy? Even from the discussions of A. Fick, and further from those of Roux, and particularly of his student Lange, it is evident that for the occurrence of hypertrophy, work and work are not the same thing. For example, if two runners cover the same distance it is clear—providing their body weight is the same—that they accomplish the same amount of work (total work [sum of work], absolute quantity of work). Now if the first were to take much less time than the second, he would accomplish a much greater quantity of work in the same unit of time than the other.

$\dfrac{\text{Work}}{\text{Time}}$ = Effort. That is, the first runner has put forth greater effort than the second.

As I have already suggested in an earlier writing, the observations of Roux and Lange imply that in respect to the occurrence of hypertrophy, a strong differentiation must be made between increased activity as a result of increase in total work (sum of work) on the one hand, and increased activity as a result of increase in effort, on the other, and only the latter plays an important role. Frequently this differentiation is not observed well enough. In contemporary writing about sports, the views concerning the influence of increase in activity on hypertrophy are quite varied.[1] The reason for these contradictions is obviously to be found in the many difficulties which are encountered in attempting to determine the effect of sports on the development of muscle. For one thing, one can seldom find ideal conditions where it would be possible to study the influence of one and the same activity. Returning to running as an example: the runner training for short distances would not practice only the 100-yd dash, but would alternate between sprints and long distante. Thus, greater and smaller amounts of effort are expended alternately. Besides, those who are active in sports usually do not limit their activity to only one branch of sports—running in this case. As a rule, they take part in swimming, jumping, etc., as well.

This greatly confuses the situation. Muscle changes that are caused by one kind of activity can be modified by other activities.

Furthermore, the thickness of the muscle can be determined only indirectly by measuring the circumferences of the extremities. Aside from differences in the thickness of skin and primarily of fat, there is another disadvantage to this method, in that only complex muscle groups can be measured, the individual components need not have been equally involved in the activities. These difficulties can be circumvented by the use of experiments on animals. Thus, I carried out experiments with laboratory rats which were forced to carry out a certain amount of running work in an electrically propelled drum.

Roux and Lange worked with both variables: effort and total work. In

order to determine the validity of their conclusions experimentally, one of these variables must be held constant while the other is varied. In one of the first series of experiments, the total work of all animals was held constant, and the effort was varied by the use of different running speeds. The animals were killed at the end of the experiments (one-half year) and their hearts as well as the skeleton muscles, which were particulary involved in the work of running, were weighed. The results of these experiments have been published earlier. It was found that in the same total work the hearts as well as the skeletal muscles (gastrocnemii) of the animals which had put forth the greatest effort were heavier.

In the second series of experiments, the effort was to be held constant while the total work was varied. As in the first series, rats from the same litter, and when possible with the same weight, were divided equally into three groups. The animals in Group A (9 animals) ran 1 hr a day for 3 months; those in Group B (8 animals) 3 hr a day for 3 months: and those in Group C (8 animals) 3 hr a day for 6 months. The speed, thus the effort, was the same for all, that is 9 m per min. At the end of the experimental periods the animals were killed and processed in the same way as in the first series. The average weights are shown in table on p. 232.

The relationships were essentially the same for all three groups. No increase in musculature was to be found in the experiments as a result of increased length of activity and thus of total work. The dry substances of the gastrocnemii did not show any dissimilarity. (Average for Group A, 24.10; for Group C, 23.92.)

Although it was shown experimentally, in agreement with Roux and Lange, that the effort, not the sum of

---

[1] Only Herzheimer's discussions of the behavior of the skeletal muscle in running are completely in agreement with Roux and Lange.

Group	Length of activity	Body Weight	% Body Weight Heart	Gastro-cnemius
A	1 hr per day for 3 months	221	3.57	6.10
B	3 hr per day for 3 months	226	3.57	6.26
C	3 hr per day for 6 months	230	3.55	6.20

the work or the length of the activity, is the deciding factor in the occurrence of hypertrophy; there is, of course, a certain minimal amount of total work as well as length (duration) or, in other words, repetition of effort necessary for the full development of the muscle substance. To this extent the length (duration) does play a part.

However if this minimal measure is exceeded, an increase in hypertrophy occurs only with an increase in effort, not with a simple continuation of the hitherto existing effort.

In my experiments, I did not determine this minimal measure, since its value was irrelevant to my inquiry. Instead, I chose as minimal work an amount which I assumed would exceed the minimal measurement. The results of the experiments which were just described show that this choice was correct because in these experiments the muscles were not altered any further by the further continuation of the running.

In the discussion so far, we have related work as a term of physical measurement to the occurrence of hypertrophy. We have said nothing about the state of the muscle as it takes part in this activity.

It is also interesting to study the different types of physiological activity in respect to their effect on hypertrophy. It is principally a matter of the two main types: isotonic and isometric muscular activity, that is, the activity of the organism with and without the possiblilty of contraction, with and without the possibility of change in

tension. Each of these types of activity occurs in isolation only in experiments, since the natural motions we execute in daily life are composed of varying amounts of each type.

Moritz indicated in respect to the heart muscle that hypertrophy occurs especially following an activity with a fairly large isometric component. This may not be true in the case of skeletal muscle, since the conditions that apply to the heart may not be simply transferable. But much of what Moritz said seems to hold true for the skeletal muscle as well. For example, it is known that a noticeable increase in the circumference of the muscle can be obtained simply by the innervation of the arm muscles if the limbs are held outstretched. Some training systems, for instance that of Sandow, use the phenomenon mentioned above to develop especially thick muscles.

However, an exact comparison of isometric and isotonic contractions is possible only if the strength and frequency of the impulses which are introduced are held constant. I carried out this comparison in an experiment with animals, in fact, with frogs, whose gastrocnemii were electrically stimulated. The muscle on one side was put into action isometrically, that on the other side isotonically, and both were done by means of a current of equal intensity and duration. Nothnagel had already used electrical stimulation in the study of hypertrophy, but he was not concerned with a comparison of isometry and isotony.

The frogs were carefully tied onto an

operating slab. I effected (approximate) isometry by fixing the foot joint in a position of dorsal flexion and fixing the knee joint in an extended position, so that no contraction could occur. In the isotonic action the muscle was allowed all possible contraction. One electrode was attached directly to the calf which was to be stimulated, the other was placed as close as possible to the ischiadicus on the upper part of the thigh. The stimulation was induced with the same voltage and frequency of impulse in both the isotonic and isometric actions: induction current 2 v, distance between coils 10 cm, short tetanic stimulation of 3 sec each, then 3 sec pause, then 3 sec stimulation again, etc. Twenty min a day for each leg. The experiments were carried out for 14 days. The animals die when the experiments are of longer duration. After the last electrical stimulation, the frogs were given 3 days' rest. They were then killed and the carefully prepared gastroenemii were weighed.

RESULTS:

Isom. stim. muscle	Isoton. stim. muscle	Isom. > Isoton.
g	g	%
1.0330	0.8198	26
0.7240	0.6927	4
0.8431	0.7273	15
1.1830	1.1053	7
0.9634	0.8623	11
0.9650	0.7998	20
0.9243	0.8383	10

The isometric muscles, therefore, weighed 4 to 26 per cent (average 13 per cent) more than the isotonic.

I performed the same type of experiment on a number of rats that I had performed on the frogs. The duration of the stimulation in this case was twice daily for one-half hour for one-quarter year. Unfortunately a considerable number of the subjects of the experiment could not be used in gathering of

data, since rats are not so easily stimulated electrically and put up quite a fight even with their limbs tied down. However, in those rats which did not resist, the isometrically active muscles weighed more than the isotonic.

Thus, the statement by Moritz concerning the heart muscle applies to the muscles of the extremities as well.

The objection could be raised in the relatively short experiments with the frogs that the increase in weight does not necessarily result from hypertrophy but could simply be caused by an increase in fluids. Since the time of Ranke, increase in water content has been repeatedly found in tired muscle. (Buglia, Schwarz, *et al*).

However, as was found by Embden and Jost, this water disappears completely after a period of rest. These writers found weight differences of 1 per cent—at the most—between stimulated and unstimulated muscles.

In the results of our experiments with frogs, definite weight differences (to 26 per cent) are found 2 to 3 days after the experiments, thus, after a lapse of time long enough for us to assume complete recuperation of the muscles. If this change in weight is caused by an increase in fluid, then it is not the same type of increase as that described by Ranke; it would be a matter of a persistent condition of endema, which we could assume to be closely related to a true hypertrophy. Rössle himself called our attention to the "increased saturation" in the beginning of the process of hypertrophy, as has often been shown by the very close relationship between the processes of endema and growth. By way of an example, I am referring to the investigations of Walter on plant material and to the findings of Davenport and Schaper on animal material (tadpoles). Pertinent here is the observation that at the suckling stage, that is at a time of extremely fast growth, the tissues are particulary saturated with fluid (see Rubner, Czerny, *et al.*).

I do not intend to make the generalization that increase in fluid is a growth process. However, if we encounter an increase in fluid under certain conditions (in this case under increased activity) in which definite growth occurs after a period of time, then we can assume—in view of the close relationship which has been described between the increase in fluid and growth—that we have before us the first stage of the growth process, in our case the hypertrophic process.

Hypertrophy or Hyperplasy?

In the above discussion of the anatomical changes, I left the question open as to whether the enlargement of the muscle under conditions of increased activity was due only to the enlargement of the individual fibers (actual hypertrophy) or whether fibers were also formed (hyperplasy).

This question has been answered in various ways in the literature. Among the older authors, Zenker, Klebs, Rokitansky, Roux, Zielonko, who was under the direction of Virchow, favored the idea of the increase of fibers, whereas Nothnagel, J. Loeb, Schwalbe and Mayeda, Tangl, and others assumed that it was only a matter of hypertrophy. The opinions are still so varied today that a short discussion of the matter does not seem superfluous, especially since the evidence is often difficult to obtain.

The question can be answered only by counting the fibers. Where counting the fibers in the heart muscle and in parts of skeletal muscle is concerned, a conclusion based on one part of the cross section cannot be applied to the whole cross section for various reasons

(the not-uncommon unevenness of the cross sections caused by the fact that a cut was not alway perpendicular to the direction of the fibers because of the branching of skeletal muscle, etc.). Nor is it permissable to conclude on the basis of a lack of mitoses that no formation of new materials is occurring. After the muscle has put forth an increased effort, simply continuing the activity will not cause a further increase in the size of the muscle. Consequently, if the experiment is terminated after this point, the mitoses may no longer be present, even through an increase in the organism may have occurred by the process of mitosis.

The best procedure is to cause hypertrophy in a muscle of an extremity and then to use the same muscle on the other side as a control by keeping it idle. Cross sections can then be made of both muscles at corresponding points, and all the fibers which occur in each can then be counted.

Morpurgo adhered to these conditions particularly well. He removed the sartorius from one side of each of two adult dogs and prepared a cross section from the exact midpoint of each one. After the incision had healed, the dogs were trained to run in a treadmill. Only in the beginning was the treadmill turned mechanically, from then on, the dogs ran spontaneously, according to their strength. From time to time, they took a rest and then resumed their activity. The experiments lasted for 2 months. Then the other sartorius was removed.

As a result of this incontestable method, it was found that the number of fibers was identical in both active and inactive muscles. Thus, no increase had taken place. This precise investigation stands alone in the literature since, as far as I know, no one else has ever approached the question in the same way, either before or after Morpurgo's time. Only Schiefferdecker attempted, at least partially, to substantiate the results of Morpurgo's experiments, by recounting the fibers in the original preparations, without repeating the entire experiment. He confirmed the findings of Morpurgo.

In spite of their great significance, the investigations of Morpurgo and Schiefferdecker do not completely settle the question. The work that Morpurgo's dogs accomplished was probably more of the duration type than of the effort type (as discussed earlier). The latter type of work, particularly, causes hypertrophy; and the question of whether the muscle reacts to work requiring an especially great amount of effort only with hypertrophy (without hyperplasy) was not decided by the experiments of Morpurgo. Besides, Morpurgo's experiments were carried out on adult animals, in which the tendency of the tissues to separate is generally less than it is in young animals.

In my own experiments, both points are considered.

I will present the results of experiments on two young animals from a series of experiments, which I will describe in more detail later, also considering the behavior of the other components of the muscle.

The dogs were trained in work of the effort type. At the beginning of the experiment, the two animals from the same litter were 3 to 4 months old. For 3 weeks I kept them in a narrow stall as inactive as possible. The sartorius was then removed from one side, using ether as an anesthetic, and great care was taken, with the help of a special holding device, to prevent the shortening of the muscle in the process of taking it out. The muscles were fixed during 2 24-hr periods in a trichloroacetic acid mixture (15cc of trichloroacetic and acetic acids in equal parts

in 100cc of 85 per cent alcohol). After processing it through the increasing alcohol series and the celloidin–paraffin bath, I prepared a cross section of 10 μ from the middle of the muscle, which had been determined and marked previously *in situ*. The work was carried out on an inclined treadmill. The effort was increased slowly until it reached a maximum of 10 km in one and one-half hours at an inclination of 33 per cent carrying a ballast which constituted 20 per cent of the body weight. The animals were fed mixed foods; sufficiently but not excessively. The experiment lasted for 6 months. After the conclusion of the work period, the animals were left undisturbed for 3 days. I then removed the sartorius from the other side in the same manner as before and prepared it in the same way I had the first.

Microphotographs were made of the cuts which were colored according to the method of Heidenhain, visual field by visual field, and were greatly enlarged so that each fiber cross section was clearly visible. Negatives made on light-sensitive paper are sufficient for making an exact count. Of the chosen enlargements 40 to 45 pictures of the 24 × 30 cm size were required for one muscle cross section. These were assembled to show the entire corss section, in order to determine which areas had been photographed twice, in order to eliminate the possibility of counting them twice. Then each picture was examined and a dot was placed in each fiber cross section. The counting was done with constant reference to the slide, which was in a microscope set up next to the pictures.

The results of the counting were:

Dog 1: inactive muscle 58,017 fibers; active muscle 61,561 fibers.

Dog 2: inactive muscle 66,782 fibers; active muscle 69,941 fibers.

The differences (approximately 6

and 5 per cent) are within the limits of normal variation, and even though both seem to favor the active muscle, they are still no proof of fiber increase.

Thus, the skeleton muscle itself hypertrophies only by simple enlargement of cells, as a result of excessive work. Consequently, in its reaction to increased demand it is different from many other organs—liver, kidneys, marrow, circulatory system—which can also form new cells under the same conditions.

In spite of the lack of new cell for-mation, this muscle enlargement pro-cess is correctly considered a part of the actual growth process—as Rössle emphasized specifically. New cell formation is probably an important but not an obligatory sign of growth, especially in the muscle. From certain embryonic months until the end of the extrauterine body development—a length of time that certainly represents a period of growth—the muscle mass increases only by enlargement and not by multiplication of the cells (Mor-purgo, McCallum).

THOMAS L. DELORME

Restoration of Muscle Power by Heavy Resistance Exercises

Reprinted from *The Journal of Bone and Joint Surgery*, **27** (1945), 645–67.

Conscious application of Siebert's findings, namely that muscle hypertrophy was dependent upon intensity rather than duration of effort, came slowly. However, the tremendous growth of rehabilitation work precipitated by World War II stimulated thinking in the direction of better techniques. DeLorme's heavy-resistance exercises were an attempt to restore systematically the atrophied muscle as quickly as possible using relatively brief exercise sessions. His system and the concept of 10 R.M. (repetitions maximum) have been widely accepted, both in theraphy and athletics.

The attention of the reader is drawn to DeLorme's use of the word "power." For those accustomed to the strict definition of power as work per unit of time, DeLorme's definition of maximum power is "maximum weight that can be lifted with one repetition, the knee going into complete extension." Since time is not a factor here, his maximum power more closely approximates maximum work or isotonic strength, using maximum resistance.

Although DeLorme's article is not a research paper per se, it does provide some case histories showing the results of his procedure, which clearly illustrate the wide range of possibilities of his method.

Exercise is essential in restoring function to muscles, weakened and atrophied as a result of injury and disease. Therapeutically, exercises may be classified according to the quality developed in the exercised muscle,—namely, power, endurance, speed, and coordination. Failure to discriminate between these classes of exercises leads to the employment of the wrong type of exercise to develop the quality needed in the muscle; inevitably the result is poor. Commonly the attempt is made to restore power by exercises to build endurance; this is a mistake.

This paper deals with the redevelopment of muscle power, chiefly in the quadriceps, although some consideration will be given to other muscles.

Preliminary Considerations

Most injuries of the thigh and knee result in atrophy of the quadriceps of varying degree. When the local injury has healed, redevelopment of quadriceps power is the most important factor in restoring normal function to the extremity. The method here presented for developing muscle power by exercise is founded on the principle of heavy-resistance and low-repetition exercises, whereas the generally accepted principle is low-resistance and high-repetition exercises—such as stationary-bicycle riding, lifting light sandbags or other weights through ropes and pulleys, stairclimbing, etc.—which develop endurance rather than power. The fatigue that results from the latter is not due so much to overcoming resistance, as to the sheer number of repetitions; therefore, such exercise does not develop power. If low resistance is used for a low number of repetitions, no significant increase in either power or endurance results, and the only value lies in increasing slightly the joint motion. On the other hand,

in our method we employ heavy resistance that calls forth all the potential strength of the muscle, Since the rate and extent of muscle hypertrophy is usually proportional to the resistance the muscle must overcome, strength returns faster than in the low-resistance exercises. We believe this to be true, because we have seen many patients fail to obtain any appreciable quadriceps hypertrophy during several months of low-resistance exercises; whereas, with the heavy-resistance exercises, we have uniformly recorded rapid hypertrophy (in several instances 2 in. to $2\frac{1}{2}$ in. of hypertrophy of the thigh muscles within 6 to 8 weeks). Power is developed in the affected thigh until it equals that in the normal. When the strength of the limbs is approximately equal, then endurance exercises may be begun. Rather than attempt to develop endurance in an atrophied, weakened muscle, it seems more logical to restore muscle strength to normal, and then build endurance by means of low-resistance, high-repetition exercises.

The quadriceps exercise described is particularly valuable, for it develops maximum power without weight-bearing. Since it is a non-weight-bearing exercise, it is especially useful in redeveloping the musculature following meniscectomy, and in unstable knees. In these two conditions, particularly when there is quadriceps atrophy, weight-bearing exercises (such as bicycling, stair climbing etc.) frequently cause swelling and fluid. Except in rare instances, we have seen neither swelling nor fluid on maximum exertion with these non-weight-bearing exercises. In most of our cases, these symptoms have actually completely subsided on exercise. After these patients have succeeded in restoring normal power to their injured limbs, they are able to do the light weight-bearing exercises mentioned without either symptom developing.

Program of Exercises

In this program of heavy-resistance exercises, the patient exerts his maximum power only once a week. The maximum quadriceps power for clinical purposes is taken to be the maximum poundage that can be raised to the point of complete extension of the leg for one repetition. It is recorded in pounds. Once each week the patient exerts the maximum effort of which he is capable for one repetition. On the other days, no weight heavier than that which is maximum for ten repetitions is used. This program of periodic maximum muscular exertion is used even on the most atrophied muscles. Contrary to the popular belief that after injury the quadriceps should never be exercised to its limits, we have never produced chronic muscle sprains or failed to achieve return of muscle power.[1] On the basis of clinical observations in 300 cases in which this program of exercises was used, we firmly believe that even extremely atrophied muscles should exert their maximum effort at regular intervals.

Description of exercise

The patient is seated on the table with his knees flexed at an angle of 90°, and the boot is strapped on the foot. A folded blanket or pad is placed under the knees. The patient is now in the starting position, as illustrated in Fig. 1. The leg is extended as completely as the disability will permit. The leg should be extended and lowered at the same rate. The movements are done smoothly, rhythmically, and without haste, but not so slowly that the mere holding of the weights will tire the patient. Quick or sudden motions while exercising are to be avoided. A momentary pause at the end of each repetition is advocated.

The importance of complete extension with each repetition cannot be overemphasized. The vastus medialis functions chiefly by carrying the leg through the last 15° of extension. The disproportionately rapid atrophy of

Fig. 1. Quadriceps exercise, using one boot.

this muscle following injuries of the lower extremity and prolonged immobilization with resultant inability to completely extend the leg is a familiar clinical picture. Restoration of strength to the vastus medialis is a major problem to orthopedists and physical therapists. If there is sufficient strength present to carry the leg either partially or completely through the last 15° the problem is not too great. However, if there is complete inability to extend through the last 15° the problem calls for more strenuous measures. In these cases it would be impossible to redevelop vastus medialis power, if the only function of this muscle were extension in the terminal 15°; but the muscle also functions through a much larger range of motion when the leg must overcome a very heavy load. This fact makes it possible to exercise the vastus medialis actively in the available range of extension, thereby building power that will eventually make it possible to completely extend the knee. Sufficient vastus medialis power to produce complete extension can be built by using heavy resistance through the available range of motion. On each repetition, when the patient has reached his maximum extension, he should be taught to expend an extra effort at this point to attain even more extension.

At the beginning of the exercise and until the limbs are approximately equal in strength, only the affected extremity is exercised. Only one boot and a short bar are used, as shown in Fig. 1. When the limbs are approximately equal in strength, then they are exercised simultaneously, using two boots attached to a long bar as shown in Fig. 2. It is advisable for the patient to use two boots for a while to increase strength in the unaffected extremity, since this extremity becomes considerably weakened from disuse. When both boots are used, the principles of exercise, poundage increase, repetitions, etc., remain the same as when one boot is used.

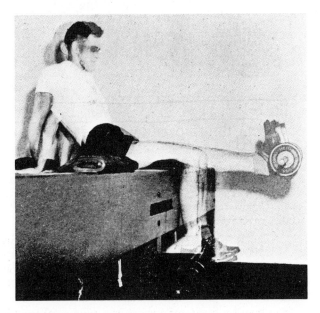

Fig. 2. Quadriceps exercise, using two boots.

Fig. 3

Fig. 4. Quadriceps-exercise table. The weight stands (*A*) are to rest the weight upon between sets of exercises.

Apparatus

Resistance is offered in the form of iron plates, graded from 1¼lb to 25 lb each. These plates are attached to an iron boot by means of a short iron pipe which fits into the boot. This boot is made especially for leg exercises. The iron boots, plates, and bars are shown in Fig. 3.

The exercises are performed on a table which should be 36 in. high and at least 50 in. wide. The legs and top of the table should be of heavy material and reinforced, since it will be subjected to considerable strain. The edge should be raised 2 in. to 3 in. so that, when the leg is completely extended, the entire limb will be parallel to the floor. The quadriceps-exercise table is shown in Fig. 4.

Repetitions and weight

Fifteen is the maximum number of repetitions ever performed in series, regardless of the amount of weight lifted. Ten or twelve is the number generally performed. The total number of repetitions for an average exercise period varies from 70 to 100—that is, seven to ten series of exercises with ten repetitions in each.

The ten-repetition maximum (10 R. M.)

The amount of weight lifted by the patient at any single extension during his first week of exercise is determined at the time of his initial workout, as follows: Starting with the weight of the boot (5 lb), and increasing by small amounts ($1\frac{1}{4}$lb to 5lb), the patient lifts each weight ten repetitions. That weight which requires maximum exertion to perform ten repetitions is thus determined. For the remainder of the week, no weight heavier than this ten-repetition maximum (10 R.M.) is used. Once each week the patient makes an attempt to increase this 10 R.M., and, when this amount is determined, no heavier weight is used during the ensuing week. For example, a patient in his first workout finds that the heaviest weight with which he can perform ten repetitions is 20 lb. Thus, during his first week, he uses nothing heavier than 20 lb. At the end of the first week, the 10 R.M. is again determined, and found to have increased to 30 lb. Then thirty is the maximum poundage used during his second week of exercise, etc.

Since 70 to 100 repetitions must be performed in each workout, and each poundage is done ten repetitions, the workout must be begun with a weight considerably less than the 10 R.M., so that when the 10 R.M. has been reached, 70 to 100 repetitions will have been performed. The example given can be continued to illustrate this. The 10 R.M. for the first week was 20 lb. By starting with $2\frac{1}{2}$ lb, plus the weight of the boot, and increasing $1\frac{1}{2}$lb after each series of ten repetitions, 80 repetitions will have been performed when 20 lb is reached.

The one-repetition maximum (1 R. M.)

As previously stated, once a week the patient exerts his maximum quadriceps power (maximum weight that can be lifted with one repetition, the knee going into complete extension). This one-repetition maximum (1 R.N.) is determined on the same day as the 10 R.M., in the following manner: When the 10 R.M. has been determined, the increases in weight are continued. With each increase beyond the 10 R.M., fewer repetitions can be done until finally that weight which can be extended only for one repetition with maximum exertion is reached. This is recorded weekly as the index of quadriceps power.

As strength returns to the muscle, the weight increases may be 5 lb to 10 lb, rather than $1\frac{1}{4}$ to $2\frac{1}{2}$, thus keeping the number of repetitions for a workout within the range of 70 to 100.

Of course there are many patients who, because of severe quadriceps weakness, have an initial 10 R.M. of less than 5 lb. In these cases, the procedure is altered, and we use two or three series of ten repetitions each without any weight, add $1\frac{1}{4}$ lb, and give two or three series more. Then, by increases of $1\frac{1}{4}$ lb, his 10 R.M. is finally determined. (When the patient is unable to begin the exercises with the weight of the boot, the exercises with the weight of the boot, 5 lb, the smaller weights are attached to the foot by means of a leather strap.)

In those cases where there is incomplete extension due to muscle weakness, the program is further altered. After the patient has performed ten repetitions with maximum poundage which can be extended to the same degree as when no resistance is being applied, he then continues to increase the poundage at the sacrifice of extension. The poundage increase is continued until the knee can be extended only a few degrees. Exercising in this way through the available range of motion is necessary where muscles are extremely atrophied, in order to build enough power eventually to effect complete extension. This is especially true when the vastus medialis is weak.

Frequency and length of workout periods

The patient exercises once a day, 5 days a week, the workout period usually lasting $\frac{1}{2}$ hr. He is encouraged to rest his leg as much as possible during the 2 days he does not report for the exercises. Since the exercise periods are short and come only once daily, the patient does not tire of the program, as is often the case when an exercise must be practised hourly or several times a day.

Data recorded

The following measurements are recorded weekly:
1. Range of motion,
   a. Extension,
   b. Flexion,
2. Thigh circumference,
3. Power,
   a. 1 R.M. (one-repetition maximum),
   b. 10 R.M. (ten-repetition maximum).

The weekly determination of the 1 R.M. and the 10 R.M. is made on the same day. For convenience, we designate Friday as the day on which the quadriceps power is determined. There should be a 2-day rest following this day of maximum exertion, and this arrangement makes it unnecessary for the patient to exercise over the weekend.

The thigh is measured once a week, at a constant level. Silver nitrate is used to mark the level, to make sure that every measurement is taken in the same place. Daily observations are made for development of fluid, swelling, pain, etc.

The maximum quadriceps power is determined, and thigh measurements of the unaffected extremity are taken, when the exercise program is initiated. Maximum results have been obtained when both extremities are equal in power, circumference, and range of motion.

Observations

Symptoms developing as a result of exercises

The only symptom that developed as a result of exercise was soreness of the quadriceps muscle. This soreness invariably disappeared within a week. In no instance has swelling or fluid appeared in the knee joint secondary to the strenuous exercises.

Development of power in the existing range of motion

Too often the main stress is placed on increasing motion in the atrophied, weakened limb with a limited range of motion, and very little or no thought is given to developing power. Nicoll states that "range without power is worse than useless, for in its extreme form we have a flail joint."[1] The return of power should accompany return of motion. It is more desirable to have normal power in the existing range of motion than to sacrifice development of power for a wider range of motion. The exercises we advocate are planned so that return of power accompanies return of motion. We believe that range of motion increases more rapidly with increasing muscle power, except when a mechanical factor prevents return of motion.

Focal exercises versus group exercises

We are convinced from our observation of patients indulging in group exercises and games, as performed in reconditioning programs, that group exercises for focal muscle redevelopment are unsatisfactory because:

1. The mental factor governing muscle exertion is such an important one in attaining maximum results that the patient must concentrate completely, and actually watch (whenever possible) the muscle being exercised throughout each repetition. Group participation offers too many factors to divert the patient's attention.

2. If a patient is unable to perform the movements as well as others in the group, he may feel his inadequacy to such an extent that he will attempt to cover up his weakness by adopting compensatory trick movements, thus accomplishing the feat with other muscles than the one which he is attempting to redevelop.

3. For the patient who must be prodded along, it is much easier for him to conceal his half-hearted efforts in group exercises.

4. Since there are individual variations in strength, symptoms, and types of injuries, it seems illogical to give exercises to groups of patients with the same repetitions, motions, resistance, and tempo.

Endurance versus power

We feel that in the past one of the shortcomings of the conventional type of physical therapy for redeveloping musculature has been a failure to discriminate between endurance-building and power-building exercises. By "power-building" exercises we mean exercises in which heavy resistance is used for a low number of repetitions. "Endurance-building" exercises are those in which low resistance is used for a large number of repetitions. These are two entirely different types, each one producing its own results, and each being wholly incapable of producing the results obtained by the other. We feel that most current attempts to redevelop musculature are based on exercises which are, in the final analysis, endurance building and not power building in nature. We feel it is wrong, for example, to put a patient with an extremity weakened by injury on such endurance-building exercises as stair climbing, walking, bicycling, and similar low-resistance exercises, until the extremities are approximately equal in strength.

A muscle exercised solely on power-building exercises will not have the quality of endurance, whereas a muscle subjected exclusively to endurance-building exercises will not have the quality of power. However, a powerful muscle can be given endurance-building exercises, and attain the quality of endurance; likewise a muscle with great endurance can attain power through the power-building exercises. How illogical it would be for a track man to train for long-distance running events solely by doing knee bends with heavy weights on his shoulder, or a professional weight lifter to train for heavy lifts solely by running several miles a day!

It seems more logical to restore the weakened extremities to normal strength by power-building exercises and then to exercise for endurance. Endurance is a quality of normal muscle, and therefore should not be sought after until the muscle has returned to normal. We believe it unlikely that endurance can be attained in a markedly atrophied muscle, for we have seen many patients who had been on low-resistance, high-repetition exercises for months, and still complained of rapid tiring of the muscle.

Physiological aspects of the heavy-resistance exercises

It is not the purpose of this paper to discuss neuromuscular or muscle physiology. We are presenting only the clinical observations made on 300 cases in which these exercises have been employed. The splendid response in muscle hypertrophy and power, together with symptomatic relief, seems to vindicate any possible violation of physiological principles. Competent physiologists who have observed these patients and our method of exercise feel fairly certain that the fatigue produced is at the neuromuscular junction, and not of the muscle fiber itself.

The question arises as to whether it is advisable to induce maximum loads on weakened and atrophied muscle fibers. We firmly believe, on the basis of our clinical observations, that even atrophied musculature must be submitted intermittently to maximum loads, in order to obtain maximum hypertrophy. We have treated several cases of fractured femur which had been immobilized from 6 to 14 months. The thigh muscles were very hard on palpation, suggesting fibrosis, and lacked power. These responded in 4 to 5 weeks, showing an increase in thigh

circumference of 1 in. to 2 in. and a remarkable increase in power. They were under maximum loads at regular intervals from the very beginning. It was interesting to observe how quickly these muscles softened and assumed the consistency of normal muscle. This observation throws an interesting light on hypertrophy and return of power in fibrotic muscle.

We believe that, in order to produce in muscle maximum hypertrophy, the heaviest load should be imposed upon the muscle as it approaches complete contraction, and not when the muscle is stretched. It is an accepted physiological principle that the greater the initial stretch or tension on a muscle (length), the greater the contractile power of the muscle. Therefore, when the maximum load is imposed on a stretched muscle, its fibers have the initial advantage rendered by the stretched state, and fewer fibers can overcome the resistance than if the muscle were not stretched. When the muscle fiber is contracted, it does not have this advantage. In order to overcome the resistance, a greater number of fibers are called upon; more fibers are exercised and thus stimulated to hypertrophy. Also, by increasing the load as the muscle reaches the contracted state, a higher degree of coordination of the contracting muscle fibers is obtained, increasing the contractile power of the muscle as a whole. Most of the power-building exercises here described are so arranged that resistance increases as the muscle contracts.

The use of a pulley system for quadriceps redevelopment has the disadvantage that the maximum resistance comes when the muscle is stretched. The pulley system as contrasted with our method is demonstrated in Figs. 5-A, 5-B, 5-C, and 5-D. We do not mean to imply that pulleys are of no value in giving heavy-resistance exercises; on the contrary, they often

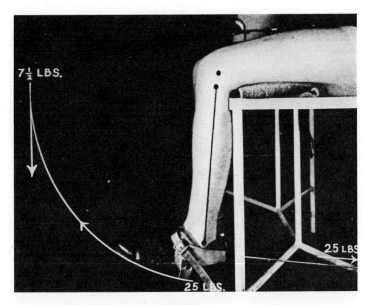

Fig. 5-A

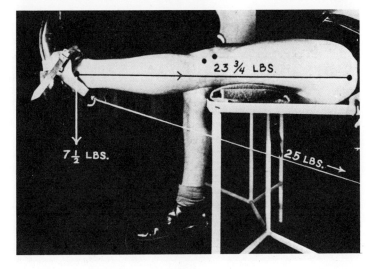

Fig. 5-B

The pulley system with knee flexed in starting position is shown in Fig. 5-A. There is 25 lb of resistance on the pulley system, applied to the leg through the rope shown attached to the foot. The long axis of the leg in the starting position is perpendicular to the rope. At this point the resistance consists of the full 25 lb. However, as the leg extends, the rope comes to lie at a more acute angle to the shaft of the leg, and the amount of resistance to be overcome decreases; so that, when the leg is fully extended (Fig. 5-B), the resistance to be overcome has decreased to only $7\frac{1}{2}$ lb. In full extension, $23\frac{3}{4}$ lb of the initial 25 lb of resistance are lost as a compression force in the direction indicated by the arrow, leaving as a resultant of forces, only $7\frac{1}{2}$ lb of resistance to be overcome by the quadriceps.

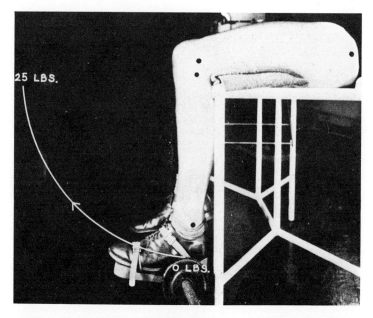

Fig. 5-C

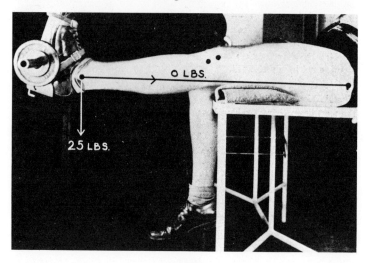

Fig. 5-D

Thus we see that the pulley system is one of decreasing resistance as the leg goes into extension. Therefore, when that part of extension controlled chiefly by the vastus medialis is reached, the resistance has greatly decreased; thus this muscle is neglected in the strenuous phase of the exercise.

When the resistance is added directly to the foot, the reverse of the above situation exists. In the starting position (Fig. 5-C), the resistance is practically nil; but, as the leg extends, the resistance rapidly increases and is maximum (25 lb) when the leg is completely extended (Fig. 5-D). There is no compression force as is present in the pulley system. The vastus medialis receives the chief benefit from this exercise.

afford the only means of exercising a certain muscle group. However, for redevelopment of such an important group as the quadriceps, it is felt that the pulley system is inadequate.

Maintenance of hypertrophy and power

The progress of several patients has been followed for 10 months after terminating this program of intensive exercise. Measurement at this time revealed no appreciable loss of muscle size or power, and there was no return of the symptoms previously noted— such as giving way of the knee or weakness of the extremity. The patient can best maintain the power gained by exercising once or twice a week for 15 to 30 min at a time. It is comparatively easy to maintain the power, once it has been attained.

Types of cases in which exercises are used

1. Unstable knees resulting from tears of the cruciate and collateral ligaments.
2. Knees following removal of the menisci—lateral, medial, or both. The program has been used vigorously following total synovectomy of the knee, with good results.
3. Fractured femora.
·4. Fractures of the patella.
5. Recurrent dislocation of the patella.
6. Fractures of tibia and fibula where prolonged immobilization has brought about quadriceps atrophy, as well as atrophy in other muscles of the extremity, and limited motion in the knee joint.
7. Knees following chondrectomy for chondromalacia of the patella.
8. Muscle weakness and limitation of joint motion, due to severe soft-tissue wounds and scarring.
9. Removal of foreign bodies from the knee joint.
10. Knees after patellectomy.

The best results have been obtained in cases of unstable knees, meniscectomies, and fractured femora. We believe the exercises are contraindicated in cases of chondromalacia, in which the disease is accompanied by pain, swelling, and fluid, and where open operation has not been performed.

Discussion of Cases

Knee instabilities

The most dramatic results have been obtained in cases of instability of the knee, of which twelve have been subjected to these exercises. In each the ligamentous injuries were old, and had not responded satisfactorily to previous treatment. Three are presented in detail, and serve to illustrate the progress made in most cases. The instabilities varied in nature: nine with injuries to the anterior cruciate and tibial collateral ligaments; one with injury to the tibial collateral ligament, with marked relaxation; one with injury of the anterior and posterior cruciate and tibial collateral ligaments; and one with injury of the anterior and posterior cruciate and fibular collateral ligaments.

The type of injury did not seem to influence the results, inasmuch as rapid gains and alleviation of symptoms occurred in the extremely loose joints as in the less unstable joints. Four of the twelve were wearing Jones knee cages when they began the exercises. Two patients discarded the braces after 14 days, one after 21 days, and another after 23 days. In other words, the average time from beginning the exercises to the time when the patients had enough quadriceps power to safely begin ambulation without the brace was 18 days. Eight of the twelve were able, after from 4 to 6 weeks, to run and play ball, without their braces and without "buckling" of the knee. Nine of the twelve had varying degrees of fluid and swelling when exercises were started; in eight of the nine these symptoms disappeared in 1 to 3 weeks. In one patient a slight amount of swelling persisted. Ten of the patients had pain on exercising and weight-bearing initially; seven lost the pain; three did not.

In all cases, after maximum benefit had been derived from the exercises, the instability persisted unchanged when the quadriceps muscle was relaxed. However, when the quadriceps muscle was contracted, it was impossible to demonstrate any looseness about the joint. A powerful quadriceps renders the knee stable only when it is contracted; but, when contracted, offers sufficient stability for ordinary activities and, as demonstrated by some of our cases, even for rather strenuous sports. It is the purpose of the exercises to build the quadriceps muscle to become powerful enough to maintain the stability of the knee, without the full help of the ligaments. Normal quadriceps power is not sufficient for this, so greater-than-normal power must be built in the involved extremity. This expalins why we use such extremely heavy resistance in cases of knee instability. In fractured femora, meniscectomy cases, etc., where the knee is stable, the purpose is to restore normal power to the injured leg; therefore, redevelopment is not pushed to such an extreme degree.

In none of the twelve cases were there any ill effects from the strenuous program of exercise.

The splendid response of these patients to exercise alone suggests that in certain types of old ligamentous injuries, surgery may not offer more.

An officer sustained an injury of the tibial collateral ligament, following which he was immobilized in a cylindrical plaster cast for 7 weeks. After removal of the cast, he received physical therapy for 7 weeks before the heavy-resistance exercises were begun. At the time the exercises were begun, he had a marked limp, walked with a cane, complained of pain about the knee, and the knee was slightly swollen. In 21 days his knee was completely asymptomatic; he had equal power in both quadriceps muscles; and had gained $\frac{3}{4}$ in. in circumference of the thigh. His maximum quadriceps power increased from 10 to 80 lb. This patient returned to limited duty with the infantry, with automatic revision to full duty.

A soldier sustained a complete dislocation of the knee when he fell from a 4-ft platform. Two weeks after injury, a meniscectomy was performed, and the patient returned to duty, but was unable to continue because of pain on weight-bearing. Five months after the initial injury, another arthrotomy was done, a partial tear of the anterior cruciate ligament being sutured and a fascial flap placed at the site of the tibial collateral ligament. Instability persisted, and 11 months after the initial injury, a third operation was done, at which time a fascial reconstruction of the tibial collateral and anterior cruciate ligaments was undertaken. Again the instability persisted, and the patient was fitted with a Jones knee cage. Three and one-half months after the last operation, the patient undertook the heavy-resistance exercises. At this time there was atrophy of the thigh of $2\frac{1}{2}$ in., flexion of 58°, maximum power of $2\frac{1}{2}$ lb, and moderate swelling of the knee joint. In 52 days of exercise, the patient made the following gains: a power increase of $62\frac{1}{4}$ lb in quadriceps, an increase of 2 in. in circumference, and a gain of 42° in range of motion. By the end of the third week of exercise, he had discarded the knee cage. Pain and swelling rapidly disappeared. The patient was discharged from the Army because of his knee injury, took a job as a truck driver, and his knee has remained asymptomatic.

Another soldier sustained injury to the tibial collateral and anterior cruciate ligaments while skiing. Fig. 6 shows the increase in the medial joint space due to injury of the tibial collateral ligament. Fig. 7 shows the positive drawer sign for tear of the anterior cruciate ligament. Following the injury, the patient had pain, thickening, and fluid in the knee. For $4\frac{1}{2}$ months he had conventional physical therapy, without improvement.

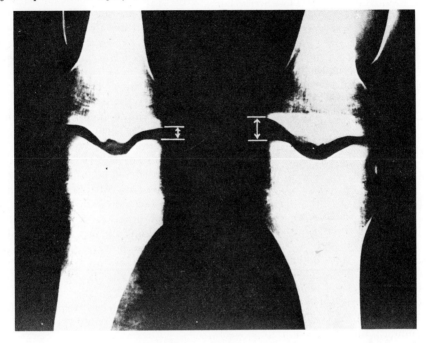

Fig. 6. Roentgenographic studies for tear of the tibial collateral ligament, showing positive abduction spread.

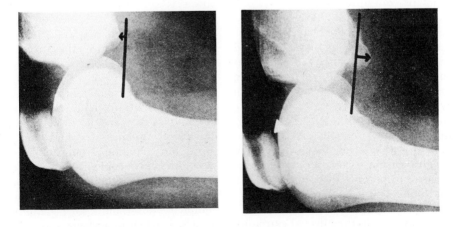

Fig. 7. Positive drawer sign for tear of anterior cruciate ligament.

After this period, a Jones knee cage was worn. Even with the brace, and while walking on level surfaces, he frequently would fall, because of the instability and muscle weakness. After using the knee cage for 7 weeks, he undertook the program of heavy-resistance exercises. Two weeks later, his quadriceps power had increased to such an extent that he felt secure enough to give up his knee cage. The symptoms of pain, fluid, and thickening had completely subsided by this time. After 1 month of the exercises, the patient had gained $1\frac{1}{2}$ in. in circumference of the quadriceps, with increased power in that muscle of from 20 lb to 80 lb, and he could sprint over uneven terrain at full speed without difficulty.

Meniscectomy cases

These patients were given quadriceps-setting exercises for several days preoperatively, and the exercises were resumed as soon after operation as possible, usually in 24 to 48 hr. Quadriceps setting was continued until the synovitis had largely subsided, and the discomfort from weight bearing was minimal; this required 3 to 4 weeks. They were then started on the heavy-resistance exercises, and, with maximum exertion on these exercises, the synovitis continued to disappear.

Twenty patients have exercised postoperatively by the heavy-resistance method. Seventeen of the twenty had definite synovitis of the knee joint at the time exercise was begun, and in only two of them did the degree of synovitis fail to decrease. In no instance was there exacerbation of synovitis due to the strenuous exercise. No patient was allowed to participate in weight-bearing exercises until the quadriceps power had been restored in the limb operated upon.

The average time required to restore normal power to the affected extremity was 19 days. Only two of the twenty patients failed to regain normal quadriceps power, and these two developed their quadriceps power to within 80 per cent of normal. Restoration of normal power and thigh circumference can be expected to occur at a much more rapid rate following meniscectomy than in cases of fractured femur, fractured patella, ligamentous injuries, etc., where the period of immobilization is usually more prolonged. It must be stressed that, following meniscectomy, the quadriceps-setting exercises given postoperatively are as important as the heavy-resistance exercises in obtaining good end results.

Restoration of a normal range of motion offered no problem in any of the twenty cases. All patients had normal knee-joint motion on completion of the exercise program. A few had difficulty in obtaining the last 15° or 20° of flexion. These, however, responded rapidly to treatment on the leg-exercising apparatus (Fig. 8).

Weight-Bearing and Non-Weight-Bearing Quadriceps Exercises

At this point it is appropriate to discuss briefly these two types of exercises. As far as increasing muscle power is concerned, both types have equal possibilities. They differ, however, in the symptoms they produce in knee joints controlled by weak, atrophied muscles.

We believe that the development of pain, thickening, and fluid on weight-bearing exercises in many of the cases of meniscectomy and unstable knees is due largely to the increased laxity in the joint, resulting from quadriceps weakness and atrophy. We have seen many of these patients with marked synovitis in the knee joint, in whom complete alleviation of knee symptoms occurred, when quadriceps power was restored to normal by non-weight-bearing, heavy-resistance exercises. The instability results in repeated strains which produce a traumatic synovitis[2] with fluid, thickening, and pain.

Of the twenty patients who had meniscectomies, seventeen had fluid, swelling, or both, of varying degree, when they began these exercises 3 or 4 weeks after the operation. On the exercise regimen outlined here, fifteen of the seventeen showed improvement. Of these fifteen patients, eight became completely asymptomatic, both subjectively and objectively; six retained only an insignificant amount of synovial thickening; and one finished the exercise program with a small amount of fluid still present in the joint. This patient had had a meniscus removed from the same knee prior to Army service, following which there developed a chronic synovitis, with marked thickening and induration of the synovia. Before the exercise program was instituted in meniscectomy cases, exercise in the gymnasium was started 3 or 4 weeks postoperatively, in an attempt to redevelop quadriceps power in these patients by the conventional methods—such as stair climbing and bicycling. On this routine, the hitherto smooth postoperative course of rapidly subsiding synovitis was not only interrupted, but in many cases there was a marked exacerbation of synovitis, which usually subsided as soon as the patient was taken off the weight-bearing exercises. It was then found that, when these same patients were given only non-weight-bearing exercises, synovitis did not recur, and the synovitis, which had previously developed, subsided during the course of exercise. It must be assumed that there is some factor in the weight-bearing exercises that produces synovitis, and that this factor does not exist

in the non-weight-bearing exercises. These findings can be explained on the basis of relative knee instability. The quadriceps muscle is as important in maintaining knee stability as are the cruciate and collateral ligaments; and, when this muscle group is atrophied and weak, the maintenance of stability rests almost entirely on the ligaments. The ligaments alone cannot maintain as high a degree of stability as when aided by the quadriceps muscle. When, as in cases of meniscectomy, quadriceps power is low, there is abnormal motion in the knee joint. It is this abnormal motion that is indirectly responsible for the development of synovitis in weight-bearing exercises. The twisting, turning, and jarring of the weight-bearing exercises in a relaxed joint probably traumatizes the synovia by nipping and stretching, causing a synovitis; whereas, if the exercises were performed sitting down, the motion in the joint would be in a normal plane, and the knee would not be under the strain of the body weight. Thus instability is precluded as a source of synovial irritation during convalescence.

Fractured femora

Charts I and II show the gains made by two patients with fracture of the femur, after they had been discharged from general physical therapy. These two represent the average response in twenty cases of fracture of the femur. The gain in circumference for those patients who had obtained flexion of the knee to approximately 90° ranged from 1 in. to 2 in. in the first 4 weeks of exercise. When flexion was less than a right angle, the gains were not so rapid, since the quadriceps could not be as thoroughly exercised through this limited range. A few patients who worked exceptionally hard increased

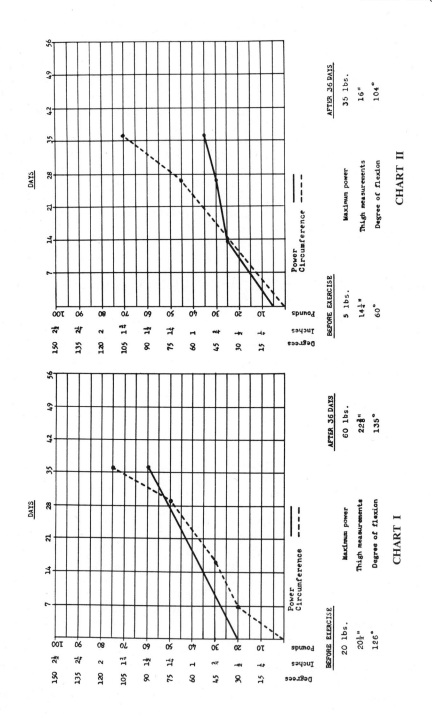

CHART I

BEFORE EXERCISE		AFTER 36 DAYS
20 lbs.	Maximum power	60 lbs.
20½"	Thigh measurements	22⅛"
126°	Degree of flexion	135°

Power ─────
Circumference ─ ─ ─

CHART II

BEFORE EXERCISE		AFTER 36 DAYS
5 lbs.	Maximum power	35 lbs.
14½"	Thigh measurements	16"
60°	Degree of flexion	104°

Power ─────
Circumference ─ ─ ─

their thigh measurements by 2 in. to $2\frac{1}{2}$ in. in from 6 to 8 weeks.

Frequently, after immobilization, the muscles of the thigh, especially the quadriceps group, are hard in consistency, due to fibrotic changes, which have occurred during the period of inactivity. Immediately after these strenuous exercises have been begun, these same muscles begin to soften, and in a few weeks have regained their normal consistency. This rapid softening of hard fibrotic muscles has been one of the most interesting aspects of this program, and has further substantiated our belief that weakened, fibrotic, atrophic muscles should not be "pampered" because of their subnormal condition, but should be exercised against heavy resistance. In the case of one patient who was immobilized for 14 months, the thigh muscles of the injured leg showed atrophy of 2 in., and had the consistency of hard rubber. After 2 months of exercise, the thigh had increased $1\frac{1}{2}$ in. in circumference, and the consistency was that of normal muscle.

Restoration of motion

Attaining a normal range of knee-joint motion, following immobilization incident to a fracture of the femur, is often a difficult and perplexing problem. After prolonged immobilization, especially in fracture of the lower third (more especially those involving the femoral condyles), there is often a marked limitation of flexion. When some of these patients first begin physical therapy (consisting of heat, massage, and exercises with mild forcing) they often rapidly regain flexion of about 30° to 50°, and then during weeks and months of a similar routine make no further progress. For these cases a leg-exercising apparatus (Fig. 8) has been constructed.

Fig. 8. Leg-exercising apparatus.

Leg-exercising apparatus

This machine was designed to allow the patient to exercise the leg against resistance in a position most conducive to the bending of the leg by such resistance. Because the patient himself is in complete control at all times of the amount of resistance, and can remove and apply resistance as pain and fatigue dictate, he will allow the leg to flex more than if a physical therapist were applying the same amount of resistance by hand. The patient cannot control the pressure or movements of the operator, and will not relax the antagonistic muscles sufficiently to permit the knee to bend to a point of discomfort. However, if he himself can apply the resistance, he will allow the knee to bend to the point of pain, without complaint. In order to attain flexion in stubborn cases, it is necessary to exercise to the point of discomfort, even pain.

The apparatus is used in the following

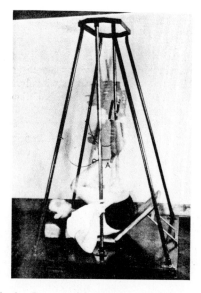

Fig. 9. Leg-exercising apparatus being used to regain flexion. The pins (*A*) fit into the metal guides at different levels, to limit downward motion of the central plate.

manner: The exercise begins with knees completely extended (Fig. 9). The pins labeled *A* are removed, thus freeing the weight, which is then slowly lowered, as the knee is allowed to flex. The downward direction is continued as far as pain or tightness in the joint will permit. The knee is then completely extended; there is a momentary pause, and it is lowered again. The cycle is repeated ten to twenty times. The pins are replaced, the patient rests for a minute or so, and the cycle of ten to twenty repetitions is repeated two or three times.

Twenty patients with fracture of the femur have been given these exercises on this apparatus. All twenty had been discharged from general physical therapy as having attained maximum flexion. By the use of this apparatus, the average gain in flexion was 25° in 32 days. However, these figures include eight patients who had frac-

tures about the femoral condyles or who had had prolonged immobilization because of slow union or refracture. They showed an average gain of 21° in 42 days. Twelve patients with uncomplicated fracture of the middle and upper thirds showed an average gain of 27° in 21 days, a considerably more rapid rate of gain than that of the group first mentioned. Two of the twenty patients were treated by manipulation under anesthesia in an attempt to increase knee-joint motion; one gained 6° as a result of manipulation; in the other, no increase in flexion could be attained. Both were then placed on this apparatus; the former gained 33° more flexion, the latter 20°. It must be emphasized that the gains in flexion recorded in all twenty cases were made after these patients had received the customary physical theraphy for weeks, sometimes months, and had been discharged because no further progress could be made. Constant bending in the form of active heavy-resistance exercises will often produce more flexion than can be accomplished by a single or repeated manipulation. In a few cases, this strenuous flexion of the knee has produced slight swelling of the joint, but in no case has there been effusion. The swelling and soreness which sometimes develop usually subside by the next exercise period.

This apparatus can also be used as a muscle developer with increasing amounts of resistance, after the patient has obtained a good range of motion. When the machine is used for muscle developing alone, the same principle of exercise and method of increasing resistance are used as for the quadriceps exercises. When used for increasing flexion, the amount of weight that can be pushed back into complete extension ten to twenty times with moderate effort is employed.

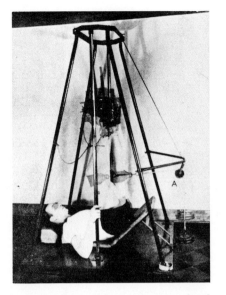

Fig. 10. Leg-exercising apparatus, showing use of the pulley system (*A*) to increase knee-joint extension.

Three patients who had flexion contractures of the knee rapidly regained complete extension by working on this apparatus. The pulley system (Fig. 10) brings pressure to bear immediately above the patella by means of the leather cuff. The pressure is directed towards extension. On each repetition, as the knee reaches its maximum extension, the cuff aids the thigh extensors in effecting further extension. Strenuous quadriceps exercises were also given in these cases.

If the injury was a simple fracture of the patella, or if the lower pole of the patella had been removed, the return of motion, strength, and size was usually rapid. However, if the patella was highly comminuted, or if there developed chondromalacia following fracture, the high-resistance exercises usually caused much pain, and occasionally fluid and swelling, and had to be abandoned.

After the immobilization period following dislocation of the patella, these exercises were begun and a rapid return to normal was noted. By building an exceptionally powerful vastus medialis, it might be possible to prevent redislocation of the patella, when the dislocation was due chiefly to weakness of that muscle.

Two patients had chondrectomies for chondromalacia of the patella; following operation, both patients had moderate synovitis of the knee. In each, the synovitis subsided, and smoothing of the patellofemoral articulation occurred as a result of these exercises.

There were many patients with soft-tissue wounds about the knee and thigh. In these, loss of flexion or extension, due to muscular weakness, scarring, or both, was the usual problem. In many cases, where the loss of active motion was a result of muscular weakness, due to loss of muscle substance, the remaining muscle tissue could be overdeveloped sufficiently to compensate for the lost tissue, thereby restoring almost normal strength to the extremity.

Many patients had a limited range of motion because of scarring about the knee joint. Unless bound hopelessly to bone or other deep structure, these scars in most instances underwent remarkable softening, allowing for normal joint motion. The constant flexing in the leg-exercising apparatus (Fig. 8) was sufficient in many cases to restore flexion to normal. The quadriceps exercise usually rapidly restored enough quadriceps power to make possible complete extension.

Results following removal of foreign bodies from the knee were similar to those in the meniscectomy patients, unless there had been considerable joint damage.

In order to gain full extension following patellectomy, it is essential to have a powerful quadriceps. We have

Fig. 11. Adductor exercise.

Fig. 12. Abductor exercise.

used this program of heavy-resistance exercises in only two of these cases. The patients rapidly obtained complete extension, without development of synovitis; and quadriceps power was restored to within 90 per cent of that in the unaffected extremity.

When quadriceps power has increased sufficiently to permit weight-bearing exercises, the patient is given heavy-resistance exercises for the other muscles of the extremity.

Development of Other Muscles of Body by Same Exercise Principle

The following are some of the other exercises we have used in redeveloping other muscles of the body by the same principle. The type of apparatus, however, varies considerably, and is designed specifically to obtain the desired results. The repetitions, method of weight increase, frequency and length increase, frequency and length of workout are exactly the same as described for the quadriceps exercises.

I. Lower extremity

A. *Adductor exercise.* This exercise is shown in Fig. 11.

B. *Abductor exercise.* See Fig. 12.

C. *Hamstring exercise.* This is an extremely important exercise, and should be diligently performed, especially by patients attempting to regain flexion in stiff knees.

D. *Stair-climbing exercise.* This exercise is not used to develop the quadriceps; it is not used at all, until the patient has built nearly full quadriceps power by the use of previously described quadriceps exercise. Resistance is added to a metal yoke, and the patient goes over and back five times with one weight, rests a minute or so, adds more weight, and then repeats. By use of the yoke, the hands are free to grasp the rail (Fig. 13). This exercise was thought necessary because, even though a patient may have good quadriceps power, he may still have some difficulty in stair climbing, if all the other muscles involved are not proportionately developed. The exercise develops, in the low-repetition, high-resistance manner,

Fig. 13. Stairclimbing exercise.

Fig. 14. Ankle exercise. Resistance can be added at points *A, B, C,* and *D,* thus giving resistance in dorsiflexion, plantar flexion, eversion, and inversion, respectively. This apparatus has 180° of motion in all four directions, thus also making possible rotary ankle motion.

all of the muscles involved in stair climbing.

E. *Calf exercise.* The resistance in this exercise is applied by adding weight to the yoke. The use of the yoke permits the hands to remain free,

and the patient can use his hands to steady himself, and maintain balance by grasping a bar in front of him. As strength increases, more weight can be added; and, as ankle-joint motion increases, the wooden block can be made higher.

F. *Ankle exercise.* The apparatus shown in Fig. 14 was devised to exercise the ankle in both dorsiflexion and plantar flexion, in eversion and inversion. Resistance may be added to the hook at *A, B, C,* or *D.* The apparatus is also used to help restore ankle-joint motion.

II. Arm and shoulder

A. *Pectoral exercise.* Amazing hypertrophy of the pectoral muscles can be attained in 2 or 3 weeks through the practice of this exercise (Fig. 15). Two patients, who sustained machine-gun-bullet wounds through the axilla with resultant damage to the pectoralis major and limitation of abduction because of scar tissue, were able to loosen the scar sufficiently to obtain a complete range of shoulder motion by use of this exercise. In both cases, after a month of exercise, the patients had increased the size of the atrophied

Fig. 15. Pectoral exercise. Arms may be kept straight or slightly bent at the elbow.

pectoralis so that it was larger than the corresponding uninjured muscle.

B. *Deltoid exercise.* This is well known.

C. *Biceps exercise.* This is an important exercise, as there exists usually an inch or so of atrophy of the arm following immobilization for fracture of the humerus. It is important, not only because it redevelops biceps power, but also because of its value in increasing elbow-joint motion. We believe that exercising for biceps power will do more to restore elbow-joint motion than all efforts to increase motion of that joint while neglecting biceps power. In this we must except instances where there is a mechanical block or where severe irreparable capsular and pericapsular changes have occurred. On each repetition the patient should make every effort to obtain as much flexion and extension as possible. Triceps exercises should also be used in conjunction with the biceps exercise.

D. *Supine press.* See Fig. 16 for illustration of the exercise. This is extremely good for loosening up the elbow and shoulder joint.

E. *Pulley exercise.* Restoring normal scapulohumeral motion following a fracture of the humerus is often

Fig. 17.   Shoulder-pulley exercise.

difficult. We have obtained, in most instances, good results through use of this pulley exercise, combined with the pectoral, biceps, and deltoid exercises. It is essential that the pulley be an extremely high one, so that the arm can go into complete abduction (Fig. 17). On each repetition the arm should be allowed to abduct as far as comfort will permit the weights to pull it; then the arm is brought back to the side, there is a momentary pause, and the exercise is repeated. This is done ten times, more weight is added, and it is repeated another ten times, etc. An effort should be made to abduct the arm a fraction further on each repetition. This exercise has produced good results, where scapular motion is limited because of fractures of the scapula and large soft-tissue defects. The constant forcing, in the form of active, heavy-resistance exercises, steadily increases the motion of the joint.

F. *Parallel bars.* This is a good exercise for the shoulder and arm (Fig. 18). Resistance is added to the weight pan strapped to the back. The width of the bars can also be varied.

Fig. 16.   Supine press

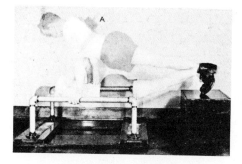

Fig. 18. Parallel bars. Resistance is added to the weight pan (*A*), strapped to the patient's back. The bars can be slid further apart as power and motion increase.

Fig. 20. Exercise for internal rotators of the arm.

Fig. 19. Exercise for external rotators of the arm. The pronator and supinator muscles of the forearm are exercised on the attachment labeled *A*, to which resistance is applied on the weight pan *B*. Resistance for the shoulder exercise is applied to the weight pan *C*.

G. *Arm-exercising table.* This table is designed to exercise the pronators and supinators of the forearm, and the external (Fig. 19) and internal (Fig. 20) rotators of the shoulder.

III. Trunk

A. *Back exercise.* Hyperextension exercises are done on the apparatus

shown in Fig. 21. This apparatus offers several improvement over the method in general use. The weight pan attached to the back makes possible increases in accurately graded resistance. This cannot be accomplished, as was attempted in the old method, by progressively extending the patient farther over the table edge. Our method does not require an operator to hold the patient's feet. The position of the patient is more stable and comfortable; and, since he is not quite parallel to the floor, it is much easier for him to hyperextend more completely.

B. *Abdominal exercise.* By maintaining the knees and hips flexed (Fig. 22), more of the load falls on the abdominal muscles and less on the iliopsoas muscle. This makes possible development of the abdominal muscles without concurrent development of the iliopsoas. Since the lumbar spine is flexed by the abdominal muscles and extended by the iliopsoas, the selective redevelopment of the abdominals brings about stronger pelvic control, which is of great value in the treat-

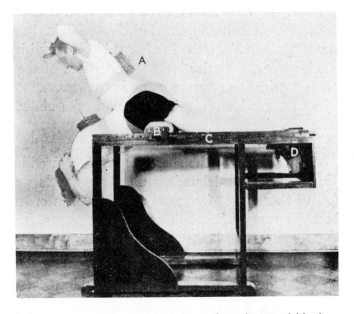

Fig. 21. Hyperextension exercise being performed on special back exerciser. Resistance is increased by adding weights to the weight pan A. The body rest B is adjustable on track C to accommodate an individual of any height. The feet are securely immobilized in two iron boots D attached to the frame.

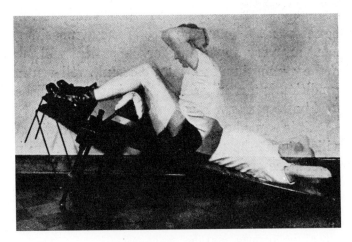

Fig. 22. Abdominal exercise.

ment of certain back ailments. Many patients who have received injuries to the anterior abdominal wall, with resultant loss of muscle tone and tissue, have exercised on this apparatus with considerable improvement. Graded resistance increases are made by increasing the incline of the board.

Only a few of the exercises actually used have been mentioned. With the equipment illustrated, several hundred different exercises can be worked out. We have shown only a few of those most frequently used, but in order to conduct exercise programs properly, both for range of motion and muscle power, in a great variety of injuries, a therapeutic gymnasium must be equipped with the apparatus described.

The Therapeutic Gymnasium

The therapeutic gymnasium should not be a place of amusement or for keeping fit. It should be a place in which a treatment, prescribed after thorough examination by the medical officer, can be properly given. The gymnasium should be supervised by the medical officer, but it is not necessary that he actually attend the exercises. The gymnasium should be planned and constructed as specifically for its purpose as is the operating room for its purpose. All pieces of exercise apparatus should be designed to produce a desired result in a specific type of case. Accurate notes on the progress of each patient should be made at regular intervals. The patient should work by appointment, and his attendance should be recorded. The appearance of the gymnasium and the working condition of the equipment are very important, for the patient will maintain much more interest in his exercise if the gymnasium is bright, colorful, well ventilated, and well kept. Equipment in poor condition is not only dangerous, but it also disheartens the patient, and makes it difficult for him to perform his exercises.

It is a good policy to work out several different ways of doing the same exercise. This will prevent the patient's losing interest from monotony. The greater the variety of exercises, the greater the patient's interest.

It has been our experience that greater cooperation is achieved, when the patient understands the nature of his injury. Anatomical charts are kept, and are exhibited on the walls, to give him a clear conception of his disability and its location. He also can see what muscles have to be redeveloped or what joints must be loosened up, before he can attain maximum benefits. A chart with the normal ranges of motion for all the joints of the body should be displayed, and the patient should be taught the normal range of the joint upon which he is working. He should become familiar with the measurements of his affected part, the power of that part, and the exact number of degrees of motion present; then, each week, when new measurements are taken, he will know in inches, degrees, and pounds the gains he has made. This will do much toward maintaining the patient's interest.

The instructor should be efficient, thoroughly familiar with each patient's disability, know what he is trying to accomplish in the patient and, above all, display interest in the work. A patient cannot be expected to show any more enthusiasm than the one who supervises his exercise.

Conclusions

1. Low-repetition, high-resistance exercises produce power.

2. High-repetition, low-resistance exercises produce endurance.

3. Each of these two types of exercise is incapable of producing results obtained by the other.

4. Weakened, atrophied muscles should not be subjected to endurance-building exercises, until the muscle power has been restored to normal by power-building exercises.

5. Restoration of muscle power with return of motion in a limb has been neglected in the past. It is, in most instances, preferable to have a limited range of motion with good power than

a normal range of motion with inadequate power.

6. Games and group exercises, as practiced in reconditioning programs, are unsatisfactory for producing focal muscle development.

7. In order to obtain rapid hypertrophy in weakened, atrophied muscle, the muscle should be subjected to strenuous exercise and, at regular intervals, to the point of maximum exertion.

8. In cases of meniscectomies and unstable knees, quadriceps power should be obtained by the use of strenuous, non-weight-bearing exercises. Weight-bearing exercises can produce pain, thickening, and fluid in knees, which do not have adequate muscle support.

References

1. Nicoll, E. A., "Principles of Exercise Therapy," *Brit. Med. J.* **1** (1943), 745.

2. Watson-Jones, R., *Fractures and Joint Injuries* (3rd ed.), **2**, Baltimore: The Williams & Wilkins Co., 1943, 702.

T. L. HETTINGER / E. A. MULLER

Muscular Performance and Training

Reprinted from the *Arbeitsphysiologie*, **15** (1953), 111–26. Translated from German.

The "strength" of concern to DeLorme and later Hellebrandt and Houtz was of a dynamic, or isotonic nature. Recognizing the difference between maximum work done by several submaximal contractions of a muscle group and maximum force resulting from a single maximal contraction, two German physiologists have concentrated upon the latter, or "isometric" strength. Their work has produced some startling findings. Hettinger and Muller showed that the maximum force which can be applied voluntarily to an immovable object was less a function of the number of repetitions than the intensity of effort. This observation was not unlike those associated with the maximal development of isotonic strength (cf. Siebert, Hellebrandt and Houtz). Their often-quoted 1953 article presented here concluded that a single daily contraction of 6-sec duration produced results equivalent to multiple contractions until exhaustion (45 sec). This procedure resulted in an average gain in strength of 5 per cent a week.

The results of such a finding have had widespread effects upon physical education in the United States, and to some extent, throughout the world. Despite the fact that isometric training appears to have little influence upon dynamic strength or cardiorespiratory endurance (the latter being more important for health and success in most strenuous athletic events), the findings of Hettinger and Muller have precipitated the development of a wide variety of static exercise programs; some requiring expensive equipment, others needing none, but each reputed to be beneficial for athletes and executives alike—beneficial, not only for increasing strength, but also for the development of power and speed. However, such claims, for the most part, have yet to be substantiated. It is interesting to recall that a similar technique called, surprisingly enough, "dynamic tension," was recommended many years earlier as the solution to the social problems faced by the "97-lb weakling."[1]

Since the 1953 report, considerable work has been done which clarifies the phenomenon of isometric strength. In 1962 Muller[2] indicated that several daily maximum contractions of 4- to 6-sec duration produce results superior to a single 1-sec contraction. In a more recent publication Muller and Rohmert[3] concluded that the rate of increase in strength from isometric training depends on the disparity between the subject's present level of strength and his maximum potential strength called "Endkraft." The closer the subject comes to his Endkraft, the slower his progress from isometric training. Some of the earlier generalizations concerning isometric training will have to be reevaluated because of these more recent findings. The need for reevaluation of the research on isometric training provides additional evidence for a cautious approach in accepting and utilizing research findings.

High athletic achievements are obtained through training, i.e. through exercises, which are chosen so to demand an increasingly greater capacity. Usually these achievements, which are executed as training exercises, remain below the maximum potential. In Helsinki in 1952, Steinhaus discovered that the majority of the Olympic winners did not practise to the point of exhaustion, not did they participate in any competitive effort during their training. Thus, for example, the weight lifters practised at only 60–80 per cent of their potential. The training system called "Progressive Resistance Exercise," which was developed in the last few years by De Lorme and his co-workers[2,3,7,8] for therapeutic purposes, systematically increases the exercise demand from week to week in a constant ratio to the maximum potential. These athletic and clinical training systems were developed purely experimentally. They do not answer the questions which are interesting from the physiological standpoint, as to 1) the minimum exercise stimulus necessary to attain an increase in muscle strength, 2) the relationship of effort, duration and frequency of exercise to the speed at which strength increases and the maximal potential of the strength increase of the muscle, 3) necessity or desirability of great fatigue and exhaustive effort of the muscle during muscle-training exercise.

In the following study, these questions have been experimentally tested

---

[1] For a brief portrait of Angelo Sciliano ("Charles Atlas") see "Muscle Business," *Fortune*, **17**, No. 1 (January, 1938), 10, 14, 24.

[2] E. A. Muller, "Physiology of Muscle Training," *Rev. Can. Biol.*, **21** Nos. 3 and 4 (1962), 303–13.

[3] E. A. Muller and W. Rohmert, "The Rate of Muscle Strength Increase in Isometric Training," *Intern. angew. Physiol.* (formerly *Arbeitsphysiol.*), **19** (1963), 403–19.

on human beings. In order to obtain physically well-defined exercise conditions, we used only isometric muscle contractions. Effort, duration and frequency were varied. The amount of effort required was always chosen so as to represent a definite percentage of the maximal strength. Thus, the amount of effort was determined after each measurement of the maximal strength. Duration and frequency, on the other hand, remained constant within each series of exercises. In the majority of our experiments, only small muscle groups were exercised, for short periods of time, so that we did not run into an involvement of the total organism, as can happen in everyday athletic training. Therefore, we refer to our exercises not as training in the general sense of the word, but we limit it to "muscle training."

Procedure

A modified Dynamometer, created by E.A. Muller (Fig. 1), was used to determine the maximum strength and to train the muscles which bend and extend the arm. A closed U-frame stands on a foundation and is held by wires. There is a pivot in the middle of the upper and lower horizontal bars, on which a lever A with arms of equal length turns. The corresponding sides of the lever arms are connected by chains, which run vertically through the whole frame. The spring balance C is hung in one chain. The arm sling B can be adjusted to different heights on the other chain, the chain that is pulled, by means of a carbine hook. The chain which is pulled is some what longer than the other. When the chain is pulled up—by the arm flexor, Fig. 1—the upper arm on the side of the chain which is being pulled meets the upper horizontal bar of the frame sooner than does the opposite end of the lower arm meet the lower horizontal bar. The chain which is being pulled thus transfers the strength of the pull to the spring balance by way of the lower arm. When the chain is pulled down—by the arm extensor—there is a corresponding transfer of strength to the upper arm. On the pulling side of the vertical bar of the frame there is the

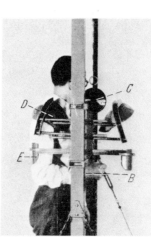

Fig. 1. Arm strength dynamometer (explanation in text).

supporting structure. This can be adjusted to any height. On it there is a padded shoulder support D for each arm, which encompasses the shoulder from above, in front and from the outside, and which receives the forces exerted by the shoulder in these directions. The supporting structure consists also of a padded upper arm support E, which receives the forces which are exerted by the upper third of the arm in a backwards or sidewards direction. The examination of the right arm is shown in the picture. In order to examine the left arm, the subject must step through the frame and turn 180 degrees. All four of the supports can be moved and fixed parallel on the median plane. The apparatus is adjusted so that the subject stands with his upper arm held vertically and his lower arm held horizontally with the wrist sling vertically over or, respectively, under the the place where the chain is attached to the arm A. Measurements at each position insure the same position of the subject in repeated experiments. The spring balance extends 0.2 mm for each kg of exerted strength, so that the contraction follows essentially isometrically. A pointer is used to show the maximum strength.

In order to measure the strength of and to train the muscle groups shown in Table 4, a sturdy structure was built, on which, with the help of chains, spring balances and paced slings in fixed positions (see footnotes in Table 4), the rotary moments of the separate limbs could be determined. To measure the strength of the finger flexors a hand-dynamometer was used, for the foot extensors, a stepping-dynamometer was used.

In order to determine the maximal strength, the subject is told to contract the flexor or extensor muscles of the lower arm as much as possible. These measurements were taken two consecutive times, and the higher score was recorded. In order to train the muscles, a specific exercise strength was marked on the spring balance and the subject was asked to hold this position for a definite period of time (until told to "halt!") or as long as possible (to the point of "not being able to continue"). This period of time is the duration of the exercise, while the number of exercises in one day is referrred to as the frequency of the exercise. Each week there were five days of exercise. On the sixth day, the maximal strength was measured, and the seventh day was a day of rest. The greatest circumference of the upper arm and the diameter of the M. biceps in the stage of maximum contraction were measured several times during the individual series of experiments. Taking into consideration the thickness of the skin and of the subcutaneous

TABLE 1

Name	Years of Age	Height in cm	Weight in kg	Muscle Groups Tested
Be.	25	176	68.0	Lower Arm Pronators
Ha.	27	171	64.5	Arm Flexor and Extensor
Het.	29	178	76.0	Arm Flexor and Extensor
Ol.	25	178	75.0	Arm Flexor and Extensor
Qui.	22	171	67.0	20 Different Muscle Groups
Re.	28	170	64.5	Lower Arm Pronators
Sch.	22	192	83.7	20 Different Muscle Groups
Th.	37	185	74.0	Arm Flexor and Extensor
We.	29	171	71.0	Arm Flexor and Extensor

fat, the area of the cross section could be calculated. The amount of strength exerted by the muscle itself was determined by considering the ratios of the levers. The strength in relationship to the area of the cross section (kg/cm^2) served as basis of comparison for the specific strength of the muscle. The result of the partial contraction of the flexor was not identical to the "absolute muscle strength," the actual cross section of the active fibers.

The experiments were carried out from 2/19/51 to 8/16/52. Nine male subjects took part in the experiments; their ages are in Table 1. Seventy one different muscle groups were trained.

Results

If one wants to compare the strength increase of the muscle in different methods of exercise, that is, the effect of different types of exercises, there are the following possibilities:

I. One can carry out a particular method of exercise for several weeks and then determine the increase of strength. Then when the strength has returned to the original level, the exercise is repeated using a different method, and the strength increase is compared. This procedure is impractical, because even when the same method is used, repetition of the exercise does not always lead to the same increase of strength. As is shown in Fig. 2, this is not only true for different subjects, but also holds true for the same subject.

2. One can change the method of exercising a particular muscle during the course of the training, in order to determine the value of the exercise on the basis of the change in the amount of strength increase. In doing this, one would have to assume that the strength increase would remain constant during the course of a training period, if the

same method is used throughout. This is usually the case only during a limited number of weeks. But if the rate of increase remains the same for several weeks after the change in method, it can be assumed that the methods which were being compared are of equal value.

3. One can train the corresponding muscle groups on each side of the same subject by a different method. This method is undoubtedly the best, since we found only small differences in beginning strength and increase of strength of the corresponding muscle groups on the left and right sides of a large number of subjects when the same method was used. The only drawback is that only two exercise methods can be compared.

4. One can train different muscle groups on the same person by different methods. However, different muscle groups show different strength increases when the same method is used, although this increase is in a specific proportion to the maximum rotary moment at the beginning of the training. However, a comparison of the value of different methods of exercise is not possible by this approach.

Therefore, we limited ourselves in the evaluation of the curves to changing the methods in the course of an exercise period or to the comparison of the left and right sides.

TABLE 2

Male Subject	Training Condition	Maximal Muscle Strength in kg	Maximal Muscle Tension kg/cm^2
Ha.	untrained	180	6,4
	trained	228	6,5
Het.	untrained	192	6,6
	trained	336	6,7
We.	untrained	194	6,7
	trained	288	6,6

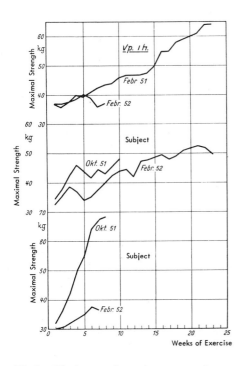

Fig. 2. The increase in maximum strength as a result of repetition of training with the same method, starting with the same strength level. The dates on the curves represent the beginning of the exercise period. Subject Th.: right arm flexor, 0.67 (parts) of the maximal strength, three times daily, 2 min total time of holding. Subject We.: right arm flexor, 0.67 (parts) of the maximal strength, once daily, 15 sec. Subject Het.: right arm flexor, 0.67 (parts) of the maximal strength, five times daily, 15 sec each.

First we experimented with a group of subjects to determine if the difference in arm-flexing strength as a result of training in the same subject—or from person to person—is always in the same ratio to the cross section of the bicep. (The participation of the M. coracobrachialis in the flexing of the arm was disregarded.) In Table 2 the results are listed.

One can see that the maximal tension of the biceps in people of different strength and different training is prac-

tically equal. Muscle strength and cross section increase proportionately. Thus, if one exercises with a stress that is always a definite part of the maximal strength, 0.33, 0.67, or 0.75, then one is exercising with a constant cross-sectional stress.

First we will discuss the affect of constant exercise stress on the increase of strength. The exercise program for the subjects 01. and Sch. are reproduced. Subject 01. exercised the left and right arm flexors with different stress, while the frequency of exercise remained constant. The stress of exercise remained constant in the given relationship to the maximal strength. The duration of the exercise with the different stresses was 50 per cent of the possible holding time to the point of exhaustion. With subject Sch. the stress of exercise on the same muscle was changed during the course of the exercise. The exercise lasted to the point of "not being able to do any more." It took place two to three times daily. The value of the exercise can be determined from Figs. 3 and 4.

The strength increase of Subject 01. is represented in Fig. 3. In exercising the arm flexor at 0.67 and 0.75 parts of the maximal strength, the rate of strength increase is almost the same. The maximal strength of the arm flexor reaches its maximum in eight to nine weeks when exercised at 0.33 parts of the maximal strength, while the increase of strength continues to the end of the series of experiments when exercised at 0.8 (parts) of the maximal strength. The very definite wave-like dips in some of the charts are in part a result of indispositions (the loss of strength on the tenth week was the result of a cold) and in part a result of the fact that the muscles were used in everyday life by the subjects and were therefore not always completely rested when they were tested.

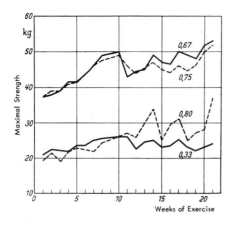

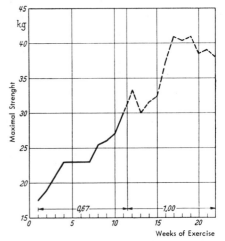

Fig. 3. The increase of maximal strength in subject 01. when varied strength of exercise was used (frequency and duration of exercise are constant). The numbers on the curves give the strength of exercise in fractions of the maximal strength. The upper curves refer to the right and left arm flexor, the lower ones to the right and left arm extensors (right———, left----).

Fig. 4. The increase of maximal strength of the left arm extensor of subject Sch. when the demand of the exercise is varied in the course of the experiment (frequency and duration of exercise are constant). The numbers under the curve give the demand (stress) of the exercise in fractions of the maximal strength.

Figure 4 shows the effect of exercise on the left arm extensor of subject Sch. During the first eleven weeks he exercised at 0.67 of the maximal strength, the following weeks, at the maximal strength itself. One can see that the increase of the muscle strength after the change reaches the same slope as before. The value of the exercise seems to be equal whether one exercises at the maximal strength or at a fraction of the maximal strength, down to 0.67.

Even at 0.33 of the maximal strength, an increase of strength can be achieved, which is, however, slower and comes to an earlier standstill.

From Table 3 and Figs. 3 and 4, it can be seen that the relatively smallest exercise value corresponds to the longest exercise duration, and that the difference between 2 and 2.5 sec exercise duration has no effect on the

TABLE 3

Subject	Trained Muscle Group	Demand of Exercise in Fraction of Maximal Str.	Duration of Each Exercise in Sec.	Frequency of Exercise Each Day
01.	Right Arm Flexor	0.67	22.5	1
	Left Arm Flexor	0.75	14.0	1
01.	Right Arm Extensor	0.33	75.0	1
	Left Arm Extensor	0.80	10.0	1
Sch.	Left Arm Extensor	0.67	50.0	3
	Left Arm Extensor	1.00	ca. 2.0	2

increase of strength. In order to investigate systematically the effect of the duration of exercise when the strength of exercise was held constant, the duration of exercise was varied between 6 and 45 sec when 0.67 of the maximal strength was used at a constant frequency (5 times or once daily).

Forty-five seconds represents the maximum possible length of time of holding before reaching the point of exhaustion. The effect of exercise with a duration of 10 and 15 sec, 6 and 34 sec, and 22.5 and 45 sec, respectively, in three left-side-right-side comparisons of the same muscle groups in subject We. in Fig. 5 shows that the rate of increase of the maximal strength is approximately the same in all six curves. The greatest rate of increase for four consecutive weeks is 2.15 kg/week in the

middle of the six curves. (Boundaries: 1.75–2.50 kg/week).

Figure 5 shows in the four lower curves that the change from five practices daily to only one does not result in a decrease in the rate of increase of the maximal strength.

This fact was further substantiated in Fig. 6, where the increase in strength of the right or left arm flexor, respectively, under 1 and 5 daily practices, and the increase in strength of the right and left arm extensor, respectively, under 3 and 7 daily practices was compared. Even though the curves are very spread out, they do show that in the long run there is a relationship between the daily frequency of exercise and the rate of increase of the maximal strength.

These results mean that holding at

Fig. 5. The increase in maximal strength in subject We. under varied exercise duration (demand and frequency of exercise are constant). The numbers on the curves represent the corresponding holding times in seconds. The four upper curves refer to the arm flexor, the two lower curves, the arm extensor (right ——, left – – – –). The Roman numerals give the number of daily exercises.

Fig. 6. The increase in maximal strength in subject Het. under varied frequency of exercise (demand and duration of exercise are constant). The two upper curves refer to the arm flexor, the lower curves, the arm extensor (right ——, left – – – –). The Roman numerals on the curves represent the number of daily exercises.

Fig. 5.   Fig. 6.

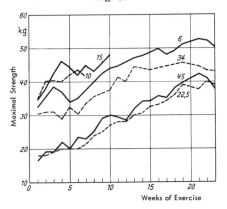

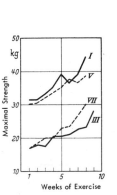

0.67 of the maximal strength for 6 seconds once a day would lead to a weekly increase in strength of 1–2 kg, but that an increase in frequency and duration as well as demand of exercise would not lead to any faster increase of the maximum strength.

In any training, one reaches a point where no further effect of training can be expected. The maximal strength has been reached. If one still continues the muscle training, the maximal strength that has been achieved usually remains the same. However, in a few cases, there is a rapid decrease in strength accompanied by painful sensations that probably point to damage of the musculature. Figure 7 shows this behavior in two training curves for the arm flexors for two different subjects. It is characteristic of this phenomenon, also referred to as over training, to occur especially when the strength has increased quickly and steeply during muscle training.

Fig. 7.

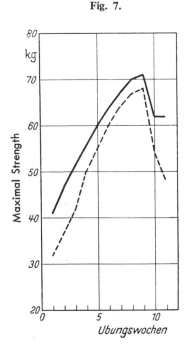

Ubungswochen

If we compare the maximal increase of strength on different muscles of the same person as to the rate of increase and the greatest potential strength, we will find considerable differences. Table 4 shows the median values of strength for two subjects who trained 20 muscle groups daily for 9 weeks at two-thirds of the maximal strength and another 24 weeks at the maximal strength. The table contains the median values for the arms and legs of both the left and right sides. In the table, column 1 represents the muscle group; column 2, the rotary moment at the beginning and the end of the training; column 3, the maximum increase of these values in per cent of the value at the beginning of training; column 4, the greatest rate of strength increase in four consecutive weeks in the course of the exercise period, expressed for each week in per cent of the value at the beginning of the first week. The muscle groups were arranged so that the percentage increases in strength increase from top to bottom. The increase was between 33 and 181 per cent of the original value contained in column 2. It would be appropriate to relate the quality of the training of the different muscle groups to the already existing strength. This latter would be expected to depend on the demands put on the muscles in everyday life. The small amount of trainability of the finger flexors, the arm flexors, and the leg flexors, and the great trainability, on the other hand, of the hip and back muscles, would seem to substantiate this theory. However, it is naturally not possible to give exact values for the daily demands on the muscles.

The results of calculations based on Table 4 have shown the relationship of the maximum percentage of the potential strength increase to the greatest rate of increase in four consecutive

TABLE 4

Muscle Group	Maximal Moment of Muscle Rotation Training		Maximal Strength Increase in % of Original Value	Greatest Increase in Strength in % for Consecutive Wks. Each Week
	Beginning	End		
Finger Flexor[1]	0.96	1.28	33	3.2
Knee Extensor[3]	23.4	31.7	36	6.7
Arm[4]	10.9	15.0	38	6.5
Leg[6]	16.6	25.1	51	6.9
Arm Flexor[2]	8.2	12.5	52	4.8
Arm[4]	5.5	8.7	58	8.8
Arm[5]	10.3	16.5	60	7.3
Arm[2]	1.05	1.9	81	10.8
Arm[5]	9.8	17.9	83	13.4
Arm Extensor[2]	4.9	9.6	96	7.6
Leg[6]	2.3	4.6	100	13.9
Leg[6]	14.3	28.9	102	9.1
Knee Flexor[3]	4.4	10.1	129	11.8
Leg[6]	2.5	5.8	132	14.1
Arm[2]	1.3	3.1	138	18.8
Thigh[6]	17.9	42.9	140	10.1
Thigh[6]	18.3	44.5	143	8.5
Hip[7]	16.3	43.3	166	11.7
Hip[7]	15.1	41.8	177	22.1
Foot Extensor[6]	11.8	33.2	181	15.9

[1-7] Hand Dynamometer

weeks. The correlation turned out to be +0.77. The rate of increase is greater, the further the maximal training condition is from the original condition. The regression between the maximal percentage increase of strength and the percentage rate of increase is 7.87, that is, with a training effect that increases the original strength by 100 per cent, an average of 8 per cent is gained in strength each week. In 11 subjects, whose arm flexors and arm extensors were trained simultaneously, that extensors always showed the higher percentage increase, corresponding to the smaller demand made of them in every day life.

In the literature a differentiation is made between the so-called strength and endurance training. DeLorme states that infrequent contractions with great resistance increases the strength of the muscle, while frequent contractions with little resistance increases the endurance. In Table 5, experiments with little resistance and a long holding period are compared with experiments with great resistance and a short holding period. Column 2 shows the exercise tension, column 3 the daily holding time in minutes. Column 4 shows the final strength in per cent of the original strength. In column 5 the percentage of change in maximal holding time for a muscle tension of 3.3 kg/cm^2 is shown.

If the holding time does not increase for the same muscle tension with the increase in size of the muscles in the course of the training, that is, the final value is 100 per cent of the original value, as in the case of subject Ha., this obviously means that the circulation for each unit of cross section was

TABLE 5

Subject	Muscle Tension kg/cm²	Daily Holding Time in min	Final Value of Maximal Strength in % of Original Value	Final Value of Max. Holding Time for Muscle Tension of 3.3 kg/cm² in % of Original Value
Ha.	2,2	8–10	164	100
Het.	4,4	2	197	110
Th.	4,4	2	173	75

not changed by the increase in thickness of the muscle. In the case of subject Het. the circulation even improved by 10 per cent. Only in subject Th. does the vascularization seem to have remained behind the growth in thickness. However, the differences are still within the range of possible error.

Discussion

V. Gertten[7] and E.A. Muller[11] carried out training experiments with static muscle contractions. In both series of experiments the results of the training were shown as an increase in the muscle strength as a result of static contractions; V. Gertten also traced the increase in the total strengths which were attained through isometric contractions which were repeated several times to the point of exhaustion. On the other hand, Muller evaluated the increase in holding time to the point of exhaustion in repeated holds at a certain strength. Since V. Gertten was exercising at the respective maximum strength, he automatically increased the demand of the exercise progressively with the increase in maximal strength as a result of training, while Muller kept the demand of exercise constant, with increasing muscle diameter, that is, with increasingly smaller muscle tension. No quantitative relationships between the demand of exercise, the duration of exercise, the frequency of exercise, and the increase in strength can be derived from either study. Perhaps one could conclude from Muller's study that only about half the maximum strength is sufficient as demand of exercise in training. Also, both series of experiments show that an increase in strength can be achieved through purely static contractions.

From our results we can draw quantitative relationships between the maximal muscle tension, the tension of exercise, and muscle training. As is shown in Table 2, the maximal tension of the M. bicep was always about 6.6 kg/cm². We have the following relationships between the exercise tension and the effect of the exercise: An increase in the effect of exercise with tension of exercise takes place only between a threshold value, which is less than 2 kg/cm², and a limit value that is to be found between 2 and 4 kg/cm². Beyond this limit value, an increase in tension of exercise does not speed up the muscle training. Below the threshold value, there is no training. Between the threshold and the limit values, a greater tension of exercise leads to a faster and greater increase in muscle strength. The effect of the exercise did not depend on the duration of the exercise between 6 and 45 sec or on the frequency of exercise (1–7 times daily).

This lack of dependence of the effect of the exercise on the frequency was also determined in the electrical treatment of paralyzed rat muscles by

Fleisch, Estoppey, and Hofstetter. The effect of the exercise was the same for a daily period of stimulation of between 1 and 45 min. Even 5 sec daily stimulation was enough to attain 20 per cent of the maximal effect of exercise.

Can the reason for the muscle training be derived from our results? One could consider the following three reasons for an increase in muscle strength:

1. The muscle tension exceeds a certain threshold.

2. The degree of exhaustion of the muscle reaches a certain value in the unit of time.

3. The transfer of energy in the muscle exceeds a definite threshold.

In 1 if the "all-or-nothing rule" holds true, each fiber is contracted maximally in the course of the alternating contraction of the individual muscle fibers. In this case, there would be no possibility of a graded tension demand on the individual fibers and therefore no dependence of growth on the tension.

In 2 the degree of exhaustion, the level of the by-products of reaction collected in the muscle fibers, could also cause the training stimulation. In the experiment with subject We. (Fig. 5), who exercised statically at 0.67 of the maximal strength, there must have been a large degree of cutting off of the blood vessels, which would lead to poor disposal of the products of reaction. In spite of this, we find the same increase in maximal strength per week in holding to the point of exhaustion as in holding for 1/9 of this time, during which only 1/9 of the total by-products that were present at the point of exhaustion could form. Thus, the concentration of these products could increase in proportion to the duration of exercise, without influencing the training effect. Therefore, we conclude that the degree of exhaustion—as far as the accumulation of by-products is concerned—is not a decisive factor in the effect of the exercise.

In 3 the remaining possibility is that the size of the muscle determines the effect of the exercise. This size always leads to a muscle training, when performance is demanded, that is not possible for an extended period of time, that is for a period of hours. From earlier experiments (E. A. Muller), one can calculate that approximately 20 per cent of the static maximal strength can always be held, while 33 per cent just barely has a training effect. Thus, one could say that when the oxygen requirement of the muscles is not completely satisfied during exercise, there is always a training effect (strengthening effect?). If this hypothesis is correct, then, especially in static work, a form of work which causes especially poor conditions for circulation with only a small transfer of material, training stimulation should arise. In repeated isometric contractions, which according to E. A. Muller produce much better conditions for circulation, and especially in short dynamic contractions, a higher exercise tension and a correspondingly higher threshold value should be necessary to attain the same training success. One could argue that in some of our exercises a daily isometric contraction at maximal strength produced a fast training. However, this contraction lasted about 2 sec, that is, much longer than the duration of contraction of 0.1–0.2 sec in rapid work and thus resulted in a greater intensity of change of matter. Thus, it could be traced to an oxygen requirement that was not satisfied. We have begun to compare the training effect of exercises with different oxygen supplies to the muscles.

We have assumed that an incompletely satisfied oxygen requirement coincides with the threshold value of the training stimulation. The exercise effect, which increased with the demand of exercise above this threshold value, could then be correlated with the corresponding increasing deficit in oxygen supply. However, this would leave unexplained the fact that the exercise effect does not increase above a certain limit, although the oxygen lack must increase. On the other hand, we could assume that exceeding the limit of the aerobic change of matter releases a constant training stimulus, regardless of how great the oxygen lack becomes and that an "all-or-nothing rule" applies to the training stimulus in the case of the muscle fibers.

We still must explain, however, why in an intermediate range the effect of the exercise is determined by the demand of the exercise. In order to do this, one must imagine that in the different arrangements of the muscles in the different muscle groups and in the different directions of pull of the fibers in the interior of the muscle and on the surface of the muscle, that some of the fibers are already working with insufficient oxygen and others are not, at the threshold of the effective exercise strength. Thus there must be a range of exercise demand at the lower limit of which all fibers obtain enough oxygen and thus no training stimulus arises, while at the upper limit all fibers obtain too little oxygen and thus are stimulated to grow. Between these two limits, the growth would then be a function of the demand of the exercise. This is exactly the behavior we found.

We must stress once again that according to our interpretation, it is not the level of the total deficit of oxygen, but the fact that the change of matter (reaction) takes place partly anaerobically at all, that produces the training stimulation. Training and training stimulus must therefore be considered separately for each fiber. This follows also from a statistical study by Linzback on the percentage distribution of the thickness of the muscle fiber in a heart muscle.

Table 4 shows the dependence of the muscle growth and the maximal muscle strength attained as being dependent on the already present strength. The relative strengths of different muscles which have been mentioned take on another aspect, if we consider the coincidental daily demands put on them, if we consider it is not a matter of the muscle tension alone but also of the degree of the satisfaction of the oxygen requirement during the demand. Muscles which perform a relatively static function of the body should reach a greater strength as a result of the daily demand relative to those whose function it is to carry out quick movements. In general we must allow that the maximal strengths which can be reached are at least three times as great as the more frequently occurring demands.

There is a certain contradiction in the fact that in Table 4 the more the muscle is already trained, the less the strength of the muscle increases, while in Fig. 7 in most instances, there is a linear increase in the maximal muscle strength in the course of the training. This could mean that the longer the muscle is maintained at a high level of training, the less is its capacity to be strengthened. In Fig. 2, we showed that there are different degrees of trainability in the same person. It usually happened that the trainability of the muscle decreased after several training experiments, even if loss of strength caused a return to the original strength. We are investigating these questions with systematic experiments.

The experiments of DeLorme and colleagues have denied the possibility that muscles will increase differently in strength and speed according to the training method. From our experiments it is apparent that the thickness and blood vessel supply of the muscle increase in proportion to each other. Thus there is no basis for the assumption that endurance and the capacity to recuperate increase to a lesser degree than the muscle strength in the training method we have chosen. The observation that either strength or speed or endurance can be improved preferentially in sport training is probably based on a greater or lesser degree of improvement of the coordination or training of the central mechanism responsible for the supply of oxygen which occurs simultaneously.

The practical value of these results for orthopedics is discussed in another place (E.A. Muller and Hettinger[14,15] and Hettinger[3]).

Summary

The increase in the maximal static holding power in different methods of exercise, different demand, duration, and frequency of exercise, was studied in 71 series of experiments on 9 male subjects. The demand of the exercise was increased in proportion to the growth in thickness of the muscle from week to week in such a way as to keep the tension of the muscle training constant in the course of the exercise. Since the increase in the cross section of the muscle was related to the maximal strength in such a way that the maximal muscle tension, that is, the muscle strength for each unit of cross section, remained constant, the constancy of the tension of the exercise was assured by the fact that a constant fraction of the maximal strength was retained.

The increase in maximal stength, which was equal to an average of 5 per cent of the original value each week, began at a threshold value of exercise tension that was below 1/3 of the maximal tension. The effect of the exercise could not be improved by increasing the tension of the exercise from 2/3 to 1/1 of the maximal tension. Only in the range of 1/3 of the maximal tension did the tension of the exercise influence the rate of training and the potential end value of the muscle growth. Exercising once a day for 6 sec had the same exercise effect as repeated exercise to the point of exhaustion (45 sec). The actual training stimulus is thus not to be found in the degree of exhaustion or the amount of reaction (change) each day, but probably in exceeding a particular speed of change of the muscle fibers. Since the amount of the change coincides with a demand that can be sustained for a considerable time, the training stimulus is assumed to be the speed of change of the individual fibers, whose oxygen need cannot be fully satisfied. This speed of change leads to growth speed of the muscle fibers which is independent of the strength of the stimulation.

The greatest possible increase on strength through training and the speed of this increase in different muscle groups showed a correlation of +0.77.

The endurance and the muscle strength increase in practically the same proportion in muscle training. With the same muscle tension the greatest holding time remains unchanged throughout the training.

Static exercise affords rapid muscle training with very little use of time and energy.*

References

1. Fleisch, A. J. Estoppey, and J. R. Hofstetter, *Helvet. Physiol.* **10** (1952), 93.
2. Gallagher, J. R., and T. L. DeLorme, *J. Bone Surg.* **31** (1952), 847.
3. Gertten, G. V., *Skand. Arch. Physiol.* **28** (1913), 13.
4. Hellebrand, F. A., A. M. Parrisch, and S. J. Houtz, *Arch. Physic. Med.*, **28** (1947), 76.
5. Hettinger, T., *Münch. med. Wschr.*, (1953), 728.
6. Linzbach, A. J., *Verh. dtsch. Ges. Kreislaufforsch.* **16** (1950), 13.
7. DeLorme, T. L., *J. Bone Surg.*, **27** (1945), 649.
8. DeLorme, T. L. and A. L. Watkins, *Progressive Resistance Exercise.* New York: Appleton-Century-Crofts.
9. DeLorme, T. L., B. G. Ferris, and J. R. Gallagher, *Arch. Physic. Med.* **33** (1952), 86.
10. Muller, E. A., *Arbeitsphysiol.* **5** (1932), 608.
11. ———, *Arbeitsphysiol.* **11** (1940), 43.
12. ———, *Arbeitsphysiol.* **5** (1932), 605.
13. ———, *Arbeitsphysiol.* **9** (1935), 62.
14. Muller, E. A, and T. Hettinger, *Z. Orthop. Verh. dtsch. orthop. Ges.* **40** (1952), 256.
15. ———, *Z. Orthop.*, **83** (1953), 617.
16. Steinhaus, A., *Persönliche Mitteilungem*, 1952.

E. A. MULLER

Physiology of Muscle Training

Reprinted from the *Revue Canadienne de Biologie*, **21** (1962), 303–13.

Muscle strength is defined as the maximum strength of an isometric contraction done voluntarily against a firm and unsurpassable resistance. At a given muscle length, the isometric maximum strength is always greater than the strength against which the muscle is able to shorten.[23] That is why a quantitative investigation of the physiological conditions of muscle training can only be done with isometric (static) contractions and measurements of strength. If muscles are trained by shortening contractions (dynamic contractions) and if the increase in strength is derived from the increase of the mechanical work performed, no attention is paid to the facts that mechanical work is improved not only by muscle strength, but also by a better blood supply to the muscles, by a better oxygen utilisation, or by a quicker removal of the acids from the blood. These accessory training effects, as important as they are for the practical increase in physical work capacity, disturb, however, the scientific research of muscle-strength training.

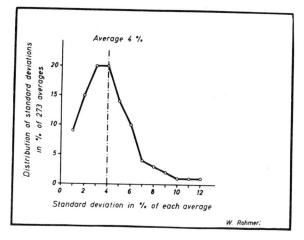

Fig. 1. Dispersion of measurements of maximal strength on 51 subjects and 12 muscle groups.

The Reliability of the Measurement of Maximum Strength

The measurement of the maximum strength by voluntary maximal contractions of muscles is not only a technical but also a psychological problem. The maximum strength cannot be obtained if the subject is not willing to do his best. A subject interested in appearing weak, e.g., during an inspection, will always give misleading results.[2, 25] Ikai and Steinhaus[11] studied the "psychological limits" of muscle strain. They found that gunshots or screaming during the contraction increase the muscular strength by 7 to 12 per cent. The strength could be altered about 30 per cent by hypnotic suggestion of strength or weakness, too. An increase in strength was interpreted as a central relief. Most of the control experiments of Ikai and Steinhaus, in which no extreme extra-stimulation was present, show a very good reproduction of the strength measurements. Therefore, the level of motivation is nearly constant in subjects who are prepared to undergo training experiments voluntarily and who are not deliberately disturbed during the strength measurement.

Recently Rohmert[24] investigated the dispersion of repeated maximum strength measurements carried out in our laboratory. The evaluation of 273 averages of 10 to 40 single strength measurements on 12 groups of trunk-, log-, and arm-muscles of 51 subjects are given in Fig. 1. The standard deviation of the single values of each of the averages is produced on the abscissa. The ordinates show the frequency of each deviation in percent of the 273 averages. The mean standard deviation is ± 4.0 per cent. In not more than 5 per cent of the cases is the standard deviation higher than 8.5 per cent. These are the limits in which errors are found due to technical deficiencies of the measurements, to changing physiological conditions, and to varying motivation.

The Evaluation of the Increase in Muscular Strength by Training

It will be shown later on that the gain in muscle strength gets smaller and smaller in the course of training until it finally ceases. This gain can be evaluated in a different way. In most cases, the increase in strength was related to the strength present at the beginning of training, called the initial strength. If you call P_0 the initial strength, P_t the strength at time t of the training, and V the speed of increase in strength, the weekly increase in strength related to the initial strength is:

$$V_{P_0} = \frac{100\%}{\text{week}} \left(\frac{P_t}{P_0} - 1 \right) (\% / \text{week})$$

The strength limit that cannot be surpassed by a given way of training was called P_E by Muller and Rohmert.[18] In the course of their studies, it was found to be of interest to express the speed of increase between initial strength and strength limit in relation to the latter.

$$V_{P_E} = \frac{100\%}{\text{week}} \left(1 - \frac{P_0}{P_E} \right) (\% / \text{week})$$

From 265 curves taken from a paper of Kirsten[12] showing the increase of strength over 8 training weeks with one daily maximum contraction of 1 sec, the following type of curves can be evaluated (Table 1). In the majority

TABLE 1

type of curve (speed of increase in strength)	% of cases	
	of 127 boys	of 138 girls
rising	11	3
constant	25	15
falling	44	56
zero or not scorable	20	26

of the curves, the weekly increase in strength falls with the course of training. Since training was exerted with maximum strength in the experiments evaluated in Table 1, the intensity of training increased steadily in the course of training (progressive training). In spite of the progressive training, the speed of increase in strength falls in the course of training until the

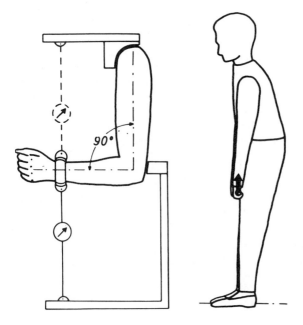

Fig. 2. (left) Dynamometer for measuring the isometric strength of the forearm flexors and extensors.

Fig. 3. (right) Position for measuring the isometric strength of the trunk extensors. Arrow indicates the direction of the pull on a dynamometer fixed on the ground floor between the feet.

TABLE 2

Muscle groups	sex	age	number of exp.	number of subj.	strength limit (kg) range	mean	SD	initial strength in percent of limit mean	SD
forearm flexors	M	15–32	32	20	21.1– 42.0	32.2	± 4.7	88.0	±5.6
(Fig. 2)	F	7–45	16	12	9.9– 23.0	16.3	± 3.8	87.3	±4.2
forearm extensors	M	9–59	32	20	11.4– 32.0	20.8	± 5.7	80.0	±9.0
(Fig. 2)	F	10–58	12	9	9.7– 20.1	13.8	± 3.0	75.5	±9.9
trunk extensors	M	11–16	39	39	70.0–232.5	118.5	±39.6	81.6	±5.7
(Fig. 3)	F	11–16	49	49	48.5–177.5	101.9	±26.3	81.3	±6.5

training contraction becomes ineffective. Evidently, the threshold of training ·rises steeper than the maximum strength during training. In the earlier experiments of Muller and Hettinger in 1953[8] this fact was not realized. They made the mistake of fixing a general threshold for the strength and duration of an effective contraction. They did not study, however, the total increase in strength attainable by training, which is important in athletics. Neither did they take into consideration whether contractions of a higher strength and duration are able to increase the strength even further. In recent years Muller and Rohmert[18] have worked on these problems. They have investigated the following questions:

1. How does the speed of increase in strength while training with one daily maximum contraction of 1 sec react if the intial strength makes up a varying proportion of the strength limit?
2. How does the speed of increase in strength while training with submaximum contractions of varying duration react if the initial strength makes up a varying proportion of the strength limit?
3. Is it possible to increase the strength limit reached with one daily maximum contraction of 1 sec even

further by prolongation of the frequency and the duration of the contractions?

The Increase in Strength Per Week Related to the Initial Strength in Per Cent of the Strength Limit while Training with One Daily Maximum Contraction of One Sec

From earlier investigations performed with Hettinger and more recent ones with Rohmert on the forearm flexors and extensors (Fig. 2) and from investigations of Kirsten on trunk extensors (Fig. 3), experiments were chosen in which isometric training with one daily maximum contraction of 1 sec was continued until muscle strength reached a plateau because the strength limit had been attained. Table 2 gives the number of subjects, the muscle groups, sex, and age. It also shows the range and average, with their standard deviation, of the strength limit and the average initial strength in per cent of the strength limit, with its standard deviation, for the different groups. The initial strength in per cent of the strength limit present at the beginning of the experiments is greatest at the forearm flexors (87–88 per cent), smallest at the forearm extensors (76–80 per cent), and in between at the trunk extensors (81–82 per cent).

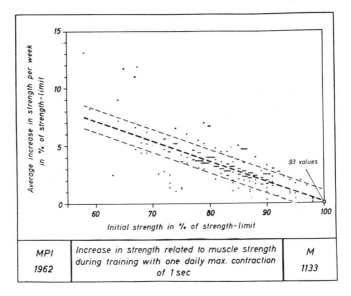

Fig. 4.

These significant differences reflect the stronger use of the forearm flexors in daily life. No significant difference due to sex can be seen in the initial strength in per cent of the strength limit. Nor is the correlation between age and initial strength in per cent of the strength limit significant. ($r = 0.214$, $b = 0.022$. The dispersion around the regression line is ± 7.59.) Thus, all the investigations that studied the initial strength related to age and sex[1, 5, 7] are also valid for the strength limit. On the other hand, all the comparisons of strength of different muscle groups using the initial strength accidently present instead of the strength limit are uncertain. It is necessary to compare the strength limits reached under equal training conditions, in order to get a true classification of the strength of different muscles corresponding to their inherent disposition.

In Fig. 4, the 180 experiments of Table 2 and 93 other experiments with

no increase in strength by training were evaluated. The initial strength in per cent of the strength limit is reproduced on the abscissa; the mean weekly rise in the maximum strength in per cent of the strength limit, on the ordinate. This mean is calculated for the total time of strength increase from initial strength up to the strength limit. It is obvious that the rise in strength is greater the more the initial strength differs from the strength limit. The correlation between initial strength and average rise in strength, both in per cent of the strength limit, is very significant, -0.88. In Fig. 4, the regression line, $b = -0.177$, is given with its dispersion. The dispersion is ± 1.00. The regression line shows the average increase in strength for the group of subjects examined, for different initial strengths. If regression lines are scored separately for the three muscle groups and for both sexes, straight lines are found parallel to and identical with one another and with the drawn straight line. There is no statistically significant correlation between the absolute level of the strength limit and the average rise in strength from initial strength to the strength limit on both sexes for the three muscles groups. Calculation of the correlation between age and weekly change of strength in per cent of the strength limit in 177 training-experiments resulted in $r = -0.325$. The regression line was $b = -0.08$. The dispersion of this regression line was ± 1.79. It is concluded that there is only an insignificant influence of age on the increase in strength per week with increasing strength.

This independence of the increase in strength of age, sex, level of strength limit, and type of muscles examined makes it probable that the dispersion around the mean regression line (see Fig. 4) is not caused by variations in individual trainability, but by errors in the measurements. These errors originate from the fact that the exact moment of reaching the strength limit cannot be fixed very well for the gradually ceasing increase of strength. The trainability of different muscles of different people is supposed to be about the same, if the initial strength has the same percentage relative to the strength limit. It follows from the straight-line curve drawn in Fig. 4 that the relation of the weekly increasing strength to the difference between strength limit and initial strength given in percent of the strength limit is constant. That means the training time from the initial strength to the strength limit is of equal length in all cases. This assumption, however, is not correct. The average training time for 75 per cent of initial strength was 5 weeks on the average, for 90 per cent about $3\frac{1}{2}$ weeks, and for 98 per cent about 2

weeks. Thus, the straight line in Fig. 4 is not straight but of a very narrow range. The true course in its limits of dispersion should be slightly upward-convex, in order to correspond with the decrease in training time with increasing initial strength. It is possible to derive the true course of the instantaneous speed of increase in strength as a function of the initial strength directly from the original curves of the increase in strength during the training time. From the 88 curves of the paper of Kirsten (used in Table 2 as well as in Fig. 4), the average increase in strength per week was calculated in steps of 5 per cent to 5 per cent of the initial strength; and the instantaneous increase in strength in per cent of the strength limit was interpolated. Related to the strength limit in per cent per week it was 8.6 for 80 per cent initial strength, 7.5 for 85 per cent, 5.6 for 90 per cent, 3.6 for 95 per cent and 2.0 for 98 per cent. The course of the curves can be seen in Fig. 10 for Training *I*. This curve drops to zero more steeply the more the initial strength approaches the strength limit. It this curve is extrapolated in direction to the smaller initial strength values, it stays nearly constant at about 11 per cent increase per week below 60 per cent of initial strength.

Rasch et al.[22] found, in 1961, that an isometric training of the forearm flexors has a training effect upon the arm extensors at the same time. In Fig. 4, experiments were used in which both muscle groups were trained simultaneously. Since the curves of the forearm flexors and extensors are parallel to and identical with the curve of the trunk extensors, it is unlikely that training of antagonists distorted the results.

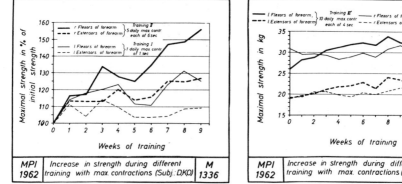

Fig. 5.

MPI	Increase in strength during different	M
1962	training with max. contractions (Subj.:D,K,O)	1336

Fig. 6.

MPI	Increase in strength during different	M
1962	training with max. contractions (Subj.:M)	1337

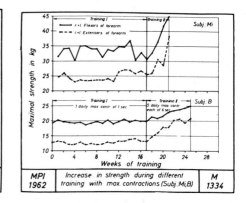

Fig. 7.

MPI	Increase in strength during different	M
1962	training with max. contractions (Subj.:R)	1335

Fig. 8.

MPI	Increase in strength during different	M
1962	training with max. contractions (Subj.:Mi,B)	1334

The Dependence of the Increase in Strength from the Initial Strength by Training with Submaximum Contractions

Twenty-eight training experiments were chosen out of earlier investigations with Hettinger, in which the forearm flexors and extensors were progressively trained by daily 67 per cent maximum contractions of various duration and in which a constant strength limit was reached in several weeks. A further training stimulus was caused by the maximum strength, which had to be measured once a week. These experiments were evaluated by Muller and Rohmert[18] in the same way as the experiments given in Fig. 4. For each experiment, V_{P_E} was calculated as a function of the initial strength in percent of the strength limit. The 28 values show a significant correlation of -0.80, the regression line $b = -0.09$ and has a dispersion of ± 0.81. The regression line passes zero near the limiting strength. The fall of the line for 65 per cent maximum contractions is about half as steep as for training with 100 per cent maximum contractions. Thus, at the same initial strength, the average speed of increase corresponds roughly to the strength of the training contractions. Duration of the contractions in the range of 5 to 45 sec was not found to influence the results. No experiments have been done with 67 per cent maximum-contractions of less than 5 sec. The number of experiments is too small to compare the strength limit for 67 per cent and 100 per cent maximum strength as a training stimulus. The courses of the respective curves point to the same strength limit.

The Effect of a Greater Duration and Frequency of Contractions on the Increase in Strength in Training with Maximum Contractions

The question of how the speed of increase in strength and the strength limit depends on the duration of the contractions in training with maximum contractions was investigated by Muller and Rohmert.[18] The results of these investigations are given in Figs. 5 to 8. Figures 5 and 6 concern experiments in which the muscles of the right and the left arm were trained simultaneously with contractions of different durations. Figure 5 shows the mean values for three girls aged between 17 and 20 yr, Fig. 6 the values of a 62-year-old man. Figures 7 and 8 concern experiments in which after a fading increase in strength by one daily maximum contraction of 1 sec, training was intensified to 5 contractions per day of 6 sec each. In Fig. 7, it can be seen that the strength of a 31-year-old man increased 28 per cent in 9 weeks by 1-sec-training, but remained constant at strength limit over 6 weeks, in spite of continued training. Only an intensified training led to a further increase in strength. The four muscle groups of the two subjects in Fig. 8 (upper curve of a

man aged 21, lower curve of a woman aged 22) did not increase in strength by a 1-sec-training for 16 to 17 weeks; but intensified training was immediately followed by an increase. A quantitative evaluation of these experiments is given in Table 3. It is evident that a more intensive training stimulus causes a more intensive increase in strength. The few values available make it probable that the strength limits for Training I and Training II have no fixed relation, but vary individually. Whether the prolonged contraction-duration or the fivefold repetitions of the contractions per day are responsible for the greater training effect is undecided.

The Training Interval

Considering the interaction between the training contraction on the one hand and the increase in strength of the muscle on the other, it is not possible to take the contraction as the direct stimulus of the increase in muscle mass and strength. The contraction, if it surpasses a certain strength and duration, is rather the cause of a lasting excitation in the muscle, which does not diminish before 24 hr. This lasting excitation, the nature of which is unknown, causes a gradual increase of the cross section and the maximum strength of the muscle. This excitation can be taken as the actual training stimulus of the muscle. The only measure of this stimulus can be derived from its effect on muscle strength. The training stimulus caused by a muscle contraction is fully effective for about one day according Muller and Hettinger.[17] It fades from day to day, and becomes ineffective after 7 days. In order to keep up the maximum increase in strength, one daily contraction of sufficient strength is necessary. Following the earlier results of Muller and

Hettinger[12] it is not possible to increase the training stimulus by shorter intervals than 24 hr, i.e., by frequent daily contractions. They combined their results of 21 training experiments on seven subjects in a curve reproduced in Fig. 9. The exact course of this curve has to be retested for in their experiments, also, the increase in strength was not related to the strength limit. It seems sure, however, that with only one or two maximum contractions per week the increase in strength takes place more slowly. If the intervals between two contractions are too long, it is not possible to prevent a fall of the muscle strength. The muscle becomes more and more atrophic. The term "atrophic," however, can only be defined in relation to the strength limit. Since different strength limits for each muscle are possible according to different sorts of training, the same initial strength can be evaluated as a different level of atrophy. Evidently, the term "atrophy" can only be used under the point of view of the respective demands of daily life on the muscles. If, for example, some of the main muscles of a greater number of subjects have a muscle strength of 80 per cent of their strength limit, owing to their daily activities, they would not be able to manage these activities with 60 per cent of the same strength limit. They could be called "relatively atrophic." Thus, this judgment leads to the opinion that with decreasing demands of daily life upon the muscle, caused by technical improvements, the group of men classified as "nonatrophic" will get weaker and weaker. This is unsatisfactory from a biological point of view. If would be worthwhile to try to find out which daily minimum contractions would keep up the minimum muscle strength that is indispensable for our health.

The question of training intervals is

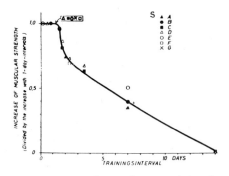

Fig. 9. Increase of muscular strength in relation to interval between two training contractions.

related to the finding described by Muller and Hettinger 1954[16] and confirmed and completed by Hettinger 1961[7] that muscle strength after the end of training is lost more slowly when the training intervals during the training have been of long duration. This phenomenon cannot be discussed here at length.

Discussion

The investigations of Muller and Rohmert[18] have altered the concept about the conditions of muscle training put forward by Muller[15] and Hettinger.[7] The fact remains unchanged that the majority of people are able to increase their muscle strength with one daily maximum contraction of 1 sec. This, however, increases the initial muscle strength of the main muscle groups of the body merely by about 20 per cent in 5 weeks. Contrary to the findings of Muller and Hettinger, it was possible to get a bigger increase in strength by prolongation of the contraction duration and by more frequent contractions per day. Muller and Hettinger suggested a general threshold at 30 per cent of the "normal" strength of muscles, which had to be surpassed by the training contraction in order to get an increase in strength. Atrophic muscles attained "normal" strength, again by contractions with merely 20 per cent of "normal" strength. The strength of a muscle was called "normal" by Muller and Hettinger if the muscle did not increase in strength by contractions between 20 and 30 per cent of normal strength. If the muscle did increase in strength, it was considered to be atrophic. If it did not react to contractions between 30 and 100 per cent of "normal" strength, it was called "untrainable." According to the new experiments and deliberations of Muller and Rohmert, the muscle never has a "normal" strength. All it has is the disposition to respond to repeated contractions of a certain strength, duration, and frequency with an increase in strength. Each increase in strength by training diminishes the efficiency of the acting-training stimulus, even of a so-called "progressive" stimulus, which is increased in proportion to the muscle strength. The threshold of the training stimulus rises with increasing strength to a point where the stimulus becomes ineffective. This is the point of the strength limit.

Figure 10 shows an attempt to express our present knowledge in schematic form. The abscissa gives the

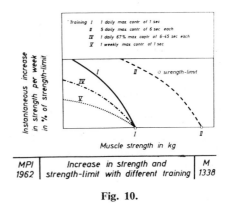

Fig. 10.

strength of any muscle group of any subject in kg, the ordinate gives, for each curve, the increase in strength per week in per cent of the strength limit. Four curves are drawn for four different ways of training. The intersection of the curves with the abscissa marks the strength limit valid for the respective training stimulus. If the training stimulus of one daily maximum contraction of 1 sec (Training I) is increased to a stimulus of several daily contractions of 4 to 6 sec (Training II), the speed of increase and the strength limit both rise. An exact quantitative

TABLE 3

Method of comparison	Subj.	Sex	Age	Intensified training	Increase in strength per week from initial strength up to strength limit in per cent of initial strength				Strength limit with Training II or III in per cent of the strength limit reached by Training I	
					with Training I		with Training II or III			
					flexors	extensors	flexors	extensors	flexors	extensors
Simultaneous and	Mu	M	62	III	0.3	1.3	3.9	3.4	107	110
different training	D	F	20	II						
with right and left	K	F	17	II	3.9	1.0	6.3	3.0	—	—
arm	O	F	17	II						
Training II or III	R	M	31	II	—	0	—	5.7	—	117
after cessation of	Mi	M	21	II	0	0	8.9	11.5	>135	>145
the effect of Train-	B	F	22	II	0	0	3.2	7.3	>125	>158
ing I										

Training I   = 1 daily maximum contraction of 1 sec
Training II = 5 daily maximum contractions of 6 sec each (interval 2 min)
Training III = 10 daily maximum contractions of 4 sec each (interval 2 min)

description of the effect of increased training stimuli is not yet possible. Some preliminary figures are given in Table 3. If the training stimulus is reduced to 67 per cent of the maximum strength and a contraction duration of 5 to 45 sec (Training IV) or to a maximum contraction of 1 sec, repeated only once a week (Training V) the speed of increase in strength gets slower. The strength limit probably does not change in these two latter cases (Fig. 10). The fact that a drop in strength by atrophy arising from a gain in strength by training, however, lowers the speed of increase in strength, prevents a greater deviation of the strength upwards and downwards in daily life. It regulates the present strength of a greater number of subjects in the relatively narrow limits given in Table 2 at about 80 per cent of the strength limit for Training I. This percentage will naturally vary with more or less daily activity (sports, occupation, illness).

The new experiments have changed the meaning of the term "trainability," entirely. Muller and Hettinger defined trainability as the weekly increase in initial strength. Since it is now known how much this increase depends on the intensity of the training stimulus, there is a temptation to define trainability as the increase in strength per week relative to the intensity of the training stimulus. But it has been proved that this increase in strength drops more and more as the strength rises up nearer to its limit. The findings of Muller and Rohmert make it unlikely that the trainability is influenced by age, sex, or muscle group, if the strength limit is taken into consideration. All the earlier experiments about a different trainability under varying conditions, in which the relative position of the initial strength to the strength limits was not verified, should be repeated, therefore. This would include studies by Het-

tinger and Muller,[9] concerning the trainability in various seasons; by Hettinger and Seidl,[10] on the trainability of muscles influenced by ultraviolet radiation; by Kraut, Muller and Muller-Wecker,[13] on the effect of protein in nutrition upon muscletraining; and the work of Hettinger,[6] concerning the effect of testosterone on the muscle.

The training effect attainable with one daily maximum contraction of 1 sec being small and slow, specially on main muscle groups and on students doing athletics, the negative results of Rasch and Morehouse,[21] of Petersen and co-workers,[19,20] and of Hansen,[4] are not unexpected. The quick rise of the hand strength with isometric maximum contractions of 6 sec in the experiments of Vanderhouse et al.[27] indicates a relatively atrophic strength of the hand. Very good results with isometric training were achieved on arm pronators and supinators by Darcus and Salter[3] and Salter.[26] Unfortunately, the strength limits were not reached or not indicated in these investigations. The best confirmation of this theory is given in the paper of Liberson and Asa.[14] They purposely selected a very atrophic muscle for training, namely, the abductor of the little finger. The training started at an initial strength of 37 per cent of the strength limit, lasted 7 weeks for the increase in strength up to strength limit, and was conducted with an average speed of increase in strength of 9 per cent per week. The course of the trainability corresponds to that given in Fig. 10. The findings concerning the question of the isotonic training and its effects on the maximum strength and duration are still so contradictory that it would be premature to try to put them into a proper order.

Summary

Irrespective of the method used for training with progressive isometric contractions, the muscular strength rises more slowly from week to week. The increase in strength ceases if an individual strength, different for different muscle and ways of training, is reached, the so-called strength limit. Only the strength limit makes comparison of the inherent disposition of different muscles possible. The speed of increase in muscular strength from initial strength up to strength limit, expressed in per cent of that limit, is not influenced by individual factors, such as sex, age, muscle group, level of the strength limit. The speed of increase and the limit of strength are determined, however, by the intensity of training. The main muscles of the body show 83 per cent (group-average 76–88 per cent), muscles rarely used as little as 37 per cent, of the strength limit in physically untrained people, when training with one daily maximum contraction of 1 sec.

References

1. Asmussen, E., and K. Heerboll-Nielsen, "Isometric Muscle Strength of Adult Men and Women," *Communication No. 11* of the Danish National Assoc. for Infantile Paralysis, Hellerup, Denmark (1961).
2. Beck, W., and Th. Hettinger, *Monatschr. Unfallheilk.*, **59** (1956), 116.
3. Darcus, H. D., and N. Salter, *J. Physiol. (London)*, **129** (1955), 109.
4. Hansen, J. W., *Intern. Z. angew. Physiol.*, **18** (1961), 474.
5. Hettinger, Th., *Arbeitsphysiol.*, **15** (1953), 201.
6. Hettinger, Th., *Intern. Z. angew. Physiol.*, **18** (1960), 213.
7. Hettinger, Th., *Physiology of Strength.* Springfield, Ill.: Charles C. Thomas, Publisher, 1961.
8. Hettinger, Th., and E. A. Muller, *Arbeitsphysiol.*, **15** (1953), 111.
9. Hettinger, Th., and E. A. Muller, *Intern. Z. angew. Physiol.*, **16** (1955), 90.
10. Hettinger, Th., and E. Seidl, *ibid*, **16** (1956), 177.
11. Ikai, M., and A. H. Steinhaus, *J. Appl. Physiol.*, **16** (1961), 157.
12. Kirsten, *Intern. Z. angew. Physiol.*
13. Kraut, H., A. E. Muller, and Muller-Wecker, *ibid.*, **17** (1958), 378.
14. Liberson, W. T., and M. M. Asa, "Brief Isometric Exercises" (Appendix I), in *Therapeutic Exercises*. New Haven, Conn.: E. Light, 1958.
15. Muller, E. A., *Rehab.*, **11** (1957), 41.
16. Muller, E. A., and Th. Hettinger, *Arbeitsphysiol.*, **15** (1954), 452.
17. Muller, E. A., and Th. Hettinger, *Intern. Z. angew. Physiol.*, **16** (1956), 184.
18. Muller, E. A., and W. Rohmert, *ibid.*, **19** (1962).
19. Peterson, B. F., *Acta Physiol. Scand.*, **48** (1960), 406.
20. Peterson, B. F., H. Graudal, J. W. Hansen, and N. Hvid, *Intern. Z. angew. Physiol.*, **18** (1961), 468.
21. Rasch, P. J., and L. E. Morehouse, *J. Appl. Physiol.*, **11** (1957), 29.
22. Rasch, P. J., W. R. Pierson, and G. A. Logan, *Intern. Z. angew. Physiol.*, **19** (1961), 18.
23. Reichel, H., *Z. Biol.*, **97** (1936), 429.
24. Rohmert, W., *Intern. Z. angew. Physiol.*, **19** (1961), 35.
25. Rohmert, W., and W. Sieber, *Med. Sachverständige*, **56** (1960), 174.
26. Salter, N., *J. Physiol. (London)*, **130** (1955), 109.
27. Vanderhoof, E. R., C. J. Imig, and H. M. Hines, *J. Appl. Physiol.*, **16** (1961), 873.

F. A. HELLEBRANDT / S. J. HOUTZ

Mechanisms of Muscle Training in Man: Experimental Demonstration of the Overload Principle

Reprinted from *The Physical Therapy Review*,
36 (1956), 371–83.

The principle of overload, although already established empirically, continued to be poorly understood. More research of a definitive type was required to discover its best application. This report sets forth a series of carefully controlled experiments whereby the investigators were able to test both theory and practice. They have shown in humans what Siebert demonstrated in frogs: that to extend the maximum limits of performance, the critical variable is intensity, or "the amount of work done per unit of time."

In addition to providing a better understanding of the overload principle, this article is important in other respects. It represents a careful and much needed test of current clinical procedures (including those of DeLorme) for combating disuse atrophy. Also, the suggestion that changes in the central nervous system contribute to improved performance, and that such changes are best facilitated in the "overload" state, has led to regarding strength development as a motor learning phenomenon. Further examples of this thinking can be seen in Hellebrandt's later work.

The investigators have added still more evidence of the remarkable capacity of the muscle tissue to withstand stress with no apparent harm. Although the type of performance studied is somewhat different from that associated with athletic events requiring cardiorespiratory endurance, a parallel can be seen between the training procedures recommended by Hellebrandt and Houtz and the popular "interval" training procedures used by runners and swimmers today.

The reader should note that the inquiry is not restricted to strength, in a narrow sense, but considers also such concomitant variables as power, endurance, and work. Insofar as the subject is dynamic *strength, these additional variables are usually a part of any maximum performance task.*

Introduction

The success of orthopedic surgery is affected to a significant degree by the management of the patient postoperatively. The procedures performed frequently demand either immobili-zation of the parts subjected to surgery or diminution in their use. Skeletal muscles thus prevented from normal activity undergo atrophy.

Cuthbertson, Howard *et al.*, and Stevenson have discussed the disturbance in mineral metabolism after fractures, prolonged bed rest and

288

skeletal operations. Loss of muscle protoplasm accounts for the negative nitrogen balance. The latter develops rapidly following trauma to bones and is only gradually reversed, even in the presence of high protein feeding. If bed rest is necessary, deconditioning of the body as a whole also occurs as Keys, Taylor *et al.*, and Deitrick, Whedon, and Shorr have shown. There is deterioration of the cardiovascular system characterized by a diminution in heart size, reduction in plasma volume, and a long lasting decrease in the ability of the vasomotor system to combat the hydrostatic effects of gravity. These various changes may be ameliorated by massage (Cuthbertson), the oscillating bed (Whedon *et al.*), or exercise (Vail), but apparently cannot be wholly prevented.

The evidence briefly reviewed suggests that the postoperative rehabilitation of the orthopedically disabled offers an ever-present challenge, especially in relation to the selection of methods for the restoration of strength, power, and endurance to skeletal muscles weakened by disuse. Exercise per se is reparative to a considerable degree, even when the activity program is left to the judgment and discretion of the patient. The curative powers of Nature unaided provide the orthopedic surgeon with a powerful ally, especially if the disabled person is in good general health and is motivated by a desire to resume normal activity. Many factors may supervene, however, which mitigate against spontaneous recovery, prolong convalescence, and lead to baffling degrees of chronic disability.[14]

The widespread use of various exercise regimes following orthopedic surgery suggests that end results may be improved appreciably by the judicious control of postoperative activity programs. It is important, therefore, that the mechanisms of muscle training be understood; only thus may aftercare be individualized to meet the particular needs of every patient. The rational application of the principles of muscle training is superior to rote adherence to any one of the systems of exercise described in the literature. The latter readily become so stereotyped as to be rendered more or less ineffective.

The physiological principle upon which the development of strength is dependent is in itself simple. Recently it was put succinctly by Dr. Roger Bannister,[24] the first man in human history to run the 4-min mile. "The art of record-breaking is the ability to take more out of yourself than you've got," said Bannister. "You punish yourself more and more, and rest between spells." Physiologically this is known as the *overload principle*. Clinically it has been incorporated in DeLorme's[10] progressive resistance exercises. It is also an integral part of the Kabat techniques of muscle reeducation, all of which utilize maximal resistance. Both methods are involved technically. Thus the basic idea which gives them their validity is easily overlooked or perverted. The DeLorme system in particular has undergone several procedural modifications which all but nullify the physiological principle upon which the development of strength is based.

The original DeLorme procedure, described in 1945, called for seven to ten bouts of repetitive exercise. From day to day the patient tried to step up the magnitude of the increments by which the load was increased systematically to the maximum selected for each week of training. Thus in actual practice less and less of the per diem exercise time was devoted to "warming up" contractions. Maximal resistance was increased at weekly intervals.

Appraising the original DeLorme procedure, it may be commended on several counts. The dosage of exercise prescribed is greater than that usually used in the clinic. It approximates that deemed obligatory in the training of athletes. The persistent pushing of effort to limits beyond those met easily is also a device common to athletic training. There is no a priori reason why the same methods cannot be applied in the treatment of simple disuse atrophy, providing the stress imposed can be tolerated by the bones and joints, and the patient is otherwise healthy. This appears to have been DeLorme's initial view for he concluded that in order to obtain rapid hypertrophy, "the muscle should be subjected to strenuous exercise and at regular intervals to maximum exertion."

In 1948 DeLorme and Watkins reported that further experience had shown that "in most cases" two or three bouts of exercise were "far more satisfactory" than the seven to ten previously advocated, and that furthermore, only one need be pitched to the level of maximal effort. It was recommended that the resistance be adjusted to one-half maximal on the first bout and stepped up to 75 per cent of full load on the second bout. Thus two-thirds of the daily workout was relegated to "warming up" activity, and the per diem dosage of overload exercise was held to only ten repetitive contractions.

As far as we have been able to determine the only evidence in support of this radical modification in the original DeLorme procedure is that supplied by clinical experience. No systematic attempt appears to have been made to test the validity of the sharp diminution in the magnitude of the effort exacted for training purposes. Reasoning from first principles suggests that some point must exist below which reduction in the dosage of exercise defeats the purpose for which it has been administered.

Expediency may have contributed to the downgrading of the work demanded from the disabled person. Under the exigencies of scheduling treatment for large numbers of patients it may have appeared to the hard-pressed physical therapist and the responsible clinician that as much was accomplished through application of the automatically graded shortcut procedure as by the original method which not only took more than three times as long to administer, but which also required the exercise of considerable judgment to gauge the limits to which the handicapped person could be pushed with safety each time he presented himself for treatment. It is easy to understand why the stereotyped short method rapidly became the standard practice of most physical therapy departments in this country. By so doing it was forgotten that the method had developed in the hospitals of the armed forces where physical therapy was only a small part of the patient's total treatment program, which often included reconditioning exercises, swimming, sports, manual arts, and occupational therapy. These adjuvants to general rehabilitation are not commonly available in civilian installations.

The "Oxford Technique" is another curious modification of DeLorme's original method of training. In 1951 Zinovieff proposed that the maximal resistance be introduced at the onset of exercise and then reduced systematically, pari passu with the development of fatigue, instead of increasing the stress imposed during the course of each practice session. This is contrary to the whole theory of overload training. Indeed, it violates the basic concept on which overload training is based. We ourselves demonstrated as early as 1946 that the DeLorme 10 R.M. (ten repetition maximum) could be carried from the onset of exercise and suggested that the "warming up" bouts might thus be eliminated. This would simplify the technique of administering heavy resistance exercise without defeating the purpose of the method if the power developed by the contracting muscles was sustained at the highest possible level in spite of fatigue. Our objective was to carry the 10 R.M. throughout the entire practice session before upgrading the maximal resistance. This is the only way the human machine can be driven to attain higher and higher peaks of all-out effort. Determination not to reduce the rate of working when the stress imposed seems insuperable is the *sine qua non* of overload training.

The overload principle is as important in the rehabilitation of the disabled as it is in the training of athletes. Restoration of function is possible only if the limits of performance are persistently extended. The rate at which improvement progresses then depends primarily on the degree to which the person is willing to punish himself. There is no short cut, effortless technique of muscle training; and no reason why physiological degrees of fatigue are contraindicated in the orthopedically disabled if cardiovascular-respiratory mechanisms operate normally and general health is unimpaired.

The purpose of this paper is twofold: *First*, to present an experimental demonstration of the overload principle. To our best knowledge this has never been done on man. *Second*, to evaluate the efficacy of some of the clinical techniques of applying strength developing exercise popularized in the last decade. As indicated previoulsy, the evidence in support of these is almost wholly empiric.

Material and Methods

The subjects of the investigation were all normal young adults. The ma-

jority had had experience in vigorous competitive athletics and professional training in physical education. They were thus already inured to the discomforts of severe exercise and knew how to extend the limits of performance by systematic training. Between 1950 and the summer of 1954 observations were made on 17 subjects, 8 male and 9 female. *In toto* 620 experiments were conducted in the course of 7 different training procedures.

All exercise was performed on the Kelso-Hellebrandt modification of the Mosso ergograph.[16] Observations were limited to wrist flexion or extension. The exercise prescribed was repetitive. It was executed to the rhythm of an audiovisual metronome. The cadence was kept constant throughout the series of experiments. The work assignment was divided into bouts consisting of 25 lifts. Each bout was followed by a rest pause equal in duration to the period of exercise. The number of bouts varied in relation to the degree of overloading.

The design of the individual experiments in presented in Tables 1 and 2. In all of these the subject had only one objective—to make each repetitive lift against a measured degree of resistance the maximal attainable under the exigencies of the conditions imposed. Thus the study called for highly trained and cooperative subjects, familiar with the disciplined behavior required for controlled laboratory experimentation.

Clinical conditions were simulated in the MCV experiments (Table 1). Training by the limit day procedure is an approximate ergographic equivalent of the original DeLorme technique of heavy resistance exercise. In the overload and underload experiments both groups of subjects performed the same number of contractions; both made an all-out effort. The only dif-

TABLE 1

Design of the MCV Experiments

Constants: No. contractions per bout, 25; cadence, 2 count rhythm with metronome at 100; duration of bout, 1/2 min; rest pause between bouts, 1/2 min; extent of contraction, maximal attainable by concentrated volitional effort; end-point of performance, failure to develop enough tension to produce a measurable lift of the assigned load in the prescribed rhythm, or completion of the assigned number of contractions.

Training by the Limit Day Procedure:

1. Begin with a light load (♀ 0.5 kg, ♂ 1 kg).
2. Increase load with each successive bout by a predetermined increment (0.25 kg or 0.5 kg).
3. Continue to complete exhaustion. Load is the independent variable and this determines the number of bouts to the end-point of performance.

MCV Overload Procedure:

1. Determine pretraining limit day performance on preferred side.
2. Repeat on contralateral side.
3. Compute work done per bout and *graph* against load.
4. From the *curve of work* thus obtained, select the initial training load. This is greater than the optimum but less than the failing load.
5. Train 3 times weekly (M.W.F.).
6. Begin with the preferred side and lift the prescribed load through the fullest possible range 250 times, dividing the work assignment into 10 bouts of 25 contractions each.
7. Repeat on the contralateral side. Both the load carried on any given day and the number of contractions are held constant. The independent variable is the extent of the contraction under the conditions imposed.
8. Compute the work done per bout and graph against time. Assess the magnitude of the stress from the fatigue curve thus obtained. When the decrement in performance is less than 20 to 25 per cent, increase the degree of overloading.

MCV Underload Procedure: Exactly like the above except that the load selected falls well in the underload zone and remains constant throughout the training period.

ference in procedure was the magnitude of the loading.

In the Illinois overload and underload experiments the total work done by all subjects was comparable since the resistance imposed and the duration of the effort were varied in inverse relation one to the other (Table 2). The independent variable was the rate of working or the power developed by the contracting muscles. Although the total work done in lifting a light load 1,000 times might not exceed significantly that done in lifting a heavy load 250 times, the amount of work done per unit time is vastly different. Thus the conditions of the Illinois experiments were set to permit direct appraisal of the efficacy of the overload principle.

A small group of experiments was also devised to assess the validity of the reduction, for clinical purposes, of the total amount of exercise performed per diem. These experiments are also described in Table 2.

TABLE 2

Design of the Illinois Experiments

Constants: Same as those in Table 1.

Illinois Overload Procedure: Same as MCV with the following exceptions—

1. Train daily, 5 days per week. (M.T.W. T.F.).
2. Train only on one side, right or left (R/L).
3. Overload to the maximum (i.e., 25 R.M.).

Illinois Underload Procedure:

1. Exactly like the above except that one subject carried 1/2 the 25 R.M. twice the number of times (500 contractions divided into 20 bouts).
2. Two subjects carried 1/4 the 25 R.M. four times as frequently as in the standard

procedure (1,000 contractions daily divided into 40 repetitive bouts).

Ergographic Equivalents of Modified DeLorme Procedures:

1. Two subjects carried the 25 R.M. for 3 bouts daily instead of 10 (75 contractions instead of 250).
2. Two subjects performed 3 bouts daily instead of 10, but carried 50 per cent of the 25 R.M. on the first bout, 75 per cent on the second bout, and the full 25 R.M. only on the last bout.
3. One subject reversed the above procedure. This is the so-called Oxford Technique. The number of bouts is limited to 3 but the full 25 R.M. is carried on the first bout, 75 per cent on the second, and 50 per cent on the third.
4. One subject trained strictly in accord with Zinovieff's original Oxford Technique. Ten bouts were performed daily, beginning with the 25 R.M. and reducing the load by 1/8 kg with each bout. After each daily workout, the subject was given a brief rest pause and then attempted to upgrade the 25 R.M. Thus the starting load was pushed *daily* to higher and higher levels.

Results and Their Interpretation

The scope and extent of the experimental data are summarized in Table 3.

Training by the limit day procedure

The work done per bout in the limit day procedure may be computed and graphed against load. This is known as the *curve of work* (Fig. 1-A). The optimum load is that resistance at which most work is done. Any resistance less than this falls in the underload zone; that greater than the optimum falls in the overload zone. Thus overload is a relative term with a fixed minimal connotation but a variable terminal value.

Overload exercise need not be exhausting. The degree to which fatigue develops varies directly with the magnitude of the stress imposed over and above optimum. The extent of contraction also varies. The greater

TABLE 3

Summary of Experimental Data*

Type of Training	Wrist Movement	R/L Side	No. of Subjects	No. Days Training	No. Training Days per Week	No. of Experiments
MCV Experiments						
1. Limit Day	Ext	R & L	6	15	5	180
2. Overload	Flex	R & L	4	20	3	160
3. Underload	Flex	R & L	3	20	3	120
ILL. Experiments						
1. Overload	Flex	R/L	4	10	5	40
2. Underload	Flex	R/L	3	10	5	30
3. Short Methods	Ext	R/L	5	15	5	75
4. Oxford Technique	Ext	R	1	15	5	15

* The early experiments were performed in the Division of Clinical Research, Baruch Center of Physical Medicine and Rehabilitation, Medical College of Virginia. Luz Maria Lopetegui and Anna Scott Hoye rendered invaluable assistance. The electromyographic equipment was made available through a grant from the Pope Foundation. The technical assistance of Miriam J. Partridge, Ted Y. Okita, and Dr. C. Etta Walters is gratefully acknowledged.

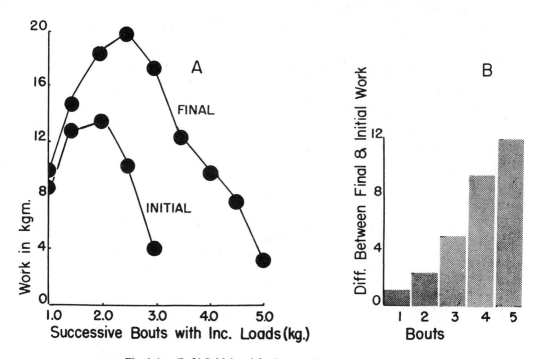

Fig. 1-A. (Left) Initial and final curve of work of one subject training by the limit day procedure.

Fig. 1-B. (Right) Column diagram illustrating the magnitude of the difference in performance on successive bouts.

the overloading the smaller the range of motion.

The influence of six practice periods during which one subject worked against increasing resistance until the load could no longer be lifted the requisite number of times in the prescribed rhythm is shown in the first illustration. Comparison of the initial and final curves of work (Fig. 1-A) indicates a substantial gain in strength, power, and endurance. However, when the absolute difference in initial and final performance on each successive bout is graphed as a column diagram (Fig. 1-B) it may be seen that whereas improvement was comparatively small in the underload bouts, it was larger when the resistance was optimal, and

strikingly sharp when the stress imposed exceeded that which could be overcome easily. This fundamentally important point is illustrated in another way in Fig. 2. Improvement is now expressed in relative terms to make all observations comparable. Here we see the efficacy of overload training simply and clearly demonstrated.

When the limit day procedure is used as a training device a substantial proportion of the total exercise period is wasted in preparatory contractions which may or may not be needed for "warming up" purposes. One-half to two-thirds of the contractions performed require less than maximal tension. It is not surprising, therefore, to find that 3 weeks of training by the

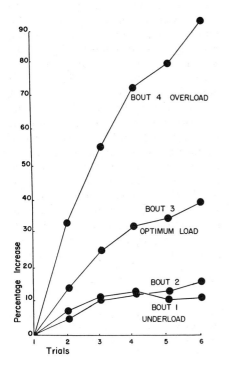

Fig. 2. Training curves for each individual limit day bout.

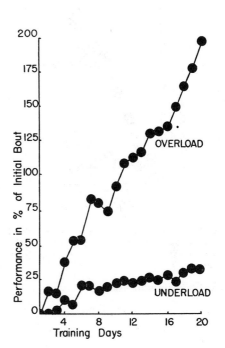

Fig. 3. Mean training curves of two groups of subjects performing the same number of contractions per diem under different conditions of loading.

limit day procedure led to only a modest improvement in performance (67.07 per cent).

> *Comparison of the influence of overloading and underloading when duration of exercises is constant*

Two hundred fifty contractions per diem three times a week for 8 weeks failed to increase strength more than minimally when the resistance against which tension was developed fell in the underload zone (Fig. 3). The same number of contractions performed against moderate overloading resulted in a dramatic gain in functional capacity (Fig. 3). The tension developed was sufficient at all times to maintain almost full range of motion. Fatigue, therefore, was minimal.

The slope gradient of the training curve rose sharply. The mean gain performance was 188.75 per cent on the right and 208.20 per cent on the left. This is far superior to training by the limit day procedure. It is also well over three times greater than that demonstrated by McMorris' and Elkins' normal subjects who performed a shortened version of the DeLorme or Oxford techniques once daily 5 days a week for 12 weeks. Indeed, the progress made by our subjects training in underload closely parallels that of McMorris' and Elkins', albeit on a lower level, when the two are graphed on the same time scale. The Mayo Clinic subjects contracted only 40 times per diem, and of these, only 10

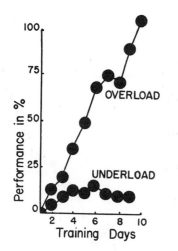

Fig. 4. Mean training curves of two groups of subjects performing equivalent total work. The duration of the effort varied inversely with the load.

the total demand on the neuromuscular system was 5 min of maximal effort per diem against maximal resistance. At the end of the practice session the muscle group primarily involved was invariably tense, painful, and swollen. Approximately 1 hr elapsed before the swelling and discomfort subsided. Recovery was always complete in 24 hr. An incapacitating degree of muscle soreness never developed. This brief intense exercise (250 contractions in 10 bouts) against maximal resistance, repeated daily for 2 weeks, yeilded remarkable increases in functional capacity (Fig. 4). One well-developed highly trained subject gained 161 per cent in ten practice sessions.

contractions were performed against maximal resistance.

Comparison of the influence of overloading and underloading when the duration of exercise is related inversely to the resistance imposed

The Illinois overload and underload experiments differed from the MCV series in two ways. First, by adjusting the variables of load and duration inversely in relation to an intraindividual criterion of functional capacity (the 25 R.M.), the total amount of work done per diem was held constant. Second, the overload resistance was upgraded to the maximal which could be overcome in 25 repetitions and it was maintained persistently at that level. Performance therefore approached complete exhaustion at the termination of the 10-bout practice sessions. The objective was to push overloading to the highest level tolerated without the development of adverse symptoms.

Since it required only 30 sec to execute each bout of 25 repetitive contractions,

Fig. 5. The influence of variations in the frequency of practice and the degree of overloading on the slope gradient of the training curve.

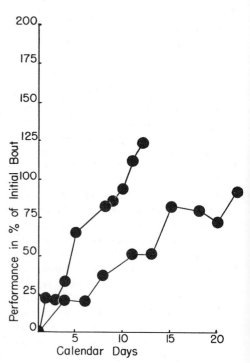

The slope gradient of the mean training curve is practically identical with that of the first overload experiment (Fig. 3). However, since as much was gained in 12 days in the Illinois experiments as in 22 days in the MCV experiments the gradient of improvement was significantly greater in the former. This may be demonstrated by graphing work output against time instead of training days (Fig. 5). There is no way of discerning from the evidence at hand whether training was accelerated in the Illinois experiments because of the greater frequency of practice, the greater degree of overloading, or both.

When the resistance was reduced to one-half 25 R.M. and the duration of exercise was doubled (500 contractions in 20 bouts), the gain in performance was negligible (9.88 per cent). When the resistance was dropped to one-quarter 25 R.M. and exercise time was quadrupled (20 min) there was little change in work output (Fig. 4). One thousand repetitive contractions per diem (40 bouts) had virtually no effect on muscle strength. The slight increase in functional capacity with training was due to the extensive mobilization of the wrist joint. This increased the range of motion and hence the height to which the assigned load could be lifted. Thus performance was augmented for physical reasons, since work

Fig. 6-A. Typical ergograms of one subject performing 10 bouts of repetitive exercise in overload (25 R.M.).

Fig. 6-B. First and last 5 ergograms of one subject performing 40 bouts of repetitive exercise in underload (1/4 25 R.M.).

Fig. 6-C. Numerical data for the underload experiment demonstrating that there is no evidence of fatigue in the course of 1,000 repetitive contractions.

Fig. 6-D. Numerical data confirming decrement in performance during overload exercise illustrated in Fig. 6-A.

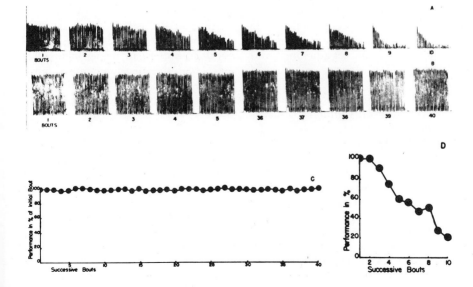

is the product of the load and the distance through which it has moved, rather than change in the contractile mechanism per se.

One subject was eliminated from the Illinois overload training curve because of persistent inability to gauge total capacity and distribute strength potential over the number of contractions assigned per diem (250). There was minimal evidence of fatigue for three or four successive bouts, after which the load selected could not be raised through full range for more than a few strokes per bout. The ability to develop tension then dropped precipitously. The ergograms of the terminal bouts were erratic and feeble in spite of exhortation to supreme effort. Although the subject continued to contract isometrically until the full 250 lifts had been attempted, performance improved only 56 per cent in 3 weeks of diligent training. This suggests that overloading which is so extreme that the extent of shortening is curtailed is less effective than training with lesser degrees of stress.

In 1944 Eccles presented evidence indicating that disuse atrophy is best counteracted by allowing muscles to shorten during their contraction. He considered both range of motion and the alternation of lengthening and shortening which occur in natural movements to be important. In an earlier work[11] he had pointed out that a few powerful voluntary contractions per day would probably be sufficient to prevent any large disuse or immobilization atrophy. Whether there is a limit beyond which the number and/or extent of contractions cannot be reduced without jeopardizing the success of the treatment is a question which remains yet to be answered. Another point frequently overlooked is whether powerful voluntary contraction is possible through

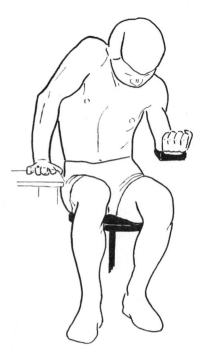

Fig. 7. Line drawing of one of a series of photographs taken during wrist flexion against maximal resistance, illustrating involuntary changes in the alignment of the head, neck, shoulder girdle, vertebral column, and non-participating extremities.

exercise of the will if no resistance to movement is provided. The Illinois overload-underload experiments suggest that the development of maximal tension is absolutely dependent on the imposition of maximal resistance.

Typical overload and underload ergograms are presented (Figs. 6-A and 6-B). It is remarkable that attention can be mobilized so effectively that 1,000 repetitive contractions could be performed in a single practice session without any sign of fatigue (Fig. 6-C). In contrast the decadence in performance was profound when the stress imposed approximated the maximum which could be tolerated under

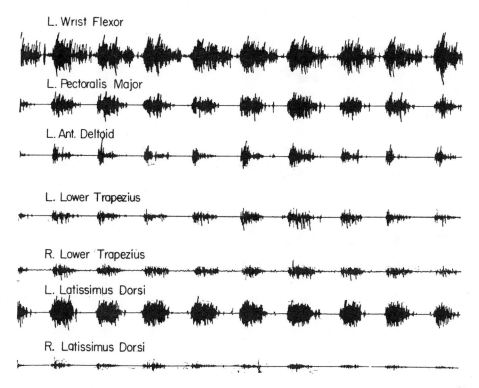

Fig. 8. Electromyograms illustrating the degree of reflex activity evoked by repetitive volitional flexion of the left wrist against heavy resistance.

the conditions of the overload experiments (Fig. 6-D). Fatigue of this magnitude is indicative of maximum exertion. It cannot be simulated by the malingerer. It never occurs in underload exercise. In our experience it is a reliable indicator of the type of performance needed to augment the ability to develop and sustain high levels of tension.

Maximal contraction against maximal resistance is accompanied by overt changes in the positioning of parts of the body far removed from the exercising appendage (Fig. 7). Lesser variations in muscle tension may be recorded electromyographically (Fig. 8). They are never haphazard. On the contrary, the responses elicited reflexly

appear to be definitely patterned and highly repeatable. We have described elsewhere[15] the influence on the positioning of the head of the proprioceptive barrage emanating from the limbs during heavy-resistance exercise in man. The tonic neck reflexes thus secondarily elicited facilitate to a high degree, augmenting the functional capacity of the limb musculature. No such neuromuscular irradiation accompanies underload exercise. Devoid of significant feedback stimulation during such activity the central nervous system appears to be incapable of increasing the flow of impulses descending from the motor cortex sufficiently to develop maximum tension.

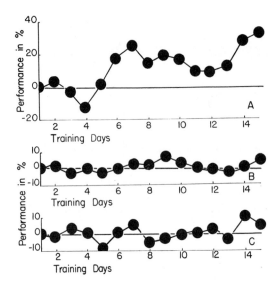

Fig. 9-A. Mean training curve of two subjects carrying the 25 R.M. for three successive bouts per practice session.

Fig. 9-B. Mean training curve of two subjects performing three successive bouts per practice session carrying $\frac{1}{2}$, $\frac{3}{4}$, and the full 25 R.M.

Fig. 9-C. Training curve of one subject performing three successive bouts per practice session carrying 100 per cent, 75 per cent, and 50 per cent of the 25 R.M.

Assessing the validity of currently popular techniques of applying heavy resistance exercise for the development of strength

Simple reduction of overload exercise to 3 instead of 10 bouts was associated with a mean increase in performance of 33.35 per cent in 15 training days (Fig. 9-A). This value falls far short of the gains recorded by the subjects who pushed performance to 10 full bouts, carrying the 25 R.M. throughout the exercise period (Fig. 4).

Simulation of the DeLorme-Watkins short method by adjusting the ergographic load to 50, 75, and 100 per cent of the 25-RM had virtually no effect on performance (Fig. 9-B). Reversal of this procedure, the so-called "Oxford Technique," likewise produced negligible changes in functional capacity (Fig. 9-C).

In our hands a downgrading of the severity of the ergographic work assignment by an amount equivalent to that introduced clinically by De-Lorme and Watkins did not prove superior to the more protracted ex-

ercise. Indeed, our evidence suggests that the living machine operates under such wide margins of safety that it is difficult to deplete hidden reserves of power in short periods of exercise consisting of small numbers of contractions. Thus stress is never introduced. A controlled experiment could be designed which would present direct evidence on this point under routine clinical conditions. It would seem important that this be done before physical therapists adopt the shortcut method as the preferred technique.

The Oxford Technique embraces two modifications of DeLorme's original procedure, one of which appears to have been generally overlooked. As previously described, the heaviest load is introduced at the onset of the practice session and is then reduced systematically to offset such fatigue as might develop. Having performed the work assignment the patient attempts to increase his 10 R.M. by a constant increment daily. If the patient is successful, the new 10 R.M. is used as the starting resistance

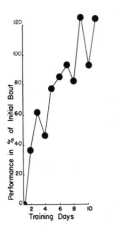

Fig. 10. Training curve of one subject exercising in accord with Zinovieff's "Oxford Technique."

for the next day's exercise session which consists of 100 lifts in 10 successive bouts. This is a vastly different procedure from the one with which the term "Oxford Technique" is usually associated. It is highly probable that the daily building up of maximal resistance might keep the degree of overloading pitched to a sufficiently high level to nullify the influence of decreasing the load in order to prevent the development of stress. The two modifications in procedure introduced by Zinovieff are therefore physiologically antithetic. Thus the Oxford Technique should be neither better nor less effective than the original DeLorme procedure.

One subject exercised strictly in accord with the recommendations of Zinovieff. The ergographic equivalent of this procedure is described in Table 2. Improvement in performance was prompt and dramatic (Fig. 10). It had reached 124.61 per cent by the ninth day of training. Beyond that point the daily increase in the 25 R.M. made the exercise so severe that total work

output began to decline. The experiment was terminated on the eleventh day at which time the number of kilogram-meters of work done in 250 repetitive contractions exceeded initial performance by 123.36 per cent.

Comment

Siebert demonstrated in animal experiments that the mere repetition of prevailing performance does not lead to the hypertrophy of skeletal muscles. Hypertrophy appears only when the rate of working is increased. Power is the decisive factor, not the total amount of work done.

Christensen found that the limits of adaptation of the heart in man can be extended only by continually increasing the intensity of the work, not by the performance of work of uniform intensity throughout the period of training. Stress apparently releases compensatory mechanisms which augment the functional capacity of any organ system.

Little has been said thus far about the nature of the changes occurring in the machinery of the human body by virtue of which the ability to perform work is enhanced. The rapidity with which overload stress increases the capacity for severe exercise suggests that this must be due in large measure to changes in the central nervous system related to motor learning. It cannot be due, initially at any rate, to alterations in anatomical structure.

Almost no attention has been directed at differentiating the functional from the morphological concomitants of therapeutic exercise. It is of signal importance to appreciate that the performance of purposive movements is a neuromuscular act, and that of the two components, the one concerned with the evoking of appropriate volitional impulses must be primary. Too much attention has been focused on the contractile tissue and not enough on the mechanisms which drive the skeletal musculature.

When muscle is required to perform heavy work for a protracted interval of time it increases in volume. Although the cause of this change has not yet been proven unequivocally, it is generally conceded to be due to the hypertrophy of existent fibers rather than an increase in their number (Adams *et al.*). Strength and endurance augment proportionally with physiologic hypertrophy, but these qualities of performance depend also on changes evolving concurrently in the central nervous system.

Proprioceptive excitation and inhibition modulate the innervation of muscle autonomously. Granit in particular has emphasized the reflex self-regulation of muscle contraction. Autogenetic inhibition serves as a "governor" of the innervation and protects the muscle against the development of traumatizing degrees of tension. Inhibition of central origin provides another line of defense. Thus voluntary contraction is essentially self-limiting, at least in the normal adult working under the conditions operating in the experiments herein reported. The imposistion of heavy resistance apparently functions as a braking device which activates servomechanisms that keep performance within the tolerance limits of the contractile tissues. The evidence suggests that normal muscle cannot be harmed by volitional effort when range of motion and cadence are controlled. In our experience overloading per se is incapable of damage to the integrity of the normal muscle fiber, when the stress imposed consists of increases in resistance, which must be overcome volitionally.

Summary and Conclusions

The end results of many orthopedic procedures are affected significantly by measures introduced postoperatively to prevent or alleviate disuse atrophy of skeletal muscles. To elucidate the mechanisms of muscle training in man 620 experiments were performed on 17 normal adult subjects. The evidence presented supports the following conclusions: *First,* strength and endurance increase when repetitive exercise is performed against heavy resistance. *Second,* the slope gradient of the training curve varies with the magnitude of the stress imposed, the frequency of the practice sessions, and the duration of the overload effort. *Third,* mere repetition of contractions which place no stress on the neuromuscular system has little effect on the functional capacity of the skeletal muscles. *Fourth,* the amount of work done per unit time is the critical variable on which extension of the limits of performance depends. *Fifth,* the speed with which functional capacity increases suggests that central nervous system changes contribute an important component to training. *Sixth,* the ability to develop maximal tension appears to be dependent on the proprioceptive facilitation with which overloading is associated. *Seventh,* no evidence was forthcoming in support of the validity of currently popular techniques of administering progressive resistance exercise clinically.

References

1. Adams, R. D., D. Denny-Brown, and C. M. Pearson, *Diseases of Muscle. A Study in Pathology.* New York: Paul B. Hoeber, Inc. (Med. Book Div. of Harper & Row, Publishers), 1953, pp. 208–10.

2. Christensen, E. Hohwu, "Minute Volume and Stroke Volume of the Heart During Severe Muscular Work," *Arbeitsphysiol.*, **4** (1931), 470-502.

3. Cuthbertson, D. P., "The Influence of Prolonged Muscular Rest on Metabolism," *Biochem. J.*, **23** (1929), 1328–45.

4. Cuthbertson, D. P., "Observations on the Distrubance of Metabolism Produced by Injury to the Limbs," *Quart. J. Med.*, **25** (1932), 233–46.

5. Cuthbertson, D. P., "Certain Effects of Massage on the Metabolism of Convalescing Fracture Cases," *ibid.*, **25** (1932), 401–3.

6. Cuthbertson, D. P., "Further Observations on the Disturbance of Metabolism Caused by Injury, With Particular Reference to the Dietary Requirements of Fracture Cases," *Brit. J. Surg.*, **23** (1936), 505–20.

7. Deitrick, J. E., D. Whedon, and E. Shorr, "Effects of Immobilization Upon Various Metabolic and Physiologic Functions of Normal Men," *Am. J. Med.*, **4** (1938), 3–36.

8. DeLorme, T. L., "Restoration of Muscle Power by Heavy-Resistance Exercise Program." Physical Therapy Dept., Gardiner General Hospital, Chicago, 1950.

9. DeLorme, T. L., and A. L. Watkins, "Techniques of Progressive Resistance Exercise," *Arch. Phys. Med. Rehabil.*, **29** (1948), 263–73.

10. DeLorme, T. L., and A. L. Watkins, *Progressive Resistance Exercise. Technique and Medical Application.* New York: Appleton-Century-Crofts, 1951.

11. Eccles, J. C., "Disuse Atrophy of Skeletal Muscles," *Med. J. Australia*, **2** (1941), 160–64.

12. Eccles, J. C., "Investigations on Muscle Atrophies Arising From Disease and Tenotomy," *J. Physiol. (London)*, **103** (1944), 253–66.

13. Granit, R., "Reflex Self-Regulation of Muscle Contraction and Autogenic Inhibition," *J. Neurophysiol.*, **13** (1950), 351–72.

14. Hellebrandt, F. A., "Physical Medicine and Rehabilitation in the Prevention of Chronic Invalidism," *J. Am. Med. Assoc.*, **142** (1950), 1353–6.

15. Hellebrandt, F. A., S. J. Houtz, M. J. Partridge, and C. E. Walters, "Tonic Neck Reflexes in Heavy-Resistance Exercise in Man," *Federation Proc.*

16. Hellebrandt, F. A., H. V. Skowlund, and L. E. A. Kelso, "New Devices for Disability Evaluation. I. Hand, Wrist, Radioulnar, Elbow, and Shoulder Ergographs," *Arch. Phys. Med. Rehabil.*, **29** (1948), 21–28.

17. Houtz, S. J., A. M. Parrish, and F. A. Hellebrandt, "The Influence of Heavy-Resistance Exercise on Strength," *Physiotherap. Rev.*, **26** (1946), 299–304.

18. Howard, J. E., W. Parsons, K. E. Stein, H. Eisenberg, and V. Reidt, "Studies on Fracture Convalescence. I. Nitrogen Metabolism After Fracture and Skeletal Operations in Healthy Males," *Bull. Johns Hopkins Hosp.*, **75** (1944), 156–68.

19. Howard, J. E., J. Winternitz, W.

Parson, R. S. Bigham, Jr., and H. Eisenberg, "Studies on Fracture Convalescence. II. The Influence of Diet and Post-Traumatic Nitrogen Deficit Exhibited by Fracture Patients," *ibid.*, **75** (1944), 209–24.

20. Kabat, H., "Sutdies on Neuromuscular Dysfunction. XI. New Principles of Neuromuscular Reeducation," *Perm. Found. Med. Bull.*, **5** (1947), 111–23; "XIII. New Concepts and Techniques of Neuromuscular Reeducation for Paralysis," *ibid.*, **8** (1950), 121–43.

21. Keys, A., "Deconditioning and Reconditioning in Convalescence," *Surg. Clin. North Am.* (1945), 442–54.

22. McMorris, R. O., and E. C. Elkins, "A Study of Production and Evaluation of Muscular Hypertrophy," *Arch. Phys. Med. Rehabil.*, **35** (1954), 420–26.

23. Siebert, W. W., "Investigation on Hypertrophy of the Skeletal Muscles," *Z. klin. Med.*, **109** (1928), 350–59.

24. Snyder, J., and P. Knauth, "The Tip That Led Bannister to Victory," *Sports Illustrated*, **1** (1954), 6–9.

25. Stevenson, F. H., "The Osteoporosis of Immobilization in Recumbency," *J. Bone Joint Surg.*, **34-B** (1952), 256–65.

27. Taylor, H. H., A. Henschel, J. Brozek, and A. Keys, "The Effect of Bed Rest on the Blood Volume of Normal Young Men," *J. Appl. Physiol.*, **2** (1949), 227–32.

28. Vail, E. M., "The Influence of Exercise on Nitrogen Metabolism Following Severe Trauma in Adult Male Patients." Unpublished Master's thesis, Medical College of Virginia, Richmond, Va., 1952.

29. Whedon, G. D., J. E. Deitrick, and E. Shorr, "Modification of the Effects of Immobilization Upon Metabolic and Physiologic Functions of Normal Men by the Use of an Oscillating Bed," *Am. J. Med.*, **6** (1949), 684–711.

30. Zinovieff, A. N., "Heavy-Resistance Exercises. The 'Oxford Technique,'" *Brit. J. Phys. Med.*, **14** (1951). 129–32.

Motor Learning and Motor Performance

For decades teachers, athletic coaches, and other observers of motor performance have held, for the most part, that motor skill is a general trait. This misconception was based upon the observation that some persons seemed to perform well at a wide variety of physical activities whereas others seemed hopelessly inadequate at anything they tried. Moreover, there was a tendency to categorize people and label them "all-around athletes" or "motor morons." In the 1920's and 1930's the expression *general motor ability* was frequently used to describe the degree to which one was "generally" skilled. It was suggested that the discovery of a suitable method for measuring "G.M.A." would benefit physical education programs in many ways, including the homogeneous classification of students and the assessment of curriculum outcomes. Consequently, it is not surprising to find that initially investigators paid more attention to definition and measurement than to the identification of the mechanisms that underlie motor skill.

Early studies[1] were heavily influenced by the developments in mental tests designed to measure the trait "intelligence" which was held to be largely innate. If intelligence could be measured through the use of unfamiliar mental tasks, why not predict motor ability in a similar way, using a variety of unfamiliar *physical* tasks? Research in this direction raised a number of questions. Was it of interest to measure (*a*) present motor status (usually called general motor ability), and if so, was this simply a reflection of present sports skill or something fundamental to all motor skills; (*b*) to determine the rate at which new motor skills could be learned (so-called motor learning ability or motor educability); or (*c*) to ascertain the ultimate development of motor skill (general motor capacity)?

---

[1] D. K. Brace, *Measuring Motor Ability* (New York: A. S. Barnes & Co., 1927).

The development of operational definitions for the constructs "ability," "educability," and "capacity" led to the construction of a variety of tests, some of which showed promise. However, subsequent work revealed a complexity of great magnitude. The intercorrelation of test items and the correlation of tests scores with various criteria soon disclosed that the motor skills of a given person were possessed to different degrees and acquired with unequal facility. The adjective "general," when applied to motor ability, thus came under suspicion.

Influenced by contemporary developments in mental testing, considerable factor analytic work in the 1930's[2] and 1940's[3] led to the development of tests to measure the components of motor ability. Despite the combining of scores for each component into a "total" score, it was recognized that "general motor ability," "motor educability," and "general motor capacity" were misnomers if thought to be general qualities present or absent to some degree.

Later, there appeared several studies extending the multidimensional nature of motor characteristics to the realm of physical fitness. Also, the postwar period has seen the publication of a variety of sports skill tests which would assess present status and curricular outcomes.[4] Although several of these have achieved satisfactory reliability they invariably consume considerable time to administer and are based largely upon face value.

Despite the work to date in the definition and measurement of motor traits, further significant progress will be dependent, to a large extent, upon the discovery of the mechanisms underlying motor learning and motor performance. That motor skill is a neuromuscular phenomenon was established long ago. However, it is not clear how the nervous system controls a skilled movement. It would appear however, that what is now known about overt motor performance (e.g., the phenomenon of motor specificity) should provide a source for hypotheses regarding the mechanisms underlying the near infinite number of human movements.

Included in this chapter are papers that should illustrate the diversity of inquiry in the field of motor learning and motor performance. No attempt has been made to include studies dealing with so-called "fine" motor skill. The papers of McCloy and Brace reflect the beginning of serious study of the character and measurement of "gross" motor skill. The Harmon and Miller paper is representative of the many studies of practice patterns and massed vs. distributed learning. The relation between intellectual and motor aptitude is the subject of the Francis

———————
[2] C. H. McCloy, "An Analytical Study of the Stunt-Type Test as a Measure of Motor Educability," *Res. Quart.*, **8** (1937), 46–56.

[3] C. H. McCloy, "A Preliminary Study of Factors in Motor Educability," *Res. Quart.*, **11** (1940), 28–39.

[4] For examples, see H. H. Clarke, *Application of Measurement to Health and Physical Education* (3rd ed., Englewood Cliffs, N. J., Prentice-Hall, Inc., 1959), 528 pp. or C. E. Willgoose, *Evaluation in Health Education and Physical Education* (New York, McGraw-Hill Book Company, 1961) 478 pp.

and Rarick study. The work of Franklin Henry, among the most productive of contemporary students of motor skill, is represented by two related papers.

C. H. McCLOY

A Preliminary Study of Factors
in Motor Educability

Reprinted from the *Research Quarterly*, **11**
(1940), 28–39.

The paper by McCloy and the one following by Brace are similarly oriented. Both men were attempting to measure motor aptitude or related qualities, and by doing so provided a better understanding of the phenomenon. Both men were influenced by comparable work in mental measurement, and both were well aware of each other's work: for example, McCloy borrowed heavily from Brace to further his inquiry into the characteristics of motor educability.

In an earlier paper McCloy[1] represents an attempt to use stunt-type items to measure motor educability or "ability to learn new skills." He reasoned that to use the Brace Test for this purpose would require the elimination of items that measured strength, body size, maturity, and power. It is interesting to note that Brace himself followed a similar approach in his 1946 paper, showing that the "stunt-type skills" require different attributes than the "sports-type skills." McCloy's second paper, presented here, is an attempt to identify the components of motor educability. After reviewing the literature, he deduced 15 tentative factors in "motor educability and athletic educability." He was careful to point out that further research may show lack of independence of two or more of the factors, i.e., there may be some correlation among factors; an observation that subsequently has been verified.[2]

McCloy's call for further research has not gone unanswered. Other scientists have attempted to measure the components of "physical fitness" or some subdomain of physical fitness like "balance" or "coordination."[3]

With the frequent use of factor analysis (and the expectation of finding two or more relatively uncorrelated dimensions representing a "universe of content,") together with Henry's work in motor specificity, such terms as "motor educa-

[1] C. H. McCloy, "An Analytic Study of the Stunt-Type Test as a Measure of Motor Educability," *Res. Quart.*, **8** (1937), 46–55.

[2] For example, see Franees Z. Cumbee, "A Factor Analysis of Motor Coordination," *Res. Quart.*, **25** (1954), 412–28.

[3] *Ibid.*

bility," "general motor ability," or "general motor aptitude" are seldom seen in today's literature other than in an historical sense. However, the absence of the "generalists" must not be taken as to suggest the "specialists" have provided all the answers. On the contrary, the structure of physical performance is far from clear. A period of time comparable to that spent in the serious study of the components of abstract intelligence has yet to pass. Thus, intellectual traits, complex as they are, may prove to be of no greater complexity than motor characteristics, and perhaps less so.

McCloy brought to physical education literature technical sophistication (e.g., factor analysis, multiple and partial correlation) and a keen imagination, the likes of which were seldom seen in the 1930's. It is interesting to note, however, that he did not restrict his activities to the laboratory; he was also active in professional associations, both in promoting and applying research. His awareness of educational goals and the problems of the teacher are well known through his wide variety of nontechnical writings. His sensitivity for the problems of teaching becomes evident in the closing paragraph of his paper where he points out the implications of differential motor abilities and capacities.

For many years educators have been seeking the keys with which to unlock the problems connected with an adequate measurement of intelligence. Originally these problems were thought to be less complex than they are now known to be. For a long period of time the term *intelligence* was used as though it concerned ability only of the type usually associated with scholastic achievement. It is now known that there are many kinds of intelligence, such as abstract intelligence, concrete intelligence, social intelligence, a kind of intelligence usually called common sense, esthetic intelligence, athletic intelligence, motor intelligence, and a number of others.[20]

The earliest work in this area was associated with attempted measurements of abstract intelligence, probably because the psychologists studying this field were "book scholars," and hence most interested in abstract intelligence. Among the early important studies of this type were those of Binet, who made very significant contributions over the years 1905–11. These were later refined in the Stanford Revision of the Binet test, first in 1916 and later in 1937. These tests are important for the consideration of the physical educator because of the fact that they developed the method of measuring intelligence or mental age by the number of objective test items passed. These, with the exception of a test of vocabulary, were almost all *pass* or *fail* items. The subject in each case succeeded in passing a test, or he did not. This type of test set the method for investigating motor intelligence a number of years later.[4]

In 1917 Pintner and Paterson[26] published a performance test, which was the first of the nonverbal tests, again being composed of test items or stunts, as it were, which were passed or failed. The advent of America's entrance into World War I added impetus to the mental testing program and produced a nonverbal abstract intelligence test, which was used with illiterates and foreigners—the so-called *Army Beta Test.*

In 1927 Spearman[32] proposed a method of statistical analysis of test items in which he believed it possible to divide tests into two kinds of factors or components. The first kind was a factor common to all of the variables, which he called a general factor. He postulated that all other factors were specific to each variable. This theory was soon found to be untenable for many test batteries as it was found that there were numerous common or group factors in addition to the specific factors. In 1931 Thurstone proposed a method of analyzing for multiple factors. This method has later been refined and published in his *Vectors of Mind*.[33] Others have presented similar methods of analysis, but we shall utilize only the Thurstone method in this presentation.

By means of this method of multiple factors Thurstone has recently[34] made notable strides in the analysis of abstract intelligence in which he progresses from the attempt to get one general average measurement of this kind of intelligence to a measurement of various factors or components of intelligence. Thurstone finds 12 factors in abstract intelligence[1] of which he has been able to identify only 9, and only 7 of the 9 are readily measurable at the present time. The nine are (1) number facility, (2) word fluency, (3) visualization of spatial relationships, (4) memory, (5) perceptual speed, (6) induction, (7) deduction, (8) verbal reasoning, and (9) restrictive thinking. These methods of study are all applicable to the study of motor intelligence and are presented here primarily as historical background.

The earlier theories of intelligence tended to assume that abstract intelligence was an innate, hereditarily determined quality which could not change appreciably during life. More recent studies, particularly those by Skeels[30] and Wellman,[36] have indicated that abstract intelligence can be markedly developed or retarded by the

___
[1] Personal communication.

presence or absence of relevant environmental stimuli. McGraw[22] has shown that this is also true for infants in the field of motor development.

Progress in Motor Educability

This progress in the field of abstract intelligence has been intriguing to the physical educator and leads us to make inquiry as to whether comparable progress cannot be made in the various fields of motor intelligence.

In writings and discussions of this problem, the author has chosen to use the term *motor educability*. Intelligence, as such, may be defined as the ability to learn or to adapt oneself to his environment in such a way as to accumulate what we think of as an education. Hence we shall use the term *motor educability* to indicate this type of motor intelligence, and *athletic educability* to indicate the type of educability characterized by what might be called the "smart player" as contrasted with that inept individual who has a perfect genius for doing the wrong thing.

In his study of general motor ability, Brace[4] produced the first important test in the field of motor educability. McCloy[16] attempted to refine the Brace test by removing most of the test variables which had to do only with motor ability, particularly strength, and by adding others which seemed more directly related to motor educability. Johnson[13] added the test which is perhaps the best test of general motor educability we have today, which test was validated in the field of motor educability by Koob.[14] The present author, using Thurstone's method of analyzing for multiple factors, has in the last few years attempted to analyze many of these test variables and has attempted to discover as many as possible of the primary factors in motor and athletic educability. These studies have been conducted in a number of ways: (a) Stunts and test variables of the Brace type and the Johnson type, and various games skills have been analyzed by the method of factor analysis. (b) A number of simple test elements have been studied by correlating them with relatively valid criteria of general motor excellence in which factors of strength and speed have been held constant. (c) A number of elements have been adopted from the studies of others, as in Griffith's studies[10, 11] of peripheral vision, where such a factor has been clearly demonstrated.[4] A few are suggested which are at present not thoroughly confirmed by objective studies but which seem to the author to be confirmed by experience and by other logical considerations. These are in every case indicated by reference 19.

The factor analysis studies, especially those of the Brace type of stunts, have been far too extensive to report here in detail. Hence, after briefly discussing the techniques used, we shall simply report the results.

Factor Analysis Studies

At this point we shall first discuss these various kinds of studies in somewhat greater detail, and later present the results of all the studies in as logical an order as possible.

I. Factor studies[2, 5, 7, 17, 23, 40, 41]

The factor analysis frequently enables the student to determine the primary factors or components of which a given battery of tests may be composed.[33] Obviously, the results are limited by the test variables analyzed; that is, if some factor which may be present in certain tests of motor educability happens to be absent in the battery of tests analyzed, this factor, of course, will not appear; nor will it appear if present in only one of the tests analyzed: it must be present in at least two variables.

Factors are, in general, uncorrelated. This assumption can usually be validly made for the factors obtained in one factor analysis. Occasionally certain compound or mixed test factors appear as single (oblique) factors, just as in certain chemical combinations the OH radical behaves like a single atom with a valence of one. Such compound factors may be broken down into their elements if proper precautions are taken. "Factors" obtained in one study, however, may possibly be correlated with factors of slightly different constitution obtained from another study.

Factor studies of continuous test variables, as those found in the Johnson test,[13] are usually much more reliable than those of the stunt, or pass-or-fail, type. This particular kind of variable (the Johnson type), however, is limited in content, and usually not more than two factors of educability appear.[5]

The Brace or stunt type[4, 12, 16] of test variable cannot be analyzed as adequately by this technique. The reliabilities of this type of test element are relatively low, and since they are usually intercorrelated by the tetrachloric method of correlation, the results are not quite comparable to the product moment correlations ordinarily used with the other variables, and the probable errors are larger. Hence the sampling errors will increase, and the results will be less consistent. For research purposes, usually the better procedure is to select stunts that are similar and to combine the scores of several of these, rather than to depend upon the success or failure of one trial in a single stunt. In the factor studies of this type presented here, it has been found rather difficult to interpret some of the results because of this inconsistency, but since we obtained practically the same results in five different studies of the same type,[17] we feel that we are justified in naming certain factors with relative confidence.

II. Test factors based upon correlations with other criteria[1, 3, 4, 12, 14, 15, 24, 27, 28]

These studies have largely been based upon the following types of criteria:

A. Correlations with ratings by competent judges of motor educability or of athletic educability.

B. Correlations of ratings of general motor ability with variables commonly recognized as being associated with motor educability.

C. Studies of speed of learning. In this type of study the existence of a factor as such must be inferred from a logical, but subjective analysis of the correlated variable. Frequently, however, there has been some substantiating evidence from factor analyses.

III. Factors inferred from the studies of others[6, 8, 10, 11, 27, 28, 34]

Some of these are studies in which the nature of the existence of the factor is established by the nature of the variable, as in the studies of peripheral vision. Others will be cited below.

IV. Factors inferred largely form subjective evidence but not as yet supported by objective experimentation[19]

We shall now list what we believe to have been found in this series of studies, discussing each under its own heading.

Prerequisites to Effective Learning

In connection with the various studies, especially with those involving the factor analysis, a number of factors and other items stand out which, while not factors of motor educability as such, might be termed prerequisites to effective learning. These will be listed below with brief comment.

1. *Muscular strength.*[7, 12, 17, 21, 23, 41] This stands out in almost all factor analyses of motor variables, and we believe that it is difficult for an individual who does not possess an adequate amount of muscular strength (at least a desirable minimum standard) to learn at an optimum rate. Several studies seem to indicate that strength of arms is especially important.[21]

2. *Dynamic energy.*[7, 17] This has appeared in four of six factor studies of the stunt variety. What is meant by the term is that physical constitution or muscular energy which is characterized by the ability to throw oneself into a performance with full vigor. This does not seem to be particularly correlated with strength as such.

3. *Ability to change direction.*[9, 29, 41] In one study, particularly 41, it has been shown that there is such a thing as a factor of *change of direction* which is relatively independent of the strength and speed factors.

4. *Flexibility.*[7] The ability to learn some types of activities, such as certain tumbling stunts, etc., is dependent upon flexibility of muscles, joints, and ligaments.

5. *Agility.*[7, 9, 12, 17, 29] This is the ability to move the body rapidly from one position in space to another, involving quick changes of direction. This element probably has much in common with the factor *change of direction* mentioned above in 3.

6. *Peripheral vision.*[10, 11] This has been proved by Griffith to be a potent factor in certain types of athletic ability.

7. *Good vision.*[19]

8. *Concentration.*[10, 11, 19] The ability to keep the mind on the game and, literally and metaphorically speaking, the eye on the ball.

9. *Understanding of the mechanics of the techniques of the activities.*[6]

10. *Absence of disturbing or inhibiting*

emotional complications. (Such as fear of water in learning to swim.)

Definite Factors in Motor Educability

The following are proposed as definite *factors* in motor and athletic educability. Not all of them are uncorrelated each with the other. Some are probably intercorrelated, and some of these are probably partially synonymous with slightly different factors found in other studies of the same abilities. Since they have come from different studies, however, and in these different researches seem to show slightly different characteristics, we have listed them for the sake of completeness, hoping that further studies of the specific items will determine their relatedness or independence.

1. *Insight into the nature of the skill.*[6,7,12,17] This insight may be of different types. In one study[6] it was obviously an understanding of the mechanics of the techniques of the activity. In others[7,12,17] it seemed to be primarily just "catching on to" the nature of the activity in such a way as to learn it more quickly. This may also be related to the item listed under 13c below.

2. *Ability to visualize spatial relationships.* In these studies we have used Thurstone's paper and pencil tests for this ability, and the two studies made show the following results. In one study[24] these test results correlated 0.778 with football coaches' ratings of the athletic "smartness" of their players. These ratings were made on a five-point scale, which varied from "almost always does the smart thing" to "almost always does the dumb thing." When these test results were combined with a knowledge of the strategy of the game (a multiple choice questionnaire), a multiple correlation of 0.898 was obtained.

The second study[1] was a correlation of this ability to visualize spatial rela-

tions, measured by the same tests, with ratings of two types: (*a*) Judgments by the instructors of the sports abilities of high school girls; in this case, *r* equals 0.510. (*b*) Ratings of the athletic intelligence of high school girls in sports in general; *r* equals 0.522. Incidentally, this same quality of visualizing spatial relations correlated 0.342 with the Iowa Revision of the Brace test,[16] and 0.527 with the Johnson test.[13] It seems to be an extremely important factor in the field of motor and athletic educability.

3. *The ability to make quick and adaptive decisions.* This might be thought of as psychomotor response speed. In one study[1] a test was devised which required the subject to respond as rapidly as possible to a quickly changing series of events. The correlation with general motor sports ability of high school girls was 0.527, and with athletic educability or smartness, 0.367. A similar test has been devised by Seashore[28] but has not been studied from this point of view. Griffith (C.R.)[2] reported similar results with a more ambitious test.

4. *Sensory motor coordination I.* This is the coordination of eye with head, hand, or foot, and is particularly seen in relation to the heading, catching, striking, or kicking of balls. It has been found in one factor analysis,[40] and in another study[28] it has been shown to be correlated with motor ability. Wendler found a correlation of this factor with the sum of several baseball test scores of 0.67, with fielding flies in baseball 0.58, with catching a soccer ball, 0.48, and with batting, 0.40.

5. *Sensory motor coordination II.* This type of sensory motor coordination is the adaptation to weight and force.[19] It is illustrated by what happens when an individual catches a tossed ball which he thinks to be a 12-lb shot but which turns out to be an indoor base-

---

[2] Personal communication.

ball, or the type of thing that happens when one lifts a suitcase that he thinks to be heavy and finds that it is empty. It is the adaptation of force to resistance or weight. This type of ability in its more refined forms probably accounts for much of the accurate response which is responsible for good form in motor performance.

6. *Judgment of the relationship of the subject to external objects (whether inanimate objects or people) in relation to the following:* (a) time,[40] (b) height, as in catching flyballs,[40] (c) distance,[2,40] and (d) direction.[19] These elements are all of the kind that are related to such activities as "leading" another individual in passing a ball, in judging flyballs or line drives in baseball, and in judging a thrown ball in batting or in catching forward passes. The evidence is not clear as to whether each of these is a factor in itself or whether they are combined in a minor Gestalt. The evidence for their being different is largely experimental; for example, many throwers of balls throw accurately, so far as direction is concerned, even in leading the receiver, but they may make mistakes in the height at which they throw the ball in their effort to make it, after being pulled downward by gravity, reach the receiver at the proper height. Others whose errors of height are negligible make errors of direction and time.

7. *Accuracy of direction and small angle of error.*[35] Voigt experimented with a light gun in which a beam of light struck a target constructed of ground glass. The place at which the target was struck by the light beam was marked by an assistant standing behind the target. It was found that the size of the error, which should increase directly with the distance from the target, did not increase this rapidly. In other words, the angle of error was reduced as the shooter stood farther away. The present author found that the same thing was true in shooting

baskets in basketball. The errors at 35 ft are not proportionately as great as are the errors at 20 ft.[18] The present author also has found that, when practicing over a season, any given individual appears to improve only to a certain point, and the degree of accuracy possible with one individual is apparently not possible with all others. Further evidence to substantiate this was offered by Oliphant.[25]

8. *General kinesthetic sensitivity and control.* This is the sort of thing that is apparently governed by muscle-joint-sensory proprioceptive mechanisms. This matter is adequately discussed in almost any of the larger physiologies. Further evidence has been brought to bear upon this particular item in connection with balance by Bass[2] [See 12d below].

9. *Ability to coordinate a complex unitary movement.*[4,8] This type of coordination is seen where an individual does a complex activity in which several parts of the body function in different ways at the same time. This type of thing ranges all the way from such party stunts as that of patting the head and rubbing the abdomen at the same time, to activities like a back somersault with a full twist and the complicated movements of the eurythmics of Dalcroze.[8] This type of activity apparently requires a different type of learning than the next one described. The Brace test type of stunt is usually of this type.[4,16]

10. *Ability to coordinate a complex series or combination of movements which follow one another in rapid succession.* This type of activity may be illustrated by such as the pole vault, the pivot and dribble in basketball, or a round off, back handspring, and back somersault in tumbling. Most of the test variables of the Johnson test[13] fall under this category.

11. *Arm control.*[7,17,19] The successful execution of many activities seems to depend upon the control of the arms.

This is illustrated by many tumbling and diving stunts, particularly those involving twister exercises, but is also illustrated by the use of the arms in jumping and balance.

12. *Factors involved in the functions of balance.* [2,7,12,17]

a) The general contribution made by the eyes to balance. Bass found that there was a vast difference in any balance exercises between doing it with the eyes opened and with the eyes closed. [2]

b) The use of the eyes in balance, where the movement involved is forward and backward, such as balancing crosswise on a narrow beam. [2] This factor may be one involving accommodation or convergence of the eyes which would imply an accuracy of discrimination in the proprioceptive sense organs in the muscles controlling the eyes.

c) The use of the eyes in balance which involves motion sidewise. [2] This is illustrated by balancing on a narrow beam running lengthwise of the feet. It may be a function of a change of the head angle in relationship to the vertical plane, or it may be related to a parallax effect. Further study is needed on this subject.

d) Kinesthetic sensitivity and control in balance. [2] This is probably the same as 8 above.

e) The balance function of the two vertical sets of semicircular canals. [2] These two sets of canals seem to function together and in forward, backward, and sidewise motion.

f) The balance function of the horizontal semicircular canals. [2] This type of sensitivity is involved largely in exercises where the head rotates in a horizontal position or in the plane of the horizontal set of canals, such as the pirouettes or spinning in the dance or skating, in balance stunts on a narrow beam running lengthwise of the foot

where the body is bent forward 90°, and in similar activities.

g) "Tension giving reinforcement." [2] Bass found a factor that was common to all balance activities when the subject was standing on a very narrow beam, which was not present when the subject was standing on the floor. She interpreted this to be the result of a heightened sensitivity of the balance mechanisms brought on by the increasing tension on the sole of the foot. This needs further confirmation.

13. *Timing.* Timing apparently involves several types of response for which eventually we should probably have more than one term.

a) The eye-motor type of timing. This is probably related to the *sensory motor coordination I* given above under 4.

b) A kind of timing that might be thought of as being characterized by a feeling for duration of time. This is illustrated by the timing of an apparatus exercise, such as the upstart on the horizontal bar where the intervals betweeen parts of the activities must be exactly timed. This may be related to motor rhythm (14*b* below).

c) The present author believes that there is a kind of timing that might be referred to as "insightful timing." This is the kind of timing in which the individual does it properly with minimum practice because he understands the activity. This may be a combination of the understanding of the mechanics of the activity (see 9 above under prerequisites), factor 1 under insight, and 13*b* under this heading.

14. *Motor rhythm.* [3,16] Blix, studying gymnastic ability, found a correlation of 0.42 between the Seashore test of motor rhythm [28] and ability to perform in apparatus work and tumbling. Others have found that there is a rhythmical element to success in the Koerth pursuit test in the Seashore

battery,[28] and Blix found a correlation of 0.41 between this ability and gymnastics.

Lemon[15] found a correlation of 0.46 between the Seashore motor rhythm test and a practical test of rhythm in dancers. This type of motor rhythm may be partly synonymous with timing (13 above), and there seem to be two types: (*a*) One may be called the "beat type" in which the individual can keep step or maintain a constant rhythm. (*b*) This is the type of motor rhythm exhibited in apparatus work (see also 13*b* above) in which the individual reacts at the rhythmical time intervals necessary to success in the performance.

15. *Sensory rhythm.*[3,15,27]   Much work has been done in this field in connection with tests of musical talent.[27] So far as applications to physical education are concerned there seem to be the following items: (*a*) A feeling for beat or regularity of interval. This would be related to 14*a* as the sensory function is related to the motor function. (*b*) What might be spoken of as a harmony of rhythmical feeling—knowing when it is right. When it is not, one feels a "rhythmical discord," as it were. (*c*) A feeling for the proper timing. This again would be related to 13*b* and 14*b* as the sensory function is related to the motor function. (*d*) A feeling for interval or duration.[27] (*e*) A feeling for stress or intensity.[27] Lemon,[15] using the Seashore tests[27] for the sense of rhythm, obtained a correlation of 0.46 with a practical rhythms test, and a multiple correlation of 0.61 between the sensory and the motor rhythm test and the practical test of rhythm (not available in Lemon's study but computed from her data).

16. *Esthetic feelings.*[19]   In physical activities, as in many other fields of art, some individuals have a greater feeling than do others for pure perfection of movement, as in the dance, in diving, in the golf swing, and in many other activities. No attempt is made to analyze this ability here. It may be a compound of a number of others, or there may be a number of subfactors. We believe it sufficiently important to be recommended for further study and analysis.

The Need for Further Research

The list of probable factors in motor educability presented here shows the need for much further research. It is presented in this preliminary form primarily to stimulate such further study. Just as the measurement of abstract intelligence has achieved its present status as the result of studies conducted over a period of 35 yr by dozens of laboratories and competent students, and is only now beginning to differentiate between specific factors of abstract intelligence, so we believe that it will take many years of careful study by research students in many of our laboratories to refine, add to, and eliminate from, this list of factors, and to learn to measure them accurately. It would seem to the author that the next steps should be, specifically:

1. To see whether some of these factors as here presented should not be further divided. It is believed that this may be true of factors 1, 2, 3, 4, 6, 8, 10, 13, 14, 15, 16.

2. To see whether some are not perhaps the same masquerading under different disguises and found in different company. This may be true of, particularly, 13, 14, 15, and of 8 and 12*d*.

3. To attempt to devise tests for each of these in its relatively pure form and to explore the possibilities that each

may make at each of the important age levels.

4. To discover which factors are related to each important type of physical education activities.

5. After this stage in the relatively pure science research in motor educability has been reached, to attempt to devise simple and successful ways to measure the more practical and important factors, and to put some of these tests into batteries. The first four of these stages will be stages of complication and detailed exploration for purposes of scientific understanding. This fifth stage is the stage of simplification —to adapt our tests for practical usage.

6. To explore the relationships of these factors of motor educability to other important life activities in industry, the professions, etc. At this stage we might well attempt to cooperate with students of engineering and other professional groups. The author feels that, if an adequate battery of tests of this type is developed, it may be possible to measure these abilities in all pupils at about the beginning of the junior high school, and on the basis of the results to advise more intelligently as to the program to be elected. To give one illustration, an individual may be badly lacking in ability to control his angle of error (factor 7) but be almost perfect in timing and motor rhythm (factors 13 and 14). Because of his inaccuracy he may never be able to play a satisfactory game of golf but because of the larger margin of error permitted, he may become exceedingly expert in badminton or tennis. Where golf might provide him with a soul-disturbing irritant for his middle age, badminton or tennis might provide him with the satisfactions that go with a thorough mastery of some skill, and the physical educator might be well advised to take such test results into account.

References

1. Anderson, Theresa, and C. H. McCloy, "The Measurement of Sports Ability in High Schools." Unpublished study.

2. Bass, Ruth I., "An Analysis of the Components of Tests of Semicircular Canal Function and of Static and Dynamic Balance," *Res. Quart.*, **10** (1939), 33–52.

3. Blix, Hamlin, "Tests for Use in the Prediction of Potential Gymnastic Ability." Unpublished Master's thesis, State University of Iowa, 1933.

4. Brace, D. K., *Measuring Motor Ability.* New York: A. S. Barnes & Co., 1927.

5. Carpenter, Aileen. Unpublished study.

6. Combs, Lex V., "A Comparison of the Efficacy of the Whole Method and of the Whole-Part-Whole Method of Teaching Track Activities." Unpublished Master's thesis, State University of Iowa, 1932.

7. Cope, Esther E., "A Study of the Component Factors of the Iowa Revision of the Brace Motor-Ability Test." Unpublished Master's thesis, State University of Iowa, 1938.

8. Cross, T. J., "A Comparison of the Whole Method, the Minor Game Method, and the Whole-Part Method of Teaching Basketball to Ninth Grade Boys," *Res. Quart.*, **8** (1937), 49–54.

9. Gates, D. D., and R. P. Sheffield, "Tests of Change of Direction as Measurements of Different Kinds of Motor Ability in Grades Seven to Nine." Unpublished thesis, State University of Iowa, 1940.

10. Griffith, C. R., *Psychology and Athletics.* New York: Charles Scribner's Sons, 1928.

11. Griffith, C. R., *Psychology of Coaching.*

New York: Charles Scribner's Sons, 1929.

12. Hill, Kenneth, "The Formulation of Tests of Motor Educability for Junior High School Boys." Unpublished thesis, State University of Iowa, 1935.

13. Johnson, G. B., "Physical Skill Tests for Sectioning Classes into Homogeneous Units," *Res. Quart.*, **3** (1932), 128–37.

14. Koob, Clarence G., "A Study of the Johnson Skills Test as a Measure of Motor Educability." Unpublished Master's thesis, State University of Iowa, 1937.

15. Lemon, Eloise, "A Study of the Relationships of Certain Measures of Rhythms Ability and Motor Ability in College Women." Unpublished Master's thesis, State University of Iowa, 1932.

16. McCloy, C. H., "An Analytical Study of the Stunt-Type Test as a Measure of Motor Educability," *Res. Quart.*, **8** (1937), 46–56.

17. McCloy, C. H., "Factor Analyses of the Stunt-Type Test Variables." Five unpublished studies.

18. McCloy, C. H. Unpublished study.

19. McCloy, C. H. This group of references is presented by the writer on logical and experiential grounds alone.

20. McCloy, C. H., and Norma D. Young, *Tests and Measurements in Health and Physical Education*. New York: Appleton-Century-Crofts, 1954.

21. McCloy, C. H., "The Apparent Importance of Arm Strength in Athletics," *Res. Quart.*, **5** (1934), 3–11.

22. McGraw, Myrtle B., *Growth—A Study of Johnny and Jimmy*. New York: Appleton-Century-Crofts, 1935.

23. Metheny, Eleanor, "Studies of the Johnson Test as a Test of Motor Educability," *Res. Quart.*, **9** (1938), 105–14.

24. Moser, Jake H., "An Attempt to Devise a Simple Method of Measuring Potential Football Intelligence." Unpublished Master's thesis, State University of Iowa, 1938.

25. Oliphant, H. A., "A Study of Improvement in Shooting Baskets as Related to the Amount of Practice." Unpublished Master's thesis, State University of Iowa, 1939.

26. Pinter, R., and D. G. Paterson, *Scale of Performance Tests*. New York: Appleton-Century-Crofts, 1917.

27. Seashore, C. E., *The Measurement of Musical Talent*. New York: G. Schirmer, Inc., 1915.

28. Seashore, R. H., "Stanford Motor Skills Unit," *Psychol. Monographs*, **30**, No. 2 (1928), 51–66.

29. Sierakowski, Frances, "A Study of Tests of Change of Direction as Measurements of Motor Ability." Unpublished Master's thesis, State University of Iowa, 1940.

30. Skeels, H. M., "Mental Development of Children in Foster Homes," *J. Consulting Psychol.*, **2** (1938), 33–43.

31. Skeels, H. M., and H. B. Dye, "A Study of the Effect of Differential Stimulation on Mentally Retarded Children," *Proceedings and Addresses, Am. Assoc. Mental Deficiency*, **44**, No. 1 (1939), 114–36.

32. Spearman, C., *The Abilities of Man*. New York: The Macmillan Company, 1927.

33. Thurstone, L. L., *The Vectors of Mind*. Chicago: University of Chicago Press, 1935.

34. Thurstone, L. L., "A New Concept of Intelligence, and a New Method of Measuring Primary Abilities," *Suppl. Educ. Record*, **17** (1936), 124–38.

35. Voigt, Günter, "Über die Richtungspräzision einer Fernhandlung," *Psychol. Forsch.*, **16**, Nos. 1 and 2. Berlin: Springer Verlag, 1932.

36. Wellman, Beth L., "Growth in Intelligence Under Differing School Environ-

ments," *J. Exptl. Educ.*, **3** (1934), 59–83.

37. Wellman, Beth L., "Mental Growth From Preschool to College," *ibid.*, **6** (1937), 127–38.

38. Wellman, Beth, L., "Our Changing Concept of Intelligence," *J. Consulting Psychol.*, **2** (1938), 97–107.

39. Wellman, Beth L., "Guiding Mental Development," *Childhood Education* (November, 1938), 108–12.

40. Wendler, A. J., "A Critical Analysis of Test Elements Used in Physical Education," *Res. Quart.*, **9** (1938), 64–76.

41. Young, Kathryn E., "An Analytic Study of the Tests of Change of Direction." Unpublished Master's thesis, State University of Iowa, 1937.

D. K. BRACE

Studies in Motor Learning of Gross Bodily Motor Skills

Reprinted from the *Research Quarterly*, **17** (1946), 242–53.

Probably the best example of the thinking of D. K. Brace can be seen in his Measuring Motor Ability, *published in 1927.[1] His 1946 paper presented here provides an opportunity to compare his work with that of McCloy. Both men seem to have been studying the same traits, yet there exist differences in opinion. For example, McCloy referred to the Brace Motor-Ability Test as being "the first important test in the field of motor educability."[2] Upon examination of McCloy's factors it is clear that he considered the Brace stunts as motor educability items, where motor educability is "the ability to learn."[3] Yet Brace, in the paper following, was concerned with the identification of traits "responsible for individual differences in ability to learn motor skills. . . ." [italics added]. In his summary of findings he states that his items proposed to measure motor learning were not good enough for predictive purposes and that the Brace Motor-Ability Test ". . . does not measure motor learning to an extent that would justify the test being classified as a test of motor educability." He concludes further that the Brace Test is slightly superior to the Iowa Revision of the Brace Test as a measure of motor learning. This had the effect of contradicting McCloy's findings*

---

[1] D. K. Brace, *Measuring Motor Ability: A Scale of Motor-Ability Tests* (New York: A. S. Barnes & Company, 1927), p. 138.

[2] See p. 000.

[3] *Loc. cit.*

if one were to accept the apparent similarity of meaning of the terms "motor learning" and "motor educability."

The confusion exemplified by the papers of McCloy and Brace is probably typical of what can be expected in the early investigation of any complex phenomenon. Hindsight suggests that in this case the confusion stemmed from (a) unclear constructs precipitated by lack of knowledge, (b) inadequate operational definitions of constructs, (c) a lack of awareness of the difficulties faced by those who would measure change over time, and (d) the failure, particularly by Brace, to appreciate fully the concept of differential motor skill or motor specificity.

The study being reported is one of a series in which the general purpose has been to try to identify traits responsible for individual differences in ability to learn motor skills involving more or less total bodily activity. The procedure followed has included selecting physical performances (called learning tests) which involve general body coordinations, securing scores on the learning tests made during a series of 90 repeated trials, computing per cent of improvement or learning, by two special methods, and correlating the amount of learning with various physical tests.

The subjects were 100 junior high school girls. Six learning tests were used of which four could be classified as of sport type, one of stunt type, and one of motor-rhythm type, as follows:

1. The Tangle. This is a stunt-type performance involving balance control and dexterity. It involves regaining the feet from a prone position with the legs crossed and feet held by opposite hands. From this position the subject must roll to the back, sit up, stand, and uncross the legs without releasing the hands. Score on the test was the number of trials required to perform the stunt correctly.

2. Rhythm test. The test involved performance of a "dance" step using arm and leg movements, devised for this purpose, and done to rhythm. The score was the number of trials required to perform the step correctly.

3. Wall volley. The test involved bouncing a volleyball against a wall, and was scored in terms of the number of consecutive bounces up to 10 that could be made on each of 30 different trials.

4. Ball bounce. This test required the subject, while standing in a 6-ft circle, to bounce a volleyball on the side of a baseball bat. The score was the number of bounces made on each of 30 trials.

5. Kick test. In this test a soccer ball was kicked, indoors, at a rectangular target on a wall 30 ft away. Thirty trials, each of which involved three kicks, were allowed.

6. Target toss. This involved tossing a basketball over a net, $8\frac{1}{2}$ ft above the floor so that the ball would fall on a target on the floor on the other side of the net. Thirty trials of three tosses each were allowed, with the score being recorded for each trial.

These tests were devised so as to sample eye-hand-foot and general bodily coordinations in movements involving gross bodily activity of a sort that had not been previously practiced specifically as such. The wall volley, ball bounce, kick, and target toss tests involve coordinations typical of sports and may be referred to as sport-type tests. The assumption is that those girls having the greatest ability to learn the sorts of motor skills involved would make most improvement. Scores on all tests were converted into standard scale scores using the *T*-scale technique.

Reliability of the four sport-type learning tests are shown in the following table.

TABLE 1

Reliability Coefficients of Learning Tests

Learning Test	First 6 trials		Total 30 trials	
	r	*P.E.*	*r*	*P.E.*
Wall Volley	0.614	0.042	0.863	0.017
Kick Test	0.227	0.064	0.519	0.049
Ball Bounce	0.504	0.050	0.805	0.024
Target Toss	0.605	0.043	0.775	0.027

Reliability of the stunt-type and rhythm-type learning tests was not established because of the nature of the tests, and must be assumed in terms of the tests themselves.

It will be noticed that the wall volley, ball bounce, and target toss tests had good reliability when computed on the basis of 30 trials but only fair reliability when computed on the basis of the first 6 trials. Because per cent of improvement involved use of scores on the first 5 trials as an initial score, results must be interpreted in light of these reliabilities. The low reliability of the kick test warranted eliminating this test in some parts of the study.

Method of Scoring Improvement

Three methods of scoring the learning taking place in the "learning tests" were used. The tangle and rhythm tests were of such a nature that the only score that could be used was the number of trials required to perform the test correctly. Scores on all these tests indicate a wide range of individual differences.

Three methods of scoring the other

4 tests were: (*a*) the total score on all 30 trials; (*b*) "the per cent-of-possible-gain method," namely, the per cent that the actual gain, after the first 5 trials, was of the possible gain after the first 5 trials; and (*c*) "the difference-in-per cent-of-gain method," namely, the difference between the per cent of the total possible score made on the first 5 trials and the per cent that the score on the final 5 trials is of the remaining possible score before the last 5 trials (this may be expressed also as the difference between the initial per cent of gain and the final per cent of gain).

Per cent-of-possible-gain method of scoring learning tests. This method of scoring involves obtaining:

1. The maximum possible score that could be made on a given learning test, for example, 300.

2. The score made on the first 5 trials called the initial score, for example, 15.

3. The total score on all trials, for example, 117.

4. The actual gain made after the first 5 trials, i.e., the total score made minus the score on the first 5 trials, for example, $117 - 15 = 102$.

5. The maximum possible gain, i.e., the maximum possible score minus initial score, for example, $300 - 15 = 285$.

6. The per cent gain, i.e., the actual gain after the initial score divided by the maximum possible gain, for example, $102 \div 285 = 35.8$ per cent.

Difference-in-per cent-of-gain method of scoring learning tests. The "difference-in-percent-of-gain method" interprets improvement or learning on the learning tests in terms of the difference between the per cent that the actual score made at the beginning is of the maximum possible total score, and the per cent that the final score is of the possible score remaining after the initial score and before the final score. The method uses the maximum score that could be made on all 30 trials in finding the per cent that the initial score (score on first 5 trials) is of the possible maximum total score. The remaining possible score used in getting the per cent that the actual score on the last 5 trials is of the possible remaining score was obtained by subtracting the score on the last 5 trials from the total score made on all 30 trials, and then subtracting this remainder from the total score possible on all 30 trials. This remaining possible gain was then divided into the actual score on the last five trials to give the per cent that the score on the last five trials is of the remaining possible score. This method of determining the remaining possible score takes into consideration the sum of the actual scores made and therefore gives the subject credit for previous scores. The per cent gain on the first five trials was subtracted from the per cent gain on the last five trials, and this difference was used as the measure of learning taking place.

An illustration of the procedure is as follows: Subject A made an initial score of 15 on the first 5 trials. The total maximum possible score for one test on all 30 trials was 300. The per cent that the initial score is of the maximum possible score was found by dividing 15, the initial score, by 300, the maximum possible score, thus giving the per cent of initial gain as 5.0. The total score on all 30 trials made by Subject A was 117; her final score was 19; the actual total score minus her final score was 117 minus 19, or 98. This 98 was then subtracted from the maximum possible score of 300, to obtain in this case, 202, which was used as the remaining possible score at the beginning of the last 5 trials. It will be seen that actually the possible score on the last 5 trials would

be 60, but in order to include credit for all previous scoring the final remaining possible score was computed as explained above. The percent that the score on the last 5 trials is of the remaining possible score was then found by dividing the final score of 19 by the remaining possible score of 202, in this case, 9.4 per cent. The next and final step was to obtain the difference between the per cent of initial gain and the per cent of final gain, or in the case of Subject A by subtracting 5.0 from 9.4 giving a difference of 4.4 per cent, or, in other words, a score of 4.4. This was the learning score used in the method of scoring referred to as "the difference-in-percent-gain method."

This is a rather complicated method of scoring the amount of learning taking place. This method and several other per cent procedures, however, were used by the author and Carpenter with other similar data and, by comparing coefficients of correlation between learning tests data and various methods of scoring improvement, was selected as the best method of scoring.

The two methods of computing per cent gain used in studies of motor learning by the author make possible expressing improvement (learning) in terms of a comparable measure, a per cent. They also have the effect of neutralizing differences of initial ability because each learner's score is expressed in terms of the ratio of her actual improvement to the possible improvement that she could make following her initial five trials.

These methods of computing per cent of gain in performance are believed to be a marked improvement over the customary method of dividing the gain by the initial score. By this customary method a beginner may appear to make a large gain merely because his initial score is low.

Measures Correlated With Learning Scores

Learning scores computed by the different methods mentioned above were compared with certain standard tests by correlation. The standard test items were:
1. Brace Motor-Ability Test.
2. Balance items in Brace Test.
3. Agility items in Brace Test.
4. Iowa Revision of the Brace Test.
5. Athletic ability (measured by three tests comprising an athletic index).
6. Physical performance level tests (seven tests of physical fitness nationally approved for high school girls).
7. McCloy's general motor-ability score, general motor-capacity score, general motor-achievement quotient, and motor quotient.

Findings

Intercorrelations between the learning tests were all low except in the case of the tangle with the rhythm test which correlated 0.601 ±0.043.

Relationship between total scores on the six tests (total score method) and the individual tests are given in Table 2.

TABLE 2

Relationship Between Industrial Learning Tests and Sum of Scores on All Learning Tests

Learning Tests	Sum of Scores on All Learning Tests (Total score method)	
Tangle Test	0.377	0.058
Rhythm Test	0.380	0.057
Ball Bounce	0.698	0.035
Target Toss	0.615	0.042
Wall Volley	0.731	0.031

The sum of scores on the four sport-type learning tests, scored by per cent-of-possible-gain method correlate with the tangle-plus-rhythm test 0.140 ± 0.066, but with the total scores on all six learning tests, 0.796 ± 0.046, thus indicating that motor learning of the stunt or rhythm type may differ from motor learning of sport-type skills.

A comparison of three methods of scoring motor learning is shown in Table 3.

TABLE 3

Intercorrelation Between Methods of Scoring Learning

Methods of Scoring Learning	Coefficient of Correlation
Total score method vs. per cent of possible gain	0.796
Total score method vs. difference between initial and final per cent gain	0.554
Difference between initial and final per cent of gain vs. per cent of possible gain	0.734

It would appear that of the two methods of computing per cent of gain the per cent-of-possible-gain method more nearly corresponds to the sum of all scores on learning trials (total score method) than does the other per cent method.

The relationship of motor learning to measures of motor ability is shown in Table 4.

Motor learning as measured in this study correlates more closely with the original Brace Motor-Ability Test than with the Iowa Revision of the Brace Test, but in neither case is the relationship sufficiently close to warrant classifying either the Brace test or the Iowa revision as a test of motor educability (motor learning). This same finding has been borne out by other previous studies made by the writer.[1]

TABLE 4

Measures of Motor Ability Correlated with Measures of Motor Learning

Measures of Motor Ability	Measures of Motor Learning (Sport-type skills)	Coefficient of Correlation
Brace Motor Ability	Per cent possible gain	0.357
Brace Motor Ability	Difference between initial and final gain	0.318
Brace Balance Items	Per cent possible gain	0.238
Brace Balance Items	Difference between initial and final gain	0.483
Brace Agility Items	Difference between initial and final gain	0.280
Iowa Revision of Brace Test	Difference between initial and final gain	0.299
Iowa Revision of Brace Test	Brace Test	0.707

TABLE 5

Relationships Between Motor Learning of Sport-Skill Type and Athletic Ability and Physical Performance Level Tests

Measures of Motor Learning	Measures of Athletic Ability and Physical Fitness Tests		
	Athletic index	Athletic index plus jump and reach	Physical Fitness Tests
Per cent-of-possible-gain method	0.667	0.660	0.567
Difference between initial and final per cent gain	0.553	0.555	0.500

Motor learning as measured correlates substantially with athletic ability and with physical performance level tests as shown in Table 5.

From these findings it would appear that there is a substantial relationship between motor learning of the sport-skill type and athletic ability, and between such motor learning and physical fitness as measured by physical performance level tests. The relationship with athletic ability, however, is slightly closer than with physical fitness.

These findings substantiate those of previous studies in indicating that learning of gross bodily motor skills of the sport-skill type relates more closely to the qualities measured by tests of running speed, jumping, and throwing than with motor ability tests (the Brace Test), or with other standardized tests proposed as measures of motor learning.[2]

Two of the six learning tests, the tangle and rhythm test, differed from the other four in that they involved performance of new coordinations not related to sport skills. The tangle involves dexterity and balance and calls for ability to analyze movement and make corrections in performance. The rhythm test calls for recognition of a movement pattern and "motor memory" in performance at a set rhythm. The learning scores on these two tests consisted of the number of trials required to master the movements.

The relationship between scores on the tangle and rhythm tests with scores on the sport-type learning tests[1] is very low as shown by a correlation of 0.140 ± 0.066 with learning measured by the per cent-of-possible-gain method. The two tests have a self correlation of 0.601 ± 0.043. Both the tangle and rhythm tests have low correlations with three of the other four learning tests, as follows:

tangle vs. ball bounce = 0.128 $\pm$ 0.066
tangle vs. wall volley = 0.132 $\pm$ 0.066
tangle vs. target toss = 0.101 $\pm$ 0.066
rhythm vs. ball bounce = 0.168 $\pm$ 0.065
rhythm vs. wall volley = 0.106 $\pm$ 0.066
rhythm vs. target toss = 0.124 $\pm$ 0.066

The tangle and rhythm tests show lower correlations with other measures of general motor ability than do the sport-type learning tests.

From these findings, in conjunction with other results reported previously in this paper, it begins to appear that there may be a type of motor learning which functions in gross bodily activities involving throwing, batting, or kicking an object which differs from motor learning involved in learning bodily movements not requiring control of an object by body coordinations. If this is true it may explain the closer relationship between motor learning of sport-type skills and athletic ability and "physical fitness" tests.

An Analysis by Partial and Multiple Correlation to Show an Apparent Difference in Types of Motor Learning

Further substantiation of the writer's belief that there are at least two types of motor learning is obtained from partial and multiple coefficients of

---

[1] Correlation with the kick test was not computed because of low reliability of the latter.

correlation obtained for four variables, namely:

1. Motor learning of sport-type skills (scored by the per cent-of-possible-gain method).
2. Motor learning measured by the tangle plus the rhythm learning tests.
3. The Brace Motor-Ability Test.
4. Athletic index (50-yd dash + basketball throw + standing broad jump).

For these four variables the zero order coefficients of correlation are:

$r\ 12 = 0.140$ $r\ 23 = 0.465$
$r\ 13 = 0.357$ $r\ 24 = 0.288$
$r\ 14 = 0.667$ $r\ 34 = 0.533$

Partial coefficients of correlation are:

$r\ 12.3\ =\ -0.031$ $r\ 23.4\ =\ 0.384$
$r\ 13.2\ =\ \ \ 0.346$ $r\ 24.1\ =\ 0.264$
$r\ 13.4\ =\ \ \ 0.002$ $r\ 24.3\ =\ 0.180$
$r\ 14.2\ =\ \ \ 0.749$ $r\ 34.1\ =\ 0.425$
$r\ 14.3\ =\ \ \ 0.603$ $r\ 34.2\ =\ 0.460$
$r\ 23.1\ =\ \ \ 0.450$
$r\ 12.34 =\ -0.270$ $r\ 23.14 = 0.399$
$r\ 13.24 =\ \ \ 0.003$ $r\ 24.13 = 0.090$
$r\ 14.23 =\ \ \ 0.708$ $r\ 34.12 = 0.356$

Coefficients of multiple correlation of significance are:

$R\ 1.23\ \ = 0.370$
$R\ 1.34\ \ = 0.667$
$R\ 1.234 = 0.756$

It will be seen that motor learning of sport-type skills has practically no relationship to motor learning as measured by the tangle and rhythm tests (stunt-type tests); and that as the Brace Test and athletic index are partialed out the relationship even becomes negative.

The relationship between sport-type learning and athletic index increases from 0.667 to 0.749 when the stunt-type learning is partialed out. This high degree of relationship between motor learning of sport-type skills and an athletic index made up of a sprint, a throw, and a jump is highly significant.

The relationship between the Brace Test and motor learning of sport-type skills drops from 0.357 to 0.346 to zero when the stunt-type learning scores and the athletic index are partialed out. This would appear to indicate that the relationship of the Brace Test to sport-type learning is due to those parts of the test which measure speed, strength, and power. This is further shown by the fact that relationship between the Brace Test and athletic index remains about the same regardless of the effect of the other two variables, a relationship varying from 0.356 to 0.533. Likewise the relationship between the Brace test and the tangle and rhythm learning tests remains fairly constant, varying from 0.465 to 0.384, and is at its lowest when the athletic index only is partialed out.

The multiple correlation between sport-type motor learning and the Brace Test and athletic index of 0.667 is raised to 0.756 when the tangle and rhythm learning tests are added. The best combination of the tangle and rhythm tests with the Brace Test produces a multiple correlation of only 0.370.

The results of this analysis of partial and multiple coefficients lead the writer to feel confident that we can distinguish at least two types of motor learning, and should suspect the existence of still other types. One type of ability to learn gross bodily motor skills is referred to by the writer as "sport-type" learning. This type of learning relates to performances involving the use of speed, strength, power, and dexterity in manipulating the body in control of some object such as a ball. There is a close relationship between this type of learning and fundamental measurements of speed, strength, and skill. Although the relationship is close, however, an adequate measure of ability to learn sport-type skills will involve supplementing measurements of such fundamental qualities as speed, strength, power, and dexterity with other measures not yet adequately identified. A revision of the Brace-type test of motor ability to eliminate items which reduce the correlation between sport-type learning tests and the fundamental qualities named above should produce a higher multiple correlation than the one reported here.

The performance of gross bodily motor activities required in daily living involves performances of the stunt type, namely, the manipulation of the body without relation to the control of some object or of a marked use of strength, speed, or power. Ability to learn such performances cannot be adequately measured by tests so far proposed, judged by the results of this and similar studies previously reported. The writer believes that the best approach yet made to this problem is the use of stunt-type tests.

Relationship of Motor Learning to Combinations of Tests Proposed to Measure General Motor Capacity and General Motor Ability[2]

Certain combinations of physical tests have been proposed by McCloy as measures of general motor capacity including ability to learn motor skills.[4] Other combinations have been proposed such as general motor-ability score, general motor-achievement quotient, and motor quotient.

The items in these measures are:
1. General motor-capacity score = 3.516 (Sargent jump in cm) + 2.20 (Brace Test T-score) + 19.12 (Burpee Test) + 119.
2. General motor ability = 0.42 (total points of dash, broad

---

[2] From a study. See reference 3.

jump, and throw) + 9.6 number of chins (pull-ups).

3. General motor-achievement quotient = general motor-ability score ÷ general motor-capacity score.

4. Motor quotient = general motor-capacity score ÷ norm for general motor capacity (by age).

The relationship between motor learning and the measures proposed by McCloy as measures of general motor capacity, general motor ability, general motor-accomplishment quotient, and motor quotient are shown in the following table.

From the data in Table 6 it would appear that the McCloy measures do measure learning of "sport-type" motor skills to some degree, but not to a degree that would warrant using any of the measures of general ability as measures of motor learning (as measured in this study). The relationship with motor learning as evidenced in the tangle and rhythm tests is quite low.

The relationship between the Mc-Cloy measures and the physical performance levels is substantial, ranging from 0.678 to 0.760. The findings appear to indicate that the McCloy measures test strength, speed, agility, and power to a greater extent than they test ability to learn even the sport-type motor skills.

These findings do not necessarily detract from the merit of the McCloy measures of general motor capacity but they do indicate to the writer that the general motor-ability score, the general capacity score, general motor-accomplishment quotient, and the motor quotient do not justify being referred to as measures of motor learning. None of these measures should be used to predict ability to learn gross bodily

TABLE 6

Relationship Between Motor Learning and McCloy Measures of
General Motor Ability and Capacity

Measures of motor learning or related tests	General Motor-Ability Score	General Motor-Capacity Score	General Motor-Achievement Quotient	Motor Quotient
Total learning score	0.468	0.488	0.339	0.477
Difference between initial and final per cent gain	0.436	0.430	0.431* 0.274	0.435
Tangle plus rhythm	0.256	0.318	0.245	0.312
Brace motor ability	....	0.674** 0.653	....	0.658
Gain on physical performance levels (omitting potato race, pull-ups, 30-sec squat thrust)	....	....	0.086	0.003
Physical performance levels	0.704	0.595	0.578	0.760
General motor-ability score	....	0.618	0.953	....
General motor-capacity score	....	....	....	0.861

* Using different pull-up scores.
** With Iowa revision + jump and reach + Burpee.

motor skills, and could, therefore, hardly be used to predict capacity for learning.

It will be noted that the correlation between learning ability, as measured in this study, and athletic ability is higher, with each method of computing learning, than is the correlation between motor learning and the McCloy measures of general ability.

Summary of Findings

Four "sport-type" learning tests were given to 100 junior high school girls to measure their ability to learn a variety of gross bodily motor skills in a designated number of trials involving 90 performances in each test. Two additional learning tests requiring mastery of complex coordinations were given to the same subjects and measured in terms of the number of trials required for mastery.

Two methods of computing per cent of gain (learning) which had the effect of neutralizing initial differences in ability were used.

The relationship between motor learning, and tests of athletic ability, physical fitness, motor ability, and certain measures proposed as measures of general motor capacity (including motor learning) were studied.

Findings appear to warrant the following conclusions:

1. There are marked individual differences in ability to learn gross bodily motor skills.

2. The learning of "sport-type" skills involves somewhat different abilities from those required to learn to manipulate the body in stunt-type or rhythm-type coordinations.

3. Ability to learn "sport-type" motor skills is related rather closely to athletic ability and to speed, strength, agility, and power, and very little to ability to learn stunt-type skills.

4. The Brace Motor-Ability Test does not measure motor learning to an extent that would justify the test being classified as a test of motor educability.

5. The Brace Test is slightly superior to the Iowa Revision of the Brace Test as a measure of motor learning.

6. Certain measures proposed to measure motor learning, namely, the general motor-ability score, general motor-capacity score, general motor-accomplishment quotient, and motor quotient do not appear to measure motor learning to a sufficient extent to be used to predict motor learning, as measured in this study.

7. Because of its low relationship with motor learning there is grave question of the validity of the McCloy general motor-capacity score as a measure of motor capacity, if such capacity is understood to involve ability to learn.

8. Of the two methods used for computing per cent of learning the per cent-of-possible-gain method relates rather closely to the total achievement recorded on the learning tests, and rather closely to athletic ability and to physical fitness.

9. The method of computing learning which is referred to as the difference between initial and final per cent of gain relates more closely than does the other per cent method to performances involving balance and less closely to athletic ability and physical fitness.

10. Further research is needed on methods of computing per cent of learning taking place, and study of different types of motor learning.

11. Perhaps the greatest contribution of this study has been to indicate that there are probably different types of motor learning, and that motor learning of "sport-type" skills is dependent to a considerable extent upon physical fitness expressed in terms of strength, speed, agility, and power.

References

1. Brace, D. K., "Studies in the Rate of Learning Gross Bodily Motor Skills," *Res. Quart.*, **12** (1941), 2.

2. Brace, D. K., *loc. cit.*

3. Burch, Geraldine. Unpublished thesis for M. Ed. degree, University of Texas, 1945.

4. McCloy, C. H., and Norma D. Young, *Tests and Measurements in Health and Physical Education*. New York: Appleton-Century-Crofts, 1954.

F. M. HENRY

Specificity vs. Generality in Learning Motor Skill

Reprinted from the *Proceedings, College Physical Education Association* (1958), pp. 126–28.

Franklin Henry is one of the most prolific reporters of research in the entire field of human movement. His sophistication in the design of experiments and his attention to detail are well known. Although basic research has been his primary concern, he is careful to note its function as a prerequisite to the improvement of teaching and learning gross motor skills. The impact of his findings in this area are just beginning to be felt by teachers, test developers, curriculum planners, as well as other research workers. His influence upon those who have worked in his laboratory has been profound; some of the best contributions to recent research literature have come from former students.

Two papers are reproduced to illustrate Henry's work in motor learning and motor performance. Since he probably is known best for his work in motor specificity, the first paper concerns that subject. It is not a research report but rather a plea to pay more attention to the tremendous implications of gross motor specificity.[1] The components of motor educability, or motor ability as described by Brace and McCloy are no longer considered sufficiently specific to describe accurately the phenomenon of motor skill.

The Henry-Rogers paper is, on the one hand, an example of theory formulation to explain already known facts, and on the other, the testing of a hypothesis generated by the theory. As a consequence, the term "motor memory" referred to

---

[1] See also, F. M. Henry, "Coordination and Motor Learning," *Proc. Coll. Phys. Educ. Assoc.*, **59** (1956), 68–75.

by Brace in his 1946 paper becomes more meaningful, and for this reason provides the basis for formulating and testing hypotheses regarding the mechanisms underlying skilled movement. Although of secondary importance perhaps, the paper gives further support to the phenomenon of motor specificity.

In a review of trends in research on coordination and motor learning reported to this group two years ago, it was found that the factual data were establishing with increasing clarity that motor skills and large muscle psychomotor abilities are far more specific than had previously been realized.[3] Our curriculum planners should become aware of the research findings—it is no longer possible to justify the concept of unitary abilities such as coordination and agility, since the evidence shows that these abilities are specific to the task or activity.

The present paper is concerned with the status of our knowledge of *generality* vs. *specificity* in the area of motor learning and transfer of training under carefully controlled conditions. In agreement with an earlier study by Lindeberg,[6] a thesis project by Blankenship in 1952[1] showed that a semester of streamlined gymnastics and "response to command" training emphasizing speed and versatility of varied motor actions failed to improve measured ability in a standardized choice reaction test designed to measure discrimination reaction and speed of movement.[5] In this test, the subject either hit a ball with a table tennis paddle using a backhand stroke in response to visual stimulus A, or dropped the paddle and reached forward to grasp a ball in response to visual stimulus B. Adequate amounts of learning *did* occur in the test itself, thus establishing its justification for use in a transfer experiment.

Subsequently, a thesis study by Gaylord Nelson[7] showed that there was some generality of motor learning ability in 10-year-old boys, since transfer of training could be demonstrated at this age if the interpolated task was similar to the tested motor act. However, at age 15, or at college age, no transfer could be detected unless the interpolated task was substantially *identical* with the original learning task. The test apparatus has recently been improved by additional timing equipment, so that reaction time and movement time are separated. Additional standardized motor learning tasks have been developed, namely, balancing on a stabilometer, caroming a light ball from a flat surface to strike a wall target, and the Lambert motor learning test.[1] Preliminary experiments with several other motor learning tests, e.g., dart throwing, had shown their unsuitability because of low individual difference reliability in the learning scores.

Three independent samplings of subjects have been studied with this group of motor learning tests. The results of one of these is available in a thesis by Edward Hart;[2] the data from the other two have been analyzed and are being prepared for publication. The findings are essentially the same in all three studies.

In one of them, the sampling was intentionally heterogeneous in order to maximize the amount of intercorrelation between learning scores in the various tasks, under the assumption that there was such a trait as general motor learning ability. The odd-even

---

[1] *Res. Quart.*, **22** (1951), 50–57.

trial reliabilities of the improvement scores were not high ($r = 0.41$ to 0.82), although they were adequate for the present purpose. The intercorrelations between learning scores in the different tasks ranged from -0.25 to $+0.24$, and none was significant even when corrected for attentuation due to unreliability.

Of particular interest is the intercorrelation between improvement in net speed of movement in the ball hit and the ball grasp, namely $r = 0.12$. The reliabilities for the improvement scores are 0.64 and 0.59, respectively. Fully corrected for attenuation the intercorrelation is still below $r = 0.20$. Yet these scores were obtained in the same units and on the same apparatus, involve a very similar task, and exhibit highly significant improvement ($t = 7.9$ and 7.3; $n = 40$). The initial raw time scores were about 50 per cent larger in the ball grasp (since the distance was about 50 per cent greater), but when converted to speed in inches per second there is no significant difference in either initial speed or improvement in speed in the two tasks. Adjusted learning scores[4] give similar results.

The theory of specific motor abilities implies that some individuals are gifted with many specific abilities and others have only a few;[3] it follows that there will inevitably be significant correlations between total test battery scores when tests involving many abilities are lumped together. The general motor factor which thus makes its appearance is a sample, fundamentally, of how many specifics the individual has, and

general motor ability does exist in this sense. This is not a question of definition; it is, on the contrary, a matter of basic theoretical insight into the problem. Failure to appreciate this distinction has beclouded our thinking in the past, and has erroneously led us to expect that practicing a motor skill would improve general coordination. However, there is no general coordination ability except perhaps in the very young.[7] Repetition of a motor act improves the specific skill that is practiced, but individual differences in ability to profit by practice are specific to that skill and definitely do not predict the ability to improve by practice in some other skill. Provided that other factors such as differential motivation and differential physiological development are excluded in the design of crucial experiments, the data seem to permit no other conclusion. Transfer of improvement due to learning is also remarkably specific.[7,8]

Acceptance of a new point of view seldom occurs without trauma. This particular manifestation (i.e., motor specificity) has been on the horizon for years. We cannot continue to shrug it off; it is no longer distant, but in clear focus and must be recognized in our curricular philosophies. Let us recall that education *gained* in strength when it discarded the doctrine of formal discipline. We do not even need to search for a new set of values to justify the teaching of specific motor skills. Athletic games, sports, and dance are already an integral and accepted part of the American culture.

References

1. Blankenship, William C., "Transfer Effects in Neuromuscular Responses Involving Choice." Master's thesis, University of California, Berkeley, 1952.

2. Hart, Edward A., "Specificity of Individual Differences in Motor Learning." Master's thesis, University of California, Berkeley, 1957.

3. Henry, Franklin M., "Coordination and

Motor Learning," *Proc. Coll. Phys. Ed. Assoc.*, **59** (1956), 68–75.

4. Henry, Franklin M., "Evaluation of Motor Learning when Performance Levels Are Heterogeneous," *Res. Quart.*, **27** (1956), 176–81.

5. Henry, Franklin M., and A. Gaylord Nelson, "Age Differences and Inter-relationships Between Skill and Learning," *ibid.*, **27** (1956), 162–75.

6. Lindeburg, Franklin A., "A Study of the Degree of Transfer Between Quick-ening Exercises and Other Coordinated Movements," *ibid.*, **20** (1949), 180-94.

7. Nelson, Gaylord A., "Differences Between 10- and 15-Year-Old Boys in Motor Learning and Specificity of Transfer." Ed.D. thesis, University of California, Berkeley, 1955.

8. Nelson, Dale O., "Studies of Transfer of Learning in Gross Motor Skills," *Res. Quart.*, **28** (1957), 364–73.

F. M. HENRY / D. E. ROGERS

Increased Response Latency for Complicated Movements and A "Memory Drum" Theory of Neuromotor Reaction

Reprinted from the *Research Quarterly*, **31** (1960), 448-58.

Abstract

The theory proposes a nonconscious mechanism that uses stored information (motor memory) to channel existing nervous impulses from brain waves and general afferent stimuli into the appropriate neuromotor coordination centers, subcenters, and efferent nerves, thus causing the desired movement. A consequent hypothesis requires that the simple reaction time will become longer when the response movement is required to be of greater complexity. Data obtained on college men and women, and 12- and 8-year-old boys, are in agreement with the hypothesis. Replacing a very simple finger movement with an arm movement of moderate complexity slows the reaction by about 20 per cent; additional complexity produces a further slowing of 7 per cent. The speed of the arm movement is considerably faster in college men than in younger boys or in college women. The correlation between reaction time and speed of movement averages approximately zero. Individual differences in ability to make a fast arm movement are about 70 per cent specific to the particular movement being made; "general ability for arm speed" occurs only to the extent of 30 per cent.

The time required for a muscle to begin to respond to direct stimulation is about 0.015 sec. A simple reflex response such as the eye wink is made in 0.04 sec, while the reflex to a blow on the patellar tendon requires about 0.08 sec. The simplest voluntary response to a stimulus (simple RT) requires 0.15 sec under the most favorable circumstances; 0.20 to 0.25 sec may be considered more typical. When complications such as discrimination between several stimuli and/or choice between several possible movements are introduced (disjunctive RT), the required time increases and may be as long as 0.50 sec. It should be noted that RT "is not the time occupied in the execution of a response; rather, it is the time required to get the overt response started".[12]

Theoretical Considerations

Early experimental psychologists considered RT to be a measure of the cumulated time required for a series of mental processes, including stimulus perception and the willing of the movement. This concept was gradually discarded during the period 1873–93 in favor of the idea that the stimulus simply triggered off a prepared reflex, the voluntary mental phase of the process being limited to the preparation, i.e., the development of a state of readiness to make a specific planned movement. This is essentially the same as the modern view. A reaction cannot be broken up into a series of successive mental and motor acts. The response is a total reaction in which perception of the stimulus runs concurrently with the motor response, with much of the perceptive process and all the overt movement occurring after the reaction, i.e., following the true RT, which is defined as the latent period between the stimulus and the first beginning of physical movement. Woodworth has traced the historical development of these ideas in considerable detail.[11]

While the traditional prepared reflex theory of RT may be accepted in its general aspects, the present writer proposes considerable modification designed to recognize current knowledge of the neuromotor system and its control by the cephalic nervous centers. There is no reflex in the modern physiological use of the term, since a reflex must be nonwillful and not voluntary. There is probably not more than a minimal involvement of the cerebral cortex in the RT response, because the neuromotor coordination centers and pathways are chiefly cerebellar or subcortical without cortical termination.[10] Perhaps in consequence of the neuroanatomy, neuromotor perception is extremely poor, although neuromotor coordination or kinesthetic adjustment (with the absence of perceptual awareness) is exceptionally well developed in humans.[5]

Performance of acts of skill (even though relatively simple) may be assumed to involve neuromotor memory. This may be operationally defined as improved neuromotor coordination and more effective response, the improvement being the result of experience and practice, possibly accumulated over a period of many years. An implication of the neuroanatomy of the system as outlined above is that such memory must be different from ideational or perceptual memory, since conscious imagery is indefinite and largely excluded.

Nevertheless, a rich store of unconscious motor memory is available for the performance of acts of neuromotor skill. Added to this are innate neuromotor coordinations that are important in motor acts. The tapping of the store may be thought of broadly as a memory storage drum phenomena, to use the analogy of the electronic computer. The neural pattern for a specific and well-coordinated motor act is controlled by a stored program that is used to direct the neuromotor details of its performance. In the absence of an available stored program, an unlearned complicated task is carried out under conscious control, in an awkward, step-by-step, poorly coordinated manner.[1]

Voluntary consideration of a particular movement that has already been learned, and is to be accomplished at maximum speed, occurs during the classical foreperiod (an interval of readiness while the subject is attentively waiting for the reaction-causing stimulus). Such consideration may involve visual imagery of the specific intended movement, but it is chiefly the development of a strong intent to start that movement in immediate response to the stimulus. It is not concerned (and indeed cannot be) with the actual formation of the already learned or structured specific program that will guide the released outburst of neural impulses through the proper centers, subcenters, and nerve channels so that it will produce the intended movement. The crucial willful act in the simple reaction is the release of the outburst of neural impulses that will result in the movement. Normally this act is voluntary and intentional rather than reflex, although in special circumstances it may become almost reflex. The term "release" is used advisedly; impulses are already present in the cephalic nervous system in the form of brain waves and afferent neural discharges from various sources and are directed and channeled rather than created.

---

[1] Subsequent to the preparation of this article the writer has become aware of an interesting observation by J. E. Birren:[1] "When skills are acquired the component movements appear discrete and are then gradually combined into a continuous pattern. Furthermore, as a skill deteriorates (because of aging) it may again assume the quality of separate movements."

This is another point of distinction between a voluntary reaction and a simple automatic stimulus-response reflex.

The above concepts can lead to a number of testable predictions in the area of motor coordination. Keeping in mind that the programming of the movement can constitute only a part of the total latency (because synaptic conduction in and of itself requires time) it might, for example, be expected that a minor program change for a simple movement would be easy to accomplish, whereas a long or rather complicated program should be difficult to change after it starts organizing the channels. Various implications of the theory will be examined in subsequent articles.

Problem Investigated

One of these implications, which will be investigated in the present study, is the theoretical requirement that there should be a longer reaction latency for a complicated movement than for a simpler movement. This is because a more comprehensive program, i.e., a larger amount of stored information, will be needed, and thus the neural impulses will require more time for coordination and direction into the eventual motor neurons and muscles.

The voluntary decision to make a movement when the stimulus occurs is thought to cause a state of readiness to respond to (and be triggered by) the stimulus. During this foreperiod, there is some amount of preliminary neuromotor response. It is known that some premovement tension may develop in the muscles that are to make the overt response, but such tension is sometimes absent and sometimes of an inappropriate nature.[10] Action potentials, however, reveal fairly consistent foreperiod excitation of both the reacting and noninvolved muscles. It is argued here that this may indicate alertness rather than implicit or partial reaction.[12] Whether this interpretation is correct or not, it seems obvious that when the movement is complicated and requires considerable skill, it is not possible for the tension during the foreperiod to be related to more than the very first phase of the overt movement. Moreover, a complicated movement necessarily involves several muscle groups and several specific areas of neuromotor coordination centers; more extensive use of learned and stored neuromotor patterns are surely required to initiate the overt motor action in this case. Thus it may be hypothesized that with richer and more complicated patterns involved, a longer latent time for the more complicated circulation of neural impulses through the coordination centers is inevitable. The situation is probably analogous to (but not identical with) the events, whatever they are, that cause greater response latency when there is a choice of movement in the reaction.[11]

The hypothesis can be tested experimentally by observing the simple RT required for the initiation of movements that vary from simple to complex. Note that there can be a simple RT for a complex movement. If the situation for a particular response involves no discrimination as between two or more stimuli, and no choice (at the time of reaction) between which of two or more movements is to be made, the RT is simple regardless of the complexity of the movement itself.

Review of Literature

While there has apparently been no investigation which approached the problem from the point of view stated above, there have been, over the years, a few researches that are pertinent.

The first was a study by Freeman in 1907, which reported that in drawing geometric figures such as a straight line, a circle, and a pentagon, the RT became longer as the figure increased in complexity.[4] In explanation, it was contended that the cause was antagonistic muscular tensions originating from anticipation of the necessary movement reversals. Unfortunately, the data were only secured on four individuals, so although the results are statistically inconclusive, they are in the anticipated direction.

On the other hand, Fitts[3] stated in 1951 that "the latent time is independent of the rate, extent, or direction of the specific movement required by the stimulus," basing his interpretation on the 1949 experiment of Brown and Slater-Hammel,[2] although he cites some other references that are less directly related. It may be noted that the experiment in question involved only the variation of the length or direction of a simple movement; complexity was not studied.

Several reports from our laboratory have included data on the RT for movements that differ in complexity. Unfortunately, with respect to the present issue, the experimental designs were oriented to the problems that were being investigated; no attempt was made to control or balance out the practice effect. The most recent of these was by Mendryk,[8] who used two movements that differed considerably in length and slightly in complexity. In subjects of three age groups (N = 50 in each), the RT's were 0.002, 0.004 and 0.009 sec faster for the longer and more complex movement. However, each subject had been given 50 trials with the short movement and 30 practice trials with longer movement before the tabled values for the latter were recorded, so there may have been a considerable practice effect acting to decrease the RT and thus occlude the complexity effect.

Mendryk has made available to the writer his data for the last 20 trials with the short movement and the first 20 trials with the subsequent longer and more complex movement, which makes possible a comparison involving less of the practice effect. In his 12 year-old group the RT for the longer movement is 0.004 sec slower than for the short movement ($t = 1.2$), in the 22-year-old group it is 0.009 sec slower ($t = 3.8$), and in the 48-year-old group it is 0.006 sec slower ($t = 2.2$). Thus while the effect is small, and not completely controlled as to practice, it is in the anticipated direction and is statistically significant for the two adult groups.

Methodology

Apparatus and movements. A reaction key was mounted at the forward end of the flat foundation board of the instrument. This was a sensitive key; the weight of the subject's finger was sufficient to keep it closed. At the back end of the board an upright supported a red warning light at eye level. A silent control switch was operated by the experimenter out of sight of the subject. When it was turned to its first position, the warning light came on. After a lapse of 1 to 4 sec (in chance order), the switch was turned to the second position, which sounded the stimulus gong and simultaneously started the RT chronoscope. When being tested with Movement A, the subject simply lifted his finger a few millimeters, which permitted the reaction key to open and stopped the chronoscope.

Movement B was more complicated. A tennis ball hung by a string which placed it about 15 cm above the reaction key and 30 cm further back, away from the subject. In response to the stimulus signal, he reached forward to grasp the ball. When the ball was touched, the upper support end of the string pulled out of a switch clip, thus freeing the ball to permit a follow-through. A second chronoscope, which also connected to the reaction key, recorded movement time (MT). It stopped when the string pulled out of the switch clip.

Movement C was somewhat more complicated; it included a series of movements and reversals. A second tennis ball (C), also supported by a string and clip, was hung 30 cm to the right of ball B. In response to the stimulus, the subject moved his hand from the key, reaching forward and upward to strike ball C with the back of the hand, then reversed direction to go forward and downward, touching a dummy push button on the baseboard to the left of the reaction key, and finally reversed again to go upward and forward, striking down ball B. This two-ball apparatus was illustrated in an earlier publication from this laboratory,[6] which listed references to detailed descriptions of the device. It should be mentioned that the circuits included provision for using an auditory stimulus (an electric gong), and this was used in the present study.

Experimental design. There were two experiments. In the first, designated Exp. 1, there was continuous rotation of conditions, trial-by-trial, with Movement A required for the first trial, B for the second, C for the third, A for the fourth, and so on. Before each trial, the subject was reminded as to which movement was to be made; moreover, he could see from the way the apparatus was set up that there were no balls, or one, or two, to be hit. Fifteen practice trials were given, followed by 30 trials (10 for each movement) which were used for the statistical analysis. While this design offered the advantage of very exact balancing out of possible practice and fatigue effects, there was a remote possibility that even though the instructions were carefully given, and the nature of the required movement for a particular trial was obvious, some cases may have occurred in which there might have been some element of choice of movement.

Experiment 2 involved one practice trial with Movement A, followed by ten trials with that movement. After a brief rest, a practice trial was given on B, followed ten trials with that movement. After another rest, one practice trial was given on C, followed by ten trials with that movement. A third of the subjects followed the A-B-C sequence, another third the sequence B-C-A, and the final third the sequence C-A-B. Each person had 30 trials (10 on each movement) in addition to the practice before each series of 10. All subjects used in Exp. 2 were well practiced in the movements, since they had gone through Exp. 1 aproximately one week earlier.

Subjects. Group I consisted of 30 undergraduate college men. Group II was composed of 30 undergraduate college women. In each group approxi-

mately half were physical education majors. These groups were tested only under the conditions of Exp. 1. Group III consisted of 20 young men ranging in age from 19 to 35 yr (average 24), and included college students, high school teachers, and others. Group IV was made up of 20 eighth-grade boys, age 11 or 12, and Group V was composed of 20 fourth-grade boys age 8 9. Not one of these 120 individuals was (or could be) selected in any way, either intentionally or unintentionally, with respect to the possibility that he would do better with one of the movements than with another one. In other words, the samples are completely unbiased with respect to the variable under consideration, which is the RT for Movement A compared with B or C.

Results and Discussion

Reaction time vs. complexity. The data of Table 1 show that all groups react more slowly as the movement becomes more complex. The reaction preceding Movement B is about 20 per cent slower, on the average, than

TABLE 1

Mean Reaction Times of the Various Groups

GROUP		MOVEMENT A		MOVEMENT B		B-A	MOVEMENT C		C-B
		M (sec)	σ	M (sec)	σ	$t*$	M (sec)	σ	$t*$
I(1)	Men	0.163	0.018	0.195	0.026	8.6	0.204	0.031	2.9
II(1)	Women	0.174	0.027	0.205	0.026	8.3	0.219	0.034	3.8
III(1)	Age 24	0.158	0.025	0.197	0.034	9.4	0.213	0.034	5.3
IV(1)	Age 12	0.178	0.023	0.214	0.035	8.1	0.226	0.033	3.4
V(1)	Age 8	0.238	0.038	0.275	0.042	8.4	0.295	0.026	4.9
III(2)	Age 24	0.144	0.019	0.186	0.031	10.1	0.199	0.032	3.4
IV(2)	Age 12	0.159	0.015	0.201	0.031	7.5	0.214	0.033	3.8
V(2)	Age 8	0.214	0.031	0.253	0.024	7.0	0.270	0.039	4.0

* A *t*-ratio of 1.70 is significant at the 5 per cent level for Groups I and II (N = 30), while 1.73 is required for Groups III, IV, and V (N = 20). The statistical hypothesis is single-tailed, since the direction of the differences is predicted by the experimental, i.e., alternative, hypothesis. It will be noted that all of the *t*-rations are significant and quite large; the smallest is 2.9.

the RT for A, and the reaction preceding Movement C is about 7 per cent slower than the RT for B. Even though the groups are relatively small, the differences between the RT's are without question statistically significant in each, as may be seen by the *t*-ratios in Table 1. Moreover, the differences are approximately as large and significant under the conditions of Exp. 2 as under the conditions of Exp. 1.

Since the findings are positive in each of five groups of subjects that differ in age and sex, and are positive under both of the experimental conditions, the evidence seems adequate to claim that the hypothesis of slower RT for movements of increased complexity, based on the memory drum theory of reaction latency, has been confirmed. It should be emphasized that the simple movement was very simple indeed. Furthermore, the amount of movement required to actuate the reaction key was only a fraction of a millimeter; in other words, the RT did not involve movement in the ordinary meaning of the word. (Some experiments that have purported to measure RT have actually included considerable amounts of movement.) The additional serial elements and reversals of direction in Movement C, as compared with B, caused only about a third as much change in RT as did the type and amount of complexity difference of B as compared with A.

The determination of the crucial elements of the complexity effect, and of just how much of a change in complexity is required to produce a noticeable change in RT, will require further investigation. It seems reasonable to expect that increased movement complexity occurring early in a movement will have a much greater influence on RT than if the complexity appears late in a movement that was simple in its early phases. Whether increased demand for accuracy and precision of movement, and increased involvement of feedback, will slow RT as implicitly predicted by the theory, are among the important questions that remain to be answered.

Secondary Problems Investigated

Age and sex differences in reaction time. It will be noticed that RT is slower in the younger age groups (Table 1), although no statistical evaluation of the differences has been made because the influence of age on RT is already well established.[12] This is not true in the case of MT. Data on that problem have only become available recently;[8, 9] the current results will be given in the next section of the report.

In the present set of experiments, the RT's of men and women subjects do not differ significantly. The *t*-ratios for the differences are 1.7 for A, 1.5 for B, and 1.7 for C; these are within the expectations of random sampling variability. As might have been hoped, the two samples of adult males have very similar RT's, the differences within each movement condition being nonsignificant ($t = 0.8$, 0.3, and 0.9). It may be seen in Table 1 that RT's are faster for all ages in Exp. 2 as compared with Exp. 1; this is of no consequence because these subjects necessarily had practice in the reactions and movements before doing Exp. 2 (since they had already done Exp. 1), and would be expected to profit by that experience. The amount of practice was of course equal for all three movements.

Age and sex differences in movement time. The mean movement times are given in Table 2. In Movement B the 8-year-old boys are 52 per cent slower than the 12-year-olds in Exp. 1, and 27 per cent slower in Exp. 2. In the case of Movement C, the figures are 54 and 33 per cent. All these differences are significant. However, the differences between the 12-year-old boys and the 50 adult males are not significant; the t-ratios are 0.9 for B and 1.1 for C and hence fail to overthrow the null hypothesis. The two samples of adult males do not differ significantly one from the other, either for Movement B ($t = 1.9$) or Movement C ($t = 1.6$). It will be recalled that Movement A was not timed, because it was simply a finger withdrawal.

The college women are 40 per cent slower than the college males in Movement B and 14 per cent slower in Movement C. These differences are clearly significant, as evidenced by large t-ratios (Table 2).

Intercorrelations. The correlation between RT and MT varies considerably among the five groups of subjects, which is not unexpected because the number of cases in any one group is rather small for this type of analysis. The relationship has been examined for Exp. 1 only. For Movement B, the values range from -0.323 to $+0.212$, with the average (using the z transformation) at $r = 0.064$. In the case of Movement C, the values range from -0.088 to $+0.420$, with the average at

$r = 0.180$. There seems to be no particular tendency for the amount of correlation to vary systematically with age or sex. These results are in agreement with the findings of others, which have recently been reviewed.[7,8] The problem here is not really whether the correlation is or is not statistically significant, since it might or might not be found significant in one particular study. Rather, the concern is whether the real correlation is low (tending to be close to zero), or substantial, i.e., moderate, or relatively high. Evidence is accumulating that it is a very low order relationship, having little or no predictive value.

The correlation of MT itself as between the B and C types of movement is somewhat higher. It is true that for age groups 8 and 12 the values are very low, namely, 0.084 and -0.002. However, in the adults the figures are 0.562 for the women, 0.489 for the college males, and 0.427 for the group of 20 men. When the five groups are averaged (using the z transformation), $r = 0.329$. While the correlation may be considered significantly different from zero for each group of adults, their average value (0.493) certainly

TABLE 2

Mean Movement Times of the Various Groups

GROUP		MOVEMENT B			MOVEMENT C		
		M (sec)	σ	t(groups)	M (sec)	σ	t (groups)
1(1)	Men	0.093	0.024		0.481	0.079	
2(1)	Women	0.130	0.027	5.6(#2-#1)*	0.552	0.094	3.1(#2-#1)*
3(1)	Age 24	0.078	0.029		0.437	0.103	
4(1)	Age 12	0.097	0.023	2.1(#4-#3)*	0.493	0.108	1.6(#4-#3)
5(1)	Age 8	0.147	0.043	4.5(#5-#4)*	0.762	0.131	6.9(#5-#4)*
3(2)	Age 24	0.081	0.013		0.391	0.161	
4(2)	Age 12	0.091	0.021	1.8(#4-#3)	0.438	0.208	0.9(#4-#3)
5(2)	Age 8	0.117	0.026	10.3(#5-#4)*	0.582	0.103	2.7(#5-#4)*

* t-ratio of 2.0 is significant at the 5 per cent level.

does not indicate a high degree of relationship.

The odd-even MT reliability coefficients (S-B corrected) for the three groups of adults are 0.982, 0.919, and 0.796 for Movement B and 0.988, 0.966, and 0.684 for Movement C. Using these values to correct the correlations between the two movements is r^2, which is 0.326, 0.269, and 0.335 in the above three relationship after the influence of error variance (unreliability) has been removed.

Now the amount of common variance of individual differences as between the two movements in r^2, which is 0.326, 0.269, and 0.335 in the above three groups of adults. (These values may be multiplied by 100 to convert them to per cent). It follows that the amount of individual difference variance that is not common to the two movements, and is not error variance, is given by the squared coefficient of alienation k^2, which is defined as $l-r^2$. It is obvious that k^2 is to be identified as the specificity of individual abilities in the two movements, while r^2 is the generality of individual abilities. The values of k^2 for the three groups are 0.674, 0.731, and 0.665, and may be converted to per cent by multiplying by 100. The relatively large values for k^2 justify the statement that ability to make a fast arm-hand movement of the type used is quantitatively determined to a greater extent (69 per cent) by abilities that are specific to one or the other of the two movements, and to a lesser extent (31 per cent) by a general speed ability that is involved in both movements. This analysis has, moreover, presented the most favorable case for generality, since it has been limited to the three groups of adult subjects; the correlation between movements approximated zero in the younger groups. The results with adults agree with those of a recent study that utilized other types of arm movements, finding 74 per cent specificity and 26 per cent general arm speed ability.[8]

Summary and Conclusions

Following a consideration of prevailing concepts of reaction time and modern knowledge of the operation of the neuromotor nervous system, a theory has been developed which places heavy reliance on nonperceptive use of motor memory in voluntary acts involving motor coordination. Innate and particularly learned neuromotor coordination patterns are conceived of as stored, becoming accessible for use in controlling the act by a memory drum mechanism that requires increasing time for its operation as the motor act becomes more complex.

To test the hypothesis that the simple reaction time becomes lengthened with increased movement complexity, data were secured on 120 individuals, including both sexes and (in the case of males) 3 age groups. Sixty of the subjects were tested with two experimental procedures in order to improve the adequacy of the control conditions. Three types of movement varying in complexity were used; both reaction time and movement time were measured.

The data were also examined with respect to several problems secondary to the main study. These included the influence of age and sex on net movement time, and the amount of generality and specificity of individual differences in speed of arm movement ability.

Results of the statistical analysis of the data seem to justify the following conclusions:

1. Under controlled conditions, simple reaction time becomes longer

when the type of movement which follows the reaction is varied from very simple to relatively complex. Further increase in complexity produces additional slowing, but to a lessened degree.

2. College women have less arm speed ability than college men.

3. Eight-year-old boys have less arm speed ability than 12-year-old boys.

(While the data suggest that 12-year-olds are slower than young adults, the statistical results are inconclusive.)

4. Individual differences in speed of arm movement ability are predominately specific to the type of movement that is made; there is only a relatively small amount of general ability to move the arm rapidly.

References

1. Birren, J. E., *Psychological Aspects of Aging*. Washington: American Psychological Association, 1956, p. 100.

2. Brown, J. S., and A. T. Slater-Hammel, "Discrete Movements in the Horizontal Plane as a Function of Their Direction and Extent," *J. Exptl. Psychol.*, **38** (1949), 84–95.

3. Fitts, P. M., "Engineering Psychology and Equipment Design," *Handbook of Experimental Psychology*, ed. by S. S. Stevens. New York: John Wiley & Sons, Inc., 1951.

4. Freeman, F. N., "Preliminary Experiments on Writing Reactions," *Psychol. Monographs*, **8**, No. 34 (1907), 301–33.

5. Henry, F. M., "Dynamic Kinesthetic Perception and Adjustment," *Res. Quart.*, **24** (1953), 176–87.

6. Howell, M. L., "Influence of Emotional Tension on Speed of Reaction and Movement," *ibid.*, **24** (1953), 22–32.

7. Lotter, W. S., "Interrelationships Among Reaction Times and Speeds of Movement in Different Limbs," *ibid.*, **31** (1960), 147–55.

8. Mendryk, S., "Reaction Time, Movement Time, and Task Specificity Relationships at Ages 12, 22, and 48 Years," *ibid.*, **31** (1960), 156–62.

9. Pierson, W. R., "The Relationship of Movement Time and Reaction Time From Childhood to Senility," *ibid.*, **30** (1959), 227–31.

10. Wenger, M. A., F. N. Jones, and M. H. Jones, *Physiological Psychology*. New York: Holt, Rinehart & Winston, Inc., 1956.

11. Woodworth, R. S., *Experimental Psychology*. New York: Holt, Rinehart & Winston, Inc., 1938.

12. Woodworth, R. S., and Harold Schlosser, *Experimental Psychology* (rev. ed.). New York: Holt, Rinehart & Winston, Inc., 1954.

J. M. HARMON / A. G. MILLER

Time Patterns in Motor Learning

Reprinted from the *Research Quarterly*, **21**
(1950), 182–87.

Numerous research studies have treated of the phenomenon of motor learning. Some investigators, for example, McCloy and Brace, have been interested in measuring motor performance, whereas others have been more concerned with the nature of motor learning per se. As one might expect, much of the research has been stimulated and strongly influenced by the study of mental learning. Consequently, it is not surprising to see many studies concerned with the relative merits of "the whole" vs. "the part" method of teaching, or the relative effectiveness of "massed" vs. "distributed" learning. Too frequently such research has been simply a series of arbitrarily structured observations of a convenient physical skill, simple or complex. The following paper by Harmon and Miller is representative of the all-too-few studies that have some theoretical orientation, in this case learning as neurological growth.

Every research study has its weaknesses, often in connection with the treatment of data. With respect to the following paper, the reader should note the use of several critical ratios for a design more properly calling for an analysis of variance.[1] However, their choice of the 1 per cent level of significance would probably offset any possibility of wrongly rejecting a null hypothesis, i.e., differences reported significant at the 1 per cent level, when using the multiple critical ratios, likely would be significant at the 5 per cent level or better had an analysis of variance been used.

The major objective of this research is to find a basis for improvement in methods of teaching. Teachers have been quite subjective in determining the frequency of practices in the teaching of motor skills or other school subjects. Only a few research efforts have been reported on the subject of time psychology. The old adage "practice makes perfect" seems to have much less meaning in the light of present research. The length of time intervals between practice periods may prove to be just as important as the length of practice periods.

The unique phase of this research is the inclusion of a time pattern that has not been used in other research, and which is found significantly more advantageous than the other three patterns used. The unique time pattern is herein called the additive pattern. It should be noted that this pattern follows a five-eight ratio and is suggested or borrowed from the field of botany. The relationship to botany is

---

[1] A. E. Edwards, "Multiple Comparison in the Analysis of Variance," *Experimental Design in Psychological Research* (New York: Holt, Rinehart & Winston, Inc., 1960), pp. 136–57.

through philotaxy, which is a law of growth of plants involving a five-eight ratio.

More and more psychologists are concluding that the learning process is a neurological growth process, therefore, more research should be encouraged in which the known laws of growth, or related factors, are applied to learning situations. In the opinion of the authors, the field of physical education offers excellent laboratories for research in which major contributions may be made that are important to all fields of education, and especially in studies of the learning process.

This research is upon the level of basic or beginning skills, in which problems of reliability of performance may be solved or better understood. One follow-up study herein reported by Lawrence[11] indicates that reliability may be determined, at least in part, by the time pattern upon which basic or beginning skills are learned.

Other research is going forward in which studies are being made of the most efficient time patterns for coaching the various sports. In other words, how long are optimum practice periods in various sports and upon what days of the week in relation to scheduled contest? Such questions may possibly be answered through experimental research in time psychology.

Experiment in Time Psychology

Physical education includes many skills which lend themselves to research in the field of time psychology due to the fact that they can be isolated, controlled and evaluated while maintaining the interest of the subjects.

Billiards was used as the motor skill to be learned because set shots could be standardized for use by all subjects, the table could be made available to all participants and an interest created and maintained in the experiment.

College women who had had no previous experience in playing pool or billiards were used as subjects for the experiment. The players were divided into four groups. The units of practice, number of practices, and length of practice periods were kept constant for all groups. The time intervals between the practice periods were varied for each of the four groups and produced the following time patterns:

1. The first group carried on their nine practice sessions 3 days per week for 3 weeks in a row—i.e., Monday, Tuesday, Wednesday of the first week, Monday, Tuesday, Wednesday of the second week, and Monday, Tuesday, Wednesday of the third week. Listing the days by numbers gives the following practice days: 1st day, 2nd, 3rd, 8th, 9th, 10th, 15th, 16th, 17th. This group was called the *Three-Days-Per-Week Group*.

2. The second group carried on their practice periods on an additive basis— i.e., adding the first two numbers or days to make the third number or day (first day plus second day equals third day); the second and third numbers or days to make the fourth number or day, etc., up to and including the fifty-fifth day which was the ninth practice session. Listing the nine practice periods by numbers, gives days on which the practices occurred: 1st day, 2nd, 3rd, 5th, 8th, 13th, 21st, 34th, 55th. This group was called the *Additive Group*.

3. Practice for the next group was conducted on a daily basis including Saturday and Sunday. The time pattern may be described as follows: 1st day, 2nd, 3rd, 4th, 5th, 6th, 7th, 8th, 9th. This group was called the *Daily Group*. From a relative point of view this group most nearly approached massed learning as far as this experiment was concerned.

TABLE 1

Summary of the Data for the Second Practice Period for the Four Groups

Groups	Number	Ranges	Means	S.D.
I—Three days per week......	18	19–41	29.2	6.96
II—Additive...............	18	20–40	29.1	6.85
III—Daily.................	18	17–43	29.3	7.41
IV—One day per week......	18	18–42	29.2	6.92

4. The last time pattern was established on the basis of practice once per week. The number of the nine respective days when the practice periods were conducted include: 1st day, 6th, 15th, 22nd, 29th, 36th, 43rd,*, 57th, 64th. The exception (*) to the one day per week schedule was made between the seventh and eighth practice periods because of vacation week. The group was called the *One-Day-Per-Week Group.*

A group of set shots were developed by the authors and tried out by two women subjects who had never played billiards or pool. During this testing period, which was conducted over a period of 2 months, 11 set shots were established and arranged more or less progressively in their order of difficulty. The first 5 of the 11 set shots were then selected for the first practice period. Number one set shot was attempted five times on the right side of the table. The same set shot was repeated on the left side of the table. This procedure was carried on with set shots 2, 3, 4, and 5, thus making a total of 50 shots per practice period. During each succeeding practice period, a new shot was added while dropping the first set shot of the previous practice. This procedure was carried on until all 11 set shots were used.

One exception to this procedure was the retention of one set shot for all practice periods. A constant was thus provided to show the effect of time on learning a single set shot.

The first practice period was used for instruction. Starting with the second practice period and continuing on throughout the ninth practice session, no corrective suggestions were given.

Analysis of The Data

The scores from the second practice period were selected as the basis for equating the four groups. These scores are presented in Tables 1 and 2.

TABLE 2

Correlation Coefficients Between Groups

Groups	Correlation Coefficients	Groups	Correlation Coefficients
I–II	0.986	II–III	0.955
I–III	0.981	II–IV	0.955
I–IV	0.973	III–IV	0.989

At the end of the experiment the statistical differences between the four groups were determined. A critical ratio of 2.50 (approximately the 1 per cent level) was considered indicative of a statistically significant difference. Table 3 shows the differences in the mean scores for the four groups for the last practice period.

1. The results of the three consecutive days per week pattern (Group I) were inferior to those of the additive pattern. However, it produced better results than the daily and the one-day-per-week patterns, respectively, but the differences were not statistically significant.

TABLE 3

Difference in Means Between the Four Groups for the Ninth Practice Period

Group Practice	No.	M	S.E.	Dmlm²	S.E.d	C.R.
I	18	31.6	1.26	3.0	1.20	2.50
II	18	34.6	0.88			
I	18	31.6	1.26	1.0	1.50	0.66
III	18	30.6	1.33			
I	18	31.6	1.26	2.0	1.56	1.28
IV	18	29.6	1.06			
II	18	34.6	0.88	4.0	1.48	2.71
III	18	30.6	1.33			
II	18	34.6	0.88	5.0	1.38	3.63
IV	18	29.6	1.06			
III	18	30.6	1.33	1.0	1.47	0.68
IV	18	29.6	1.06			

2. The additive time interval pattern (Group II) produced the best results. There were statistically significant differences in the mean gains and resulting critical ratios of this group over those of the other three groups.

3. The results of the daily time pattern (Group III) were better (but not better, statistically significantly) than those for the one-day-per-week time pattern (Group IV) but inferior to the results of the other two patterns.

4. The one-day-per-week pattern (Group IV) proved to be the poorest of the four patterns.

5. The results of the one set shot which was used in all practice periods for the four groups were similar to the results of all set shots for the groups. In other words, as far as results were concerned, the research might have been limited to one set shot for all four groups.

Conclusions

1. There were no statistically significant differences between the patterns through the sixth practice period. Significant differences thereafter occurred and were probably due to the various time patterns used from the beginning of the experiment. Therefore, in conducting research in this field, practices should be carried on beyond six practice periods.

2. There were no statistically significant differences in the final results between the nine consecutive days pattern, the three consecutive days per week for three weeks pattern, and the pattern of one day per week for nine weeks.

3. There were statistically significant differences in the final results in favor of the additive pattern over the other three patterns.

4. A good base or foundation should be established in learning a new skill such as billiards. Relative massing at the beginning of the learning process is to be preferred over widely spaced time intervals at the beginning. From three to five practice periods were found satisfactory for establishing beginning skills.

5. After the foundation has been laid, greater spacing between practice periods has a more favorable effect upon learning than continued massing.

6. Progressively lengthening the time intervals between the practice periods

(the additive pattern) proved beneficial in learning a new motor skill. The additive pattern may not be the best time pattern to be used in learning, but should be considered as a point of reference from which further research may be undertaken in finding such a pattern.

Further Research

In a follow-up study Longley[12] used a "Massed-evenly spaced" time pattern[1, 2, 3, 8, 15, 22, 29, 36, 43] which, when compared with Miller's[15] four time patterns gave the following results:

The improvement of the "Massed-evenly spaced" group (Longley's) was slightly inferior to the Additive group (Miller's Group II), although the result was not statistically significant. There were statistically significant differences in favor of the "Massed-evenly spaced" group over Miller's other three groups —i.e., Daily group, Three-day-per week group, and One-day-per-week group. These results were similar to the Additive group's statistically significant superiority over the other three groups.

The results of these two studies seem to indicate that some form of a massed-spaced time pattern should be used in learning a new motor skill.

Lawrence,[11] using over 60 per cent of the subjects used in the original study, made a reliability check of the Additive group (Miller's Group II) and the Daily group (Miller's Group III). The check was to be considered indicative of the degree of retention between the two groups.

The results of the study showed a statistical significance (a critical ratio of 2.87) in favor of the Additive group over the Daily group.

A conclusion which may be drawn from this study is that the retention in a massed-interpolated-spaced learning pattern (Additive group) was superior to the retention in a massed learning pattern (Daily group). Further research should be conducted before any final conclusions may be made as all of the original subjects were not used in the reliability check.

There are many unsolved problems in the field of time psychology, some of which are now in the process of being solved by other research workers.

References

1. Arnold, F., "The Significance of an Additive Time Pattern in Learning Motor Skill." Unpublished Master's thesis, Boston University, 1949.

2. Bunch, M. E., "Cumulative Transfer of Training Under Different Temporal Conditions," *J. Comp. Psychol.*, **32** (1941), 217–31.

3. Cook, T. W., "Factors in Massed and Distributed Practice," *J. Exptl. Psychol.*, **34** (1944), 325–33.

4. Dore, L. R., and E. R. Hilgard, "Spaced Practice as a Test of Snoddy's Two Processes in Mental Growth," *ibid.*, **23** (1938), 359–74.

5. Dunohy, Pierre, *Biological Time*. New York: The Macmillan Company, 1937.

6. Gagne, R. M., "The Effect of Spacing of Trials and the Acquisition and Extinction of a Conditioned Operant Response," *J. Exptl. Psychol.*, **29** (1941), 201–16.

7. Hilgard, E. R., and M. B. Smith, "Distributed Practice in Motor Learning: Score Changes Within and Between Daily Sessions," *ibid.*, **30** (1942), 136–46.

8. Humphreys, L. G., "The Factor of Time

in Pursuit Motor Learning," *J. Psychol.*, **2** (1937), 429–36.

9. Kingsley, H. L., and R. Garry, *The Nature and Conditions of Learning* (2nd ed.). Englewood Cliffs, N. J.: Prentice-Hall, Inc., 1957.

10. Lashley, K. S., "The Acquisition of Motor Skills in Archery," *Carnegie Inst. Wash., Papers Marine Biol.*, **7** (1915), 105–28.

11. Lawrence, D. P., "A Reliability Check of Two Interpolated Time Patterns in Motor Learning." Unpublished Master's thesis, Boston University, 1949.

12. Longley, G. F., "The Effect of Massed Followed by Evenly Spaced Practice on Learning a Motor Skill." Unpublished Master's thesis, Boston University, 1949.

13. Lorge, I., *Influence of Regularly Interpolated Time Intervals Upon Subsequent Learning*. New York: Bureau of Publications, Teachers College, Columbia University Press, 1930.

14. Lyons, D. O., "The Relation of Length of Material of Time Taken for Learning and the Optimum Distribution of Time, Part III," *J. Ed. Psychol.*, **5** (1914), 155–63.

15. Miller, A. G., "The Effect of Various Interpolated Time Patterns on Motor Learning." Unpublished Ph.D. dissertation, Boston University, 1948.

16. Murphy, H. H., "Distribution of Practice Periods in Learning," *J. Ed. Psychol.*, **7** (1916), 150–62.

17. Robinson, E. S., "The Relative Efficiencies of Distributed and Concentrated Study in Memorizing," *J. Exptl. Psychol.*, **4** (1921) 327–43.

18. Ruch, T. C., "Factors Influencing Relative Economy of Massed and Distributed Practice in Learning," *Psychol. Rev.*, **35** (1928), 19–45.

19. Smith, F. O., "The Influence of Variable Time Intervals on Retention of Meaningful Material," *J. Exptl. Psychol.*, **30** (1942), 175–79.

20. Snoddy, G. S., *Evidence for Two Opposed Processes in Mental Growth*. Lancaster, Pa.: Science Press, 1935, p. 103.

21. Snoddy, G. S., "Evidence for Universal Shock Factors in Learning," *J. Exptl. Psychol.*, **35** (1945), 403–17.

22. Snoddy, G. S., "Reply to Dore and Hilgard," *ibid.*, **23** (1938), 375–83.

23. Travis, R. C., "Practice and Rest Periods in Motor Learning," *J. Psychol.*, **3** (1937), 183–87.

24. Travis, R. C., "The Effect of Length of Rest Period on Motor Learning," *ibid.*, **3** (1937), 187–97.

25. Troy, Jr., J. J., "A Study of Peak Performances in Relation to the Practice Periods." Unpublished Master's thesis, Boston University, 1948.

R. J. FRANCIS / G. L. RARICK

Motor Characteristics of the Mentally Retarded

Reprinted from the *American Journal of Mental Deficiency*, **63** (1959), 792–811.

The relationship between mental and physical characteristics of children and adults has been of interest to professional and lay persons for many years. The antithesis brain vs. brawn, when contrasting athletes and "bookworms," suggests to many that a negative correlation must exist between physical and mental traits. Needless to say, several investigators have attempted to verify or refute what appears to be a commonly held opinion. As pointed out by Francis and Rarick in their review of the literature, the existing evidence suggested ". . . that when observations extend beyond the bounds of normality, motor proficiency and intelligence are related," although little or no relationship appears to exist for children in the "normal" range of intelligence.

The Francis-Rarick findings were somewhat contradictory in that they found that the motor proficiency of retarded children was considerably less (2–4 yr) than that of normal children, yet correlations between intelligence and motor perform-ance ". . . were generally low and of approximately the same order as other investigators have reported with normal children." This apparent paradox might be accounted for by the rather narrow range of IQ scores among the retarded children used in this study.

What is, perhaps, of greater interest are two additional findings: the dis-crepancy between the motor proficiency of the retarded and that of the normal child tends to increase with age; and mental retardation does not appear to upset the pattern of interrelation among motor traits.

It is interesting to note that this study was one of the first to be supported by the Cooperative Research Branch of the U.S. Department of Health, Education and Welfare.

A considerable body of information is available concerning the physical and mental development of mentally re-tarded children, but only a limited number of investigators have made observations on the motor characteris-tics of the slow-learning child. It has been a common practice in the past to relegate the slow learner to those aspects of the curriculum which utilize primarily manual pursuits under the assumption that the motor capacities of these children are more nearly normal than their mental powers. While slow-learning children do appear to enjoy the more tangible pursuits which in-volve both small and gross muscle activity, insufficient data are at hand to guide curriculum workers in respect to the motor needs and abilities of mentally retarded children.

Purpose and Scope of the Study

The present investigation was de-signed to obtain information on the gross motor abilities of a group of mentally retarded children assigned to special classes in the public schools of Madison and Milwaukee, Wisconsin. The more specific purposes of the study were:

1. To determine age and sex trends in certain gross motor abilities of mentally retarded children.

2. To compare the motor achievement levels of the mentally retarded with normative data on normal children.

3. To determine if the interrelationships among gross motor functions of the mentally retarded are different than the interrelationships among those traits of children of normal intelligence.

4. To determine the extent to which the degree of mental retardation is related to the motor achievement levels of the slow learner.

The subjects for the investigation included 284 mentally retarded children attending the public schools of Madison and Milwaukee, Wisconsin. The IQ's of these children were between 50 and 90 with a chronological age range of 7.5 yr to 14.5 yr. To this group a battery of 11 motor performance tests designed to measure strength, power, balance, and agility was administered. Normative data on normal school children are available on most of these tests so that comparisons could be made between the motor achievement levels of normal and mentally retarded children.

Background of the Investigation

Much has been written concerning the relationship between intelligence and motor ability. With normal humans the evidence shows that measures of intelligence and scores on motor performance tests are not closely related. For example, the work of Johnson[9,10] and Miles[18] demonstrated that

intelligence is not related to measures of physical skill, the latter investigator including observations from early life to late maturity. Keller[13] using the Johnson skill test found that physical skill increased with chronological age and school grade, but not with mental age or IQ. Ray[21] reported correlations of 0.09 to 0.26 between physical skill and mental achievement for groups of children of different levels of intelligence with IQ ranges of approximately 15 points in each group. It is interesting to note that the highest of these correlations was in the IQ range of 81 to 95. Likewise when scores on mental achievement and physical achievement were correlated for the cases in that IQ range a positive correlation of 0.76 was found, the highest for any of the IQ categories. This would suggest that relationships between motor functions and intelligence are higher in the low normal range than in IQ ranges of higher intelligence.

The fact that general observation of mentally defectives often discloses marked tendencies toward infantile motor behavior has led investigators to give more detailed study to the motor characteristics of the child of low mentality. In describing the motor characteristics of these children, Tredgold[28] points out that while the most pronounced motor deficiency of the mentally defective is in the finer hand and finger movements, the grosser functions involving body balance and locomotion are usually clumsy and ungainly also. Tredgold[29] holds the point of view that even with training the mentally defective has difficulty in developing manual dexterity and body balance, and movement tends to remain uncoordinated. On the other hand, Sherman[24] believes that mentally retarded children have the capacity to learn the more simple sensory-motor skills as easily as normal children provided they are given the opportunity. In reviewing the work of other investigators, Doll[4] concludes that the evidence points to a deficiency in motor proficiency which is characteristically associated with mental defectiveness.

More recently Sloan[25] presented comparative data on the motor proficiency of 20 feebleminded and 20 normal children matched by age and sex. The Lincoln adaptation of the Oseretsky test of motor proficiency[26] was administered to the subjects in both groups. Reliable differences favoring the normal children were found on all six of the subtests of the Oseretsky scale. The author concluded that motor proficiency cannot be considered as an isolated function, but rather as another aspect of the total behavior of the organism. The study clearly indicates that when observations extend beyond the bounds of normality, motor proficiency and intelligence are related. This supports the point of view of most observers that certain minimum levels of intelligence are required if the organism is to perform effectively the sensory-motor tasks common to our culture.

Method of Procedure

General methodology

The general methodology of the investigation was directed to (a) obtaining motor performance data on the mentally retarded boys and girls by age and sex so that comparisons could be made with the motor behavior of normal children, and (b) providing data for a study of the interrelationships among motor abilities of the mentally retarded. In describing the motor characteristics of mentally retarded children, the investigators utilized for the most part motor performance tests which

have been successfully used with normal children for the age range encompassed by this study. The use of measures for which normative data are available permitted comparisons of the performance of the mentally retarded with that of normal children by age and sex. Furthermore previous studies using these tests had evolved standardized procedures for test administration and had indicated the type of ability which the test was designed to measure. The use of tests which have been routinely employed with normal children also permitted the investigators to examine sex differences in motor performance of the mentally retarded and to determine if such differences were of the same magnitude as the differences observed in normal children. Since studies[22] on normal humans have indicated that motor abilities are more specific than general, the extent of specificity of motor functions could also be investigated with the mentally retarded through the use of these measures.

Selection of the measures

Since only limited observations have been made on the motor proficiency of the mentally retarded through the use of gross motor skill tests, the following guides were employed in the selection of the measures:

1. Tests which sampled different kinds of abilities. Previous work[22] on normal humans has shown that the average intercorrelation among motor tests approximates 0.30. Therefore care was taken to sample those kinds of abilities which previous research had indicated as being important in predicting over-all motor ability—events involving the elements of strength, speed, power, agility, and balance. The run, the jump, and the throw are activities common to the play experiences of all children and with normal children a weighted

combination of these events plus a measure of strength has been shown to be a good predictor of "general motor ability."[14]

2. Tests which were easy to administer and simple to score. Since the testing operations were moved from school to school, tests were needed which required only a limited amount of equipment.

3. Tests which could be administered under well standardized conditions.

4. Tests which were simple enough for the slow learner to comprehend.

5. Tests which gave promise of providing high reliabilities with children of below-normal intelligence.

The measures which most nearly satisfied the above criteria and which were used are listed in the appropriate categories as follows:

1. Measures of Static Strength:
    a. Dynamometric strength of right grip
    b. Dynamometric strength of left grip
    c. Pulling dynamometric strength
    d. Thrusting dynamometric strength
2. Measures of Running Speed:
    a. 35-yd dash for time
    b. 30-yd dash for time (with 5-yd starting time deducted)
3. Measures of Power or Dynamic Strength:
    a. Vertical jump (jump and reach)
    b. Standing broad jump
    c. Ball throw for distance
4. Balance:
    a. Balance beam (10 ft)
5. Agility:
    a. Burpee Test (squat thrusts)
    b. Agility run

Description of tests and testing procedures

All children were tested individually on each event although 10 to 15 children were brought into the testing area together. Fatigue was reduced by testing all members of the groups on one item before moving to the next. In most instances all tests were given to a particular child on one day.

Measures of static strength. A Stoetling hand dynamometer was used in testing the strength of grip of the right and left hand and a manuometer of the rectangular type inserted in the frame of a push-pull attachment was employed for measuring the strength of pull and thrust. For all static strength measures the procedures recommended by Jones[11] were followed. Three trials were given on each item and the best of the three efforts was used as the child's strength score.

Measures of running speed. Running speed was measured by the time taken to run a distance of 35 yd from a stationary standing position (gross time) and also by the time required to negotiate the last 30 yd of the same run (net time). The administration of the test necessitated two timers, one of whom timed the runner from the signal go until he crossed the 35-yd finish line. The second timer timed the runner from the moment he crossed a point 5 yd from the start until he crossed the finish line. Signals for starting and stopping the watches were given by the two timers, one of whom stood at the finish line and the other at a point 5 yd from the starting position. Two trials on the same day were given to each subject, the better of the two trials being considered as the subject's speed on this event.

Measures of power or dynamic strength. The vertical jump was administered according to standard directions using the jump and reach method. To motivate the children the body of a giraffe was painted on a large cardboard and the children attempted to touch designated markings on the giraffe's body with the finger tips. The difference between the child's standing reach and the highest point touched in the jump was taken as the measure of the vertical jump. Three jumps were given, the best effort being used as the subject's score.

The standing broad jump was administered on the gymnasium floor, the distance between the take-off mark and the landing point of the heel nearest the take-off mark was used as the distance jumped. The best of the three jumps was taken as each subject's score.

In the throw for distance a tennis ball was used for the 8- and 9-year-olds and a standard softball was used with the older children. All children were asked to perform the overarm throw. All throws were made from a point behind a restraining line, the subjects using a single step in executing the throw. The distance was measured by steel tape from the restraining line to the point at which the ball first struck the ground. Three trials were given and the distance of the fathest throw was used in subsequent computations.

Measure of balance. A 10-ft balance beam with a breadth of 1-5/8 in. (top surface 9 in. from the floor) was used in the measurement of dynamic balance. The child was asked to walk the beam heel-to-toe, a distance of ten steps. A score of ten was given for executing the distance with no step-offs. If the child stepped off the beam prior to completing the ten steps, he was credited with a score equal to the number of steps he had completed prior to the step-off. Two trials were given on the balance beam, the better effort being recorded as the balance score.

Measures of agility. The squat thrusts were administered and scored according to procedures described by Mc-Cloy.[14] The children were given a demonstration of the technique and in many instances several trials were needed before many of the subjects were able to perform the movements correctly. This test seemed to be the most difficult one for the largest number of subjects to comprehend and execute and for some children appeared to be as much a test of understanding as of agility. Therefore, the validity of the test for slow-learning children is open to question.

The agility run was devised as a measure of bodily orientation involving the skills of quick rising, quick starting, quick stopping, and rapid acceleration in the run. The subject started the test from the supine position on the floor. At the signal go the subject rose as rapidly as possible, traversed a distance of 20 ft, picked up a small ball on a table and ran back to the starting line as rapidly as possible. The subject's score was the time in seconds from the signal go until he returned to the starting point. Two trials were given, the best being used as the subject's score.

Description of the sample. No attempt was made to draw a random sample of mentally retarded children from the Madison and Milwaukee school systems. All physically normal children in special classes for slow learners in two Madison schools were included in the study. This constituted a group of 69 children, 41 boys and 28 girls. In Milwaukee, children from special classes of 11 schools were included in the study comprising 215 children, 140 boys and 75 girls.

Means for height, weight, chronological age, and IQ are given in Tables 1 and 2. In comparing the mean heights and weights of the boys and girls included in the sample with published norms[27] on Iowa school children, the means for the children under observation at each age level approximated the figures for the Iowa children. The mean IQ of the boys was highly similar from one chronological

TABLE 1
Means and Standard Deviations of Age, Height, Weight, and IQ of Mentally Retarded Boys

Chron. Age	N	AGE (YEARS)		HEIGHT (INCHES)		WEIGHT (POUNDS)		IQ	
		Mean	S.D.	Mean	S.D.	Mean	S.D.	Mean	S.D.
8	15	8.1	0.36	50.9	3.05	68.3	21.75	70.3	8.07
9	30	9.0	0.39	52.2	2.56	65.0	10.09	69.6	10.36
10	31	9.9	0.35	54.0	3.49	73.7	13.92	70.2	7.22
11	26	11.0	0.39	57.1	4.12	84.0	19.57	69.1	7.26
12	24	11.9	0.34	58.0	3.65	88.4	22.74	68.6	7.99
13	28	12.9	0.32	61.5	2.87	101.7	20.10	69.2	8.09
14	27	13.9	0.37	62.7	4.70	110.2	28.67	68.2	10.25

TABLE 2
Means and Standard Deviations of Age, Height, Weight, and IQ of Mentally Retarded Girls

Chron. Age	N	AGE (YEARS)		HEIGHT (INCHES)		WEIGHT (POUNDS)		IQ	
		Mean	S.D.	Mean	S.D.	Mean	S.D.	Mean	S.D.
8	12	8.0	0.40	50.5	3.41	58.1	11.87	64.3	5.80
9	22	9.1	0.29	53.2	3.19	66.8	15.29	66.2	7.34
10	13	9.8	0.28	54.4	2.29	81.2	14.27	69.9	5.46
11	12	11.0	0.32	59.0	3.16	84.8	15.55	69.7	9.95
12	15	12.0	0.35	58.0	3.35	91.5	19.55	69.7	7.69
13	15	13.0	0.37	60.4	3.57	111.4	31.93	65.9	6.28
14	14	13.9	0.33	61.6	3.17	103.5	16.75	64.6	6.42

age group to another ranging between 68 and 70. With the girls the IQ range was slightly greater falling between 64 and 70. It should be noted that the number of cases is limited at each age level, particularly for the girls, and hence the findings presented here should be viewed in this light.

Reliabilities of the measures

As mentioned earlier the accepted performance score for each child on a particular event was the best of the two or three trials administered. In those events where three trials were given, reliability coefficients were computed by correlating the child's best performance score with the average of the other two. Where only two trials were given the best score was correlated with the other score. Reliability coefficients were obtained on each event for each sex at each age level.[1]

Static strength measures. All reliability coefficients for the four static strength measures were above 0.857. The fact

[1] Reliability coefficients for all measures by age and sex may be obtained from the investigators at the University of Wisconsin, Madison.

that 53 of the 56 coefficients were above 0.91 gave evidence that the mentally retarded children were capable of performing reliably on this type of strength measure. The reliabilities obtained here differed little from those obtained by Jones[11] on the same measures given to adolescent children in which reliabilities ranging from 0.932 to 0.964 were reported. Neither chronological age nor sex appeared to affect the reliability of the static strength measures for this group of mentally retarded children.

Measures of dynamic strength. The standing broad jump, the vertical jump and the throw for distance have been shown to be highly reliable measures when administered to normal children. In the present investigation these measures proved to be highly reliable when used with the mentally retarded children. Only 2 of the 42 coefficients were below 0.928, the broad jump with the 13-year-old boys being 0.812 and the vertical jump with the 13-year-old girls being 0.708. On the basis of the coefficients reported here the mentally retarded children performed with acceptable reliability on the tests of dynamic strength.

Measures of running speed. Reliabilities were determined for both the 35-yd dash (gross time) and for the 30-yd dash (excluding time for the first 5 yd). The reliabilities obtained with the mentally retarded children compare favorably with those reported by Espenschade[5] on normal children. At ages 8, 9, and 10 the reliabilities on the dash for boys and girls were similar with none for either sex lower than 0.912. At the older age levels the boys performed more reliably than the girls with all coefficients for the boys above 0.933 whereas with the girls four of the coefficients were below 0.90. At ages 13 and 14 three of the four reliabilities for girls were below 0.90.

This indicates that reliability of performance in the dash may in part be a function of chronological age with mentally retarded girls just as it is with normal girls. Problems of motivating adolescent girls in the dash have been reported by Espenschade,[5] and it appears likely that the lower reliabilities found in this event with the mentally retarded girls is indication of a similar tendency with this group.

Measures of balance and agility. The reliability coefficient for the measures of balance and agility were the lowest of any of the tests administered. In the case of the balance-beam test the low reliabilities were perhaps due to the scoring system utilized which restricted the range of scores to a maximum of ten and forced the clustering of scores to a narrow range at each age level. Even so, the reliabilities for this event ranged from 0.669 to 0.999, which permitted the use of the scores for group analysis. In the case of the squat thrusts the reliabilities were affected in part by the difficulty many of the children had in correctly executing the event which introduced considerable subjectivity in scoring. However, the girls performed quite reliably on this test with only one of the correlation coefficients falling below 0.911. In the case of the boys, two of the coefficients were above 0.93 with the other five ranging from 0.726 to 0.892. The agility run proved to be more reliable with 10 of the 14 coefficients being above 0.90.

Findings of the Study

In presenting and discussing the findings of the study, the material has been organized under four headings, namely: (*a*) age and sex trends in motor proficiency; (*b*) comparisons of motor proficiency of normal and mentally retarded children; (*c*) interrelationship among gross motor functions of the

TABLE 3

Means and Standard Deviations of Grip Strength of Mentally Retarded Boys and Girls

Chron. Age	GRIP STRENGTH RIGHT (IN KG)				GRIP STRENGTH LEFT (IN KG)			
	Boys		Girls		Boys		Girls	
	Mean	S.D.	Mean	S.D.	Mean	S.D.	Mean	S.D.
8	13.4	3.42	7.8	2.42	12.1	3.56	7.6	2.85
9	14.4	3.45	12.3	3.90	13.0	3.20	12.0	3.19
10	15.6	3.45	12.3	3.04	14.1	2.99	12.5	3.12
11	17.7	4.62	17.1	4.13	16.7	4.75	15.7	4.27
12	18.6	4.97	17.9	3.90	17.5	4.77	16.9	3.98
13	24.0	6.68	18.9	4.87	23.7	6.93	18.6	4.97
14	26.4	8.66	22.2	5.49	24.8	7.70	22.9	5.17

mentally retarded; and (d) relationship of IQ to motor performance of the slow learner.

Age and sex trends in motor proficiency

Static dynamometric strength. The data on right and left grip strength grouped according to chronological age for both sexes are given in Table 3. It should be noted that both right and left grip strength increase with age. The greater increments in strength between the 12th and the 13th year suggest the approach of puberty which is also reflected in the increases in body weight for both sexes at this age level. At each age level the boys on the average are stronger in both right and left grip than the girls. This coincides with the findings of other studies on normal children at these age levels.[11, 15, 16] For the boys, the right hand is stronger at each age level than is the left, whereas with the girls at two age levels the left hand is the stronger. These data are somewhat different from reports on normal humans in which it has been shown

TABLE 4

Means and Standard Deviations of Pull and Thrust of Mentally Retarded Boys and Girls

Chron. Age	PULL (IN POUNDS)				THRUST (IN POUNDS)			
	Boys		Girls		Boys		Girls	
	Mean	S.D.	Mean	S.D.	Mean	S.D.	Mean	S.D.
8	22.4	8.02	14.8	5.37	24.5	9.89	14.8	6.15
9	27.3	9.62	24.1	5.59	29.9	11.95	21.4	7.03
10	31.0	8.40	23.0	7.36	33.6	11.57	24.4	9.04
11	36.4	8.69	30.6	10.21	38.5	14.11	28.9	10.40
12	34.5	12.02	34.4	10.00	40.2	15.54	35.0	13.23
13	44.6	13.68	34.9	11.46	52.2	18.41	33.7	15.54
14	48.5	14.16	33.4	12.18	55.9	17.10	33.7	15.69

that right grip is about 12 per cent stronger than the left in girls and only about 6 per cent stronger in boys.[11]

The data on strength of pull and thrust for the mentally retarded boys and girls are presented in Table 4. The same pattern of increase in strength as was observed in gripping strength is seen in the case of both pull and thrust for boys, namely, a rather constant increment in strength by chronological age up to age 12 and then a substantial increase. For girls this pattern does not hold, for maximum strength in both pull and thrust appears to be achieved at approximately 12 yr of age, followed thereafter by little if any change. It is interesting to note that Jones[11] found with normal girls a tendency for strength of pull and thrust to continue to increase through the years 12, 13, and 14. For boys thrusting strength is higher at every age level than pulling strength, whereas with girls the differences are slight throughout.

Dynamic strength. The application of maximum muscular effort in propelling the body or body segments with maximum velocity in a single burst of activity is generally held to be a measure of dynamic strength or power. Jumping performance and power throws have frequently been used to measure dynamic strength. It should be recognized that these skills require more than a simple application of muscular force, since the skills of jumping and throwing require the coordination and proper timing of many body segments. Therefore performance of these skills is in a large measure a reflection of previous experience in activities involving these skills.

Means and standard deviations of performance in the standing broad jump and the vertical jump for boys and girls are shown in Table 5. It will be noted that the boys on the average excelled the girls in both jumping skills at six of the seven age levels. With normal children, the male shows on the average a rather marked superiority in jumping performance at every age level. The year-to-year changes in performance scores in the standing broad jump of the mentally retarded do not show a regular and gradual increase with chronological age as is typical with normal children, nor are these increments of as great a magnitude. For example, Kane and Mere-

TABLE 5

Means and Standard Deviations of Dynamic Strength Measures of Mentally Retarded Boys and Girls

| | BROAD JUMP (IN INCHES) | | | | VERTICAL JUMP (IN INCHES) | | | |
| | Boys | | Girls | | Boys | | Girls | |
Chron. Age	Mean	S.D.	Mean	S.D.	Mean	S.D.	Mean	S.D.
8	36.7	14.20	18.4	11.77	6.9	2.78	3.8	2.44
9	33.4	13.22	35.0	11.58	7.6	2.39	6.9	2.52
10	36.6	11.71	29.7	12.79	7.1	2.24	6.4	2.06
11	40.5	10.76	34.7	15.09	8.4	2.24	8.5	2.10
12	39.1	10.38	35.8	10.60	8.4	2.87	8.2	1.73
13	45.7	9.73	38.1	10.58	9.9	2.05	8.8	1.24
14	44.7	14.92	38.3	9.98	11.0	3.95	8.5	2.76

TABLE 6

Means and Standard Deviations of Ball Throw for Distance Measures
of Mentally Retarded Boys and Girls

| Chron. Age | SOFTBALL THROW (IN FEET) | | | | TENNIS BALL THROW (IN FEET) | | | |
| | Boys | | Girls | | Boys | | Girls | |
	Mean	S.D.	Mean	S.D.	Mean	S.D.	Mean	S.D.
8					41.0	15.20	19.0	6.55
9					53.2	24.10	31.3	10.51
10	55.8	23.47	33.9	22.33				
11	66.9	21.57	36.5	16.48				
12	71.3	26.70	50.4	20.96				
13	93.4	32.70	61.0	17.94				
14	92.4	29.12	47.4	20.49				

dith[12] found that between 7 and 9 yr of age boys showed an increase in mean broad jumping performance of 8.2 in. and an increase of 10 in. between 9 and 11 yr. For the mentally retarded boys there was no change in performance between 8 and 10 yr and a gain of only about 3 in. between 10 and 12 yr of age. It should be noted that the greatest age difference in broad jump performance for boys was observed between the ages 12 and 13 which followed the pattern of change noted in static strength. It should be noted also that between ages 9 and 14 the difference in broad jumping performance for the mentally retarded girls was only 3 in. as compared to differences of approximately 14 in. reported by Kane and Meredith for normal girls between the ages of 7 and 11 yr. In the vertical jump the sex differences are of the same order as for normal children, although the scores for both sexes are markedly lower than the performance levels of children of normal intelligence.

The data for the distance throw by age and sex are give in Table 6. It will be noted that the boys were superior to the girls at every age level, which follows the typical pattern for normal children. The approximately two to one superiority of the boys at age 14 is similar to that reported by Espenschade.[5] Age trends for both sexes show a rather consistent yearly increment with the performance of boys reaching a plateau at 13 yr of age and the girls showing a decline after this age level. The stabilization or decline of performance in the throw at this age level is typical of normal girls, but normal boys continue to show improvement in the throw during the adolescent years.

Speed of running. Mean times for performance in the 30- and 35-yd dashes for both sexes at each age level are given in Table 7. With advancing age improved performance for both sexes may be observed for most age levels. Perhaps the best indication of running speed is provided by examining the data for net time for 30 yd which excludes both the reaction time of the performer at the start and the time required for acceleration during the first 5 yd of the run. With this as a measure of running speed, the boys showed progressively faster times with advancing age whereas the performance for the girls was less regular with increasing age. For example, the per-

TABLE 7

Means and Standard Deviations of Performance Times of Mentally
Retarded Boys and Girls in the 30- and 35-Yard Dashes

Chron. Age	35-YD DASH (GROSS TIME IN SECONDS)				30-YD DASH (NET TIME IN SECONDS)			
	Boys		Girls		Boys		Girls	
	Mean	S.D.	Mean	S.D.	Mean	S.D.	Mean	S.D.
8	7.2	1.11	9.6	1.37	5.8	0.85	7.7	1.38
9	7.3	0.90	7.6	1.02	5.8	0.78	6.1	0.88
10	7.1	0.84	8.0	0.78	5.7	0.70	6.2	0.84
11	6.9	1.05	6.7	0.57	5.5	0.84	5.4	0.51
12	6.4	1.57	7.2	1.10	5.1	1.21	5.8	0.94
13	6.3	0.86	6.7	0.70	4.9	0.75	5.2	0.59
14	6.1	0.74	6.5	0.70	4.8	0.69	5.1	0.77

formance times of girls at age 9 were better than would be expected on the basis of the mean performance at ages 8 and 10 yr. It should be recalled that the number of cases of girls at the lower age levels was small and chance may have introduced a disproportionate number of good performances at this age level. High performance of girls at this age level was also noted in the jumping events which suggests a clustering of motor talent within this age group.

Balance-beam performance. Studies of body balance in children have been directed primarily to the study of (*a*) the ability of children to maintain balance in a stationary position on one foot (static balance) and (*b*) the ability of children to maintain balance while moving (dynamic balance). Most authorities agree that positioning of the body while in motion is more closely related to the kind of balance required in most of the physical skills of childhood than is static balance. Hence in the present investigation a balance beam was employed as a measure of dynamic balance. Mean scores of boys and girls by chronological age are

TABLE 8

Means and Standard Deviations of Balance-Beam Performance of Mentally
Retarded Boys and Girls

Chron. Age	BALANCE BEAM (NO. OF STEPS)			
	Boys		Girls	
	Mean	S.D.	Mean	S.D.
8	8.1	3.18	5.8	3.34
9	8.1	3.14	8.1	3.18
10	7.9	2.97	7.1	3.34
11	8.8	2.58	7.5	3.50
12	8.3	2.98	8.5	2.70
13	9.4	1.99	8.7	2.67
14	9.1	2.29	7.8	2.88

shown in Table 8. The scores represent the average number of steps taken before the subject stepped off the beam. In general, average performance scores for both boys and girls show an increase with advancing age, the boys being superior at most age levels. Studies of balance-beam performance by Seashore[23] have shown that there is a gradual increase in performance from 7 yr to 12.5 yr, with a slight decline during early adolescence. With the mentally retarded group under investigation, the decline in performance in both sexes occurred at age 14. Espenschade[6] reported that adolescent boys show a reduction in gain in performance on beam-walking tests in the years 13 to 15, which the investigator attributed to an "adolescent lag" in the development of dynamic balance. It would appear that in this respect the mentally retarded are similar to normal children.

Age and sex differences in agility. Means and standard deviations of performance on the agility run and the Burpee test are shown in Table 9. It will be noted that improved performance in the agility run occurred with boys as age increased. While a similar trend was noted with the girls, the mean scores at ages 10 and 14 were poorer than at ages 9 and 13, respectively. At each age level the boys were superior in performance to the girls which follows the general trend for agility-type runs with normal children. In the Burpee test (squat thrusts) the boys were superior in performance to the girls at all ages with the exception of the 12-year-old age level. The trend of performance on the Burpee test did not show clear-cut differences with chronological age which is rather typical of the performance of normal children also.

Comparison of motor proficiency of mentally retarded and normal children

Static dynamometric strength. In order to present a graphic account of the differences in manual strength between normal and mentally retarded children, the mean strength of right grip is presented in Fig. 1 by age and sex for normal and mentally retarded boys and girls. It will be noted that the slope of the strength curves are similar for the normal and mentally retarded children, although at each age level the normal children for a given sex are substantially

TABLE 9

Means and Standard Deviations of Agility Measures for Mentally
Retarded Boys and Girls

	AGILITY RUN (IN SECONDS)				BURPEE			
	Boys		*Girls*		*Boys*		*Girls*	
Chron. Age	*Mean*	*S.D.*	*Mean*	*S.D.*	*Mean*	*S.D.*	*Mean*	*S.D.*
8	6.2	0.89	7.5	1.40	3.6	1.04	2.8	0.95
9	6.0	1.17	6.3	0.99	4.0	1.14	3.7	0.90
10	5.9	0.65	6.7	0.79	4.2	1.04	3.4	0.88
11	5.7	0.65	6.0	0.67	4.0	0.74	3.7	0.72
12	5.7	0.87	5.9	0.78	3.7	0.98	3.7	1.00
13	5.4	0.68	5.8	0.70	4.2	1.05	3.6	1.19
14	5.2	0.60	5.9	0.84	4.4	0.98	3.3	0.88

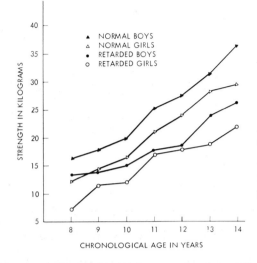

Fig. 1. Mean strength of right grip for normal and mentally retarded boys and girls. Data on normal boys and girls adapted from Meredith,[15] Metheny,[16] and Jones.[11]

stronger than the mentally retarded. While the sex differences in manual strength are reasonably large for both groups at each age (ages 11 and 12 in the mentally retarded excepted), it should be noted that normative data on normal girls show a superiority of the normal female over the mentally retarded male at all age levels above 9 yr of age. The general slope of the curve for both normal males and females is somewhat greater than that for the mentally retarded, indicating that the slow-learning child on the average loses ground in terms of acquiring manual strength. It is also interesting to note that in manual strength the normal 8-year-old male shows a gripping strength on the average equal to that of the 10-year-old slow learner. While the manual strength of the normal 8-year-old boys was approximately 2 kg greater than the mentally retarded 8-year-old, the difference was almost 10 kg at 14 yr of age. Although the differences were in the same direction

for the girls at these ages, the magnitude of the differences was not so great.

The data on shoulder girdle strength (pull) for normal and mentally retarded boys and girls are shown in Fig. 2. Unfortunately, normative data on normal boys and girls on this measure are not available under 11 yr of age. As was true of manual strength, normal boys and girls were substantially stronger than the mentally retarded children of the same sex. The drop in pulling strength of the mentally retarded boys at 12 yr of age can be explained in part by the fact that the group at this age level was somewhat atypical in both height and weight, being only slightly taller and heavier than the 11-year-olds. Since strength and weight correlate rather highly, this may account for what appears to be inconsistent data. A similar trend, although not as great, may be observed in manual strength at this age level (Fig. 1) and may also be noted with thrusting strength (Fig. 3). It is inter-

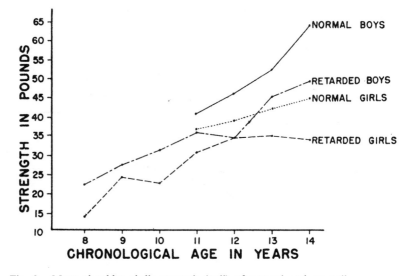

Fig. 2. Mean shoulder girdle strength (pull) of normal and mentally retarded boys and girls. Data on normal boys taken from Jones.[11]

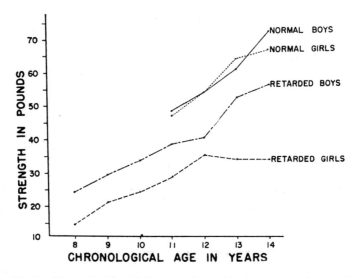

Fig. 3. Mean shoulder girdle strength (push) of normal and mentally retarded boys and girls. Data on normal boys and girls taken from Jones.[11]

esting to note that the sex differences in pulling strength are of about the same magnitude for the normal and mentally retarded children at 11 yr and again at 14 yr of age. Apparently the factors associated with puberty which affect strength development in the two sexes function to about the same degree in normal and mentally retarded children. Why the trend in pulling strength for the mentally retarded girls should reach a plateau at 12 yr of age and then decline at 14 yr cannot be explained. With normal girls the upward trend continues through 14 yr of age with the slope of the curve being approximately the same as that for the three previous years.[11]

Age differences in thrusting strength for normal and mentally retarded boys and girls are shown in Fig. 3. Here again the normal children are markedly superior to the mentally retarded at those age levels for which normative data are available. Why the sex differences in thrusting strength should be so much greater in the mentally retarded than in the normal children is not apparent. With normal children the data presented by Jones[11] indicated that at 13 yr of age girls were on the average stronger in thrusting strength than boys. With the mentally retarded the sex differences were greater at this age than at the younger age levels.

In summarizing the data on static dynamometric strength of normal and mentally retarded children, the evidence clearly showed that the mentally retarded children included in this study were markedly inferior in strength to normal children at every age level. In general, this inferiority became more noticeable with advancing age. The reason for this tendency to lose ground is not readily apparent, but it cannot be due to growth failure, since at almost every age level the mentally retarded children were at or exceeded published height and weight norms. It is perhaps due to a tendency for the mentally retarded to use his body less than the normal child in activities which require the development of maximum muscular force. This may in part be due to a lower level of energy expenditure in the mentally retarded child, hence the drive to move into activities demanding the use of muscular force has little appeal.

Dynamic strength. Comparative data on normal and slow-learning children in the standing broad jump are given in Fig. 4. In this measure the differ-

Fig. 4. Comparison of mean performance scores in the standing broad jump for normal and mentally retarded children by chronological age. Data on normal boys and girls adapted from Neilson and Cozens,[19] Espenschade,[5] and the Highland-Mendota Beach Research Project, University of Wisconsin.

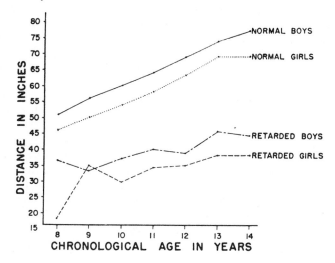

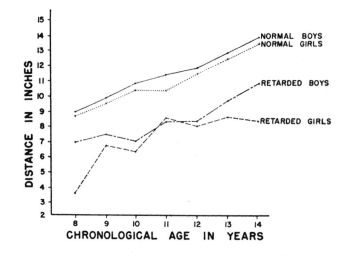

Fig. 5. Comparison of means in the vertical jump for normal and mentally retarded children by chronological age. Data on normal boys and girls adapted from Meyer,[17] McCloy,[14] and Neilson and Cozens.[19]

ences between the groups are great at every age level. The performance of the mentally retarded in the standing broad jump at 14 yr of age for both boys and girls does not equal the mean performance of the normal 8-year-old of either sex. In comparison with normal children, the slope of the performance curves for the slow learners indicates that these children are losing ground with advancing age. It should be kept in mind that the standing broad jump is a complex skill and is readily subject to learning effects. The data would suggest that either the slow learner has not had as much experience with this kind of skill as the normal child or that the learnings associated with this skill are too involved for him to master readily.

Performance curves of mentally retarded and normal boys and girls for the vertical jump are shown in Fig. 5. It is interesting to note that the difference in mean performance in the vertical jump between the ages of 8 and 14 yr for the normal boy was on the average approximately 5 in., whereas with the mentally retarded boy it was slightly less than 4 in. Likewise the normal girls showed a differential of almost 5 in. in mean performance between 8 and 14 yr, whereas the difference for the mentally retarded girls amounted to $4\frac{1}{2}$ in. In the standing broad jump the differences between the scores at 8 and 14 yr were of the order of 25 in. for the normal boys and only 7 in. for the mentally retarded boys. Apparently the problem of organizing the body for the skills required in the broad jump is of a higher order than that required for the vertical jump and hence less improvement is to be expected in the broad jump with the slow learner.

Observations on the throwing behavior of normal boys and girls has universally demonstrated the marked superiority of the boys in this event at all age levels, the difference becoming greater with advancing age. As is shown in Fig. 6, the same general pattern of performance holds true for

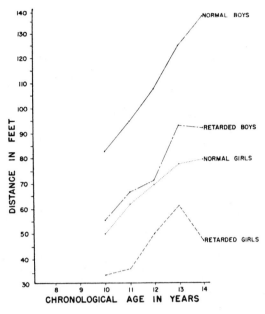

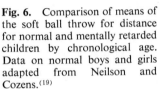

Fig. 6. Comparison of means of the soft ball throw for distance for normal and mentally retarded children by chronological age. Data on normal boys and girls adapted from Neilson and Cozens.[19]

the mentally retarded children included in the present study, although the mean performance of the mentally retarded boys and girls is substantially lower than that of normal children at each age level. The sex factor in this event is the most striking of all the performance tests given, for it is the one event in which the mentally retarded boys exceeded the normal girls at every age level. It is interesting to note that at 13 yr of age, the peak level of average performance for mentally retarded boys, this group had achieved the level attained by the normal 11-year-old boy. Likewise, the mentally retarded girls at 13 yr of age (their peak level of performance in this event) were at the average performance level of normal 11-year-old girls. It can also be seen that the difference in mean performance between normal and mentally retarded children of the same sex is greater at the older age levels than at the younger. For example, with the boys, the difference at 10 yr of age in the distance throw was approximately 27 ft, while at 14 yr of age the difference was 45 ft; with the girls these differences at 10 and 14 yr were 16 ft and 35 ft, respectively. Whether this is related primarily to differences in learning ability or to differences in practice and opportunity to perform this skill is not known. Observations of the mechanics of performance of both boys and girls in the study group disclosed that the movement patterns of large numbers of children of both sexes were poor and indicated unfamiliarity with the correct manner of executing this skill.

Running speed. The age trends for average speed of running expressed in yards per second for normal and mentally retarded boys and girls are shown in Fig. 7. The typical trend of superiority of performance of the normal children over that of the mentally retarded is again demonstrated in this event. The superiority of the normal children is so great that at no age level do the means of the mentally retarded children approximate the mean performance of the normal child of the

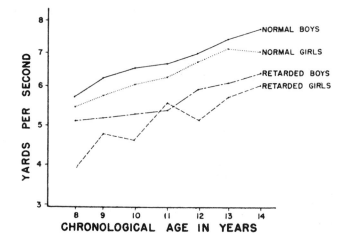

Fig. 7.   Speed of running data for normal and mentally retarded children by chronological age. Data on normal boys and girls adapted from Espenschade,[5] Meyer,[17] and Neilson and Cozens.[19]

same sex. It will be noted that the normal girls achieve the greatest speed of running on the average at approximately 13 yr of age with performance declining thereafter, whereas the mentally retarded girls continue to show improvement between 12 and 14 yr. The mean performance of the normal boys and girls is on the average closer at 12 than at 14 yr while that of the mentally retarded is closer at 14 than at 12.

Measure of agility. The Burpee test, or the number of squat thrusts executed in a 10-sec period, is presumed to be an index of general body coordination or agility. It will be noted that the normative data given in Table 8 for normal children show only modest changes with advancing age. As indicated earlier, this test did not prove to be entirely satisfactory with the slow learners due to problems of learning the correct execution of the event. Hence, caution should be exercised in interpreting the curves presented for the mentally retarded boys and girls as given in Fig. 8. Even so, it is safe to say that in

agility, as measured by the Burpee test, the slow learners were at no age level equal to the standard of performance of the normal 8-year-old boy or girl.

General summary on performance of normal and mentally retarded children

From the data presented herein, it is clearly evident that the mentally retarded boys and girls included in this study were well behind published standards of motor performance of normal children. In certain events such as the squat thrusts and the standing broad jump, the mentally retarded at age 14 failed to reach the standard of the normal 8-year-old child of the same sex. In running speed the standard for the normal boy and girl of 10 yr of age is superior to the average performance of the mentally retarded 14-year-old of the same sex. In tests of strength the mentally retarded lag 1 to 3 yr behind the standards for normal children. In the vertical jump, a measure of explosive muscular power, the slow learner is as much as 4 yr retarded

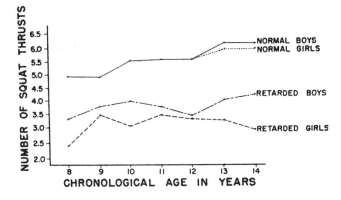

Fig. 8. Comparison of mean performance scores on the Burpee test for normal and mentally retarded children by chronological age. Data on normal boys and girls adapted from Carpenter,[2] and McCloy.[14]

in development when viewed in the light of published norms on normal children. These data provide rather definite evidence of the extent of motor retardation of the slow learner. However, the basic factors underlying the cause of the retardation must await further investigation. The fact that at certain age levels the performance curves show some unusual peaks, as for example the rather consistently high performance of the 9- and 11-year-old mentally retarded girls, suggests that the sample drawn at these age levels contained some rather high quality performers. This would suggest that the potential for higher levels of motor achievement is attainable with the slow learner.

Interrelationships among motor functions

As pointed out earlier, studies on normal human beings have shown that both gross and fine motor skills are rather specific in nature, although certain types of motor skills have been shown to be more highly correlated than are others. In general, it has been shown that events which purport to measure the same general kind of ability tend to give reasonably high intercorrelations. The data in the present study offered the opportunity to determine whether known interrelationships among motor functions in the normal tend to hold true also for the mentally retarded. Therefore intercorrelations among all performance tests by age and sex were computed. The general trend of interrelationships among the performance variables has been taken from 14 intercorrelation tables[2] (one intercorrelation table for each of the seven age levels for each sex) and is discussed in the following sections.

Static dynamometric strength. Most studies are in agreement that intercorrelations among measures of static dynamometric strength range between 0.50 and 0.90 for adults and adolescents. For example, Jones[11] in a study of 72 adolescent boys found that the intercorrelations among measures of strength of grip, pull, and thrust ranged from 0.72 to 0.83. With the mentally retarded boys at the 12-, 13-, and 14-

---

[2] The intercorrelation tables may be obtained upon request from the authors at the University of Wisconsin, Madison.

year-old age levels, the intercorrelations among these measures ranged from 0.54 to 0.88 with the majority of the coefficients clustering around 0.70. Thus, it would seem that with the older boys the interrelationships among the strength variables are of about the same magnitude for mentally retarded boys as for normal boys. At the lower age levels with the mentally retarded boys, there is greater evidence of specificity of strength with many of the correlations in the range 0.40 to 0.50. These correlations are of about the same size as the majority of the correlations reported by Irish[8] in a study of interrelationships among eight strength variables in children 6 to 9 yr of age. With the mentally retarded girls all correlations among the strength variables are positive, but the correlations for the three older age groups range from 0.16 to 0.92. At the lower age levels the correlations among the strength measures are still lower with several coefficients approximating 0.10 or less. Therefore, it is evident that with the group studied static strength as measured here is more specific in character for girls than for boys. The same sex difference tends to be true with normal children. However, the correlations between right and left grip strength and between strength of pull and thrust are reasonably high for both sexes at almost all age levels. It is not surprising to find that the strength of muscle groups which are closely related anatomically and functionally are highly correlated.

Measures of power. For the purposes of the present discussion speed of running is included as a power type of event along with the vertical jump, standing broad jump, and the throw for distance. This is done because studies on normal humans have shown that the scores on these events show reasonably high intercorrelations, and factor analysis studies have indicated

that these events are strongly weighted with the "speed factor."[3,20] The magnitude of these intercorrelations with normal adolescents is illustrated by the findings of Espenschade[5] in which intercorrelations among power-type events were reported ranging from 0.44 to 0.82 for boys and 0.29 to 0.78 for girls. The highest correlations reported by Espenschade between any two single events for both sexes were between the standing broad jump and the dash with coefficients of 0.82 and 0.78 for boys and girls, respectively. With college men, however, Brown[1] reported a correlation of only 0.457 between the broad jump and the 60-yd dash. Hester[7] in a recent study on junior high school boys reported inter-correlations among the four power events ranging from 0.59 to 0.76, the latter correlation being between the broad jump and the dash. With the mentally retarded boys, the intercorrelations among the four events were on the average only slightly lower than those reported on normal boys, ranging at most age levels between 0.35 and 0.80. For the girls in the age groups below 12 yr the majority of the correlations fell in the range of 0.30 to 0.60 which are similar to the correlations reported by Espenschade.[5] However, in the age groups 13 and 14 yr the intercorrelations, while still positive, were somewhat lower (0.20 to 0.40). In general, it would seem safe to conclude that with the sample of mentally retarded subjects studied, the intercorrelations among the tests designed to measure power were not greatly different than those found with human beings of normal intelligence.

Measures of balance and agility. Many gross motor skills require elements of body balance and among these are the skills involving rapid changes in body direction. Therefore one might expect measures of balance and agility to be positively correlated. Some evidence of this is given by the work of Brown[1] in which he obtained a correlation on college men of 0.431 between a dodging run and a measure of body balance. With the mentally retarded boys, correlations between the balance-beam test and the agility run ranged from 0.25 to 0.73 and with the girls from 0.06 to 0.74. For both sexes the majority of the correlations were in the range 0.30 to 0.60 indicating that these abilities are correlated in the mentally retarded in much the same way as in normal persons. It is interesting to note that the broad jump which is an event requiring considerable balance and agility as well as power gave correlations with the balance test of 0.31 to 0.79 for the mentally retarded boys and from 0.33 to 0.70 for the girls (the 14-year-old group excepted). This compares favorably with the correlation reported by Brown[1] on college men of 0.36 between these two events.

The data on this group of mentally retarded children indicate rather strongly that the clustering of motor traits and abilities of the mentally retarded is not greatly different from that which has been observed on normal adolescents and adults.

Intelligence and motor performance

Observations on normal children of school age have shown that when measures of intelligence and measures of motor skill are correlated, the coefficients are low and in many instances approximate zero. When the tables of intercorrelations were examined, it was noted that of the total of the 84 correlations of motor performance variables with IQ (12 correlations at 7 age levels for each sex), 82 of the coefficients for the boys were positive. While most of the correlations were low, the fact that they were so consistently positive suggests that intelligence may play a role in

the motor performance of the mentally retarded boy. With the girls the findings are less clear with many of the coefficients negative and others close to zero. Of the 84 correlations at all age levels for the girls, a total of 56 were positive and 28 negative. However, there is neither a clear-cut nor consistent pattern of interrelationship of the motor performance variables with IQ for either boys or girls, since variables giving reasonably high correlations at one age level drop close to zero at another age. Therefore, it can be stated that although the relationship between motor performance and IQ tended to be positive, the intercorrelations were low and not greatly different from what one would expect to find with normal children.

Summary and Conclusions

This investigation has been concerned with describing certain motor characteristics of mentally retarded children. The subjects for the investigation included 284 mentally retarded boys and girls in special classes in the public schools of Madison and Milwaukee, Wisconsin. A battery of 11 gross motor tests was given to all subjects and observations were made on age and sex trends for each skill tested.

In order to obtain a picture of the status of the motor development of the slow learner, comparisons were made between the motor achievement levels of the mentally retarded by age and sex with published norms on normal children. In addition the study was concerned with investigating the interrelationships among motor abilities of the mentally retarded and comparing these results with similar information on normal children. Observations were also made on the relationship between intelligence and the motor abilities of the mentally retarded child.

The findings indicated that the age trends in strength for each sex followed approximately the same pattern as those for normal children, although at a lower level at every age. On the power measures (standing broad jump, vertical jump, and the distance throw), age and sex differences were similar to the differences reported on normal children, although in the standing broad jump the differences between age groups for both sexes were markedly different from those reported on normal children. In running speed, balance, and agility, the differences between the levels of performance of the mentally retarded by age and sex followed the same general pattern as those observed on normal children.

Direct quantitative comparisons between the motor proficiency scores of the mentally retarded and published data on normal children resulted in more definite conclusions. In general, it can be stated that with the mentally retarded children studied, the means of both boys and girls on most measures were 2 to 4 yr behind the published age norms of normal children. Furthermore, the discrepancy between the normal and the mentally retarded tended to increase with each advancing age level.

Apparently motor functions in the mentally retarded cluster to approximately the same degree as in normal humans, for when the interrelationships among scores on the specific motor tests were examined, the interrelationships among particular variables were similar to those reported for persons in the normal range of intelligence. While most of the intercorrelations among tests purporting to measure similar gross motor functions were in the range 0.40 to 0.70, the size of these coefficients is sufficient to indicate that these abilities tend to cluster in the mentally retarded to about the same extent as in the normal.

The findings of the study clearly demonstrated that intelligence as measured by standardized intelligence tests was positively correlated with most of the motor performance tests. However, the coefficients were generally low and of approximately the same order as other investigators have reported with normal children.

In conclusion it can be stated that the mentally retarded children included in this investigation were markedly inferior to normal children in all motor performance tests and that with advancing age the deviations from the normal tended to become greater. However, the general pattern of change by age and sex was similar to that reported on normal children, as were the intercorrelations among the specific motor tests. Although the findings would indicate that the poor quality of motor performance was a function of low intelligence, the relationships between measures of intelligence and motor performance were similar to correlations obtained between these variables on normal humans. The great differences in motor proficiency between the normal and the mentally retarded, as demonstrated here, clearly shows that the degree of motor retardation of these children is perhaps greater than had been previously supposed.

References

1. Brown, Howard Steven, "A Comparative Study of Motor Fitness Tests," *Res. Quart.*, **25** (1954), 8–19.

2. Carpenter, Aileen, "The Measurement of General Motor Capacity and General Motor Ability in the First

Three Grades," *ibid.*, **13** (1942), 444-65.

3. Coleman, James W., "The Differential Measurement of the Speed Factor in Large Muscle Activities," *ibid.*, **8** (1937), 123–30.

4. Doll, Edgar A., "The Feebleminded Child," in *Manual of Child Psychology*, ed. by Leonard Carmichael. New York: John Wiley & Sons, Inc., 1945, pp. 845–85.

5. Espenschade, Anna, "Motor Performance in Adolescence," *Monographs Soc. Res. Child Develop.*, **5** (1940). 1–126.

6. Espenschade, Anna, Robert R. Dable, and Robert Schoendube, "Dynamic Balance in Adolescent Boys," *Res. Quart*, **24** (1953), 270–75.

7. Hester, Robert A., "The Relationship Between Performance of Junior High School Boys in the Standing Broad Jump and Achievement in Selected Tests of Motor Ability." Unpublished Master's thesis, University of Wisconsin, Madison, 1955.

8. Irish, Helen, "A Study of the Within Year and Between Year Interrelationships Among Measures of Static Dynamometric Strength Used With Lower Elementary School Children." Unpublished Master's thesis, University of Wisconsin, Madison, 1957.

9. Johnson, Granville B., "Physical Skill Test for Sectioning Classes Into Homogeneous Units," *Res. Quart.*, **3** (1932), 128–37.

10. Johnson, Granville B., "A Study of the Relationship That Exists Between Physical Skills as Measured, and the General Intelligence of College Students," *ibid.*, **13** (1942), 57–59.

11. Jones, Harold E., *Motor Performance and Growth*. Berkeley: University of California Press, 1949, p. 181.

12. Kane, Robert J., and Howard V. Meredith, "Ability in the Standing Broad Jump of Elementary School Children 7, 9, and 11 Years of Age," *Res. Quart.*, **23** (1952), 198–208.

13. Keller, Lindsey D., "The Effect of Maturation on Physical Skill as Measured by the Johnson Physical Skill Test," *ibid.*, **9** (1938), 54–58.

14. McCloy, Charles H., and Norma D. Young, *Tests and Measurements in Health and Physical Education*. New York: Appleton-Century-Crofts, 1954.

15. Meredith, Howard V., "The Rhythm of Physical Growth: A Study of Eighteen Anthropometric Measurements on Iowa City White Males Ranging in Age Between Birth and Eighteen Years," *University of Iowa Studies in Child Welfare*, **11**, No. 3 (1935), 128.

16. Metheny, Eleanor, "The Present Status of Strength Testing for Children of Elementary School Age," *Res. Quart.*, **12** (1941), 115–30.

17. Meyer, Margaret. Unpublished data on Randall School Children. Madison, Wis., 1956.

18. Miles, Catherine C., and Walter R. Miles, "The Correlation of Intelligence Scores and Chronological Age From Early to Late Maturity," *Am. J. Physiol.*, **44** (1932), 44–78.

19. Neilson, N. P., and Frederick W. Cozens, *Achievement Scales in Physical Education Activities, for Boys and Girls in Elementary and Junior High Schools*. New York: A. S. Barnes & Co., 1935.

20. Rarick, G. Lawrence, "An Analysis of the Speed Factor in Simple Athletic Activities," *Res. Quart.*, **8** (1937), 88–105.

21. Ray, Howard C., "Interrelationships of Physical and Mental Abilities and Achievements of High School Boys," *ibid.*, **11** (1940), 127–41.

22. Seashore, Harold G., "Some Relationships of Fine and Gross Motor Abilities," *ibid.*, **13** (1942), 246–59.

23. Seashore, Harold G., "The Development of a Beam-Walking Test and Its

Use in Measuring Development of Balance in Children," *ibid.*, **18** (1947), 246–59.

24. Sherman, Mandel, *Intelligence and Its Deviations*. New York: The Ronald Press Company, 1945, p. 286.

25. Sloan, William, "Motor Proficiency and Intelligence," *Am. J. Mental Deficiency*, **55** (1951), 394–406.

26. Sloan, William, "The Lincoln-Oseretsky Motor Development Scale," *Genet. Psychol. Monographs*, **55** (1955), 183–252.

27. Stuart, Harold C., and Stuart S. Stevenson, "Physical Growth and Development," in *Mitchell-Nelson Textbook of Pediatrics*, ed. by Waldo E. Nelson. Philadelphia: W. B. Saunders Co., 1950. pp. 59–71.

28. Tredgold, A. F., *A Textbook of Mental Deficiency* (6th ed.). Baltimore: William Wood (Division of the Williams & Wilkins Co.), 1937.

29. Tredgold, A. F., *A Textook of Mental Deficiency* (7th ed.). Baltimore: The Williams & Wilkins Co., 1947.

VI

Ergogenic Aids

Ergogenic aids are substances or factors that are thought to influence work output. Work output has been the object of the panaceas and nostrums of scientists and quacks alike throughout the ages. Observation of the rituals carried out by some athletes, coaches, and trainers before and during athletic contests might lead the viewer to believe that he were in another age of mankind. True, the more modern advances of science have reached into most of the locker rooms and gymnasiums of the world, but even here many of the potential aids are used uncritically or incorrectly. The studies presented in this chapter are examples of the attempts of researchers to differentiate between fact and fiction.

In each of the areas presented, smoking, oxygen inhalation, drugs, and breakfast intake, there have been differences of opinion among physiologists and physical educators, due, in part, to the difficulty in designing studies on ergogenic aids. One of the major problems in research of this type is the so-called psychological effect of any special substance or procedure. Some of these studies show that attempts have been made to control the psychological effect. Another problem in studying ergogenic aids is the fact that the physical condition or rate of training of the individual might modify some relationships found with untrained subjects. Variability in human physical performance is a natural phenomenon and, although controlled in experiments by statistical and other means, might account for differences in response to laboratory situations.

The matter of ergogenic aids still requires much additional study. More rigorous research designs, including selection of a large enough number of different types of subjects and replication of experiments, are a must if more valid information is to be made available to coaches and physical educators. The studies presented in this chapter certainly should provide some interesting points of departure.

R. G. BANNISTER / D. J. C. CUNNINGHAM

The Effects on the Respiration and Performance During Exercise of Adding Oxygen to Inspired Air

Reprinted from the *Journal of Physiology* (*London*),
125 (1954), 118–37.

Dr. Bannister confounded the pundits of the sports world in 1954 when he became the first human to run the mile in less than 4 min. The 4-min mile was the sonic barrier of the distance runner. Bannister showed that it could be done! Although the first 4-min mile was an accomplishment of courage, persistence, and great athletic ability, it was also a feat of the intellect. For Bannister learned how the body could be pushed to even greater limits of performance by extending the cardiorespiratory mechanisms of the body, through research conducted at Oxford while he was working on his thesis for an M.D. degree. This study is one of several he conducted at that time.

The study revealed that the addition of oxygen to inspired air increased the subject's maximum work performance. Bannister found that performance was improved more by adding 66 per cent and 100 per cent oxygen than by 33 per cent, and that the optimum result was obtained at 66 per cent oxygen in inspired air. The study postulates that the reason for the effectiveness of oxygen inspiration in improving performance was the abolition of arterial anoxemia which is present when atmosphere air is breathed during exhausting work. Through these studies, Bannister found that it was possible to push the organism to higher extremes of oxygen consumption and carbon dioxide output. The application of these findings opened the doors to higher levels of athletic achievements.

There have been several reports in the literature of the effects of oxygen on the respiration and performance during heavy work. The most extensive of these was by Asmussen and Nielsen[3] who showed, among other things, that during moderately severe exercise on the bicycle ergometer the addition of oxygen to the inspired air resulted in a marked and sudden depression of the respiration. To explain their findings they postulated that muscle working under partially anaerobic conditions liberated into the blood stream an unknown substance which stimulated the respiration and which was rapidly destroyed by high concentrations of oxygen. This was in addition to any effects which might be ascribed to the production of excess lactate. More recently, Miller[46] has reported that he could detect no effect on any of the quantities which he measured when oxygen was added to the inspired air of athletic and nonathletic subjects performing moderate and severe exercise on a treadmill.

It therefore seemed worthwhile to see whether the effects described by Asmussen and Nielsen[3] could be produced during hard exercise on the treadmill and to consider the possibility that these effects, if present, might be explained without invoking the intervention of an unknown hypothetical substance.

Methods

The methods used and the four subjects employed have been described in a previous paper by Bannister, Cunningham, and Douglas.[6]

Results

Exercise to exhaustion while breathing air enriched with oxygen

Four experiments were carried out on each subject. An intensity of exercise was chosen for each subject such that

the breaking point was reached in 6–9 min when breathing atmospheric air. The subjects then ran to exhaustion in three further experiments during which they breathed 33, 66, and 100 per cent oxygen, respectively. The CO_2 output when breathing higher concentrations of oxygen was about the same as when breathing air. The oxygen consumptions were recorded, but were obviously unreliable for the reasons discussed by Hill, Long, and Lupton.[33] The results of 20 such runs by 4 subjects are shown in Fig. 1 and the duration of the exercise and breaking points in Table 1.

The addition of oxygen to the inspired air always improved performance considerably and often resulted in the establishment of a steady state during exercise which would normally produce rapid exhaustion (Table 1).

Substitution of 66 per cent or 100 per cent oxygen for air reduced the pulmonary ventilation by 5–25 l per min in all subjects. In the air-breathing experiments on P.J.P. and N.D.McW. the breaking points occurred so early that only one or two measurements of ventilation were possible. These were almost certainly not steady-state values, and the ventilation was probably still rising rapidly. It is likely that had the maximum ventilation been recorded with these two subjects, the differences between the air and oxygen

TABLE 1

Duration of Exercise During the Inhalation of Different Air-Oxygen Mixtures.
Speed in All Experiments $6\frac{1}{4}$ mi per hr

		DURATION OF EXERCISE WHEN BREATHING			
		21% O_2	*33% O_2*	*66% O_2*	*100% O_2*
Subject	*Gradient*	*min sec*	*min sec*	*min sec*	*min sec*
R. G. B. (1)	1 in 7	8 45	8 45	*17 15	*16 32
R. G. B. (2)	1 in 7	8 26	15 17	23 40	20 40
D. J. C. C.	1 in 10	8 58	11 20	*24 48	20 45
N. D. McW.	1 in 8	6 35	13 25	*23 0	17 18
P. J. P.	1 in 16	6 25	10 15	13 50	11 55

* Denotes breaking point not reached.

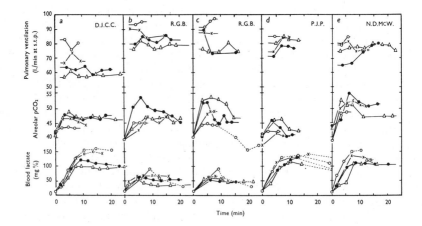

Fig. 1. *a-e*: Effect of different concentrations of oxygen in the inspired air on respiration and blood lactate during very heavy standardized exercise. Speed in all experiments, $6\frac{1}{4}$ ○——○, breathing atmospheric air; x —— x, breathing 33% O_2; ○——○, breathing 66% O_2; ○—○, breathing 100% O_2. Points obtained during exercise joined by full lines; points obtained during recovery at rest joined by broken lines. a, subject D.J.C.C., gradient, 1 in 10; b, c, subject R.G.B., gradient 1 in 7; d. subject P.J.P., gradient, 1 in 16; e, subject N.D. McW., gradient 1 in 8.

experiments would have been greater than is indicated in Fig. 1*d* and *e*. The blood lactate response was reduced by one-third to a half in three subjects and by one-seventh in the other by the inhalation of the higher concentrations of oxygen. The magnitude of the differences in blood lactate in three subjects is masked by the fact that they were completely exhausted before the blood lactate reached its highest level when breathing air, whereas the lower concentrations recorded during oxygen inhalation were steady-state or near-steady-state values. When inspiring 66 per cent or 100 per cent oxygen the alveolar pCO_2 was from $\frac{1}{2}$ to 9 mm higher than when air was breathed; in the two athletes figures as high as 54 and 55 mm were recorded, 14 and 15 mm above the preliminary resting values. The alveolar pCO_2 showed a tendency to fall slightly as the exercise continued.

The effects of 33 per cent oxygen were intermediate between those of air and of the higher concentrations of oxygen.

66 and 100 per cent oxygen. The experiments showed that the inhalation of 100 per cent oxygen during severe exercise at sea level resulted in complete exhaustion within 12–21 min, whereas three of the subjects, when they breathed 66 per cent oxygen, had not reached their breaking points when they stopped running after 23 min; the fourth reached his breaking point 2 min later than in the experiment when he breathed 100 per cent oxygen. There were no clear-cut differences between the pulmonary ventilations or the blood lactate and alveolar pCO_2 levels with 100 per cent and 66 per cent oxygen. A small difference in one direction with one subject was usually offset by a difference in the opposite direction with another.

The subjective effects were impressive. Three of the four subjects found the exercise much easier when breathing 66 per cent oxygen. R.G.B. noticed with surprise that he felt mentally elated when breathing 66 per cent, but not when breathing pure oxygen. The exercise was incomparably easier than in any of the previous runs at this intensity; breathing was effortless and he stopped running more from boredom than from exhaustion. In the second series of experiments when he ran for 24 min on 66 per cent oxygen he again noticed these effects, although he had completed a run to exhaustion on the previous day. D.J.C.C. felt breathless when breathing 100 per cent oxygen, although the pulmonary ventilation was 19 1 per min less than when breathing air. With 66 per cent oxygen his breathing was comfortable, and he felt that he could continue to run indefinitely. The other subjects did not know the composition of the inspired air. P.J.P. ran on 66 per cent oxygen on the day after his run to exhaustion on pure oxygen, and although he made no comments he lasted for 2 min longer than on the previous day. N.D.McW. ran on 66 per cent oxygen one morning having completed a run to exhaustion on 100 per cent oxygen the evening before. As he stopped running he said, "You don't have to tell me that there was more oxygen that time!" His breathing seemed easier than during other runs. He thought that there was a definite elation which he distinguished from the mere absence of discomfort. He would have been prepared to run indefinitely had he not had to catch a train.

Sudden changes in the oxygen content of the inspired air during less severe exercise

In these experiments the subjects R.G.B. and D.J.C.C. exercised at slightly lower intensities. Running at $6\frac{1}{4}$ mi per hr up a gradient of 1 in 12 (R.G.B.) and on the level (D.J.C.C.), intensities at which their oxygen consumptions were 3,390 and 1,970 cc per min, respectively, no perceptible change in pulmonary ventilation or alveolar pCO_2 occurred when the inspired gas was suddenly changed from air to 66 per cent oxygen. The subjects were presumably free from oxygen lack during these runs. When they ran at the same speed up gradients of 1 in 10 and 1 in 16, respectively (oxygen consumptions, 3,860 and 2,500 cc per min), definite effects were observed on raising the concentration of oxygen in the inspired air. The subjects breathed atmospheric air for the first 20 min, then 66 per cent oxygen for 10 min, then air for another 10 min. After this R.G.B. stopped running, but D.J. C.C. was switched to 33 per cent oxygen for a further 10 min and finally back to air for 5 min. Blood samples for the estimation of lactate were withdrawn at intervals, the alveolar pCO_2 was measured very frequently with the carbon dioxide meter and the pulmonary ventilation was determined immediately before and after the changes. The results are shown in Fig. 2a and b. In the case of R.G.B. the pulmonary ventilation changed extremely quickly after the switches from 74 to 64 and from 72 to 80 1 per min. The collection of expired air was started after only a few seconds and by that time the changes must have been almost complete. Had there been a significant delay the first bag determination would have given a value intermediate between those for the steady states before and after the switch. However, it showed a changed in ventilation greater than that finally established. The CO_2 meter recorded changes of alveolar pCO_2 from 41.5 to 43 and from 44 to 38 mm. They started about 20 sec after the switch, and there was a large overshoot before a steady value was achieved, particularly after the change from 66 per cent oxygen back to air. The latency of the response of the alveolar pCO_2 to the altered alveolar pO_2 must have been extremely short in view of the length of tubing from the alveolar air sampler to the meter (about 6 ft), the time taken for the alveolar pO_2 to change, and for the alveolar pCO_2 to alter following a change in pulmonary ventilation. The experiment on D.J.C.C. was carried out before the rapidity of the changes was appreciated and measurements were not made sufficiently quickly, but the latency in his case was also small and the changes similar in magnitude.

Alterations of ventilation and alveolar pCO_2 in the same directions occurred later in the same experiment on D.J.C.C. when he was switched to 33 per cent oxygen and back to air, but the effects were not so great. Trotter (personal communication) has provided some evidence that there may be fluctuations in the CO_2 meter reading following large changes in the nitrogen and oxygen contents of the mixture analyzed. This may have contributed to the effects reported here, but the magnitude of the changes in alveolar pCO_2 reflected the changes in ventilation. In five out of six subjects investigated in another connection these rapid changes have been observed

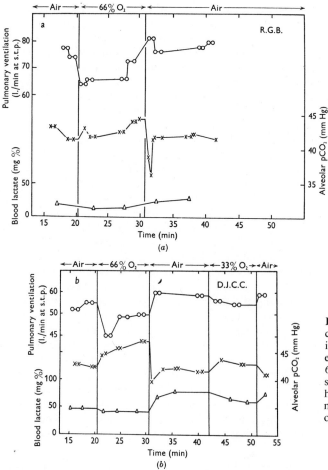

Fig. 2. *a-b*; effects of rapid changes of oxygen content of inspired air during severe exercise. *a*, subject R.G.B., speed $6\frac{1}{4}$ mi per hr, gradient, 1 in 10; *b*, subject, D.J.C.C., speed $6\frac{1}{4}$ mi per hr, gradient, 1 in 16. Inspired gas mixtures are indicated at the top of the figure.

following sudden changes in the inspired oxygen concentration.

The blood lactate changed comparatively slowly after each switch and could not have been responsible for the rapid alterations in ventilation and alveolar pCO_2.

Marked subjective effects were also present. The slight pain in D.J.C.C.'s legs which was present when he breathed air disappeared when 66 per cent oxygen was inspired. When the switch back to air occurred 10 min later he became much more aware of his breathing. After a further 10 min he was getting very tired, but 20 sec after the switch to 33 per cent oxygen his breathing became easier and his vision became suddenly brighter. He was reminded of the change which occurs when normal atmospheric air is suddenly inspired after a period of breathing air deficient in oxygen at rest. Ten minutes later, when he started breathing air instead of 33 per cent oxygen, he became dyspnoeic and was forced to change his respiratory rate from 30 to 45 breaths per min.

Discussion

Respiratory effects of adding oxygen to the inspired air

The difference in the concentrations of lactate in the blood which were observed when gas mixtures enriched with oxygen were breathed during work are in general agreement with the findings of Asmussen and Nielsen[3] and of Lundin and Ström.[43]

The significance of the changes in alveolar pCO_2 produced by oxygen are discussed elsewhere (Bannister *et al.*[6]). The mode of action of oxygen in producing the results reported here requires further consideration.

The effects of adding oxygen to the inspired air during exercise was studied by Hill, Long, and Lupton.[34] During heavy work of approximately constant severity they found that the pulmonary ventilation was not always reduced. However, the capacity for maximal exertion was considerably increased when 50 per cent oxygen was inspired. The oxygen consumptions were about 20 per cent greater than when air was breathed and higher concentrations of lactate in the blood could be tolerated. They thought that the differences were too great to be explained in terms of the increased oxygen content of the arterial blood alone, and postulated that during maximal work breathing air there might be a fall in the oxygen tension of the arterial blood which might affect the heart and brain. The abolition of the anoxemia by the addition of oxygen to the inspired air would result in an increase in cardiac output and possibly in the tolerance of the brain for acid metabolites.

Haldane and Priestley[25] reported that during moderate exercise in untrained subjects the alveolar pCO_2 rose to higher levels and the work seemed easier when oxygen was inhaled. They did not detect this difference during moderate exercise in a subject who led a more active life. Briggs[10] made similar observations on the pulmonary ventilation and CO_2 content of the expired air. In 1934, Chirstensen, Krogh, and Lindhard summarized their studies on heavy work. In particular they found that when the exercise was so severe that it could not be maintained for 2 min, the addition of oxygen to the inspired air had no effect on the performance. With work of slightly lower intensity oxygen increased the endurance and the capacity for work. When, breathing oxygen, the subject started with moderate exercise and the intensity was subsequently increased by stages, he was able to maintain rates of work which had previously exhausted him within 2 min. Evidently time was required for the adjustment of the respiratory and circulatory systems to the new conditions if the extra oxygen was to produce its effect. There are no contradictions between any of these findings and our own.

Asmussen and Nielsen[3, 4] and Asmussen[1] were the first to show conclusively that during prolonged heavy work on a bicycle ergometer the addition of oxygen to the inspired air produced a considerable reduction in the pulmonary ventilation, an increase in the alveolar pCO_2, and a reduction in the blood lactate. They could not detect such an effect with light or moderate work and concluded that it was present only above certain intensities. They showed that the effect was graded in that the reduction in ventilation was small with 30 per cent, large with 60 per cent, and maximal with 100 per cent oxygen. They also found that if a sudden switch was made from atmospheric air to oxygen during the work, the change in ventilation occurred much more rapidly than the alterations in the concentration of lactate or pyruvate in the blood. All our findings are, generally speaking, in agreement with theirs, except that in two of our four subjects the depression of ventilation was greater with 66 per cent than with 100 per cent oxygen and that the differences at these levels were probably insignificant. However, our main experiments were different in that the work resulted in exhaustion within 6–9 min when breathing air. We did not investigate the relative values of 66 per cent and pure oxygen during prolonged exercise at the slightly lower intensity used by Asmussen and Nielsen.

Hickam, Pryor, Page, and Atwell[32] have shown that the substitution of pure oxygen for air reduces markedly and suddenly the ventilation during heavy exercise in untrained subjects. This is accompanied by the abolition of a previously existing slight arterial desaturation with oxygen. Unlike Asmussen and Nielsen, they conclude that the effect is due to the removal of an anoxic stimulation of the carotid chemoreceptors. It is a pity that such short experimental periods were used. The subjects could hardly have been in a steady state in any part of these experiments, and so the large numbers of measurements made cannot be compared quantitatively with our own or others in the literature. However, their results are in qualitative agreement with many of ours.

Miller[46] was unable to record any important subjective or objective differences either in untrained subects or in athletes running to exhaustion when 100 per cent oxygen was substituted for air. No respiratory measurements were made. This is in complete contradiction to our findings and to those of the earlier workers. He reports that when subjects were told that they were to run on oxygen their performance improved. We can scarcely believe that the differences which we and many others have observed were entirely subjective. In particular, the inspired air mixtures were unknown to two of our subjects, and we were still able to detect effects which varied in magnitude with the amount of oxygen added to the inspired air.

Asmussen and Nielsen[3, 4] did not think that a reduction of the arterial pO_2 during heavy exercise when breathing air was responsible for the effects they observed on the grounds that if it occurred at all it was too small to stimulate the chemoreceptors. They also pointed out that the further depression in ventilation which occurred when pure oxygen was substituted for 60 per cent could not be explained on the basis of an abolition of arterial anoxemia. They excluded changes in blood lactate, which were too slow to be responsible. Subsequent experiments in which they trapped blood in the legs with pneumatic cuffs during work and observed the effects produced when the circulation was reestablished during the subsequent rest led to the postulation of a substance closely related to the "hyperpnoein" of Yandell Henderson.[31] This substance was supposedly produced by ischemic muscle; it stimulated the chemoreceptors and was rapidly destroyed in the presence of oxygen. Further evidence for their view was provided by the observation that during heavy work with the arms alone, similar effects were obtained from the substitution of oxygen for air. This occurred at relatively low metabolic rates, when the cardiovascular and respiratory systems were not working to capacity.

However, our data and those of Asmussen and Nielsen are not incompatible with a more orthodox explanation in terms of arterial anoxemia. If the arterial pO_2 is depressed during heavy exercise, the addition of oxygen to the inspired air would be expected to raise the arterial pO_2 to values in excess of the threshold of the carotid and aortic chemoreceptors and to lower the ventilation. In addition, a lowered arterial pO_2 might result in cardiac embarrassment, which would be relieved by breathing oxygen. This is another possible means by which arterial anoxemia might affect the pulmonary ventilation, and is briefly considered later in this paper. For the theory that the effects were due to arterial anoxemia acting by way of the chemoreceptors to be satisfactory by itself, certain requirements must be met: (a) The part of the hyperpnoea in heavy exercise which may be ascribed

to anoxic stimulation of the chemoreceptors (i.e., the increase which is recorded when air is substituted for 66 per cent or 100 per cent O_2) should be comparable to the increase in ventilation when the subject is exposed to a similar degree of anoxia at rest. (b) The arterial pO_2 in heavy exercise should be depressed to levels which would stimulate the chemoreceptors. (c) If possible, satisfactory explanations for the depression of the arterial pO_2 should be available. It might be the result of limitations in the rate of diffusion of oxygen across the pulmonary epithelium or of fairly gross irregularities of distribution of blood flow and air flow in different parts of the lungs, or of both. (d) If these requirements are met, it has to be decided whether the graded effect of 33 and 66 per cent O_2 on the ventilation may be explained in similar terms: in other words, is it possible that the inhalation of 33 per cent oxygen is insufficient to abolish completely the arterial anoxemia which exists when air is breathed? The theory must also account for the effect of oxygen on the ventilation during work with the arms alone. We have no data on this point. These requirements must now be considered in some detail.

Response to oxygen lack at rest

Recent accounts of the causes of hyperpnoea during strenuous exercise have rejected the suggestion that a lowering of the arterial pO_2 may be a factor in normal subjects (Comroe;[13] Pitts;[49] Gray;[23] Grodins[24]). This is presumably due to the widespread belief that the ventilatory response of normal subjects to anoxia of short duration at rest is relatively small (e.g., Dripps and Comroe[19]). Such data, though correct in themselves, do not take account of the inhibitory effect of the accompanying acapnia. When this acapnia is reduced to a minimum by the process of acclimatization, the effectiveness of quite small reductions in the arterial pO_2 in stimulating the ventilation becomes apparent (Fitz-Gerald;[21] Boothby[8]). Haldane, Meakins, and Priestley[25] showed that when oxygen lack is added to the effects of an excess of carbon dioxide, as occurs when a subject rebreathes air from a confined space at rest, the effects of the anoxia appear earlier and more powerfully than when the subject rebreathes air and the pO_2 falls at a similar rate, but the CO_2 is not allowed to accumulate. Nielsen and Smith[48] and Gee[22] have produced evidence to show that the effects of the two stimuli combined need not necessarily be strictly additive, as has been assumed by Gray.[23] Gee's results agreed with those of Haldane et al.[25] in suggesting that in the presence of an excess of CO_2 stimulation of the breathing by anoxia may occur with only slight depressions of the alveolar oxygen tension. Hill and Flack,[35] Douglas and Haldane,[17] and DuBois[20] in breath-holding experiments showed that the breaking point was reached later and at a higher alveolar pCO_2 when oxygen was added to the inspired air. It appeared that anoxia played some part in advancing the breaking point even when the alveolar pO_2 was well above 100 mm. Recent experiments in this laboratory (Cormack, Cunningham, and Gee, unpublished) on rebreathing at rest from a 6 l spirometer containing either air or oxygen indicated the same thing, namely, that in the presence of a large excess of CO_2 a very powerful stimulation of respiration from "oxygen lack" may occur when the alveolar pO_2 is still well above 100 mm. In contrast, when the same rebreathing experiments are carried out following a period of acapnia induced by the inhalation of 10 per cent oxygen for 30 min, no effect

from oxygen lack alone may be detected until the alveolar pO_2 falls to 60 or 55 mm. It will be seen from Fig. 1 that in our exercising subjects there was a considerable rise in alveolar pCO_2 and blood lactate, and hence in the arterial hydrogen-ion concentration. It is therefore possible that a considerable anoxic stimulus existed even though the arterial pO_2 may not have fallen very much. The mechanism of this response is obscure since Åström[5] and Metz and Bernthal[45] have shown that acapnia potentiates and CO_2 excess reduces the stimulant effects of anoxia on the respiration of anesthetized animals. At present there is no obvious explanations for these contradictory findings but for our purposes the experiments of Nielsen and Smith[48] of Gee[22] and of Cormack et al. (unpublished) on unanesthetized man are more directly applicable. We may therefore conclude that the ventilatory response to simple oxygen lack may be quantitatively adequate for the present purpose.

The arterial oxygen tension in severe exercise

It has been known for a long time that at high altitudes the performance of very severe exercise results in a reduction in the saturation with oxygen of the arterial blood (Douglas, Haldane, Henderson, and Schneider[18]). At sea level the position is not so clear. Several workers reported a fall in the arterial oxygen percentage saturation during severe exercise (e.g., Harrop;[29] Himwich and Barr[36]). Most of these observations were based on determinations of saturation with the Van Slyke apparatus, which, as used in those days, gave rise to a small systematic error (Roughton, Darling, and Root[53]). The data are unsuitable for the present purpose since changes in oxygen tension rather than saturation are responsible for chemoreceptror stimulation (Comroe and Schmidt [14]), and only large changes of tension can be detected by measuring saturation at sea level. This criticism applies to determinations with the oximeter and also to those reported by Asmussen and Nielsen.[3] The only direct measurements of arterial oxygen tension during heavy exercise at sea level of which we are aware are those of Lilienthal, Riley, Proemmel, and Franke.[42] They found that it fell from 94 mm at rest to 73 mm during three experiments on one subject who exercised at an intensity which was rather less than that reported in this paper. Hickam *et al.*[32] found a fall of about 2 per cent saturation during fairly heavy exercise in 11 untrained subjects. This would correspond to a fall in tension of about 20 mm if the oxygen dissociation curve remained unchanged. However, there was also a considerable alteration of serum pH which may account for part of the change in saturation.

The causes of anoxemia in heavy exercise

(a) *Limitations in the rate of diffusion of oxygen across the pulmonary epithelium.* Little can be said on this subject since we have no relevant data and the figures given for the diffusion coefficient of the lung (DO_2) are conflicting. It is agreed that the DO_2 is increased during exercise, but the absolute values are not known for certain. Marie Krogh[40] gave figures of about 25 at rest and 50 to 60 in moderate exercise. Bøje[7], using the same method, got slightly higher values at rest and figures of up to 57 in very severe exercise. Lilienthal *et al.*[42] obtained similar figures at rest and during moderate exercise, but recorded a value of 75 in one subject who performed severe exercise of a slightly lower relative intensity than

we used. On the other hand, Hartridge and Roughton[30] suggested that the CO method might give low values, and Roughton[52] pointed out that a DO_2 of 200 would be required to explain the data from a single experiment of Asmussen and Chiodi[2] on exercise at high altitude. The comments on this work by Lilienthal *et al.*[42] assumed a large error in the measurement of the arterial percentage saturation with O_2 by Asmussen and Chiodi. Schmidt, Lambertsen, Aviado, Pontius, Barker, and Moyer[54] found that the DO_2 at rest was in excess of 60, which is more in keeping with Roughton's calculations. Making reasonable assumptions for the cardiac outputs of our two subjects, R.G.B. and D.J.C.C., almost complete equilibrium between the oxygen of the alveolar air and the pulmonary capillary blood would be reached if their DO_2's exceeded 100 and 75, respectively. In the circumstances the question must be left open, but in either case we think that the major part of the arterial anoxemia was produced by the factors considered in the next subsection.

(b) *Imperfect distribution of blood and air within the lungs.* Imperfect distribution of the blood and air was first suggested by Haldane, Meakins, and Priestley[26] as cause of arterial anoxemia. Their views were summarized by Haldane and Priestley.[27, p. 208 ff.] The effects of such local inequalities of air supply and blood flow have recently been worked out quantitatively by Riley and Cournand.[50, 51] They express in terms of a complete "venous shunt" the combined effects of local underventilation and overperfusion in parts of the lung proper, together with the addition of true venous blood to the blood in the left side of the heart, such as probably occurs through the bronchial and Thebesian veins. Their data suggest that this "shunt" probably amounts to about 3 per cent of the total blood flow in normal subjects at rest. So far there are no data relating to rapidly exhausting exercise. The nature of the extremely efficient mechanism which probably regulates the distribution of air and blood to various parts of the lungs during rest is incompletely understood. It would not be surprising if it were to become less effective during the severe strain of maximal physical work. It is possible to calculate the limits within which such an "effective venous shunt" must lie in order to produce a low arterial pO_2 with 33 per cent, but a normal or raised arterial pO_2 with 66 per cent oxygen. Certain numerical assumptions are made in the calculation. For the subject R.G.B., with an oxygen consumption of 4.4 l per min it is assumed that the mixed venous blood was 40 per cent saturated with oxygen and that the oxygen capacity of his blood was 20 volume per cent. These figures would give a cardiac output of about 37.5 l per min,

a figure which seems reasonable in view of the work of Christensen.[11] The blood which passed through adequately ventilated alveoli probably came very near to equilibrium with the alveolar oxygen. During the experiments in which 33 and 66 per cent oxygen were breathed, it would take up oxygen in excess of that required to raise its pO_2 to 100 mm, and the surplus would be available to oxygenate the blood from the "effective venous shunt." The relative magnitude of a shunt which could be oxygenated to a pO_2 of 100 mm may be found from the equation:

$$\frac{\text{Surplus } O_2 \text{ (vol. \%)}}{\text{Arteriovenous difference (vol. \%)}} =$$

$$\frac{\text{effective venous shunt (\% of cardiac output)}}{100 - \text{effective venous shunt (\% of cardiac output)}}$$

The calculation is shown in Table 2. The dissociation curve of Courtice and Douglas,[15] extrapolated to high

TABLE 2

Calculation of the Magnitude of the " Effective Venous Shunt " Which Would Produce an Arterial pO_2 of 100 mm Hg When Gas Mixtures Other Than Air Are Breathed

	Inspired oxygen		
	21%	33%	66%
Alveolar pO_2	100	193	428
O_2 content of blood from normally ventilated alveoli:			
Combined, HbO_2%	97.5	99.69	100
Combined, vol. %	19.5	19.95	20.0
Dissolved, vol. %	0.29	0.56	1.24
Total, vol. %	19.79	20.51	21.24
Mixed arterial O_2, vol. %	19.79	19.79	19.79
"Surplus" O_2, vol. %	0	0.72	1.45
O_2 content of mixed venous blood:			
Combined, HbO_2 %	40	40	40
Combined, vol. %	8	8	8
Dissolved, vol. %	0.07	0.07	0.07
Total, vol. %	8.07	8.07	8.07
Arteriovenous difference, vol. %	11.72	11.72	11.72
"Effective shunt," % total flow	0	5.8	11.0

values of pO_2, and the Bohr coefficients of solubility have been used.

If the cardiac output were lower and the arteriovenous difference greater, a smaller shunt would suffice. Under the conditions specified, a shunt of 6 per cent when air was breathed would have resulted in an arterial pO_2 of 67 mm, which is a little lower than the figure found by Lilienthal et al.[42] It is therefore quite possible that occurrences of this type were responsible for a depression of the arterial pO_2 to levels which would produce a strong stimulation of the chemoreceptors. We would like to emphasize once more that this 6 per cent "effective venous shunt" does not mean that 6 per cent of the cardiac output bypasses the lungs altogether. The Thebesian vein component of the true shunt may well increase considerably, but a large part of the "effective venous shunt" would probably be made up of blood which passes through regions of the lungs where the air supply is relatively deficient, but not completely absent. Such an effect might result from a cessation of pulmonary vasoconstrictor activity in the interests of the maximum possible blood flow. In this case, active regulation of blood distribution would cease.

The graded effect of 33 and 66 per cent oxygen on the ventilation

The full effect of oxygen in reducing the ventilation was achieved with 66 per cent but not with 33 per cent oxygen. In order to explain these findings in terms of arterial anoxemia alone, the arterial pO_2 would have to be less than 100 mm even when 33 per cent oxygen was breathed. This would occur if the "effective venous shunt" were between 6 and 11 per cent of the total blood flow, which seems rather large. It may be that the depression of the arterial pO_2, if present at all, was insufficient to account for the whole of

the difference between results with 33 and 66 per cent oxygen. However, the difference between the blood lactate levels may have been sufficient to increase the ventilation considerably. To be certain that this was not the cause, it would be necessary to show that the ventilation changed *abruptly*, from, for example, 85 to 75 l per min in the case of R.G.B. if he were switched suddenly from 33 to 66 per cent oxygen. No such experiment is on record. The same considerations apply to the differences between 60 and 100 per cent oxygen which were found by Asmussen and Nielsen[3] but which we failed to confirm, and also to the difference between work with the arms alone on air and pure oxygen. It seems, therefore, that the effects observed may be explained tentatively in terms of known factors, namely arterial anoxemia and acidosis resulting from the accumulation of lactate. Further experiments of the type suggested should provide an answer to some of the problems, and direct measurement of the arterial pO_2 would settle them all. It seems likely that a fall in the arterial pO_2 would affect the breathing by way of the carotid and aortic chemoreceptors. In addition, it is possible that cardiac function might be limited by anoxia, as was suggested by Hill et al.[34] and this might influence the breathing. Little is known about the way in which such a relatively small cardiac insufficiency would produce dyspnoea, but it would probably allow the pressures on the right side of the heart to rise, and this in turn might initiate reflexes from the great veins, right heart, or pulmonary vessels. Such respiratory reflexes have been demonstrated in cats by Harrison, Harrison, and Marsh[28] and by Megibow, Katz, and Feinstein,[44] and in man by Mills.[47]

It has been mentioned elsewhere (Bannister et al. [6]) that when the oxygen want of severe exertion is abolished, the pulmonary ventilation is not much greater than that produced by the application of an equivalent CO_2 stimulus at rest. We think that the greater part of the hyperpnoea of severe exercise can be explained in terms of oxygen lack, lactate accumulation, and CO_2 excess. The thresholds for these are probably lowered by the rise of body temperature. We do not discard altogether the effects of nervous stimuli from the working limbs, but we think they contribute comparatively little to the ventilation in the steady state, though they are probably of importance in producing the rapid adjustments to the changing conditions which occur at the beginning of exercise.

The difference between the effects of 66 and 100 per cent oxygen

These experiments differ from others reported in the literature in showing that there is an optimum level for the alveolar oxygen tension in heavy exercise and that if this is exceeded performance suffers. The limits between which this optimum value lies have not been determined. It may be that the inhalation of about 50 per cent would be sufficient to produce the benefit which resulted from 66 per cent oxygen, and that the disadvantages which result from an excess do not become apparent until considerably more oxygen is added to the inspired air.

The reasons for this optimum value are obscure. At rest adverse effects do not occur until pure oxygen has been breathed for many hours, unless the pressure is greatly increased. With 100 per cent oxygen the symptoms experienced by our subjects were generalized rather than local. This, together with the fact that a small excess of lactate accumulated in the blood, suggests that the working muscles were not responsible. There is no reason to think that the heart was adversely affected when pure oxygen was substituted for 66 per cent. The load on the heart was reduced since there was probably no increase in the oxygen consumption and the arterial blood was carrying nearly an extra volume per cent of dissolved oxygen. The situation differs from that described by Hill et al.[34] when they postulated a considerable increase in the cardiac output to explain the large increases in oxygen consumption of which their subjects were capable when 50 per cent oxygen was breathed. In their experiments the intensity of the work was increased when oxygen was inhaled, while in ours it was kept constant. On our hypothesis oxygen lack was slight or absent in the two cases, and the stimuli from pH and pCO_2 were similar. The chemoreceptors could scarcely have been responsible for the difference. Irritation of the respiratory tract by the oxygen or from the dryness of the gas, inhaled as it was straight from storage cylinders, cannot be excluded. However, when 66 per cent oxygen in nitrogen was supplied direct from cylinders it did not have this effect, and in any case not all the subjects complained of respiratory distress. The comments of three of the subjects suggested that the effect was nervous. When breathing 66 per cent oxygen they felt an elation which was strikingly absent when breathing pure oxygen. It may have been due partly to the absence of the expected unpleasant sensations which normally accompany exercise of this severity and partly to the unexpected feeling of enhanced physical capability. However, the known factors which produce distress were not increased when pure oxygen was inspired, yet the subjects felt depressed rather than elated. Dautrebande and Haldane[16] noticed that the respiration was increased when oxygen at slightly increased pressure was breathed at rest and explained this in terms of a slowing of the cerebral circulation. Dripps and Comroe[19] and Asmussen and Nielsen[3] have reported similar findings, though Dripps and Comroe attributed them to irritation of the respiratory tract. Kety and Schmidt[37] found that the inhalation of pure oxygen reduced the cerebral blood flow by about 13 per cent. Lambertsen, Kough, Cooper, Emmel, Loeschcke, and Schmidt[41] have shown that when pure oxygen at a pressure of 3.5 atm is inspired by subjects at rest, the slowing is sufficient to result in an almost normal pO_2 in the jugular venous blood, in spite of the heavy load of extra oxygen carried in solution by the arterial blood. As a result by no means the whole of the brain is exposed to high pressures of oxygen. Under these circumstances the subject usually experiences the convulsions of oxygen poisoning after an exposure of 1 hr. When the subject inspires CO_2 at a pressure of about 52 mm (Kough, Lambertsen, Stroud, Gould, and Ewing[39]), or takes mild exercise (Lambertsen, personal communication), the convulsions occur much earlier. CO_2 probably acts by increasing the cerebral blood flow, and thereby reducing the protection from high tensions of oxygen afforded to the brain by circulatory changes; Lambertsen was unable to show a similar increase in blood flow during mild exercise (oxygen consumption, 1,200 cc per min), but Kleinerman and Sokoloff[38] found an increase which was almost significant when their subjects performed mild exercise breathing air. In our subjects breathing 100 per cent O_2 at atmospheric pressure during very severe exercise the alveolar and probably also the arterial CO_2 tensions were considerably elevated. We would

suggest tentatively that the adverse effects which we experienced were caused by the exposure of large parts of the central nervous system to abnormally high tensions of oxygen. If the "effective venous shunt" in the pulmonary circulation, which was mentioned earlier, was of the magnitude suggested, the inhalation of 66 per cent oxygen would not have resulted in substantial increases of arterial pO_2 so an increased circulation to the brain would have produced no ill effects. If, as a result of the very high arterial pO_2 when 100 per cent oxygen was breathed the hemoglobin passing through the brain were not reduced, the buffering capacity of the blood for CO_2 would be impaired. The data of Lambertsen et al.[41] are contrary to the view that oxygen poisoning results from the failure of the blood to transport CO_2, but a modest rise in the tissue CO_2 pressure might contribute to the other adverse effects of oxygen at high pressure. There is, however, no positive evidence for these views; the absence of an increase of cerebral blood flow during Lambertsen's experiments on exercise does not support them, though it must be borne in mind that the exercise was not comparable to that performed by our subjects.

These considerations bring us back to the respiratory effects of 66 and 100 per cent O_2. It might be thought from the data of Lambertsen and his colleagues that the increased pO_2 in the blood vessels of the brain when 100 per cent O_2 is breathed would produce a small further rise in the pCO_2 of the respiratory center and hence a small increase in pulmonary ventilation, compared with the experiments using 66 per cent O_2. We did, in fact, record a small difference in two subjects, but, as already mentioned, the other two subjects showed small changes in the opposite direction. It may be that this effect was sometimes masked by slight differences in other variables, e.g., the blood lactate. It is clear from Fig. 1 that there was no systematic difference between the respiratory effects of 66 and 100 per cent O_2.

Summary

1. Two athletes and two nonathletic subjects ran on a motor-driven treadmill up various gradients. The intensity of the work was adjusted so as to ensure that each individual reached his breaking point between the 7th and the 10th minute when he breathed atmospheric air. In other experiments he performed the same exercise while breathing 33, 66, or 100 per cent O_2.

2. Pulmonary ventilation, alveolar pCO_2 and pO_2, and blood lactate were measured frequently during each run. The time taken to reach a breaking point was also recorded.

3. In all instances, addition of oxygen to the inspired air increased the time required to reach a breaking point. The performance was improved more by 66 per cent and 100 per cent than by 33 per cent O_2.

4. With 66 per cent O_2 three of the subjects did not reach a breaking point within 23 min. The discomfort which they had experienced when breathing air was replaced by a feeling of positive well-being. In contrast, when breathing 100 per cent O_2 they never felt elated, and all reached breaking points within 21 min.

5. Oxygen reduced the pulmonary ventilation and the blood lactate response, and allowed the alveolar pCO_2 to rise to higher levels. Thirty-three per cent O_2 had a smaller effect than 66 per cent or 100 per cent O_2. No systematic difference could be detected between the effects of 66 per cent and 100 per cent O_2 on respiration.

6. Two subjects exercised at a slightly lower intensity of work. Sudden changes were made in the inspired gas mixtures, from air to 66 per cent or 33 per cent O_2 in the course of the runs. These changes were followed extremely rapidly by reductions in the pulmonary ventilation and increases in the alveolar pCO_2. Subjective improvement occurred over the space of a few breaths. On switching back to air, the reverse changes in the pulmonary ventilation and the alveolar pCO_2 followed very rapidly. These effects were not observed during moderate exercise.

7. Reasons were presented for regarding the respiratory effects of inhaling high concentrations of O_2 as being due to the abolition of an arterial anoxemia which was thought to be present when air was breathed during exercise of more than a critical intensity. Relief of the anoxemia might exert its effects through the carotid and aortic chemoreceptors, or by improving cardiac function, or both.

8. It was thought unnecessary to postulate the existence of an unknown respiratory stimulant liberated by muscles working under partially anaerobic conditions, though the possibility was not excluded.

9. The depressant action of 100 per cent when compared with 66 per cent O_2 was discussed. It was tentatively suggested that it might be due to increases in the cerebral circulation resulting from the excess of circulating CO_2 and lactate. Such an increase would nullify the protection from the deleterious effects of high-pressure oxygen afforded to the brain by the cerebral vasoconstriction which occurs at rest when pure oxygen is breathed.

References

1. Asmussen, E., "Blood Pyruvate and Ventilation in Heavy Work," *Acta Physiol. Scand.*, **20** (1950), 133–36.

2. Asmussen, E., and H. Chiodi, "The Effect of Hypoxemia on Ventilation and Circulation in Man," *Am. J. Physiol.*, **132** (1941), 426–36.

3. Asmussen, E., and M. Nielsen, "Studies on the Regulation of Respiration in Heavy Work," *Acta Physiol. Scand.*, **12** (1946), 171–98.

4. Asmussen, E., and M. Nielsen, "The Effect of Autotransfusion of 'Work Blood' on the Pulmonary Ventilation," *ibid.*, **20** (1950), 79–87.

5. Åström, A., "On the Action of Combined Carbon Dioxide Excess and Oxygen Deficiency in the Regulation of Breathing," *Acta Physiol. Scand. Suppl.*, **27** (1952), 98.

6. Bannister, R. G., D. J. C. Cunningham, and C. G. Douglas, "The Carbon Dioxide Stimulus to Breathing in Severe Exercise," *J. Physiol. (London)*, **125** (1954), 90–117.

7. Bøje, O., "Über die Grösse der Lungendiffusion des Menschen während Ruhe und körperlicher Arbeit," *Arbeitsphysiol.*, **7** (1933), 157–66.

8. Boothby, W. M., "Effect of High Altitudes on the Composition of Alveolar Air," *Proc. Mayo Clin.*, **20** (1945), 209–13.

10. Briggs, H., "Physical Exertion, Fitness and Breathing," *J. Physiol. (London)*, **54** (1920), 292–318.

11. Christensen, E. H., "Beiträge zur Physiologie schwerer körperlicher Arbeit. V Mitteilung: Minutenvolumen und Schlagvolumen des Herzens während schwerer körperlicher Arbeit," *Arbeitsphysiol.*, **4** (1931), 470–502.

12. Christensen, E. H., A. Krogh, and J. Lindhard, "Investigations on Heavy

13. Muscular Work," *Quart. Bull. Health Org. League of Nations*, **3** (1934), 388–417.

13. Comroe, J. H., "The Hyperpnoea of Muscular Exercise," *Physiol. Rev.*, **24** (1944), 319–39.

14. Comroe, J. H., and C. F. Schmidt, "The Part Played by Reflexes From the Carotid Body in the Chemical Regulation of Respiration in the Dog," *Am. J. Physiol.*, **121** (1938), 75–97.

15. Courtice, F. C., and C. G. Douglas, "The Ferricyanide Method of Blood-Gas Analysis," *J. Physiol. (London)*, **33** (1947), 345–56.

16. Dautrebande, L., and J. S. Haldane, "The Effects of Respiration of Oxygen on Breathing and Circulation," *ibid.*, **55** (1921), 296–99.

17. Douglas, C. G., and J. S. Haldane, "The Regulation of Normal Breathing," *ibid.*, **38** (1909), 420–40.

18. Douglas, C. G., J. S. Haldane, Y. Henderson, and E. C. Schneider, "Physiological Observations Made on Pike's Peak, Colorado, With Special Reference to Adaption to Low Barometric Pressures," *Phil. Trans. Roy. Soc. (London)*, **B203** (1912), 185–318.

19. Dripps, R. D., and J. H. Comroe, "The Effect of the Inhalation of High and Low Oxygen Concentrations on Respiration, Pulse Rate, Ballistocardiogram and Arterial Oxygen Saturation (Oximeter) of Normal Individuals," *Am. J. Physiol.*, **149** (1947), 277–91.

20. DuBois, A. B., "Alveolar CO_2 and O_2 During Breath-Holding, Expiration and Inspiration," *J. Appl. Physiol.*, **5** (1952), 1–12.

21. FitzGerald, M. P., "Further Observations on the Changes in the Breathing

and the Blood at Various High Altitudes," *Proc. Roy. Soc. (London)*, **B88** (1914), 248–58.

22. Gee, G. B. L., "Some Factors in the Control of the Respiration in Man." B.Sc. thesis, Oxford University, 1949.

23. Gray, J. S., *Pulmonary Ventilation and Its Physiological Regulation*. Springfield, Ill.: Charles C. Thomas, Publisher, 1950.

24. Grodins, F. S., "Analysis of Factors Concerned in Regulation of Breathing in Exercise," *Physiol. Rev.*, **30** (1950), 220–39.

25. Haldane, J. S., J. C. Meakins, and J. G. Priestley, "The Respiratory Response to Anoxemia," *J. Physiol. (London)*, **52** (1918), 420–32.

26. Haldane, J. S., J. C. Meakins, and J. G. Priestley, "The Effects of Shallow Breathing," *ibid.*, **52** (1918), 433–53.

27. Haldane, J. S., and J. G. Priestley, *Respiration* (new ed.). New Haven, Conn.: Yale University Press, 1935, p. 232; p. 208 ff.

28. Harrison, T. R., W. G. Harrison, and J. P. Marsh, "Reflex Stimulation of Respiration From Increase in Venous Pressure," *Am. J. Physiol.*, **100** (1932), 417–19.

29. Harrop, G. A., "The Oxygen and Carbon Dioxide Content of Arterial and Venous Blood in Normal Individuals and in Patients with Anemia and Heart Disease," *J. Exptl. Med.*, **30** (1919), 241–57.

30. Hartridge, H., and F. J. W. Roughton, "The Rate of Distribution of Dissolved Gases Between the Red Blood Corpuscle and Its Fluid Environment. Part I: Preliminary Experiments on the Rate of Uptake of Oxygen and Carbon Monoxide by Sheep's Corpuscles," *J. Physiol. (London)*, **62** (1927), 232–42.

31. Henderson, Y., *Adventures in Respiration*. Baltimore: The Williams & Wilkins Co., 1938, p. 56.

32. Hickam, J. B., W. W. Pryor, E. B. Page, and R. J. Atwell, "Respiratory Regulation During Exercise in Unconditioned Subjects," *J. Clin. Inv.*, **30** (1951), 503–16.

33. Hill, A. V., C. N. H. Long, and H. Lupton, "Muscular Exercise, Lactic Acid and the Supply and Utilization of Oxygen. Part IV: Methods of Studying the Respiratory Exchanges in Man During Rapid Alterations Produced by Muscular Exercise and While Breathing Various Gas Mixtures," *Proc. Roy. Soc. (London)*, **B97** (1924), 84–95.

34. Hill, A. V., C. N. H. Long, and H. Lupton, "Muscular Exercise, Lactic Acid and the Supply and Utilization of Oxygen. Part VII: Muscular Exercise and Oxygen Intake," *ibid.*, **B97** (1924), 155–67.

35. Hill, L., and M. Flack, "The Effect of Excess of Carbon Dioxide and of Want of Oxygen Upon the Respiration and the Circulation," *J. Physiol. (London)*, **37** (1908), 77–111.

36. Himwich, H. E., and D. P. Barr, "Studies in the Physiology of Muscular Exercise. Part V: Oxygen Relationships in the Arterial Blood," *J. Biol. Chem.*, **57** (1923), 363–78.

37. Kety, S. S., and C. F. Schmidt, "The Effects of Altered Arterial Tensions of Carbon Dioxide and Oxygen on Cerebral Blood Flow and Cerebral Oxygen Consumption of Normal Young Men," *J. Clin. Inv.*, **27** (1948), 484–92.

38. Kleinerman, J., and L. Sokoloff, "Effects of Exercise on Cerebral Blood Flow and Metabolism in Man," *Federation Proc.*, **12** (1953), 77.

39. Kough, R. H., C. J. Lambertsen, M. W. Stroud, R. A. Gould, and J. H. Ewing, "Role of Carbon Dioxide in Acute Oxygen Toxicity at $3\frac{1}{2}$ Atmospheres Inspired Oxygen Tension," *ibid.*, **10** (1951), 76.

40. Krogh, M., "The Diffusion of Gases Through the Lungs of Man," *J. Physiol. (London)*, **49** (1914), 271–300.

41. Lambertsen, C. J., R. H. Kough, D. Y. Cooper, G. L. Emmel, H. H. Loeschcke, and C. F. Schmidt, "Oxygen Toxicity. Effects in Man of Oxygen Inhalation at 1 and 3.5 Atmospheres Upon Blood Gas Transport, Cerebral Circulation and Cerebral Metabolism," *J. Appl. Physiol.*, **5** (1953), 471–86.

42. Lilienthal, J. L., R. L. Riley, D. D. Proemmel, and R. E. Franke, "An Experimental Analysis in Man of the Oxygen Pressure Gradient From Alveolar Air to Arterial Blood During Rest and Exercise at Sea Level and at Altitude," *Am. J. Physiol.*, **147** (1946), 199–216.

43. Lundin, G., and G. Ström, "The Concentration of Blood Lactic Acid in Man During Muscular Work in Relation to the Partial Pressure of Oxygen of the Inspired Air," *Acta Physiol. Scand.*, **13** (1947), 253–66.

44. Megibow, R. S., L. N. Katz, and M. Feinstein, "Kinetics of Respiration in Experimental Pulmonary Embolism," *Arch. Internal Med.*, **71** (1943), 536–46.

45. Metz, B., and T. Bernthal, "Interaction of Respiratory Drives," *Federation Proc.*, **12** (1953), 99.

46. Miller, A. T., "Influence of Oxygen Administration on Cardiovascular Function During Exercise and Recovery," *J. Appl. Physiol.*, **5** (1952), 165–68.

47. Mills, J. N., "Hyperpnoea in Man Produced by Sudden Release of Occluded Blood," *J. Physiol. (London)*, **103** (1944), 244–52.

48. Nielsen, M., and H. Smith, "Studies on the Regulation of Respiration in Acute Hypoxia," *Acta Physiol. Scand.*, **24** (1941), 293–313.

49. Pitts, R. F., "Regulation of Respiration," in William H. Howell, *A Textbook of Physiology* (16th ed.), ed. by John F. Fulton. Philadelphia: W. B. Saunders Co., 1949, p. 858.

50. Riley, R. L., and A. Cournand, "'Ideal' Alveolar Air and the Analysis of Ventilation-Perfusion Relationships in the Lungs," *J. Appl. Physiol.*, **1** (1949), 825–47.

51. Riley, R. L., and A. Cournand, "Analysis of Factors Affecting Partial Pressures of Oxygen and Carbon Dioxide in Gas and Blood of Lungs: Theory," *ibid.*, **4** (1951), 77–101.

52. Roughton, F. J. W., "The Diffusion Constant of the Lung," *Am. J. Med. Sci.*, **208** (1944), 136–37.

53. Roughton, F. J. W., R. C. Darling, and W. S. Root, "Factors Affecting the Determination of Oxygen Capacity, Content, and Pressure in Human Arterial Blood," *Am. J. Physiol.*, **142** (1944), 708–20.

54. Schmidt, C. F., C. J. Lambertsen, D. M. Aviado, R. G. Pontius, E. S. Barker, and J. H. Moyer, "The Pulmonary Diffusion Coefficient for Oxygen (DO_2)." *Abstr. XVIII Intern. Physiol. Congr.*, 1950, p. 434.

P. V. KARPOVICH

The Effect of Oxygen Inhalation on Swimming Performance

Reprinted from the *Research Quarterly*,
5 (1934), 24–30.

The success of the Japanese Olympic swimming team in the 1932 Olympic games led to questions about the effect of oxygen inhalation on performance, for it had been reported that the Japanese took oxygen for 5 min about half an hour before competition. Karpovich used the Springfield College swimming team as subjects for his experiments. He found that when oxygen is inhaled before swimming, it increases speed in the 100-yd swim. But, since its effect is of short duration—the body cannot store oxygen—it must be breathed immediately before the exercise. Consequently, Karpovich concluded that the Japanese Olympic victories could not have been due to the inhalation of oxygen because of the half-hour interval involved.

Karpovich acknowledges that the study does not control the psychological effect in its design, but he maintains that the effect might have been neutralized because the first few subjects did not perform as well when they inhaled oxygen. The results of this study have been confirmed by other investigators who found that although oxygen inhalation before exercise does not assist performance of much duration, it does assist recovery from exercise.

The fact that the Japanese Olympic swimming team used oxygen inhalation before the contest and was so victorious aroused general interest in the effects of oxygen breathing upon athletic performance. As far as it could be learned the Japanese took the oxygen for 5 min about half an hour before the competition. Could such a procedure affect the speed in swimming? Some American coaches immediately decided that it could and stated that the Japanese swimmers were thereby "doped" and by means of this "unethical" method were able to make such a successful showing. This question has been presented to the writer on many occasions. In order to answer this and other concomitant questions the present investigation has been undertaken.

Historical Findings

M. Pembrey and F. Cook[7] found that after exercise it was much easier to breathe oxygen than air. The subjects in each case were unaware of what they were breathing. Leonard Hill and Martin Flack[4] experimented with the effect of oxygen breathing upon the pulse, blood pressure, respiratory rate, athletic performance, and recovery from fatigue. The oxygen was administered for 3 min immediately before the exercise and also for 4 or 5 min during the recovery. The exercises used were running up and down a flight of 26 stairs 8 or 9 times, as fast as possible, and boxing. The subjects did not know when ordinary air and when oxygen was given to them. These investigators came to the conclusion that the effect of the oxygen breathing was a greater speed in running, lower pulse rate, and higher blood pressure. The subjective feeling was better and there was a quicker relief from dyspnoea. In the case of boxing they stated that "oxygen given at the end of the third round to a 'done' man sends him back to the ring full of fire and energy."

C. G. Douglas and J. S. Haldane[2] compared the effect of forced breathing of ordinary air with that of quiet breathing of oxygen. The duration of each type of breathing was 3 min. The exercise used was running up and down 40 ft of stairs twice in 70 sec. Their conclusions were in favor of the forced breathing. The pulse rate was slower and came to normal more quickly with forced breathing than after oxygen breathing. The quiet inhalation of oxygen had a very slight effect if any.

Leonard Hill and J. Mackenzie, challenged by the above paper, investigated the effect of a forced breathing of air and a deep breathing of oxygen. They used three kinds of respiration: (*a*) quiet breathing of ordinary air; (*b*) forced breathing of air; and (*c*) deep breathing of oxygen. The duration of the latter two types was 3 min. After each of the respiratory preliminaries, the subjects lifted a weight of 60 lb to a height of 19 in. while holding the breath. Although the possible effect of fatigue was against the exercise with oxygen, because this was the last in the series, the results were definitely in favor of oxygen breathing, since the men could perform more foot-pounds of work. The subjective feelings

were also better after oxygen. Experiments performed with runners were in favor of oxygen, because the men were able to run faster. Oxygen inhalation half an hour after the first run proved advantageous for the speed of the second run as compared with breathing of the ordinary air. It was also easier to hold the breath in a resting position after taking oxygen. After a forced respiration the record of breath holding was 3 min, whereas after oxygen breathing for 5 min, it reached 9 min and 3 sec.

Leonard Hill and Martin Flack[5] found that a man after taking oxygen was able to run, holding his breath, 470 yd in 110 sec. At the end of this run he continued wobbling about in an unconscious condition. They think that the preliminary oxygen breathing can be useful for running short distances only, not more than half a mile. They also state that the beneficial effect of oxygen inhalation may last for 15 min, citing for their proof that it was easier for a bicyclist to climb a hill so many minutes after taking oxygen.

Israel Feldman and Leonard Hill[3] found that a preliminary inhalation of oxygen had a marked effect upon the amount of lactic acid voided with the urine after exercise. After a brief period of stair climbing there was almost no lactic acid and after a prolonged climbing there was very little, provided the oxygen had been given before the exercise.

Henry Briggs[1] determined the amount of oxygen consumed by different persons while doing physical work and breathing either normal air or almost pure oxygen. He found that the thoroughly trained man received no advantage from breathing oxygen if the load was small or moderate, but, if the load was excessively large so that the work could be performed for a short time only, oxygen inhalation was beneficial and the subject was able to do more work. The nontrained man was helped a great deal by breathing oxygen even with small loads. The well trained man used less oxygen and gave off a higher per cent of carbon dioxide, indicating a better utilization of oxygen.

Experimental Findings

The effect of oxygen inhalation immediately followed by swimming. After a deep expiration the subject made two deep inhalations of pure oxygen and immediately plunged into water, holding his breath. The varsity swimmers were used as the subjects.

From Table 1 it can be seen that in 11 out of 17 cases men broke their own unofficial records. In two cases they bettered their usual time and in four they made their usual time.

Of the six men who could not break their own records, four did not follow the instructions and exhaled the oxygen before they hit the water, and one was not in good shape. (There was no account for the sixth man.) In this experiment the men knew that they were breathing oxygen and the criticism can be advanced that it was a purely psychological effect. This is a logical criticism but it cannot be applied to this experiment for this reason. Three out of the first four men in the series did not break their records and this created a skeptical attitude among the men who followed; yet as soon as the

TABLE 1

The Speed in Swimming Immediately After Taking Oxygen

Name		Stroke	Usual time in sec	Best time in sec	Oxygen time in sec	Distance swum without breath
*1	Br.	Crawl	61.0	59.0	59.3	135 ft.
2	De.	. . . . .	60.0	58.0	57.7	135 ft.
*3	Ja.	. . . . .	57.2	57.0	57.2	120 ft.
*4	Si.	. . . . .	58.6	58.0	58.6	135 ft.
5	Li.	Breast	72.0	70.8	69.3	120 ft.
6	Ko.	Crawl	58.0	57.5	56.3	100 ft.
*7	Sc.	Back	71.0	70.0	71.1	20 ft.
8	Ho.	Crawl	55.0	53.8	53.1	100 ft.
9	Su.	Back	68.2	67.8	65.8	105 ft.
10	So.	Crawl	65.0	63.0	62.8	130 ft.
†11	Lo.	Breast	83.0	81.0	83.0	105 ft.
‡12	Wu.	. . . . .	73.2	71.5	72.6	160 ft.
13	Gr.	Crawl	70.0	68.6	68.3	90 ft.
14	Pa.	. . . . .	59.0	58.8	58.4	120 ft.
15	Ha.	. . . . .	72.0	70.0	68.0	190 ft.
16	Pr.	. . . . .	61.0	60.0	59.0	100 ft.
17	We.	. . . . .	58.0	56.8	56.2	95 ft.

* Did not follow the instructions, exhaled the oxygen before hitting water.
† No account.
‡ Was not in good shape. On the same day made 100 yd in 76.5 sec without oxygen.
A flying start was used throughout. The length of the tank was 60 ft.

swimmers obeyed the instructions explicitly, the results became apparent.

The effect of oxygen given several minutes before the swim. Swimmers inhaled oxygen for a period of from 3 to 5 min and discontinued it 4 to 5 min before a 100-yd swim, using ordinary air in that interval. This procedure had no noticeable effect upon the speed of swimming.

The effect of preliminary oxygen breathing upon running in place while holding the breath. In order to find the effect of preliminary oxygen breathing with an interval of ordinary respiration before the exercise, the following experiments were conducted. Men ran in place, holding the breath. The rhythm and the leg action were uniform. After a preliminary inhalation of oxygen *immediately* before the exercise the men were able to run for a longer period than after breathing ordinary air. When oxygen inhalation was followed by a 1-min interval of ordinary respiration the beneficial effect was very marked. After a time interval of 2 min the effect was slight in some cases and indefinite in most of the cases. After a period of 3 min or longer no effect was noticed.

The effect of oxygen breathing upon the recovery. After a 100-yd swim, the men rested for 10 min, then took pure oxygen for 5 min, then had another rest for 5 min, and then swam another 100 yd. This procedure was not sufficient for a complete recovery, but 28 min of rest including 5 min of oxygen breathing were sufficient for a complete recovery; however the same period of time *without oxygen* was sufficient for recovery of some men. There was one marked advantage in oxygen breathing used immediately after a strenuous exercise: the men got quicker relief from the symptoms of distress.

The effect of preliminary oxygen inhalations on speed in actual competition. This was tried in four different intercollegiate meets, three times in the Springfield tank and once elsewhere. During the meet outside of Springfield all of the men but two showed a rather slow time regardless of whether they had taken oxygen or not. There were probably several reasons for that. One reason was that the weather was exceptionally cold and the men traveled in a small bus, practically without any ventilation, so that at the end of the trip 7 men out of 16 swimmers complained of headache. The second reason lies

TABLE 2

The Performance in Running One Minute After Taking Oxygen

	Vo.	Bu.	Ki.	Mi.	Pa.	Ur.	Vi.	Ka.
	NAMES OF THE SUBJECTS							
Without O$_2$								
Time in sec	29	33	38	38	49	38	41	40
With O$_2$								
Time in sec	52	36	48	49	62	68	80	51

The exercise used was a running in place holding the breath.
The figures represent the average time of several trials.

probably in overeating. On the day of competition some men had a slight case of diarrhea.

During the home meets, although some of the official pool records were broken, it is difficult to state what bearing this inhalation of oxygen had on the records. Only in two cases, when men started a relay race not many seconds after oxygen inhalation, was it possible to attribute part of their success to oxygen. Yet one man who lowered his time 2 sec in a 100-yd swim had had no preliminary oxygen inhalation. In analyzing the time records during the competitive meets we unfortunately do not know how fast the men would have swum on those occasions if they had had no oxygen.

Discussion and Conclusion

There is no doubt that oxygen taken immediately before strenuous exercise does benefit the person. It enables him to run or swim faster or perform more work in the same period of time. If the time interval between the oxygen inhalation and the exercise is short, say, 1 min, the effect may still last; with an increase in the length of the interval, the effect disappears very rapidly.

The nature of this phenomenon has often been misunderstood. Although L. Hill thought that oxygen could be stored in the body tissues, this was definitely disproved by numerous investigators. We now know that the breathing of oxygen does not increase oxygen consumption in normal people. Only when the partial pressure of oxygen in the alveolar air becomes too low and the rate of the blood circulation becomes too rapid and there are symptoms of want of oxygen will breathing of pure oxygen increase the consumption of this gas. The main purpose of preliminary oxygen brea-

thing is to wash out carbon dioxide from the lungs and retain in the lungs as much pure oxygen as possible.

Suppose a man's vital capacity of the lungs is 500 cc and his residual air is 1,000 cc, then the oxygen content of his lungs after a deep breath of air will be approximatly 1,100 cc. The same man, after a thorough oxygen inhalation, will have almost 6,000 cc of pure oxygen. Since the oxygen consumption at rest is about 225 cc per min, there is enough oxygen to last for 25 min. In reality the man will be able to hold his breath not longer than 10 min due to accumulation of carbon dioxide.

If, after oxygen inhalation, the person starts to breathe ordinary air in the normal manner, he will wash out the excess of oxygen from the lungs. This undoubtedly will take more than 1 min. It can be verified mathematically. Suppose the tidal air is 250 cc and the dead space is 150 cc; then on every inhalation only 200 cc. of air enter into the alveoli and the same amount leaves the alveoli. If the respiratory rate is 10 per min it is evident that it would take more than 1 min to wash out the excess oxygen. Actual analyses of the expired air showed that there was, after 1 min, 50.4 per cent and, after 2 min, 20.3 per cent of oxygen.

It is a well-known fact that quiet breathing with a fully expanded chest is extremely difficult. Consequently after a full inhalation there is a tendency to exhale about 1,500 to 2,000 cc. This leaves from 3,600 to 3,100 cc of oxygen in the lungs. The above calculations hold true, in general, even for these figures.

The variation in the depth and respiratory rate explains why the effect of a preliminary oxygen breathing varies in different people and may vary in the same person, but there is no reason whatever to believe that its effect would last 15 min as was suggested by L.

Hill. Since there is no storing up of oxygen in the tissues, a prolonged oxygen inhalation is wasteful. The best results are achieved after several deep and rapid respirations. Some of the students in the writer's laboratory were able to hold the breath for 6 min and 30 sec after three breaths.

The beneficial effect of the oxygen inhalation upon the speed in swimming may be explained in the following manner. In the first place, it is a fact of common knowledge that respiratory movements retard the speed. Now oxygen inhalation makes respiration unnecessary for a certain length of time. Therefore the speed is increased.

In the second place, there is more oxygen available; therefore more vigorous movements can be maintained longer. All the swimmers noticed that they could swim the first 60 yd much more easily. A. V. Hill suggested in this connection that a covered track filled with the oxygen would make for better records in running.

The effect of the preliminary oxygen breathing will be more noticeable in 100- and 220-yd swims. The 50-yd swim is too short and can be taken care of by a normal oxygen debt. In the longer distances, such as the 440, one should be careful because in this case the swimmer has a tendency to swim the first 100 faster than usual and this may upset the pace and increase fatigue at the end of the race. Ordinarily oxygen taken before a 100-yd swim reduces fatigue and lessens the stiffness in the arms, legs, and muscles of the jaw after the race.

The question has been asked as to the safety of oxygen breathing. It can be stated definitely that a few minutes of oxygen breathing cannot cause any harm. To call oxygen a "dope" is unwarranted.

Although it is beyond the scope of a physiological paper to go into a discussion as to what is ethical and what is not, nevertheless it might be asked that if the use of sugar is allowed in competition, why should oxygen be excluded?

In view of the fact that the Japanese took oxygen more than 5 min before swimming, it is safe to assume that the oxygen was not responsible in any way for their phenomenal speed.

Summary

1. Oxygen inhalations immediately followed by swimming increase the speed in the 100-yd dash.

2. Oxygen given 4 to 5 min before a 100-yd dash has no noticeable effect upon the speed.

3. Oxygen breathing in actual competition, unless given at the start, is hardly worthwhile.

4. Inhalation of oxygen for 5 min after a 100-yd swim has little effect upon the recovery, judging from a second 100-yd swim 20 min later.

5. Oxygen breathing immediately after a severe exercise gives quicker relief from respiratory and circulatory embarrassment.

6. The effect of preliminary oxygen breathing lasts at least 1 min, if the person remains quiet.

7. After three inhalations of oxygen a person can hold the breath in lying position up to 6 min and 30 sec.

References

1. Briggs, H., *J. Physiol.* (*London*), **37** (1919), 41.

2. Douglas, C. G., and J. S. Haldane, *ibid.*, **39** (1909), 1.

3. Feldman, I., and L. Hill, *ibid.*, **42** (1911), 439.

4. Hill, L., and M. Flack, *ibid.*, **38** (1909), 28.

5. Hill, L., and M. Flack, *ibid.*, **40** (1910), 347.

6. Hill, L., and J. Mackenzie, *ibid.*, **39** (1909), 33.

7. Pembrey, M., and F. Cook, *ibid.*, **37** (1908), 41.

W. W TUTTLE / M. WILSON / K. DAUM

Effect of Altered Breakfast Habits on Physiologic Response

Reprinted from the *Journal of Applied Physiology*, **1** (1949), 545–59.

This study, conducted at the State University of Iowa, shows that the cliché, "An army travels on its stomach," has some basis in fact. The experiments involved examination of the maximum work output, reaction time, and tremor of a group of six female subjects over a 9-week period. During this time a breakfast regimen in four classifications was prescribed ranging from omission of breakfast to a heavy breakfast.

The results showed that the omission of breakfast caused a decrease in maximum work output and an increase in reaction time and tremor. On the other hand, a light breakfast of 400 cal was associated with a significant improvement in maximum work output and reaction time and a decrease in tremor magnitude when compared to an 800-cal breakfast. These findings tend to confirm the recommended practice of a moderate breakfast intake for individuals who do not perform vigorous physical work. Certainly, the results do not give comfort to those who advocate the omission of breakfast for the average person.

The problem of eating habits has demanded considerable attention and investigation both from the standpoint of health and industrial efficiency. Many ideas based on purely theoretical grounds have been suggested as rules to follow in the matter of eating habits. For example, the athlete has been cautioned against eating heavy meals and certain types of food during competition days. It is generally accepted that heavy work should not be attempted with the stomach full of food, and that water should not be ingested during the intermission between strenuous bouts of exercise, except in small quantities. The data which seem to support many of these ideas appear to be observations and experiences obtained by those engaged in strenuous work.

Meal spacing is usually arranged from the standpoint of convenience rather than as an attempt to meet the optimum physiologic demands of the body for energy. Haggard and Greenburg[7,8,9,10] pursued the idea that the maintenance of a high blood sugar level was conducive to high work efficiency. If true, it seemed reasonable to assume that if the characteristic drop in blood sugar which occurs between meals could be avoided by between-meal feeding, work efficiency would be improved. Haggard and Greenburg[8] also reported that the consumption of a meal increased muscular efficiency significantly, but a repetition of this work by Haldi et al.[11] failed to confirm this effect. In a subsequent experiment, Haldi and Wynn[12] failed to find any beneficial effects in work output resulting from midmorning and midafternoon feeding of factory workers regardless of the amount or kind of the food eaten at these times. When rest periods were substituted for food, the results were also negative.

Supercharging the body with food seems to fall into the same category as supercharging it with vitamins, in that nothing is gained as far as capcity to do work is concerned. However, in considering meal spacing, other factors such as the distraction of hunger, boredom with the task at hand, as well as available fuel for work, must be taken into account. This is suggested by the report of Mann[16] which states that the greatest percentage of industrial accidents occurs between 11 a.m. and 12 noon.

Breakfast habits deserve special consideration from the standpoint of irregularity and the omission of the morning meal. This is especially true because irregularity of breakfast habits, in many instances, is caused by a poorly arranged morning schedule.

Where the breakfast is omitted or eaten under the pressure of time, inefficiency may result from an accentuation of any tendency toward nervous reaction to the forenoon tasks.

In the present study an attempt has been made to show the effects of altered breakfast habits on (a) maximum work output, (b) simple and choice reaction time, and (c) neuromuscular tremor.

Method

Maximum work output. In measuring maximum work output one must recognize the fact that the results represent the amount of work a subject will do rather than the amount he is capable of doing. This situation calls for careful experimental management and planning so as to avoid variable motivation during the work period. Another problem which must be considered in the measurement of maximum work output is that as a result of each preceding bout of exercise the subjects improve, and continue to do so over a rather long period of time. This improvement phenomenon has been shown in this laboratory by Wilson et al.[20] and by others, among them Karpovich and Pestrecov.[15] This leaves two alternatives in studying the effect of any variable on maximum work output. The first is subjects may be trained by performing daily bouts of exercise until they cease to improve, that is, reach a plateau, and the second alternative is to allow the element of improvement to operate but recognize it as an influencing factor. Suppose, for example, that during a 9-week period subjects work for 3 weeks under normal conditions, 3 weeks under altered conditions, followed by a 3-week control period. If the maximum work output gradually increases during the first control period, decreases or remains unchanged during the period

of altered conditions but again improves during the second control
period, it is quite safe to conclude
that the experimental conditions
imposed caused a decrease im maximum work output. This later procedure
was followed in the experiment herein
reported.

In this, as in any experiment involving the measurement of maximum
work output, the first problem is the
selection of an amount of work which
the subjects can perform well and at the
same which will differentiate between
small changes in work capacity.
Experience has shown that to measure
small changes (or large ones) in maximum work output an exercise must be
adopted which provides sharp end
points if quantitative data are to be
calculated. The bicycle ergometer (as
described by Tuttle and Wendler [19])
is satisfactory for this type of measurement of maximum work output.

The work consisted of riding the
bicycle at maximum effort for 1 min.
A work record is shown in Fig. 1. One
minute of work was selected since
experience showed that by extending
the work some subjects showed exhaustive reactions such as nausea, vomiting,
dizziness, and muscle soreness. These

symptoms had to be avoided, because
the exercise had to be repeated at
regular intervals and the subjects re-
sented these reactions. By limiting the
work period the subjects are more apt
to exert greater initial effort because of
the absence of psychologic reactions to
the effects of exhaustive exercise. It
was proven in this laboratory that an
extension of the work period did not
markedly improve the test validity
since the maximum work output for
1 min correlated 0.94 with maximum work output for 2 min. The
amount of work done in the 1-min
period was found by laying off 12 5-
sec intervals on the work record as
shown in Fig. 1. The mean voltage for
each 5-sec interval was calculated and
written on the work record. With the
use of a calibration table constructed
by Tuttle and Wendler, [19] the work
equivalent to the voltage reading was
recorded for each 5-sec interval. The
average maximum work output for the
12 5-sec intervals is the work performed
in 1 min.

Reaction   time.   Since   it   is   well
established that reaction time is sensitive to changes in physiologic condition,
this test was adopted as a possible
means of detecting changes brought

Fig. 1. Record of maximum work output for 1 min recorded in volts.
The mean work equivalent to the voltage generated for each 5-sec interval
is written on the record.

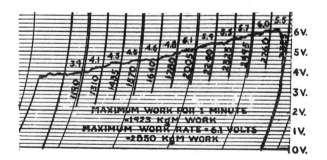

about by altered breakfast habits. In this experiment reaction time is defined as the interval elapsing between the appearance of a light stimulus and the response to it made by pressing an acrosnap switch with the index finger. The reaction time was recorded in milliseconds by means of a Dunlap chronoscope, specially arranged for this purpose. Electric circuits were arranged so that simultaneously with the flash of the stimulus light the chronoscope hand started. The chronoscope hand stopped when the subject closed the switch with the index finger.

So as to provide for the measurement of choice reaction time the stimulus light was placed as number 1 in a bank of five. The lamp bank was so arranged that light 1 could be lit without starting the chronoscope hand. This arrangement provided means whereby practice trails and a variety of patterns could be given without resetting the chronoscope after each trial. Both simple and choice reaction times were employed in this experiment. In case of the former the subject was shown light 1 only and she responded to it as fast as possible. The choice reaction time pattern consisted of flashing any or all the lights in a promiscuous fashion, the subject being instructed to respond to light 1 only.

The subjects were alone in a room equipped with a dim red light. The room was some distance from the chronoscope. Before each experiment the subject was allowed time for dark adaptation. Not only was each subject given several practice periods before experimentation started but also she was allowed several practice trials before each set of measurements was taken. Each subject performed 50 trials of simple and 30 trials of choice reaction time. Since no rest period was allowed in the reaction time series the choice reaction time responses were limited to 30.

Tremor. The presence of tremor in man is recognized as a normal physiologic phenomenon. Wolfenden and Williams[21] were the first to make systematic records of tremor. Aside from pathologic implications, the tremor studies reported have dealt with its character, factors influencing it, origin, rate and amplitude, and classification. Eshner[5] concluded from his studies that tremor was characterized by irregularity and that frequency and extent were inversely related. Binet[2] proposed what he called "The Law of Tremor" in an attempt to classify factors influencing it. The origin of tremor has been investigated by Jasper and Andrews,[14] Travis and Hunter,[18] Fulton, Liddell, and Rioch,[6] Aring and Fulton,[1] and Sollenburger.[17] The consensus seems to be that tremor is a result of postural contraction inherent in the simplest reflex arc. It is independent of the higher centers for its origin although it is modified by the activity of higher centers. The rate at which tremor occurs has been studied by Herren[13] and Bousfield[3] who conclude that for the upper extremity the rate varies from 5 to 12 per sec. Clinically, Bucy[4] divides tremor into two main groups which he designates as tremor at rest, that is, those which occur in parts which are supported but which are not at the time involved by voluntary muscular contractions, and intention tremor, also known as action tremor, which occurs in the part when its musculature is being voluntarily contracted. Static tremor is a manifestation of intention tremor and is present when an extremity is being held still unsupported except by voluntary resistance against the force of gravity.

The investigation herein reported is designed to show the effect of alteration of breakfast habits on the nature of static tremor.

Static tremor was recorded from the outstretched right arm, unsupported except by voluntary resistance against the force of gravity both before and after a 1-min bout of strenuous exercise on a bicycle ergometer. The index finger of the unsupported arm barely touched an electric generator. The generator consisted of a permanent magnet loudspeaker, with a button attached to the armature, which was in contact with the finger. The generator was supported on a ring stand adjusted to the proper height. The tremor of the outstretched arm activated the speaker by generating voltage in the armature. In order to amplify the voltage generated in the armature of the speaker, advantage was taken of one channel of an Offner E. E. G. The voltage was amplified sufficiently to activate a crystograph recorder. Before each experiment the recorder was standardized so that a test signal of 3000 v caused a pen swing of 14 mm. A tremor record is shown in Fig. 2. The recording paper was pulled past the pen at a rate of 10 cm per sec. The tremor score was determined as follows. A strip of tremor record 10 cm long was measured off. A line was

Fig. 2. Neuromuscular tremor record. The score is found by determining the area under the curves occurring during the period of 1 sec as set off by the vertical lines.

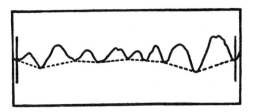

drawn from trough to trough of each consecutive tremor contained in the 10-cm (1 sec) strip. The total area of the tremor for 1 sec was used as the score. This was found by tracing the boundary of the tremor with a planimeter. The scores take into account both amplitude and rate. By multiplying the planimeter readings by 16.77 the score is expressed in square centimeters.

Subjects. Six healthy, normal women ranging in age from 22 to 27 yr were used in this study. The subjects were housed as a unit in an attempt to minimize temptation during periods of abstinence from breakfast. To our knowledge no subject broke the dietary regime during any of the experiments. The subjects were fed the specified breakfasts by trays prepared in the diet kitchen of the University Hospitals under the supervision of the Department of Nutrition. All subjects were graduate students and were relatively consistent in eating, sleeping, and exercise habits.

The subjects pursued their regular schedule in all respects except that their breakfast habits were controlled, and they spent the hour immediately preceding luncheon (11:00 a.m. to 12 noon) in the laboratory performing the experimental routine.

Breakfast classification. Four breakfast classifications were used to vary experimental conditions, viz. a heavy breakfast, a light breakfast, coffee only, and omission of breakfast. The heavy breakfast consisted of fruit, cereal and cream, one egg, bacon (one slice), toast (two slices) and jam, milk, and coffee if desired. The caloric value was approximately 800. The light breakfast consisted of fruit, one slice toast, butter, milk, and coffee if desired, and had a caloric value of approximately 400. Omission of breakfast was defined as abstinence from food intake between 6:00 p.m. (dinner) and 12 noon (lunch) the following day. The "coffee" breakfast was regulated the same as omission of breakfast except that one cup of coffee with one ounce of cream and no sugar was taken in the morning at the breakfast hour.

A series of three experiments were performed to show any effects that altered breakfast habits might have on the physiologic responses described.

EXPERIMENT 1. This experiment was undertaken as an exploratory study to determine if it were possible to demonstrate differences in physiologic responses to heavy breakfasts and no breakfast. The experiment consisted of three consecutive 3-week periods. During the first period all six subjects ate the heavy breakfast; during the second period three subjects ate the heavy breakfast and three subjects omitted breakfast; during the third the procedure for the second period was rotated. Thus, "no breakfast" status could be compared with "heavy breakfast" status both for individual subjects and for groups of subjects. Behavior changes, which were extraneous to the breakfast variable, also could be detected. Data were collected once each week for three performance tests: work output, reaction time, and tremor pattern. The testing period for all three experiments was limited to the hour preceding the noon lunch and was kept constant as to time of day and day of the week for a given subject.

The results of this experiment showed sufficient differences in subject behavior to heavy breakfasts and no breakfast to warrant a continuation of the study. Although there was no change in work output, reaction time responses showed a group tendency toward an increase when breakfast was omitted and the tremor magnitude was significantly increased in every case when no breakfast was eaten.

EXPERIMENT 2. This experiment, which is actually a repetition of a part of Exp. 1, was designed to meet two specific purposes: (*a*) to determine whether the tendencies and positive changes in Exp. 1 could be repeated and (*b*) to determine whether all differences would be significant if data were collected more frequently. The experiment consisted of two consecutive 3-week periods. During the first period all subjects ate the heavy breakfast and during the second all subjects omitted breakfast. Data were collected between 11:00 a.m. and 12 noon, twice each week from each subject for the three tests. This procedure insured ample data for analysis of each test investigated, that is, work output, reaction time, and tremor pattern.

1. *Maximum work output.* The summary of the six records per subject of work output for each period and the analysis there of are shown in Table 1. Five of the six subjects showed a highly significant decrease in maximum work output when breakfast was omitted. The scores of the other subject remained practically unchanged.

2. *Reaction time.* The summary of reaction time data for Exp. 2 (both simple and choice responses), collected biweekly for each of the six subjects, is tabulated by periods in Table 2. Reaction time for each subject increased during the no-breakfast period; five of the six subjects showed a significant change in the simple responses but only three subjects showed a true increase in choice response time.

3. *Tremor.* As in Exp. 1 each of the six subjects demonstrated a highly significant increase in the magnitude of tremor pattern before exercise when breakfast was omitted. After exercise only five subjects demonstrated this

TABLE 1

Effect of Altered Breakfast Habits on Maximum Work Output of Six Subjects During Two Periods of Three Weeks' Duration Each. Experiment 2, Breakfast vs. No Breakfast

	1	2	3	SUBJECTS 4	5	6	Av.
Period I							
Heavy Breakfast							
M (kg-m)	1869	2053	2300	1641	1916	2215	1999
S. D.............	50.0	36.1	41.9	54.5	51.9	42.0	17.6
Period 2							
No breakfast							
M (kg-m)	1767	1917	2017	1511	1725	2194	1855
S. D.............	28.9	65.6	49.5	61.9	96.9	67.6	28.8
t (1 vs. 2)	3.81	3.73	9.10	3.30	3.56	0.54	8.78
Signif. level	1%	1%	0.1%	1%	1%	60%	0.1%

TABLE 2

Effect of Altered Breakfast Habits on Simple and Choice Reaction Time of Six Subjects During Two Periods of Three Weeks' Duration Each. Experiment 2, Breakfast vs. No Breakfast

	1	2	3	SUBJECTS 4	5	6	Av.
		Simple Reaction Time					
Period 1							
Heavy breakfast							
M (sec)	0.299	0.302	0.249	0.246	0.238	0.227	0.260
S. D.............	0.016	0.010	0.011	0.016	0.022	0.004	0.009
Period 2							
No breakfast							
M (sec)	0.315	0.325	0.264	0.268	0.277	0.237	0.281
S. D.............	0.013	0.014	0.006	0.009	0.021	0.008	0.005
t (1 vs. 2)	1.78	2.63	3.00	2.75	2.79	2.50	4.00
Signif. level	20%	5%	2%	5%	2%	5%	1%
		Choice Reaction Time					
Period 1							
Heavy breakfast							
M (sec)	0.335	0.388	0.316	0.280	0.272	0.308	0.317
S. D.............	0.012	0.030	0.005	0.009	0.008	0.027	0.005
Period 2							
No breakfast							
M (sec)	0.366	0.391	0.340	0.301	0.284	0.330	0.335
S. D.............	0.010	0.010	0.008	0.009	0.025	0.027	0.009
t (1 vs. 2)	4.43	0.21	6.00	3.50	1.00	1.29	3.60
Signif. level	1%	90%	0.1%	1%	40%	30%	1%

TABLE 3

Effect of Altered Breakfast Habits on Magnitude of Neuromuscular Tremor of Six Subjects During Two Periods of Three Weeks' Duration Each, Both, Before and After One Minute of Maximum Work. Experiment 2, Breakfast vs. No Breakfast

	SUBJECTS					
	1	*2*	*3*	*4*	*5*	*6*
			Before Exercise			
Period 1						
Heavy breakfast						
M (sq cm)	1.6	1.5	1.4	1.3	1.6	1.7
S. D............	0.38	0.36	0.39	0.34	0.24	0.36
Period 2						
No breakfast						
M (sq cm)	2.5	2.2	2.3	2.1	2.6	2.4
S. D............	0.29	0.29	0.41	0.64	0.29	0.34
t	4.21	3.38	3.56	2.47	5.96	3.17
Signif. level	1%	1%	1%	5%	0.1%	1%
			After Exercise			
Period 1						
Heavy breakfast						
M (sq cm)	3.4	2.3	2.6	2.3	2.7	3.0
S. D............	0.71	0.43	0.68	0.53	0.48	0.83
Period 2						
No breakfast						
M (sq cm)	3.7	3.4	3.4	2.9	3.4	4.0
S. D............	0.41	0.39	0.39	0.43	0.48	0.83
t	0.82	4.23	2.28	1.97	2.30	1.90
Signif. level	50%	1%	5%	10%	5%	10%

significant change. The summary and analysis of these data are given in Table 3.

EXPERIMENT 3. This experiment consisted of three consecutive 3-week periods. During the first period all subjects ate the heavy breakfast, during the second all subjects consumed coffee only for breakfast, and during the third all subjects ate the light breakfast. Data were collected twice a week, as in Exp. 2, for work output, choice reaction time, and tremor pattern.

1. *Maximum work output.* The summary of data given in Table 4 is compiled from four records per subject during period 1, five per subject during period 2, and four per subject during period 3. Five work records were lost during this 9-week experiment because of temporary mechanical failure of the bicycle ergometer. The group means for each test of work output are plotted in chronological order in Fig. 3B.

A comparison of the means (by subjects) for the heavy breakfast period with those for the coffee period (Table 4) shows that five of the six subjects did less work during the coffee period. Only three of these differences were statistically significant. If coffee represented an adequate breakfast, each subject would be expected to demon-

TABLE 4

Comparison of Maximum Work Output During Three-Week Periods of Heavy Breakfast, Coffee Only, and Light Breakfast. Experiment 3

				SUBJECTS			
	1	2	3	4	5	6	Av.
Period 1							
Heavy breakfast							
M (kg-m)	1850	2102	1986	1529	1876	2275	1937
S. D.............	35.7	13.9	53.1	79.2	47.8	21.9	16.7
Period 2							
Coffee only							
M (kg-m)	1831	1952	1924	1604	1728	2236	1877
S. D.............	30.0	89.5	67.9	113.5	39.6	26.9	35.1
Period 3							
Light breakfast							
M (kg-m)	1878	2161	2283	1612	1945	2339	2036
S. D.............	27.3	35.1	68.4	52.3	44.0	70.6	15.5
t (1 vs. 2)	0.77	2.93	1.16	0.99	4.47	2.06	2.76
Signif. level	50%	5%	30%	40%	1%	10%	5%
t (2 vs. 3)	2.15	3.88	6.08	0.12	6.85	2.65	7.43
Signif. level	10%	1%	0.1%	—	0.1%	5%	0.1%

TABLE 5

Comparison of Choice Reaction Time of Six Subjects During Three-Week Periods of Heavy Breakfast, Coffee Only, and Light Breakfast. Experiment 3

				SUBJECTS			
	1	2	3	4	5	6	Av.
Period 1							
Heavy breakfast							
M (sec)	0.339	0.365	0.290	0.283	0.262	0.313	0.309
S. D.............	0.015	0.007	0.018	0.016	0.007	0.008	0.005
Period 2							
Coffee only							
M (sec)	0.355	0.366	0.295	0.289	0.253	0.292	0.308
S. D.............	0.018	0.014	0.009	0.007	0.004	0.021	0.004
Period 3							
Light breakfast							
M (sec)	0.334	0.340	0.273	0.268	0.246	0.268	0.288
S. D.............	0.009	0.017	0.011	0.006	0.005	0.016	0.005
t (1 vs. 2)	1.45	0.14	0.56	0.75	3.00	2.10	0.33
Signif. level	20%	90%	60%	50%	2%	10%	80%
t (2 vs. 3)	2.33	2.60	3.67	5.25	3.50	2.00	6.67
Signif. level	5%	5%	1%	0.1%	1%	10%	0.1%

strate a gradual increase in work output proceeding from the level established at the end of period 1 (Fig. 3B). Instead, there was a precipitous drop in work efficiency at the beginning of the coffee period. Although there was subsequent improvement, the level of efficiency at the end of the coffee period never reached that which maintained at the end of the heavy breakfast period.

When the individual means for period 3 (Table 4, light breakfast) are compared with the respective means for period 1 and 2, it will be noted that, without exception, the mean outputs

for period 3 are greater than those for either of the preceding periods, i.e., each subject regained or surpassed her original work status while eating a light breakfast. These progressive changes through the three periods are more strikingly demonstrated when consecutive group means are plotted (Fig. 3B). Statistical comparison of the individual means for periods 2 and 3 show that five of the six subjects improved significantly when changed from coffee to a light breakfast. Individual work output differences between heavy and light breakfasts could not be compared statistically because (*a*)

Fig. 3. Graphic representation of three measures of physiologic response, as indicated, to altered breakfast habits during three 3-week periods of experimentation. The scores plotted are means derived from responses of six subjects.

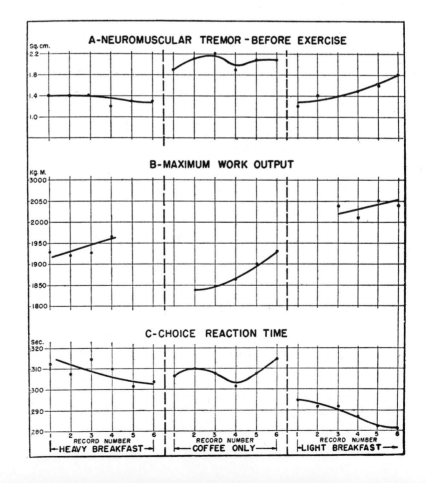

there was no way of establishing the residual effects of the coffee period and (*b*) the expected normal increase during the last three of the 9 weeks of experimentation on the bicycle ergometer was not established for these subjects.

2. *Reaction time.* Choice reaction scores for each subject for the six records taken biweekly during each of the three experimental periods are summarized in Table 5. Each record score represents an average of 50 responses, all of them being given without interruption during the same test. In an attempt to accentuate any difference which might exist in choice reaction times, the number of responses was increased from 30 to 50. The choice reaction time score tends to improve with repetition as is demonstrated by the group scores plotted for periods 1 and 3 in Fig. 3C. However, during period 2, when breakfast consisted of coffee, *subjects 5* and *6* only (Table 5) showed this characteristic improvement; all others tended to decrease in efficiency. A comparison of the group means for periods 1 and 2 gives a *t* of 0.33 which is an indication of no change in choice reaction time status for the entire group (Table 5).

During period 3, when subjects were eating a light breakfast, there was an abrupt improvement of choice reaction time scores over both periods 1 and 2. This was evidenced by the first record (Fig. 3C, period 3). When individual means for period 3 (light breakfast) are compared with the respective means for period 2 (coffee) all subjects show a significant improvement in reaction time scores. Simple reaction time was not measured during this experiment.

3. *Tremor.* Since tremor pattern is not affected by learning or repetition no progressive decrease in tremor magnitude is expected as the experiment progresses. A summary of the data for the three periods (heavy breakfast, coffee, and light breakfast)

relative to the magnitude of the tremor pattern, taken both before and after strenuous exercise, is given in Table 6. A graph of the group means for consecutive records taken before exercise during the three 3-week periods is presented in Fig. 3A. After-exercise data are omitted from the graph since they show the same trend.

Each subject showed a significant increase in tremor magnitude when coffee was substituted for the heavy breakfast for records taken both before and after exercise. A comparison of period 2 (coffee) with period 3 (light breakfast) shows a direct reversal, i.e., subjects tend to return to their heavy-breakfast tremor magnitude status. The latter changes are highly significant for five subjects both before and after exercise. The subjects show a tendency for an increase in tremor magnitude during the last week and one half of the experiment (Fig. 3A). This increase may be the result of final examinations, graduate orals, and similar nervous strain encountered by students at the end of the school year.

Discussion

We have every reason to believe that all subjects followed the prescribed breakfast menus explicitly. In spite of this fact there are numerous individual variations from the general patterns established by the group. These individual differences are no doubt basic, especially where the nervous system is involved. During an experiment extending over a rather long period of time, there are environmental situations arising which cannot be controlled. For example, during the examination periods, there was an alteration in tremor and reaction time among the subjects, the extent depending on their basic responses to such situations.

In experiments where women are used as subjects, menstruation some-

TABLE 6

Comparison of Tremor Magnitude in Six Subjects During Three-Week Periods of Heavy Breakfast, Coffee Only, and Light Breakfast. Experiment 3

| | SUBJECTS | | | | | | |
	1	2	3	4	5	6	Av.
			Before Exercise				
Period 1							
Heavy breakfast							
M (sq cm)	1.4	1.2	1.6	1.2	1.2	1.4	1.3
S. D............	0.26	0.31	0.28	0.23	0.15	0.38	0.08
Period 2							
Coffee only							
M (sq cm)	2.1	2.1	2.1	1.8	1.8	2.5	2.1
S. D............	0.29	0.73	0.26	0.41	0.48	0.23	0.12
Period 3							
Light breakfast							
M (sq cm)	1.5	1.4	1.6	1.4	1.6	1.4	1.5
S. D............	0.26	0.12	0.31	0.26	0.28	0.23	0.19
t (1 vs. 2)	4.02	2.54	3.07	2.86	2.67	5.53	12.31
Signif. level	1%	5%	2%	2%	5%	0.1%	0.1%
t (2 vs. 3)	3.45	2.11	2.76	1.84	0.80	7.59	6.00
Signif. level	1%	10%	5%	10%	50%	0.1%	0.1%
			After Exercise				
Period 1							
Heavy breakfast							
M (sq cm)	2.4	2.0	2.4	1.7	2.1	3.6	2.4
S. D............	0.41	0.24	0.14	0.15	0.31	0.79	0.14
Period 2							
Coffee only							
M (sq cm)	4.3	3.2	3.5	3.0	3.4	4.7	3.7
S. D............	0.86	0.53	0.58	1.04	0.76	1.04	0.49
Period 3							
Light breakfast							
M (sq cm)	2.8	2.4	2.5	2.3	2.5	2.7	2.5
S. D............	0.39	0.24	0.46	0.33	0.48	0.56	0.26
t (1 vs. 2)	4.46	4.49	3.78	2.77	3.54	1.88	5.70
Signif. level	1%	1%	1%	2%	1%	10%	0.1%
t (2 vs. 3)	3.55	3.00	3.02	1.43	2.24	3.78	4.84
Signif. level	1%	2%	2%	20%	5%	1%	0.1%

times causes a variability of reactions, the extent depending on the individual involved. In some cases, work output was noticeably affected.

In evaluating data relative to measures such as maximum work output and reaction time, it must be recognized that there is an improvement in performance caused by repetition at regular intervals. This improvement continues for a relatively long period of time and becomes progressively less until a plateau is reached. In drawing conclusions, this fact must be taken into account. For example, in Exp. 3, the group averages for reaction time were the same during the heavy breakfast period and the coffee period. If coffee had represented an adequate breakfast, one has a right to expect that there would have been a progressive decrease in choice reaction time scores.

Summary

Data collected twice each week, between 11:00 a.m. and 12 noon, relative to the effect of altered breakfast habits on physiologic response justify the following conclusions.

1. The omission of breakfast caused a decrease in maximum work output, an increase both in simple and choice reaction time, and an increase in tremor magnitude.

2. When coffee alone is substituted for a heavy breakfast there is a decrease in the level of performance in maximum work output, and choice reaction time; there is an increase in tremor magnitude.

3. When a light breakfast is substituted for coffee alone the level of performance of maximum work output and choice reaction time improves significantly; there is a decrease in tremor magnitude.

4. There are considerable individual differences in response to altered breakfast habits.

5. Because the breakfast period of coffee only occurred between heavy breakfast and the light breakfast periods a direct comparison of the physiologic responses during the light and heavy breakfast periods could not be made.

References

1. Aring, C. D., and J. F. Fulton, *J. Neurol. Neurosurg. Psychiat.* (formerly *Journal of Neurology and Psychiatry*), **35** (1936), 439.

2. Binet, L., *Lancet*, **1** (1920), 265.

3. Bousfield, W. A., *Am. J. Psychol.*, **15** (1932), 104.

4. Bucy, P. C., *The Precentral Motor Cortex.* Urbana, Ill.: University of Illinois Press, 1944.

5. Eshner, A. A., *J. Exptl. Med.*, **2** (1897), 301.

6. Fulton, J. F., E. G. T. Liddell, and D. McK. Rioch, *J. Neurol. Neurosurg. Psychiat.* (formerly *Journal of Neurology and Psychiatry*), **28** (1932), 542.

7. Haggard, H. W., and L. A. Greenburg, *Science*, **79** (1934), 165.

8. Haggard, H. W., and L. A. Greenburg, *Diet and Physical Efficiency.* New Haven, Conn: Yale University Press, 1935.

9. Haggard, H. W., and L. A. Greenburg, *J. Am. Dietet. Assoc.*, **15** (1939), 435.

10. Haggard, H. W., and L. A. Greenburg, *ibid.*, **17** (1941), 753.

11. Haldi, J. G., C. Eusor, and W. Wynn, *Am. J. Physiol.*, **121** (1938), 123.

12. Haldi, J., and W. Wynn, *Federation Proc.*, **7** (1948), 48.

13. Herren, R. Y., *J. Exptl. Psychol.*, **15** (1932), 87.

14. Jasper, H. H., and H. L. Andrews, *J. Neurophysiol.*, **1** (1938), 87.

15. Karpovich, P. V., and K. Pestrecov, *Am. J. Physiol.*, **134** (1941), 300.

16. Mann, J., *Ind. Med. Surg.*, **13** (1944), 368.

17. Sollenburger, R. T., *J. Exptl. Psychol.*, **21** (1937), 579.

18. Travis, L. E., and T. A. Hunter, *Am. J. Physiol.*, **81** (1927), 355.

19. Tuttle, W. W., and A. J. Wendler, *J. Lab. Clin. Med.*, **30** (1945) 173.

20. Wilson, Marjorie, W. W. Tuttle, Kate Daum, and Helen Rhodes, *J. Am. Dietet. Assoc.*

21. Wolfenden, R. N., and D. Williams, *Brit. Med. J.*, **1** (1888), 1049.

P. V. KARPOVICH / C. J. HALE

Tobacco Smoking and Physical Performance

Reprinted from the *Journal of Applied Physiology*,
3 (1951), 616–21.

The principal concern about smoking at present is its relationship to lung cancer and cardiovascular disease. Prior to the lung cancer studies, interest was directed mainly toward the effect of smoking on physical performance. This study, conducted in 1950, attempted to investigate the problem experimentally. Eight smokers and five nonsmokers were studied in experimental situations in which performance on the bicycle ergometer was determined during periods of smoking and periods of nonsmoking. Despite the fact that the authors expected to find significantly lower performance during the smoking periods, they found that the difference in performance between the smoking and nonsmoking periods was not statistically significant.

The authors report that there is considerable variation in the subjects' performance under conditions of tobacco use. Some individuals apparently are more sensitive to tobacco than others. As a result, the paper suggests that the no-smoking rule for athletes is probably a wise precaution. Of course, recent lung cancer studies have provided a much more cogent reason for refraining from smoking.

Although the effect of tobacco smoking upon athletic performance is widely discussed among coaches and athletes, our knowledge regarding this topic is rather inadequate. References often are made to athletic records made by smokers and nonsmokers. These references usually furnish material of either a conflicting or inconclusive nature. There is, moreover, no convincing proof of an immediate harmful effect of smoking upon athletic performance.

A frequently quoted report of Kennedy[5] showing that nonsmokers were more proficient in cross-country running than smokers, may be contrasted with the Pittsburgh marathon race,[1] in which four of the first five winners were smokers. To this we should also add personal observations by athletes themselves who continue to smoke either openly or surreptitiously without any apparent detrimental effect. It is quite possible that there may not be any uniformity in the effect of smoking upon different people because of several variables—individual differences, amount of smoke inhaled, speed of smoking, and frequency of smoking. Moreover, man's physical performance may vary independently of smoking. For this reason, more experimental work is needed regarding this problem.

Recently Henry and Fitzhenry[2] showed that smoking before exercise had no effect upon oxygen intake, oxygen debt, net oxygen cost of exercise, and rate of recovery. Reeves and Morehouse[6] could not observe any effect of preliminary smoking upon performance in Sargent jump test, Harvard step test, speed of tapping, or strength of grip. The lack of effect of smoking on grip strength was also reported by Kay and Karpovich.[4]

Although in theory experimentation of this sort appears to be simple, in practice it is difficult to find a large number of smokers who would be willing to stop smoking and nonsmokers who would be willing to start smoking and inhale smoke. Thus an experimental group cannot be too large and should be composed of thoroughly dependable men. This condition necessitates numerous tests on each individual over a relatively long period of time.

Preliminary Observations

In the preliminary investigation[3] one of the writers had several men excellently trained on bicycle ergometers. Their endurance was well established by numerous tests. Three of these men, who could ride in excess of 4 hr performing 6,000 and 7,150 ft-lb of work per min, were allowed to smoke cigarettes while riding. One man, after smoking a cigarette, declined further smoking because of throat dryness. The other two men smoked in 4 to 5 hr 14 and 18 cigarettes, respectively (inhaling the smoke into the lungs), and broke their previous records.

On another occasion a bicycle rider, habitual smoker, stopped smoking for 1 week and then on a testing day he was given a cigarette which he smoked in 1 min and 30 sec. This made him so sick that he could hardly ride.

These observations are mentioned here to illustrate difficulties of interpretation. It must be confessed that during the first test, the investigators as well as the subjects expected endurance to be lowered by smoking; however, this did not happen. Should this be interpreted then that smoking increased

endurance or endurance increased in spite of smoking?

The second observation demonstrates the effect of speed of smoking. Even a nonabstainer may be made sick if he attempts to smoke too fast. When a cigarette is smoked in 10 min, only 0.2 mg of nicotine is inhaled, but if a cigarette is smoked in 2 min, 6.5 mg of nicotine is inhaled.[7]

Present Investigation

The present investigation includes two series—one conducted in 1948–1949 on habitual smokers and the other conducted in 1949–1950 on smokers and nonsmokers. The exercise used in both series consisted of completing a prescribed amount of work on a bicycle ergometer in the shortest possible time with the subjects trying to break their records each time.

Before the actual experimentation began, each subject had to practice riding from 1 to 2 months, two or three times a week, in order to become familiar with pacing and to reach a semblance of a performance plateau.

The smoking was controlled by requiring the smokers on some days or weeks to abstain from smoking, and the nonsmokers to smoke on certain days or weeks.

First Experimental Series

The subjects were five college students who smoked habitually, averaging ten cigarettes a day. For four of them, the exercise consisted of 425 pedal revolutions with a load of 8 lb, the total distance being 6,116 ft and work done, 48,928 ft-lb. One of the subjects for whom this rate of work was too difficult performed only 234 pedal revolutions, thus covering only 4,086.8 ft, the total amount of work being 32,964 ft-lb. All men had a preliminary training period of 2 months, after which the experiment continued for $3\frac{1}{2}$ months. Each man rode the ergometer twice a week, thus each subject received between 24 and 31 tests, with the exception of one man who became ill and was forced to withdraw after 8 tests. During the entire investigation, the subjects continued to indulge in their habitual smoking. On the test days, however, they did not smoke before the test except on "smoking" days, when they were allowed to smoke one cigarette in about 6 to 7 min (the usual smoking time). The smoke was inhaled into the lungs. The exercise was started approximately one minute after smoking. Riding time was recorded. Notes of subjective reactions were also made.

Results

The essential statistical data are presented in Table 1. Examination of this table shows that the average time of all subjects was better on nonsmoking days; however, this was statistically significant for two men only.

Reports made by subjects regarding how they felt before, during, and after rides had no bearing on their riding times.

Second Experimental Series

The second series was undertaken because of the inconclusiveness of the results obtained in the first series. The method, however, was modified in order to determine the effect of smoking upon physical performance of non-smokers, and also to determine the effect of complete abstinence from tobacco on the performances of habitual smokers.

The subjects were eight college students, three of whom were habitual smokers, who used on the average ten cigarettes a day and five nonsmokers. The exercise used was the same as in the first series. The subjects spent 4 weeks on preliminary training in riding the ergometer, after which the experiment proper began. It continued from 7 to 10 weeks with subjects riding twice a week. Smoking was controlled in such a manner that the subjects had alternately a "smoking" week and a "non-smoking" week. During a smoking week, the smokers used tobacco in

TABLE 1

Effect of Smoking Upon Riding Time on Bicycle Ergometer

SUBJECT	SMOKING TESTS			NONSMOKING TESTS				*t*-VALUE
	N	*Mean* *min-sec*	*S.D.* *sec*	*N*	*Mean* *min-sec*	*S.D.* *sec*	DIFFERENCE *sec*	
1	13	4–48.6	10.62	19	4–41.3	10.21	7.3 ± 3.72	1.96*
2	14	4–48.1	6.01	14	4–41.0	7.99	7.1 ± 2.77	2.56*
3	13	4–39.0	6.20	14	4–37.0	6.37	2.0 ± 2.44	0.82
4†	12	3–50.0	7.31	12	3–45.7	8.40	4.3 ± 3.36	1.28
5‡	5	5–12.0	12.00	3	5–09.8	10.10	3.2 ± 3.60	0.89

* Statistically significant (minimum *t* value for significance at 0.05 level is 1.70).
† Subject rode shorter distance than the others.
‡ Subject had to withdraw from the experiment because of illness.

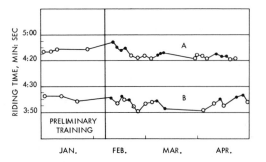

Fig. 1. Performance curves on a bicycle ergometer for two tobacco-sensitive subjects: *A*: Habitual smoker; *B*: nonsmoker. ●: Performance after smoking; ○: performance without smoking.

habitual manner and also had to smoke one or two cigarettes immediately preceding their rides. The non-smokers smoked during that week only one cigarette before their rides. Smoking time was 6 to 7 min. During the nonsmoking week, all subjects completely abstained from tobacco. In addition to these weekly periods, the nonsmokers alternated smoking and nonsmoking days. Figure 1 represents performance curves plotted for two

tobacco-sensitive subjects, one of whom was a habitual smoker and the other a nonsmoker. During the preliminary training, time trials were held only once a week although men rode three times a week.

Results

Data obtained in this series were treated in two ways in order to determine individual and group effects of smoking. From Table 2 it may be seen that there was a statistically significant deleterious effect of smoking on one smoker and two nonsmokers, which substantiates findings in the first series. The average riding time on nonsmoking days was better than on smoking days for all men but one (*subject 5*).

In order to determine the effect of smoking on the group, the data obtained were pooled. Although the average riding times for each group were better without smoking than with smoking, the differences were not statistically significant; they may be considered at the most as an indication of a trend.

TABLE 2

Effect of Smoking Upon Riding Time on Bicycle Ergometer

| SUBJECT | SMOKING TESTS | | | NONSMOKING TESTS | | | DIFFERENCE | *t*-VALUE |
	N	*Mean* min–sec	*S.D.* sec	*N*	*Mean* min–sec	*S.D.* sec	sec	
Smokers								
1	10	4–31.7	9.38	10	4–24.2	4.07	7.5 ± 3.42	2.19*
2	8	4–26.6	10.94	5	4–21.7	8.70	4.9 ± 6.28	0.78
3	10	4–16.8	4.76	8	4–14.4	6.43	2.8 ± 2.89	0.97
Nonsmokers								
1	8	4–10.4	7.06	9	4–01.4	7.58	9.0 ± 3.81	2.36†
2	9	4–22.0	5.84	11	4–14.7	3.11	7.3 ± 3.07	2.38*
3	5	4–15.2	6.28	6	4–13.8	8.40	1.4 ± 5.00	0.28
4	8	4–11.3	10.00	10	4–05.1	8.22	6.2 ± 4.53	1.37
5	8	4–48.2	8.00	9	4–53.1	8.49	−4.9 ± 4.30	1.14

*, † Statistically significant (minimum *t*-values for significance at 0.05 level are 1.73 and 1.75, respectively).

Discussion

The obtained results undoubtedly indicate that an individual's resistance to tobacco varies. While some men can smoke with seeming impunity, others exhibit a deleterious effect.

Although the number of subjects in this study was small, one may observe a rough consistency of the ratio of those who were affected by smoking to those who were not. In the first group of five, this ratio was 2 : 3; in another group of three, it was 1 : 2; and in the last group of five, it was 2 : 3. Thus for all 13 subjects used in this study, the ratio was 5 : 8. Whether this ratio will hold true on larger groups may not be answered without further experimentation. The fact remains, however, that there are some, and probably relatively large numbers of men, who are slowed down in performing an athletic feat similar to a mile run. For this reason, the no-smoking rule imposed by coaches and trainers on their teams is a wise one.

One may wonder why the deleterious effect of tobacco was not more noticeable on nonsmokers than smokers. The answer may be found in the fact that although the nonsmokers tried to inhale smoke, they did not do it very well.

Although the average riding times for all experimental groups were better on nonsmoking days, these improvements were not statistically significant. Evidently the presence of men relatively nonsensitive to tobacco, offset the large gains made by tobacco-sensitive men, and the average for the group sank below the threshold of statistical significance.

Summary

Thirteen college students were used as subjects, eight of them were habitual smokers, and five nonsmokers. Exercise consisted of performing on a bicycle ergometer a prescribed amount of work, comparable to a 1-mi run on the track, in the shortest possible time. Each subject served as his own control by either smoking or abstaining from smoking. The period of abstinence from smoking was from 7 to 10 days.

The average riding times for all subjects but one were better when they did not smoke. This however, was statistically significant for only three smokers and two nonsmokers, and was not significant for the group. Abstinence from smoking for 1 week showed improvement in a tobacco-sensitive subject, and no effect in nonsensitive ones. Reports made by the subjects regarding how they felt before and during the rides had no apparent connection with their performances.

Since a relatively large proportion of an athletic team may consist of tobacco-sensitive men, the no-smoking rule is a wise precaution.

References

1. Dawson, P. M., *The Physiology of Physical Education*. Baltimore: The Williams & Wilkins Co., 1935.

2. Henry, F. M., and J. R. Fitzhenry, *J. Appl. Physiol.*, **2** (1950), 464.

3. Karpovich, P. V., and K. Pestrecov, *Am. J. Physiol.*, **134** (1941), 300.

4. Kay, H. W., and P. V. Karpovich, *Res. Quart.*, **20** (1949), 250.

5. Kennedy, T. F., *J. Roy. Army Med. Corps*, **57** (1931), 451.

6. Reeves, W. E., and L. E. Morehouse, *Res. Quart.*, **20** (1950), 245.

7. Sollmann, T. A., *A Manual of Pharmacology and Its Applications to Therapeutics and Toxicology*. Philadelphia: W. B. Saunders Co., 1948.

P. V. KARPOVICH

Effect of Amphetamine Sulfate on Athletic Performance

Reprinted from the *Journal of the American Medical Association*,
170 (1959), 558–61.

In the late 1950's several reports appeared in the press about "doping" athletes. Some professional athletes openly admitted that they took "pep pills." The situation became so serious that the American Medical Association commissioned two studies on the effect of the most potent of the "pep pills," amphetamine sulfate. The paper presented here is one of these studies; it was conducted at Springfield College by Dr. Karpovich; the other was conducted at Harvard University by Drs. Beecher and Smith.[1] The latter study used larger doses of amphetamine than the Karpovich study and hence found that performance was improved in about 75 per cent of the trained athletes studied. Karpovich found improvement in only 3 of 54 performers with a mild dosage. In this experiment Karpovich used a placebo in a double-blind procedure to control the psychological effect of the taking of a drug.

As a result of these experiments the ad hoc *Committee on Amphetamines and Athletics of the A.M.A. recommended the use of amphetamines in athletic competition be condemned on dual grounds: their use was considered a violation of the canon of sportsmanship, and amphetamines could also have harmful effects and result in habituation.*

Recently there has been a great deal of agitation regarding the use of amphetamines in athletics. This agitation has been based mainly on rumors or secondhand information regarding one or two athletes who reportedly have admitted the use of amphetamine (Benzedrine) sulfate. It is, however, not known how these athletes would have performed with and without this drug under conditions of a controlled experiment.

While it is well known that amphetamines can cause euphoria and various degrees of insommia which prolong wakefulness which might be used for activity, no reliable evidence exists that amphetamines are effective in increasing either endurance or speed in activities. For this reasons, the present study was undertaken. This study was so designed that it would be possible to detect the effect of the drug on endurance, recuperative ability, and speed of athletic performance under two conditions: "laboratory" conditions and under emotional stress during actual athletic competition.

---

[1] G. M. Smith and H. K. Beecher, "Amphetamine Sulfate and Athletic Performance," *J. Am. Med. Assoc.*, **170** (1959) 102–16.

Methods

Activities. The following activities were included: (*a*) running to exhaustion on an electrically driven treadmill at 7.2 mi per hr and 5-degree inclination twice in succession with a 10-min rest in between the runs, (*b*) swimming 100 yd as fast as possible twice in succession with a 10-min rest in between, (*c*) swimming 220 and 440 yd once on each testing day (*d*) running 220 yd on an outdoor track for time trials, and (*e*) running various distances (from 100 yd to 2 mi) during competition. Altogether 532 tests were used for statistical analysis.

All "laboratory" experiments consisted of six tests done on six different days, three times with the drug and three times with a placebo. Experiments during actual contests were planned so that each subject would run from four to eight times, one-half of the runs with amphetamine and one-half without. However, since it was not always possible to know ahead of time what subject would take part in the contest, the number of tests and the order of administration of the drug and placebo varied.

Medication. From the standpoint of medication, this study may be divided into two parts. In 1958 all but four subjects were given a capsule of 10 mg of amphetamine sulfate one hour before the test. These four subjects received 20 mg 30 min before the test. The drug and the placebo were administered from six coded bottles and given to subjects in rotating order. Neither I nor my assistants knew the code, which was kept in the A.M.A. headquarters on my request.

In 1959, although the drug and the placebo were administered from coded bottles, I, but not my assistants, knew the code. This was done in order to expedite the detection of individuals who were affected either beneficially or deleteriously by the drug so that they could be subjected to additional tests. In 1959 all subjects received 20 mg of amphetamine or placebo 30 min before the test. In both series, the placebo was made of calcium lactate.

Subjects. All subjects were male college students. Most swimmers and all trackmen were varsity men. All the treadmill runners, some of whom were also varsity men, received preliminary training in running on the treadmill. Twenty-five men were used on the treadmill, 18 in swimming, and 11 in track time trials during competition. Altogether, 54 subjects were used. All subjects had a medical examination. Blood pressure and pulse rate were taken on several occasions one-half hour and one hour after medication. Since no particular variations were observed, this procedure was discontinued.

Results

Treadmill runs. Tests with 10 mg of amphetamine given to 11 subjects one hour before the run showed no evidence of either a beneficial or deleterious effect of the drug on the endurance and recuperation from fatigue. From the table it may be seen that the average times for the first runs were 391.06 sec with the drug and 398.24 sec with the placebo. The duration of the second run was 281.63 sec with the drug and 279.72 with the placebo. The average total times were 672.69 sec and 677.96 sec, respectively. Analysis of variance of times showed that the differences between the figures in each pair were not statistically significant.

Tests with 20 mg of amphetamine given to ten subjects one-half hour

TABLE 1

Mean Time (in Seconds) of Performance With and Without Amphetamine *

	Swimming 100 yd (11 Men)			Swimming		Track			Treadmill (11 Men)			Treadmill (10 Men)			Treadmill (Special Group of 4 Men)		
	1st Swim	2nd Swim	Difference	220 Yd. (16 Men)	220 Yd. (11 Men)	440 Yd. (9 Men)	220 Yd. (9 Men)	Competition† (12 Men)	1st Run	2nd Run	Difference	1st Run	2nd Run	Difference	1st Run	2nd Run	Difference
Amphetamine	62.34	62.81	0.47	168.62	151.2	311.6	25.13	99.4	391.06	281.63	109.43	241.40	232.79	8.61	232.2	169.8	62.4
Placebo	62.33	63.20	0.87	169.64	151.6	311.0	25.15	100.0	398.24	279.72	118.52	258.60	227.44	31.16	249.7	148.2	101.5
Amphetamine minus placebo	0.01	−0.39	−0.40	−1.02	−0.4	0.6	−0.02	−0.6	−7.18	1.91	−9.09	−17.20	5.35	−22.55	−17.5	21.6	−39.1
Amphetamine, 1st plus 2nd	125.15								672.69			474.19			402.0		
Placebo, 1st plus 2nd	125.53								677.96			486.04			397.9		
Amphetamine total minus placebo total	−0.38								−5.27			−11.85			4.1		

* Subjects in each group, except "Treadmill (10 men)," received at least six tests. In this group only four tests were given. Analysis of variance of performance time and also of variance in time differences between first and second "runs" in swimming and treadmill running showed no statistically significant differences between effects of amphetamine and placebo.

† Varsity meets, 100, 220, and 440 yd; 1/2, 1, and 2 mi. Time of running with the placebo was taken as 100 per cent.

416

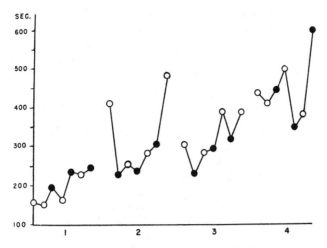

Fig. 1. Effect of amphetamine (20 mg taken one-half hour before test) on treadmill running time. Speed, 7.2 mi per hr; angle of inclination, 5 degrees. (Solid dot, amphetamine; open dot, placebo.)

before the run also gave no statistically significant difference (see Table 1).

Tests with amphetamine on a special group: Four men, highly interested in the experiment and therefore highly motivated to do their utmost, were each tested seven times. Most of the subjects felt a sense of euphoria after taking the capsule containing 20 mg of amphetamine, the effect being noticeable about 30 min after taking the capsule. They also thought that they could run longer when they felt this effect, but they did not.

It may be observed from Fig. 1 that the best times for the first runs were obtained by all subjects during the last session regardless of the chemical taken: two of the subjects had taken amphetamine and the other two a placebo. The psychological effect of the knowledge that it was the last test was obvious. Although the average results obtained for the entire group are the same as those obtained in other treadmill experiments, there was a definitely different reaction on the

part of one of the subjects. *Subject 3* (Fig. 1) exhibited a deleterious effect of amphetamine. His drug times were shorter than the placebo times. The average drug time was only 284 sec, whereas the placebo time was 357 sec. Unfortunately this subject was not available for further experimentation. *Subject 2* showed a puzzling behavior occasionally observed in experiments involving endurance testing and not related to the chemicals consumed. His first and last runs were the best. Since the improvement in the last run had psychological reason, a similar interpretation may be suggested regarding the first run.

Swimming. Tests were made with 10 mg of amphetamine given to 11 subjects 1 hr before swimming 100 yd. The average time for the first swim was 62.34 sec with the drug and 62.33 with the placebo. For the second swim the times were 62.81 and 63.20 sec, respectively (see table). Analysis of variance showed that these differences were not statistically significant. Thus no beneficial or deleterious effect of amphetamine was observed on either the speed of swimming or recuperation from fatigue.

Tests were also made with 20 mg of amphetamine given 30 min before swimming. Nine subjects swam 440 yd. The average drug time was 311.6 sec and the placebo time 311.0. Two groups of subjects swam 220 yd. In one group, consisting of 16 men, the average drug time was 168.62 sec and placebo time was 169.64 sec. In the second group, consisting of 11 men, the times were 151.2 and 151.6 sec, respectively. Statistical analysis showed that the difference between each pair of figures was not statistically significant.

Inspection of the time graphs made for each subject showed that there were three subjects whose speed was increased by the amphetamine. Figure 2 shows a time graph prepared for one of these subjects. This graph consists of two parts. Part one was obtained when the subject was at the peak of condition. During this period, one can see a trend. The two fastest times were made with the drug during part two, after the swimming season was over, and the subject's speed fluctuated 8 sec instead of 2 sec as in part one. The effect of amphetamine was observed each time he took the drug. The second man, a much faster man whose time varied from 143 sec to 146 sec, swam faster each time he took amphetamine. Without the drug, his average time was 146 sec; with the drug it was 143.3 sec. One subject swam 440 yd faster each time with amphetamine than with placebo. This average drug time was 301.6 sec, and placebo time was 303.3 sec. His swimming time for 220 yd, however, was not affected.

Track running with amphetamine taken one hour before test. Nine varsity men were tested six times, after 10 mg of amphetamine, each in time trials for 220-yd runs. The average running time after taking amphetamine was 25.13 sec and after taking the placebo 25.15. Analysis of variance showed that there was no statistically significant difference between the times.

Competitive track runs. Twelve men made 65 runs in seven events: 100 yd, 220 yd, 220 yd with low hurdles, 440 yd, $\frac{1}{2}$ mil, 1 mil, and 2 mil. If the time of running after taking the placebo is given a value of 100 per cent, the average time of running after taking the drug is 99.4 per cent. The best time was made 11 times with the drug and only 9 times with the placebo. There were two ties. This observation, however, cannot be accepted as even an indication of a trend.

Fig. 2. Effect of amphetamine (20 mg taken one-half hour before the test) on speed of swimming 220 yd. Part 1 was obtained during the swimming season and part 2 after season. (Solid dot, amphetamine; open dot, placebo.)

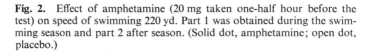
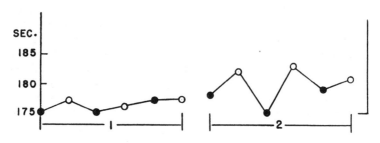

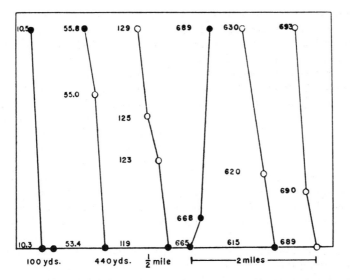

Fig. 3. Time graphs obtained during intercollegiate track meets. Running time of some subjects improved and that of some deteriorated regardless of the chemical taken. (Solid dot, amphetamine [20 mg, one hour before the run]; open dot, placebo.)

An inspection of the individual time graphs shows a disturbing fact (Fig. 3). Some runners showed a consistent improvement in speed and some a consistent deterioration in performance regardless of the chemical taken.

Looking at the 100-yd record, one may assume that this man improved under the influence of the amphetamine. The 440-yd man improved also, even though before his second run he received the placebo. The half-miler kept on improving while getting placebos, and one may suppose that he would have improved during his last run if the placebo instead of amphetamine had been given (as happened with the last two-miler). The first two-miler's performance became steadily worse in spite of or because of amphetamine.

Comparison of weather and track conditions with the records failed to show any relation. If by chance tests were made only on subjects 1, 3, or 5, conclusions could be drawn that amphetamine increases the speed of running. The graphs 4 and 6 in Fig. 3 will make one wonder. It is quite possible that these steady changes in performance are not related to the effect of the drug at all.

Subjective Reports

Subjects were asked to report any unusual sensation, comfortable or otherwise, and whether they slept well or not. When 10 mg of amphetamine was given, the placebo was blamed or praised as often as the drug. When 20 mg was given, the subjects were 75 per cent correct in guessing when they had been given the "pep pills." Some complained of difficulty sleeping. The latter was remedied equally well by a sedative or another capsule of placebo. The four subjects in the special treadmill group usually guessed correctly when amphetamine was administered.

In this group there was a man from India who had never taken any drugs in his life and was at first reluctant to join in the experiment. He could always guess correctly whether it was a drug or a placebo that had been taken. However, this did not affect his running time.

Comment

During the experiment subjects did not know what drug was being investigated. Their guesses ranged from amphetamine to tranquilizers. The medication schedule was adhered to strictly except in one instance when a man, after taking the drug, ran half an hour later than scheduled. When, on one occasion, trackmen did exceptionally well, they begged for more of the "miracle pills." Subsequent examination of records revealed that some of these "miracle pills" were placebos.

Examination of individual records of competitive runs shows that for no known reason some athletes steadily improved and some steadily declined in proficiency during the last three meets. If by chance, only certain men had been used in this study, results could have been either definitely in favor of or definitely against amphetamine.

Four subjects in the special treadmill group gave their best performance during the last test. It was fortunate that two of them had received amphetamine and two the placebo. If they all had received the same chemical, interpretation of the results would have been more difficult.

There are other stumbling blocks which may be encountered. On one occasion, a subject improved his endurance 88 per cent (from 402 sec to 756 sec) after taking 10 mg of amphetamine. However, a few days later another man, running after taking 10 mg of placebo, improved his endurance more than 132 per cent (from 860 sec to 2,000 sec). He ran on three more occasions, twice with the drug and once with the placebo, but his time never surpassed 958 sec. This particular man was a good distance runner and very cooperative. He could not offer any acceptable explanation of his phenomenal run. Such unusually long running times immediately arouse a suspicion that these two men were not always running to the limit of their ability, a suspicion easily aroused when tests depend on maximum voluntary performance. However, there was no other tangible evidence on which to suspect these two subjects of shirking their pledges, and they were retained in the experiment.

Observations similar to this have been made by me during other experiments involving endurance. No suitable explanation has ever been found.

The results obtained during track contests were different from those obtained on the same men during the 220-yd trials. Whereas during the trials no effect on performance was discovered, the data obtained during athletic competitions could be interpreted in a manner fitting the fancy of the interpreter. All reports regarding the ergogenic action of chemicals obtained from studies of single individuals or small groups should be regarded with extreme caution. It is also advisable to plot performance graphs for each subject, so that any unusual reaction can be discovered immediately and followed up with additional tests.

Summary and Conclusions

In an investigation of the effect of amphetamine sulfate on the athletic performance of 54 male college students, the drug was given in doses of 10 and 20 mg, either one hour or one-half hour before the test. Activities used were as follows: running to exhaustion on a treadmill twice in succession with a 10-min rest in between, running 220-yd track time trials, running distances from 100 yd to 2 mi under competitive conditions, swimming 100 yd twice in succession with a 10-min rest in between, and swimming 220 and 440 yd. Altogether 532 tests were statistically analyzed.

All subjects but four showed neither beneficial nor deleterious effect of 10 or 20 mg of amphetamine. Three of the four subjects definitely improved in swimming 220 yd, while one improved in swimming 440 yd. One treadmill subject showed a deleterious effect of amphetamine. He ran longer after taking the placebo than after the amphetamine. Thus, three of the subjects were definitely benefited by the amphetamine, and one man was affected deleteriously. All these men received 20 mg of amphetamine.

The Effect of Exercise on Health

In view of the popularity of reports on the effect of exercise on health, three studies have been selected as examples of work in those areas. One study deals with weight control and exercise, another is concerned with cardiovascular disease and exercise, and the third, the longevity of college athletes. The studies are all of the ex post facto design in that the groups are self-selected. Accordingly, the findings should be viewed with caution until it is possible to design experiments or some prospective surveys on these phenomena. The studies are interesting both from the standpoint of research design and their findings. Ex post facto studies of this type often provide excellent leads for further work of an experimental nature.

J. MAYER / P. ROY / K. MITRA

Relation Between Caloric Intake, Body Weight, and Physical Work; Studies in An Industrial Male Population in West Bengal

Reprinted from the *American Journal of Clinical Nutrition,*
4 (1956), 169–75.

Mayer and his associates have long held the position that it is not so much what you eat that makes you fat, but the relative amount of exercise performed. This study which is based on the analysis of weight, caloric intake, and occupation of 213 mill workers in West Bengal, shows that although the subjects who do the hardest physical work eat more, they weigh the same as those who do light work and who eat less. Persons in sedentary occupations tended to eat more and weigh more. Mayer does not deny that other factors influence obesity, but he believes that urbanization and mechanization may be responsible for a decrease in activity which ultimately contributes to the increased incidence of obesity.

It has been stated—or implied—by many workers that the regulation of food intake functions with such flexibility that an increase in energy output due to exercise is automatically followed by an equivalent increase in caloric intake. This view, usually accompanied by a minimization of the energy expenditure due to exercise, has often led to the disparagement of physical activity as a factor in weight control. The fallacies inherent in such an attitude have been discussed previously.[10,12] It has been shown that when rats are exercised for increasing durations on a treadmill, intakes vary linearly with exercise only within certain limits of activity.[14] Below this level, in what can be termed the "sedentary" range, a further decrease in activity is not followed by a decrease in food intake but, on the contrary, by a slight but significant increase. The animals increase both their weight and fat content. Enforced total inactivity in the rat can even lead to a considerable degree of obesity.[7] It has also been shown that spontaneous inactivity is a major factor in the development of genetic obesity in the mouse.[11] Enforced exercise decreases weight gain even when food is available ad libitum in other types of animal obesity.[9,13] These findings appear related to the well-known practice among farmers to restrict the activity of animals (e.g., hogs, geese) which they want to fatten.

It appeared of interest to see whether these experimental results could be extended to man. The availability for study of a large population of male subjects demonstrating extreme differences of physical activity made it possible to attempt to correlate work with food intakes and body weight.

Subjects

The subjects constituted a sample of 213 workers out of a total of 800 on whom height and weight data were obtained. All were employees (or, in the case of the "stall holders" or bazaar shopkeepers, licensees) of the Ludlow Jute Co., Ltd., at Chengail, West Bengal. The mill is situated on the Hooghly (Ganges) about 20 miles south of Calcutta, and it and the "labor lines" (workers' quarters) have been described by Chernin[3] on the occasion of his studies of parasitic infestations in the population of this mill. The total number of workers is in the neighborhood of 7,000.

The study was carried out on individuals 5 ft 2 in. to 5 ft 4 in. tall, the most usual range among the male workers of the mill. They were reasonably healthy individuals, free of obvious signs of malnutrition, of which those most frequently encountered in this population were anemia, angular stomatitis, and other riboflavin deficiency symptoms, and ocular and skin anomalies probably referable in part to vitamin A deficiency.

The subjects, some 50 per cent of whom were indigenous Bengalis, also included persons from other parts of India as well, in particular Orissa, Madras, Bilaspuri (Central Province), Bihar, and United Province. Bengalis, although almost equally divided between Hindus and Moslems in the workers' population as a whole, were preponderantly Hindu in this sample, as were workers from other provinces. These men were engaged in 16 occupations, which involved varying degrees of physical activity. In addition, the large clerical group was split into four subgroups depending essentially on the distance from their homes to the mill. Unemployment is widespread among people of this degree of education in Bengal and, as a result, "babus" (clerks) will commute considerable distances to a place of work—in this case, because of the lack of roads fit for buses, on foot and more exceptionally on bicycles.

Methods

Food intakes were obtained by exhaustive dietary interviews using a preestablished questionnaire based on cross checks (by meals and by foodstuffs). The interviews were generally conducted in Bengali or Hindustani. In a few cases, interviews were conducted in English or by way of a reliable interpreter with individuals who spoke Telegu. Because most individuals interviewed lived away from their families, had little facility for storing food, and had a very uniform diet, additional checks could be obtained by questions on the amounts of food bought daily and weekly and on the amount of money spent on edibles (lists and prices of foods locally purchasable in one bazaar and in the village were obtained and checked). Repeated interviews and cross checks on individuals chosen at random, conducted at several weeks' intervals gave good agreement. A few random checks by direct weighing also confirmed the general reliability of the data; in fact, the extraordinary uniformity of the diet from day to day, and the monotony of living conditions gave a much higher degree of reproducibility than could be obtained in a Western population.

The results were analyzed using the Indian Food Composition Table established by the Coonoor Nutrition Laboratory,[1] and the following values calculate for each individual and averaged for each group (with standard deviations): animal protein, vegetable protein, total protein, fat, carbohydrate, calories, thiamine, riboflavin, niacin, and vitamin C. Activity was evaluated by a combination of methods. A detailed observation of each occupation was undertaken, with particular care given to "microschedule" (pauses, intervals between movements, etc.). Secondly, a thorough analysis conducted by an efficiency engineers' firm was available.

In this survey, "physical demand" was characterized on the following basis: "Physical demand is defined as the amount and continuity of physical endurance needed and for which allowances must be made to compensate for the degree of fatigue involved. Work necessitating awkward bending, stretching, reaching, and other unusual postures must be recognized and rewarded. Also, the muscular effort required in excessive walking, standing on hard floors . . . must receive rating attention." A number of examples were used to illustrate the attribution of ratings: e.g., hand lifting weight up to 10 lb—infrequently, none, frequently, very low; up to 50 lb—infrequently, low, frequently, medium; up to 75 lb —infrequently, high, frequently, very high. Eighty-one occupations were analyzed in this fashion.

Oxygen consumption and carbon dioxide production data pertaining to a number of occupations in the jute industry as obtained by Sen Gupta and Ferris[16] were also available. While it was obviously impossible to calculate energy expended as work as such, the foregoing information seemed to permit a classification of the occupations in order of increasing caloric cost. At any rate, broad classes of activity could be differentiated with a reasonable certainty as to differences in energy cost. The following classes and groups were studied (ranged in order of increasing activity):

1st Class: *sedentary*. Thirteen *stall holders*, constituting a group of extraordinarily inert mode of life, who sat at their shop all day, except for one day a week and on occasional buying forays; 8 *supervisors* who lived on company premises and who either sat at desks or confined their walking to the precincts of one department; 22 *clerks* (called clerks I in Table 1) who lived on company premises and who did not engage in any sport. Their walking was confined, during most of the week, to company premises.

2nd Class: *light work*. Three groups of *clerks*, 13 in group II and 10 in group III, who were differentiated by the fact that group II and III lived outside of the mill compound, with group II commuting at least 3 mi and group III at least 6 mi. Group IV engaged in athletic activities (soccer) besides commuting. There was also a group of 22 *mechanics*, whose job was relatively standard except inasmuch as they did not have many power aids at their disposal.

3rd Class: *medium work*. *Drivers* (10 men) drove either electric tractors or steam locomotive, and did some coupling and uncoupling of wagons. The other groups, 10 *winders*, 10 *weavers*, and 10 *bagging twisters*, were composed of individuals driven at a steady pace by the nature of the machines they were operating. A number of operations involving some strength (lifting of rolls, pushing on large levers, etc.) were involved.

4th Class: *heavy work*. Eleven *mill waste carriers* who carried small bales of 50 to 75 lb. The work of *pilers* (10 men) and *selectors* (10 men) involved the handling of heavy bales (150 to 200 lb) at intervals and on relatively short stretches, as well as the opening of bales, lifting of fractions thereof, etc.

5th Class: *very heavy work*. *Ashmen* and *coalmen* (15 men) shoveled ashes and coal in tending furnaces. The work of *blacksmiths* corresponded to the classic occupation without power aids (15 men). *Cutters* (10 men) swung heavy cleavers and hacked steadily at jute fibers, a particularly hard and tiring procedure. Finally, 19 carriers

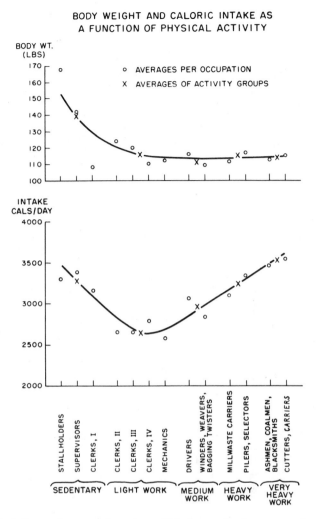

BODY WEIGHT AND CALORIC INTAKE AS A FUNCTION OF PHYSICAL ACTIVITY

Fig. 1

were divided between 9 *Bojha carriers* (190 lb per man) and 10 *bale carriers* (400 lb for 3 men).

Additional information which was obtained included: height and weight (by means of portable scales and height-measure with sliding headpiece), religion and caste, income, numbers of dependents, regular payments on loans, amount of money sent home weekly, amount of money spent on items other than food, and educational level. Age had to be estimated, from questions and from physical appearance, as the absence of a system of

registration of births results in a general ignorance of one's own age, even among clerks and supervisors.

Results

The relation of caloric intake to physical activity is given in Fig. 1. Differences in caloric intakes between classes were statistically significant; differences between groups within classes generally were not. Caloric intakes were adequate to satisfy hunger, and for the "light work" and more active classes agreed well with the caloric requirements which could be

TABLE 1

Average Daily Nutrient Intake * and Median of Money Spent per Week (Exclusive of Loan Repayments and Money Sent Home)†

Occupational Group	Animal Protein g	Vegetable Protein g	Fat g	Thiamine µg	Riboflavin µg	Niacin mg	Vit. C mg	Money spent per week Rupees
Stall holders	38.2 ± 18.7	54.6 ± 11.8	102.9 ± 44.1	1630 ± 331	1169 ± 351	14.6 ± 5.6	57.6 ± 34.3	12(8–15)
Supervisors	29.3 ± 21.2	59.7 ± 16.1	81.2 ± 36.3	2150 ± 696	1237 ± 452	14.4 ± 5.5	76.6 ± 43.3	70(28–144)
Clerks I	23.5 ± 17.7	52.5 ± 12.6	45.8 ± 35.9	1435 ± 453	848 ± 329	11.7 ± 3.7	53.6 ± 28.2	
Clerks II	17.1 ± 10.0	59.3 ± 17.5	42.5 ± 22.4	1672.4 ± 493	997 ± 391	11.6 ± 4.7	50.1 ± 21.2	50(26–168)
Clerks III	26.3 ± 16.6	56.4 ± 15.6	46.3 ± 23.6	1703 ± 517	1100 ± 436	12.0 ± 4.2	50.3 ± 11.0	
Clerks IV‡	28.0 ± 19.9	63.1 ± 24.6	54.3 ± 27.1	1851 ± 655	1053 ± 467	13.7 ± 5.5	60.3 ± 30.7	
Mechanics	8.1 ± 7.0	53.1 ± 14.5	19.3 ± 9.7	1499 ± 366	616 ± 196	10.1 ± 2.3	37.8 ± 10.8	8(4–11)
Drivers	16.2 ± 6.8	67.6 ± 15.5	38.3 ± 16.7	1903 ± 550	904 ± 331	15.3 ± 6.5	37.7 ± 12.7	7(3–15)
Winders	5.6 ± 5.0	62.7 ± 7.2	17.3 ± 4.7	1677 ± 209	727 ± 355	11.2 ± 2.1	37.1 ± 14.3	3(2–4)
Weavers	10.3 ± 6.3	68.4 ± 15.2	23.5 ± 6.3	1829 ± 482	887 ± 219	13.5 ± 3.0	37.0 ± 5.2	10(2–18)
Bagging twisters	12.5 ± 5.7	65.9 ± 11.2	37.9 ± 16.9	1809 ± 304	779 ± 303	15.0 ± 3.3	33.3 ± 9.7	5(2–9)
Mill waste carriers	9.9 ± 3.6	71.2 ± 8.9	29.2 ± 10.3	1892 ± 199	749 ± 96	15.2 ± 2.6	29.4 ± 10.3	4(2–8)
Philers	16.0 ± 5.4	72.2 ± 9.3	51.3 ± 9.6	1449 ± 948	973 ± 187	17.5 ± 2.5	43.6 ± 18.5	8(3–16)
Selectors	15.6 ± 7.1	77.9 ± 11.2	53.2 ± 12.0	2150 ± 697	1238 ± 452	14.4 ± 5.4	76.7 ± 43.3	6(2–12)
Ashmen, coalmen, blacksmiths	12.2 ± 6.2	80.3 ± 17.1	51.6 ± 10.6	2301 ± 730	1081 ± 315	19.8 ± 8.8	32.2 ± 13.4	12(2–27)
Cutters	13.1 ± 7.7	90.1 ± 16.1	50.3 ± 15.1	2845 ± 760	1193 ± 332	25.7 ± 8.2	56.9 ± 62.2	7(1–11)
Carriers	16.2 ± 7.5	88.2 ± 11.3	58.1 ± 12.1	2108 ± 335	732 ± 187	18.9 ± 3.3	31.2 ± 9.5	6(2–17)

Figures after ± are standard deviations. One rupee = 0.21 dollar. Figures in parentheses give range.

* Main sources of animal protein are (in order of decreasing importance): fish, eggs, buffalo and cows' milk, meat, curds, and cheese; of vegetable proteins: rice, lentils; of fat: vegetable oil, ghee, invisible animal fat; of thiamine: rice (undermilled); of riboflavin: leafy vegetables; of niacin and vitamin C: vegetables and fruits.

† Difficulties are encountered when computing real income due to the communal family and living systems; thus the very low incomes reported for some workers are compatible with life because they feed themselves as members of a community of similarly situated individuals. Loan repayments have been excluded from incomes, because of the colossal interest rates (up to 30 or 40 per cent per month) often exacted by money lenders. Only medians and ranges are given for incomes; the degree of accuracy obtained, for the reasons given above, does not warrant elaborate statistical treatment. On the average, stall holders and supervisors had five dependents over the age of 10 years, three dependents in the 1–10 year range, and one half in the 0–1 year bracket. Clerks had six dependents over 10 years of age, four in the 1–10 bracket, and three-fourths under 1 year. Workers had four dependents above 10 and four under 10 (infants included).

‡ This group was the most heterogeneous in terms of physical activity because of the differences in athletic schedules between members. At least one of the men could qualify as "heavy worker" and several as "medium workers" because of their athletic activity. This variability is reflected in the larger standard deviations.

calculated on the basis of the FAO Committee report.[4] The major proportion of calories was derived from carbohydrates in all groups, with an increasing proportion of fat in the higher intake groups (stall holders and supervisors, pilers, selectors, and "very heavy work" class), all of which consumed more than 50 g of fat per day (Table 1). Protein intakes were at or above 70 g per day, but the major part of the protein (at least three-fourths) was derived from vegetable sources. Only two men were total vegetarians, but the amount of animal products generally consumed was so low that for several groups (mill waste carriers, winders, weavers, mechanics) the daily intake of animal protein was on the average of less than 10 g. It may be noted that the weavers and mechanics were among the better paid groups, so that their lower animal protein intake did not represent a more stringent economic necessity. Weavers were predominantly Moslems, so that religious practices were not involved in this avoidance of animal products. Clerks had on the whole the largest intake in animal proteins, in spite of their being predominantly Hindu with an appreciable proportion of Brahmins among them.

Daily thiamine intakes were adequate (above 1.4 mg on the average for all groups, and generally in the 1.6–1.9 mg range, as were niacin (above 12 mg) and vitamin C (30–60 mg range), but riboflavin intakes were very low (generally in the 0.6–1 mg range) (Table 1). Carotene-vitamin A and calcium levels were low but were difficult to estimate on a group basis because of the widespread practice of chewing lime-treated green leaves wrapped around betel nuts.

Caloric intakes were not correlated with income (clerks, mechanics, and weavers had higher incomes than men in the "heavy work" and "very heavy work" categories); nor were caloric intakes correlated with religion or caste. The differences in religion had, as a matter of fact, very little correlation with nutrient intakes, except as regards the source of animal proteins. Similarly, age did not appear to be a factor in the differences in intake noted between groups. As regards physical status, the variation of weight as a function of exercise (average height 5 ft 3 in., average weight 119 lb) is given in Fig. 1. Differences in average weight between the "light work," "medium work," "heavy work," and "very heavy work" classes were not significant. The "sedentary" group was on the average much heavier. The "stall holders" and "supervisors" were obviously much fatter than the other occupation groups. Although the group "Clerks I" (very sedentary individuals) was relatively light, it may have been actually a relatively "fat" group where the visibly poor degree of muscular development obscured, from the point of view of weight, a relatively greater adiposity than in the "work" groups.

Discussion

Inasmuch as it is legitimate to draw a parallel between purely experimental results and the results of a population study, there is a striking parallelism between the findings in animals[14] and those in man. In both cases it appears that food intake increases with activity only within a certain zone. By analogy with previously used terminology,[10,12,14] this zone can be called the "normal activity range." Below that range, in what has been termed the "sedentary" zone, a further decrease in activity is not followed by a decrease in food intake but, on the contrary, by an increase. It may be at first surprising to note that a fundamental mechanism, that of the regulation of food intake, ceases to respond in a certain interval to variations of energy expenditure. This may be interpreted by considering the fact that, in this hundreds of thousands of years of evolution, man did not have any opportunity for sedentary life except very recently. An inactive life for man is as recent (and as "abnormal") a development as caging is for an animal. In this light, it is not surprising that some of the usual adjustment mechanisms would prove inadequate.

The increase in weight associated with inactivity appears to be of significance in relation to the problem of obesity. The importance of inactivity in various forms of experimental obesity has already been recalled. As regards human obesity, Greene[6] has reported on more than 200 overweight individuals in whom the beginning of obesity could be traced to a sudden decrease in activity. Bruch[2] has emphasized the frequency of the coexistence of physical inertia and obesity in children. Peckos[15] and Fry[5] have questioned the role of hyperphagia in the positive energy balance leading to obesity in children. Finally, in collaboration with Johnson and Burke, one of

us (J.M.) has found that the average caloric intake of obese high school girls in Boston suburbs was no greater than that of the normal-weight individuals of similar age, height, and school grade, but their physical activity was very much less.[8] The fact that mechanized, urbanized modern living may well be pushing an ever greater fraction of the population into the "sedentary" range may thus be a major factor in the increased incidence of obesity.

Summary

The relation between caloric intake, body weight, and physical work was established in a group of 213 mill workers in West Bengal. These workers covered a wide range of physical activity, from sedentary to very hard work. It was found that caloric intake increases with activity only within a certain zone ("normal activity"). Below that range ("sedentary zone") a decrease is activity is not followed by a decrease in food intake but, on the contrary, by an increase. Body weight is also increased in that zone. The picture is similar to that previously found in experimental animals.

References

1. Akroyd, W. R., V. N. Patwardhan, and S. Ranganathan, "Nutritive Value of Indian Foods and the Planning of Satisfactory Diets," *Health Bull. No. 23* (4th ed.), Government Printer, Simla, 1951, p. 79.

2. Bruch, H. "Obesity in Childhood. IV: Energy Expenditure of Obese Children," *Am. J. Diseases Children,* **60** (1940), 1082.

3. Chernin, E., "Problems in Tropical Public Health Among Workers of a Jute Mill Near Calcutta. I: Malaria

in the Labor Population. II: A Study of Intestinal Parasites in the Labor Force. III: Intestinal Parasites in the European Supervisory Staff and Their Food-Handler Servants. IV: Hemoglobin Values and Their Relation to the Intensity of Hookworm Infections in the Labor Force. V: Eosinophile Levels and Their Relation to Intestinal Helminthiasis in the Labor Force," *Am. J. Trop. Med. Hyg.,* **3** (1954), 74, 94, 107, 338, 348.

4. Committee on Caloric Requirements

(A. Keys, Chairman, J. Mayer, Technical Secretary), *Food Agr. Organ. Nutr. Studies No. 5*, Washington, D. C., 1950.

5. Fry, P. C., "A Comparative Study of 'Obese' Children Selected on the Basis of Fat Pads," *J. Clin. Nutr.*, **1** (1953), 453.

6. Greene, J. A., "Clinical Study of the Etiology of Obesity," *Ann. Inst. Med.*, **12** (1939), 1794.

7. Ingle, D. J., "A Simple Means of Producing Obesity in the Rat," *Proc. Soc. Exptl. Biol. Med.*, **72** (1949), 604.

8. Johnson, M. L., B. S. Burke, and J. Mayer, "Relative Importance of Inactivity and Overeating in the Energy Balance of Obese High School Girls," *Am. J. Clin. Nutr.*, **4** (1956), 37.

9. Marshall, N. B., and J. Mayer, "Energy Balance in Goldthioglucose Obesity," *Am. J. Physiol.*, **178** (1954), 271.

10. Mayer, J., "Genetic, Traumatic, and Environmental Factors in the Etiology of Obesity," *Physiol. Rev.*, **33** (1953), 472.

11. Mayer, J., "Decreased Activity and Energy Balance in the Hereditary Obesity-Diabetes Syndrome of Mice," *Science*, **117** (1953), 504.

12. Mayer, J., "The Physiologic Basis of Obesity and Leanness. Parts I and II," *Nutr. Abstr. Rev.*, **25** (1955), 597, 871.

13. Mayer, J., R. G. French, C. Y. Zighera, and R. J. Barrnett, "Hypothalamic Obesity in the Mouse: Production, Description, and Metabolic Characteristics," *Am. J. Physiol.*, **182** (1955), 75.

14. Mayer, J., N. B. Marshall, J. J. Vitale, J. H. Christensen, M. B. Mashayekhi, and F. J. State, "Exercise, Food Intake, and Body Weight in Normal Rats and Genetically Obese Adult Mice," *ibid.*, **177** (1954), 544.

15. Peckos, P. C., "Caloric Intake in Relation to Physique in Children," *Science*, **117** (1953), 631.

16. Sen Gupta, A., and B. G. Ferris, Jr., "Assessment of Metabolic Cost in Different Types of Jobs in Jute Industry" (to be published). Published in preliminary form by A. Sen Gupta, Working Paper XII, *Indian Council on Medical Research Symposium on Industrial Health*, Bombay, September, 1953.

H. J. MONTOYE / W. D. VAN HUSS / H. OLSON
A. HUDEC / E. MAHONEY

Study of the Longevity and Morbidity of College Athletes

Reprinted from the *Journal of the American Medical Association*,
162 (1956), 1132–34.

This study was a part of a larger national research project that was sponsored by the physical education honorary fraternity, Phi Epsilon Kappa. Questionnaires were sent to over one thousand athletes and to an equal number of nonathletes who had formerly attended Michigan State University. The results showed that the longevity of athletes was not significantly different from that of the non-athletes and that the causes of death were very similar. Although the selection of the subjects was fairly well controlled, and the results of this study agreed with studies done by Dublin in 1932 and Rook in 1954, it fails to provide adequate evidence on the type of activity patterns of the subjects, related data on diet, occupation, and heredity—information needed to draw more definitive conclusions. Further exploration using the prospective approach in study design should prove very helpful in clarifying the relationship between physical activity and longevity.

The effects of intensive athletic competition on the heart and other organs and on bodily resistance to disease has long been a subject of controversy. Previous to the work of Morgan[9] in 1873, the viewpoint prevailing in England was that competitive oarsmen did not live beyond 50 yr of age and that this reduced longevity was directly caused by athletic competition. The studies of Morgan[9] and Meylan[8] in 1904 refuted this concept. Attempting to gain further insight into the longevity of athletes, Anderson[1] and Greenway and Hiscock[5] compared the longevity and causes of death of Yale University athletes with use of insurance tables. Dublin,[3] Knoll,[7] Hartley and Llewellyn,[6] and Wakefield[13] similarly compared their data on athletes with insurance company or general population statistics. Bickert,[2] Van Mervennee,[12] and Schmid[11] added to the

body of information available on the longevity and morbidity of athletes but presented no control data. Hartley and Llewellyn[6] point out that athletes are a select group and that, therefore, comparisons with data of life insurance company tables are open to serious criticisms. Dublin[3] stated that a comparison of athletes with their classmates might yield more valid information.

Dublin's[4] second study in 1932 and Rook's[10] work in 1954 represent perhaps the best analyses in the literature on the longevity and causes of death among athletes and nonathletes. Dublin's results show the expectation of life in years at age 22 for honor men (47.73) to be greater than for either the average graduate (45.71) or the athlete (45.56). All college groups, however, showed greater life expectation at age 22 than was listed in tables covering the period 1900-1915 for American men

(44.29) or was given for American white males listed in the 27 registration states of the United States for 1919-1920 (43.35). Rook's results as to longevity varied from Dublin's, in that the average age of sportsmen at death (67.97) exceeded that of the randomly selected group (67.43) in his study. The intellectual group again, however, had the greatest longevity (69.41). In all studies in which causes of death were investigated, deaths by external violence among athletes markedly exceeded those among controls. Typically, Wakefield[13] in 1944 found 34 per cent of all deaths among former basketball players were due to external violence, as compared with 17.3 per cent for the general population of the state of Indiana. Rook found the death rate due to external violence to be 97.9 per thousand for sportsmen, as compared with rates of 46.7 for intellectuals, and 70.4 for his random group.

The results of studies regarding comparative rates of death due to cardiovascular causes do not indicate clear trends. In Rook's[10] study for instance, 27.3 per cent of the deaths before age 65 among controls were due to cardiovascular conditions, as compared to 22.5 per cent among sportsmen. Wakefield's[13] results, on the other hand, showed 25 per cent of all deaths caused by disease to be due to cardiovascular-renal diseases, as compared to only 16 per cent for the general population of Indiana. Dublin's[3] results in 1928 showed that, of all deaths among athletes over 45 yr of age, 32 per cent were due to heart disease, as compared with a rate of about 20 per cent of the total deaths among insured groups from this cause.

Present Study

The present study was undertaken as a pilot study of the larger national research project inaugurated in 1951 and sponsored by the physical education honorary fraternity, Phi Epsilon Kappa. Questionnaires prepared by a national study committee were sent out to 1,130 former athletes and 1,130 others not former athletes, individually matched as to years of attendance at Michigan State University and ranging in dates of birth from 1855 to 1919. (For purposes of this study, athlete is defined as a letter winner in a varsity sport.) Of the 2,260 questionnaires sent out, 1,212 were returned with sufficient information to be included. Six hundred twenty-nine, or 55.66 per cent, of the questionnaires sent to athletes were returned, as were 583, or 51.59 per cent of those sent to the control group. The distribution of returns by year of birth shown in Fig. 1 would seem to indicate that comparisons are justified with respect to longevity or causes of death. Data from the questionnaires were tabulated, punched onto IBM cards, and analyzed, insofar as possible by IBM techniques. The data have been statistically analyzed where appropriate (Tables 1 and 2). One hundred twenty-three, or 9.85 per cent, of the total returned questionnaires were for deceased subjects, of whom 67 were athletes and 56 controls. Since this was a questionnaire study and, hence, subject to response error, particularly with regard to cause of death, it was decided to determine the validity of the responses. Therefore, data from the death certificates were obtained in 104 cases. List B of the "Manual of the International Statistical Classification of Diseases, Injuries, and Causes of Death"[14] was used for the classification of the causes of death. Errors in the causes of death were classified as major, minor, and those of insufficient information. A major error was listed when the questionnaire response was not pathologically related to the cause of death on the death certificate. A minor error indicated that the response

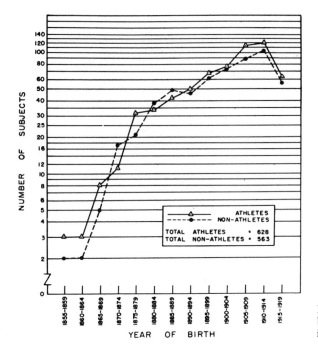

Fig. 1. Distribution of years of birth of athletes and nonathletes included in study.

TABLE 1

Comparison of Athletes and Nonathletes, by Selected Characteristics

Characteristic	Athletes, %	Nonathletes, %
Service in armed forces*	66.4	55.8
Branch of service*		
Army	70.1	82.7
Navy	23.2	13.9
Marine Corps	2.8	...
Other	3.9	3.4
Activity in service		
Mild	13.7	18.9
Moderate	50.4	53.9
Vigorous	35.9	27.2
Married	96.9	97.0
Drinker*	77.6	66.5
Smoker*	68.7	60.2
Weight in college*	164 lb	153 lb
Weight gain since college	9.7 lb	10.4 lb

*These differences are statistically significant, i.e., it is unreasonable that chance would account for them.

and the actual cause were related pathologically although classified differently in the international classification.

The validation results, in which the data from death certificates and the questionnaires were compared, were as follows: 1. In dates of birth, agreement was very good. Only 10 discrepancies were noted, with a mean error of 0.35 yr, which was not statistically significant. 2. In ages at death, agreement was good. Twenty-two discrepancies were noted, with a mean error of 0.32 yr, which also was not statistically significant. 3. Nineteen discrepancies were noted in causes of death. Two were major errors, 13 minor errors, and 4 were cases in which insufficient information was available to make a decision. Most of the errors noted concerned cardiovascular causes, particularly heart disease. While the layman is apparently oriented to the term "heart disease," the death certificate might list the cause of death as coronary thrombosis or angina pectoris, which technically, for classification purposes, is erroneous. Because of this, fine classifications of causes of death from conditions of the cardiovascular area were not possible. Coarse classifications, however, were affected very little when questionnaire and death data were compared (Fig. 2).

The age at death of the athletes and nonathletes is compared in Table 2. The difference in actual and expected age at death is not surprising, when we consider how highly select the men in attendance at college were during these years. Also, since the percentages of returns of the questionnaires in the two groups were 55.66 and 51.59, it is quite probable the sample became even more select due to the difficulty in obtaining data on those who died in the earlier years. What is of interest here, however, is that there is little

TABLE 2

Comparison of Age at Death of Athletes and Nonathletes

	Mean Life Expectancy, Yr.*	Mean Age at Death, Yr.†	Difference, Yr.
All deaths included			
Athletes	65.96	73.86	7.90
Nonathletes..	65.97	74.24	8.27
Excluding accidental deaths			
Athletes	65.96	74.43	8.47
Nonathletes....	65.99	74.59	8.60

*Computed for the time when the athlete or nonathlete was in college, using the appropriate mortality tables.

†Actual ages of death were used where death had occurred. Otherwise this represents the individual's present age plus remaining years of life predicted from current mortality tables.

Fig. 2. Comparison of data on cause of death received from questionnaires used in study and of data from state health department records.

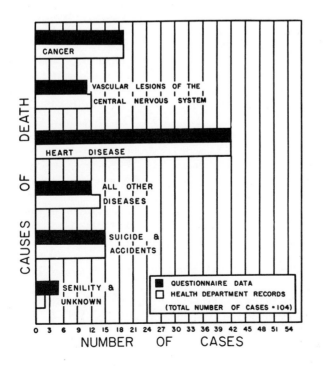

difference existing between the two groups. This is in agreement with the studies by Dublin[14] and Rook.[10] Differences between the athletes and nonathletes in the distribution of causes of death, type of death (sudden or lingering), and causes of death of parents were statistically insignificant.

Summary

The questionnaire method was employed in securing data on former college athletes (letter winners) and nonathlete controls. The results indicated that the longevity of athletes was approximately the same as that of controls and the distribution of causes of death was very similar. A significantly greater percentage of former athletes served in the armed forces and, of those serving, a significantly larger proportion served in the Navy and Marine Corps. A significantly greater percentage of former athletes smoked and drank, and their weight in college was appreciably greater. There were no significant differences in the number married, weight gain since college days, or strenuousness of activity while in the armed services.

References

1. Anderson, W. G., "Further Studies in Longevity of Yale Athletes," *Med. Times*, **44** (1916), 75–77.

2. Bickert, F. W., "Einfluss des wettkampf-mässig betriebenen Sport auf die Lebensdauer und Todesursache: Eine statistische Studie," *Deut. med. Wochschr.*, **55** (1929), 23–25.

3. Dublin, L. I., "Longevity of College Athletes," *Harper Hosp. Bull.*, **157** (1928), 229–38.

4. Dublin, L. I., "College Honor Men Long-Lived," *Statist. Bull. Metropolitan Life Insurance Company*, **13** (1932), 5–7.

5. Greenway, J. C., and I. C. Hiscock, "Preliminary Analysis of Mortality Among Athletes and Other Graduates of Yale University," *Yale Alumni Weekly*, **35** (1926), 1086–88.

6. Hartley, P. H. S., and G. F. Llewellyn, "Longevity of Oarsmen: Study of Those Who Rowed in Oxford and Cambridge Boat Race From 1829–1928," *Brit. Med. J.*, **1** (1939), 657–62.

7. Knoll, W., "Welches Lebensalter erreichen die Ruderer von 'Oxford-Cambridge'? (Eine Richtigstellung)," *Med. Klin.*, **34** (1938), 464–66.

8. Meylan, G. L., "Harvard University Oarsmen," Harvard Grad. Mag., 9 (1904), 362–76.

9. Morgan, J. E., "University Oars, 1873," in P. V. Karpovich, "Longevity and Athletes," *Res. Quart.*, **12** (1941), 451–55.

10. Rook, A., "Investigation Into Longevity of Cambridge Sportsmen," *Brit, Med. J.*, **1** (1954), 773–77.

11. Schmid, L., "How Long Sportsmen Live, in Sport and Health," Royal Norwegian Ministry of Education, Oslo, Norway, 1952, pp. 100–107.

12. Van Mervennée, C. J., "Life Span of Athletes," *Ned. Tijdschr. Geneesk.*, **85** (1941) 535–43.

13. Wakefield, M. C., "Study of Mortality Among Men Who Have Played in Indiana High School State Final Basketball Tournaments," *Res. Quart.*, **15** (1944), 3–11.

14. World Health Organization, "Manual of International Statistical Classification of Diseases. Injuries, and Causes of Deaths" (Adopted 1948). *Bull. World Health Organ.* Suppl. 1, Vol. **1** (1948), Vol. **2**, Alphabetical Index (1949).

H. L. TAYLOR

Coronary Heart Disease in Physically Active and Sedentary Populations

Reprinted from the *Journal of Sports Medicine and Physical Fitness*,
2 (1962), 73–82.

This paper presents a review of several types of data used to assess the relationship of coronary heart disease and amount of physical activity. Taylor raises many questions about the validity of epidemiological studies which compare groups on the basis of a given variable without serial observations. While the data generally tend to show lower death rates due to coronary heart disease among active populations, Taylor suggests possible selective factors and other sources of bias that might have affected these results. A great deal more precision is required in these types of studies before definitive conclusions can be reached.

The possibility that physical activity continued at a moderate level through middle age might be protective against the development of coronary heart disease has been studied seriously for only a decade. Most of the effort up to the present time has been put into trying to establish that coronary heart disease does in actual fact occur less frequently among physically active men than among their sedentary contemporaries. To establish this fact, certain conditions were required. In the first place, since coronary heart disease in middle age is essentially a male disease, observations on or records of disease in men in large numbers were wanted. Furthermore, since it was known that coronary atherosclerosis develops slowly over a period of perhaps 10 to 25 yr, men whose physical activity over this period could be reliably described without undue expenditure of funds were also desired. It was felt that if lack of physical activity was in fact to be a consequential factor in the epidemic of coronary heart disease that is currently afflicting middle-aged males in the United States and Great Britain, it would be profitable to look for groups of truly sedentary males and males who were required to perform work at only a moderate level of intensity.

These and other considerations have led investigators to examine occupations which require different levels of physical activity. Data bearing on the question of whether occupations requiring moderate physical activity are associated with less coronary heart disease among males than strictly sedentary occupations have been gathered by several methods and can be classed as several kinds of information.

Historically, the first important investigations were concerned with obtaining data on the rate of appearance of new cases of coronary disease (incidence) in active and sedentary populations. Investigations of this type are summarized in Table 1.

Morris and his collaborators[9] made use of two stable employed populations in which it was possible to have information on all serious disease reported to a central office over a period of 18

TABLE 1

Physical Activity and Coronary Heart Disease. The Ratio of the Incidence in
Occupational Groups

Author	Occupations Compared	Population	Time Interval	Method	Active / Sedentary
Morris *et al.* (1953)	Bus drivers vs. Conductors	31,000	2 yr	reports	0.70
Morris *et al.* (1953)	Telephonists vs. Postmen	110,000	2 yr	reports	0.75
Chapman *et al.* (1957)	Classified Civil Servants	2,252	2½ yr	exam.	0.90

months to 2 yr. All cases that might be coronary heart disease were investigated and in this way new cases were determined. Morris reported that not only was coronary heart disease less frequent in the active population but that, in this population, it also appeared in less serious and virulent forms. In both groups studied by Morris, walking was an important activity of the physically active population and provides some assurance that the physical activity of the two groups was different although reasonable estimates of the physical activity level of the several groups are lacking and it is also clear that the inactive group (bus drivers) was not completely sedentary.

This system of collecting data regarding disease can be relied on to give good relative estimates of the appearance of new disease in its more advanced form in the groups compared. But it must be admitted that the appearance of coronary heart disease in its mildest forms will not be detected. Since the milder forms of the disease, particularly angina, occurred more frequently in the active population, there is a possibility that the incidence in the inactive population was underestimated. This kind of information can be obtained in a more elegant way which ensures the finding of the milder cases when a population is examined

to identify all disease at a given date and then reexamined after a suitable length of time. This was the methodology used by Chapman and his colleagues[2] when they studied employees of the city of Los Angeles. Here, however, the investigators used a list adapted by the National Office of Vital Statistics from a U.S. Department of Labor coding and there is some doubt that this list properly separated the physically active employees of the city of Los Angeles from those who are essentially sedentary. Nevertheless, we must take note of the fact that these investigators failed to find a significant difference in the incidence of coronary heart disease among males in sedentary and physically active occupations.

The next type of information available is concerned with the prevalence of coronary heart disease (the number of cases per unit of population existing within a group at any given time) in active and sedentary occupations. Data of this type are summarized in Table 2. Brown and his associates[1] examined 85 per cent of the men 60-69 yr old on 11 panels of English physicians in the neighborhood of Birmingham. The physical activity of the occupation was classified and the prevalence of coronary heart disease calculated for three levels of physical activity. Only 85 per cent of the men in the populations were

TABLE 2

Physical Activity and Coronary Heart Disease. The Ratio of the Prevalence in Occupational Groups

Author	Occupations compared	Population	Age	Method of Data Collection	Active/Sedentary
Brown et al. (1957)	Classified medical panelist	85% of 1,243	60–69	Exam.	0.61
Zukel et al. (1959)	Farmers vs. "Others"	19,830	35–75	Physician reports	0.68

examined and the distribution of activity in the "no shows" was not determined. If we assume that the type of occupation was randomly distributed among the men who were not examined and undue "selection against the study" by people with coronary heart disease did not exist, we can consider the data confirmatory of Morris' original hypothesis. Zukel and his colleagues of the public health service[10] used the cooperation of the physicians in the Grand Forks, North Dakota area as a means of locating cases of coronary disease among farmers and men employed in the other occupations. The difference in physical activity between the two groups is not known but it is believed that the farmers were more active. But it is quite possible that some cases of coronary heart disease among far-

mers were missed by the method of data collection. The differences in prevalence between farmers and others is large and may be considered consistent with Morris' hypothesis.

A third type of data bearing on this question comes from death rate information. Data of this kind are presented in Table 3. An important question here is whether it is possible to properly classify the physical activity required by the occupation of the deceased and whether the man in question had actually been employed for a reasonable number of years in the same occupation or one demanding a similar level of physical activity.

It is likely that British society is organized in a way that makes classification of occupations on death certificates more reliable than in the

TABLE 3

Physical Activity and Coronary Heart Disease. Death Rates Ascribed to Arteriosclerotic Heart Disease in Occupational Groups

Author	Population	Occupations compared	Age	Physical Activity Class	Death Rate No. per 1,000	Active/Sedentary
Stamler (1960)	City of Chicago	Clerical	45–54	Light	5.6	
		Sales		Heavy	8.13	1.45
Morris (1959)	England	Laborers		Light	5.28	
		Classified	55–64	Moderate	4.22	0.80
		Occupations		Heavy	3.99	0.64

United States. At least it is recognized that occupational mobility is much higher in this country than in England, Wales, and Scotland. Finally, death rate figures are always open to the problems associated with the reliability of the diagnosis on the face of the death certificate.

The British death rate figures support the hypothesis of Morris while the American figures do not.

A fourth method of obtaining information on the relationship of coronary disease to physical activity is illustrated by the work of Forssman and Lindegard[6] at the University Hospital in Malmo, Sweden. The investigators began with 62 male coronary patients who had been referred to their hospital. For controls, they chose to take the next entry of the same age and sex in the Malmo City register. This kind of enforced randomization of selection of controls makes comparison of controls and patients a good deal more meaningful. When the two groups were classified by serum cholesterol level as high, medium, and low, an excess of coronary patients were found in the high and medium categories. On the other hand, when the patients and controls were classified according to daily physical activity, eight patients and seven controls were found in the

high category. In the medium activity class there were 30 patients and controls while 24 patients and 24 controls were in the low activity class.

The final major method that has been used to examine the question under discussion is that of studying consecutive autopsies and classifying the physical activity of the last recorded occupation. Morris and Crawford[8] obtained the cooperation of the pathologists in 206 hospitals in the British National Health Service who agreed to provide information on the state the myocardium and the coronary arteries found at 25 consecutive autopsies along with information on the last occupation.

Table 4 summarizes the findings on the amount of coronary artery atherosclerosis with respect to the intensity of activity. It is very clear that the degree of atherosclerosis in the coronary arteries is not affected by the physical activity of occupation. The reader should remember that the figures are in cases which did not die of coronary disease, so prevalence of coronary artery disease cannot be estimated from these figures. However, the observations of lesions of the myocardium yielded a different picture. The pathologists were asked to describe the macroscopic lesions. In order to eliminate individuals

TABLE 4

British Necropsy Survey. The Proportions of Coronary Artery Disease* in 3,800 Noncoronary Deaths by Activity of Occupation. Males Aged 45–70 (After Morris and Crawford)

Classification of Coronary Artery Lesion Observed	Light	Active	Heavy
Population	1,440	1,429	862
Coronary Atherosclerosis present	87*	84*	83*
Severe Coronary Disease	14	11	13
Calcification present	23	20	21
Focal Obstruction	25	19	22

* All figures are in numbers per hundred.

TABLE 5

British Necropsy Survey. Proportions of Ischemic Myocardial fibrosis Arranged by Activity of Occupation found in 3,800 Noncoronary Deaths, (After Morris and Crawford)

Lesion Observed	Item	Light	Active	Heavy
	Population	1,440	1,429	862
Small	No	142	96	49
Multiple			6.7	5.7
Scars*	%	9.9		
Large Fibrous	No	51	28	10
Patches†	%	3.5	2.0	1.2

* Considered to be the product of a less severe and more slowly developing coronary insufficiency and myocardial ischemia.

† Considered to be large healed myocardial infarcts.

in whom fibrosis might occur that was not the result of coronary artery disease, cases with rheumatic heart disease were discarded along with cases of any of the collagen vascular diseases or syphilis. It was then found that there were two general types of fibrosis which were presumed to be the result of ischemia of the myocardium produced by coronary artery disease. The first type consisted of large fibrous patches which were usually transmural. This findings was classified as a large healed infarct. The second type of myocardial fibrosis consisted of small multiple scars which were judeged to be the product of lesser and more slowly developing coronary insufficiency and myocardial ischemia. The relationship of these findings to the physical activity of occupation are presented in Table 5. In contrast to the relationship with measures of the degree of atherosclerosis, it is clear that a high degree of relationship exists. The differences between activity groups in the multiple diffuse scarring are not as large as those found in the large fibrous patches. When people who had evidence of hypertension were studied separately, it was found that a more marked relationship exists. In the hypertensive group of the men whose jobs required light physical activity, 21 per

cent showed small multiple scars while men whose job required heavy physical activity had only 4.9 per cent. It is not surprising, then, to find that people with no evidence of hypertension prior to death showed little or no relationship between the small multiple scars and the physical activity required by the job.

Morris and Crawford have properly pointed out that postmortem data are notoriously difficult to deal with in a way which guarantees that bias does not exist. It is well known that hospital post-mortem rates are low; that the population of a hospital is biased by the rules of the admitting officer; and finally, it is generally conceded that many biases exist in autopsy data which are not recognized. Nevertheless, the autopsy data reported by Morris and Crawford are important confirmatory evidence which must be viewed as giving strong support to the hypothesis that coronary heart disease occurs less frequently in men in occupations requiring physical activity.

There appears to be, then, a number of studies—none of which is perfect—indicating that there is less coronary heart disease among men in occupational groups requiring physical activity. The imperfections of each study are characeristic of epidemiology since it is practically impossible to find a perfect situation for examination. The data are more consistent for groups in Great Britain than in the United States. It is one of the cardinal tenets of epidemiological work of this kind to search for evidence from as many, as various and as independent sources as possible.

Accordingly, the staff of the Laboratory of Physiological Hygiene felt that there was a need for a careful examination of the relationship between physical activity and coronary heart disease in an American population in which there could be some real security regarding the history of physical activity of men over a period of 10 to 20 yr during middle age. For this purpose, the railroad industry offered certain unique advantages. Railroad occupations can be graded with regard to job responsibility and also to physical activity. The physical activity required by railroad occupations ranges from the completely sedentary job of the male stenographer and the bill clerk to the moderate activity level of the switchman to the heavy activity of the section man laying new track. Furthermore, the labor agreements between the brotherhoods and management place great emphasis upon seniority and define seniority rights in such a way that it is not easy to transfer from one craft to another. The seniority and retirement rights of railroad crafts tend to encourage men to enter the railroad industry early in life and to hold them in it after they have been there for a few years. The result of all this is that the 50-year-old switchman who has 20 yr of employment in the railroad industry has rarely held any other job in the railroad industry and the majority of fellow workers who are 40 yr of age or more have 10 yr or more of service. Thus we can say with some confidence that switchmen represent a group of people whose physical activ-

ities on the job can be reasonably classified over a considerable period of time.

Furthermore, the Railroad Retirement Board maintains records on railroad employees for the purpose of administering retirement and death benefit programs which offer larger financial advantages than social security. Death certificates are required for payment of death benefits. It is believed that only a small percentage of families of railroad employees fail to apply for death benefits since the railroad employee characteristically spends a large part of his life employement on the railroad industry and the brotherhoods carefully indoctrinate the members of their rights under the Railroad Retirement Act. A turnover rate among railroad employees who have had more than 10 yr of service is one of the lowest in the country. So the railroad employees represent a stable working population. It was found possible to interest not only the authorities of the Railroad Retirement Board but also management and brotherhood officials in cooperating in a study of heart disease among railroad employees.

These considerations led to a study of death rates among physically active and sedentary railroad employees.[13] Clerks were chosen as examples of men holding a sedentary job. Switchmen were selected as men whose job required moderate physical activity and section men were studied as individuals whose job requires heavy labor. The death rate study was an integral part of a larger epidemiological study of physical activity and coronary heart disease.

It happens that for the purpose of calculating collections, credits, retirement reserves, etc., the Railroad Retirement Board prepares a punch card on every one employed during each calendar year in the railroad industry. A set of such cards was obtained for male clerks, yardmen (switchmen), and track men (maintenance of way employees). These cards were arranged in social security number sequence. A cohort was set up which required that men have a record of 10 yr of service in 1951 and employment by the railroad industry in 1954. Deaths among both men in active service and in retirement were collected from the Railroad Retirement Board. The social security numbers on the death certificate were matched against the cohort eligible listing of men in service in 1954.

This method of handling the data meant a well-defined population was set up and that the only deaths admitted to the study were deaths of men in the original groups. Errors then were confined to under-reporting of deaths. It is believed that such instances were few since real finacial reward to the relatives resulted by placing a claim with the Railroad Retirement Board for a death benefit payment.

Death rates were worked out for the years 1955 and 1956. There were 191,609 man years of exposure to risk and 1,978 deaths were reported. The results are summarized in Table 6 where age adjusted deaths for arteriosclerotic heart disease are presented. It is possible to show that the differences between the clerks and switchmen and between the clerks and section men are highly significant in a statistical sense. However, we may inquire whether they are believed to be valid. Here it should be pointed out that there were only a few deaths among the people who retired in 1955 or 1956. After the age of 55, the yardmen retire more rapidly than the clerks and it is of some consequence to see whether a large number of cardiac deaths will appear from this source. Such an event is referred to as a delayed reaction and it is known that this can change the picture markedly. It is possible then that in a few years the death rates from arteriosclerotic heart disease in the active groups may begin to approach the rate reported for the clerks. It is planned to follow this group in the Railroad Retirement Board for 2 to 3 additional years before coming to a firm conclusion on this matter.

On the other hand, the ratio between the death rate in active and sedentary groups is of the same order of magnitude as that found in the British studies of incidence, prevalence and death rates. The data presented here with the reservations expressed above must be regarded as supporting the hypothesis that less coronary heart disease appears in men in occupations requiring a moderate amount of physical activity than in those whose occupations are sedentary.

Up to the present time, there has been little or no information on the characteristics of men employed in the several occupations under consideration. Knowledge of certain personal characteristics is of great importance since the work at Framingham[4] has shown that men who have (a) excess weight for age and height, or (b)

TABLE 6

Physical Activity and Coronary Heart Disease. Death Rates Ascribed to Coronary Heart Disease Among Selected Railroad employees, ages 40 to 60 (After Taylor et al)

Occupations compared	Physical Activity Class	Man Years of Observation	Death Rate No/1000 (Age adjusted)	Active Sedentary
Clerks	Sedentary	85,112	5.7	
Switchmen	Moderate	61,630	3.9	0.68
Section men	Heavy	44,867	2.8	0.49

TABLE 7

The Physical Characteristics of American Truck Drivers and Normal Groups
(After Damon and McFarland)

	U.fl. Selective Service 1943	Sheldon (1954)	Truck Drivers	Champion Truck Drivers
Number	3,000,000	46,000	269	103
Age (years)	26		37	34
Weights (lb)	152		167	167
Stature (cm)	173.9	174	173.6	175.3
Chest circum.	90.8		97.8	98.3
$Hg./\sqrt[3]{Wgt.}$	12.8		12.48	12.57
Endomorphy		3.34	3.58	
Mesomorphy		4.11	4.61	
Ectomorphy		3.42	2.45	

elevated blood pressure, or (c) elevated serum cholesterol concentration have a larger risk of developing coronary heart disease than the balance of the population. Indeed, if men whose values are considered elevated in two of these three characteristics are compared to men who are considered to be normal in all three, it is found that the former group develops 12-15 times as much coronary heart disease as the latter group. It is clearly of importance to know whether these characteristics are evenly distributed among active and sedentary groups of males.

If we agree that sufficient documentation exists to accept the hypothesis that men in physically active jobs do have less coronary heart disease than their contemporaries in sedentary jobs, we are still faced with uncertainty in regard to whether the observed difference in the incidence of the disease is caused by the physical activity.

The possibility exists that men with specific characteristics prefer and therefore select when possible, the outdoor job which requires physical activity. We must know whether such selection carries with it factors which are associated with high coronary disease rates.

That such selection does influence personal characteristics can be illus-

trated with data presented in Table 7. This is a study of the characteristics of truck drivers carried out by Damon and McFarland.[3] The data for men taken into U.S. Selective Service and studied by Sheldon are not well matched controls but are the best approximation of a sample of U.S. males available. The characteristics of a group of truck drivers working in the northeastern part of the United States appear next and finally the characteristics of champion truck drivers appear in the last column. Damon and McFarland estimate that the average male age 37 in the United States weighs 163 lb. Accordingly, truck drivers in the United States are judged to be heavier and have a larger chest circumference than other males. Furthermore, in regard to somatotype, the truck driver has a high mesomorphic score, is low in ectomorphy, and about normal in regard to endomorphy. If we now compare this datum with that obtained in the army by Newmann and White,[10] we find a different picture. These authors reported that 2,500 army truck drivers could not be distinguished from 25,000 members of the Armed Forces with regard to both body measurements and somatotypes. In the army, men are assigned jobs and there is not as great an opportunity for selection of job by the individual to occur. The inference is clear that with regard to truck drivers selection with a segregation of specific physical characteristics, does take place. It will be remembered that Morris and his colleagues studied bus drivers and conductors. If bus drivers turned out to be more mesomorphic than their conductor contemporaries, one would indeed have food for thought since Spain[11] has shown that among the accidental deaths brought to the coroner's office in New York City, the mesomorphs showed the most advanced atherosclerosis of the coronary arteries.

The death rate study of clerks, switchmen and section men by the staff of the Laboratory of Physiological Hygiene is only on aspect of a larger study which includes physical examination and measurement of a large number of clerks, switchmen, dispatchers and executives drawn from the employees of 20 cooperating railroads operating in the northwestern part of the United States. This work will provide a great deal of information as to the personal characteristics of clerks and switchmen.

Studies of this type will eventually firmly establish the relationship of the physical activity required by occupation and the development of coronary heart disease. It will be important to examine this relationship· in as many different occupational and biological situations as possible so that general relationships can be developed. It will be useful to know whether physically active groups have a better life expectancy and less coronary heart disease than sedentary groups in areas where low fat diets are eaten.

It is generally agreed among epidemiologists that establishing a relationship between groups which differ in the presence or absence or in the degree of presence of an etiological agent is merely a start (and not a very good start)

in establishing the agent as an important factor in the etiology of a disease. A next step is serial observation. Do men who are known to be physically active develop less coronary heart disease than men who are known to be sedentary when both groups are followed for a few years? Such a procedure eliminates, among other things, the possibility that some active men who develop symptoms of coronary heart disease drop out of the active group and are lost to any study of prevalence or death rates.

Note that dropouts of this kind need not be very large to change both the prevalence and the death rate. But while this demonstration reduces the area of uncertainty regarding the role of an agent in the etiology of a disease, the effects of experiment must be introduced. Here one can start with experiments with animals and the demonstration by Eckstein[5] that exercise promotes collateral circulation around a narrowing in the coronary artery of the dog is of extreme interest. But more species must be studied before a suggestion can be made in good faith that a similar situation holds in man. Finally, experiments must be carried on man in terms of both treatment and prevention. If exercise is really useful in preventing an initial attack of coronary thrombosis, it is reasonable to ask whether it is not also useful in reducing the probability of a second attack. This hypothesis can be tested by properly designed therapeutic trials in which the experience of a group of ambulatory patients are placed on carefully graded exercise some months after their first attack, and compared to a properly selected group of comparable patients who are not exercised. If such a therapeutic trial were carried out and it was shown that exercise improved the prognosis of coronary patients after their first attack, the case for exercise as part of a prophylactic program to reduce coronary heart disease would indeed be strong. Under ideal circumstances, one would like to see a physical fitness program started in middle-aged males with properly matched controls in order to see if such a program reduced the coronary heart disease attack rate but the magnitude of this task is so large that is is not likely to be carried out.

In the meantime, one must view the hypothesis that exercise is a protective measure against coronary heart disease in middle-aged men with caution and admit that there is only presumptive evidence for this concept.

References

1. Brown, R. G., L. A. G. Davidson, T. McKeown, and A. G. W. Whitefield, "Coronary Artery Disease: Influence Affecting Its Incidence in Males in the Seventh Decade," *Lancet*, **273** (1957), 1073.

2. Chapman, J. M., L. S. Goerke, W. Dixon, D. B. Loveland, and E. Phillips, "The Clinical Status of a Population Group in Los Angeles Under Observation for Two to Three Years," *Am. J. Public Health*, Spec. Suppl. **47** (1957), 33.

3. Damon, A., and R. A. McFarland, "The Physique of Bus and Truck Drivers With a Review of Occupational Anthropology," *Am. J. Phys. Anthropol.*, **13** (1955), 711.

4. Dawber, T. R., F. E. Moore, and G. V. Mann, "Coronary Heart Disease in the Framingham Study," *Am. J. Public Health* (Part 2), **47** (1957), 4.

5. Eckstein, R. W., "Effect of Exercise and Coronary Narrowing on Coronary Collateral Circulation," *Circulation Res.*, **5** (1957), 230.

6. Forssman, O., and B. Lindegaard, "The Postcoronary Patient, a Multidisciplinary Investigation of Middle-Aged Swedish Males," *J. Psychosomatic Res.*, **3** (1958), 89.

7. Morris, J. N., "Health and Social Class," *Lancet*, **1** (1959), 303.

8. Morris, J. N., and M. D. Crawford, "Coronary Heart Disease and Physical Activity of Work," *Brit. Med. J.*, **2** (1958), 1485.

9. Morris, J. N., J. A. Heady, P. A. B. Raffle, C. G. Roberts, and J. W. Parks, "Coronary Heart Disease and Physical Activity of Work," *Lancet*, **2** (1953). 1053, 1111.

10. Newman, R. W., and R. M. White, "Reference Anthropometry of Army Men," *Environmental Protection Section Report No. 180*. Office of the Quartermaster General, U.S. Army, Lawrence, Mass.

11. Spain, D., V. A. Bradess, and I. J. Grunblutt, "Postmortem Studies on Coronary Atherosclerosis, Serum Beta-Lipoproteins and Somatotypes," *Am. J. Med. Sci.*, **229** (1955), 294.

12. Stamler, J., M. Kjelsberg, and G. Hall, "Epidemiological Studies on Cardiovascular-Renal Disease. I: Analysis of Mortality by Age-Race-Sex-Occupation," *J. Chronic Diseases*, **12** (1960), 440.

13. Taylor, H. L., E. Klepetar, A. Keys, W. Parlin, H. Blackburn, and T. C. Puchner, "Death Rates Among Physically Active and Sedentary Employees of the Railway Industry," *Circulation* (Part 2), **22** (1960), 822.

14. Zukel, W. J., R. H. Lewis, P. E. Enterline, R. C. Painter, L. S. Ralston, R. M. Fawcett, A. P. Meredith, and B. Peterson, "A Short-Term Community Study of the Epidemiology of Coronary Heart Disease," *Am. J. Public. Health*, **49** (1959), 1630.

Prediction of Human
Physical Performance

Man has shown curiosity about his destiny for probably as long as he has been a thinking organism. Manifestations of this have been seen in many forms, including philosophy, religion, art, and science. Our concern in this chapter is to present examples of attempts to predict the limits of physical performance.

The problem of predicting human performance has fascinated people from all walks of life, yet most statements concerning the physical capacity of man have been in the realm of conjecture. However, the successes of the nineteenth-century scientists (and their dreams of absolute determinism) coupled with the growing number of armchair reflections upon world records, motivated many investigators to pursue a scientific course for the answer. It is interesting to note that many of those who have contributed to the literature on the subject have done so by taking time out from the study of other phenomena.

In the nineteenth century the "perfect man" was characterized by a variety of static measures such as height, weight, muscle girths, segment lengths, etc. This anthropometric approach has its adherents in the twentieth century, not as an end in itself but as a corollary of physical performance. In the articles presented here, Sargent for example, in his "The Physical Test of a Man" considered the importance of height and weight in determining maximum performance. Lookabough, using several body measures, attempted to predict "total potential strength." More recently, Sills and Mitchem related gross body type to performance on physical fitness tests.[1]

With so much attention being given to performance measures, the

---

[1] See also H. H. Clarke, "Relation of Physical Structure to Motor Performance of Males," *Profess. Contrib.* No. 6, American Academy of Physical Education, November, 1958, pp. 63–74.

method of fitting curves to existing performers became relatively popular. Kennelley's article was remarkable in this respect, in both its breadth and depth of insight. However, his approach did not answer the question "why?" or "how?" Consequently, some researchers looked to exercise physiology for an explanation of the mechanism underlying maximum performance, of which the work of Hill and Henry is representative.

Much of contemporary research attempts to explain *current* performance records or to predict new ones in weight or time-over-distance events where present records are below values expected from curves fitted to related performance data.[2] Efforts of this kind seem to come from a desire to identify the factors that underlie maximum physical achievement. Increasing the accuracy of predicting present records, or predicting potential performance of particular persons will, in all likelihood, depend upon the development of models that include a wider variety of variables, including those associated with psychology, kinesiology, anthropology, genetics, and sociology.

Fitting curves to existing records is one thing; what levels of performance man will ultimately achieve is quite another, and is probably more the concern of the poet than the scientist. Inasmuch as the evolution of man as an organism has become, for the most part, the responsibility of man himself, only the naive or the mystic will have sufficient courage to make precise prognoses. Serious armchair predictions such as the famous performance ceilings described by Brutus Hamilton[3] are seldom heard today. Yet in the face of the sub-four minute mile, the 7-ft high jump and the 17-ft pole vault, one cannot help but wonder, "Where will it stop?" Perhaps the only safe statement regarding man's eventual physical prowess is the one which disregards all limits except one; ultimately, the best time over a distance A to B will be "nothing flat."

The papers for this section were selected to represent three approaches to prediction: the use of anthropometry (Sargent; Lookabough; and Sills and Mitchem), the development of equations for curves fitted to existing record performances (Kennelly), and the consideration of physiological variables in the development of predictive equations (Hill; Henry).

---

[2] For an example of a maximum performance "lag" in weight lifting see P. V. Karpovich, "The Mighty Muscle," *ibid.*, pp. 59–63.

[3] B. Hamilton, *Amateur Athlete*, 1937.

A. E. KENNELLY

An Approximate Law of Fatigue in the Speeds of Racing Animals

Reprinted from the *Proceedings of the American Academy of Arts and Sciences,*
42 (1906), pp. 275–331.

This paper represents an early, yet remarkable attempt to develop curves predicting maximum physical performance from existing records of the time. Kennelly has shown that his "approximate law of fatigue" as expressed in a logarithmic function holds up rather well ". . . with horses as with man, in air or on water, as indicated by the records analyzed in this paper." However, as is to be expected with pioneer work, subsequent writers have pointed out weaknesses in Kennelly's 1906 study.[1] Nevertheless, it would seem that Kennelly should be given credit for the time-distance approach to predicting world records, a procedure that several others have used but with different mathematical relations.

Some of Kennelly's observations find support in the literature today. For example, his recommendation that record-breaking performances will be those where the athlete maintains a uniform speed throughout a race has been upheld by contemporary exercise physiologists. Also, his suggestion, that those who would establish new records should select an event or distance in which the present record is below the curve, can also be found in later work by Henry, Karpovich, and Lietzke.

Races between swift men, or between swift horses, have been of the greatest interest in all times. Olympia and Epsom Downs are known to fame by the races they have witnessed. Olympian races, recently revived, are of international interest.

It is strange that, judging from encyclopedias and textbooks on athletics, there is very little published information concerning the speeds at which races are run. Apparently, all that is known by our books on these matters is that short races are run at higher speeds than long races. Every one knows that a contestant in a mile or kilometer race runs at a lower speed than a sprinter in a 100-yd or 100-m dash.

There has, however, been accumulated during the last century, and particularly during the last 50 years, a considerable fund of publicly recorded information concerning the record times in which races of stated length have been run. Athletes are, for example, generally familiar with the records of the 100-yd and the mile runs; namely, 9.6 and 252.75 sec, respectively. A reduction of either of these record times by even 1 per cent would be a matter

---

[1] See **M. H. Lietzke,** "An Analytic Study of World and Olympic Racing Records," *Science,* **119** (1954), 333–36; and comments on Lietzke's work by Henry (1955).

of worldwide importance and the hero of the new record would be famous among the inhabitants of the temperate zones.

This paper presents the data which the writer has been able to collect upon record speeds in various kinds of racing, as well as the conclusions that seem to be warranted thereby. It will be seen that the records align themselves closely to a simple mathematical relation. It is not pretended that the records conform rigorously to this mathematical relation. Such a condition could hardly be expected from the performances of different animals at different times and in different parts of the world. It is claimed, however, that any one who will analyze the records presented will be able to satisfy himself that they approximate to the said mathematical relation for practical purposes within satisfactorily small limits of deviation.

We may commence with horseracing records.

Horses Trotting

Table 1, the data of which are taken from p. 259 of *The World Almanac and Encyclopedia* for 1906, gives in column I the data of the record, in column II the distance run, or length of the course, and in column III the best record time. For these data *The World Almanac* is made responsible. These data have been checked, however, by those given in the same publication for preceding years. No event has been rejected. The best records for 1, 2, 3, 4, 5, 10, 20, 30, 50, and 100 mi of trotting are taken. They are stated to be world's records, and at least one—the 4-mi event—is stated to have been made in England.

Commencing with the above data, column IV shows the distances expressed in meters. The meter and kilometer are so much simpler to deal with numerically than the foot, yard, furlong, and mile, that it is worthwhile to

TABLE 1

Analysis of World's Trotting Records (Harness Racing)

I. Date.	II. Distance, miles.	III. Time, seconds. T	IV. Distance L, meters.	V. Speed V, $\frac{\text{meters}}{\text{seconds}}$	VI. log. L.	VII. log. T.	VIII. log. V.	IX. log T' computed.	X. T' computed.	XI. deviation, $T' - T$.	XII. Per cent $100\left(\frac{T'-T}{T}\right)$
1905	1	118.5	1,609.3	13.58	3.2066	2.0737	1.1329	2.0774	119.5	1.0	0.8
1902	2	257.0	3,218.7	12.52	3.5077	2.4099	1.0978	2.4162	260.7	3.7	1.4
1893	3	415.5	4,828.0	11.62	3.6838	2.6186	1.0652	2.6143	411.4	−4.1	1.0
1899	4	598.0	6,437.4	10.77	3.8087	2.7767	1.0320	2.7548	568.6	−29.4	4.9
1893	5	750.75	8,046.7	10.72	3.9056	2.8755	1.0301	2.8638	730.8	−20.0	2.8
1893	10	1,575.0	16,094.0	10.22	4.2066	3.1973	1.0093	3.2024	1,594.0	19.0	1.2
1865	20	3,505.0	32,187.0	9.18	4.5077	3.5447	0.9630	3.5414	3,477.0	−28.0	0.8
1857	30	6,479.0	48,280.0	7.45	4.6838	3.8115	0.8723	3.7393	5,484.0	−995.0	15.0
1846	50	14,140.5	80,467.0	5.69	4.9056	4.1504	0.7552	3.9888	9,746.0	−4394.5	31.0
1853	100	32,153.0	160,930.0	5.01	5.2066	4.5072	0.6994	4.3274	21,250.0	−10,900.0	34.0

reduce all distances to meters. Column V gives the average speed at which the record was made, expressed in meters per second. Thus, taking the first event, the mile (1,609.3 m) was trotted in 118.5 sec. This represents an average speed of 1,609.3 ÷ 118.5 = 13.58 m per sec (30.4 mi per hr; or 44.5 ft per sec).

Turning now to Fig. 1, the abscissas are laid off both in miles and in kilometers, as far as 20 mi (32.2 km). The ordinates represent speeds both in meters per second and in miles per hour. Another scale of ordinates gives the record time of each run in seconds. It is seen that the speeds, taken from column V, drop from 13.58 m per sec (30.4 mi per hr) at 1 mi (1,609 m) to

9.18 m per sec (20.6 mi per hr) at 20 mi. The average speed of the trotting horse that made the 20-mi record was therefore 67.6 per cent, or about two-thirds of that of the trotting horse which made the 1-mi record.

Taking next the time ordinates, the rising line in Fig. 1 closely follows the first six successively increasing times. It is evident that both the speed-distance line and the time-distance line are curves, when thus plotted. The curvature of these curves is greatest near the start, or over the short courses, and diminishes as the course increases.

If, however, the speed and the time with respect to distance be plotted on logarithm paper, as in Fig. 2, instead of on ordinary cross-section paper, as in

Fig. 1. World's trotting records.

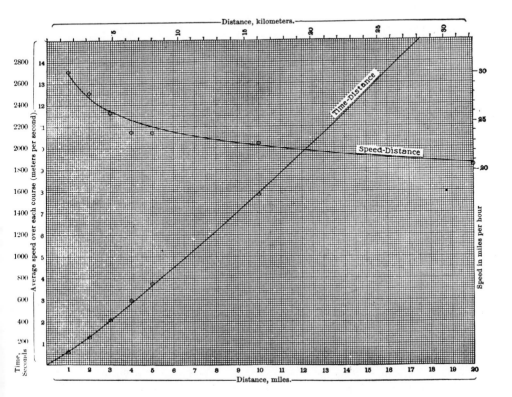

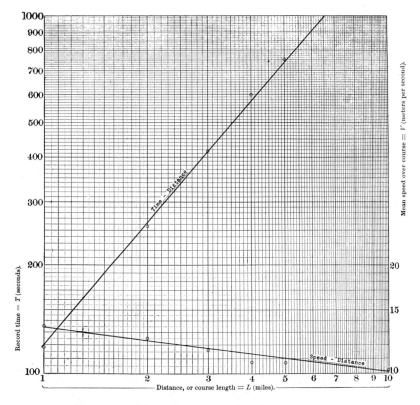

Fig. 2. World's trotting records plotted on logarithm paper.

Fig. 1, the points fall approximately upon straight lines.

The above fact is the gist of this paper. That is to say, if we consider the three quantities L, T, and V, or length of course, record time, and average speed of the run, in a series of events, any one, say T, plotted against either of the others, say L, the observations are found to fall approximately upon a straight line, with logarithm paper. In other words, the curves plotted on plain rectangular paper from the same records are approximately simple exponential curves, of the type $y = x^n$.

Instead of plotting the quantities in the ordinary way upon logarithm paper to produce straight lines, we may perform the equivalent operation

of plotting the logarithms of the quantities upon ordinary scaled paper, and produce similar straight lines. That is, we may plot any one of the quantities $\log L$, $\log T$, and $\log V$ against either of the other two. For some purposes the latter method is to be preferred, although it takes more time. Its application is presented in Fig. 3, where $\log T$ and $\log V$ are both plotted as ordinates against $\log L$ as abscissas for all of the data of Table 1. Columns VI, VII, and VIII in the table contain the common logarithms of the entries in columns IV, III, and V, respectively. It is seen in Fig. 3 that the speeds fall closely upon the descending straight line, as far as the 20-mi distance, as already seen in Fig. 2. Beyond the 20-mi distance, the speeds fall off markedly and are much too low to meet the line. Table 1 indicates, however, that these long-distance records of 30, 50, and 100 mi, respectively, were made about 50 years ago, whereas the short-distance records are of recent date. At the dates indicated (1846, 1853, 1857) the short-distance trotting records were by no means so good as they are today. It is reasonable to assume that if these deviating long distances were attempted today, their records would be materially improved.[1]

The ascending line in Fig. 3, connecting log T and log L, represents the sequence of record times with satisfactory precision, as far as 20 mi, with the exception, perhaps, of the 4-mi

---

[1] Since this paper was written, the writer has been indebted to Prof. E. L. Mark for a photographic curve sheet pertaining to a paper presented by Prof. Francis E. Nipher to the St. Louis meeting in 1903 of the American Association for the Advancement of Science. The curve sheet shows the steady reduction in the record times of the trotting-horse mile and also of the running-horse mile at different dates between 1840 and 1903. The curves indicate a final limit to the trotting mile at 98 sec and a final limit to the running mile at 91.5 sec. The equations to the curves do not appear on the sheet, but have been computed by the writer, from the curves, as follows:

At any epoch y years after 1840, the trotting-horse mile record approximates to

$$T_y = 98 \, (1 + 0.56 \times 10^{-0.00526y}) \text{ sec} \quad \text{(a)}$$

and for the running-horse mile record:

$$T_z = 91.5 \, (1 + 0.154 \times 10^{-0.00993z}) \text{ sec (b)}$$

where z is the epoch in years after A.D. 1863.

From formula (a) or from the curve sheet, the ratios of reduction in the trotting-horse mile record time to 1905 are,

at 1846	0.82
” 1853	0.844
” 1857	0.858

Using these correcting ratios, the 30-mi trotting record is brought on to the logarithmic straight line in Fig. 3; while the 50-mi and 100-mi records are only brought about halfway toward that line, as indicated on the figure.

event, in which the time is long and the speed low. As shown in Fig. 1 or Table 1, the speed in the 4-mi trot is only half of 1 per cent greater than the speed in the 5-mi trot. It should be relatively faster by more than this amount, to judge by the speeds in the other events, and this means that it should lie nearer the straight line of time-distance in Fig. 3.

Beyond 20 mi, the points deviate markedly from the rising straight line of Fig. 3 in the direction of excessive time, or low speed, as already considered.

The rising straight line of Fig. 3 represents the equation

$$\log T = \tfrac{9}{8} \log L - 1.53 \quad (1)$$

while the falling straight line of speed-distance corresponds to

$$\log V = 1.53 - \tfrac{1}{8} \log L. \quad (2)$$

That is, the rising line makes with the axis of abscissas an angle of 48° 22′, whose tangent is $\tfrac{9}{8}$; while the falling line makes with the same axis an angle of −7°7′30″, whose tangent is −$\tfrac{1}{8}$.

Equation (2) implies that at $L = 1$, or upon a course 1 m long, the speed of trotting would be 33.9 m per sec, the logarithm of this number being 1.53. It would be impossible for a horse to reach any such speed on such a very short course, even with flying start, if only owing to inertia and the large effort required for initial acceleration. The initial velocity of Eq. (2) is therefore a fictitious quantity of merely theoretical interest. The speed curve of Fig. 1 and the straight speed lines of Figs. 2 and 3 mark a satisfactory application of Eq. (2) between the limits of 1 mi and 20 mi. Columns IX and X of Table 1 give the computed time for each event, as determined by Eq. (1) or the rising lines in Figs. 1, 2, and 3. Column XI gives the deviation or discrepancy between the computed record time T'

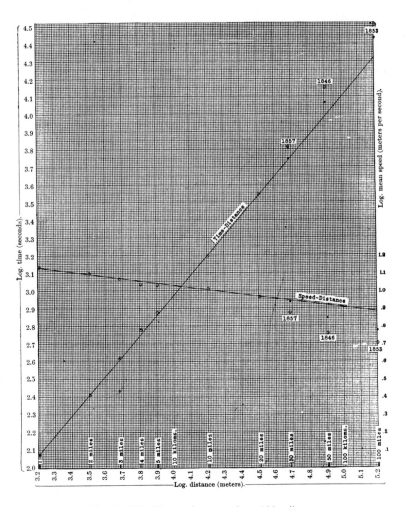

Fig. 3. World's trotting records to 100 miles.

sec and the published record time T sec, while column XII expresses this discrepancy in percentage of the record time T. Thus, the 4-mi event should have been trotted in 568.6 sec by the formula, as against the published record of 598 sec, a discrepancy of 29.4 sec or 4.9 per cent of the published record. It is seen that between the limits of 1 mi and 20 mi (1.61 and 32.2 km) the average discrepancy between the recorded time and the time taken from the Eq.

(1) or the ascending lines in Figs. 2 and 3 is 1.8 per cent. The discrepancy is much greater in the three longest events and reaches 34 per cent in the 100-mi trot. Owing to the age of these three records, however, it is submitted that they may properly be set aside. At all events, between the limits of 1 mi and 20 mi the straight logarithmic line of times agrees with the published records to an average of 1.8 per cent. If the suspected 4-mi record were set aside,

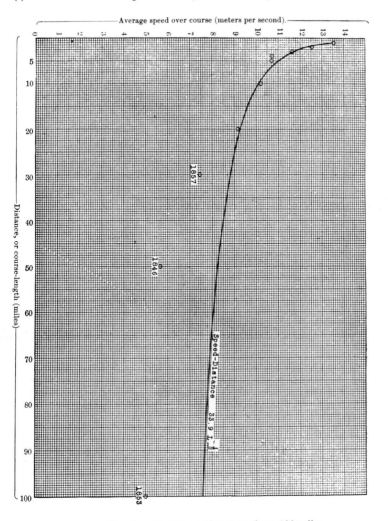

Fig. 4. World's trotting records to 100 miles.

the average discrepancy without regard to sign would come down to 1.1 per cent.

In Fig. 4, drawn to uniform scale, the average speeds are continued to 100 mi of course-length, or beyond the limits of Fig. 1. The curve of speeds corresponds to Eq. (2) or to

$$V = \frac{33.9}{L^{\frac{1}{8}}} \text{ m per sec.} \qquad (3)$$

The figure shows the discontinuity which exists between the speeds over the three longest courses and those over courses up to 20 mi, as taken from column V, Table 1.

Horses Running

The records for running-horse races appear in columns I and II of Table 2. They are taken from p. 258 of *The World Almanac* for 1905, which gives the records for 33 courses be-

TABLE 2

Horses Running

Analysis of Record Performances on American Turf.

I.	II.	III.	IV.	V.	VI.	VII.	VIII.	IX.	X.	XI.	XII.
Distance, miles	Time T, seconds	Distance L, meters	Speed V, meters/seconds	log T	log L	log V	log T' computed	T' computed, seconds	T' − T discrepancy, seconds	$100\left(\dfrac{T'-T}{T}\right)$ per cent discrepancy	Mean per cent
0.25	21.25	402.3	18.93	1.3274	2.6046	1.2772	1.3028	20.08	−1.17	5.5	
0.375	34.0	603.5	17.75	.5315	.7807	.2492	.5009	31.69	−2.31	6.8	
0.4375	40.5	704.1	17.38	.6075	.8476	.2401	.5761	37.68	−2.82	7.0	
0.5	46.0	804.7	17.49	.6628	.9056	.2428	.6414	43.79	−2.21	4.8	
0.5625	51.6	905.2	17.54	.7126	.9567	.2441	.6990	50.01	−1.59	3.1	
0.625	56.75	1005.8	17.72	.7540	3.0025	.2485	.7504	56.29	−0.46	0.8	
0.6875	62.5	1106.4	17.71	.7959	.0439	.2480	.7970	62.66	0.16	0.3	
0.75	68.0	1207.0	17.75	.8325	.0817	.2492	.8395	69.10	1.10	1.6	
0.8125	78.4	1307.6	16.68	.8943	.1165	.2222	.8787	75.63	−2.77	3.5	
0.875	83.5	1408.1	16.86	.9217	.1486	.2269	.9148	82.19	−1.31	1.6	
0.9375	92.2	1508.9	16.37	.9647	.1787	.2140	.9486	88.84	−3.36	3.6	
1.0000	95.5	1609.3	16.85	.9800	.2066	.2266	.9800	95.50	0	0	
1.0114	100.0	1627.6	16.28	2.0000	.2115	.2115	.9855	96.72	−3.28	3.3	
1.028	101.2	1655.0	16.35	.0052	.2188	.2136	.9937	98.56	−2.64	2.6	
1.040	102.6	1673.3	16.31	.0111	.2236	.2125	.9990	99.98	−2.62	2.6	
1.0625	104.6	1709.9	16.35	.0195	.2330	.2135	2.0097	102.2	−2.4	2.3	
1.125	111.0	1810.5	16.31	.0453	.2578	.2125	.0376	109.0	−2.0	1.8	
1.1875	117.4	1911.1	16.28	.0697	.2813	.2116	.0741	118.6	1.2	1.0	1.9
1.25	122.8	2011.7	16.38	.0892	.3036	.2144	.0891	122.8	0	0	
1.3125	133.0	2112.3	15.88	.1239	.3248	.2009	.1131	129.7	−3.3	2.5	
1.375	137.6	2212.9	16.08	.1386	.3450	.2064	.1357	136.7	−0.9	0.7	
1.5	150.25	2414.0	16.07	.1768	.3827	.2059	.1781	150.7	0.45	0.3	
1.625	165.2	2615.2	15.83	.2180	.4175	.1995	.2273	168.8	3.6	2.2	
1.75	177.0	2816.3	15.91	.2480	.4497	.2017	.2535	179.3	2.3	1.3	
1.875	199.0	3017.5	15.16	.2989	.4796	.1807	.2871	193.7	−5.3	2.6	
2.000	206.5	3218.6	15.59	.3149	.5077	.1928	.3188	208.4	1.9	0.9	
2.125	222.0	3419.8	15.40	.3464	.5340	.1876	.3483	223.0	1.0	0.5	
2.25	229.2	3621.0	15.80	.3602	.5588	.1986	.3762	237.8	8.6	3.8	
2.5	264.5	4023.3	15.21	.4224	.6046	.1822	.4278	267.8	−3.3	1.2	
2.625	298.5	4224.5	14.15	.4749	.6258	.1509	.4516	282.9	−15.6	5.2	
2.75	298.75	4425.7	14.82	.4753	.6460	.1707	.4743	298.1	−0.65	0.2	
3.00	324.0	4828.0	14.90	.5105	.6838	.1733	.5169	328.8	4.8	1.5	
4.00	431.0	6437.0	14.93	.6345	.8087	.1742	.6574	454.4	23.4	5.4	

tween $\frac{1}{4}$ mi (402.3 m) and 4 mi (6,437 m) on American turf, revised to December 1, 1904. Column III gives the distances in meters and column IV the average speed of each run. The times and the speeds are plotted against distance to uniform scale in Fig. 5 and to logarithmic scale in Fig. 6. In the latter case the entries in columns V, VI, and VII are used. It is to be noticed that in Fig. 5, with uniform ruling, the observations follow curves, whereas in Fig. 6, with logarithmic ruling (or logarithms of the quantities on uniform ruling), the observations fall substantially on straight lines. The two curves drawn in Fig. 5, respectively, correspond mathematically to the two straight lines drawn to meet the observations in Fig. 6.

Referring to Fig. 6, it is to be observed that the record speeds are low, or the

Fig. 5. Running horses, speeds, and record times.

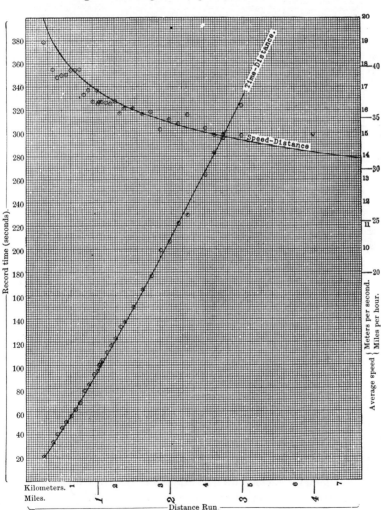

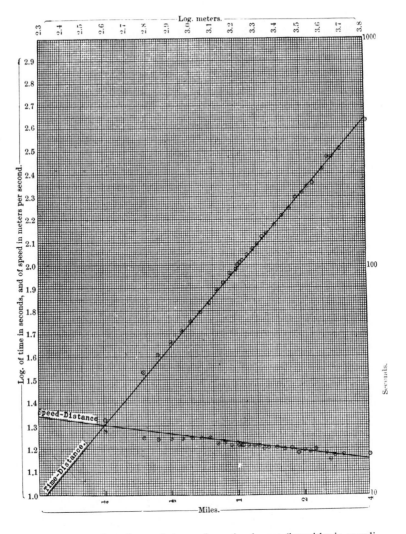

Fig. 6. Speeds and record times of running horses (logarithmic coordinates).

times high, with respect to the straight lines up to 1,000 m (0.62 mi). It is possible that this discrepancy on the short courses be due to the inertia of the horses; that is to say, the horses may be supposed to lose time, or to miss attainment of speed, over the short runs below a kilometer, owing to the effort required to start their bodies into motion from rest. This time lost in acceleration is ignored in the straight-line logarithmic law, which assumes that the animal starts with full speed. For courses of over 1 km, the discrepancy disappears.

Moreover, horse races are stated to be rarely run over distances less than 5 furlongs (1,006 m), so that the question of the discrepancy over short courses is of but little practical importance.

The ascending straight line in Fig. 6,

drawn to meet the points as fairly as may be, is carried through the 1-mi record, and makes an angle with the axis of distance of 48°22′, whose tangent is $\frac{9}{8}$. The falling line is also carried through the 1-mi record and makes an angle with same axis of $-7°\ 7'\ 30''$, whose tangent is $-\frac{1}{8}$.

The straight lines of Fig. 5 correspond to, or determine, the following equations:

$$\log T = \tfrac{9}{8} \log L - 1.6274 \qquad (4)$$

and

$$\log V = 1.6274 - \tfrac{1}{8} \log L. \qquad (5)$$

These are also respectively equivalent to:

$$T = \frac{L^{\frac{9}{8}}}{42.4} \text{ sec} \qquad (6)$$

and

$$V = \frac{42.4}{L^{\frac{1}{8}}} \text{ m per sec.} \qquad (7)$$

By comparing Eqs. (7) and (3) it appears from them that the record speeds of trotting horses is less than the record speeds of running horses over a given distance in the ratio of 33.9 to 42.4, or by 20 per cent of the latter.

On courses longer than 1 km, the straight lines of Fig. 6 fit the observations of Table 2 with satisfactory precision, some observations lying on one side and others on the other. The greatest discrepancies are at $2\frac{1}{4}$ mi and at 4 mi. Figure 5 shows in its upper line that both of these performances were remarkable. The speed over the $2\frac{1}{4}$-mi course appears from the data to have been greater than the speed in the 2-mi event. Again, the speed in the 4-mi race was actually higher than the speed in the 3-mi race.

Column IX of Table 2 gives the time that should correspond to each event, according to formulas (4) or (6). Column X gives the deviation from the record time. Column XI expresses the deviations in percentage of the record time. The mean percentage deviation

between observed and computed record times between the limits of 1 km (5 furlongs) and 6.44 km (4 mi) is shown in column XII to be 1.9 per cent. Consequently, we may expect by following the ascending straight line of Fig. 6 to predict the record time of any race between these limits to within 2 per cent on the average.

The mean percentage deviation between observed and computed record times for the entire series of events, i.e., between $\frac{1}{4}$ mi and 4 mi (0.4 to 6.44 km), is 2.4 per cent.

Horses Pacing

The record data for pacing-horse races in harness on American turf appear in columns I, II, and III of Table 3. They are taken from p. 260 of *The World Almanac* for 1906. The entries in the succeeding columns, IV to VIII, are then found in the manner previously described. In Fig. 7 the logarithm of the time, or log T in column VII, is plotted against the logarithm of the distance, or log L in column VI. The logarithm of the mean speed in each event, or log V in column VIII, is also plotted. Taking the ascending time-distance line, it is a straight line ruled through the 2-mi record point, so as fairly to conform with the other record points. It makes an angle with the distance axis of 48° 22′ or $\tan^{-1}\frac{9}{8}$. Referring to the descending speed-distance line, it is a straight line drawn through the 2-mi record point, so as fairly to conform with the other record points. It makes an angle with the distance axis of $-7°\ 7'\ 30''$ or $\tan^{-1} -\frac{1}{8}$. The two straight lines include between them an angle of approximately 55° 30′ 30″.

The straight lines of Fig. 7 correspond respectively to the following equations:

$$\log T = \tfrac{9}{8} \log L - 1.5363 \qquad (8)$$

TABLE 3

Analysis of Pacing Horse Records in Harness on American Turf

I. Date	II. Distance, miles	III. Time T, seconds	IV. Distance L, meters	V. Speed V, $\frac{meters}{seconds}$	VI. $\log L$	VII. $\log T$	VIII. $\log V$	IX. $\log T'$ computed	X. T' computed, seconds	XI. $T' - T$, deviation	XII. $100\left(\frac{T'-T}{T}\right)$ per cent deviation	Means.
1903	$\frac{1}{2}$	56.0	804.7	14.37	2.9056	1.7482	1.1574	1.7325	54.0	−2.0	3.5	
1905	1	115.25	1609.3	13.97	3.2066	2.0616	1.1450	2.0711	117.8	2.55	2.2	1.9
1903	2	257.0	3218.7	12.53	3.5077	2.4099	1.0978	2.4099	257.0	0.0	0.0	
1891	3	453.25	4828.0	10.65	3.6838	2.6563	1.0275	2.6080	405.5	−47.75	10.5	
1891	4	610.0	6437.4	10.55	3.8087	2.7853	1.0234	2.7485	560.4	−49.6	8.1	5.4
1874	5	783.5	8046.7	10.27	3.9056	2.8940	1.0116	2.8575	720.3	−63.2	8.1	

$$\log V = 1.5363 - \tfrac{1}{8} \log L. \qquad (9)$$

These in turn correspond respectively to the following:

$$T = \frac{L^{\frac{9}{8}}}{34.38} \text{ sec.} \qquad (10)$$

$$V = \frac{34.38}{L^{\frac{1}{8}}} \text{ m per sec.} \qquad (11)$$

An inspection of column X, Table 3,

containing the computed record times according to formulas (8) and (10), shows that the $\tfrac{1}{2}$-mi record was 2 sec longer than the computed time, the mile $2\tfrac{1}{2}$ sec shorter, and the 3-mi, 4-mi, and 5-mi events considerably longer. These deviations appear in column XI, and are given in percentages of the respective actual records in column XII. The $\tfrac{1}{2}$-mi deviation of $3\tfrac{1}{2}$

Fig. 7. Pacing records plotted to logarithmic coordinates.

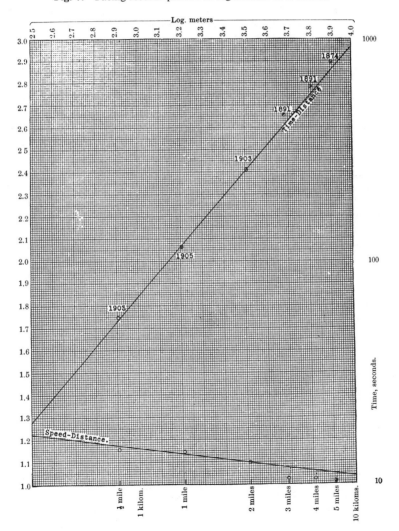

per cent may be explained by inertia on short courses. The deviations of $10\frac{1}{2}$, 8, and 8 per cent on the long distances are not explainable in such a manner. The 3-mi and 4-mi records date from 1891, and the 5-mi record from 1874. Reference to the records of 1892, as given on p. 273 of *The World Almanac* for 1894, shows that at that time the pacing records were low by comparison with those at the present date. Thus the mile record (1.6 km) in pacing was 124 sec, and the 2-mi record (3.2 km) was 287.75 seconds, which are in deviation from the modern records of those events, according to Table 3, by 7.6 and 11.9 per cent, respectively. Consequently, it seems fair to say that these records of 3, 4, and 5 mi, which are 8 to 10.5 per cent off the straight lines in Fig. 7, would have been close to similar lines drawn for records in 1894. In other words, the 1-mi and 2-mi records have steadily improved since 1891, whereas the 3-mi 4-mi, and 5-mi records remain as they were at that date.

If we eliminate the 3-mi, 4-mi, and 5-mi records from consideration, the average discrepancy between the computed and observed record times is seen in column XII to be 1.9 per cent. If, however, we have to consider all of the events, the average discrepancy is 5.4 per cent.

Summing up the analysis of horse racing as presented in Tables 1, 2, and 3 with their accompanying curve sheets, it is submitted that the logarithmic straight lines meet the observations, within reasonable limits of range, to 2 per cent of average discrepancy. Moreover, these corresponding straight logarithmic lines are parallel to each other for running, pacing, or trotting. This means that there is a similar law of fatigue in each of these styles of progression.

Men Running

The first two columns of Table 4 give the world's records of running races. The first four events, up to 45 yd inclusive, are taken from the Amateur Athletic Union records, as given on p. 262 of *The World Almanac* for 1906. The remaining events, up to 623 miles inclusive, are taken from p. 242 of *The World Almanac* for 1904. For each event the best record has been selected, whether the holder was amateur or professional. Amateur records are indicated in column II by the letter A. The last eight events are taken from records of the Olympian Games, as published in the Boston *Transcript* for May 12, 1906. These international contests have been held in 1896, 1900, 1904, and 1906. The best of these four records has been taken for each event.

In Fig. 8, log T (see column VI, Table 4) is plotted as ordinates against log L (column V) as abscissas. The circles mark the world's records and the crosses the Olympian records. In order to keep the chart within reasonably small dimensions, retaining a fairly extended scale, the observations are made to cross the chart twice, by employing dual scales of ordinates and abscissas. The straight line is drawn through the 500-yd record to meet the remaining observations. It runs off the sheet the first time at log $T = 2.71$ and log $L = 3.5$. It then recommences at the left hand of the upper line and finally leaves the sheet at log $T = 4.9$ and log $L = 5.45$. These parts of what would be a single straight line on a larger sheet make an angle of 48°22' or $\tan^{-1}\frac{9}{8}$ with the axis of abscissas. The record points conform closely to this line, swinging slightly from one side of it to the other. They lie above it

TABLE 4

Men Running

Analysis of Best Professional and Amateur World's Records.

I. Distance, yards	II. Time T, seconds		III. Distance L, meters	IV. Speed V, meters/seconds	V. log L	VI. log T	VII. log V	VIII. T' computed	IX. T'−T deviation, seconds	X. $100\left(\dfrac{T'-T}{T}\right)$ deviation per cent
20	A	2.8	19.5	5.188	1.2622	0.4472	0.7150	1.55	−1.25	−44.5
35	A	4.0	32.0	8.000	.5052	.6021	.9031	2.90	−1.1	−27.5
40	A	4.4	36.6	8.312	.5632	.6435	.9197	3.37	−1.03	−23.5
45	A	5.2	41.2	7.914	.6144	.7160	.8984	3.85	−1.35	−26.0
50		5.25	45.7	8.706	.6600	.7202	.9398	4.33	−0.92	−17.5
60	A	6.4	54.9	8.572	.7393	.8062	.9331	5.32	−1.08	−16.9
70	A	7.2	64.0	8.890	.8062	.8573	.9489	6.33	−0.87	−12.1
75		7.25	68.6	9.458	.8362	.8604	.9758	6.84	−0.41	−5.7
80	A	8.0	73.2	9.145	.8643	.9031	.9612	7.36	−0.64	−8.0
100		9.6	91.4	9.524	.9611	.9823	.9788	9.5	−0.1	−1.0
110		11.0	100.6	9.144	2.0025	1.0414	.9611	10.5	−0.5	−4.5
120	A	11.4	109.7	9.625	.0403	.0569	.9834	11.6	0.2	1.8
125	A	12.4	114.3	9.207	.0580	.0934	.9646	12.2	−0.2	−1.6
130		12.125	118.9	9.804	.0751	.0837	.9914	12.7	0.6	4.8
131.5		12.4	120.2	9.696	.0800	.0934	.9866	12.9	0.5	4.0
135		13.2	123.4	9.352	.0915	.1206	.9709	13.3	0.1	0.8
140		13.5	128.0	9.482	.1072	.1303	.9769	13.8	0.3	2.2
150		14.5	137.2	9.458	.1372	.1614	.9758	14.9	0.4	2.8
180	A	18.0	164.6	9.144	.2164	.2553	.9611	18.3	0.3	1.7
200		19.5	182.9	9.380	.2622	.2900	.9722	20.6	1.1	5.7
220	A	21.2	201.2	9.490	.3036	.3263	.9773	23.0	1.8	8.5
250	A	24.6	228.6	9.294	.3591	.3909	.9682	26.5	1.9	7.7
300		30.0	274.3	9.144	.4382	.4771	.9611	32.5	2.5	8.3
350	A	36.4	320.0	8.792	.5052	.5611	.9441	38.7	2.3	6.3
400	A	42.2	365.8	8.668	.5632	.6253	.9379	45.0	2.8	6.6
440	A	47.0	402.3	8.561	.6046	.6721	.9325	50.1	3.1	6.6
500	A	57.8	457.2	7.910	.6601	.7619	.8982	57.8	0	0
600	A	71.0	548.6	7.727	.7393	.8513	.8880	71.0	0	0
660	A	82.0	603.5	7.361	.7807	.9138	.8669	79.0	−3.0	−3.7
700		89.0	640.1	7.203	.8069	.9494	.8575	86.5	−2.5	−2.8
800	A	104.4	731.4	7.007	.8642	2.0187	.8455	98.0	−6.4	−6.1
880		113.5	804.7	7.089	.9056	.0550	.8506	109.2	−4.3	−3.8
1000	A	133.0	914.4	6.874	.9611	.1239	.8372	126.0	−7.0	−5.3
1320	A	182.8	1207.0	6.602	3.0817	.2620	.8197	172.2	−10.6	−5.8
miles										
1		252.75	1609.3	6.367	.2066	.4027	.8039	238.1	−14.6	−5.8
1.25		330.0	2011.6	6.095	.3035	.5185	.7850	299.0	−31.0	−9.4
1.5		403.5	2414.0	5.997	.3837	.6058	.7779	376.7	−26.8	−6.6
1.75	A	488.2	2816.0	5.768	.4496	.6886	.7610	446.8	−41.4	−8.5
2		551.5	3218.7	5.837	.5077	.7415	.7662	519.4	−32.1	−5.8
2.5	A	726.0	4023.0	5.542	.6046	.8609	.7437	667.6	−58.4	−8.0
3		859.5	4828.0	5.618	.6838	.9342	.7496	819.6	−39.9	−4.6
3.5		1004.2	5633.0	5.607	.7507	3.0020	.7487	974.6	−29.6	−3.0
4		1165.6	6437.0	5.525	.8088	.0665	.7423	1133.0	−32.6	−2.8
4.5	A	1345.0	7242.0	5.385	.8599	.1287	.7312	1293.0	−52.0	−3.9
5		1480.0	8047.0	5.436	.9056	.1703	.7353	1456.0	−24.0	−1.6
5.5	A	1662.6	8851.0	5.150	.9470	.2208	.7262	1621.0	−41.6	−2.5
6		1790.0	9656.0	5.394	.9848	.2529	.7319	1787.0	−3.0	−0.2
6.5	A	1976.4	10,462.0	5.293	4.0196	.2959	.7237	1956.0	−20.4	−1.0
7		2085.0	11,265.0	5.404	.0518	.3191	.7327	2126.0	41.0	2.0

Prediction of Human Physical Performance

TABLE 4—Continued.

I.	II.	III.	IV.	V.	VI.	VII.	VIII.	IX.	X.
Dis-tance, miles	Time T, seconds	Distance L, meters	Speed V, $\frac{meters}{seconds}$	log L	log T	log V	T' computed	T'−T deviation, seconds	$100\left(\frac{T'-T}{T}\right)$ deviation per cent
7.5	A 2298.0	12,070	5.252	4.0817	3.3614	0.7203	2297	−1	0
8	2420.0	12,875	5.320	.1097	.3838	.7259	2470	50	2.1
8.5	A 2613.0	13,680	5.236	.1361	.4171	.7190	2645	32	1.2
9	2721.0	14,484	5.322	.1608	.4347	.7261	2820	99	3.7
9.5	A 2931.0	15,289	5.217	.1844	.4670	.7174	2998	67	2.3
10	3066.6	16,094	5.248	.2066	.4866	.7200	3175	108.4	3.5
10.5	3229.0	16,900	5.214	.2279	.5097	.7182	3355	126	3.9
11	3388.0	17,703	5.225	.2480	.5299	.7181	3534	146	4.3
11.5	3543.0	18,508	5.224	.2674	.5494	.7180	3716	173	4.9
12	3722.5	19,312	5.187	.2858	.5709	.7149	3898	175.5	4.7
13	4231.0	20,922	4.946	.3206	.6264	.6942	4266	35	0.8
14	4572.0	22,531	4.928	.3528	.6601	.6927	4637	65	1.4
15	A 4804.6	24,140	5.023	.3827	.6817	.7010	5010	205.4	4.3
16	5286.0	25,750	4.872	.4108	.7231	.6877	5389	103	1.9
17	5655.0	27,360	4.838	.4371	.7524	.6847	5768	113	2.0
18	A 6010.0	28,970	4.819	.4619	.7789	.6830	6147	137	2.3
19	A 6360.0	30,580	4.807	.4854	.8035	.6819	6537	177	2.8
20	A 6714.0	32,190	4.794	.5077	.8270	.6807	6926	212	3.1
21	A 7570.0	33,790	4.464	.5288	.8791	.6497	7315	−255	−3.4
22	A 7968.0	35,410	4.444	.5491	.9013	.6478	7709	−259	−3.2
23	A 8390.0	37,010	4.411	.5683	.9238	.6445	7918	−472	−5.6
24	A 8825.0	38,620	4.377	.5869	.9457	.6412	8504	−321	−3.6
25	A 9224.0	40,240	4.363	.6047	.9649	.6398	8904	−320	−3.5
30	11,709.0	48,280	4.124	.6838	4.0685	.6153	10,930	−779	−6.6
40	16,647.0	64,370	3.868	.8088	.2214	.5874	15,110	−1537	−8.6
50	21,304.5	80,470	3.777	.9056	.3285	.5771	19,410	−1895	−8.9
60	27,033.0	96,560	3.572	.9848	.4319	.5529	23,830	−3203	−11.9
70	32,595.0	112,650	3.456	5.0518	.5132	.5386	28,350	−4245	−13.0
80	38,030.0	128,750	3.386	.1098	.5801	.5297	32,950	−5080	−13.4
90	43,215.0	144,850	3.352	.1609	.6356	.5253	37,610	−5605	−13.0
100	48,390.0	160,933	3.325	.2066	.6848	.5218	43,320	−5070	−10.5
110	55,245.0	177,030	3.204	.2480	.7423	.5057	47,130	−8115	−14.7
120	60,490.0	193,120	3.192	.2858	.7817	.5041	51,980	−8510	−14.1
130	68,685.0	209,220	3.046	.3206	.8369	.4837	56,890	−11,795	−17.2
140	75,030.0	225,310	3.003	.3528	.8752	.4776	61,830	−13,200	−17.6
150	80,905.0	241,400	2.984	.3828	.9080	.4748	68,380	−12,525	−16.7
200	126,568.0	321,900	2.543	.5077	5.1024	.4053	92,370	−34,200	−27.0
300	209,826.0	482,800	2.302	.6838	.3218	.3620	145,700	−64,126	−25.8
383	288,625.0	616,400	2.135	.7899	.4606	.3293	192,300	−96,325	−33.4
450	343,578.0	724,210	2.108	.8599	.5361	.3238	230,000	−113,578	−33.0
500	393,509.0	804,700	2.005	.9056	.5949	.3107	258,900	−134,600	−34.1
560	451,485.0	901,200	1.996	.9548	.6547	.3001	294,100	−157,385	−34.8
623	510,030.0	1,003,000	1.966	6.0013	.7078	.2935	331,700	−179,300	−34.5
..	7.0	60	8.57	1.7782	0.8451	.9331			
..	10.8	100	9.25	2.0000	1.0334	.9666			
..	21.6	200	9.25	2.3010	1.3345	.9665			
..	49.2	400	8.13	2.6021	1.6920	.9101			
..	116.0	800	6.90	2.9031	2.0645	.8386			
..	245.8	1500	6.10	3.1761	2.3906	.7855			
5	1571.6	8047	5.12	3.9056	3.1962	.7094			
..	10,288.0	40,000	3.90	4.6021	4.0123	.5898			

as far as log $L = 2.0$. They lie beneath from log $L = 2.0$ to log $L = 2.66$, and again from log $L = 4.0$ to 4.5. In the remaining parts they lie above. In other words, the straight line hits the record path at log $L = 2.1, 2.7, 3.75,$ and 4.5.

Table 4 gives in column VIII the values of the record times corresponding to the straight line in Fig. 8. Column IX gives the deviation from the world's record for each event and column X the percentage deviation. The per-

centage deviation commences at -44.5 for the shortest run (19.5 m). It dwindles to 0 at about 110 m. It reaches a maximum of 8.5 near 200m, returns to 0 at 500 m, swings over to -8.5 at 2,800 m, returns to 0 near 10 km, swings to 4.9 at 18 km, crosses the zero point near 30 km, and then steadily increases numerically and in the negative direction until it is -34.8 at 900 km.

The large discrepancies below 100

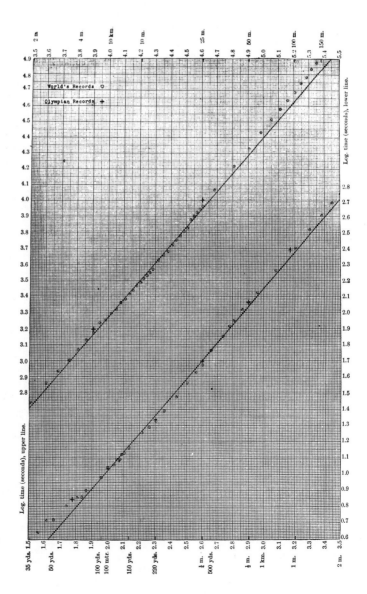

Fig. 8. World's running records.

yd may be attributed to inertia. This is indicated in Fig. 9, where the speeds of the events are plotted up to 201 m. It is evident from the dotted line following the records that runners attain their maximum apparent speed in the neighborhood of 110 m (120 yd). At shorter distances the retarding effect of inertia prevents a higher average speed in the run from being developed. At longer distances, the starting retardation is reduced in effect, but fatigue acts in its place. The simple logarithmic law, represented by the heavy line, takes no account of inertia and assumes a maximum speed

Fig. 9. Mean running speeds over short courses.
NOTE. Figure 8 expresses the relation between time and distance to logarithmic coordinates. The scale of abscissas at the top of the figure gives the logarithm of distance in meters for the upper line; that at the bottom, for the lower line.

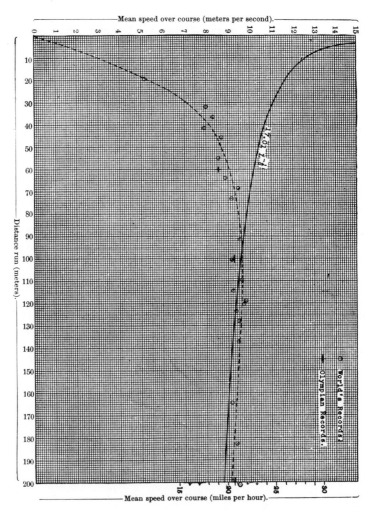

on an indefinitely short course. It is probably not worthwhile going to the complication of correcting the formula by a term or terms introducing a retardation at the start, since races below 100 yd are rare, and the deviation between the actual and computed speeds disappears beyond 100 yd.

At the other end of the line in Fig. 8 the deviations become large after log L = 5 or beyond 100 km. Beyond 150 mi the deviations exceed 20 per cent. It is possible that the discrepancy may here be accounted for by reason of the fact that somewhere in this neighborhood the runner stops at intervals to take food, or rest, and there is no longer a continuous performance enacted. According to the logarithmic straight line, the speeds on courses between 450 and 623 mi (724 and 1,003 km) are only two-thirds of what should be expected.

Summing up the entries in column X, without regard to sign, it is found that if all the events are included from 19.5 m to 1003 km, the average deviation is 8.9 per cent. If, however, the summation be limited to the range from 100 m to 100 km, the average deviation is 4.3 per cent. This appears to be a satisfactory result, considering that the range of distance is 1,000 to 1, and the range of records times 2,500 to 1.

From a practical standpoint it may be inferred from an inspection of either Table 4 or Fig. 8, that it should be easier for trained athletes to beat the world's records between 600 m and 9 km, or between 30 and 1,000 km, than to beat the records between 100 m and 600 m, or between 10 km and 30 km. Expressed in another way, we should expect the degree of physical exhaustion in record runs over the short courses up to 600 m to be more severe than on the courses from that distance up to 9 km. The existing 1-mi or 3-mi record does not seem to be so severe as the

records from 100 yd to 500 yd. Whatever mathematical conclusions may be drawn from the data, the belief seems unavoidable that a study of Fig. 8 will be useful to athletes training for running with a view to breaking records.

The crosses in Fig. 8, representing Olympian records, while useful as a check, do not serve the results in establishing the straight lines, because these Olympian records are inferior to the corresponding world's records, excepting that for the 100-m race.

The line of Fig. 8 corresponds to the following formulas:

$$\log T = \tfrac{9}{8} \log L - 1.2307 \qquad (12)$$

or

$$T = \frac{L^{\frac{9}{8}}}{17.01} \text{ sec.} \qquad (13)$$

$$\log V = 1.2307 - \tfrac{1}{8} \log L \qquad (14)$$

or

$$V = \frac{17.01}{L^{\frac{1}{8}}} \text{ m per sec.} \qquad (15)$$

Men Walking

The data for walking races are given in columns I and III of Table 5. They are taken from p. 244 of *The World Almanac* for 1904, and are world's records, amateur and professional. The best records in walking, unlike other athletic sports, seem to have been made entirely by professional walkers.

Figure 10 indicates the points found by plotting log T from column V against log L from column IV. In order to economize space, the series of points is carried twice across the sheet to two sets of scales. The straight line, seen in two segments, is drawn through the 4-mi record point, and is drawn to meet the other points fairly. It makes an angle of 48°22′ or $\tan^{-1} \tfrac{9}{8}$, with the axis of distances. The entries in column

TABLE 5

Men Walking

Analysis of World's Best Walking Records, Amateur or Professional.

I. Distance, miles	II. Distance, L, meters	III. Time, T, seconds	IV. log L	V. log T	VI. log V	VII. V, meters seconds	VIII. log T', computed	IX. T', computed	X. T' − T deviation	XI. $100\left(\dfrac{T'-T}{T}\right)$ percentage deviation
1	1,609.4	383.0	3.2066	2.5832	0.6234	4.201	2.5428	349.0	−34.0	−8.9
2	3,218.7	794.0	.5077	2.8998	.6079	.054	.8816	761.4	−32.6	−4.1
3	4,828.0	1,221.5	.6838	3.0869	.5969	3.953	3.0797	1,201.0	−20.5	−1.7
4	6,437.4	1,658.0	.8087	.2196	.5891	.882	.2202	1,660.0	2.0	0.0
5	8,046.7	2,110.0	.9056	.3243	.5813	.813	.3292	2,134.0	24.0	1.1
6	9,656.1	2,581.0	.9848	.4118	.5730	.741	.4183	2,620.0	39.0	1.2
7	11,265.0	3,064.0	4.0517	.4863	.5654	.676	.4936	3,116.0	52.0	1.7
8	12,875.0	3,517.0	.1097	.5462	.5635	.660	.5588	3,621.0	104.0	3.0
9	14,484.0	4,034.0	.1608	.6057	.5551	.590	.6163	4,133.0	99.0	2.5
10	16,094.0	4,485.0	.2066	.6518	.5548	.588	.6678	4,654.0	169.0	3.8
11	17,703.0	4,958.0	.2480	.6953	.5527	.570	.7144	5,181.0	223.0	4.5
12	19,312.0	5,434.0	.2858	.7351	.5507	.554	.7569	5,713.0	279.0	5.1
13	20,922.0	5,926.5	.3206	.7727	.5479	.531	.7961	6,253.0	326.5	5.5
14	22,531.0	6,431.5	.3528	.8083	.5445	.504	.8323	6,797.0	365.5	5.7
15	24,140.0	6,956.0	.3827	.8424	.5403	.470	.8659	7,343.0	387.0	5.6
20	32,187.0	9,597.0	.5077	.9821	.5256	.354	4.0066	10,150.0	553.0	5.8
30	48,280.0	16,494.0	.6838	4.2173	.4665	2.928	.2047	16,110.0	−384.0	−2.3
40	64,374.0	22,610.0	.8087	.3543	.4544	.847	.3452	22,140.0	−470.0	−2.1
50	80,467.0	28,456.0	.9056	.4542	.4514	.828	.4542	28,460.0	4.0	0.0
60	96,561.0	34,847.0	.9848	.5422	.4426	.771	.5433	34,940.0	93.0	0.3
70	112,650.0	41,915.0	5.0517	.6224	.4293	.687	.6186	41,550.0	−365.0	−0.9
80	128,750.0	50,513.0	.1097	.7034	.4063	.549	.6838	48,280.0	−2,233.0	−4.4
90	144,840.0	57,550.0	.1608	.7600	.4008	.517	.7413	55,120.0	−2,430.0	−4.2
100	160,940.0	65,330.0	.2066	.8151	.3915	.463	.7928	62,060.0	−3,270.0	−5.0
120	193,120.0	79,585.0	.2858	.9009	.3848	.426	.8819	76,190.0	−3,395.0	−4.3
150	241,400.0	110,188.0	.3827	5.0421	.3406	.191	.9909	97,930.0	−12,258.0	−11.1
200	321,870.0	146,790.0	.5077	.1667	.3410	.193	5.1316	135,400.0	−11,390.0	−8.3
250	402,340.0	198,744.0	.6046	.2983	.3063	.024	.2406	174,000.0	−24,744.0	−12.5
300	482,800.0	239,400.0	.6838	.3791	.3047	.017	.3297	213,500.0	−25,900.0	−10.8
400	643,740.0	348,663.0	.8087	.5424	.2663	1.846	.4702	205,300.0	−53,363.0	−15.3
500	804,670.0	470,025.0	.9056	.6721	.2335	.712	.5792	379,500.0	−90,525.0	−19.3
531	854,559.0	499,710.0	.9317	.6987	.2328	.709	.6086	406,100.0	−93,610.0	−17.8

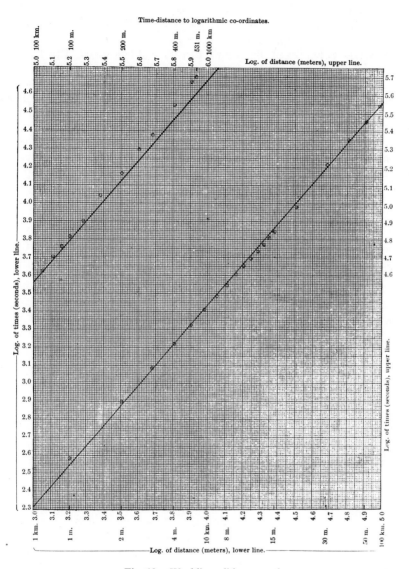

Time-distance to logarithmic co-ordinates.

Fig. 10. World's walking records.

VIII correspond to points on the straight line. The computed times T' of each event are thus obtained and set down in column IX. The last column gives the percentages of deviation between the actual and computed record. The observations commence above the line, or the record times for the 1-mi and 2-mi events are long, or the speeds low, by comparison with the 4-mi and the 50-mi records. This can hardly be accounted for by inertia, as in horse racing; because at the low speed of walking, the retardation, due to starting from rest, must disappear in less than 100 m.

The points fall below the line between 4 mi and 30 mi, representing faster speeds than the computed to the extent of nearly 6 per cent. Between 40 and 70 mi the agreement between the observed and computed times is close. Beyond 70 mi the speed falls below that computed by the logarithmic line. The deviations do not exceed 5 per cent until beyond 120 mi.

The mean percentage of deviation, without regard to sign, is 5.6 per cent over the entire series of events, and 3.4 per cent between the limits of 1 mi and 120 mi.

There seems to have been scarcely any improvement in walking records during the ten years preceding the date at which these have been selected (1904).

The straight line of Fig. 10 corresponds to the following equations:

$$\log T = \tfrac{9}{8} \log L - 1.0646 \qquad (16)$$

and

$$\log V = 1.0646 - \tfrac{1}{8} \log L \qquad (17)$$

or

$$T = \frac{L^{\tfrac{9}{8}}}{11.6} \text{ sec} \qquad (18)$$

and

$$V = \frac{11.6}{L^{\tfrac{1}{8}}} \text{ m per sec.} \qquad (19)$$

Men Rowing

Table 6 is compiled from the data contained in the article on "Rowing" appearing on p. 208, Vol. X, of the *Universal Encyclopedia* published in 1900. The entries in columns I, II, III, and V of Table 6 are taken directly from that article. The remaining columns give the deductions therefrom, as in preceding cases. The logarithms of the times are plotted against the logarithms of the distances in Fig. 11. The

8-oar line is drawn through the 4-mi record point. The 1-mi record is the only point seriously off the line, in the direction of low speed. The 1-mi speed is seen in column VI to be lower than the 4-mi speed. The 4-oar line is also drawn through the 4-mi record point. The 3-mi event is the only one seriously off this line, in the direction of high speed. The speed over this course was 5.15 m per sec, which is only about 7 per cent short of the record speed for the 1-mi event. The single-pair-of-sculls line is drawn through the 5-mi record point. The $\tfrac{1}{4}$-mi and the 1-mi events are the only ones seriously off this line. It is possible that the quarter-mile is affected by starting inertia. The mean deviation for the entire series is 6 per cent. If we discard the 1-mi 8-oar event and the $\tfrac{1}{4}$-mi singles event, the mean deviation of the remaining series is 4.3 per cent. This seems to be a good showing for the logarithmic straight line considering the extent to which both wind and tide are capable of influencing rowing speeds.

All three straight lines in Fig. 11 are drawn to make an angle of 48°22′ with the axis of distances.

The formulas deducible from the three straight lines of Fig. 11 are presented in Table 7.

It is seen that for any given distance over 1 mi, the speeds of 8s, 4s, and singles are in the ratio 15.92 : 13.02 : 12.16, or 100 : 81.8 : 76.4, to the degree of approximation supported by the analysis.

Men Swimming

The data for swimming have been taken from the world's records given on p. 252 of *The World Almanac* for 1905, setting forth 38 events from 25 yd to 4,000 yd by amateurs and by

TABLE 6

Men Rowing

Analysis of Records of American Oarsmen.

I. Type	II. Date	III. Distance, miles	IV. Distance L, meters	V. Time T, seconds	VI. Speed V, meters seconds	VII. log L	VIII. log T	IX. log V	X. log T' computed	XI. T' computed, seconds	XII. T'−T deviation, seconds	XIII. $100\left(\dfrac{T'-T}{T}\right)$ per cent deviation
8-oars	1883	1	1609.3	304.75	5.281	3.2066	2.4839	0.7227	2.4054	254.3	−50.5	−16.5
	1889	1.5	2414	400	6.035	.3827	.6021	.7806	.6035	401.3	1.3	0.3
	1891	2	3218.7	583.5	5.516	.5077	.7660	.7417	.7442	554.9	−28.6	−4.9
	1891	3	4828	867.5	5.564	.6838	.9383	.7455	.9423	875.6	8.1	0.9
	1888	4	6437.4	1210	5.320	.8087	3.0828	.7259	3.0828	1210	0	0
4-oars	1883	1	1609.3	291	5.530	3.2066	2.4639	0.7427	2.4929	311.1	20.1	6.9
	1887	2	3218.7	747	4.309	.5077	.8733	.6344	.8317	678.8	−68.2	−9.1
	1875	3	4828	937.25	5.151	.6838	.9719	.7119	3.0298	1071	133.8	14.6
	1871	4	6437.4	1480	4.349	.8087	3.1703	.6384	.1703	1480	0	0
	1860	5	8046.7	1844.75	4.362	.9056	.2659	.6397	.2793	1902	57.3	3.1
	1871	6	9656.1	2360.6	4.090	.9848	.3730	.6118	.3684	2390	29.4	1.2
single-sculls	1891	¼	402.3	57	7.058	2.6046	1.7559	0.8487	1.8352	68.4	11.4	20.0
	1872	1	1609.3	301	5.347	3.2066	2.4786	.7280	2.5224	333	32.0	9.6
	1868	2	3218.7	680	4.734	.5077	.8325	.6752	.8612	726.4	46.4	6.8
	1890	3	4828	1171	4.123	.6838	3.0680	.6152	3.0593	1146	−25.0	−2.1
	1883	4	6437.4	1677.5	3.837	.8087	.2247	.5840	.200	1585	−92.5	−5.5
	1879	5	8046.7	2036.25	3.951	.9056	.3088	.5968	.3088	2036	0	0

Time-distance to logarithmic co-ordinates.

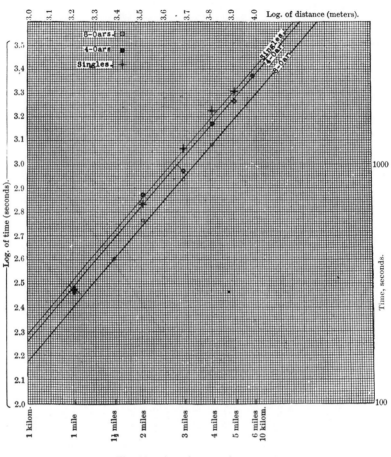

Fig. 11. American rowing records.

professional swimmers of all nations. These data appear in columns I and II of Table 8. The remaining columns work from these data as in preceding tables.

In Fig. 12, log T' is plotted against log L, and also log V against log L. The ascending time-distance straight line is drawn through the 220-yd (201.2-m) record point, and thence in a direction to conform fairly well with the other record points. It is drawn to make an angle of 48°22′ or $\tan^{-1} \frac{9}{8}$ with the axis of distances. The

descending straight line of speed-distance is likewise drawn through the 220-yd record point, and to make an angle of $-7°\ 7'\ 30''$ or $\tan^{-1} - \frac{1}{8}$ with the same axis.

Referring to the latter line, it will be observed that there is no visible retardation of speed over the short courses even down to 25 yd (22.9 m). On the contrary, the speeds for the first four events, up to 60 yd (55 m), inclusive, are higher than correspond to the logarithmic straight line. This may be accounted for by the fact that

TABLE 7

Quantitative Results of Analysis of Rowing Records

8-oars	*4-oars*	*Singles*
$\log T = \frac{9}{8} \log L - 1.202$	$\log T = \frac{9}{8} \log L - 1.1145$	$\log T = \frac{9}{8} \log L - 1.085$
$\log V = 1.202 - \frac{1}{8} \log L$	$\log V = 1.1145 - \frac{1}{8} \log L$	$\log V = 1.085 - \frac{1}{8} \log L$
$T = \dfrac{L^{\frac{9}{8}}}{15.92}$ seconds	$T = \dfrac{L^{\frac{9}{8}}}{13.02}$ seconds	$T = \dfrac{L^{\frac{9}{8}}}{12.16}$ seconds
$V = \dfrac{15.92}{L^{\frac{1}{8}}} \dfrac{\text{meters}}{\text{second}}$	$V = \dfrac{13.02}{L^{\frac{1}{8}}} \dfrac{\text{meters}}{\text{second}}$	$V = \dfrac{12.16}{L^{\frac{1}{8}}} \dfrac{\text{meters}}{\text{second}}$

Fig. 12. Swimming records.

Time-distance and speed-distance to logarithmic co-ordinates.

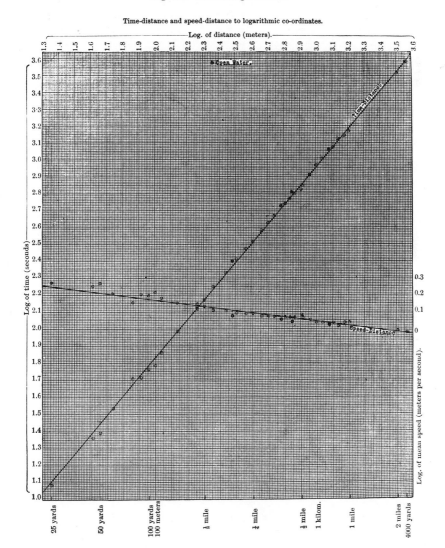

TABLE 8

Men Swimming

Analysis of Best Professional and Amateur Records

I.		II.	III.	IV.	V.	VI.
Distance, yards		Time T, seconds	Distance L, meters	V, meters/seconds	log T	log L
25	A	12.2	22.86	1.874	1.0864	1.3591
45	A	23.0	41.15	.789	.3617	.6144
50	A	24.6	45.72	.859	.3909	.6601
60	A	34.0	54.86	.614	.5315	.7393
80	P	51.0	73.15	.434	.7076	.8642
90	A	51.6	82.3	.595	.7126	.9154
100	A	58.0	91.44	.577	.7634	.9611
110	A	61.0	100.6	.649	.7853	2.0025
120	A	72.2	109.7	.520	.8585	.0403
150	A	96.6	137.2	.420	.9850	.1372
200	A	140.0	182.9	.306	2.1461	.2622
220	A	148.6	201.2	.354	.1720	.3036
250	P	177.8	228.6	.285	.2499	.3591
300	A	214.6	274.3	.278	.3316	.4382
330	O	252.3	301.8	.196	.4019	.4797
350	P	258.0	320.0	.240	.4116	.5052
400	A	297.0	365.7	.231	.4728	.5631
440	A	326.2	402.3	.233	.5135	.6046
500	A	383.6	457.2	.192	.5838	.6601
550	A	423.4	502.9	.188	.6268	.7015
600	A	465.0	548.6	.180	.6675	.7393
660	O	533.0	603.5	.132	.7267	.7807
700	A	547.4	640.1	.169	.7383	.8062
750	A	587.4	685.8	.167	.7689	.8362
770	O	642.0	704.1	.097	.8075	.8476
800	A	628.0	731.5	.165	.7980	.8642
880	P	664.5	804.6	.211	.8225	.9056
900	P	706.0	823.0	.166	.8488	.9154
1000	A	812.8	914.4	.125	.9100	.9611
1100	A	925.4	1005.8	.087	.9663	3.0025
1200	A	1011.0	1097.2	.085	3.0048	.0403
1320	O	1148.5	1207.0	.051	.0601	.0817
1400	A	1183.0	1280.2	.082	.0729	.1073
1500	A	1324.6	1371.6	.035	.1221	.1372
1650	A	1390.4	1508.7	.085	.1431	.1786
1760	A	1476.2	1609.3	.090	.1691	.2066
3520	A	3294.0	3218.7	0.9772	.5177	.5076
4000	A	3824.0	3657.0	0.9564	.5825	.5631

TABLE 8—Continued.

VII.	VIII.	IX.	X.	XI.
			$T' - T$	$100\left(\dfrac{T' - T}{T}\right)$
log V	log T' computed	T' computed seconds	deviation, seconds	per cent deviation
0.2727	1.1094	12.87	0.67	5.5
.2527	.3966	24.93	1.93	8.4
.2692	.4480	28.05	3.45	14.0
.2078	.5371	34.44	0.44	1.3
.1566	.6776	47.6	−3.4	−6.7
.2028	.7352	54.35	2.75	5.3
.1977	.7866	61.18	3.18	5.5
.2172	.8332	68.11	7.11	11.7
.1818	.8751	75.01	2.81	3.9
.1522	.9847	96.54	−0.06	−0.1
.1161	2.1254	133.5	−6.5	−4.6
.1316	.1720	148.6	0	0
.1092	.2344	171.5	−6.3	−3.5
.1066	.3121	205.2	−9.4	−4.4
.0778	.3700	234.5	−17.8	−7.1
.0936	.3988	250.5	−7.5	−2.9
.0903	.4639	291.0	−6.0	−2.0
.0911	.5106	324.0	−2.2	−0.7
.0763	.5730	374.1	−9.5	−2.5
.0747	.6196	416.5	−6.9	−1.6
.0718	.6621	459.3	−5.7	−1.2
.0540	.7087	511.3	−21.7	−4.1
.0679	.7374	546.3	−1.1	−0.2
.0673	.7711	590.4	3.0	0.5
.0401	.7840	608.1	−33.9	−5.3
.0662	.8026	634.8	6.8	1.1
.0831	.8492	706.6	42.1	6.3
.0666	.8602	724.8	18.8	2.7
.0511	.9116	815.8	3.0	0.4
.0362	.9582	908.2	−17.2	−1.9
.0355	3.0007	1002.0	−9.0	−0.9
.0216	.0473	1115.0	−33.5	−2.9
.0344	.0761	1192.0	9.0	0.5
.0151	.1098	1288.0	−36.6	−2.8
.0355	.1563	1433.0	42.6	3.1
.0375	.1887	1544.0	67.8	4.6
1.9899	.5265	3362.0	68.0	2.1
.9806	.5889	3881.0	57.0	1.5

A denotes an amateur record. P, a professional record. O, a professional record in open water. Except as indicated above, the records are stated to have been made in baths or bathing houses, as distinguished from open water.

swimming speeds are only 15.5 per cent of men's running speeds at any given distance beyond 100 m; so that the retardation at starting must be much less than in running. Moreover, it is possible that the starting plunge made by the swimmer may actually advance him, relatively speaking, on the shortest courses.

With the exception of the four open-water events, on all of which the speed is distinctly low, and the 80-yd event, which has an unduly low speed (about the same as in the 150-yd event), the observations cling closely to the straight line. The speeds at both the half-mile and the 1-mi events appear to be distinctly higher than the rest.

Fig. 13. Amateur skating records.

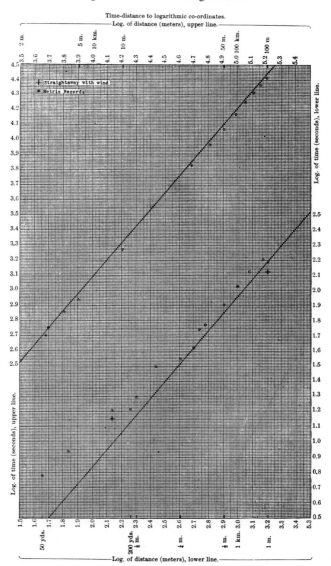

Table 8 indicates that the mean deviation, without regard to sign, of all the events is 3.5 per cent.

The formulas pertaining to the straight lines in Fig. 12 are

$$\log T = \tfrac{9}{8} \log L - 0.4196 \qquad (20)$$

$$\log V = 0.4196 - \tfrac{1}{8} \log L \qquad (21)$$

$$T = \frac{L^{\frac{9}{8}}}{2.628} \text{ sec} \qquad (22)$$

$$V = \frac{2.628}{L^{\frac{1}{8}}} \text{ m per sec.} \qquad (23)$$

Men Skating

Table 9 gives the analysis of 24 yard and mile events and also 5 metric events, between the limits of 50 yd and 100 mi. The data appearing in columns I and II of this table are taken from the records of the Amateur Athletic Union revised in 1905 and published on p. 265 of *The World Almanac* for 1906. They represent, therefore, amateur records.

In Fig. 13, log *T* has been plotted against log *L*, crossing the sheet twice for economy in space. The straight line drawn in two sections is carried through the 1-mi record point. It also runs very near to the 2-mi, 4-mi, 500-m, and 5,000-m points. There is a wide deviation of the points from the line between 50 yd (45.72 m) and 440 yd (402.3 m). Thus may be attributed to the influence of inertia in acceleration at the start. Column IV of Table 9 shows in fact that the maximum speed over a course is not reached until the 440-yd event (402.3-m), when it attains 11.43 m per sec (25.5 m per hr). The entries in column IV also reveal considerable relative variation, and do not descend with the same degree of uniformity as is manifested by the corresponding speed entries in Table 8, or other tables. Perhaps this variability

in the records is due in some measure to the influence of wind, which is particularly active on skating speeds.

Column XII of Table 9 indicates that the mean percentage deviation of the series of computed times against record times is 7.6 per cent between 500 m and 100 mi (160.9 km). If the same test is applied to the entire series between 50 yd and 100 mi, the mean percentage of deviation, without regard to sign, is 13.3 per cent.

The following formulas pertain to the straight line of Fig. 13:

$$\log T = \tfrac{9}{8} \log L - 1.4143 \qquad (24)$$

$$\log V = 1.4143 - \tfrac{1}{8} \log L \qquad (25)$$

or

$$T = \frac{L^{\frac{9}{8}}}{25.96} \text{ sec} \qquad (26)$$

$$V = \frac{25.96}{L^{\frac{1}{8}}} \text{ m per sec.} \qquad (27)$$

Men Bicycling

The data for bicycling have been taken from pp. 267 and 268 of *The World Almanac* for 1906, and are embodied in columns I and II of Table 10. The first five events are professional, paced records against time. The next series of events, from 2 mi to 100 mi, inclusive, are professional motor-paced records, in competition. The remainder are stated to be American competition, professional, paced, hour records. The average speeds over the distances are set down in column V. It will be seen that the speed between 2 mi (3.22 km) and 30 mi (48.28 km) was almost precisely uniform at 23.5 m per sec. In fact, it appears from the table in *The World Almanac* that all of these records were made by one and the same individual, on one and the same day (May 31, 1904), at Charles River Park, Mass. Again, from 31 mi (49.89 km) to 50 mi (59.59 km), the speeds are nearly

TABLE 9

Men Skating

Analysis of Amateur Skating Records

I. Distance, yards	II. Time T, seconds	III. Distance L, meters	IV. Speed V, meters/seconds	V. log L	VI. log T' computed	VII. log T	VIII. log V	IX. T', seconds, computed	X. T'−T deviation, seconds	XI. $100\left(\dfrac{T'-T}{T}\right)$ deviation per cent	XII. Mean percentage deviation
50	6.0	45.72	7.62	1.6601	0.4533	0.7782	0.8819	2.84	−3.16	−52.0	
75	8.6	68.58	7.974	.8362	.6514	.9345	.9017	4.48	−4.12	−48.0	
150	15.88	137.16	8.635	2.1372	.9901	1.2009	.9363	9.78	−6.1	−38.3	
200	16.4	182.88	11.150	.2622	1.1307	.2148	1.0474	13.51	−2.9	−17.8	
220	19.8	201.2	10.160	.3036	.1773	.2967	.0069	15.04	−4.8	−24.0	
300	31.4	274.3	8.736	.4382	.3287	.4969	.9413	21.32	−10.1	−32.1	
440	35.2	402.3	11.43	.6046	.5159	.5465	1.0581	32.8	−2.4	−6.8	
600	55.25	548.6	9.929	.7393	.6674	.7423	.9970	46.5	−8.8	−15.8	
880	80.4	804.6	10.01	.9056	.8545	.9053	1.0003	71.5	−8.9	−11.1	
1,320	133.0	1,207.0	9.075	3.0817	2.0526	2.1239	.9578	112.9	−20.1	−15.1	
miles											
1	156.0	1,609.3	10.32	.2066	.1931	.1931	1.0135	156.0	0	0	
2	342.6	3,218.7	9.395	.5077	.5319	.5348	.9729	340.3	−2.3	−0.7	
3	503.0	4,828.0	9.598	.6838	.7300	.7016	.9822	537.1	34.1	6.8	
4	720.5	6,437.4	8.934	.8087	.8705	.8576	.9511	742.2	21.7	3.0	
5	864.0	8,046.7	9.314	.9056	.9795	.9365	.9691	954.0	90.0	10.4	
10	1,871.2	16,093.0	8.600	4.2066	3.3181	3.2721	.9345	2,080.0	208.8	11.1	
30	6,800.0	48,280.0	7.100	.6838	.8550	.8325	.8513	7,161.0	361.0	5.3	
40	9,286.0	64,374.0	6.932	.8087	.9955	.9678	.8409	9,897.0	611.0	6.6	
50	11,759.4	80,467.0	6.842	.9056	4.1045	4.0704	.8352	12,720.0	960.0	8.2	7.6
60	14,820.6	96,561.0	6.515	.9848	.1936	.1709	.8139	15,620.0	800.0	5.4	
70	17,715.6	112,654.0	6.358	5.0517	.2689	.2483	.8034	18,570.0	854.0	4.8	
80	20,515.0	128,748.0	6.275	.1097	.3341	.3121	.7976	21,580.0	1,065.0	5.2	
90	23,157.6	144,841.0	6.254	.1608	.3916	.3647	.7961	24,640.0	1,482.0	6.4	
100	25,898.0	160,935.0	6.213	.2066	.4531	.4133	.7933	28,390.0	2,492.0	9.6	
meters											
500	41.8	500.0	11.95	2.6990	1.6221	1.6218	1.0772	41.9	0.1	0.2	
600	59.6	600.0	10.07	.7782	.7112	.7752	1.0030	51.4	−8.2	−13.8	
1,000	107.0	1,000.0	9.346	3.0000	.9607	2.0294	.9706	91.4	−15.6	−14.6	
1,500	160.8	1,500.0	9.328	.1761	2.1588	.2063	.9698	144.1	−16.7	−10.4	
5,000	565.4	5,000.0	8.843	.6990	.7471	.7524	.9466	558.6	−6.8	−1.2	

TABLE 10

Men Bicycling

Analysis of Professional Bicycling Paced Records

I.	II.	III.	IV.	V.
Distance, miles	Time, h. m. s.	Distance L, meters	Time T, seconds	Speed V, meters seconds
0.25	20.0	402.3	20.0	20.12
0.33	27.8	536.4	27.8	19.3
0.5	41.0	804.7	41.0	16.92
0.66	58.6	1,072.8	58.6	18.30
1	1 06.2	1,609.3	66.2	24.30
2	2 19.0	3,218.7	139.0	23.16
3	3 31.6	4,828.0	211.6	22.82
4	4 43.0	6,437.4	283.0	22.75
5	5 51.0	8,046.7	351.0	22.93
6	7 00.2	9,656.1	420.2	22.98
7	8 07.6	11,265.4	487.6	23.10
8	9 14.2	12,874.8	554.2	23.23
9	10 22.0	14,484.1	622.0	23.28
10	11 29.2	16,093.0	689.2	23.35
11	12 36.2	17,703.0	756.2	22.88
12	13 43.0	19,312.0	823.0	23.46
13	14 50.4	20,921.0	890.4	23.50
14	15 57.2	22,531.0	957.2	23.54
15	17 03.4	24,140.0	1,005.4	24.00
16	18 10.6	25,749.0	1,090.6	23.61
17	19 17.4	27,359.0	1,157.4	23.64
18	20 24.2	28,968.0	1,224.2	23.66
19	21 30.8	30,577.0	1,290.8	23.68
20	22 37.6	32,187.0	1,357.6	23.71
21	23 44.6	33,796.0	1,424.6	23.72
22	24 51.8	35,406.0	1,491.8	23.73
23	25 59.0	37,015.0	1,559.0	23.75
24	27 07.6	38,624.0	1,627.6	23.73
25	28 14.2	40,234.0	1,694.2	23.75
26	29 22.6	41,843.0	1,762.6	23.73
27	30 30.2	43,452.0	1,830.2	23.74
28	31 37.4	45,062.0	1,897.4	23.75
29	32 48.0	46,671.0	1,968.0	23.72
30	33 52.6	48,280.0	2,032.6	23.77
31	36 26.0	49,890.0	2,186.0	22.82
32	37 37.2	51,499.0	2,257.2	22.81
33	38 48.8	53,109.0	2,328.8	22.81
34	39 57.6	54,718.0	2,397.6	22.82
35	41 07.6	56.327.0	2,467.6	22.82
36	42 18.2	57,937.0	2,538.2	22.83
37	43 28.2	59,546.0	2,608.2	22.83
38	44 39.2	61,155.0	2,679.2	22.82
39	45 49.4	62,765.0	2,749.4	22.83
40	47 00.0	64,374.0	2,820.0	22.83

TABLE 10—Continued.

I. Distance, miles		II. Time, h. m. s.			III. Distance L, meters	IV. Time T, seconds	V. Speed V, meters/seconds
41			48	10.8	65,983.0	2,890.8	22.82
42			49	21.2	67,593.0	2,961.2	22.82
43			50	31.2	69,202.0	3,031.2	22.83
44			51	41.2	70,811.0	3,101.2	22.83
45			52	20.8	72,421.0	3,170.8	22.84
46			54	23.8	74,030.0	3,263.8	22.68
47			55	49.6	75,639.0	3,349.6	22.58
48			57	21.2	77,249.0	3,441.2	22.45
49			58	43.2	78,858.0	3,523.2	22.38
50			59	59	80,467.0	3,599.0	22.36
100		2	48	11.8	160,930.0	10,091.8	15.58
miles	yds.						
50	3	1			80,470.0	3,600.0	22.35
77	440	2			124,322.0	7,200.0	17.27
106	900	3			171,409.0	10,800.0	15.87
137	275	4			220,728.0	14,400.0	15.33
168	910	5			271,198.0	18,000.0	15.07
197	220	6			317,241.0	21,600.0	14.69
199	220	7			320,456.0	25,200.0	12.71
218	440	8			351,230.0	28,800.0	12.20
246	440	9			396,300.0	32,400.0	12.23
265		10			426,480.0	36,000.0	11.84
289		11			465,100.0	39,600.0	11.75
312	880	12			502,920.0	43,200.0	11.64
335	1540	13			540,535.0	46,800.0	11.55
355		14			571,314.0	50,400.0	11.33
372		15			598,670.0	54,000.0	11.09
397	220	16			639,100.0	57,600.0	11.09
403	440	17			649,000.0	61,200.0	10.60
416		18			669,500.0	64,800.0	10.33
432		19			695,200.0	68,400.0	10.16
450	1540	20			725,600.0	72,000.0	10.08
466	660	21			750,600.0	75,600.0	9.928
485	220	22			780,700.0	79,200.0	9.858
507	1320	23			817,100.0	82,800.0	9.870
528	925	24			850,600.0	86,400.0	9.846

uniform at 22.8 m per sec (51 mi per hr), and these appear to have been likewise made at Charles River Park by the same rider on the same day (September 1, 1903). There is very little fall of speed between the 50-mi event and the 2-mi event, or apparently but little fatigue as far as 50 mi.

Beyond 50 mi, however, the speeds fall off and fatigue is indicated.

Figure 14 shows log T plotted against log L, as in preceding cases. The observations fall near to a straight line AB, BC as far as 50 mi. This line makes an angle of 45° with the axis of distances. For the purposes of com-

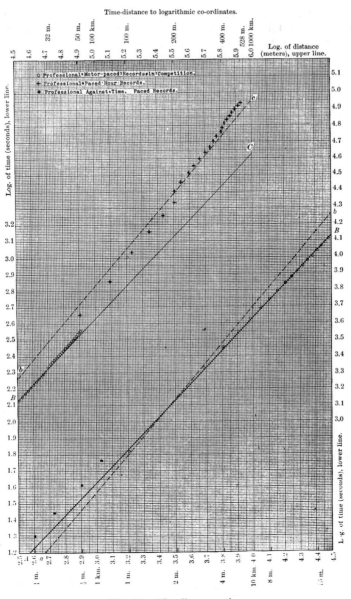

Fig. 14. Bicycling records.

parison a broken line *ab, bc* is drawn through the 2-mi record point at an angle of 48°22′ to correspond with the lines in all of the other figures. The contrast is very noticeable. Beyond 100 mi (160.9 km) the points tend to follow the direction of the broken line, but not with any degree of precision.

The inference to be drawn from Table 10 and Fig. 14 is that we have no means of discovering from these records what the highest speed of a bicycle rider may be. It is inconceivable that there should be no fatigue for 50 or 30 mi. If the record speed over 30 mi be 23.77 m per sec, the speed over 2 mi should be much greater. If the same law of fatigue held for bicycle riders as for runners, walkers, swimmers, and skaters, the speed at 2 mi should be approximately $\sqrt[8]{15}$ or 1.40 times greater; viz., 33.3 m per sec, or 74.4 mi per hr. There is no proof, however, that the same law of fatigue applies, and the air resistance at such high speeds might influence the results. It is, however, evident that the speed at 2 mi, or similar distances, is kept down abnormally to that at 30 mi. The explanation suggests itself that the records are all made on a circular track of considerable lateral inclination. The cyclist, on short runs, perhaps attains the highest speed that he dares and not the highest speed that his muscles could develop. When traveling at 23.75 m per sec (53 mi per hr), careful steering must be needed to keep on the track, and perhaps the records indicate the limit of steering nerve rather than the limits of speed and endurance below 30 or 50 mi. The case is somewhat similar to that of automobiles in this respect. The track records of heavyweight gasoline automobiles, as given in *The World Almanac* for 1906, indicate speeds of 30 m per sec (67 mi per hr) at 1 mi, and hardly any reduction up to 10 mi, or no sensible fatigue within those limits. At 1,000 mi (1,609 km) the speed is 20.35 m per sec (45.5 mi per hr). But on the straightaway courses, as distinguished from track courses, the speed averaged 46.77 m per sec (104.5 mi per hr) at 1 mi, and fell off distinctly with distance at a rate very similar to the fatigue rate of racing animals. Until, therefore, we have a wide straightaway course, say 5 km long, provided for cyclists, of as good quality throughout as is

presented in circular tracks, the cyclist's maximum speed will remain a matter of doubt.

Summary of Results

A summary of the results of the various analyses in regard to accuracy is presented in Table 11. Column I refers to the table considered; column II, the character of the race. The total number of records in each table appears in column III. The range of distances covered is given in column IV, both in miles and in kilometers. The sum total of the percentage deviations, without regard to their sign, as found for each table, including every record, is given in column V. The quotient of the sum in column V, by the number of records in column III, gives the mean percentage deviation for each table in column VI, or the mean difference between the computed record time and the actual record time in percentage of the latter. Reasons have been given in connection with each table why certain records should be left out of consideration. The remainder are discussed in columns VII, VIII, IX, and X. These contain what may be called the net results, while columns III, IV, V, and VI contain the gross results.

In the net results, horses come out the best, and nearly equally well for trotting, running, or pacing, viz., 1.9 per cent mean deviation. The horses come out much better than the men in this comparison. It should be observed, however, that the ranges of distances covered by the horse races are relatively small—20, 6.4, and 4—whereas with men the ranges are successively 1,320, 120, 6, 185, 300—much greater. Perhaps if the ranges covered in the horses' performances had been similar to those covered in the men's performances, the disparity in precision would disappear. In the

TABLE 11

Summary of Deviations

I. Table	II. Racers	III. Total number of Records	IV. Range of Distances Miles	Kilometers	V. Sum total of percentage Deviations without regard to Sign	VI. Average percentage Deviation over entire series of Records	VII. Number of properly acceptable Records	VIII. Range of Distances Miles	Kilometers	IX. Total percentage Deviations	X. Average percentage Deviations
I	Horses trotting	10	1–100	1.61–161	92.9	9.29	7	1.00–20	1.61–32.2	12.9	1.84
II	Horses running	33	$\frac{1}{4}$–4	0.40–6.4	80.3	2.43	28	0.63–4	1.00–6.4	53.1	1.89
III	Horses pacing	6	$\frac{1}{2}$–5	0.80–8.0	32.4	5.40	3	$\frac{1}{2}$–2	0.80–3.2	5.7	1.90
IV	Men running	92	$\frac{1}{80}$–623	0.02–1000	807.1	8.77	69	$2\frac{1}{2}$–60	0.07–96.5	286.3	4.15
V	Men walking	32	1–531	1.60–855	178.8	5.59	25	1.00–120	1.60–193	83.7	3.35
VI	Men rowing	17	$\frac{1}{4}$–6	0.40–9.7	101.5	5.97	15	1.00–6	1.60–9.7	65.5	4.36
VIII	Men swimming	38	$\frac{1}{70}$–2.3	0.02–3.7	133.8	3.52	38	$\frac{1}{70}$–2.3	0.02–3.7	133.8	3.52
IX	Men skating	29	$\frac{1}{35}$–100	0.05–161	384.7	13.26	22	$\frac{1}{3}$–100	0.55–161	165.7	7.53
		257			1811.5	7.05	207			806.7	3.9

men's performances the net average deviation is about 4 per cent, except in skating, where it is 7.5 per cent. The net average deviation of all the 207 records is 3.9 per cent.

Considering the gross results of columns III, IV, V, and VI, the lowest deviation is found in trotting horses (2.43 per cent) followed by men swimming (3.52 per cent). The greatest deviation is in skating (13.26 per cent). The mean deviation of the whole series of 257 records, rejecting none, is 7.05 per cent.

It is submitted that the summary in Table 11 demonstrates the proposition that the records in races of men and of horses approximately follow straight lines when plotted on logarithm paper; because the average percentage deviation of all the records is only 7 per cent from the line, and excluding 50 of the records as unreliable for reasons assigned, this average deviation falls to 4 per cent. The record time that should belong to any given distance within the usual limits, and for any of the events considered, except bicycling,

Fig. 15.   Speed-distance and time-distance lines.

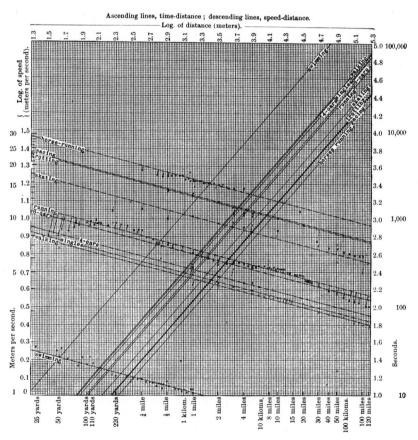

EXPLANATION.   At the right of the figure the numerals 1.0 to 5.0 are logarithms of time (seconds).

can thus be assigned with these probable degrees of accuracy.

It is not so remarkable that the records of any one event, such as men running, should approximately conform to a logarithmic straight line; but it is remarkable that the straight lines should be parallel, or substantially parallel, in all of these eight classes of events, including three gaits in quadrupeds and three gaits in bipeds, besides motion in the water and over ice. Figure 15 collects all of the logarithmic straight lines on one sheet to a reduced scale. The ascending parallel straight lines are time-distance lines. The descending parallel straight lines are speed-distance lines. The mean speeds of the various events in Table 1 to 9 inclusive are plotted with relation to the descending lines in such a manner as to reveal their deviations as clearly as possible.

Deductions from the Results

Starting with the approximate equation

$$T \cong \frac{L^{\frac{9}{8}}}{c} \text{ sec} \qquad (28)$$

as borne out in the preceding discussions of records in eight different kinds of races, where c is a constant for each type of race, it follows that as the length L of the course increases, the time occupied in the race will increase according to Table 12.

Thus, if Eq. (28) is correct, doubling the distance means increasing the time by 118 per cent, and increasing the the distance 60 times increases the time 100 times. Since Eq. (28) is not set up as a rigid law, but as a statistical approximation, or approximative law, we cannot expect to find the relations of Table 12 accurately presented by all the events. For instance, if we limit ourselves to the first statement that twice the distance should be covered in 2.18 times the time, we can examine all the cases of pairs of such events in the records already considered and find what the ratios of time are when the distances are as $2:1$. The answer to this question is contained in Table 13.

TABLE 12

Effect of Increase of Distance Upon Increase in Time

Increase in Distance	Increase in Time	Increase in Distance	Increase in Time
2	2.181	70	119.1
3	3.442	80	138.4
4	4.757	90	158.0
5	6.114	100	177.8
6	7.506	200	387.8
7	8.928	300	770.5
8	10.38	400	845.9
9	11.85	500	1087.0
10	13.33	600	1335.0
20	29.08	700	1588.0
30	45.90	800	1845.0
40	63.43	900	2106.0
50	81.54	1000	2371.0
60	100.1		

TABLE 13

Analysis of Time Ratios Over Pairs of Courses in Ratio of 2:1

Table	Type of Racers	No. of Pairs	Range of Distances covered		Sum of Ratios	Mean Ratio	High-est Ratio	Low-est Ratio
			Miles	Kilometers				
I	Horses trotting	5	1–100	1.61–161	11.092	2.218	2.327	2.098
II	Horses running	19	0.25–4.0	0.4–6.4	40.523	2.133	2.244	2.000
III	Horses pacing	3	0.5–4	0.8–8.0	6.662	2.221	2.374	2.058
IV	Men running	57	0.03–300	0.02–483	123.754	2.171	2.593	1.818
V	Men walking	18	1–500	1.61–805	39.678	2.204	2.375	2.073
VI	Men rowing	8	0.25–6	0.4–9.6	17.950	2.244	2.518	1.981
VIII	Men swimming	23	0.014–2	0.023–3.2	50.337	2.189	2.436	2.016
IX	Men skating	13	0.03–100	0.05–161	27.198	2.092	2.556	1.760
	General average	146	...	...	317.194	2.173	2.593	1.760

Taking, for example, the case of running men with reference to Tables 4 and 13, there are 57 pairs of records in which one distance is just double the other, commencing at 20–40 yd and ending with 150–300 mi. The sums of all the time ratios for these 57 pairs of events is 123.754, representing an average value of 2.171, as against 2.181 required by Table 12 from Eq. (28). The highest ratio in any of these pairs is 2.593, and the lowest 1.818.

It will be seen that men running and men swimming come nearest in their averages to the ratio 2.181; while men skating deviate the most (4 per cent). Taking all the 146 pairs of double distances presented in the entire set of records, and without rejecting any, the average ratio of all is 2.173, which is within 0.4 per cent of the value 2.181 required in Eq. (28). This result constitutes an independent demonstration of the approximate accuracy of that equation. If pairs at short distances affected by starting retardation, or at very long distances, had been rejected, the agreement would have been still closer.

Equation (28) leads to the following:

$$T \cong \frac{c^8}{V^9} \text{ sec} \qquad (29)$$

or the time varies approximately inversely as the ninth power of the speed in the race. If we assume that the racer reaches the winning post virtually exhausted, so far as affects racing effort, then the time of exhaustion varies inversely as the ninth power of the speed. The computed effect of increasing speed is given in Table 14.

Table 14 shows that if a racer increases his speed 10 per cent, he brings down his running time from 100 to 42.4, or 2.36 times; and if he doubles his speed, he becomes exhausted in 0.195 per cent of the original time, or 512 times more quickly.

The records do not show that any one racer would be exhausted 512 times as soon if he doubled his speed, because there is no evidence at hand as to the behavior of any single individual at doubled speeds. If, however, any one racer could be trained to take the record speed at each event in the entire series—that is to say, if a runner could be trained to take every race from the 20-yd dash to the 50-mi run

TABLE 14

Computed Influence of Speed Upon the Time of Exhaustion

Speed	Time	Reciprocal	Speed	Time	Reciprocal
1.0	1.000	1.0	1.5	0.0260	38.4
1.01	0.915	1.09	1.6	0.0146	68.7
1.1	0.424	2.36	1.7	0.00843	119
1.2	0.194	5.16	1.8	0.00504	198
1.3	0.0943	10.6	1.9	0.00310	322
1.4	0.0484	20.7	2.0	0.00195	512

at world's record speeds in each—then this ideal athlete would be exhausted in a time approximately as the inverse ninth power of the speed. It is reasonable to assume that what would be true of this ideal athlete also tends to be true of any normal athlete, even though his range of speeds and distances be limited.

As an example of this rapid rate of exhaustion, take the 29-mi (32.19-km) running event in Table 4. The speed at which this race was run averaged 4.794 m per sec as shown in column IV. At twice this speed or 9.588 m per sec, there is no exact distance in the table; but the nearest is 131.5 yd (120.2 m) at 9.696 m per sec. The time of the 20-mi event was 6,714 sec in column II. The time of the 131.5-yd event was 12.4 sec, or 541 times less, as against 512 times in Table 14.

Again, consider the last event in Table 8 of swimming records. The 4,000-yd (3,657-m) event was finished in 3,824 sec at a speed over the course of 0.9564 m per sec. If we take a speed 1.5 times greater than this, or 1.4346 m per sec, we find one near to it in the table; namely, 1.420 m per sec (column XI) in the 150-yd (137-m) event. According to Table 14, the time of exhaustion at 1.5 times greater speed is 38.4 times less than the original. The time should therefore be 3824 ÷

38.4 = 99.6 sec. The actual time of the event is given as 96.6 sec.

Distance

Equation (28) leads to the following expression for L:

$$L \cong c^{\frac{8}{9}} T^{\frac{8}{9}} \text{ m.} \qquad (30)$$

That is, as more and more time is allowed for racers to occupy in an event, the distances they will travers will not be directly proportional to the time, but will vary as the eighth power of the ninth root of the time, approximately. A few numerical values are given in Table 15.

It is thus indicated that with 500 times more time, the distance covered will be only 251 times greater. As an example, we may take the 4-mi (6.44-km) walking event of Table 5. It occupied 1,658 seconds. If we increase the time 20 times, or to 33,160 sec, we should expect from Table 15 that the distance covered would be 57.2 mi (92 km). The nearest event to this in Table 5 is the 60-mi (96.6-km), occupying 34,847 sec or 21 times the original time, which is a satisfactory agreement.

Another consequence of Eq. (28) is expressed:

$$L \cong \frac{c^8}{V^8} \text{ m} \qquad (31)$$

TABLE 15

Distances Traversed with Increasing Racing Time

Time	Distance	Time	Distance
1	1	20	14.3
2	1.85	50	32.4
3	2.66	100	60.0
4	3.43	200	111.0
5	4.18	500	251.0
10	7.74	1000	464.0

or the distance covered in a race varies approximately as the inverse eight power of the speed adopted. That is, if an athlete could be trained to take any distance from the shortest to the longest at the record speed for the event; then the distance which this athlete would be able to run before being exhausted would be as the inverse eighth power of his speed over the course. A few numerical values are given in Table 16.

The table shows that if the speed is doubled, the distance that can be run, before exhaustion, is reduced 256 times according to (31).

As an instance, the 20-mi (32.19-km) running event of Table 4, already referred to, may be selected. The speed over the course was 4.794 m per sec. At 9.588 m per sec the distance should be $\frac{20}{256} = 0.0781$ mi $= 125.7$ m. Table 4 shows that at 9.696 m per sec, the

nearest to the required speed, the distance run was 131.5 yd, or 120.2 m.

Speed

Equation (28) leads to the expression for speed:

$$V \cong cL^{-\frac{1}{8}} \cong \frac{c}{L^{\frac{1}{8}}} \text{ m per sec} \quad (32)$$

already illustrated in formulas (3), (7), (11), (15), and (19). It means that the speed of racing over courses of different lengths varies inversely as the eighth root of the length, approximately. Table 17 gives a few numerical applications of this rule. According to these results the speed has to be reduced 1.33 times to race 10 times the distance, and 1.78 times to race 100 times the distance. Thus, taking the 100.6-m event (110 yd) in Table 4, the speed over the course is

TABLE 16

Distances Capable of Being Traversed as the Speed Is Increased

Speed, V	Distance, V^{-8}	Reciprocal, V^8	Speed, V	Distance, V^{-8}	Reciprocal, V^8
1.0	1.	1.	1.5	0.0390	25.6
1.01	0.923	1.08	1.6	0.0233	43.0
1.1	0.467	2.14	1.7	0.0143	69.8
1.2	0.233	4.30	1.8	0.00907	110.0
1.3	0.123	8.16	1.9	0.00589	170.0
1.4	0.0678	14.8	2.0	0.00391	256.0

TABLE 17

Effect of Increasing Distances Upon the Speed Over the Course

Distance, L	Speed, $L^{-\frac{1}{8}}$	Reciprocal, $L^{\frac{1}{8}}$	Distance, L	Speed, $L^{-\frac{1}{8}}$	Reciprocal, $L^{\frac{1}{8}}$
1	1.	1.	100	0.562	1.78
2	0.917	1.09	200	0.516	1.94
3	0.872	1.15	300	0.490	2.04
4	0.840	1.19	400	0.473	2.12
5	0.815	1.22	500	0.460	2.17
6	0.799	1.25	600	0.449	2.23
7	0.784	1.28	700	0.441	2.27
8	0.771	1.30	800	0.433	2.31
9	0.760	1.32	900	0.427	2.34
10	0.750	1.33	1000	0.422	2.37
20	0.688	1.45	2000	0.387	2.59
30	0.654	1.53	3000	0.368	2.72
40	0.631	1.59	4000	0.355	2.82
50	0.613	1.63	5000	0.345	2.90
60	0.599	1.67	6000	0.337	2.97
70	0.588	1.70	7000	0.331	3.02
80	0.578	1.73	8000	0.325	3.08
90	0.570	1.75	9000	0.320	3.12

9.144 m per sec. At 96.56 km (60 mi), nearly 1,000 times greater distance, the speed has fallen to 3.572 m per sec, or to 39.1 per cent of the former. According to Table 17, the speed should fall to 42.2 per cent on increasing the distance thousandfold.

Another consequence of formula (28) is expressed thus:

$$V \cong c^{\frac{8}{9}} T^{-\frac{1}{9}} \cong \frac{c^{\frac{8}{9}}}{T^{\frac{1}{9}}} \text{ m per sec} \qquad (33)$$

or the speed over the course approximately varies inversely as the ninth root of the racing time.

In Table 18 the speeds of the various racers are set down as computed for courses of 1 km and of 1 mi. Thus over 1-km courses the speed of the running horse is 17.88 m per sec (column VI), and the time for the race 55.9 sec. At the end of the series come swimmers, with a speed of 1.108 m per sec and an inferred kilometer-time of 902.4 sec.

Table 8 shows that the time for 1.006 km was 925.4 sec. Turning to the mile range, the speed of the running horse is 37.7 mi per hr over the 1-mi range. His mile-time is 95.5 sec, both computed and recorded. The speed of the swimmer is 2.336 mi per hr, and the mile-time 1,544 sec as computed, and 1,476.2 sec as observed. The speed of a running man is almost precisely half that of the trotting horse, for distances above 1 km where starting retardation ceases to affect the horse. The speed of a professional walker is very nearly the speed of a professional rower (singles).

It is to be noted that all these speeds are average speeds over the courses. There is no evidence among the records to show what the speed was at different points in the course. So far as concerns anything appearing in the data, the speed of a runner, for example, which averages 7.17 m per sec over a 1-km course, might be 10 m

TABLE 18

Speeds Over Courses at 1-Kilometer and 1-Mile Distances

I. Table	II. Racers	III. log c	IV. c	V. Speed at 1 Kilometer	VI.	VII. Computed Time for 1 Kilometer, seconds	VIII. Speed at 1 Mile	IX.	X.	XI. Computed Time for 1 Mile, seconds	XII. Record Time for 1 Mile, seconds
				log	meters/seconds		log	meters/seconds	miles/hours		
II	Horses running	1.6274	42.4	1.2524	17.88	55.9	1.2266	16.85	37.70	95.5	95.5
III	Horses pacing	1.5363	34.38	1.1613	14.50	68.98	1.1355	13.66	30.56	117.8	115.25
I	Horses trotting	1.53	33.9	1.155	14.29	70.0	1.129	13.46	30.13	119.5	118.5
IX	Men skating	1.4143	25.96	1.0393	10.95	91.35	1.0135	10.31	23.08	156.0	156.0
IV	Men running	1.2307	17.01	0.8557	7.173	139.4	0.8299	6.759	15.12	238.1	252.75
VI	Men 8-oars ⎫ rowing	1.202	15.92	0.827	6.714	148.9	0.8012	6.327	14.15	254.3	304.75
VI	Men 4-oars ⎬	1.1145	13.02	0.7395	5.489	182.2	0.7137	5.173	11.57	311.1	291.0
VI	Men singles ⎭	1.085	12.16	0.710	5.129	195.0	0.6842	4.833	10.81	333.0	301.0
V	Men walking	1.0646	11.6	0.6896	4.893	204.4	0.6638	4.611	10.32	349.0	383.0
VIII	Men swimming	0.4196	2.628	0.0446	1.108	902.4	0.0188	1.044	2.336	1544.0	1476.2

per sec in the first part and 5 in the last part, or vice versa. Evidence is lacking to show what the facts are, and they are of great importance to the science of athletics. The speed of a world's-record type of trained runner might be determined at any or all points of a course, either by securing a light recording chronograph on the back of his belt, with a thread payed out as he ran, or by pacing the runner with a light motorcar carrying an automatic speed recorder, or by noting on a chronograph the times of the runner's passage past a suitable number of fixed points along the track.

Although nothing can be stated directly from the data in this paper as to the degree of uniformity or of variation in the speed of a record-making trained racer, yet if it is proper to apply the inference drawn from a long series of complete races to the speed conditions during the operations of any one taken singly, then it should follow that the speed of a record-maker is very nearly uniform throughout the whole course. If, as appears from the whole series, the time of exhaustion varies inversely as the ninth power of the velocity, and this condition applies within the limits of any single race, then it is easily seen that the quickest way to reach the winning post is to take at the outset that speed which will just produce exhaustion at the goal, and keep to that speed throughout the course. The penalty for raising the speed at any part would be a degree of untimely exhaustion far outweighing the benefit gained. Trainers commonly direct practicing athletes to spurt, or accelerate, near the end of the run. This advice must be sound on any theory, because to slacken speed at the end, if there is any balance of running energy left, would be absurd. The runner naturally expends all the available energy balance on the last

lap; but if he is able to accelerate to any appreciable extent, it must mean that he has kept too much energy in reserve, and he would have done better to adopt a higher general speed. If, on the contrary, his pace falls to any appreciable extent at the end, he would have economized time by maintaining a lower general speed. Experimental evidence to test this theory would be of great interest. If the theory is correct, athletes, in training for a given event, ought to be motor-paced, the speed of the pacing motor being set uniform. In the earlier practice, this motor speed should be, say, 15 per cent less than the desired record speed, and the athlete should train to keep close to the motor. As the training progressed, the uniform speed of the motor over the course should be raised, say, 1 per cent at a time. Of course these suggestions advance beyond the warrant of evidence at this time.

Conclusions

An analysis of the various national and international appended racing records, as detailed above, leads to the following conclusions, for trotting, pacing, and running horses, as well as for running, walking, rowing, skating, and swimming men:

(a) The time varies approximately as the ninth power of the eighth root of the distance. Doubling the distance means increasing the time 118 per cent (Table 13).

(b) The time occupied in a record-making race varies approximately inversely as the ninth power of the speed over the course. Doubling the speed cuts down the racing time 512 times (Table 14).

(c) The distance covered increases approximately as the eighth power of the ninth root of the time. Doubling the time of the race allows of increasing the course length by 85 per cent (Table 15).

(d) The distance covered increases approximately as the inverse eighth power of the speed over the course. .Doubling the speed cuts down the distance that can be covered 256 times (Table 16).

(e) The speed over the course varies approximately as the inverse eighth root of the distance. Doubling the distance brings down the speed about 8.3 per cent (Table 17).

(f) The speed over the course varies approximately as the inverse ninth root of the racing time.

It may be noted that all of the statements (a) to (f) are different aspects of one and the same fact.

(g) If any of the three quantities L, T, and $V = L/T$ be plotted on logarithm paper as ordinates to either of the other quantities as abscissas, the record points will fall on, or near to, a straight line (Figs. 2, 3, 6, 7, 8, 10, 11, 12, 13, and 15).

(h) Athletes aspiring to break racing records might succeed better in attacking those whose points fall below the straight lines of speed against distance, or above the straight lines of time against distance, rather than those whose points fall on the opposite sides of those lines.

(i) The records presented on bicycling do not determine the proper highest speed of cycling below 30 mi (48 km), since there is apparently no reduction in speed by fatigue up to that distance.

(j) With the exception of bicycling, as noted above, the law of fatigue in racing is the same, or very nearly the same, with horses as with men, in air or in water, as indicated by the records analyzed in this paper.

D. A. SARGENT

The Physical Test of a Man

Reprinted from the *American Physical Education Review*,
26 (1921), pp. 188–94.

During the late nineteenth century and the early twentieth century the results accrued from the various physical training programs of the time were assessed by taking a large number of body measurements. Anthropometry was a significant element of the program advocated by the leaders of that epoch, such as Hitchcock, Sargent, and Seaver. Measuring techniques were standardized and charts published giving dimensions for the typical man and woman. The correlation between static measurements and performance were thought to be strong enough to warrant this practice. However, in the beginning of the twentieth century questions were raised concerning the efficacy of such an assumption. Sargent's paper represents one of the early attempts to measure the capacity of man by using

a performance test in combination with static measures.[1] The "Sargent Jump,"
or a slight modification of it, is still used today as a test item in several physical
fitness batteries.

Sargent's test was not an attempt to predict ultimate levels of performance but
rather to estimate man's present "functional capacity." By present-day standards
it is a gross oversimplification despite his words, "It is so simple and so effective
. . ." However, the linking of performers with physical characteristics of the body
has become common. The paper by Lookabough, and that by Sills and Mitchem
exemplify this tendency.

One of the strongest of the natural forces with which man is constantly contending is gravity, or the tendency of his body to be attracted and held to the surface of the earth. The infant first crawls, then creeps on its hands and knees, and finally by the aid of crib or chair or mother's assistance, gets onto his feet. The raising of the head, the straightening of the spine, grasping with the hands and feet, and striking out and kicking with the arms and legs are only preliminary movements necessary to prepare for the standing position. All the twisting, rolling, wriggling, squirming, crawling, creeping, and occasional stiffening and straightening of the trunk and limbs an infant can be induced to do, the better it will be for his future development.

A child must first get a footing in the world and be able to move in the erect position before the adult may properly function as a human being. In other words, the child must pass in a few months from the animal stage of its existence where all its organic inheritances for thousands of years had fitted its body to resist the force of gravity in a horizontal plane, to a vertical position where gravity acts in a perpendicular plane. Is it any wonder that over 75 per cent of our youth of both sexes have a bad posture, and that so few ever attain the ability to meet this comparatively new strain—the ability to sit and stand erect?

If there is any doubt as to the seriousness of failing to measure up to this test of young manhood, ask your physician as to the fundamental causes of the following list of physical imperfections: spinal curvature, knock-knees, bowlegs, flat feet, drooping head, round shoulders, weak backs, varicose veins, hernia, sagging of the abdominal organs, misplacement of the pelvic organs, and many other physical weaknesses and defects which afflict mankind.

These prevailing weaknesses are mainly due to the failure of the body to make provision to resist this constant force of gravity to pull us down from our toplofty, vertical position to a horizontal plane. We pay our respect to this natural force by availing ourselves of every opportunity to lean, sit, and recline at our work throughout the day, and we finally yield to it completely by assuming a horizontal position for sleep at night.

Many of these bodily weaknesses and imperfections to which I have referred have arisen largely from civilized man's neglect to care for the form and strength of his bodily mechanism as an African Zulu or Sandwich Islander would do. Instead of priding himself upon his ability to sit straight without support

---

[1] Yet Sargent was a leading exponent of anthropometry.

for his spine and legs, as shown by many of the savage tribesmen, civilized man luxuriates in upholstered chairs and lounges molded to his physical defects—and then wonders why he has a weak back and can not stand in a vertical position.

Yet the ability to stand erect, thereby relieving the arms and hands from supporting the body, and conserving their strength to be directed into self-chosen activities constitutes man's supreme inheritance.

How is this ability attained? By gradually strengthening and developing the muscles all up and down the front and back of the trunk and legs. These muscles hold the body balanced in perfect equilibrium over the two feet, which, in length and breadth taken together, average about one-sixth the perpendicular height. When the body is thus accurately balanced on the bones of the legs and spine, gravity is acting parallel with these bones, and consequently the strain is taken largely from the muscles and thrown onto the bones and ligaments.

If one relaxes from this vertical position, and stands with the body flexed or bent forward at the knees, hips, back, and neck, the strain is then brought upon the muscles and after a little while the effort of standing becomes intolerable. But strain or pain means loss of power and energy. This is the reason why a perfect poise in standing or sitting is the most economical position that can be maintained.

Although the ability of a man to stand on his feet and maintain perfect poise is of vital importance, it is not the only requisite. He has other things to do. During the growing period of youth, while one is acquiring his stature, gravity should be used so as to stimulate the growth force, not to retard it, as is often done by keeping children too long on their feet either in working or playing. It is better to continually fall and try to rise again than to remain standing too long.

A young man having acquired full stature, and learned to stand and sit correctly in defiance of the laws of gravity, must generate still more force and let gravity act in harmony with his physiological necessities and his mental and physical desires. In other words, he must add to his weight as well as his height before he can cut any figure in the world, bear his own burdens, fight his own battles, and render service to others. This means that he must extend his growth force and developmental energies into body breadths, depths, and thicknesses as determined by given measurements, as well as into lengths or vertical directions. The only way of adding effective weight is through the development of the muscles, which constitute nearly 50 per cent of all the tissues of the normal man, and determine to a large extent the size and function of the other organs. By this use of the term "muscle," I do not refer to the large superficial voluntary muscles only, but to the muscles of digestion, circulation, respiration, glandular organs, special senses, etc. The only way that any muscle tissue may be developed is through the activities; and our responsibility for the proper training, nutrition, and consequent development of this part of our anatomy is great indeed.

The primary object of all the efforts of physical education through athletic games, sports, plays, and general gymnastics, is to add to the power and efficiency of mind and body through the agency of the muscular system. This efficiency is determined largely, I shall hope to show, through the intimate relation of body height and weight. These two factors are always taken into consideration in publishing the names of players on the great football teams, boat crews, and in other athletic organizations. Why? Simply because in a vague way, there is thought to be a correlation between the height and weight and a man's physical efficiency. Up to the normal limit, a man's strength is supposed to increase with his height and weight. Men are matched in boxing, wrestling, and tug-of-war contests according to their weights, such as lightweights, 135 lb, middleweights, 160 lb, heavyweights, 175 lb, etc. In boxing and wrestling, at least, this weight classification is further refined by having a bantamweight class of 115, a featherweight class of 125, a welterweight class of 145, and a heavyweight class for all men over 175 lb.

No team, crew, or individual contestants would be considered well-matched if they had to give or accept much difference in weight from their opponents. So we find in studying the characteristics of different types of athletes and gymnasts that variations in stature or total height, sitting height, height of knee, and relative length of trunk and limbs, tend to favor different classes of athletic performers. As a rule, the oarsman is favored by having a long body and relatively short legs; the middle-distance runner, jumper, and hurdler by having long legs and a relatively short body; the gymnasts by having short arms; and the heavy lifter by having short thighs. And so through the whole range of athletic specialists, each gains some mechanical advantage from the development that is peculiar to him.

Woman's incapacity for certain kinds of physical activities as compared with man's arises largely from the fact that she is on the average 24 lb lighter and 5 in. shorter than he is. The whole Japanese race averages only 5 ft 4 in. in stature, due largely to their relatively short legs that have undoubtedly been made so by their long-continued racial habit of sitting on their heels with their legs sharply bent under them. These facts and many more have come to us through our studies in anthropometry and the classification of physical measurements.

Age, sex, and race are rightly considered the dominant factors in evaluating any body measurements, and the height, weight, and chest girth are admittedly the most important of these measurements. Moreover, there is a probable standard of height, weight, and chest girth for every age, each sex, and all the different races. These facts are known in a general way by those whose business it is to make physical examinations, such as surgeons in the army and navy, life insurance examiners, and physicians who examine school and college students, candidates for civil service, and employees in all the different trades and industries where physical conditions are now being taken into consideration.

So, in theory at least, it may be well said in support of the relationship of bodily measurements and vital functions "that the greater advance we may make in inquiries of this nature, the more perfectly is the law of proportion that governs the typical man demonstrated; rendering it equally apparent how undue or imperfect development of any one organ or function throws the remaining organism out of gear, and constitutes a greater or less tendency to disease."

In popular estimation it takes so many inches and so many pounds and a certain size chest girth to make a man, and this estimation is borne out largely by experience. Hence, the universal interest in the physical measurements of the human body. However, those of us who are engaged in making physical measurements of men by the thousand soon learn the limitations of the information which comes to us from this source alone. While it is true that the strength and functional capacity of a part generally increases with the size of that part, other things being equal, the number of cases where other things are not equal is so numerous that the generalization should be greatly modified.

The measurements alone do not tell us anything of the texture and quality of the parts covered, i.e., how much is fat or bone, and how much muscle, nor do the measurements alone give us any information of innervation of the parts, upon which power and efficiency so frequently depend. Even if we accept the physical measurements of a man as an indication of his potential power, as so many of us almost intuitively do, we are soon taught by experience that there is in many men an unknown equation which makes for power and efficiency which has never been determined and which can only be measured by an actual test.

The important question is, what is this unknown equation and how can it be simply and practically tested and numerically expressed? With a good many others, I have been wrestling with this problem for years by the way of strength tests, endurance tests, speed tests, etc., but have never come across any one that satisfied me or quite met the demands of the situation. It is said that every pioneer or inventor or discoverer, if he lives long enough, goes through three stages in his career. The first one is where his propositions are unfounded and absurd; the second stage is where if proven true, they are not original; and the third stage is where they are so self-evident that any fool ought to have thought of them. I have now arrived at the third stage in my career, and want to share what seems to me the simplest and most

effective of all tests of physical ability with the other fools who have been looking for one. I have dwelt at some length upon gravity as a constant force to be overcome and its relation to the height and weight and other measurements of the body. The new test that I offer consists of using the constant factors of height and weight which one always has with him, in a little different way than is commonly thought of. It is so simple and yet so effective for testing the strongest man or weakest woman or child that one feels almost like apologizing to the general public for mentioning it.

The New Test

The individual to be tested stands under a cardboard disk, or paper box cover, heavy and stiff enough to hold its form, about 12 in. in dimeter, held or suspended from 10 to 20 or more in. above his head. He is then requested to bend forward, flexing the trunk, knees, and ankles, and then by a powerful jump upward, straightening the legs and spine, to try to touch the cardboard disk with the top of the head. Swinging the bent arms forward and upward at the time the legs, back, and neck are extended, will be found to add to the height of the jump. When the disk has been placed at the highest point above the head that can be just touched in jumping, this height is measured. The difference between this height and that of the total stature is of course the height actually jumped.

Now, if this height is multiplied into the total weight of the body at the time of making the jump, it will give one some idea of the amount of work done in foot-pounds as usually calculated. But it will be observed, no credit is given for lifting the full weight of the body from the deep knee or squatting position to the perpendicular standing position, which difference represents about half the height. The total work depends upon how heavy and how tall the individual is. Thus, if a man weighs 150 lb and is 70 in. tall, one-half of that height would be 35 in., which, multiplied into the full weight and divided by 12 (to reduce inches to feet) would equal 437 ft-lb, thus:

Formula $A =$

$$\frac{\text{weight} \times \text{half the height}}{12} = 437 \text{ ft-lb.}$$

In estimating work done outside of the body, this amount of energy expended is not always taken into consideration as power expended. In the new test, however, an individual must not only do a certain amount of work in physical effort in rising from the crouching attitude to the perpendicular position, but he must generate force enough to project his body 10, 20, or 30 in. into the air, above the height attained in the standing position. If this person weighing 150 lb should jump 20 in. above his height, this weight multiplied by 20 and divided by 12 would equal 250 ft-lb, thus:

Formula $B =$

$$\frac{\text{weight} \times \text{height jumped}}{12} = 250 \text{ ft-lb.}$$

This amount of work done would be acceptable according to the usual methods of estimating human power. Both the A and B formulæ are frequently used for tests of the physical basis of efficiency. The height jumped will depend a good deal upon the length of the legs and trunk that make up the total stature, the tall man being favored—therefore an exact ratio of the height jumped to the stature would seem to make the test more equitable. Thus, if the man weighing 150 lb. was 70 in. tall and jumped 20 in. above his head, the ratio of 20 to 70 would account for this advantage in height. This ratio may be obtained by

the following formula:

Formula $C =$

$$\frac{\text{height jumped} \times 100}{\text{total height}} = 28.5$$

Although the formulæ A, B, and C are interesting in enabling one to account for his efficiency or deficiency in the test, these formulæ may be dispensed with in favor of one including the three important factors which we are considering. If then, in the new test we multiply the total weight by the height jumped and divide this product by the total height of the person in inches the result will give a fair index of the effort made in the smallest number of figures. This is always an advantage in making a test and handling the data for statistical purposes.

Thus if the individual tested weighed 150 lb and jumped 20 in. above his head and was 70 in. tall, the formula for his efficiency index would be as follows:

Index $=$

$$\frac{\text{weight} \times \text{jump}}{\text{height or stature}} = \frac{150 \times 20}{70} = 42.8.$$

As an example of the way this formula works out in practice, I have selected the first ten pupils graded according to this test from the Sargent School of some four hundred pupils. It must be borne in mind that none of the girls had any preliminary practice for this particular test, other than that which comes to them in their regular school work. With the freshmen at least it was largely a question of natural ability (see Table 1).

No. 1 is a vigorous athletic girl, being 67.5 in. in height and 152 lb in weight. She jumps 20 in. above her head which is 0.300 of her height, does 253 ft-lb of work (as shown by multiplying her weight by the height jumped and dividing that product by 12), and has an energy index of 45.

No. 2 has an energy index of 43.2.

TABLE 1

First Ten Out of Four Hundred Tested at the Sargent School of Physical Education, Cambridge, Mass.

	Class	Age	Jump Inches	Height Inches	Ratio Jump to Height	Weight lb	Foot-Pounds of Work	Index
1. L. V. M.	Jun.	20	20	67.5	0.300	152	253	45.0
2. M. M. G.	Sen.	20	20	61	0.328	132	220	43.2
3. M. E. W.	Sen.	20	20.5	65.5	0.312	132	226	41.3
4. M. J. O.	Jun.	20	18.8	60.2	0.312	132	217	41.0
5. H. W.	Sen.	22	15.3	64.2	0.238	176	224	40.5
6. M. E. F.	Fresh.	19	16.9	60.6	0.260	145	204	40.5
7. J. I. J.	Fresh.	23	14	68	0.206	196	240	40.3
8. E. M. B.	Sen.	23	20.5	61.5	0.333	117.5	200	39.1
9. H. A. B.	Fresh.	23	16	68	0.236	163	217	38.2
10. B. S.	Fresh.	18	17.5	64.5	0.271	146	213	38.0
Average		20.5	17.9	64	0.279	148	221	40.95

Although she is shorter and lighter than some of her mates and does less foot-pounds of work than four others in the group, she lifts her weight higher in proportion to her height, and therefore gets a high score. She is an earnest student and a good all-around athlete, but not a star.

No. 3 is the star athlete of her class, excelling especially in running and jumping. In this test she jumps 20.5 in. above her height, but she is 4.5 in. taller than No. 2 and does not lift her weight as high in proportion to her height.

No. 4 although of the same weight as Nos. 2 and 3, and jumping the same proportion of her height as the girl above her, does not jump as high and therefore gets a little lower index.

No. 5 jumps nearly 5 in. less than those who have preceded her, but she is a strong husky girl weighing 176 lb and to raise this weight a less height requires a high index.

No. 6 has the same index as No. 5, although she is 3.6 in. shorter and weighs 31 lb less. She makes up for this difference in weight and height by jumping an inch and a half higher, and jumping a greater per cent of her height.

No. 7 is the heaviest girl in the school, weighing 196 lb, and is 68 in. in height. As might be expected she jumps the least height of any in the group, and the least percentage of her own height. But she projects 196 lb 14 in. above her head and thereby does 240 ft-lb of work, which makes her the second strongest one on the list.

No. 8, although she lacks the mechanical advantage in height that a girl of 67 or 68 in. would possess, and has the least advantage in weight of any in the group, still manages to project her 117.5 lb 20.5 in. above her head, which is the highest ratio of her own height of any in the group (0.333). This girl is quite strong for her height and weight and very energetic—she also has the distinction of being the highest ranking scholar in her class. The records of Nos. 9 and 10 are self-explanatory. They are girls of fine natural physiques, good athletes, superior to the average in height and weight, and will show a much higher index after a little more training.

I have commented upon the variations in physique as shown by the height and weight in these seven individuals, because these variations illustrate the compensating nature of the test. With a variation of 7.4 in. in height and 78.5 lb in weight, there is little difference in their physical ability as shown by the test, as all were able to make the first ten in the school. What one lacks in height and length of limb, she makes up in strength, speed, and energy; what another lacks in weight she makes up in height and energy; what still another one lacks in energy and speed she makes up in superior height, strength, and weight; while still another who lacks both in height and weight has to make up for this deficiency by greater determination, will power, nerve force, or some other unknown quality, that makes for physical efficiency. If any one of the factors chosen for the formula had been adopted as a standard, it would have brought a little different type of girl to the front. This is shown in Table 2.

It will be observed by referring to Table 2, that, if the height of the jump had been the only factor considered, M. E. W. and E. M. B. would have come to the front as 1 and 2; or if height and weight had been the prime

factors, J.I.J., who was 10 in the jump, would have been put in the first place. If the height jumped in proportion to her own height had been accepted as the final test, E. M. B. would have reached first place, though she ranked 10 in weight and strength. Then again, if foot-pounds of work done, as usually calculated, had been adopted as the standard, J. I. J. would have come up from tenth place in height really jumped and ratio of height jumped to second place. The foot-pound formula is perhaps the best test for real strength and gives the taller and heavier girls a decided advantage.

It must be admitted, however, that the three girls who come the nearest to the front in all the factors that make up the test are those that stand 1, 2, and 3, according to the index adopted. What this index as thus obtained really indicates is a question that may well engage our attention.

First, no one would deny that the ability to project one's weight 20 or 30 in. into the air, against the force of gravity requires *strength* on the part of the muscles engaged in the effort. No one would deny that the effort would have to be made with a certain degree of velocity or *speed* in order to create

TABLE 2

Relative Standing of First Ten According to Other Factors as Jump, Height, Weight, etc.

Index	Jump	Height	Ratio of Jump to Height	Weight	Foot-Pounds
1. L. V. M.	1. M. E. W.	1. J. I. J.	1. E. M. B.	1. J. I. J.	1. L. V. M.
2. M. M. G.	2. E. M. B.	2. H. A. B.	2. M. M. G.	2. H. W.	2. J. I. J.
3. M. E. W.	3. L. V. M.	3. L. V. M.	3. M. E. W.	3. H. A. B.	3. M. E. W.
4. M. J. O.	4. M. M. G.	4. M. E. W.	4. M. J. O.	4. L. V. M.	4. H. W.
5. H. W.	5. M. J. O.	5. B. S.	5. L. V. M.	5. B. S.	5. M. M. G.
6. M. E. F.	6. B. S.	6. H. W.	6. B. S.	6. M. E. F.	6. M. J. O.
7. J. I. J.	7. M. E. F.	7. E. M. B.	7. M. E. F.	7. M. M. G.	7. H. A. B.
8. E. M. B.	8. H. A. B.	8. M. M. G.	8. H. W.	8. M. E. W.	8. B. S.
9. H. A. B.	9. H. W.	9. M. E. F.	9. H. A. B.	9. M. J. O.	9. M. E. F.
10. B. S.	10. J. I. J.	10. M. J. O.	10. J. I. J.	10. E. M. B.	10. E. M. B.

impetus enough to carry the body 20 in. above its own level in the standing position. Further, no one would deny that back of the requisite strength of muscle fibers and rapidity with which they are made to contract there must be *energy*, "pep," "vim," vitality, or whatever it may be termed which drives our internal machinery. Overlapping all, of course, is the skill or dexterity with which the jump is executed.

I think, therefore, that the test as a whole may be considered as a momentary tryout of one's strength, speed, energy, and dexterity combined, which, in my opinion, furnishes a fair physical test of a man, and solves in a simple way his unknown equation as determined potentially by his height and weight. It will be observed that the parts tested, namely, the muscles of the feet, calves, thighs, buttocks, back, neck, anterior deltoid, chest, and biceps are the muscles most used in all forms of athletics, sports, track and field games, setting up exercises, posture drills, etc., and are of fundamental importance in all the active industries.

For this reason, I think it should precede any other all-around physical test in basic value.

In presenting this paper for discussion, I have intentionally narrowed myself down to a consideration of the factors involved in making the test, omitting the experience that has led up to it, and the application that may be made of it, and the method of conducting it.

To those who wish to try the experiment, I would suggest that the jump be made in gymnasium slippers or at least in shoes with low heels, and as the factors, weight, height, and height jumped are to be multiplied and divided in the calculation, that all the measurements be made with the greatest accuracy.

If the test is of any value, then the standardization of it, and the collection of different data concerning it will, of course, be of the greatest importance, and follow naturally for the benefit of those who want to make use of it.

G. LOOKABOUGH

The Prediction of Total Potential Strength of Adult Males from Skeletal Build

Reprinted from the *Research Quarterly*, **8** (1937), pp. 103–08.

This paper further illustrates attempts to link body measurements with physical performance, in this case strength. Although physical educators of Sargent's time and before had an elaborate system of anthropometry, there were few attempts to develop predictive equations using some combination of static measures. Lookabough has considered a variety of body-build measures and studied their relation to "*total strength.*" *Although some of his procedures would be questioned today, it is interesting to note his use of partial correlation and multiple regression techniques to develop predictive equations, a method still in common use.*

Introduction

The purpose of this study is to predict total potential strength of adult males from skeletal build. "Total potential strength" is not interpreted as the "absolute total" strength that one is capable of developing, but rather the total strength that would be athletically useful to the individual. This problem might be stated: *The prediction of total potential athletically useful strength of adult males from skeletal build.*

Method of Procedure

An attempt was made to get subjects who were almost as strong as they were likely ever to become. Most of them were athletes competing in sports that would tend to develop strength to a high degree in all parts of the body. Sixty such males of college age were used as subjects in this study. Many of these athletes had won national championships in sports.

All of the measurements of strength and build were made by standard anthropometric methods. Corrections for fat were made by methods used in the Iowa Child Welfare Research Station. Each subject was measured by the entire battery of strength and build tests on one day and this was repeated at a later date. The following measurements were used in computing the total strength: right grip, left grip, chest push, chest pull, thigh flexors, back lift, leg lift, chins, and dips. Chins and dips were converted into pounds by the McCloy method.[1]

In testing each subject, the best marks made in each test item, at either testing period, were added and used as the total strength for that subject. The measurements used to determine skeletal build were: weight, sitting height, standing height, arm span, shoulder width, chest width, chest depth, hip width (bi-iliac), elbow width, knee width, and chest circumference. Fat measurements were taken to be used in correcting for fat, in the hip-width and chest-circumference measurements. The average of the two measurements of each build item was used as the final measurement of that part when corrections for fat had been made. The weight of each individual was then predicted from the measurements of his standing height, chest circumference, hip width, knee width, and elbow width. This was done by a formula used in the Iowa Child Welfare Research Station.

Statistical Methods

Intercorrelations of the thirteen variables of strength and build were made. They were numbered as follows: 0, strength; 1, weight; 2, weight predicted; 3, sitting height; 4, standing height; 5, arm span; 6, shoulder width; 7, chest width; 8, chest depth; 9, hip width; 10, elbow width; 11, knee width; and 12, chest circumference. Partial correlations were then used to determine the relative strength predicting values of the variables. The results obtained were:

$$_r01.2 = 0.0542$$
$$_r03.11 = 0.0163$$
$$_r04.11 = -0.0290$$
$$_r05.2 = 0.0699$$

$_r06.2(12) = 0.0721$
$_r06.2 = -0.0979$
$_r07.(12) = 0.0027$
$_r08.(12) = 0.0863$
$_r09.(11) = 0.0912$
$_r09.2 = 0.0752$
$_r0(11).2 = -0.0605$
$_r02.(11)(12) = 0.3827$
$_r0(12).2 = 0.1600$

Multiple correlations were next tried giving the following results:

$R0.(12)(10)(11)2 = 0.6220$
$R0.(12)(10)(11)94 = 0.6200$
$R0.(12)(10)(11) = 0.6138$

This showed that chest circumference, elbow width, and knee width gave almost the same correlation with strength as any combination of build in this group of variables.

The regression equation for this group was then computed by standard statistical methods and the strength was predicted for each of the sixty subjects by this formula:

Total strength = 23.82 chest circumference + 210.5 elbow width + 102.24 knee width − 2277   (1)

Raising the Line of Regression

A judgment rating of each of the 60 subjects was made by the author, who had carefully studied each individual during the time the measurements were being taken. They were rated in three groups: 0 ratings were given those the author judged to be about as strong as they were likely to become. Those capable of bringing their total strength up by an appreciable amount were rated 1, and those capable of increasing their strength quite a bit more were rated 2.

A scattergram of the two variables— strength obtained by testing and strength predicted by Formula (1)— was drawn, and the judgment ratings of the subjects were placed in the appropriate squares. The correlation

between these two variables was 0.6370. The regression line "A" for predicting total strength from the regression values of these variables was then computed and drawn on the scattergram. This line represents the average strength for each "build category" for the 60 subjects.

A study of the scattergram shows that all but two of the subjects that had been rated 0 are above the mean line and all but two of the subjects rated 2 fell below the mean, while those rated 1 were about equally divided above and below.

According to the subjective judgment of the author, all but two of those who scored below the mean line were capable of such development as would bring their scores up to or above this line of regression. Since the purpose of this study was to predict total potential strength, it seemed desirable to raise the regression line to the place it would be if all of the subjects had been thoroughly developed when tested. It was, therefore, raised by approximately twice the standard error of estimate. This was done in spite of the fact that two of the subjects had actual strength that was slightly greater than that predicted for them, because the interpretation of the total potential strength is not the "absolute total," but rather the total amount which might be athletically useful to the individual.

The standard error of estimating strength by Formula (1) is 229.66, and the mean score of strength predicted for the 60 subjects is 2,332 lb. The mean score was divided by twice the standard error of estimate. This gave the per cent of the score at any given point along the scale that the new regression line was to be raised above the regression line used in Formula(1). This resulted in raising the new regression line two standard

STRENGTH OBTAINED IN 100 POUNDS

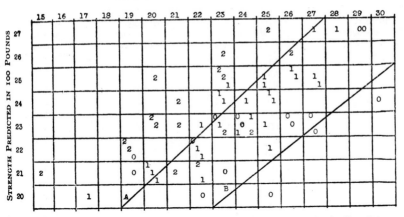

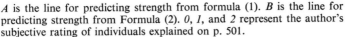

A is the line for predicting strength from formula (1). *B* is the line for predicting strength from Formula (2). *0, 1,* and *2* represent the author's subjective rating of individuals explained on p. 501.

errors of estimate for those whose predicted strength is 2,332 lb, while it is raised proportionally more for those whose predicted strength is greater than the mean, and proportionally less for those whose predicted strength is less than the mean. A subject whose skeletal measurements are great would be expected to be able to increase his total strength more than one with measurements not so great.

When Formula (1) was applied to this new regression line "B," it became Formula (2), which is:

Total potential strength = 20.02 chest circumference + 175.88 elbow width + 85.91 knee width − 1529.

Tables have been constructed to facilitate the calculation of total potential strength of adult males as predicted by Formula (2).

Method of Using Table 1

To correct chest circumference for fat: Add the fat measured on the chest front and chest back, and subtract this sum algebraically from 35, which is the average sum of chest fat. Find this difference in the left-hand column of the table and read its value directly opposite in the right-hand column. This value is added or subtracted, according to its sign, from the actual chest girth.

Method of Using Table 2

Find the corrected chest measurement in the left-hand column, and read its value directly across in the opposite column. The table values are given in centimeters; but their fractional values may be accounted for by adding two to the total score for each one-tenth centimeter.

Find the elbow measurement in the column under *elbow* and read its value in the column immediately to the right. Knee values are found in the same way under the *knee* column. The sum of chest, elbow, and knee values is the predicted total potential strength of the individual, since the constant in the formula was deducted in the construction of the table.

TABLE 1

Readings (= average) in millimeters.	Subtract (or add) in centimeters.	Readings (= average) in millimeters.	Subtract (or add) in centimeters.
1	0.1	16	2.5
2	0.3	17	2.7
3	0.5	18	2.8
4	0.6	19	3.0
5	0.8	20	3.1
6	0.9	21	3.3
7	1.1	22	3.5
8	1.3	23	3.6
9	1.4	24	3.8
10	1.6	25	3.9
11	1.7	26	4.1
12	1.9	27	4.2
13	2.0	28	4.4
14	2.2	29	4.6
15	2.4	30	4.7

TABLE 2

This Table Gives Values for Formula (2)

Chest in cm		Elbow in cm		Knee in cm	
80	602	6.0	532	8.7	747
81	622	6.1	550	8.8	756
82	642	6.2	568	8.9	765
83	662	6.3	585	9.0	773
84	682	6.4	603	9.1	782
85	702	6.5	621	9.2	790
86	722	6.6	638	9.3	799
87	742	6.7	656	9.4	808
88	762	6.8	674	9.5	816
89	782	6.9	691	9.6	825
90	802	7.0	709	9.7	833
91	822	7.1	727	9.8	842
92	842	7.2	745	9.9	851
93	862	7.3	762	10.0	859
94	882	7.4	780	10.1	868
95	902	7.5	798	10.2	876
96	922	7.6	815	10.3	885
97	942	7.7	833	10.4	893
98	962	7.8	851	10.5	902
99	982	7.9	868	10.6	911
100	1,002	8.0	886	10.7	919
				10.8	928
				10.9	936
				11.0	945

Conclusions and Recommendations

1. Within limits, total possible strength of adult males can be predicted from skeletal build.

2. The results of this study are applicable only to those whose ages range from 18 to 50 yr, which is the range of the ages of the subjects studied.

3. It is recommended that a similar study be made of boys of the junior high school and high school age range.

4. Information gained from this study should prove useful in the training of athletes for sports in which the strength element is important. By determining what strength an athlete has, and what he is capable of attaining, his training could be better directed.

5. This should serve as a guide for those who are interested in developing their strength to the maximum of their possibilities.

References

1. McCloy, C. H., "A New Method of Scoring Chinning and Dipping," *Res. Quart.*, **2** (1931), 4.

F. D. SILLS / J. MITCHEM

Prediction of Performances on Physical Fitness Tests by Means of Somatotype Ratings

Reprinted from the *Research Quarterly*, **28** (1957), 64–71.

The work of Sills and Mitchem in relating body characteristics and physical performance represents one of many studies by physical educators who utilized Sheldon's somatotyping system for classification of body types.*

As the authors point out, the significance of height and weight measures in predicting performance of college men is questionable. It is important to note that although they were moderately successful in predicting physical performance from body typology, they have attempted to predict not to some general physical fitness criterion, but rather to three aspects of fitness. This serves to illustrate the problem facing the would-be prognosticator, i.e., the existence of differential abilities in humans cannot be overlooked. Also, it becomes clear in this paper, and

---

* W. H. Sheldon, S. S. Stevens, and W. B. Tucker, *The Varieties of Human Physique* (New York: Harper & Row, Publishers, 1940).

to some extent in Lookabough's work, that precision in predicting physical performance cannot be achieved through consideration of only one or a small number of attributes of the human organism.

Abstract

Scores on three fitness tests were predicted for various body types using the body components endomorphy, mesomorphy, and ectomorphy as independent variables.

All of the somatotypes found in the sample were placed in 13 categories. The 13 categories were divided, on the basis of the scores made by the various somatotypes on each of the tests, into 4 groups. T-score tables were constructed, for each group, for each of the four tests. The same somatotypes were not placed in the same groups for all four tests. In this respect, this method of classification differs from many others that have been suggested.

A battery of four tests to measure physical fitness is included in the physical education curriculum at the State University of Iowa. This battery consists of sit-ups, pull-ups, the 100-yd pickaback run,[1] and the 300-yd shuttle run. Standard scores for each of the four tests have been determined on the basis of the performance of the male students who have participated in the basic-skills program in physical education from 1947 to 1950.

This battery of tests is important to the student since his standardized scores on the four tests are averaged and used, with other criteria, in determining his qualifications for exemption from the basic-skills course. In accordance with a procedure

---

[1] In 1954–1955, this test was replaced with the 1-min squat-thrust test.

commonly practiced in the determination of norms for fitness tests, no consideration is given to individual variations in body type.

Scoring tables have been published based upon the measurements of age, height, and weight. An example of this type of table is McCloy's Universal Scoring Tables.[4] Cozens[2] stated, "Even with college men we must recognize the superiority of certain stature groups over others." On the basis of this belief, Cozens published achievement scales for nine different stature groups. Bookwalter[1] studied body build and physical performance in elementary schoolchildren using the Wetzel Grid as a means of classification. He found "indication of a fairly systematic relationship between physique channels and developmental levels according to the Wetzel Grid and the physical fitness scores of elementary school boys in Indiana." Miller[5] observed that the Cozens classification was satisfactory for grouping college men according to size, but that the classification was of no particular value in predicting performance on a seven-item test battery. He concluded, "as far as general physical performance is concerned, it seems that height and weight are unsatisfactory elements upon which to base a classification of college men."

In a study by Willgoose,[9] the highest mean PFI score was attained by the mesomorph-ectomorph group, the next highest mean score by the extreme mesomorph group. He found that endomorphy was a limiting factor in respect to physical fitness. By means of a factor analysis, Sills[7] identified endomorphy and mesomorphy as factors, and found that the former was not related to the strength tests and motor tests included in his experiment. In another study, Sills and Everett[8] analyzed the relationship between dominant body types and performance on motor and strength tests. They concluded that excess weight was a handicap to the endomorphs and that insufficient strength was a handicap to the ectomorphs. The mesomorphs were superior to the other two types in all of the tests included in the study. Cureton and Hunsicker[3] found that, in general, mesomorphs and ectomesomorphs score higher on physical fitness tests, than do the other somatotypes.

It did not appear from a review of the related literature that a satisfactory method had been developed for classifying male university students relative to their performance on physical fitness tests. Since the authors were of the opinion that the same standards should not be required for all students, it was the purpose of this study to determine to what extent, if at all, the standards should be based upon somatotype ratings.

Procedure

Four hundred and thirty-three University of Iowa male freshmen served as the subjects for the study. Each subject was given the four physical fitness tests, photographed, and somatoscoped according to the method explained by Sheldon, Stevens, and Tucker in their text, *The Varieties of Human Physique.*[6]

The following steps were then taken: first, multiple correlation coefficients were computed to determine the relationship between the body type components and the physical fitness tests; second, equations were computed to predict scores on each of the 4 tests; third, the development of a classifica-

tion system with 13 categories that included all of the somatotypes in the population being studied; fourth, test scores were predicted for the somatotypes included in each category; fifth, the categories were ranked from the highest to the lowest according to the predicted scores for each of the physical fitness tests; sixth, adjoining categories were combined, on the basis of similar scores, to reduce the classification to 4 groups; and seventh, 514 students were assigned to the 4 groups on the basis of their somatotype ratings. T-score tables were then computed, for each of the four groups, for sit-ups, pull-ups, and the 300-yd shuttle run.

Correlations. Intercorrelations (see Table 1) for the four fitness tests and three body components were computed. The zero-order correlation coefficients for the endomorphic component with each of the four fitness tests were negative; the coefficients for the mesomorphic component with each of the four fitness tests were positive; while the coefficients for the ectomorphic component with the four tests were both positive and negative. Although none of the coefficients was very high, all except two were significant at the 1 per cent level. Multiple correlation coefficients for the three somatotype components with each of the four fitness tests were determined.

Multiple Correlations

Sit-ups $\quad R_{1.567} = 0.3464$ (6.52 P.E.est.)
Pull-ups $\quad R_{2.567} = 0.5716$ (1.98 P.E.est.)
300-yd Run $\quad R_{3.567} = 0.4937$ (2.11 P.E.est.)
100-yd Pickaback
$\qquad R_{4.567} = 0.4617$ (1.54 P.E.est.)

Prediction equations. Equations were computed to predict scores on each of the four physical fitness tests utilizing the three somatotype components as independent variables.

TABLE 1

Zero Order Correlation Coefficents*

Variables	No.	1	2	3	4	5	6	7
Sit-ups........	1	——						
Pull-ups	2	0.2879	——					
300-yd run	3	0.2988	0.4461	——				
100-yd picka-back run	4	0.3471	0.4441	0.6033	——			
Endomorphy ..	5	−0.2716	−0.4709	−0.3243	−0.3331	——		
Mesomorphy ..	6	0.1892	0.4258	0.3223	0.3917	−0.2562	——	
Ectomorphy ..	7	−0.1279	0.0373	0.1977	−0.0264	−0.2866	−0.4069	——
Means........		42.8	7.2	54.5	25.5	2.3	4.1	2.6
Standard Deviations		10.4	3.6	3.6	2.6	1.3	1.0	1.4

* E. F. Lindquist. *Statistical Analysis in Educational Research,* p. 212. For 400 subjects an *r* of 0.128 is significant at the 1 per cent level.

1. Sit-ups
$$X_0 = -2.5574X_1 + .1765X_2 - 1.6076X_3 + 52.3324$$
2. Pull-ups
$$X_0 = -.9580X_1 + 1.3112X_2 + 2.321X_3 + 3.5151$$
3. 300-yd Run
$$X_0 = +.3175X_1 - 1.5097X_2 - .8877X_3 + 62.261$$
4. 100-yd Pickaback
$$X_0 = +.4457X_1 - .8997X_2 - .1005X_3 + 28.472$$

3. Ectomorph mesomorph
4. Mesomorphic ectomorph
5. Endomorphic mesomorph
6. Moderate mesomorph
7. Endomorph mesomorph
8. Moderate ectomorph
9. Mesomorphic endomorph
10. Balanced
11. Moderate endomorph
12. Ectomorph
13. Endomorph

Classification system. Sheldon[6] has suggested that "for most experiments requiring fewer categories, it would appear advisable to combine certain of the closely related somatotypes." He then presents 19 categories that might prove useful in the design of an experiment. A modification of this suggestion has been adopted for the present study. Closely related somatotypes were combined in the development of a classification system involving 13 categories.

1. Mesomorph
2. Ectomophic mesomorph

Prediction of scores. The prediction equations were then used to predict the scores that the various somatotypes within each category would make on the four fitness tests. It was found that, when the somatotypes in one category had higher scores on one of the physical fitness tests than those in another category, the latter frequently had higher scores than the former on another of the physical fitness tests.

Ranking and grouping of categories. For each of the 4 physical fitness tests, the 13 categories were ranked from the highest to the lowest on the basis of the predicted scores. It was found that the same scores could be expected for many of the somatotypes in adjoining categories and, for this reason, the categories were combined into four groups. The groups included different combinations of categories, for the reason given in the preceding paragraph, for each of the physical fitness tests. The four groups and their predicted scores, for three[2] of the physical fitness tests, are given here:

Sit-ups

Moderate Mesomorph Mesomorph Ectomorphic Mesomorph	46-47-48- 49-50
Endomorphic Mesomorph Ectomorph Mesomorph Mesomorphic Ectomorph Moderate Ectomorph	41-42-43- 44-45
Moderate Endomorph Balanced Endomorph Mesomorph Ectomorph Mesomorphic Endomorph	36-37-38- 39-40-41
Endomorph	33-34-35

Pull-ups

Ectomorphic Mesomorph Mesomorph Ectomorph Mesomorph	9-10-11
Moderate Mesomorph Endomorphic Mesomorph Mesomorphic Ectomorph	7-8-9
Ectomorph Endomorph Mesomorph Moderate Ectomorph Balanced	4-5-6
Mesomorphic Endomorph Moderate Endomorph Endomorph	1-2-3

[2] Standards for the 60-sec squat-thrust test are being established to replace those for the pickaback test.

300-Yard Run

Ectomorphic Mesomorph Ectomorph Mesomorph Mesomorph Mesomorphic Ectomorph	51.0-52.5- 54.0
Endomorphic Mesomorph Balanced Moderate Mesomorph	53.0-54.5- 56.0
Ectomorph Endomorph Mesomorph Moderate Ectomorph	55.0-56.0- 57.0
Mesomorphic Endomorph Moderate Endomorph Endomorph	58.0-60.0- 62.0

Scoring tables. The scores of 514 students were used to compute T-score tables for the 3 fitness tests. The numbers of subjects used in constructing the four T-score tables for the sit-ups test were: Group I—196, Group II—156, Group III—147, and Group IV—15; for the pull-ups test: Group I—157, Group II—160, Group III—134, and Group IV—63; for the 300-yd shuttle run: Group I—185, Group II—177, Group III—85, and Group IV—67. In order to improve the validity of the tables, additional subjects must be tested so that each of the tables will be based upon the scores of at least 500 subjects. It is much easier, as shown by the figures given, to obtain subjects for certain of the groups than for the others.

It was possible to compute T-scores for raw scores throughout the entire range of scores on two of the tables, but for the pull-ups test this was not possible for three of the four groups. These three tables were arbitrarily adjusted so that a passing score could not be given unless the subject performed at least one pull-up.

An examination of the three tables indicates that they discriminate be-

TABLE 2

Sit-ups

T-Score	Group I	Group II	Group III	Group IV
5	6	5	2	1
10	11	9	6	2
15	16	13	10	6
20	21	17	15	10
25	26	22	19	15
30	30	26	23	19
35	35	30	27	23
40	40	34	32	27
45	45	38	35	32
50	50	43	40	36
55	55	47	44	40
60	59	51	48	44
65	64	55	52	48
70	69	60	57	52
75	74	64	61	57
80	78	68	65	61
85	83	72	69	65
90	88	76	74	69
95	92	82	79	74
100	95	85	82	79

TABLE 3

Pull-ups

T-Score	Group I	Group II	Group III	Group IV
5	0	0	0	0
10	0	0	0	0
15	0	0	0	0
20	1	0	0	0
25	2	1	—	—
30	4	2	1	—
35	5	3	2	—
40	7	4	3	1
45	8	6	4	2
50	10	8	5	4
55	11	10	7	6
60	13	12	9	7
65	15	14	11	9
70	16	15	13	11
75	18	17	14	13
80	20	19	16	15
85	21	21	17	17
90	23	22	19	18
95	24	24	20	20
100	25 and over	25 and over	21 and over	21 and over

TABLE 4

300-Yard Shuttle Run

T-Score	Group I	Group II	Group III	Group IV
5	64	69	70	76.5
10	63	67	68.5	74.5
15	62	65.5	67	72.5
20	60.5	64	65.5	71
25	59	62.5	64	69
30	58	61	62.5	67
35	57	59.5	61	65
40	55.5	58	59.5	63.5
45	54.5	56	58	61.5
50	53	55	56.5	60
55	52	53	55	58
60	51	51.5	53.5	56
65	49.5	50	52	54.5
70	48	48.5	50.5	52.5
75	47	47	49	51
80	46	45.5	47.5	49
85	44.5	44	46	47
90	43.5	42.5	44.5	45.5
95	42	41	43	43.5
100	41 and under	40 and under	41.5 and under	42 and under

tween the members of the four groups, and that subjects of similar body builds will be graded more fairly than would be the case if the traditional type of scoring table were to be used.

Summary

Four major steps were taken in the development of this study. The first was to predict scores on fitness tests by using the body components endomorphy, mesomorphy, and ectomorphy as independent variables. The second was that of establishing 13 categories into which all of the somatotypes found in the sample could be placed. In the next step the 13 categories were divided into 4 groups on the basis of the scores predicted for each of the 3 fitness tests. And finally, T-score tables were constructed for each of the four different groups on all three of the fitness tests.

The assumption has been made that, in placing a given subject (somatotype) in a group for one of the fitness tests, the same subject may fall into another group on one or both of the other two fitness tests. For each of the three tests, therefore, different somatotypes will be grouped together according to their ability.

The multiple correlation coefficients for body-build with sit-ups, pull-ups, and the 300-yd shuttle run show substantial relationships that may serve as a basis for classifying male college students into homogeneous groups, a procedure that makes it possible to grade the student in accord with others of similar ability.

References

1. Bookwalter, Karl W., *et al.*, "The Relationship of Body Size and Shape to Physical Performance," *Res. Quart.*, **23** (1952), 271–79.

2. Cozens, Frederick W., "A Study of Stature in Relation to Physical Performance," *ibid.*, **1** (1930), 38–45.

3. Cureton, Thomas K., and Paul Hunsicker, "Body-Build as a Framework of Reference for Interpreting Physical Fitness and Athletic Performance," *ibid.*, Suppl., **12** (1941), 301–30.

4. McCloy, C. H., *The Measurement of Athletic Power*. New York: A. S. Barnes & Co., 1932.

5. Miller, Kenneth D., "A Critique on the Use of Height-Weight Factors in the Performance Classification of College Men," *Res. Quart.*, **23** (1952), 402–16.

6. Sheldon, William H., S. S. Stevens, and W. B. Tucker, *The Varieties of Human Physique*. New York: Harper & Row, Publishers, 1940.

7. Sills, Frank D., "A Factor Analysis of Somatotypes and Their Relationship to Achievement in Motor Skills," *Res. Quart.*, **21** (1950), 424–37.

8. Sills, Frank D., and Peter W. Everett, "The Relationship of Extreme Somatotypes to Performance in Motor and Strength Tests," *ibid.*, **24** (1953), 223–28.

9. Willgoose, Carl E., and Millard L. Rogers, "Relationship of Somatotype to Physical Fitness," *J. Educ. Res.*, **42** (1949), 704–12.

A. V. HILL

The Physiological Basis of Athletic Records

Reprinted from *The Scientific Monthly*,
21 (1925), pp. 409–28.

Although record performances in various athletic events had been noted for some time, little work appeared providing an explanation of these phenomena. Obviously, such explanations required information about a variety of factors, including the physiological limits of exercise. Through the research of A.V. Hill and other physiologists, the facts about work and energy usage became better known. Applying such knowledge, and obviously influenced by Kennelly's work, Hill wrote this paper in an effort to provide a physiological explanation for maximum physical work of the kind necessary for record performance. As such it is a forerunner to the Henry paper that follows.

In the study of the physiology of muscular exercise there is a vast store of accurate information, hitherto almost unexploited, in the records of athletic sports and racing. The greatest efforts and the most intense care have been expended in making what are really experiments upon these subjects, and the results obtained represent what may justly be described as a collection of natural constants of muscular effort in the human race. It is the purpose of this address to discuss certain aspects of the data available in connection with various forms of racing, and to see how far physiological principles at present known underlie them.

Sources of Information

The most complete set of records available, for a great variety of sports, is to be found in *The World Almanac and Book of Facts*, published by the New York *World*. Much of the information here presented was obtained from the 1925 edition of that work; similar but less extensive data can be found in our own *Whitaker's Almanack*. In addition, various books on horse-racing, on swimming, and on rowing have been searched for suitable material. The study of such data is not new. In most cases, however, it has been carried out not from the physiological but purely from the statistical standpoint; insufficient knowledge of the underlying physiological principles was available to make it profitable to ask for the why and wherefore. Recent developments, however, of the scientific study of muscular effort in man have indicated certain broad lines on which some at any rate of the relations so established can be explained. I will not deal further with the statistical analysis of the facts, beyond referring to an extremely interesting and suggestive collection of them given in a paper by A. E. Kennelly, entitled "An Approximate Law of Fatigue in the Speeds of Racing Animals," published in the *Proceedings of the American Academy of Arts and Sciences*, Vol. 42, p. 275, 1906. Some,

indeed, of my data are taken directly from that paper.

Fatigue as the Determining Factor

An important and interesting problem for any young athlete is presented by the question, "How fast can I run some given distance?" The maximum speed at which a given distance can be covered is known to vary largely with the distance. What are the factors determining the variation of speed with distance? How far, knowing a man's best times at two distances, can one interpolate between them for an intermediate distance, or extrapolate for a distance greater or less? Obviously the answer to such questions depends upon the factor which in general terms we designate fatigue. Fatigue, however, is a very indefinite and inexact expression; it is necessary to define it quantitatively before we can employ it in a quantitative discussion such as this. There are many varieties of fatigue, but of these only a few concern us now. There is that which results in a short time from extremely violent effort: this type is fairly well understood; there is the fatigue, which may be called exhaustion, which overcomes the body when an effort of more moderate intensity is continued for a long time. Both of these may be defined as muscular. Then there is the kind which we may describe as due to wear and tear of the body as a whole, to blisters, soreness, stiffness, nervous exhaustion, metabolic changes and disturbances, sleeplessness, and similar factors, which may affect an individual long before his muscular system has given out. Of these three forms of fatigue the first one only is as yet susceptible of exact measurement and description. The second type may quite possibly come within the range of experiment at no distant date. The third type is still so indefinite and complex that one cannot hope at present to define it accurately and to measure it. Undoubtedly, however, all these types of what we call "fatigue" influence—indeed, determine —the results which are to be presented.

Presentation of Data

The data will be exposed throughout this discussion in graphical form, and in every case but one (Fig. 5) the quantities plotted are the speed as ordinate and the time, or some function of the time, as abscissa. The reason for taking the *time* occupied in a race as one of our variables is simple; the problem before us, physiologically speaking, is, clearly, *how long can a given effort be maintained?* The length of time is given by the abscissa as the independent variable; the magnitude of the effort, or some function of it, as represented by the speed (that is, by the average speed over the race considered), is given as ordinate. It will be shown below, as Kennelly indicated in his paper, that the ideal way to run a race, possibly not from the point of view of winning it, but certainly from that of breaking the record for the distance, is to run it at constant speed. In those performances which have attained to the dignity of a world's record it is unlikely that this criterion has been to any very large degree neglected. Apart, therefore, from the fact that there is no speed of which we have any record except the average speed, we are probably not far wrong in using the average speed as a fairly exact measure, or at any rate as a function of the effort involved.

In one case only (Fig. 6) the time occupied in the race has been given on a logarithmic scale: no great virtue attaches to the logarithm, but if 75 yd

and 100 mi are to be shown on the same diagram in a readable form it is necessary somehow to condense the abscissae at the longer times. As a matter of fact, from the standpoint of an athlete, one second in ten has the same importance as ten seconds in a hundred, as a hundred seconds in a thousand; in this sense, therefore, a logarithmic scale of time most truly represents the duration of an effort. Such a scale, however, has not been used for any ulterior reason, but only, as in Fig. 6, to get all the available data on to one diagram.

Running and Swimming : Shorter Times

In Fig. 1 all the important world's records are presented, average speed against time, for men and women running and for men and women swimming. The crosses representing men rowing in an eight-oar boat will be discussed later. It is obvious in all four cases that we are dealing with the same phenomena, a very high speed maintainable for short times, a speed rapidly decreasing as the time is increased and attaining practically a constant value after about 12 min. There are no reliable records, in the case of swimming, for times of less than about 50 sec, so that the curves can not be continued back as far as those for running. There can, however, be no doubt that the curves for running and swimming are essentially similar to one another and must depend upon the same factors. In running, starting inertia is the cause of the initial upward trend of the curves: a maximum average velocity is attained in the case of men for about 200 yd, of women for about 100 yd; after that a rapid decrease sets in, ending only when the time has become 10 or 15 min, the distance 2 to 3 mi. The phenom-

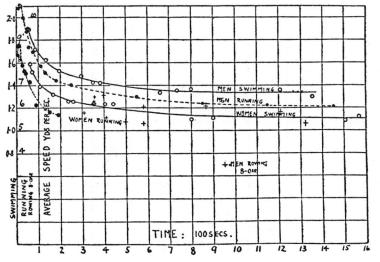

Fig. 1. World's records for men and women swimming and running: average speed in yards per second against time in seconds. *Note.* The scale for swimming is five times as great as for running. The observations for men rowing an eight-oar boat are on the same scale as running and are referred to later in the text.

ena shown in Fig. 1 are susceptible of a fairly exact discussion.

Oxygen Intake, Oxygen Requirement, and Oxygen Debt

In recent papers my colleagues and I have tried to emphasize the importance of a clear distinction between the oxygen intake and the oxygen requirement of any given type and speed of muscular effort. When exercise commences, the oxygen intake rises from a low value characteristic of rest to a high value characteristic of the effort undertaken. This rise occupies a period of about two minutes; it is nearly complete in 90 sec. The oxygen used by the body is a measure of the amount of energy expended: 1 l of oxygen consumed means about 5 cal of energy liberated, enough to warm 5 l of water one degree Centigrade—expressed in mechanical ener-

gy, enough to raise about 1 ton 7 ft into the air. It has been established, however, that the oxygen need not necessarily be used during the exertion itself. The muscles have a mechanism, depending upon the formation of lactic acid in them, by which a large amount of the oxidation may be put off to a time after the exercise has ended. The recovery process, so called, is a sign of this delayed oxidation: it is just as important to the muscle as recharging to an electric accumulator. The degree, however, to which the body is able to run into debt for oxygen, to carry on not on present but on future supplies, is limited. When an oxygen debt of about 15 l has been incurred the body becomes incapable of further effort: it is completely fatigued. In anything but the shortest races our record-breaking athlete should finish with something near a maximum oxygen debt, otherwise he

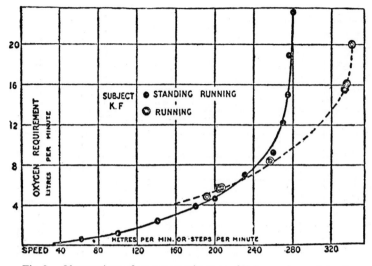

Fig. 2. Observations of oxygen requirement of K.F. running and standing-running at various speeds. Horizontally, speed: running, meters per minute; standing-running, steps per minute. Vertically, oxygen requirement per minute, liters.

has not employed all his available power, he has not done himself full justice. The maximum effort, therefore, which he can exert over a given interval depends upon the amount of energy available for him, upon (a) his maximum oxygen intake (that is, his income) and (b) his maximum oxygen debt (that is, the degree to which he is able to overdraw his account). These maxima are fairly well established for the case of athletic men of average size—about 4 l per min for the one, about 15 l for the other.

It is possible for a man to make an effort far in excess of any contemporary supply of oxygen. This effort will require oxygen afterwards, and the total oxygen needed per minute to maintain the exercise can be measured. It is what we call the "oxygen requirement" characteristics of the effort involved. Now experiments have shown (see Fig. 2) that the oxygen requirement varies very largely with

the speed: it increases far more rapidly than the speed, more like the second or third power of the speed, so that high speeds and intense efforts are very wasteful. These facts enable us approximately to deduce the general form of Fig. 1.

Imagine an athlete with a maximum oxygen intake of 4 l per min,[1] capable of running until his maximum oxygen debt has been incurred of 15 l. If he runs for 15 min the total oxygen available during the exercise and in arrears is $15 \times 4 + 15 = 75$ l: an effort can be made requiring 5 l of oxygen per min. Imagine, however, that he exhausts himself not in 15 but in 5 min: the total oxygen available during or in arrears is $5 \times 4 + 15 = 35$ l. He may exert himself more violently,

---

[1] Assumed, for the sake of simplicity in calculation, to commence as soon as the race begins. For a more accurate calculation the gradual rise of the oxygen intake at the beginning of exercise can be taken into account.

therefore, with an effort equivalent now to 7 l per min. Imagine next that he runs himself to exhaustion in 2 min: $4 \times 2 + 15$, i.e., 23 l of oxygen, are available, 11.5 per min; a correspondingly greater effort can be made. By such calculations it is possible from Fig. 1 to deduce a relation between oxygen requirement and speed. Taking the case of a man swimming, the result is shown in Fig. 3 on the assumption of a maximum oxygen debt of 15 l, a maximum oxygen intake of 3.5 l per min, and the supposition that at the end of the race the performer is completely exhausted. A similar calculated curve is given for the case of running, on the hypothesis of a maximum oxygen debt of 15 l and a maximum oxygen intake of 4 l per min. These curves are similar in character to those shown in Fig. 2 for the cases of running and standing-running, which have been investigated in the laboratory. There

can be little doubt that the factors here described are the chief agents in determining the form of the curves given in Fig. 1.

Limits of the Argument

It is obvious that we must not pursue the argument too far. A man can not exhaust himself completely in a 100- or a 200-yd race: even 300 yd is not sufficient to cause an extreme degree of exhaustion, though a quarter-mile, in the case of a first-class sprinter, is enough, or almost enough, to produce complete inability to make any immediate further effort. We have found an oxygen debt of 10 l even after a quarter-mile in 55 sec. It is obvious, therefore, that we cannot pursue our argument below times of about 50 sec, that the maximum speed is limited by quite other factors than the amount of energy available. It is not possible in

Fig. 3. Oxygen requirement, running and swimming, of record-breaking athletes, calculated from curves of Fig. 1, on the assumption that at the end of a race the performer is completely exhausted, having attained his maximum oxygen debt. Maximum oxygen debt assumed = 15 l for both. Maximum oxygen intake assumed: for running = 4 l per min; swimming = 3.5 l per min. Method of calculation described in the text.

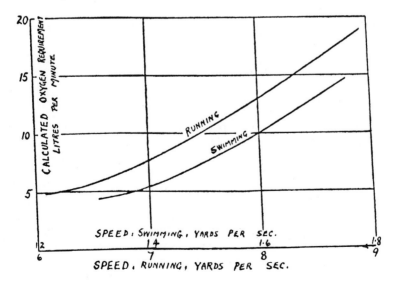

any way to release energy explosively for very short intervals of effort: other factors determine the maximum speed, factors mechanical and nervous. Neither can the argument be applied to very long races, where—as we shall see below—other types of exhaustion set in.

Comparison of Men and Women; Swimming and Running

There are certain characteristics of these curves which are of interest. In the first place those for men and women are almost precisely similar. For a given time of swimming the maximum speed for a woman appears throughout the curves to be almost exactly 84 to 85 per cent of that for a man. The curve relating oxygen requirement to speed, in the case of swimming, is not known from experiment, nor are the maximum oxygen debts and the maximum oxygen intakes known for women with any certainty. It would be very interesting to determine them, were volunteers forthcoming. If we assume what is roughly true, that the energy expenditure rises approximately as the square of the speed, we may conclude that a woman swimming is able to exert, per kilogram of body weight, about 72 per cent of the power expended by a man. Women are well adapted to swimming: their skill in swimming is presumably just as great as that of men; the difference in the maximum speed for any given time can be a matter only of the amount of power available.

In running, the same type of comparison may be made, though here not over the same range of times. For anything but the shortest races the maximum speed of a woman is almost precisely 79 per cent of that of a man running for the same time. For very short times, 5 to 10 sec, the ratio is

greater, namely, 84 per cent. Here again there would seem little reason to attribute the difference of speed, at any rate for the longer races, to anything but a difference in the maximum amount of power expendible over the period in question. Assuming again, as an approximate means of calculation, that the energy used per minute varies as the square of the speed, we see that a woman running is able to liberate in a given time only about 62 per cent of the energy expendable by a man of the same weight. It is probable that this ratio between men and women, as determined by swimming and by running, respectively, is really the same in either case, and that the apparent difference depends upon an inexactness in the simple laws we have assumed for the variation of energy expended with speed. It would seem fair to take the mean of these two values, 67 per cent— that is, about two thirds—as the ratio of the amount of energy expendable by a woman in a given time as compared with that by a man of the same weight. It would be of great interest— and quite simple—to test this deduction by direct experiment on women athletes.

Men and Women Jumping

A further interesting comparison between men and women may be found in the records of high jumps and long jumps. The world's record long jump for a man is 25.5 ft, for a woman 16.9 ft. The high jump records are, respectively, 6.61 ft and 5 ft. At first sight, when compared with running, these records for women seem extraordinarily poor: the high jump is only 75.5 per cent, the long jump only 66 per cent, of that for men. Such a conclusion, however, rests upon a misunderstanding, almost like that which makes many people believe that if a man could jump as well as a flea he could easily clear the top of St. Paul's Cathedral. It is a matter only of elementary mechanics to show, on the assumption that a woman can project herself vertically with a velocity proportional to that with which she can project herself horizontally, the constant of the proportion being the same as for the case of a man, that both the high jump and the long jump in the two sexes should be in the ratio *not of the velocities but of the squares of the velocities.* The maximum range and the maximum height of a projectile vary as the square of the velocity of projection. Thus it is right to compare, for men and women, not the height of the high jump or the distance of the long jump, but the square roots of these quantities, if we wish to study their relative performance in jumping as compared with running. This being so, we find that the high jump of a woman, as measured by its square root, is 87 per cent of that of man;[2] the long jump, measured in a similar way, is 81.5 per cent. These compare closely with their relative performances for very short times of running, where a woman, as shown above, can run 84 per cent as fast as a man. It is amusing to find simple mechanics explaining such apparent differences between the sexes.

The Characteristic Oxygen-Requirement-Speed Curve

The curves given in Fig. 2 define the economy with which movements are carried out. By such means can be shown the amount of energy required,

___

[2] It would really be fairer to compare the heights jumped, less the initial heights of the centers of gravity, say 3.1 ft and 2.8 ft, respectively. This gives 2.2/3.51 = 0.63 as the ratio of the heights, of which the square root is 0.79, a close agreement with the long jump.

in terms of oxygen used, in order, say, to run or swim for a minute at any given speed. The curves will vary largely from one individual to another. Some men move more efficiently than others at all speeds: A may be more efficient at one speed than B is, but less efficient at another. For most kinds of muscular exercises the characteristic curve of Fig. 2 is ascertainable by experiment. In some cases, as in swimming, experimental difficulties might be considerable, at any rate at higher speeds. It is obvious, however, that such a curve must exist for any person performing any kind of continuous muscular exercise. In it we have a characteristic of that given individual for that particular form of work.

Skill

Some people are much more skilled than others. To a large degree, of course, the skill and grace associated with athletic prowess is natural and inborn; to a large degree, however, it can be produced by training and breeding. All the movements required in the violent forms of muscular exertion here discussed are rapid ones, far too rapid to be directly and continuously subject to the conscious intelligence: they are largely, indeed mainly, reflex, set going by the will but maintained by the interplay of proprioceptive nervous system and motor apparatus. The nature of muscular skill can not be discussed here; possibly, however, above all other factors it is the foundation of athletic prowess. Such skill has a physiological basis as it has a psychological aspect. It is a fit subject for discussion alike by physiologists, psychologists, students of physical training, athletes, masters, and workmen. The further study of skill is likely to be most fruitful in many branches of human endeavor. Here I

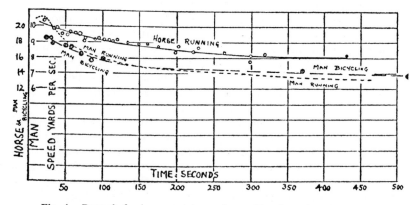

Fig. 4. Records for horse running and man bicycling; dotted curve for comparison, man running, taken from Fig. 1. Horizontally, time in seconds; vertically, average speed in yards per second. *Note.* The horse, and the man bicycling are shown on half the scale of the man running. The records for bicycling are the unpaced professional records against time. The records for horses were made in America.

would only remark that the forms of the characteristic curves of Fig. 2 depend upon the skill of the subject in ordering his movements, just as the "miles per gallon" of a motorcar depends upon the skill of those who designed and adjusted its timing gear and its magneto. Given incorrect adjustment due to lack of skill, given imperfect timing of the several parts of the mechanism, given unnecessary movement and vibration, the whole system will be inefficient. Fundamentally, the teaching of athletics for anything but the shortest distances consists in training the performer to lower the level of his characteristic curve, to carry out the same movements at a given speed for a smaller expenditure of energy.

Bicycling and Horse-Running

Not all forms of muscular exertion are so violent, involve so great an expenditure of energy, when carried out at the highest speed, as running and swimming. In Fig. 4 are two examples of this fact, horse running

and bicycling. For horse running a long succession of records on American horses are plotted on the topmost curve: below are the records of men bicycling, the unpaced professional records, made not in a race but against time. Most bicycle races are useless for our purpose: the competitors proceed in groups, trying one to ride behind the other to avoid wind resistance, and the speed may be absurdly low. Paced records are of little value because the efficiency of the wind-screen provided by the pacing apparatus is not standardized. These professional records, however, made unpaced, simply with the intention of breaking the record, are probably reliable, and they form a reasonably smooth curve. Plotted on the same diagram for comparison is a curve to represent a man running, a replica of that of Fig. 1. The first two curves are on twice the scale of the third, since a running horse and a bicycling man can go about twice the speed of a running man. It is obvious at once that neither of these two curves falls anything like so rapidly as does that of a running man; fatigue does not so soon set in: the amount of energy expended at the highest speed must be much less than in a running man. This conclusion, indeed, is obvious to any one who has tried to ride a bicycle fast. It is impossible to exhaust oneself rapidly on a bicycle: the movements are too show, they involve too little of the musculature of the body; it would require some minutes to produce by bicycling a state of exhaustion easily attainable within a minute by running. The curve for horse running is almost parallel to that for bicycling; presumably, therefore, the movements of a horse are so arranged that the extreme violence of effort possible in a human "sprinter" is unattainable: possibly the movements are too infrequent, or the qualities of the horse's muscles are so different, that the kind of fatigue rapidly attainable in man is not possible in the horse; possibly the horse will not "run himself out" so completely as a man.

Bicycle Ergometers

The curves of Fig. 4 are of interest in connection with the numberless experiments which have been made with bicycle ergometers. Nearly all the laboratory observations on man, in connection with muscular exercise, have been made with that implement. It has been obvious to my colleagues and myself during the last few years that the types of exercise chiefly adopted by us, running and standing-running, are more exhausting and require a far greater expenditure of energy than those employing the bicycle ergometer. In rowing and in pedaling a bicycle it may not be possible to attain respiratory quotients of 2 or more during or shortly after exercise. After running, or standing-running, however, very high values are attained, due to the fact

that these latter forms of exercise, at the highest speeds, are so very much more energetic than the slower movements of rowing or bicycling. It is speed and frequency of movement which determine the degree of exhaustion produced by it. To exert a powerful force in a moderate ryhthm is not anything like so tiring as to exert a much smaller force in a frequent rhythm: hence the reason for "gearing up," as in the bicycle and in the long oars of a rowing-boat.

Horse-Racing

The fact that running is not so exhausting to a horse as to a man is well shown by the records of Fig. 5. There the small circles represent the best English records of horse racing between the years 1721 and 1832. Speed in meters per second is given against kilometers distance. The larger circles represent the best of some more recent English records, from 1880 to 1905. D, O, and L represent, respectively, the Derby, the Oaks, and the St. Leger. It will be seen how little the speed falls off for the longer races: 6 or 7 km are run at the same speed as one or two. There is, indeed, a visible tendency for the curve to rise toward the left, as in Fig. 4; there is, however, no obvious further fall of the curve toward the right after about 2 km. Such a statement would seem preposterous to a human runner if applied to himself. Either the horse can not exhaust himself so rapidly as a man, or he can not be induced by his rider to go as hard as he ought. A man may be able to force himself to a greater degree of exhaustion than his rider can force a horse. An amusing incidental point brought out by Fig. 5 is the fact that the small circles and the large ones are intermingled. The horses of 150 years ago could run just as fast as

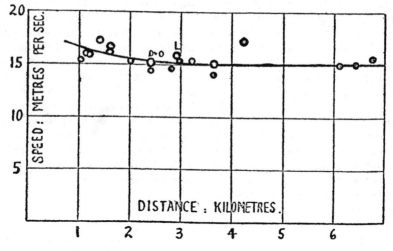

Fig. 5. Records for horse races. Small circles = old English records, 1721–1832. Large circles = later English records, 1880–1905. D = Derby, 0 = Oaks, L = St. Leger. Average speed, meters per second, against distance in kilometers.

The Logarithmic Graph

Let us pass now to a consideration of the last diagram, Fig. 6. There average speed in a race is plotted against the logarithm of the time occupied in it, the logarithm being employed, as stated above, for the purpose of including all records from 75 yd to 100 mi in the same picture. That people think, to some degree, in logarithms, although unconsciously, is shown by the fact that the records which men have thought it worthwhile to make are distributed approximately uniformly over the picture from left to right. Figure 6 presents the data of athletics perhaps more clearly than any other. The initial rise of the curve for their modern successors—a fair comment on the doctrine that the improvement of the breed of horses is the chief and a sufficient reason for encouraging the continuance of horse racing—even in time of war.

men running, which is due to starting inertia, is very obvious. The rapid fall beyond 220 yd is clearly seen. It is obvious that the 100- and the 220-yd ($\frac{1}{8}$-mi) records are better than those lying in their neighborhood, that the quarter-mile record is extremely good, the 500-yd record very bad, by comparison with its neighbors. This diagram should enable any enterprising and scientific athlete to select the records most easy to break: let him try those for 120 yd, for 500 yd, for three-quarter-mile, for 5 mi, but not for 220 yd, quarter-mile, 1 mi, and 6 mi.

Long-distance Records

In Fig. 1 we saw that the speed fell to what seemed to be practically a constant level toward the right of the diagram: this fall represents the initial factor in fatigue. On the logarithmic scale, however, where the longer times are compressed together, the curve continues to fall throughout its length.

This later fall is due to factors quite different from those discussed above. Consideration merely of oxygen intake and oxygen debt will not suffice to explain the continued fall of the curve. Actually the curve beyond 10 mi seems to some degree doubtful. Apparently the same extent of effort has not been lavished on the longer records: the greatest athletes have confined themselves to distances not greater than 10 mi. The curve A drawn through all the points has a suspicious downward bend in it, which suggests that if Alfred Shrubb or Nurmi had tried to break the longer records they would have done so very effectively. Possibly the true curve lies more like the continuation C: possibly it may be intermediate as shown at B. It would seem doubtful, indeed, whether the running curve and the walking curve are really to meet at about 150 mi. The most probable continuation of the running curve would seem to be somewhere between the lines B and C.

The continued fall in the curve, as the effort is prolonged, is probably due to the second and third types of fatigue which we discussed above, either to the exhaustion of the material of the muscle, or to the incidental disturbances which may make a man stop before his muscular system has reached its limit. A man of average size running in a race must expend about 300 g of glycogen per hr; perhaps a half of this may be replaced by its equivalent of fat. After a very few hours, therefore, the whole glycogen supply of his body will be exhausted. The body, however, does not readily use fat alone as a source of energy: disturbances may arise in the metabolism; it will be necessary to feed a man with carbohydrate as the effort continues. Such feeding will be followed by digestion; disturbances of digestion

Fig. 6. Records for men skating, bicycling, running, and walking, and for women running. Horizontally, logarithm of time occupied in race; vertically, average speed in yards per second. The same scale is used throughout, except for bicycling, where half the scale is employed, as shown in square brackets. The curve for men running appears to be somewhat doubtful beyond 10 or 15 mi, and three alternative curves are shown by broken lines.

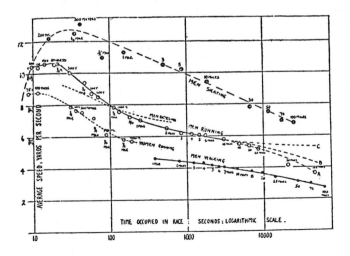

may occur—other reactions may ensue. For very long distances the case is far more complex than for the shorter ones, and although, no doubt, the physiological principles can be ascertained, we do not know enough about them yet to be able further to analyze the curves.

Women's Running Records

The women's curve, as far as it goes, is very similar to the men's. Some records again are better than others. An enterprising woman athlete who wants to break a record should avoid the 300 m; she would be well advised to try the 500 m. It would be very interesting to have an intermediate point between 100 and 220 yd.

Bicycling and Walking

As before, the curve for men bicycling, which is drawn on twice the scale vertically of the running curves, is far less steep than they are. The conclusion from this was emphasized above. The walking curve is interesting—it is approximately straight. Physiologically speaking, there is not much interest in the shortest walking races, since here walking is artificial and extremely laborious; running at a considerably higher speed is much more easy. For longer distances, however, say from 10 mi onward, we have probably in walking the most reliable data available for long-continued muscular effort. If we wish to study the exhaustion produced by exercise of long duration, walking-men may well provide the best subjects for our experiments.

Skating

There remains the top curve of all, that for men skating. The initial rise of the curve, due to starting inertia,

is very obvious. The fall of the curve beyond the maximum is nowhere near so rapid as for the case of running. Clearly in skating a man is not able to exert himself with the degree of ardor that is possible in the more primitive exercise of running. Skill and restraint are necessary, as they are in bicycling: there are limits to the output. Moreover, the effort can be continued for a long time, at comparatively high speeds. It is interesting to note that a man can skate 100 mi at almost the same speed as another man can run 1 mi. The curve falls uniformly throughout as does the walking curve. Clearly the phenomena of gradual exhaustion could be well investigated in the case of skating. Here again it is obvious which records the aspiring athlete should attempt to break.

Rowing

There are only a few records available, and those lying between rather narrow limits, for the case of rowing. Taking the case of an eight-oar boat, I have been able to obtain very few reliable data. Kennelly gives records of crews rowing, for times from 305 to 1,210 sec. Yandell Henderson, in the *American Journal of Physiology*, Vol. 72 p. 264, 1925, gives five observations made upon the Yale crew of 1924. In addition there are records for the Henley course: these, however, are usually contaminated by the speed of the water. The most reliable of the data have been plotted in Fig. 1 on the same scale as the running, on five times the scale of the swimming. The observed points, shown by crosses, are somewhat scattered. As far as they go, a mean curve through them would lie practically along the curve for women swimming, but of course on five times the scale. The interesting part of the curve to the left is lacking; it is obviously impossible to make observations on an eight-oar boat for periods of 20 sec, starting inertia is too great and no result of any value could be obtained. It would, however, be of interest to obtain data as far back as possible; certainly the records of crews rowing in still water for a minute and above should be ascertainable, and they would help to fit rowing into the scheme outlined by the other types of muscular effort.

Work and Stroke Frequency in Rowing

In rowing the movements are slow: in an eight-oar boat, from 30 to 40 strokes per min. According to observations by Lupton and myself the maximum efficiency of human muscular movement is obtained at speeds of about one maximal movement per second. In rowing, experience and tradition alike suggest that such a speed is about the optimum. In an eight-oar boat the recovery takes almost as long as the stroke, both occupying about one second. It is of interest how practical experience has gradually evolved a speed of movement which is almost exactly what a physiologist might have predicted as the most efficient. At a stroke of about 32 per min the mechanical efficiency is apparently near its maximum. An enormous amount of work has to be done in propelling a boat at speeds like 10 to 12 mi per hr. According to Henderson, each member of the crew of an eight-oar boat must exert about 0.6 of a horsepower. Clearly, if this enormous amount of external work is to be done it must be accomplished by working under efficient conditions: those conditions necessitate a stroke of a particular frequency; only when the race is very short is it permissible, in order to obtain a greater output, to work less efficiently by adopting a more rapid stroke. The stroke may rise to 40 per

min for a short distance: in such an effort the oxygen debt is accumulating rapidly and exhaustion will soon set in. The amount of work, moreover, will not be proportionately greater, probably only slightly greater, than at the lower frequency. The conditions which determine the speed of movement, the "viscous-elastic" properties of muscle, are what ultimately decide the length of the oars and the speed of movement in a racing-boat. It is interesting to find —as, of course, was really obvious— how closely athletics is mixed with physiology.

Wastefulness of High Speeds

This last discussion leads us to the question of what determines the great wastefulness of the higher speeds. Why, returning to Fig. 2, does a speed of 280 steps per min require 24 l of oxygen per min, while a speed of 240 steps per min requires only 8 l of oxygen? The answer depends upon the variation of external work with speed of muscular movement. In a series of recent papers it has been shown that in a maximal muscular movement the external work decreases in a linear manner as the speed of shortening increases. At sufficiently high speeds of shortening no external work at all can be performed. In most of these athletic exercises, apart from the case of rowing, a large proportion of the mechanical work is used in overcoming the viscous resistance of the muscles themselves. At high speeds of running only a small fraction of the mechanical energy of the muscles is available to propel the body, once the initial inertia has been overcome. The speed of shortening is so rapid that little external work can be done. The work is absorbed by internal friction, or by those molecular changes which, when the muscle is shortening rapidly, cause its tension to fall off. When working against an external resistance, as in rowing, there is an optimum speed. If an effort is to be long continued it must be made at a speed not far from the optimum. When, however, the whole of the resistance to movement is internal, as in running, there is no optimum speed: the expense of the movement increases continually as the speed goes up; the faster we move, the greater relatively the price: our footsteps are dogged by the viscous-elastic properties of muscle, which prevent us from moving too fast, which save us from breaking ourselves while we are attemping to break a record.

Uniform Speed is the Optimum

The amount of energy required per minute to run or to swim, or, indeed, to propel oneself in any way, increases more rapidly than the speed—in the cases which have been investigated, approximately as the square of the speed. This mathematical relation is not exact: the facts can only really be described by a curve such as that of Fig. 2, but it simplifies the argument. From the form of the curve of Fig. 2, or from the variation of energy output as the square of the speed, we can immediately deduce that the most efficient way in which to run a race is that of a uniform speed throughout. Imagine that a man runs a mile race in 4 min 30 sec at a uniform speed of 6.52 yd per sec: his energy expenditure is proportional to $4\frac{1}{2}$ times 6.52 squared; that is, 191.3 expressed in some arbitrary unit. Imagine now that he runs it at two speeds, 6 and 7 yd per sec, 780 yd at the lower, 980 at the upper speed: the total time is the same: the energy expended, however, is slightly greater, 192.3 instead of 191.3. This small variation of speed in the race has produced no serious increase in the energy expenditure. Let us imagine,

however, that one portion of the race, 665 yd, is run at 5 yd per sec, while another portion, 1,096 yd, is run at 8 yd per sec. The total time occupied in the race is still 4 min 30 sec. The energy expended, however, is greater, namely, 201.5 units. Even this, however, is not a very large increase; by running about half the time at 8 yd and half the time at 5 yd per sec, the energy expended has been increased only about 5 per cent as compared with that required for running at a uniform speed of 6.5 yd per sec throughout. Although, therefore, theoretically speaking, the optimum fashion in which to run a race is that of uniform velocity throughout, comparatively large variations on either side of this velocity do not appreciably increase the amount of energy expended.

Possible Advantages of a Fast Start

There may, indeed, be advantages in starting rather faster than the average speed which it is intended to maintain. The sooner the respiration and circulation are driven up to their maximum values, the greater will be the amount of oxygen taken in by the body, the greater the amount expendable during the race. It is a common practice in mile races to start very fast and to settle down later to the uniform speed: this may have a physiological basis in the quickening up of circulation and respiration achieved thereby.

The Simple Mechanics of High Jumping

One final point may be worthy of mention—this time connected with high jumping and long jumping. Recently I made a series of observations, with a stopwatch reading to 0.02 sec, of the times occupied by a number of high jumpers from the moment they left the ground to the moment they reached the ground again. With men jumping about five feet the time averaged about 0.80 sec. Calculating from the formula

$$S = \tfrac{1}{2}gt^2,$$

where t is half the total time of flight, the distance through which the center of gravity of the body was raised must have been about 2.5 ft. The men competing must have had an original height of their center of gravity of about 2.7 ft. Thus, in the high jump, their centers of gravity went about 5.2 ft high into the air. They cleared a height of 5 ft: they just managed to wriggle their centers over the bar. Now, paradoxical as it may seem, it is possible for an object to pass over a bar while its center of gravity passes beneath; every particle in the object may go over the bar and yet the whole time its center of gravity may be below. A rope running over a pulley and falling on the other side is an obvious example. It is conceivable that by suitable contortions the more accomplished high jumpers may clear the bar without getting their centers of gravity above or appreciably above it. Let us calculate, however, on the assumption that the center of gravity of a jumper just clears the bar. The world's record high jump is 6.61 ft, the center of gravity of the performer being presumably about 3 ft high at rest. He raises it therefore 3.61 ft into the air, from which we may calculate that the whole time occupied in the jump is about 0.96 sec. Seeing the amazing complexity of and the skill involved in the rapid movements and adjustments involved in a record high jump, it is striking that all those events can occur within a time of less than one second. All the characteristics of the proprioceptive system must be evoked in their highest degree in carrying out such a skilled, rapid, and yet violent movement.

Long Jumping

It is well known to athletes that success in long jumping consists in learning to jump high. It is not, of course, the case that a record long jumper performs at the same moment a record high jump. He must, however, cover a very considerable height. The world's record long jump is 25.48 ft. With the check provided by the vertical impulse in the last step we cannot well imagine the horizontal velocity to be greater, at this moment, than that of 100 yd completed in 10 sec; that is, than 30 ft per sec. Let us assume this value; then the performer remains in the air for $\dfrac{25.48}{30}$; that is, 0.85 sec: hence we may calculate that the vertical distance covered is about 2.9 ft. Assuming the center of gravity of the subject to have been originally 3 ft high, this means that it must have reached a height 5.9 ft in the air, enough, in a high jump, to enable its owner to clear 5.9 ft. It is interesting to find that the simple laws of mechanics emphasize so strongly the precepts of the athletic trainer. Not only must one jump high if one wishes to break a long jump record, but one must bring one's center of gravity nearly six feet high into the air; for one must project oneself vertically, so that one may remain for 0.85 sec above the ground.

Conclusion

The practice of athletics is both a science and an art, and, just as art and science are the most potent ties tending to draw men together in a world of industrial competition, so sport and athletics, by urging men to friendly rivalry, may help to avert the bitterness resulting from less peaceful struggles. If therefore, physiology can aid in the development of athletics as a science and an art, I think it will deserve well of mankind. As in all these things, however, the reward will be reciprocal. Obviously in the data of athletic records we have a store of information available for physiological study. Apart from its usefulness, however, I would urge that the study

is amusing. Most people are interested, at any rate in England and America, in some type of sport. If they can be made to find it more interesting, as I have found it, by a scientific contemplation of the things which every sportsman knows, then that extra interest is its own defense.

F. M. HENRY

Prediction of World Records in Running Sixty Yards to Twenty-six Miles

Reprinted from the *Research Quarterly*,
26 (1955), 147–58.

The equations derived by Henry represent the most elegant attempts thus far to predict record performance. He has improved upon previous attempts in a number of ways. An example is the addition of the "acceleration factor," whereby he accounts for the occurrence of velocity changes, particularly at the beginning of races. Heretofore others had assumed velocity to be constant for a given race. Probably a more significant contribution of Henry's equation, however, is the consideration of some of the physiological processes that determine maximum performance.

Abstract

Previous attempts to formulate the mathematical relationship between velocity and elapsed time (or distance) in running records have failed to account for the sprint events and have been empirical rather than theoretical. In the present study, a velocity equation is developed which consists of the sum of three exponential terms having fatigue constants or k's characterizing the muscle energy supply systems—the alactate and lactate oxygen debts and the glycogen reserve. A subtractive exponential term represents the acceleration factor in the sprints. Using this equation, record speeds for 100 yd and longer distances are predicted with an error of less than 1 per cent; for the 60-m—60-yd sprints, with errors of 2 and 3 per cent.

In his 1924 Herter lectures at the Johns Hopkins University, the distinguished physiologist A. V. Hill called attention to the fact that "Some of the most consistent physiological data available are contained, not in books on physiology . . . but in the world's records for running. . . ." [2, p. 98] Lietzke [8] has recently reviewed the attempts that have been made, beginning in 1905, to derive a descriptive mathematical relationship between distance and running time. None of these attempts have in his opinion been successful, although the mathematical forms used have ranged from a modified parabola to a semilogarithmic hyperbola.

Lietzke has given a more general and more accurate formulation of the relationship than any of the others. The distance y as a function of the time t is predicted through the use of the parabola

$$y = at^k, \tag{1}$$

where the units conversion factor a has the magnitude 11.72 for yard-second units and k is 0.914, within the interval between the mile run and the marathon distance of 26.2 mi. With different curve constants, he is able to use a separate form of the formula for the interval between the 440 and the mile, but has no success at all with the shorter distances. Lietzke as well as some of the other investigators cited by him have mentioned the importance of "physiological relationships," but their formulae are strictly empirical in nature.[1]

Purpose of the Study

If records in running competition are in fact determined to an important extent by physiological processes, it should be possible to derive from physiological factors a formula that will predict the runner's speed as a function of time for any of the distances used in competition—the sprints and middle distances as well as the mile events and the marathon. This would of course require adequate knowledge of the crucial physiological capabilities of the runners who made the records. Such information, unfortunately, is not available. However, it is possible to set up some generalized mathematical formulations representing the physiological factors. The resulting formula can be tested as a predictor of the time-distance records, and the underlying hypothesis can be tested as a prediction of the pattern of the records as a function of distance or elapsed time.

Theory and Method

The groundwork for the study will be found in previous articles giving mathematical expression for lactate and alactate oxygen debt [1, 3, 5] and for the time-velocity relation in "allout" running.[4] Since the *integral* or time-distance curve is notoriously insensitive as pointed out by Lietzke, and moreover is *theoretically incorrect* in this particular problem as will be explained later, the *derivative* or rate curve will serve as the basis of the analysis. It will be most convenient to plot this curve with a logarithmic ordinate, using linear or arithmetic time units for the abscissa.

Acceleration factor. The upper curve

---

[1] This statement is somewhat unfair to A. V. Hill, since his work on sprint velocity led directly to the inclusion of the acceleration factor in the present study. Moreover, he has used oxygen metabolism data to estimate speed within certain distance ranges.

"The Ultimate of Human Effort," an article by Brutus Hamilton (*Amateur Athlete*, Feb. 1935), should be added to the Lietzke reference list, and his date for the pioneer Kennelley study should be changed to 1906. George P. Meade, another pioneer in the systematic study of World Records, has kindly called the writer's attention to a later article by Kennelley (*Proc. Am. Acad. Arts and Sciences*, August, 1926) in which the 3:58 mile was predicted.

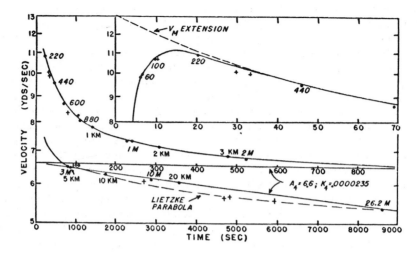

Fig. 1. Average velocity of world record times. The crosses represent "substandard" records.

in Fig. 1 gives the average velocity for the championship records for the sprints. (In the actual curve-fitting, a wider graph was used, in order to include the middle distances up to the 880-yd and 1-km records.) By drawing a smooth line through the highest points (ignoring the 300-yd and 300-m distances, plotted as crosses, because they have been largely neglected in competition), a curve is obtained which is remarkably similar to the 300-yd "all-out" velocity curve recently reported.[4]

It will be seen that the velocity (defined as speed in the forward direction) becomes progressively less as the distances decrease from approximately 200 yd. This is because it takes time to accelerate the mass of the runner; at the start, his velocity is zero. Acceleration would progress linearly and without limit, as a function of time, if it were not for the "energy loss" and viscosity factors that impose what may be considered as a counter force that is proportional to the speed of the runner. The net outcome is that the runner approaches some limiting velocity v_m

in accord with an exponential law.[4]

It is easiest to evaluate this subtractive exponential term graphically by extending the main velocity curve leftward until it reaches the ordinate. It may be seen in Fig. 1 that the intercept of this extension is 13.1 yd per sec. Now, if one substracts the observed velocities from this extended v_m curve, a series of *differences* as a function of time is obtained. These differences plot out as a straight line on a semilog graph, and it requires 2.79 sec for the initial magnitude of 13.1 to drop to half this amount. (Naturally, this plot of the differences must be made on a greatly expanded time scale. See upper right curve of Fig. 2.) From this *half-time*[4] the exponent k_1 is determined as 0.693/2.79 or 0.248, and the coefficient a_1 is of course 13.1. The observed k_1 is considerably smaller than the k_1 of 0.75 found in all-out running, but that is because the latter was determined from the *instantaneous* velocity at various time stations whereas in the present case it is determined by the *average* velocity of the runner when he sprints various distances. For that reason, it does not have a rigorous theoretical meaning, but it *is* an acceleration-energy loss component and does serve its purpose in the formula.

Glycogen depletion factor. The next step is to derive a component for the physiological factor determining the velocity at long distances of the range 3 to 26 mi. It is common knowledge that a run of only a few miles has no influence on the blood sugar level, but a 26-mi run causes a serious drop, indicating considerable depletion of the glycogen reserve. For example, Morehouse and Miller [9, p. 53] in discussing this matter, state that in the Boston marathon of 1924 the blood sugar concentration of several runners was reduced by a half. In his discussion of glycogen depletion, Karpovich (6, p. 156) mentions experiments showing marked drop in the blood sugar after 3 hours' exertion. In very rough figures, therefore, it might be expected that the half-time for glycogen depletion would be in the region of 5 or 6 hr.

The lower curve of Fig. 1 gives the average velocity for the long distances. Here, we are fortunate in having

available the remarkable records of Zatopek at distances ranging from 5 km to the 26.2-mi marathon. The latter serves as the right-hand point of the straight line drawn through or close to his other points and through the Haegg 5-km and 3-mi records. The intercept magnitude a_4 of this line is 6.6 and its half-time is 8.19 hr so k_4 (in seconds units) is 0.0000235. Considering the half-time, it seems not overly presumptuous to identify this component with the glycogen supply. Since it plots as a straight line on a semilog graph, the function is exponential.

The crosses in the figure represent existing records at intermediate distances. The velocities at the 15-mi and 25- and 30-km distances (run by others) lie on the Lietzke parabola (dashed line), but the Zatopek records for the 10-mi, the 1-hr, and the 20-km events are considerably above the parabola and on the exponential line.

Lactate and alactate energy factors. Next in importance as sources of energy are the lactate and alactate oxygen debts, the former representing a maximum store of 75 to 90 kcal and the latter

Fig. 2. Exponential curve analysis. The main figure shows the two-component composition of the residuals after subtracting the $a_4 - k_4$ component from the velocity curve. The insert figure shows the residuals after subtracting the sum of the three positive components from the sprint velocity curve. (Note that all components add vertically since these are semilog graphs.)

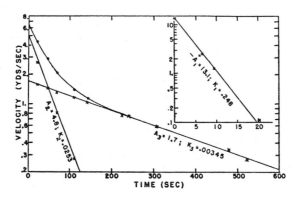

perhaps 25 or 30. Exercise metabolism studies from this laboratory [1,3,5] have reported half-times of 215 sec and 30 sec for these functions. It can be expected that they will be involved in the remaining portion of the curve analysis.

For the analysis of this part of the velocity curve, the records for the range 220 yd through 2 mi have been plotted as the middle curve in Fig. 1, including the a_4—k_4 component which appears as a straight line just below the curve. (Although that component looks like a base line due to the expanded time scale, it actually has a slight slope, dropping from 6.6 to 6.5 in 750 sec.) The first step is to draw a smooth curve through the points and then subtract the a_4—k_4 component vertically from this curve at progressive intervals of time. The differences so obtained are then plotted in a separate semilog graph (Fig. 2). The lower limb of the difference curve is accounted for by the straight line $a_3 = 1.7$, $k_3 = 0.00345$, which has a half-time of 201 sec. Subtracting this component from the difference curve gives a series of points that fall on the straight line $a_2 = 4.8$, $k_2 = 0.0253$, with a half-time of 27.4 sec.

Results

Equation for speed of runner. It is now possible to set up the rate equation

$$dy/dt = a_4 e^{-k_4 t} + a_3 e^{-k_3 t} + a_2 e^{-k_2 t} - a_1 e^{-k_1 t} \qquad (2)$$

which gives the velocity of running in yd per sec for any elapsed time within the region 5 sec to 10,000 sec. It may be noted that the subtractive component a_1—k_1 has such a short half-time that it may be neglected for distances longer than 300 yd or for times that are greater than 30 sec; also, the a_2—k_2 component contributes only 0.01 yd per sec at 1

mi and may be neglected thereafter. Somewhere between 5 and 10 km the a_3—k_3 component also drops out. The sum of the three positive components at any time t gives the dashed line leftward extension in the upper curve of Fig. 1. This is the velocity that would have been attained if the runner had not for physical reasons lost considerable time in accelerating his body mass to full speed.

Errors of prediction. Since the graphs cannot be read with sufficient accuracy to determine the errors, they have been included as part of the tabulation in Table 1. The largest errors, of the order of 2 or 3 per cent, are at the 60-m and 60-yd distances. At 800 m the observed velocity is 1.3 per cent faster than predicted by the equation. With these exceptions (and they represent rather small deviations), the errors are small—less than 1 per cent. It is interesting that the recent 3′:58″ mi run by Landy is only 0.8 per cent faster than predicted by the equation, which was set up to fit the 1954 *World Almanac* data. It is anticipated that eventually the records for other distances will also move up to lie above the curve, but it will probably be a number of years before any important modification of the curve-constants will be necessary.

Justification of exponential analysis. Any curve that is characterized by regularly decreasing curvature can be described by a mathematical function consisting of a sum of exponentials, provided that the number of terms in the polynomial approaches the number of points to be fitted. Equation (2) is not of that category.

Consider the a_4—k_4 component (the lower curve in Fig. 1). It is obvious by inspection that the Zatopek records at 5, 10 and 20 km and 10 mi establish a

TABLE 1

Predicted and Observed Velocities

Event Time (Sec)	60 yd 6.1	60 m 6.6	100 yd 9.3	220 yd 20.2	440 yd 46.0	600 yd 69.2	880 yd 109.2	1 km 141.3	1.5 km 223.0
$a_1e^{-k_1t}$	−2.89	−2.60	−1.31	−0.09	—	—	—	—	—
$a_2e^{-k_2t}$	4.12	4.06	3.79	2.88	1.50	0.83	0.30	0.13	0.02
$a_3e^{-k_3t}$	1.68	1.67	1.65	1.58	1.45	1.34	1.17	1.04	0.79
$a_4e^{-k_4t}$	6.60	6.60	6.60	6.60	6.60	6.59	6.59	6.58	6.57
Total (yd per sec)	9.51	9.73	10.73	10.97	9.55	8.76	8.06	7.76	7.38
Observed (yd per sec)	9.83	9.94	10.75	10.89	9.57	8.68	8.05	7.73	7.35
Error	−3.2%	−2.1%	−0.2%	0.7%	−0.2%	0.9%	0.1%	0.4%	0.4%

Event Time (min) (sec)	1 mi	2 km	3 km	2 mi	3 mi	5 km	10 km	10 mi	20 km	26.22 mi
(min)	4	5	7	8	13	13	29	48	59	143
(sec)	1.4	7.0	58.0	40.4	40.4	58.2	2.6	12.0	51.7	3.2
$a_3e^{-k_3t}$	0.74	0.59	0.33	0.28	0.10	0.09	—	—	—	—
$a_4e^{-k_4t}$	6.57	6.56	6.53	6.52	6.46	6.44	6.32	6.17	6.07	5.39
Total (yd per sec)	7.32	7.15	6.86	6.80	6.56	6.53	6.32	6.17	6.07	5.39
Observed (yd per sec)	7.29	7.13	6.86	6.76	6.50	6.53	6.27	6.14	6.09	5.38
Error	0.4%	0.3%	0.0%	0.6%	0.9%	0.0%	0.8%	0.5%	−0.3%	0.2%

straight line within the range 1,000 to 4,000 sec, and this line can be extended to his marathon record at 8,583 sec. (The 10-km point is about 0.9 per cent low; Zatopek remedied this minor defect in June 1954 by running the distance in 28′: 54.2″, which is rather precisely on the line.)

A series of residuals is left after this component has been removed from the observed velocities within the range from 20 sec, when the influence of the start is just dropping out as a factor, to 1,000 sec, where the straight line component began. This series forms a curve (Fig. 2). It resolves into two and only two components, as can be seen by the x symbols which represent the fractionation of the observed residual velocities into two straight-line functions. There are many events within this range. The first of the components is defined by 5 points (one of these, at 141 sec with the ordinate at 0.12, does not show on the graph). The other component is defined by 10 points. It should be remembered that a *straight* line in the semilog graph means that the component is exponential—it would not plot as a straight line on an arithmetic graph.

The insert graph of Fig. 2 gives the resolution of the residual velocities for the sprints, after subtracting the sum of the computed last three components. The x's in this figure therefore represent observed values. While these points do not fall exactly on a straight line, they are certainly not off very far. It should be realized, also, that the k's are all separated by approximately one order of magnitude (two magnitudes in the case of k_4).

Time and speed at a specified distance. Predicted time can most readily be estimated graphically, by plotting a time-distance curve similar to an integral curve, the distances on the graph being computed as the product

of time and the corresponding rate from Eq. (2). It is desirable to draw this figure on a log-by-log graph since the points will then lie very nearly on a straight line for distances greater than 220 yd as can be seen in Fig. 3. The scale of this graph is magnified about eight times as compared with the corresponding Lietzke figure, hence the errors are more noticeable. Estimation of speed in yd per sec as a function of distance can also be made graphically, but no straightforward mathematical formula is available because the exponential equation cannot be solved for t.

Discussion

Lietzke formula. Equation (1) has the advantage of flexibility. While the first derivative of this expression, namely

$$dy/dt = akt^{k-1} \qquad (3)$$

does *not* give the speed of the runner, the mathematical statement of the average speed

$$y/t = at^{k-1} \qquad (4)$$

differs from Eq. (3) only by the constant k. Moreover, the original equation is easily solved for t, since

$$t = (d/a)^{1/k} \qquad (5)$$

which provides a useful formula. Regardless of the mathematical elegance of the parabola, however, it has certain serious deficiencies. The curve constants have no physiological meaning. It is an empirical formula, and like other empirical formulae can be used only within a restricted range of data. At the practical level, it fails to predict with adequate accuracy. If the curve constants are chosen to fit the distance range 1 to 3 mi, they also fit the marathon, but the predicted velocities for the 10-, 15-, and 20-km runs lie considerably below the Zatopek records

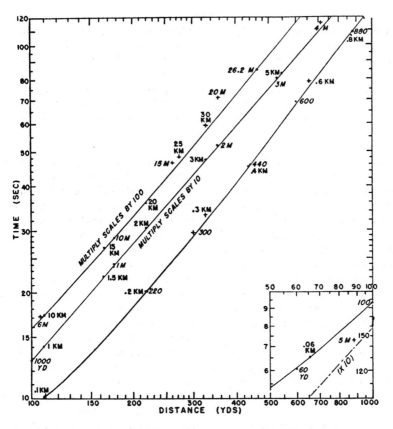

Fig. 3. Log-by-log plot of time-distance relationship. The smooth curves represent the product of time and velocity computed from Eq. (2). Note that the fragment of the curve 1200–1600 sec with the substandard 5 mi is in the lower right corner (broken line). Other substandard records are identified by crosses.

as was shown in Fig. 1 and 3. If the curve constants are chosen to fit these Zatopek records, the formula fails to predict the marathon and also the range 1 to 3 mi. It should be mentioned that while Lietzke[8] gave Eq. (4) as the rate formula, his velocity curves are simply smooth curves connecting the points and are *not* based on his rate formula.

Power output. In a recent note, Katz[7] has used a parabola to describe the energy output in horsepower of athletes during hill climbing. Velocity

(i.e., the distance traveled per unit time) can be considered as related to square root of the power output, although it does not explicitly take into account the variation in frictional resistances as a function of speed. For this reason, the k obtained in the Katz analysis would be expected to be different. It is 0.784 compared with the Lietzke k of 0.914. While Katz states that his points "fall on a surprisingly straight line" over a 5–magnitude range of time, he does not give the precision of fit of his curve.

Actually, the fit is rather poor. He

TABLE 2

Errors in Predicting Power Output in Hill Climbing by the Katz Equation

Time (sec)	2.4	4	30	44	225	342	1,320	4,110	9,060
Observed H.P...	1.70	1.32	0.94	0.87	0.44	0.57	0.45	0.27	0.24
Predicted H.P...	1.60	1.44	0.93	0.85	0.60	0.55	0.41	0.32	0.27
Error (%)......	6.25	8.26	1.08	2.36	26.70	3.64	9.77	15.62	11.12

has drawn his curve through the highest and lowest power outputs. The intermediate observations of horsepower and their per cent deviations from his curve are shown in Table 2. Since the errors are large, the points *could* be fitted by a parabola, or by some other function such as an exponential formula. Nevertheless, his analysis is of interest, since it illustrates the possibility of analyzing hill-climbing as well as level-ground performance.

Integral curve. Equation (2) can be integrated by standard methods. The resulting formula for the distance y at any time t is

$$y = \frac{a_4}{k_4}(1 - e^{-k_4 t}) + \frac{a_3}{k_3}(1 - e^{-k_3 t})$$
$$+ \frac{a_2}{k_2}(1 - e^{-k_2 t}) - \frac{a_1}{k_1}(1 - e^{-k_1 t}) \quad (6)$$

While this formula gives the area under the rate curve, and *would* give the distance y attained by the runner at time t if he ran his race in the velocity pattern described by the rate curve, the facts of the matter are that his velocity pattern is not of this form. Consider for example the recent 3 min 58 sec mile run by Landy. He ran the first quarter in 58.5 sec, the second in 61.0, the third in 60.5, and the last in 58.0, all of these being within 2.5 per cent of his average velocity of 7.4 yd per sec. Had his pattern of running been as specified by the rate curve, his average lap velocities would have been about 10.2 8.3, 7.7, and 7.4 yd

per sec and he would have reached the tape *more than a half-minute* before he actually did. Of course no runner in his right mind would attempt to pace his mile in any such manner, because it is too inefficient physiologically.[4]

Instantaneous velocities. The integral curve (Eq. [6]) and the exponential rate curve (Eq. [2]) are both effective in predicting the instantaneous distances and velocitites in *all-out* running, although the curve constants are of course somewhat different in that situation. Using only the a_1—k_1 and a_2—k_2 components, a rather good fit was secured for the curves of 24 track men and 30 other students who ran as fast as possible *throughout* a distance of 300 yd. It was observed that the velocity curve tended to flatten out somewhat during the last 80 yd. although the available data did not permit an analysis of the phenomena. It is obvious by inspection of those data[4] that the addition of the a_3—k_3 and a_4—k_4 components would give an almost exact description of this flattening of the curve.

Energy supply for 24-hour run. It is known that continuous work of many hours' duration without food intake draws on the body fat for energy supply.[6, p. 46] Theoretically, therefore, a fifth component should be added to Eq. (2) in order to describe this process. Only a few data are available to estimate the additional curve constants—

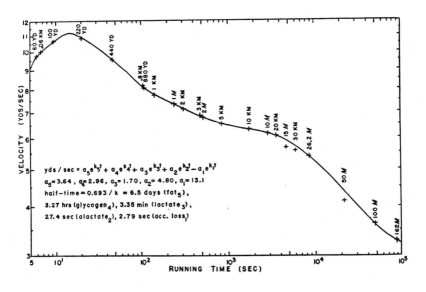

Inside the figure:

VELOCITY (YDS/SEC)

RUNNING TIME (SEC)

labels on curve: 60 KM, 106 KM, 100 YD, 220 YD, 440 YD, .8 KM 880 YD, 1 KM, 1 M, 2 KM, 2 M, 3 KM, 3 M, 5 KM, 10 KM, 10 M, 20 KM, 15 M, 30 KM, 26.2 M, 50 M, 100 M, 162M

$$yds/sec = a_5 e^{k_5 t} + a_4 e^{k_4 t} + a_3 e^{k_3 t} + a_2 e^{k_2 t} - a_1 e^{k_1 t}$$

$a_5 = 3.64$, $a_4 = 2.96$, $a_3 = 1.70$, $a_2 = 4.80$, $a_1 = 13.1$

half-time = $0.693/k$ = 6.5 days (fat$_5$),

3.27 hrs (glycogen$_4$), 3.35 min (lactate$_3$),

27.4 sec (alactate$_2$), 2.79 sec (acc. loss$_1$)

Fig. 4. Theoretical time-velocity curve. Log-by-log plot of five-component equation. The Lietzke rate formula (Eq. [4]) would plot as a straight line in this figure.

Lietzke[8] in his Fig. 10 shows a point at 162 mi with a time of 24 hr, and Hill's graph [6, p. 62] gives the times for 50- and 100-mi runs. While these data are not world records in the usual sense, they do give reasonable results when tested with a five-component exponential equation (Fig. 4).

The a_4—k_4 component of Eq. (2) should consequently be thought of as representing glycogen *and* other unresolved energy supply factors such as fat. The "fat" component is nonlimiting and unrecognized for distances shorter than the marathon, but becomes increasingly important in determining performance in very long runs of 50 mi or more. Total potential energy of each of the energy supply systems, if completely used up, would be equal to a/k (with the appropriate subscripts).

Resolution of the a_4—k_4 component into its two principal factors gives a shorter half-time (3.27 hr) for glycogen depletion. The fatigue constants thus become $k_4 = 5.88 \times 10^{-5}$ for glycogen and $k_5 = 1.234 \times 10^{-6}$ for "fat" (including possibly protein). The energy depletion rates of the other components remain unaltered.

Implications of the exponential equation. The a coefficients can be given only a very general sort of definition at the present time. They may be thought of as proportional to energy *output*, as expressed by velocity units. Because of differences in metabolic efficiency of the different physiological processes that they represent, they are probably not equivalent units of energy *input*. The k's may be visualized as time-constants governing the rate of energy depletion of each of the energy resources, and imply that the *rate* of depletion of each is always a constant proportion of the undepleted amount still available at any particular instant t after the beginning of the run. Viewed in this manner, the k's may be thought of as physiological fatigue constants governing the decrement in speed as the length of the race increases.

Estimation of possible improvements in records. Hill in 1924, after plotting the world record velocities against the distances of the events, commented on the remarkable smoothness of the velocity curve: "The relation . . . may be accepted practically as a natural constant for the human race. It would require almost a superhuman effort to change one of the points by 2 per cent."[2, p. 99] Others have since been equally venturesome. Since his statement, records speeds in the 220 and 440 have improved nearly 4 per cent; in distances of one mile and greater, the improvements have been well over 5 per cent.

In part this may be ascribed to the greater statistical probability that an unusual performance will be seen in a larger sample. Also, running surfaces as well as techniques may be better; human capabilities may have increased. Whatever the cause, we have no good reason to believe that the end of improvement is yet in sight. Although it is 30 years after Hill's classical work on the physiology of running, we still have insufficient knowledge to estimate dependably the ultimate limits of human performance.[2]

A theoretically meaningful formula that describes accurately the time-distance-velocity relationships *can* be used to pick out which events are presently being run substandard with respect to human capabilities, but this is not within itself a very important purpose. Rather, the function of the equation is to coordinate various and perhaps widespread bits of knowledge and factual observations in a more and more meaningful manner, the eventual goal being that scientific understanding which alone makes possible the correct and dependable solution of practical problems.

Conclusions

Using the known time-constants or k's for alactate and lactate metabolism, and a third k crudely estimated from the few facts available regarding glycogen depletion, an equation consisting of a series of exponential fatigue terms has been developed to describe the speed and position of a runner as a function of time. A subtractive term must be included to account for the loss from internal resistance and the development of momentum during the initial acceleration of the runner.

This rate equation makes possible the computation of the average velocity of a runner for distances ranging from 60 yd to 26 mi. World-record speeds and times in the commonly run events can be predicted accurately.

There are indications that the addition of another exponential term to account for energy supplied from body fat will extend the range of prediction to about 150 miles.

References

1. De Moor, Janice, "Individual Differences in Oxygen Debt Curves Related to Mechanical Efficiency and Sex," *J. Appl. Physiol.*, **6** (1954), 460–66.

2. Hill, A. V., *Muscular Activity*. Baltimore: The Williams & Wilkins Co., 1926.

3. Henry, F. M., Aerobic Oxygen Con-

---

[2] For a recent discussion of this matter, see "A Note on Physiological Limits and the History of the Mile Run," *Res. Quart.* 25 (1954), 483.

sumption and Alactic Debt in Muscular Work," *J. Appl. Physiol.*, **3** (1951), 427–38.

4. Henry, F. M., "Time-Velocity Equations and Oxygen Requirements of 'All-Out' and 'Steady-Pace' Running," *Res. Quart.*, **25** (1954), 164–77.

5. Henry, F. M., and Janice De Moor, "Metabolic Efficiency of Exercise in Relation to Work Load at Constant Speed," *J. Appl. Physiol.*, **2** (1950), 481–87.

6. Karpovich, P. V., *Physiology of Muscular Activity*. New York: W. B. Saunders Co., 1953.

7. Katz, L., "Comments on Power Developed by Human Beings," in Letters to the Editor, *Am. Scientist*, **42** (1954), 532.

8. Lietzke, M. H., "An Analytical Study of World and Olympic Racing Records," *Science*, **119** (1954), 333–36.

9. Morehouse, L. E., and A. T. Miller, *Physiology of Exercise*. St. Louis, Mo.: The C. V. Mosby Company, 1953.